SRINAGAR

KASHMIR

THE HIMALAYAS

Kashol 17,839

Dudang P.

Shapiyon

Islamabad

Maru

Padam

Pir Panjal Pass 11,400

Marbal Pass 11,570

Badrawar

Kistawar

Kilar

Shor

Bara Lacha Pass

CHAMBA

Chamba

Barutal

Tandi Lyelang

Chamba R.

Hanze

Dankhar

Jasrota

Pudua

Dalhousie

Baldr

Chini

Parangla

Lahul

Sialkot

Sujanpur

Nurpur

Pathankot

Chuhda

Nagar

SIALKOT

Zafarwal

Madhopur

Dharmsala

Srikanpur

Midh

Shalkar

Shipki Pass

GURDASPUR

Gurdaspur

Kangra

Baijnath

Jwalamukhi

Sujanpur

KANGRA

Banjar

BASHAHR

Marong

Majitha

Batala

Dasuya

Miani

MANDI

Mandi

Rampur

AMRITSAR

Hoshiarpur

Una

3

Suket

Bined

Hoshiarpur

Kartarpur

HOSHIARPUR

BILASPUR

SUKET

Sri Kanta

Kasur

Jullundur

Phagwara

DUB

Bilaspur

Bhagat

Simla

Rampur

JULLUNDUR

Nalagarh

SIMLA HILL

Kotgarh

A

Zira

Ludhiana

Kasauli

Solon

STATES

Firozepore

Jagraon

Raikot

Malerkotla

SIRMUR

Nahan

Sirmur

Dehra

Tehri

MEHRAJ

Nabha

Patiala

AMBALA

Chhachhrauli

Siri Kanta

PATIALA

Sangrur

Ambala

Nahan

Srinagar

Bhatinda

Dehra

Hardwar

Rori

Kaithal

Pundri

KARNAL

Ganga

Deoband

Sirsa

Fatahabad

Saffdon

Karnal

Muzaffarnagar

Bijnor

Nagna

Ellenabad

HISSAR

Jind

JIND

Panipat

Meerut

Moradabad

Hansi

Mahm

Rohtak

Sonpat

Hissar

Bhadra

Tushan

Bhiwani

ROHTAK

Sambhal

Rajgarh

Bawani

Dadri

Dujana

Delhi

DELHI

Ghaziabad

Chandausi

Loharu

JIND

Gurgaon

Faridabad

Bulandshahr

Singhana

Rawari

GURGAON

Palwal

Khurja

Mahindragarh

Sohna

ESERT

Hodal

Aligarh

ONS OF PUNJAB

LHI DIVISION

HORE DIVISION

LLUNDUR DIVISION

WALPINDI DIVISION

ULTAN DIVISION

Firuzpur Jhirka

Kishangarh

76

78

78

Longitude East of Greenwich

East of Indus

My Memories of Old Punjab

Gurnam S.S. Brard

Hemkunt

© Gurnam S. S. Brard
First Published 2007

ISBN: 81-7010-360-6

Published by:

Hemkunt Publishers (P) Ltd.
A-78, Naraina Indl. Area, Phase I, New Delhi-28
Tel.: 4141-2083, 2579-5079
Fax: 91-11-4540-4165
E-mail : hemkunt@ndf.vsnl.net.in
www.hemkuntpublishers.com

Printed and bound in India by
HEMTECH INDIA
Custom Printing & Publishing
hemtech@gmail.com
at Rakesh Press.

CONTENTS

INTRODUCTION

This book is about my early life and about my family in Punjab, India; it is also a description of many aspects of the village life during the first half of the twentieth century.

In my childhood, there were no paved roads in our part of India, but only the cartwheel ruts through the sandy soil; there was no motorized transport, but only ox-drawn wagons or animal mounts; any sources of power were provided only by humans or animals; and most people used mustard oil burning clay lamps for lighting, since we knew of electricity only as those flashes through the clouds; I saw an electric light burning for the first time after I became a teenager and went to a city. Most of the necessities of life, food, shelter and clothing, were produced from local materials right there in the village, probably as it had been done 2000 years ago.

After World War II and the partition of India, urban and modern trends started affecting the rural areas also. Not only have the old ways of life changed, most people of the generation before me have died, so the conditions of those days before the war are forgotten. On a visit to India in 2003, I went to my village as I wanted to speak to some old-timers. But even many of my contemporaries had died, and I became the old-timer now.

The first part of this book is about my family and my early life, and the later part describes the environment, the conditions of our village life and many aspects of that culture. To give the reader an idea of family interactions, I start my story with a brief history of my early ancestors and then describe the lives of the members of my extended clan. My parents and siblings impacted my own life, so I discuss their lives before describing my own. My early life was affected by my aversion to school and to education, and by my attraction to the farming life of uneducated villagers. This was not uncommon for those immersed in the village culture, where there was a slight contempt for literate people among the young. My wish to live as a simple farmer was a source of anguish for my family. Over time, my attitudes changed; after some years of farming on the family land, I did go to college in India and later on I received a Ph.D. to become a physicist in the United States.

The later part of the book is important because it provides the context of my life and portrays the conditions in which I grew up. I have described the customs and complexities in that apparently simple rural life as I saw them. Topics such as the status of women in various roles, local religious practices and prejudices, the caste system and its relationship to vocation, superstitions, marriage customs, death rituals, fairs and festivals, clothing as a religious statement, Partition and the Independence of India, crimes and laws, homes and fields, foods and drinks, recreation and sports, dance and music, performances and entertainment, holy cows and other animals, trees and crops, bedtime stories and riddles, sexual mores and taboos, are all discussed in varying detail. So this book is also a sort of ethnography, describing the way of life in the Punjab province of India in the first half of the twentieth century. My experience was mostly rural until the age of about twenty when I went to college. Since I use a number of Punjabi terms which may be unfamiliar to many people, I have included a glossary of Punjabi words at the end. In stead of adding an 's' to make the Punjabi words plural, I have usually used the same Punjabi words for singular and plural. All the words within quotation marks are my translation, as they were actually said in Punjabi.

Nothing in this book is fictional. Most of this material is from my memory. Some of the information is from conversations I have had with family members, and some from my own reading in the past. There are scores of stories of people imbedded in the book where they seemed to fit; I have described them as they occurred, since I feel that personal stories are often the best way to shed light on the workings of a society. The names in the stories are real, except for the names in the chapter on sexual taboos and mores, which were all changed to avoid identification. I have tried to avoid any factual errors in the text, but it is obvious when some of the statements are just my opinions and not absolute truth. Some of the words, expressions and statements in the text may appear politically incorrect in today's environment. My intent was to describe the conditions of 70 years ago and how people thought and talked then. Whether I describe religious differences, ethnic apartheid, caste discrimination, superstitions, or women's status, it is to state the truth of those times and not an expression of my personal feelings; so I request tolerance from those who might feel offended.

I have many friends and family members to thank for their support and encouragement while I wrote this book. I was originally motivated by my daughter Amrita and my sons Apar and Gyan, who seemed fascinated by stories about my early life in the rural Punjab, and who repeatedly asked me to write them down. I also received encouragement from my friend Judy Miller Johnson, who read one of the raw versions of this work, and said that she felt herself reliving her own early life in Wyoming as she read about my life in the Punjab village. I was also urged on by an Indian lady, Dr. P.S. Phadke, who thought that the material in the book was really captivating. An earlier version of the manuscript was edited by Kenneth Sanderson, but I changed made of it afterwards. I am grateful for the encouragement and advice of my friend R.K Janmeja (Meji) Singh, Ph.D., who reviewed the manuscript. My nephew Jatinder S. Gill, M.D., also read the manuscript and gave me some suggestions.

Gurnam Singh Sidhu Brard, Ph.D
P.O. Box 2401,
Stateline, NV 89449
email: gurnamsb@yahoo.com

CHAPTER 1

A BRIEF HISTORY OF OUR CLAN

My people, the Sidhu Brards of village Mehraj, lived some miles east of Bhatinda in the southern part of Punjab. When I was young, the province of Punjab extended from the river Indus in the west to Jumna, a tributary of the river Ganga (Ganges) in the east; it was bordered by Kashmir and the Himalayan mountains in the north and by the Rajputana desert in the south. Our village is situated about 50 miles from the river Sutlej, which is a tributary of the Indus. We were about 150 miles northwest of the City of Delhi and about 100 miles south of Lahore.

The word Punjab means "five rivers" and refers to these five tributaries of the river Indus: the Sutlej, the Beas, the Ravi, the Chneab, and the Jehlum. In ancient times, the Aryans, the Greeks, the Persians, the Afghans and the Turkic Mughal people came across the Indus River and the Indus Valley after crossing the Khyber Pass. So they named the country and its people by the name of the river, variously called the Ind, the Indus, or the Hind (hence its people: Hindu), some calling the country Hindustan, whose English name is India; eastern Hindus like to call the country Bharat. At the partition of India in 1947, the old Punjab was divided between India and Pakistan; then only the rivers Sutlej and Beas were left in India. The Pakistan boundary was chosen by the British to be close to the river Ravi in a few places; so a large part of the old Punjab went to make Pakistan.

There is quite a bit of folklore and written material about our ancestors. The main reason for this notoriety is that a man named Phul (rhymes with cool) from our clan went out and established himself as the chief of a small territory in 1654, and in the next century the descendents of Phul became the rulers of the Phulkian States. About the time I was born in 1930, our people, the Sidhu Brards of Mehraj, were just ordinary farmers. But our early ancestors had been warriors who ruled over territories around southern Punjab and in the Rajputana desert off and on. After having been defeated in several battles and losing their forts and territories, in about 1630 they came and occupied the hundred square mile of land east of the town of Bhatinda, where most of our people still live in the twenty-two villages. These villages have grown from the original village of Mehraj, and are collectively known as MehrajKe or Bahia (of twenty two villages).

Memorizing Ancestral Names.

7

One day my father said to me: "Gurnam, you are eleven years old. A *Rajputra* becomes a youth at twelve; you better start taking the responsibilities of being a man." When I asked: "What is a *Rajputra*?" it gave my father another opportunity to launch into the frequently repeated stories of his ancestors: "Gurnam, you should know that we are not just ordinary *Jat* (Punjabi pronunciation is Jutt; farmer caste). Our ancestors, the Sidhu Brards, were the *Kshatri Rajput* warriors, and our ancestor Jaisal founded and ruled the principality of Jaisalmer in Rajputana many centuries ago. The word *Rajputra* is a variation of the word *Rajput* (ruler's son)."

We heard such descriptions frequently from elders. My father would make us recite the names of our paternal ancestors up to thirty or forty generations, just as children learn multiplication tables. I still remember that I am nine generations removed from my ancestor Sandly, fourteen generations from Mehraj and twenty-one generations from Brard, who was several generations removed from Sidhu. I used to recite like this: Gurnam Singh, son of Naginder Singh, Naginder Singh son of Jagat Singh, Jagat Singh son of Sajjan Singh, Sajjan Singh son of Mahan Singh, of Dhanna, Dhanna son of Firoz, son of Chaudhry, of Sangtia, of Sandly, Roop Chand, MOHAN, Pakkho, Satto, MEHRAJ, Baryam or Behram, Sangher, Bau, Rai, Bairat, Paur, BRARD, Hameer,.... upto Bhoor, SIDHU, Khiva and beyond. Instead of telling us *baat* (night-time stories), my father would make us count these *peerhi* (generations) up to Jaisal or Bhatti and we were scolded if we mispronounced or skipped any ancestral name. My father was particularly in the habit of praising his paternal ancestors, emphasizing how they were great warriors of superior character. Maternal ancestors were not considered to be of any significance in determining one's character or abilities; they thought that a boy inherited his traits from his paternal forefathers only. In fact, calling a young boy 'Ma Jaisa' or mother-like, was a putdown and rebuke.

People in our village had the habit of fabricating tall tales to glorify their ancestors. In the days when your caste and heredity could get you special treatment, there was a tendency to inflate one's past. Some would consider themselves the descendents of mythical Rajput warriors, of ancient rulers, and even of divine beings from the epics of Ramayan and Maha Bharat. But the story of the warrior Bhatti is more credible. He is believed to have founded the town of Bhatinda and also the town of Bhatner (now called Hanuman Garh) further south in the desert. It was some centuries later that Bhatti's presumed descendent, and our ancestor, Jaisal, struggled to carve out a kingdom in the desert of Rajputana. In this effort, Jaisal tried to get help from his maternal uncle Jai Chand of Kanauj, but he was opposed by King Prithvi Raj Chauhan of Delhi. So Jaisal joined Mohammed Ghauri of Afghanistan in defeating the Delhi king in the battle of Panipat. Muhammed Ghauri in turn helped Jaisal in the capture of Ludherwa. Then Jaisal founded his capital city of Jaisalmer near Ludherwa. Later, his son Hem Mal was awarded the entire territory of Lakhi Jungle, the region of Punjab south of the Sutlej river and bordering the desert. As a result of shifting fortunes, some generations later, his descendent, and our ancestor, Khiva ruled only over the territory of Bhatinda in the Lakhi Jungle.

Khiva broke the caste rule by taking a wife from a family of the Jat caste. That action degraded the caste of his descendents from *Kshatri Rajput* (warrior ruler) to *Jat* (farmer). Other *Rajputs* ostracized Khiva for breaking the ancestral code by marrying a *Jat* woman; they would not eat with the lower caste *Jats* or relate to them socially. Khiva's son and

8

our ancestor Sidhu, the ruler of Bhatinda, and the progeny that bear his name, were forever degraded to the *Jat* caste.

The Bhattis of Bhatner, with the aid of king Ghias-ul-Din Tughlak of Delhi, pushed the sons of Sidhu out of Bhatinda; the Sidhus survived by settling in the LadhuKot and FakherSar Thehri villages of southern Punjab. It was many generations later that Sidhu's descendent Brard (originally pronounced Berard and now usually spelled Brar) tried to wrest the control of his ancestral fort of Bhatinda.

In 1399, the invasion of India by Temur the Turk (variously called Temur Lang, Teymoor the Lame or Tamerlane) had weakened the Bhattis of Bhatner. Then Brard gathered thousands of warriors and after much bloodshed, he defeated the Bhattis. There are old songs about the horsemen slain and the rivers of blood from this battle between the Bhatti Rajputs and the Sidhu Brards. It is written in the Tarikh Rajgan Punjab (history of rulers of Punjab) that Brard lost two thousand horsemen and the Bhattis lost even more. But Brard secured his capital and the fort of Bhatinda. Some time after capturing Bhatinda, Brard also established a fort at Bidowal, which had been settled by a Bhatti named Bido a hundred years earlier. Thereafter, Brard dominated the Lakhi Jungle.

When Brard died in 1415 at Bidowal, his son Dull (or Dhool), whose descendent is the Maharaja of FaridKot, became the ruler of Bhatinda while the other son, our ancestor Paur, became chief of the less important Bidowal.

Harassment by the Sidhu Brards made Bhairon, the Bhatti chief of Bhatner, take a drastic action. He gave his daughter to the Muslim king of Delhi and he himself also converted to Islam. Offering a daughter to a king, though he might already have many wives in his harem, was a way to gain his favor. With the religious ties and the kinship by marriage, the Bhatti got the help of the king's forces to slay many of the Sidhu Brards and to drive them out of Bhatinda and Bidowal. For some generations thereafter, the Brards lived in obscurity in villages like Punj Graeen and Kaonke.

The Sidhu Brards were desperate to repossess their ancestral territory. So when Baber, a descendent of Temur the Turk, came from Afghanistan to attack Ibrahim Lodhi of Delhi in 1525CE, the Sidhu Brards, led by Sangher, joined him with 5000 warriors in the Battle of Panipat. After that victory, Baber allotted the chiefdoms of Bhatinda, Bidowal, and Panj Graeen to the Sidhu Brards; Sangher's son Baryam (our ancestor) got Bidowal. But his control was not durable lasting. When Sher Shah Suri drove Humayon son of Baber out of India, the Bhatti of Bhatner, with the help of this Delhi ruler, pushed our ancestor Baryam out of Bidowal. Some years later, Humayon returned to India to attack king Sikander Suri. In that attack Baryam joined Humayon, and after the victory he regained the title to Bidowal. But getting a title from the king was not enough in those days; force was still needed to retain possession of a territory. As he reached Bidowal to assert his control, Baryam was killed; his sons Mehraj and Gharaj were also killed in that battle against the Bhattis. The loss of a great warrior like Mehraj was a big blow to the Sidhu Brards. In later years, the son and the grandson of Mehraj, named Satto and Pakkho, were also killed in the unsuccessful attempts to recapture Bidowal.

Our Village Named After The Warrior Mehraj

The newly converted Muslim Bhatti and even many Hindu rulers were stuffing the harems of the new Emperor of Delhi with their daughters to secure his favors. Emperor Akber, son of Humayon, had started accepting Hindu wives in order to strengthen his rule in the largely Hindu India; thereby he also earned the reputation of being lenient and accommodating toward the Hindus. He even started a new, tolerant religion, called Deen Ellahi. The Sidhu Brards and many Rajputs, who did not resort to such sacrifices of their daughters, lost Akber's sanction of their possessions. But if a chief in a remote area could defeat another by force, the Emperor might be reluctant to intervene, if the new chief was willing to pay tribute. So Mohan, the great grandson of Mehraj, fought several battles with the Bhattis to recapture Bidowal, but he was unsuccessful. In the year 1642, Mohan again led the clan from his Mehraj village in a campaign to recapture his ancestral Bidowal. He died in that battle along with his sons Kul Chand and Roop Chand, the latter being our ancestor and the father of Sandly and Phul. After such losses and with dim prospects, our clan abandoned thoughts of Bidowal territory, until Phul rose to power.

Mohan and his sons had tried to settle in the area east of Bhatinda where the Maan and Bhullar tribes had been dominant. But the Bhullar were opposed to any encroachment by the Sidhu Brards. At that time the Sikh Guru, Har Gobind, was engaged in battles against the forces of the Mughal General, Lalla Beg, at a site now called GuruSar near the present village of Mehraj. Mohan and his sons provided aid to Guru Har Gobind in that struggle, and later they requested the Guru's help in securing land for themselves. When the Guru asked the Bhullars for "one village worth of land" for the Sidhu Brards, their chief, Baghela, replied, "You are asking a village worth of land; we won't give them even a finger width." Then the Guru advised Mohan to move some distance away from the Bhullar stronghold, and "fix a *mohri*" (thorny tree branch, usually used to build a fence) to claim ownership. Ownership of open land used to be asserted by the fixing of a *mohri* into the ground. This mohri was the symbol of a new settlement. The Guru promised that he would help the Sidhu Brards to defend as much land as one of their horsemen could encircle in one day's ride. So a Sidhu horseman encircled and marked approximately one *lakh* (hundred thousand) acres. Mohan established this *mohri* in about 1631 under a *bunn* tree by the Ramsara pond and named the village after his great-grandfather Mehraj who had died in the battle of Bidowal. That bunn tree was still thriving at Ramsara pond in the center of our village when I was a young boy.

It is said that the Bhullars, who considered the Sidhu Brards a menace, came and uprooted the *mohri* and threw it into the Ramsara pond. Mohan complained to the Guru about this bad omen. The Guru is reported to have assured him by saying: "The roots of your *mohri* have gone deep into *pataal* (in other words, a great depth); so no one will be able to uproot your clan from here."

There is a legend about Jad Purana, who was the son-in-law of the Bhullars, and who was feared because of his strong physique. The legend says that once when he was visiting his in-laws, the girls from his in-law village started teasing him in order to test his strength; teasing, taunting, and bantering with the visiting husband of a girl, by a gathering of other girls of the village was, and still is, a social custom. The girls pointed to a wooden post in the courtyard, which was really a small tree stump and was used to tether cattle and horses. They taunted him about his strength and said, 'If you are so strong, pull that wooden post out of the ground.' Jad Purana did not know that the

10

wooden post was really a tree stump. They say that Jad Purana was so strong that he managed to pull the tree stump and all its roots out of the ground.

This legendary Jad Purana, a relative of the Bhullars and therefore an adversary of the Mehraj people, came to clash with the Sidhu Brards over the occupation of land. It is said that Guru Hargobind sent some of his Sikh horsemen in support of the Sidhu Brards and the Guru patted Kala, son of Mohan, on the back for encouragement to fight. Jad Purana advanced on them with the Bhullar supporters. There was a battle in which Kala of Mehraj slew Jad Purana at the sand dune of Gummet. That Gummet Dhora (mound) became a famous landmark and the power of Bhullars was then broken. The Guru's encouraging pat on Kala's back, followed by his victory convinced people in the area that the Sidhu Brards had the blessings of the Sikh Guru on their side. Gradually, there were no Bhullars or Maans left in that territory, and the Sidhu Brards were firmly in control of roughly one lakh acres as their domain of Mehraj, east of Bathinda in Lakhi Jungle.

When I was young, regional names like Lakhi Jungle (great forest), Puadh, Banger, Rohi (desert), Bate, etc., were used for the different regions of the sub-Sutlej Punjab. But now irrigation by canal water has reduced the contrasts between the environments; modern transportation facilities also have made the distances less significant and have created uniformity of speech and customs.

The land of Mehraj village was divided into the four *putti* (domains) of the sons of Mohan: Karm Chand, Dya Chand (Kala), Kul Chand (Saol) and Roop Chand. But since Roop Chand had died in the battle of Bidowal, his putti was named after his son Sandly, our ancestor. There were two other sons of Mohan, named Seman and Sardool, born to a less important wife; those two also were given some land, but not a significant enough tract to form a separate *patti*. In time the family settled into twenty-two villages in the four putti, and their territory came to be called *Bahia* (meaning: of twenty-two villages). We used to count the names of all twenty-two villages and the word Bahia is even now used as a family name by many of our people.

Although the descendents of Mehraj had an adequate amount of land, it only provided subsistence living. Our ancestors were warriors; they received only a portion of whatever the tenant cultivators could produce, depending on rain and subject to other agricultural calamities. There is a story about the descendent of Mehraj, named Kala son of Mohan, who went to pay respects to the Sikh Guru, Hargobind, who had made a sojourn in their territory, according to the traveling customs of holy men. Kala's young, orphaned nephews, Phul and Sandly, tagged along with their uncle to see the Guru. The two little boys were running about with bare torsos in the warm climate, and they playfully started slapping their bellies with their hands. The Guru asked Kala why the children were beating their bellies like drums. Kala casually answered "Guru Ji, my orphan nephews are usually well behaved but they may be hungry; sometimes the aunts are not as attentive to their needs as their mother would be." It is said that the compassionate Guru gave Phul and Sandly a blessing by saying "These boys will be the rulers of territories, and their horses will drink at the banks of Sutlej and Jumna rivers," implying that the extent of their territories would be vast. When Kala came home and told his wife about the Guru's blessings given to his orphan nephews, she said to him "You took these little urchins to see the Guru and got them blessings; what are you doing for your own sons?!" So the next day Kala took

11

his own sons also to the see the Guru and to get them a blessing. The Guru said, "They too will eat their own kill." The meaning of this expression is that 'no one will take from them what is theirs.' To this day there is a joke that the Phulkian princes (the descendants of Phul) got their raj because Phul was "drumming his belly" as if faking hunger before the Sikh Guru.

As the orphan brothers Sandly and Phul grew up, the adventurous Phul (born around 1632 in Mehraj) made his way out of the ancestral village of Mehraj. In 1654 he founded the village Phul (after his own name), about three miles away from Mehraj. Some people say that Phul had to pay a tribute of four camels to the governor of Sirhind in order to be recognized as the head of that territory. Phul built a fort there and in later years, a wall was built around the village of Phul. His crowning glory came in 1659 when he attacked Bidowal, slew many of the Bhatti chiefs in battle, and finally occupied Bidowal, thus avenging the blood of many ancestors. Then he brought many Sidhu families to settle there. Phul's sons established themselves as chiefs of different villages and territories. They provided military and other aid to the Sikh guru, Gobind Singh. The invitation letter of Guru Gobind Singh, written in 1696 to two of Phul's sons, Rama and Tiloka, who had settled in Bhadaur and other territories, contains the words *"Mera Ghar, Tera GharHai,"* i.e., "My house is your house." The words in that letter from the holy Sikh Guru, are still treasured by the descendents of Phul. Our clan felt a special connection to the Sikh Gurus, because the sixth Guru Hargobind helped them to establish their estate (which covered 100 square miles) and then blessed them with his word. Later the tenth guru, Gobind Singh, sought their aid and spent some restful days among them in Talwandi Sabo (now widely known as the site of the shrine of DamDama Sahib), where he devoted time to writing and reflection.

Alla Singh, who died in 1765, and who was the son of Rama and grandson of Phul, ventured out and made Barnala the capital of his newly conquered territory and later founded the city of Patiala. I understand that the Sardars of Rampura and several other chiefdoms, are also from Rama's lineage. The descendents of Tiloka (another son of Phul) founded the states of Nabha and Jind, and became the Sardars of many territories such as Badrukhan, and Dyalpura Mirza.

Alla Singh and the Phulkian *missl* (militia) had played a major part in the 1758 battle of the Sikh missls against the Afghan invader Ahmed Shah Abdali. This was a bad defeat for the Sikhs. Alla was captured by Abdali and his capital of Barnala was sacked. But after recognizing his abilities, Abdali released Alla Singh, and appointed him the governor of Barnala area, because that seemed the best way to administer the territory. A little later when the Sikhs became stronger and the Afghans weakened, the Sikh missls captured the provincial capital of Sirhind. Alla, having played the most prominent part, became the ruler of all the surrounding territories including Sirhind, which had been an important provincial capital, on the road between Delhi and Lahore. But from the Sikh view, Sirhind was a cursed city because Guru Gobind Singh's sons had been buried alive by the ruler there, so the Sikhs practically destroyed Sirhind during its capture. Instead, Alla founded Patiala some distance away, as the capital of his new kingdom, which included the Sirhind territory.

At the establishment of these princely states, whose rulers descended from our village Mehraj, our family name became prominent. The nineteenth-century English historian Sir

Lepel Griffin writes in his book, *Chiefs and Families of Note*: 'Sidhu was a scion of the royal Rajputs of Jaisalmer. Sidhu's descendents are spread all over the eastern Punjab and their blood is the oldest and bluest in the province south and east of the Sutlej river, excepting the chiefs of Simla hills.' Our people had also developed close connections with the Sikh Gurus. After the 1704 battle of Chamkaur, Guru Gobind Singh wrote the *Zafarnama* (note of victory), inviting his adversary Emperor Aurangzeb to come, containing the Persian words: *'Nahin Khatra Zarrah der Een Rah Tura Est, Hameen Qaum Berard der Hukme Mara Est..'* This translates as follows: There is not a grain of danger to you in coming this way; since the entire nation of Brards is under my order... The Sidhu Brards of Mehraj had been independent of any other rulers for some time. The old Moughal Empire maps show our area to be *bey qanoon* (without their rule). Griffin, in one of his historical notes, writes about "The Republic of Mehraj" existing up to 1835, before the British power absorbed it.

But compared to the Phul branch of the family, our people of Mehraj were insignificant; their remaining claim to fame was having the common ancestry with the Phulkian rulers. The Phulkian States survived by aligning with the British and against the strife-torn remnants of the Sikh Empire of Maharaja Ranjit Singh, before the latter were finally defeated in the second Anglo-Sikh War of 1849. From the point of view of the larger Sikh Empire, the stance of the Phulkian princes was a damaging act. But the Phulkian States had felt threatened continuously by Ranjit Singh's intent to absorb them as he had subjugated most other states and Sikh missls north of the Sutlej river. The Phulkian rulers chose to join The British and thus tilted the balance against the Sikh Empire.

Our MehrajKe (of Mehraj) family were not a part of any territory that the British conquered, but were allied with the British just like the Phulkian states. They were not big enough to form a state by themselves and they had no existing ruler who would govern in the new environment. Therefore they were given a choice about the administration of their territory, either to join the Phulkian states or the British-ruled territory. They chose to be a part of the British territory rather than be ruled by the officials of the Maharajas of Patiala or Nabha, although their small territory was totally surrounded by the territories of these princes on all sides. Their attitude was that since they were the equals of the Maharajas, and part of the same family; they would not want to be subject to any servant or the police force of a Maharaja. Our little pocket of the Mehraj territory was far away from any British territory and 70 miles from the British district headquarters of Ferozepur, with Phulkian states and other territories in between. The British gave our Mahrajke family a *sanad*: a binding agreement marked with a seal, which guaranteed that no land tax would be imposed. Unlike other farmers in the country, they were recognized as owners of the land, rather than occupying land that belonged to the crown or a prince. In my days, people still used to sing the little ditty in Punjabi: 'Oh sons of Mohan, what are you worried about? You don't have to pay any land revenue, so bring a bottle and a chicken!'

In earlier times, the Phulkian Maharajas used to come to our village Mehraj, to visit or to ask for manpower to face a threat. By the time my uncle was a young boy, only Hira Singh, the ruler of Nabha, who was popular for his intelligence and informality, ever passed through our village. My uncle told us that Raja Hira Singh used to park his elephant on our side of village Mehraj, under the big Neem tree by the pond, with his

13

horsemen and guards around him. Our Mehraj family was invited by the Phulkian Maharajas to all the important occasions, ceremonies, weddings, coronations, and festivals, just like they invited their closer relatives. But there were so many of us in the extended family of twenty-two villages of Mehraj that we had to select a person or two from each portion of the village to represent us. Sometimes the Maharaja had to arrange tents for the overflow crowd when the number of uninvited guests exceeded plans. My father had represented our *putti*, Sandly, in a wedding or two of the Maharaja's family. Liquor used to flow freely at those celebrations and people who needed opium and other such instruments of pleasure were provided for. Some village people did not really behave properly after getting drunk on unlimited free liquor, but the Maharaja was quite indulgent. He would have standing orders for the police never to arrest the misbehaving *bhaichara* (brotherhood) but just to escort them politely back to their lodging. My elder brother Kartar had gone to Patiala once to attend a celebration in the 1930s, and he received the customary gift on behalf of the Maharaja of Patiala before returning home.

My father, who was conservative in other matters, supported the Phalkion rulers with great enthusiasm; he even admired for Maharaja Bhupinder Singh of Patiala. When Maharaja Bhupinder died in 1938, I heard other people in our village say: "The great Maharaja is no more. His son the new Maharaja Yadvinder might be of impeccable personal conduct, but he is not as big-hearted as his father used to be." They didn't condone the Maharaja Bhupinder's indulgent behavior, his collecting hundreds of wives and concubines and his other extravagances, but they admired that he was passionate about sports and had a magnetic personality.

But the rumors about Maharaja Bhupinder were that any time that he saw a pretty girl, he asked his aides to find out whose daughter she was and how to obtain her. They say that some of the new sardars had received *jagirs* (land grants) from the Maharaja by offering their daughters in marriage to him. In addition, he collected other concubines when he went on trips to the mountain resorts, etc. Some such concubines that he did not want to keep anymore, he unloaded on his cronies and on lesser sardars as "gifts." They say that the Scandal Point, in the hill resort and India's summer capital city of Simla, is so named because of the Maharaja's actions. Maharaja Bhupinder was said to have picked up a niece of the English Viceroy of India at that spot. Some say that the Maharaja took the Viceroy's niece by force and kept her for many days, while others say that she was fascinated by his personality and went with him willingly as a guest.

I had heard these ancestral stories many times as I was growing up and becoming conscious of my surroundings. Bits and parts of these stories were repeated by elders and raconteurs with various degrees of exaggeration. They would mix in some fiction in the process and introduce inconsistencies about time and the characters involved. Such stories provided casual entertainment while sitting in the *sutth* (plaza), or while walking with others to the fields, to fairs and celebrations, or to the market town. Walking was a perpetual activity of life in those days and such entertainment made the trips bearable. Some landmark, or some incident recalled would lead to a connection with the ancestral stories. These stories also came from the words of the *Sansi* (who, in our village, lived on handouts), the *Mirasi* caste singers who specialized in praising people of their ancestors, and the Brahmin (priests) who depended on our people in those times. In the process of flattering the landowners, at the time of weddings, births, and celebrations, and in order

14

to receive favors, they would start with flowery exaggerations about the heritage of the Sidhu Brards. They would say, "O, noble lord, the best of Brard *bans* (dynasty), dweller of *haveli* (mansion), lord of estates, owner of *moti* (pearls), please be generous." Hearing all that praise was enough to give any child a swollen head, even though the descriptions were mostly false; there were no mansions and no pearls and the signs of poverty were plenty even among the landowners. Most of us in the village were poor farmers; the sardars and aristocrats of Punjab were elsewhere, not in our village. Those sardars lived in big mansions, rode horses, entertained themselves by hunting with friends, and never worked with their own hands. They owned villages where the hereditary tenants cultivated their lands; their women were never seen in public; and even their disabled and dysfunctional sons could receive big dowries when the parents of any girl made an offer of marriage. There were many in the Sidhu clan with opium addiction, mediocre intelligence, dysfunctional personalities, and bare subsistence lives, all around us. People used to say: 'To a frog, his pond is the entire universe.' So by recalling their history, the Sidhu Brards of Mehraj still believed that they were better than the real sardars. They just had to close their eyes to the poverty and dreary life of many of their kin.

CHAPTER 2

OUR EXTENDED FAMILY

When my father talked of our extended family, he meant all our people in the twenty-two villages of Mehraj and some more who had settled in other territories. But I will start with the descendents of my ancestor Dhanna, which included the house of Bhan Singh, the house of Aunt Harnami (Harnam Kaur), our house, and four more houses in the outer part of the village. In the 19th century the Jwanda branch of our family, lived across from our houses of the Dhanna branch, but they all moved to the outer part of the village when the space got crowded as they were more numerous than our branch. I remember three older men of the Jwanda branch who were still alive: Bogh Singh, Bhawan Singh and Phumman. Bogh Singh was a tall, gentle fellow, retired from the military. He had purchased a *Thalli Wali* (desert woman) wife. They had one baby who died soon after birth. Phumman, although big and tall, had a high pitched voice and no facial hair. He lived an odd lifestyle like a monk, mostly away from our village, coming back every six months to collect money from those who cultivated his land. Bhagwan Singh had become blind in his old age, his wife Kahno took care of him and they had a married daughter named Ranjitan. By the mid 1940s the entire male line of Jwanda died out, whereas there are more than a hundred people of our Dhanna branch alive now. Our people from the Dhanna branch acquired most of their land, depending on how well each one was able to negotiate. Their abandoned mud structures opposite our old house gradually fell down and the resulting space, which was not large or valuable, was used by our people.

Dhanna's grandsons, my great-grandfather Sajjan Singh and his brother Wazir Singh, lived in the old house in the interior of Mehraj village. That house was probably the site of the original house of our ancestor Sandly at about the time of the founding of the village since it was on the highest central spot. The houses of the three branches of his descendents started outward from that point and rainwater from that vicinity flowed down in all other directions. As they grew up and separated, great grandfather Sajjan built his own house adjacent to the ancestral house which his brother Wazir inherited, probably about the time that the British conquered Punjab in mid-19th century.

Wazir had a son, Sucha Singh, who died when I was about four years old. I remember trailing after my mother as she had gone to borrow fire from their hearth next door, in

Map of Old Punjab

Sodagar, Gurnam, Amar Nath and Harnek on March 1, 1946.

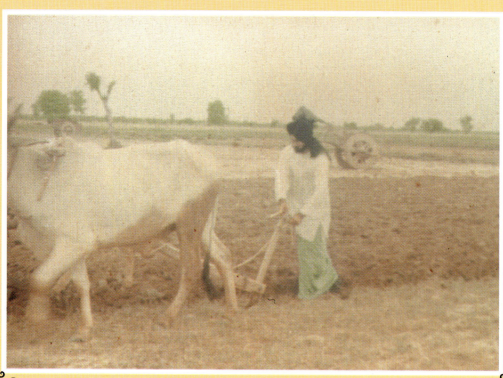

Author refreshing his plowing skills during a trip to India.

Author in Punjabi village clothes with uncle Trilok Singh.

A Farmer with Oxcart loaded with animal fodder & people.

A couple dressed up in Punjabi rural style.

A Farmer taking his camel cart to the market.

order to start the fire in our own. It was customary to borrow a sizzling tinder or cow-dung patty from the neighbor's mud stove or oven; one did not need to ask permission because such stoves and ovens were usually not behind closed doors. That day, when we found Sucha Singh lying motionless on his *charpai* in the courtyard in the middle of the afternoon my mother was concerned. As he did not appear to be breathing; she addressed him loudly "Baba Ji, Baba Ji, Baba Ji!" It was usually considered immodest for a woman to talk to a senior male in-law, but this was a serious situation, so she had no choice. And hearing no response from him, she called out to aunt Harnam Kaur (Harnami) whose house was on the other side of our own. My mother said to her, "Bebe Ji, something has happened to Baba." A few minutes later, the death of Sucha Singh was confirmed. But he was probably 60 years old; so this was not considered an untimely death in those days. Sucha Singh also had a sister, Maha Kaur, who was married into the village of TaamKot. She was important to my father and his brothers, as the closest living female relative when both of my father's parents died of plague within one week of each other (in 1903 or thereabouts).

Sucha Singh was the father of two sons, Bhag and Bhan, and two daughters, Santi and Nikki. Later on, Bhag would have two sons, Sarwan and Kulwinder with a Chinese wife whom he had married in Hong Kong. His younger brother Bhan had ten sons and two daughters. I remember having seen all of these people except Sajjan Singh, Wazir Singh and Maha Kaur, when I was young. Although our common ancestor was four generations before me, we considered the descendents of all those mentioned above as one family, for weddings and funerals. In fact for most occasions we included all the people in our extended family connected to us about eight generations back.

Shum Koo, My Chinese Aunt

The Chinese wife of uncle Bhag Singh, mentioned above, needs describing because her situation was so unusual. Like many other Punjabi Sikhs, Bhag had gone to work in Hong Kong, where he learned to read and speak the Chinese language. He married a Chinese woman there, as he was in Hong Kong for 21 years without returning to India even once. I remember the day in 1939 when he arrived and told us "It has been 21 years and 14 days since I left the village." Their son, named Sarwan, probably a year younger than me, was born in Hong Kong and was in school there before World War II. When Sarwan arrived in the village with his father, he spoke Chinese and some elementary English, but he spoke no Punjabi.

Bhag Singh, a man of high integrity and great honesty, could also be a man of wild excesses; the stories of his drinking and defiant behavior from his days before going to Hong Kong were still well known in the village. He would do things with flair and drama in Hong Kong too. The tales of his becoming wealthy in Hong Kong, being drunk, out of control, sleeping on bedspreads of currency notes to show contempt for money, gambling, eating opium, becoming poor and wealthy again, along with other tales, at least some of which were probably exaggerated, traveled to our village by word of mouth.

But Bhag Singh was totally broke when he returned from Hong Kong. His younger brother Bhan, who still lived in the village, had to send him money to Hong Kong to pay for his fare back to the village. In those days, subsistence living could always be provided by the ancestral land and there was always the ancestral house in the village for everyone to return to. A few months later his Chinese wife also came from Hong Kong. After separating his half of the family land from that of his younger brother, Bhag Singh started working on his farm. His wife provided support, but in our families women did not do actual farm work; the only farm tasks that our women could do were to feed the milk buffalo at home, to take lunch for workers in the fields, and to pick cotton during the season along with the hired women.

I knew Uncle Bhag to be very honest, straight talking, a little gruff but generous of heart; he was never petty in personal relations with other people. But he could be rude and physically violent to his wife when he was in a drunken state; so she was resentful of his behavior. In 1939 when he had decided to come back from Hong Kong to India, his wife, whose real name was Shum Koo although she was also given a Punjabi name, Ranjit Kaur, decided not to come with him to our village. He brought his son Sarwan with him; apparently a husband had more right over his children than a wife did in those days. But as the fear of war and of the Japanese occupation came upon her, she decided to travel from Hong Kong to Punjab some months later. My cousin Sarwan told me that her reason to come to India was the concern for his (her son) welfare; she feared that Bhag Singh could marry another wife who might not treat the boy properly. Our village was not a comfortable place for a lady from Hong Kong in the 1930s. Her skin was several shades paler even than that of her light-skinned husband, and with her distinctly chinese features, she stood out.

Shum Koo was a strong minded woman and coped as well as she could since she had no other good options. But her urban Chinese heart could never accept the harsh and strange life in rural Punjab. She had another son named Kulwinder in late 1941; he was nicknamed Chitta (white) because of his lighter complexion compared to others in the neighborhood. But since Shum Koo could not pronounce the Punjabi sounds exactly, she called him Cheeta. In 1948, after living through the religious massacres related to the Partition of India, she left our village to live in a Chinese community in Calcutta, 1000 miles from her sons. She wrote to them a few times, inviting them to visit, but they never saw her again.

The boys, Sarwan Singh and Kulwinder Singh, grew up to be like other Sikh men in our culture, solid citizens without any indication (except a very slight influence on features) of their Chinese heritage. The younger son Kulwinder (Cheeta) joined the Indian Army for a while, but got an early discharge and came back to dabble in electrical gadgets. Later he lived a life of leisure as a gentleman farmer in the village and became a locally influential wise man. Cheeta could quote the Sikh scriptures and ancient sayings to make his point, although he was not too religious. His older brother, Sarwan, taught in a school in Punjab for a while but then migrated to England. Having been born in Hong Kong, he was entitled to a British passport; so after 1960 he worked and lived in England. Sarwan was an intelligent and warm-hearted man like his father; he and I shared many wonderful activities together during our boyhood. Although he was about my age or a bit younger, he was three or four years behind me in school because he had to learn Punjabi and Urdu after he arrived in the village and then start school in the first grade.

18

At about this time, there were a couple of other Chinese women who also arrived in our village, following their husbands. At least one of them left a daughter with the husband's family in our village; but none of the Chinese women stayed there for life. These other Chinese women seemed to be good-humored and gregarious, not tough and rigid in attitude as Shum Koo was.

Aunt Shum Koo lived the life of a farmer's wife for a couple of years and then she opened a shop of miscellaneous goods in the front portion of her house. But she never really liked the village life. She did not smile much, or indulge in friendly idle chatter as the village people usually did. I did not see her laugh much, although she would sing Chinese songs while working. Some people said that she was cold-hearted and had no warmth in her, but it might all have been because of the language problem. Foreign races were accused of being strange by the village people, unless they made special efforts to assimilate. While an Indian face had all its owner's changing emotions written on it, you could not tell from Shum Koo's face whether she was angry or pleased with you. She was very business-like, in a culture where people were informal and shared everything, including gossip, with others of their neighborhood. She never wasted time in socializing or associating with other women of the village. There were wives from other cultures (mostly from the desert) who gradually mixed in our community, participated in community celebrations and festivities, and became just like our own people; but Shum Koo never wanted to be one of our people. She never learned to, or could not, pronounce the Punjabi sounds properly. She always wore Chinese clothes and went about with a bare head while every village wife covered her head with a veil and covered her face from their in-laws' elders. Going out with a bare head was considered immodest, brazen, and even a bad omen, but Shum Koo seemed to look at the Indians with contempt and to consider them backward. She did not want to conform to the rural ways and probably thought they were uncivilized. She did not like Punjabi food but prepared whatever she could in the Chinese style. She could slaughter chicken and other animals with her own hands, while most people in the village did not eat meat; the village women thought she had to have a tough heart to grab and kill animals. When she left in 1948, the village women would say "What kind of hearts do these foreign women have! She sent away her young son from Hong Kong in 1939; and now she is leaving two sons and her family here; no wonder she can kill an animal with her own hands so easily. These foreign people have no heart; they are too businesslike." But obviously, she missed her own culture, community, food, and the comforts of city life. Punjab rural life was quite primitive in those days and she might have felt isolated from her own people. Since she never had close associations with other women, her life must have been somewhat lonely in the nine years she spent in our village. Sometimes she would offer coins to the boys if they caught fish for her from the irrigation ditches. Village people thought that her food of various critters and weeds was so strange and she felt the same way about theirs. In everyday life, Shum Koo never showed much emotion except some annoyance and anger. Those men of our village who had known her in Hong Kong said that her temperament was unusual and that not all Chinese women were so business-like. Her husband's drinking and other habits also made her life difficult. Ironically, after her departure her husband quit drinking and other destructive habits, and became a very respected wise man.

Shum Koo may not have been sentimental and friendly, but she was very disciplined, honest, and ethical. She kept a retail shop of miscellaneous supplies in the village and would treat even ignorant customers quite fairly. Once when I was buying one measure of melons for an equal measure of wheat grain from a street hawker, she scolded me for being made a sucker by the hawker. She said in broken Punjabi "Melons are two *paisa* per *ser* (about a kilo), wheat is eight paisa per ser; you are giving four times as much as you are receiving; what kind of education are you getting in your school!" But her pronunciation of each sound was so different from normal Punjabi that the children remembered and mimicked sentences like these frequently for entertainment. She could not pronounce the Punjabi consonants correctly; so she depended mainly on vowels, and she omitted the verbs for "is," "was," and "have," in her speech. And since the neighborhood children addressed my uncle Tiloka as "Taya" (senior uncle), she also called him Taya once when she asked for help. This faux pas was a big joke in the neighborhood where women had to be careful how they talked to a senior in-law. When it was a question of taking care of farm animals or other tasks, she could act like a man, while most local wives would act a little coy and delicate. I think she was one of the best-looking Chinese women I have known: tall and slim in stature, with good skin, nice hair, a square face, and a well-shaped nose and eyes. The village kids always had anecdotes and humorous things to tell about her speech, her food habits, and her ways of working.

No Daughters for Three Generations!

My great grandfather Sajjan had no daughters, and nor did my grandfather. The fact that there were no surviving girls in our family until my sisters, is a bit suspicious but we are told that my father's mother never bore or killed any baby girls. Sajjan had three sons that lived to be adults: Jewna (or Jivna), the eldest, my grandfather Jagat Singh (Jagta), and the youngest, Bhagta. They all had died before I was born, but my oldest sister saw Jewna and Bhagta. My grandfather Jagta had died when my father was about seven years old, so none of us saw any paternal grandparents. Jewna had three daughters, two of whom had their own families in village Raiya. Since my father did not have any sisters, we would go to visit these daughters of Jewna who were my nearest paternal aunts. Jewna's older son Amolak (1869-1967) had worked in Amritsar for some time as a machinist or technician of some kind. He had been married and widowed and then had gone to work in Hong Kong. After returning from Hong Kong, he lived in our house for many years, instead of living in his own house with his brother. But then he went back to Hong Kong again in about 1937. He was stuck there during World War II and on his return after the war he related some bad experiences during the Japanese occupation. Back in the village as an unmarried adult, Amolak again ate and lived in our house and not with his brother. He wore clean clothes and was a methodical thinker. He did not do much farm work, but he would graze our cattle and he used to bring *ber* (wild fruit) for us from the fields. In principle, he would have a half share in his brother's inherited house and land, but unmarried men usually did not assert such rights; they lived with whichever relative they felt comfortable with and did whatever work they could do for that house. We already had a big family and one more person to feed made no difference. All he required was a bed somewhere;

and in a farming household, the presence of any additional man was beneficial. He kept a big *petti*, a locked wooden box about 12 cubic feet in size, in his brother's house for his special possessions, but he would visit that house only occasionally. We heard many stories from him about the younger days of uncle Amolak, who, as a young boy grazing his cattle, saw the first digging of canals and the first arrival of trains in the 1870s, a couple of decades after the British conquest of Punjab.

Jewna's younger son Channan, nicknamed Viceroy, died in about 1944; Viceroy's wife Gulabo and their five daughters all died young in the 1940s, thus ending Jewna's family in Mehraj.

CHAPTER 3

MY GRANDPARENTS LOST TO PLAGUE

My grandfather Jagat Singh (Jagta), the second of three brothers, was described as a short man with a bad temper. He had become a widower and then he was married again to Maano of village Kanganwal. My grandmother Maano was reputed to have been a beautiful woman with delicate features and great social graces, as we heard some stories about her from her contemporaries. Jagta was able to get such a second wife, obviously not because of his personal qualities or wealth; they say "People would marry their daughter even to a dog of Mehraj in those days, because of the prestige of the Sidhu Brard name." Bhagta, the third son of Sajjan, renounced worldly life and became a *sadhu* (Hindu holy man). Such sadhus did not have wives and families. So out of the three brothers, only Jagta's male offspring survived in Mehraj.

Jagta and Maano had four boys: Trilok Singh (Tiloka), Naginder Singh (my father), Inder Singh (Nikk) and Mohinder Singh. These boys were at approximate ages 9, 7, 5 and 2 when their parents died of plague within a few days of one another, around the turn of the century, probably in the year 1903. My father, Naginder Singh, did not like to discuss this much; but once he described his mother's death with great emotion to my sisters. First his father died. Sensing the house as a source of the plague, my grandmother took the young boys out of the house and moved to an open field outside the village so that her children would not get the disease. But the plague must have been incubating within her, because she developed plague symptoms within days of becoming a widow. And when she was about to die, she told her oldest son how to look after the younger ones, and where to get help. And finally she told the boys to go and bring a sadhu from the *dera* (monastery) so that she could donate grain to the holy man with her own hands, in hope that she would get a reward of grain in the next life. By the time the sadhu came, she was severely ill. She had no strength except to ritually touch the sack of grain she wanted the holy man to carry away with him, and she died very shortly thereafter.

In such situations, the most suitable and caring person for custody of the orphans would be an affluent female blood relation. But Naginder's maternal relatives had also all died at about the same time, probably of the same plague. His father had no sisters (so the boys had no aunt), which would normally be the next best situation. Fortunately, there was Maha Kaur, the daughter of Naginder's grandfather's brother Wazir, a married woman with good land holdings in the village of Taamkot, about 25 miles away. Being from the same clan was as good as an immediate relative. So this aunt was able to take two of the boys, Tiloka and Nikk, to her house in Taamkot. The other two, Naginder and Mohinder, were sent to live with their sadhu uncle, Bhagta, in the town of Bhatinda.

Baba Bhagta was not a sadhu of the nude body, ash-smeared, variety; he had his own *dera*, disciples, property, money flow from the offerings of devotees, and some esoteric learning. But according to my father, he was also a disci-plinarian and a hard taskmaster; he had a mean temper and a sadistic streak. At least this is the impression I had from my mother and father for years, although my brother Kartar thinks that is a one-sided judgment of the old holy man.

My father Naginder and his brother Mohinder were beaten frequently for any perceived lack of diligence in work, for any delay or imperfection in the accomplishment of assigned tasks, and for other faults of omission and commission. Such tasks could include cooking for the sadhu and his disciples, cleaning utensils, hauling water, and other household chores, in addition to school work. My father was a scholar by inclination but the environment and opportunities were never favorable for the realization of his potential. The situation in Bhatinda should have provided an automatic opportunity for education, as there was no farm work to be done. But being in too big a hurry to get away from his tyrannical uncle in Bathinda, he never finished high school and quit in the ninth grade. My father said that he and his brother were always wishing for an end to the daily ordeal. He would describe how he sometimes used to watch helplessly when his brother Mohinder was being beaten by the sadhu with a flexible stick that could make the blood ooze from the skin of the child, and how he would wish their parents were alive. The other two brothers, Tiloka and Nikk, lived in a relatively indulgent environment as "guests" in the aunt's household in Taamkot 25 miles away. They got used to grazing cattle and learned to plow the fields. They were not spoiled as they could have been in a maternal grandparents' household, since they actually had to work, but the aunt treated them with as much kindness as she would treat her own children. The question of any education for Tiloka and Nikk was unthinkable, however, in a place where there were no schools, and none of the farmers, even though they were landowners, were literate.

Return of the Orphans and the Rise of Tiloka

When my uncle Tiloka came into his mid-teens, he and his brother Nikk returned from Taamkot to the ancestral home and to our meager land holdings in Mehraj. In general, when someone was away for a long time or in service in a far away place, it was expected that the nearest relative would take control of his house and land without any formal agreement. On return he would start living with these relatives and slowly start taking charge of his share of the property. But since my grandfather's older brother Jewna had his separate house, our house probably had just been locked up for a few years after my grandparents died. The family land was not enough even for "two oxen and a plough." But in that society, being the son of a landowner Jat, where all the Jats were related, conferred a certain degree of standing on you. And that intangible status and standing were like capital assets. Whereas a low-caste person with the same economic assets could never go beyond where he was stuck, there was nothing to limit a Jat boy except his own initiative and hard work. So Tiloka, now back in Mehraj, started land cultivation with all seriousness. Their Sadhu uncle tried to tempt Naginder into staying with him with the offers of his wealth (yes, the holy men could accumulate wealth and property, from donations and land income). But Naginder and Mohinder had such bitter memories of so many years of abuse that they could not accept his offers and they came home to join their brother Tiloka. After some setbacks, with hard work and discipline, Uncle Tiloka started the joint family of the four brothers on a ramp to prosperity.

Uncle Tiloka was of a gentle and reflective nature, probably like his mother. He was tall, broad shouldered, of medium build, with gentle eyes, a high-bridged nose, a luxuriant beard, a broad forehead, and high cheekbones. Although totally illiterate, he would tie his turban like an educated Sikh gentleman when he was not in the midst of farm work. Other farmers would never tie their turbans like the educated people. Young village men took pride in looking rough and rude, which later became an adult habit. Tiloka had gotten into some skirmishes with men who had the reputation of being aggressive, nasty, and violent to others, but not many people were willing to tangle with him, since he was a strong young man and had three brothers. Once an elder said to a group of such violent fellows: "Don't mistake the gentle nature of our *munda* (boy) Tiloka; he will smash your bones if you mess with him." Calling the grownup man "Munda" seemed strange to the listeners, and Tiloka, the head of our large household, was teasingly called "Munda" by his friends for many years thereafter.

His reputation as a trustworthy, hardworking and upright man was soon established. Money lenders trusted and respected him. They would say "Trilok Singh, take some money and use it to rent or buy land; you can pay back when you sell the crop." But they would not lend easily to other people who really needed help. In the years before and even during the Great Depression, our family made money by growing crops and farming efficiently because of his leadership. Uncle Tiloka never learned to sign his name and always had to use his thumb print, yet he understood the use of money and took small opportunities to make things profitable. He would go to cattle fairs and buy animals that were low-priced but had the potential of increasing in value within a year or two. For example, he would buy a buffalo that was not giving milk but had possibilities after insemination and calving. He would select a calf that could become an ox in a couple of years, or a young camel that, after some training, would be able to pull a plough and carry loads and riders. It was always possible to find areas where certain kind of animals were cheaper and of better quality than in other areas. When my uncle bought new animals, we as children were fascinated and delighted to watch them as we evaluated their looks and habits. But of course actually making money was subject to many pitfalls and never easy. Although shop keeping was considered a degrading occupation for the landowner Jats, buying and selling cattle was considered a normal part of farm life. In support of trading, Tiloka himself used to cite a little rhyme telling how Temur the Lame (Temurlane, great-grandfather of Baber) grew up grazing goats, was a trader, and later became a king and conqueror: *"Temur Lang beopari; bakkri chari, paisa banaya, bana beopari"* and so on. There were other sayings he lived by, such as the Persian: *"Qatra qatra, mei shawad darya,"* i.e., "Drop by drop, it becomes a river." He gathered even small spills of grain to avoid waste. Young girls would laugh and say "If Uncle Tiloka sees a bit of cotton lying in the courtyard, he picks it up, shakes off the dirt and brings it to put into the pile in the house; he never allows any waste." Other farmers would consider such a practice to be demeaning. Being careless of little things and being wasteful was the prestigious thing to do, but Uncle Tiloka thought waste was immoral.

He would tell the story of a rich merchant who was about to pour the foundation for a new mansion. It was a custom to pour a little *ghee* into the foundation before starting construction, for good omen and to assure good fortune. But this prosperous merchant had a whole canister of ghee ready to pour into the foundation, when a fly fell into the canister of ghee. The merchant removed the fly from the ghee with his finger; but before throwing it away, he carefully squeezed the fly into the canister to recover all the ghee that was sticking to the fly. And then he poured the canister of ghee into the foundation. People who watched such a rich man squeezing ghee from the dirty fly were shocked and asked why such a wealthy man would go to such extremes to save a trivial amount of ghee, especially when the ghee was going to be poured into the ground anyway. The merchant said, "The ghee sticking to the fly was a waste, and that is why I squeezed the fly; but for an appropriate cause I am willing to expend the whole canister of ghee." Uncle Tiloka was not quite the fly-squeezer that the rich man was, but he hated any waste. In fact he could be quite generous to us and to his brothers when it was appropriate. And he believed that if you worked steadily, and accumulated little by little, you would succeed in improving your condition. He was a great advocate of hard work and progress. He would say: "In Frang (Persian name for Europe) people have made much progress and have created a paradise; they say that in the city of Paris, the roads are made of rubber and the houses are made of glass." To him, this meant that on their roads your wagon wouldn't hit ruts and bumps; and what could be cleaner and brighter than a house made of glass!

There were other village people who went to regions like Hissar, Balhotra, Parwersar and Nagaur in the desert of Rajputana to buy camels and oxen, and they brought them to Punjab for profit or for personal use. But some of those journeys could take more than a month, and only people whose presence at home was not essential, or professional traders, would go that far. Uncle Tiloka, being the head of our farming operation, could not take that much time for secondary activities like animal trading; his efforts were limited to the cattle fairs in southern Punjab. His younger brother, Nikk, who was somewhat handicapped, could do jobs like cattle grazing but not hard or skillful farm work. So keeping and raising animals for profit was also a part of Trilok Singh's way of providing suitable work for everyone. In his farming setup, these methods of buying and maintaining animals for profit worked with great difficulty and never with any spectacular success. The important part of our income was from the crops of cotton, wheat, chickpea, mustard, and barley, while corn, millet, and beans were the minor summer crops.

In the village of Mehraj, where bare subsistence was the pattern of most peoples' lives, our farming operation became one of the largest, and by the 1930s Uncle Tiloka became much respected around the area. We had not only enough land for two ploughs to cultivate with our hired workers, but also some additional land to give to independent sharecroppers. There was no serendipity, no clever methods, no windfall, or any stroke of good fortune. It was just a matter of breaking the lands with the wooden plough, sowing the seeds and nourishing the crops; we lived by economizing to the extreme, with utmost efficiency. It was continuous, bone-breaking hard work, persistence, and discipline that brought some measure of success. During the Depression, many village people who already owned enough land were actually getting poorer and losing their lands by selling it bit by bit, in order to live. But to Tiloka and his brothers, anyone who spent more than he earned was committing an economic sin and being disgraceful. There were setbacks, like a dead ox, a pregnant buffalo that aborted, or the slow, painful, withering and burning of crops for lack of rain in some years, but the steady and persevering nature of the brothers rode it all out. Real affluence was still out of reach, as the scale of operations was limited. But by the 1930s, the illiterate orphaned young man who had started from scratch had brought himself and his brothers a long way by sheer hard work and discipline. And this was at a time when many owners of land were facing poverty, incurring ever bigger debts and bankruptcies because of the worldwide economic depression.

Uncle Tiloka, the head of our household, would say *"Badda bubber, badda tubber, badda nugger"* which means that big tummy, big family, and big town can all create difficult problems. That thought was contrary to the popular thinking where big tummy, big family, and big village, were all considered desirable and prestigious. Being fat signified good health and prosperity, there was strength and safety in numbers in a large family, and there were many benefits and security in a bigger village. Uncle Tiloka was a natural leader who could gather many other men of the brotherhood in the village for any big task, if and when he needed them. In my memory, he was the quintessential patriarch. Men would willingly volunteer for a project whenever he asked them. People in the village did not respect my father the way they respected my uncle. On major decisions Uncle Tiloka would consult my father (as he himself was completely illiterate); so he worked by consensus and consultation. He decided who should be put to what work, which sharecroppers to hire for the next year, how many laborers to get for the harvest each day, what crop to plant in which field, which field needed to be gathered first, what major purchases to make that year, and when to sell the grain or cotton. In my entire life, I never heard of an incident of conflict or disharmony between my father and Uncle Tiloka. My father pretty much obeyed his older brother, a pattern that was not unusual in our society, where respecting the older person was considered a virtue.

Uncle Tiloka was in control of all of our family money and was the holder of the keys to the family safe. That safe was a steel box weighing more than a couple of hundred pounds, with multiple keys and with chambers within chambers. I remember that when Uncle Tiloka used to open the main lock and lifted the heavy door of the safe, other locking compartments were revealed, and they required separate keys to open. It had writing on it in Urdu, with the name of its manufacturer in Gujranwala (now in Pakistan). As a child I had never seen the inside of the safe, except from a distance. I used to feel that the safe and those *behi* (record books) in it were mysterious and forbidden things. I remember that Uncle Tiloka would spread a sheet on the floor near the safe and would arrange the silver rupee coins in little towers of twenty each. These towers of twenty would be arrayed in rows and columns of five or ten on each side, so he could count the total, because like every other illiterate person, he could count by twenties only. He knew that ten tens or five twenties made a hundred, and ten hundreds made a thousand. There were never any occasions to count beyond a thousand, although the village people knew the words *lakh* (hundred thousand) and *crore* (10 million).

Paper currency had not yet become common in the thirties. I remember the Victorian

26

coins of India which showed Queen Victoria with braid and crown. In later years the head of Edward VII was bare on the coins, and then coins of George V showed him with a beard, crown and jacket. I remember when Emperor George V died in 1936, Edward VIII got involved with the divorcee Mrs. Simpson; so George VI was placed on the British throne. Then the new coins had the picture of George VI, with a shaved face and his crowned head shown only above the neck; they used to call the new coins "neck cut."

Apart from counting the rupee coins, Uncle Tiloka also had to make sure that the coins were good. In those days, one in every few coins could be a counterfeit. People could easily pass the base coins to you if you were not watchful, and those coins were worthless in the hands of an honest man. The base coins could superficially look like the regular coins, with subtle differences in texture, weight, or color of the metal. The standard practice was to put the coin on the tips of the first two fingers, strike the coin with the thumb nail from below and listen for the characteristic "clean sound" as you struck it and flung the coin into the air to catch it. The base coins would have a dull or different sound and once you got stuck with them, you could go after the previous owner of the bad coin but not honestly pass the base coins to someone else. The other person could deny having passed the base coin to you and disputes could arise easily. There were some con artists who specialized in passing base coins to shopkeepers, creditors, and unsuspecting innocents by various ruses and tricks. When the rupee notes were introduced, the ignorant Jats thought they were worthless pieces of paper because they had no silver in them; but the knowledgeable Hindu shopkeepers thought they were a boon, because they did not have to fear the plague of base coins anymore.

In our safe, my uncle also kept any gold ornaments and precious things that the family owned. But whenever I tried to get a closer look inside the safe or its contents, he would say that children should stay away from such things. People were secretive about expensive things and did not want anyone else to know the extent of their possessions. The other important things that were kept in the safe were the *behi* (or *bahi*). These behi were record books that could be a more than an inch thick and somewhat long. The flexible, cloth-reinforced cardboard bindings of the behi allowed it to be folded once and tied with a string. Only the very important agreements, events, and transactions were recorded in these behi, and such recording was usually done by a banker/merchant or Brahmin. Since the farmers were illiterate, they could only put their thumb-print on the agreements in the behi, which had to be read or written by some trusted outsider. My father started recording the important agreements in the behi, as he was as educated as any Brahmin or shopkeeper in the village. There could be some Gurmukhi or Urdu writing, but the early writings by merchants/bankers could also be in Hindi or Landha or some older scripts. Things related to major money transactions, land sale pledges, things related to important events like marriage or death, *neonda* (contributions of money by relatives or community members at a marriage), and even sharecropper agreements were recorded with the thumb-prints of the individuals. We still have some behi from the nineteenth century, but they are musty and crumbling. There was always something foreboding, secret, or hush-hush about those behi; I was not old enough to be involved in business affairs or to have access to the behi, nor could I read those scripts.

To me as a little child, Uncle Tiloka felt like a benevolent monarch in whose kingdom there was no fear and no scarcity, and who would take care of me if something went wrong. He also provided little pleasures by giving me rides on the camel and by bringing some goodies for all the children when he came home from work or from the market. The children saw nothing negative or fearful in him, although we could be afraid of our own father and critical our own mother. We all loved him unconditionally, because he was sympathetic and there was never any harshness in his ways. As an old man now I feel that there is nothing I would not give up to live the life of a ten-year-old in our joint family under Uncle Tiloka's regime.

In his personal life, Trilok Singh was not a lucky man. He had been married before the age of twenty according to the customs of the day; but his wife died after only a couple of years of marriage, and his infant son died just before her. He never got married again, and in the joint family system, he treated all his nephews and nieces as his own children. After the breakup of the joint family of his brothers in 1945, Trilok Singh, his dreams broken, lived some of the time in Talwara where we owned land on the Rajputana-Punjab border. Our family had some land left there even after the old sadhu Bhagta had sold most of the acreage some decades earlier. My brother Kartar helped Uncle Trilok Singh acquire some additional land. There in Talwara, Trilok Singh still wanted to build something big for his nephews and nieces, as was always his dream. He was well known among the older men in that village. For a brief time there was a new village named Dhani Trilok Singh (Group of Trilok Singh) of farming and grazing families on his land. But during the "development projects" of the 1950s, the Government acquired that land by eminent domain. They thus took away land from everyone, and assigned them compensation or land elsewhere and forced their departure. This wiped out all traces of the Trilok Singh Village.

After moving to Talwara, Uncle Trilok Singh would come to our Mehraj village for visits. When he could simplify his affairs in Talwara, he would spend weeks and months in Mehraj. His dream of our family of 20 people growing and prospering together was never to be. The acrimony between the families of his married brothers who had wives and children, Naginder and Mohinder, never ceased over one issue or the other. Uncle Trilok Singh and Nikk, as the unmarried brothers, were then considered temporary entities; it was expected that without any heirs, their property would come to the married brothers' families automatically. So Uncle Tiloka's share of the land and house was taken by Uncle Mohinder, and my father controlled the land of Uncle Nikk after the family breakup, even though the brothers were only around 50 years old. A single brother could eat and sleep in the married brother's house and could negotiate his other needs, but his land was in the control of the married brother.

We used to think that Uncle Tiloka was a strong man with good health. But I remember that during my visit in 1967 he complained about the occasional severe pain that traveled from his chest to his shoulders and neck. That would suggest some heart or artery condition; and nowadays such a condition could be corrected. But we thought that was just pain due to old age and we were unaware that anything could be done about it. Like other village people, Uncle Tiloka thought that garlic had curative values and restored good health. So on some days when he did not feel well, he would ask my sisters to fry some garlic in about a quarter pound of ghee. Then he would drink the ghee and eat the fried garlic cloves. Drinking a bowl full of melted butter was a common practice among young men, because they thought that ghee was pure strength, as proved by the subsequent weight gain. Only now do we realize that so much butter was not good for his arteries. The grand old man Trilok Singh died in late 1967 at the age of 73, while he was sleeping in our front *bethik* (sitting room). I was in the United States at the time of his death, and I had seen my beloved uncle for the last time during my visit to India in April 1967. In my childhood many families in our village used to worship some ancestors. Uncle Tiloka would certainly be a worthy object of such ancestor worship. We have built a schoolroom in our village in his name. Although he himself never went to any school, he made it possible for me and my siblings to be educated. Without his initiative, support, and nurturing, we could never be where we are today.

Naginder Singh Joined Patiala Lancers

An unfortunate dispute between my uncle Tiloka and his sadhu uncle Bhagta led to some drastic changes in the lives of the four brothers. The sadhu had come from Bhatinda with his disciples to our family home in Mehraj, and while his nephews were out, he proceeded to take away the family safe and some other things that he wanted. This safe was a steel box weighing more than a couple of hundred pounds. It was inherited by my grandfather Jagta when he inherited the house, as his older brother Jewna had already separated from the family and built his house at the periphery of the village. Since Bhagta, the youngest, had left to become a sadhu many years earlier, his rights to take away any family property were not clear according to the prevailing customs. But as my grandfather Jagta had died many years earlier, the sadhu felt that he, and not his young nephews, should have control over the common family property.

The holy sadhu had been annoyed with my uncle Tiloka, and he was not quite detached from material acquisitions. Doors in the village were rarely locked in those days. The locked door of a substantial house in the village would be an ominous sight. One of the curses in the villages used to be: "May your house be locked for ever." Anyway, when the sadhu and his disciples were removing the family safe, someone ran to the fields and informed Tiloka of this raid on the family assets and Tiloka came home in a rage. Being a strong young man, Tiloka caught up with the carriage of the sadhu. He beat up the disciples and during the fight he broke the arm of his sadhu uncle and he brought the safe back to the family home. This led the sadhu to press assault charges and seek Tiloka's arrest and prosecution. He also asked Naginder (my father) to be a witness against Tiloka, with some threats if he refused to testify, although Naginder never saw the incident. Naginder was in a dilemma. There was no way he was going to be a false witness against his older brother, but the wrath of the powerful sadhu uncle could be damaging. Naginder went to consult his Taamkot cousins and they advised him to go away somewhere or to join the military, so that he would not be available as a witness. The First World War was in progress at the time. So he joined The Patiala Lancers as a cavalryman (In those days, the troopers still used horses to mount and were trained to use lances as well as rifles.), even though he was married at the time. Whenever a husband was absent for any length of time, it was common for his wife to go to live in her parents' village, especially if she had no grown children, as was the case with my mother, Bhag Bharii.

Trilok Singh got three months in jail for his use of force and causing injury. As revenge, the sadhu also sold the *biswa* (one-twentieth of a village) of land that we owned in Talwara, Rajputana. That was the land in which my father and his brothers had tried to settle once, but had abandoned temporarily because of the difficulties; they were planning to reclaim the land from bushes, trees and wild grass. That land would have stayed in their possession if the sadhu had not sold it. Although in those days that wild land was not of much value, it is very precious and quite productive now. The brothers also forfeited all possibilities of getting any part of the holy uncle's wealth. The sadhu would still occasionally ask Naginder Singh to come and live with him. He wanted one of the brothers to become the official disciple to control the dera (monastery) income and wealth; but none of the brothers took advantage of such offers from the holy man. The dera was in theory a holy institution, but in practice it could be the sadhu's personal fiefdom until the Gurdwara Act was passed in the 1920s. Then some of the Hindu-style deras, in which the Sikh holy book might also be recited, were made into Sikh gurdwaras. Some holy men were able to prevent the conversion of their deras into gurdwaras, by removing the Granth (the holy book of the Sikhs) and claiming that they were traditional Hindus.

World War I ended without Naginder Singh seeing any action. He was in the forces of Patiala, a princely state which, although under the influence of the British Empire, was not directly under the British rule, and this delayed deployment. After World War I, he was discharged for being too weak (thin) for his height, as only the best physical specimens among the soldiers were retained after the war was over. He said, "The doctor decided that I was not substantial enough as I had lost some weight because of a temporary illness, and they wanted to keep only the healthiest-looking men." He would tell us stories later about his days in service, about how good a marksman he was, how good a horseman he was, how his *saees* (horse groom and caretaker) massaged the horse and made its coat shine every day, how they went riding and hunting wild boars in the Maharaja's *beed* (game preserve) during their free time, and so forth. For some of this time in service, he and my mother lived in Patiala, but they did not have any children yet. My father tried to teach her to read and write Gurmukhi, but she had absolutely no aptitude or inclination to learn that.

After Naginder was discharged from the force, he and Bhagi came back to join his brothers in our village Mehraj. For a couple of years, he also tried teaching school in our village. In later years, I occasionally heard some older men calling him "Master Ji." But living in a farming family, it was easy for him to get caught up in the farm work. Finally he settled in, assisting his brothers farming, and raising his family.

Naginder Singh was about six feet tall and somewhat thinner than his older brother Trilok Singh. His other two brothers, Inder (Nikk) and Mohinder, were small in stature, more like their own father. I thought that my father, although thin and sinewy, was physically quite strong, but in reality he was just very determined, stoic, and persistent. It was customary for every rural man to boast about how strong he was, and my father made similar claims, with some facts to support his assertions. I would walk behind my father in awe of his long, thin thighs and muscular calves. I remember that sometimes my father would buy and carry home a 125-pound sack of cottonseed for buffalo feed from Phul Mandi, five miles away. This he would carry on his head; but when his neck felt tired he would lift the sack on his hands above his head for some distances, until he arrived home after covering the distance of five miles. Whether it was digging or repairing irrigation ditches, watering the fields on cold winter nights, spreading manure in the fields, harvesting, or some other farm work, it was usually a twelve to fourteen-hour workday for him. Our temporary laborers and our sharecroppers who had to work along with him were always hoping he would get tired and quit on time, but Naginder and his brothers were never the ones to finish or quit early; what they lacked in speed, they made up in endurance. My father was usually relegated by my uncle Tiloka to the hardest tasks that other adult males of the family could avoid, as they did not have any children of their own to feed. The others could just say "I don't give a damn; I am not going to kill myself; what babes of mine will cry from hunger?" But my father could not afford to neglect or avoid difficult tasks since he had a big family to feed. Any difficult or dangerous task fell to him, and I never saw him shirk any responsibility. There was nothing hard or dangerous, as far as he was concerned. As a result he developed the ability to endure great hardships. He was never put to the plough, since plowing was usually the job of our sharecroppers. Only when a sharecropper was needed for a difficult or undesirable task would my uncle himself man the plough temporarily.

In spite of his willingness to endure extreme physical hardship for long periods of time, Naginder Singh's heart was not in farm work but in reading anything he could find, in any language that was used in those parts. His brothers and his wife complained about his putting his face in the newspaper when he could be doing something useful. They would say "When he is absorbed in the newspaper, he sees nothing and hears nothing; he becomes totally absent from this world. Reading does not do any good to a farmer; reading should be the activity for the idle, for the Brahmins or the shopkeepers. The calf could be suckling all the milk out of the buffalo under his very nose and he would never notice; a herd of animals could be eating the crop, but he can be totally oblivious when he is reading something." My father had developed a thick skin to such criticism. He could pick up any book, paper, or old magazine that might be lying around and become oblivious of his surroundings and of the amount of time elapsed. He could read Punjabi in Gurmukhi script, Urdu and Persian in the Arabic script, Hindi and Sanskrit in Devnagri script and enough English in Roman script to read most books that came his way. He could even decipher the antiquated Landha script that shopkeepers/ bankers used in earlier times. Because of his experience in reading difficult writing, he could read handwritten things, which inexperienced students could not. People would say, "Those young boys may have gone through many more grades and even college, but their education is never enough to read what Naginder Singh can decipher." He could recite the holy Granth in the Gurdwara, like the trained readers called Granthi, and he understood the meaning of the scriptures better than most others did.

Naginder Singh would buy the Indian *jantri* (calendar book, or almanac), which frequently had signs of the zodiac on its cover, for each year. The jantri would also contain other information, how much rain to expect in the coming year, the positions of stars and possible events such as famines, wars, hurricanes, diseases, earthquakes, floods, crop pests, and other disasters. Brahmins had made a living for ages by telling people the auspicious times for various activities according to the configuration of the heavenly bodies. Some of that information had become standardized enough to publish predictions of likely events and natural disasters in the annual jantri, whether they came true later or not. Since my father was as educated as any local Brahmin, people would come to ask him if bad days were ahead if there were going to be adequate rains, if there were going to be dust storms, locusts, or excessive drought in summer. Some thought it might be possible to propitiate the gods by making offerings, *yugg*, charity and prayers. But my father himself looked skeptically at all such predictions. He used the jantri mainly as a calendar for upcoming events and to tell what festivals were on what days, and that sort of thing. He would say, "The astrological predictions are all fabrications of the Brahmins to loot the ignorant."

There was some disadvantage in his ability to focus his mind. He could walk from the village to the fields, remaining completely oblivious of his environment, as if he was sleepwalking or in a trance. I remember walking behind him sometimes when he was in some kind of reverie, talking with his hands, making gestures. It would appear as though he were silently making a point by pointing his finger; at other times he would wave his hand or even shake his head, as if he were in a court room. People usually made such gestures only while speaking or arguing, but my father was known to make a variety of hand and body gestures unconsciously as he walked.

Apart from his voracious appetite for reading every kind of writing, Naginder Singh had a prodigious memory and a tendency to give precepts or examples. He could quote numerous passages of prose or poetry from the scriptures of Sikh, Hindu, or other religions. He would recite poems and rhymes from famous saints, from obscure poets, or even from children's books. He could quote from folklore or from secular writings, to reinforce any point of advice or argument. After quoting in one language, he would think of the applicable rhymes and lines from other languages to reinforce his point. It could be about the virtue of hard work, about getting up early, about the value of education and learning, about keeping company with mischievous or nasty people, about the non-recoverability of lost time, about the effect of genetics on a person, about the importance of proper upbringing and instruction, about the futility of pleasures, about simplicity in living, about the power of mind over matter, or about the order of the universe. A compilation of his favorite quotations would fill a book if I could remember them all.

My father told us that he had learned to think critically because of the association with many monks and holy men who came to visit the dera of his sadhu uncle, when he himself was also living there as a youngster. Those Hindu monks would discourse on different subjects and he would sit with them and listen. From the sadhu uncle's guardianship he had learned to make some medicines from herbs and other ingredients, to take care of wounds and injuries, to diagnose and cure some diseases, to cook meals and desserts, to make ropes from hemp, to string beds, and other useful things. What he did not learn there, he had the ability to learn by himself later. None of his sons seem to have inherited the same abilities to do things with their hands, except perhaps Kirpal, but my sisters did turn out to be capable like him in such ways. Fortunately we all inherited some of his ability to memorize.

Naginder Singh's obsession to educate his children made us different from most other villagers, who usually tried to make fun of literate people. A few villagers wanted their sons to be educated, but Naginder Singh was one of the very few who advocated the education of girls and women also. He would say that you could not expect smart children unless their mothers were smart, and this fact alone was enough reason to educate girls. He believed and emphasized that general social uplift was not possible without the education of women. He would say: "A society in which women are uneducated will remain backward. If life is an oxcart, man and woman are its two wheels. How can the oxcart of life run properly if one of its wheels is smooth and rounded, while the other wheel is rough and unworkable?" While our culture recognized the position of husband as superior in a household and downplayed the intelligence of women, my father would say that wife is like a *wazir* to a king, like an advisor and counselor who makes a positive difference in making family decisions, and that a king with a stupid or ignorant wazir could have serious problems. He had a four-sentence Sanskrit rhyme for *vidya* (learning) which could be translated something like this: vidya brings light; vidya brings prestige; keep acquiring vidya, until your breath expires.

One day, after being frustrated with my resistance to education, my father started philosophizing: "There are four essentials to happiness. First is good health, and God has granted me good health. Second is prosperity; though I am not rich, by God's grace we have enough to eat. Third is having a good wife; my wife is not the best, but I will live with my lot. Fourth is good children. I have been blessed with very good children, except this son of mine, Gurnam, who has ruined my life." As a teenager I did not care if I hurt my father, but in later years I felt regret about having disappointed him and caused him anguish.

Pillar of Strength, Fountain of Knowledge

My father was a man of great convictions and not ambivalent about anything, whether the subject was education, the conduct of men and women, the importance of character, or the pursuit of a goal. His persistence in continuing to work hard even when very tired stemmed from such attitudes. He was relatively careless about his own appearance and said that excessive attention to appearance was wrong since one cannot claim too much credit or blame for one's looks. In fact he thought that rejecting people with ugly looks was like insulting God, because God had made those people that way. In our society people with black skin were considered inferior or low caste, but my father would say that "black skin was as good as light skin; even Krishn Bhagwan (the God Krishna) had black skin." It is true that Krishna is usually depicted in pictures with black, even bluish skin, while other Hindu gods are shown with light skin. My father was against all body alterations, tattoos, jewelry, or ornaments, and excessive attention to fashion in clothing. His attitude toward hair was consistent with this: God gave you hair for good reason; you should not violate His creation by cutting hair. He would say "*Saabt soort rabb di; bhannen bey imaan*," which means that the natural, whole man is the image of God; those who distort the natural look are corrupt violators. His claim was that a Sikh lives according to God's design, without cutting hair, and without mutilating or changing body parts, whereas some other religions distort God's creation. He thought that the Muslim custom of cutting the penis foreskin was against God's will and so was the removal of hair by humans. When we used to argue that cutting hair was not much different than clipping nails, my father would insist that all hair was like parts of the body and God made them all for a good reason.

He was unpretentious, but he was calm in the belief that no one was better than him and that no race, tribe, or family was better than his own. Sometimes, I would come back from college and say things like this: "We are just ordinary poor farmers with very little land and a low standard of living; we are nothing compared to the sons of the big sardars and high officials who go to school with us." To this my father would retort, "You tell those sardars that your ancestors were warriors and rulers when the ancestors of those big officials were just ordinary peasants, and that you have a rich history. Tell them your ancestors owned one lakh (hundred thousand) acres of land, but your family has grown into thousands of people over the 22 villages; so your own share has become small. Nobody has better heritage than yours." He never seemed to lack confidence, nor to have any fears. Unfortunately, I did not inherit these traits. I am neither doubtless nor fearless. The only one who came close to our father's attitudes was my younger brother Gurdial.

For all his toughness and his disciplinarian nature, Naginder Singh was also quite sentimental when it came to his children. He had no concern about himself, but constantly worried and planned for the education, health, and well-being of all seven of his growing children. Sickness was not uncommon in a big family like ours, and my father was involved in aiding every recovery. Although he knew some things about herbs and folk medicine, he believed that modern doctors had the more scientific approach.

In his old age, whenever my father received a letter from me in America, people say that he would carry the letter in his pocket for months or until the next letter arrived, just as people carry the pictures of their children or grandchildren. At any time when he was alone he would read the letter to himself again and again, and when others asked about me, he would read the letter to them if they showed sufficient interest.

When I was young, my father seemed to be a pillar of strength in mind and body, and a fountain of unlimited knowledge. He never worried too much about his physical appearance, which exasperated his wife and daughters when they wanted him to look appropriate for the occasion. He had an opinion about everything and almost never said "I don't know." He was a great believer in science and rational thought, and he never saw any contradiction between science and religious beliefs. He believed that God created the scientific laws, and one way to appreciate God was to learn how those laws operate and to act accordingly. He had learned to make some medicines from herbs and chemical compounds and also some ointments for healing wounds. He would clean the wounds with antiseptic water obtained by boiling the leaves of the *neem* tree; then he would apply the ointment he made and tie a bandage made from some turban rag. He had the confidence to prepare various concoctions for body strength, like the *panjiri* for women who had given birth. And he could prepare *prasad* (consecrated pudding) for distribution at the gurdwara. He was a firm believer in modern medicine and vaccinations, and he believed that all those people trying to heal others with *toona* (voodoo-like rituals) and with worship of various gods and goddesses were ineffective. In pain he could be quite stoic and tough. I don't remember ever seeing my father lying sick in bed. There were times when he got sick, but he would not stop work just because of illness. We heard things like this: "If fear grabs you, then you should grab the fear first." or "If hunger is bothering you, you should start bothering the hunger." or "If you want your food to taste good, keep getting really hungry for a long time; then even the dried bread will taste like desert." It was pretty hard for us to measure up.

But his rational thinking did not quite tame his temper; he could be quite uncontrollable

34

in his anger sometimes. He could be physically violent towards my mother. If a *daang* (big stick) or *ghotna* (pestle), or any heavy object came into his hands, he might strike her with it. Apparently, all that fat on my mother must have been good protection, because she never had any broken bones. Wife-beating was a common practice in many houses in the village. Such occasional beatings in our house continued until my brothers and I became teenagers and were big enough to defend our mother. I remember the first time when my brother Kartar got between him and my mother and said "I will not let you hit her ever again." And many times my father was ready to physically fight with opponents in disputes over land or water rights or other matters. Clever ways to handle relationships and business matters were not his strong suit; many times he caused conflicts in such matters, which his uneducated but more deliberate brother Tiloka had to straighten out.

Did his habit of physical abuse to his wife transfer the trait to his children, as is believed in popular psychology to be the automatic 'cycle of violence'? This did not happen in our family. It may depend upon the social norms and the marriage partners involved, as well as the example of parents. None of Naginder Singh's three daughters, married to husbands with occupations as diverse as farming, school teaching and plant genetics, were ever physically abused or even threatened with physical abuse throughout their married lives. Out of his four boys, I was the only one with an attitude that was somewhat domineering toward my wife. But I was also the child least likely to copy my father. My three brothers did not hit their wives and none of my three sisters was ever beaten by their husbands. So this theory of a cycle of violence going from generation to generation did not seem to apply to our family.

His Religious Routines

In midlife and in later years, my father had a practice of getting up three hours before sunrise (*paher da tarka*). In our society, no religious person would sleep after the morning light unless he was ill; the warm climate also made it easy to get up early. First, my father would bathe and then he would recite portions of *gurbani* (Sikh scriptures) for more than an hour. The portions of the *Granth* he would generally consider for recitation were the *Japji*, *Jaap* and *Swayye*, which he remembered by heart; sometimes he would recite *Sukhmani*. He would say "On any day that I do not complete the morning recitations, I don't feel *swatantra*; things don't go right for me that day, and some adversity or mishap may occur. When my morning recitations are complete, I feel joyful and on top of things for the rest of the day." And if any of his sons did not do well in a test or job interview, he would say "I think the reason for the bad result might be that I had been unable to complete my recitation of the scriptures that day because of another disrupting matter." I personally did not relate to this attitude when I was a teenager; I thought that religious rituals were just a pastime, akin to superstition.

In later years he claimed to have less and less interest in worldly matters and spent more and more time in reading and reciting gurbani. Some people in the village started thinking that sitting in his presence or listening to him recite the gurbani would benefit their own lives. Some would say "His good fortune and the education, health, and success of his children are all due to his immersion in gurbani. Just as 'iron floats if fastened to wood,' we may avoid drowning in misfortune by attaching ourselves to him." So some villagers would just want to come and sit in his presence when he was an old man. But it appears that other than Gurdial, none of his sons developed a religious bent of mind, and his daughters were more like their mother regarding religious matters.

My father was an enthusiastic and uninhibited singer, but only for singing the holy *shabads* (chants) or scriptures. Whenever he was not occupied with other concerns and efforts, he would spontaneously start singing some shabad. There was not any possibility of his getting bored; he could always start singing the scriptures. But secular songs were unthinkable; he sang only the songs in praise of God. Even when he would recite some romantic sounding poetry, he would say, "This word 'beloved' is really a reference to God; the poet is really writing about his love of God and not of a woman or of a man."

Our Family Culture

Naginder Singh demanded from his children the unadulterated truth in all matters. None of us children would ever dare to tell a lie. And although I was the least compliant of all my siblings in other respects, I never developed the courage to lie, as one requires a callous and unfeeling mind to be able to lie. The village people also had the custom of swearing by things dear or important to them, when they wanted to convince others that they were telling the truth. So swearing by father, by life, by the scriptures, by one's eyes, by son, and so forth, was common among the people. In addition, the Muslims would swear by Allah, Rabb, or Quran, the Hindus would swear by *Devi* (goddess) or by the cow, and the Sikhs would swear by Guru or by Granth (the holy book). Some nominally Sikh men in the village would still swear by the cow during my time. Sometimes the boys would cheat and swear by the Gods of other religions, such as a Sikh swearing by Allah or Devi. They felt that the Gods of other people were powerless and could not cause any harm if one swore falsely by them; they believed that it was only their own true God that could cause harm if they swore falsely. But in our family, no one was allowed to ever use the device of swearing to convince others that we were telling the truth. We could only add the word *satch* (truth) to whatever we said, and people thought that without swearing by something important or sacred, the word 'satch' was meaningless. Other people felt that this behavior was peculiar. They would insist, "What is the harm in swearing if you are telling the truth? It is only if you lie that swearing by your father could cause your father to drop dead or swearing by your eyes could turn you blind." But our tongues never got used to pronouncing 'the swearing words.'

The culture of our family was different from that of most other families among whom we lived in the village. So, to some extent we as children were a little odd. We could not understand how other people could use obscene and crude language in front of their women and children, and how their children could use the obscene words routinely and casually. Whereas in the American language there are only a few obscene words, in our village the graphic and pornographic quality of the words used by men and boys routinely would shock even the most jaded westerners if they knew their translated meanings. Men in the village used obscene words loudly and in public as they engaged in routine activities, cursing their children, goading their oxen to pull harder, or describing something that did not go right. But since they did this routinely and not just in anger or frustration, no one thought about the filth and salacity of the words. They would intersperse the obscene words in routine conversation, just as Americans use the expressions like "You know," or "I mean." Even little boys said those words without understanding the meanings completely. Some lower caste women used obscene vocabulary toward each other. Women in some households would call each other, *bahel* (whore), *gaddan yaddhi* (fucked by donkeys), *ghoosa maroni, ghorian di rann* and other abuses involving animal copulation, and female anatomy when they quarrelled. This pattern of language changed gradually and by the 1940s most people had moderated their habits of using obscene words.

But in our household no one would ever dare to use an obscene word. No one in our house had to be punished for lying, swearing, or using obscene word. Later, I tried, using those obscene words while grazing cattle with other boys in the fields, because that was the pattern of 'real men,' but I would feel awkward and uncomfortable. It took some practice for me to use the obscene and filthy words effectively; still I never learned to swear by Guru, by Granth, or by anything else.

Children in polite households were required to address the elders by adding the respectful suffix "Ji," after the relationship of the person to them. Thus Bapu Ji for father, Taya Ji for the senior paternal uncle, Chacha Ji for the junior paternal uncle, and Mama Ji for the mother's brother were the required forms of address in our house, even if we were in an angry and quarrelsome mood. In our house, the word "Ji" was not used for addressing my mother, but was sometimes used for addressing other women relatives. My mother added the word "Ji" to address the senior women and elders of her husband. All women of the village greeted the senior women of the community with the words, *"Bebe ji matha tekdi haa."* This literally means: "Respected lady, I put my forehead at your feet," but the actual touching of feet was infrequent and for special occasions only. In our house, respect for elders in general was emphasized, but my father was feared just like God by all his children.

My Father's Last Days

Naginder Singh (1896-1984) was quite healthy during most of his life. But one April day in 1984, he felt weak, and he was brought from the village to his son, Kirpal, who was practicing medicine in Bhatinda. Three years earlier in 1981 he had had an episode that appeared to be a heart or stomach problem after eating the sanctified pudding from the gurdwara. By chance on that day, Kirpal had been visiting my father in Mehraj and by the end of the day he noticed that my father seemed to have recovered. But on April 14th 1984, when he was brought to Bathinda, he was considerably weaker. Kirpal had him under observation and noticed that his blood pressure was lower than normal. Two more days passed, and my father took a bath at midday and went for a short walk, but felt week and came back to lie down. A little later Kirpal noticed that his father had low blood pressure, so he started conducting more tests. My mother said "Kirpal, why are you so frenetic?" Our frail and fading father remarked "He is doing his experiments on me." Still later on the same day, my father got even weaker and said to Kirpal "Try to save me if you can," and within the hour thereafter he closed his eyes and died on April 16, 1984.

From my perspective as a child, my father had a formidable mind and I thought that nobody else's father could ever have the qualities comparable to his. Like every little boy I wanted to have his abilities, and strength of mind. As I grew older I still admired him and his words still rang in my mind, but then I did not want to be quite like him in every way. And although I have inherited some of his traits, I am less like him than are any of my brothers; I came to be more like my mother in physical and emotional qualities and in fact more like my maternal uncles whom I rarely saw.

My brother Kartar was more like my father in physique and intellect and Gurdial was more like him emotionally. I feel satisfied that my father was pleased with me and was proud of me in his later life. My regrets are that I made him unhappy when I was teenager and that I did not serve my parents as well as all my brothers did. For the peace of your soul and for your Karma, service to your parents is the best thing you can do, according to the old beliefs. I have surely come up short in service to my parents.

The occasion of my father's last rites, in April of 1984 in our house in Mehraj, was one of the few times in their adult lives that all seven of his sons and daughters were together in our village. My father's death ended an era for our family. It locked the door of our house, as my mother moved in with my brother Kirpal in Bhatinda. It changed the possibilities of gatherings for our complete family; we could no longer go home like youngsters. There was no home to go to any more even though the structures were still there.

Bhag Bhari, Loaded with Good Fortune

My mother's father had died a few months before she was born and her mother died before she was a year old. They left behind two boys, Amar Singh and Sohan (Sohna) Singh and four girls: Ram Rakhi, Nand Kaur (Kauri), Chand Kaur, and Bhag Bhari (my mother) in the village of Laleana, about 15 miles south of Bhatinda. It is interesting that the names of two of the sisters are like the modern Sikhs, ending in Kaur, while the youngest and the oldest girls got the traditional Punjabi names. The oldest boy was a teenager, perhaps already married, and my mother was an infant when her parents died. They essentially had to raise themselves with some supervision from a kindly maternal uncle named Ganga Ram. I saw old Ganga Ram, usually with blue turban and long beard, for he used to visit us when I was a little boy. From his name you would think he was a devout Hindu; in reality he was a Sikh but had been born before the Singh Sabha movement, when there were relaxed attitudes rather than strict divisions between Hindu and Sikh customs. Ganga Ram divided his time between his own family in the village of Dikkhan and his deceased sister's family in Laleana. My mother, the youngest child of her family, was then raised by her older brother's wife so that her sister-in-law became like a second mother to her. But even she died when my mother was about five years old. They say that the death of that brother's wife left my mother devastated, because now she was conscious and attached to the lady. But as time went on, she learned to spin yarn and embroider under the care of her sisters. Embroidery was a requirement for all landowners' girls as they made *phulkari* (flower work) of embroidered patterns as wearable covers, shawls and veils, before they were married off. Her family had a good amount of land and later all three of her older sisters were married off into the village of TaruAna.

My maternal uncle Amar Singh, having lost his parents years earlier, had the responsibilities that a father would normally have, including finding husbands for his sisters. When he was on the lookout for a match for his youngest sister Bhag Bhari (Bhagi), he had come to attend a wedding in Mehraj. There he spotted my father, Naginder Singh, who was a *preeha*, a volunteer feeding the guests. Boys in the brotherhood

38

always volunteered to take care of the guests at the weddings of their extended clan. And people were always on the lookout for suitable matches for their daughters, sisters, and nieces. The story goes that Amar Singh asked the hosts: "Who is that tall, handsome boy? Which family is he from? How much land do they have?" He was told that the best way to approach the subject of a marriage proposal to Naginder was through his sadhu uncle in Bhatinda. This set the ball rolling for the eventual marriage of Naginder and Bhag Bhari, who according to the customs of the day never saw one another until after marriage. And although Naginder Singh would later become an *amritdhari* Sikh (one who has been formally initiated by taking the *amrit*, a ritual drink),, their marriage ceremony was performed by a Brahmin with the Hindu rites of circling around the fire, as was still the custom in that rural region of Punjab in the second decade of the twentieth century. In keeping with her brothers' status, the family contributed a lot of gold jewelry, and a *Sandooq* (bride's four-legged dowry box) full of clothing and other valuables. In the village of LaleAna, with a fair amount of irrigated land, Bhag Bhari's own family was prosperous. But she was being married into a relatively poor, struggling family of brothers trying to make a life from scratch after having been orphans. The main asset that my father's family had was the family name Sidhu of Mehraj, the illusion of wealth of the sadhu uncle in Bhatinda, and the false expectation that the nephews might benefit from that wealth.

When my mother was married, everything seemed to have gone well. That contrasted with the feelings of the family toward her when both of her parents died. At that time every one felt that Bhagi was a cursed child who had killed her father just before she was born and killed her mother soon after she was born. Years later, they even thought that she had killed her sister-in-law who was like a second mother to her. "The cursed, unfortunate one!" they thought; sarcastically they had named her Bhag Bhari, which means blessed, fortunate one. Bhag Bhari literally means loaded with blessings and good fortune. Her maternal uncle, Ganga Ram used to pray: "Oh Lalaan Wale (Glorious Lord), take this child away! If Bhagi dies I will give a *sawa munn rote* (hundred-pound cake) in your name to express my gratitude." This was not any secret wish but spoken openly in front of every family member, off and on; many people felt that such daughters were a punishment to the parents from God.

It was not uncommon for poor children in rural areas to die, but Bhagi did not die and was destined to live for nearly 99 years in good health, and to prosper like all her siblings. Years later, when she had several children and a modicum of prosperity as indicated by the number of oxen and buffaloes in her husband's household, the old maternal uncle Ganga Ram would come to visit and would express joy at her good fortune. Once during those visits, Bhagi laughingly reminded him: "Uncle, do you remember when you used to pray for my death, with the pledge to offer a hundred-pound cake to God?" The old man burst into tears and regretted thinking and uttering such thoughts, and about how wrong he was; but he was happy at how her life had turned out. Now a person could claim emotional scars from such upbringing, but people in the village culture took things stoically, especially from their parents and elders. It was just not customary to believe that a parent or elder wanted anything except what would be good for the child's future, even though the elder might curse and complain. Such curses were uttered frequently in despair and frustration, but even when they were said in anger, the children had no choice but to live with it. The children somehow did not feel alienated, as they considered such treatment to be their fate or a normal condition of life; in fact many felt guilty that they were the cause of trouble.

Bhag Bhari may not have been blessed with good looks or a clever mind, but she did enjoy naturally good health and had a very kind and conscientious disposition. She was known for her generosity to laborers, workers, and beggars, and would treat even the animals with compassion. She herself said that she was ugly compared to the women of other land-owning families and that she lacked the wiles and clever ways of the village women. She never learned to read or write even a single letter of Gurmukhi. She did not come from a religious tradition, and almost never went to the gurdwara for worship. But she believed in God and she recognized and counted all the wonders of God. She would recite God's name before starting almost every task. One of the ways in which I unconsciously imitate her is by invoking God's name when beginning any task; but I do it silently, and only for the tasks that involve risk.

My mother had an extraordinary ability to deal with physical and mental stress and to bear adverse events as the will of God, without breaking down. She was kind to people in distress but had a mind of steel when difficult circumstances arose, while most women in that society pretended to be physically and mentally fragile and delicate. She was not religious in any ritualistic way but had unflinching faith that God does all the right things. And if He did something that was bad for us, she felt that nothing could be done about it, saying only, "It is His will," or "It is your Karma." Growing up without parents; dealing with young brothers, who without the restraint of parents were prone to drinking and violence; being married into a joint family where for nearly twenty years she was the only woman, and had to deal with the whims of the husband's brothers; the dictatorial habits of her husband and occasional physical beatings; the unending and back-breaking housework and farm-related work; bearing eleven children and raising seven of them; all these extremes of hardship had tempered her mind to bear anything, and to accept God's will.

The year of my mother's birth is unknown to me; but she said she was about the same age as her husband was at their marriage, having by that time grown up and marriageable for many years. Since she might be born around 1896, and she died on Oct 29, 1995, she had a pretty long life.

After my father died in 1984, my mother intended to live in the family home in the village. Initially she resisted the idea of moving in with her son Kirpal in Bhatinda by saying "I want to live the rest of my life in this house. If I live with Kirpal, I might say some harsh or inappropriate word to his servants or to his in-law relatives who live with him frequently and that could be most awkward." But after some persuasion she went to live with Kirpal and abandoned the family home. She lived there until Kirpal left to go to America in late 1993 and then she was taken to live with my brother Gurdial in Chandigarh.

In her last days my mother was reluctant to go to the her daughters houses. She would say: "I might die there and people will say 'What kind of sons did she have, considering that she had to die at a daughter's house!' and my sons will be disgraced." It was the custom for parents in Punjab to take nothing from a daughter's house, but only to give things to her. Some people would not even drink water from a daughter's house.

When her daughter Chhoti said, "Mother, we will tell them that you died in your son's house," she said, "People find out the truth about such things; I want to die in my son's house so they will not be disgraced." In that culture, parents considered the son's house and land as their own, and they considered the daughter's house and land as belonging to her in-laws. Like other people of her time, my mother believed that boys and men were the only ones who were capable of doing important work and defending their families from harm. She would say that God created girls only because He wanted humanity to reproduce and increase, and that otherwise women were not capable of any important work.

Just before our mother's death, my brother Kartar and I arrived from America to be by her side, as our brother Gurdial had called us to say that she was ill and was not going to live much longer. She had been taken to the PGI hospital in Chandigarh, where the standard of care was the best available, though still not particularly good. But this was done more to relieve the family's anxiety than with any real hope of improving her condition. Her oldest daughter Maro, who had also come to see her, had said "Don't take her to any hospital; just recite the *gurbani* and let nature take its course." But the rest of the family wanted to try all the possibilities of medical help; they did not want the mother of a military general to die for lack of medical care. When I arrived from America to see my mother in the hospital, she had been in a state of coma for three days; but soon after my arrival she began to open her eyes. She was happy to see us and commented on my "nice turban and beautiful foreign clothes." After she had regained consciousness, the rest of the conversation went like this:

My sister Chhoti said "Mother, do you know who this is? This is Gurnam, Amrita's father; do you know who Amrita is?" Mother said: "Yes, she is Gail's daughter." Then my mother questioned me: "Do you have a wife now?" and I flippantly replied, "Oh, plenty of wives, mother; but now I am an old man." Mother said "No, you are still young; you look good; you should get married." And I said, "Mother, I am 65 years old; do you know how much 65 is?" Mother said "Yes, it is *panj* (5) and *satth* (60)." That is how our uneducated village people counted the numbers, i.e., singles, twenties, hundreds, etc.

Then we started teasing her by asking, like in the old days when she had never traveled to anywhere, "Mother, which way is Mehraj?" and she said "To the west." Then she looked at her hand and talked about having all those money lines and wealth chambers in the palm of her hand, but never having any money in her control. "Just as well that I did not have any money; where would I have hidden it?" she said.

I asked her: "Mother, what was the name of your father and of your grandfather?" She replied, "My father was Jivan Singh and grandfather was Boota Singh." I asked this to check her mental functions and also because it might be possible to find her date of birth from the records in the district headquarters, if both those names were known. But most of her talk that day was trivial, about the cooler weather, or about drinking tea twice a day. Some of her talk was incoherent or inconsistent.

As my mother lay suffering, her daughters were sometimes sad and crying, but sometimes they teased and joked with her to keep it from becoming a heavy and sad occasion. They knew that she was going to die and that they were going to lose her, but it was not a tragedy—just an inevitable passing away. When Chhoti asked, "Are you alright, mother?" she replied: "I am sorry for all the suffering that I am causing you."

41

Then Chhoti asked: "Are *you* suffering, mother?" Mother answered, "Oh, no bullet is striking me! I am speaking of the suffering I am causing for all of you, who are taking care of me."

Then I asked, "Does anything hurt, mother?" She answered "No, nothing hurts; I just feel very weak; but what do you expect when one is just one or two years less than 100 years old." Then I said: "Another question mother, when you were unconscious and nearly dead for two days, did you see any gods, angels, or devils?" She answered, "No, I never saw anything like that; sometimes I felt too weak to generate the energy to even open my eyes and other times I was unconscious." Then I jokingly asked: "Mother, where do you think you will go when you die, to heaven or to hell?" She said: "Only God knows about such things; but I think I am going somewhere nice as I have not done too many bad *paap* (sins)." And that is a nice thing for any human to be able to say at the end.

I would have liked to know exactly what was going through her mind, how sad she was feeling about leaving this world and her family, and how she felt about all her struggles and the dreams of early years—whether she felt satisfied with her life. But my mother Bhag Bhari died two days after this conversation, when I had gone out of the house.

All those who knew my mother believed she was naturally fortunate and had God's favor. They used to say, "When she was young and unmarried in LaleAna, her presence created prosperity and good fortune in their household and her brothers enjoyed the society of big sardars. When she came to the household of Sidhu Brards, she brought good fortune on them, and those four orphan brothers, without much property to depend upon, became prosperous gradually. After she left LaleAna and took away good fortune with her, her brothers' household suffered serious setbacks. Bhagi brought good fortune with her wherever she went." This was said even before the time when her sons and daughters were educated and before they established themselves in good positions.

Since my father's death in 1984, my mother had lived with my brother Kirpal in Bhatinda. My brother Gurdial and his wife would frequently ask her to live with them because everyone believed that the *punn* (good deed) of serving an aging parent was the highest blessing one could have. But she felt more comfortable with Kirpal in Bhatinda, where people would come from our village of Mehraj almost every day and chat with her, providing the village news and continuity with that community. When Kirpal decided to go to America in November 1993, Gurdial took her to his house in Chandigarh. There, Gurdial and his wife Sukhjinder also took good care of her. She always expressed the hope that Kirpal would come back from America to Bhatinda and then she would again live there with him, closer to the village. But that was never to be.

My mother's presence was always a source of comfort to me; I regret that I did not serve my parents as well as all my brothers did.

Uncle Inder Singh (Nikk; *Naggran Wala*)

Uncle Nikk's real name was Inder Singh. Inder, the Punjabi pronunciation for the Hindu God Indra, is one of the most-used appellations in modern-day Punjab, usually combined with other name parts. His nickname, Nikk, means young, little or small. Since he and his brothers had returned after the unsuccessful farming venture from their land in

Talwara village in Rajputana, and since they also had ancestral land in the villages of Kalyan and BujjoAna, some people started calling Nikk by the name Naggran Wala (owner of many villages). This was flattery and teasing exaggeration, which is common in the villages. So if someone in the village wanted to get on his good side, he addressed Nikk by the name Naggran Wala.

But the unfortunate Nikk did not have a good personal life. Like his youngest brother, he was somewhat shorter than the average, although he had a handsome face. Nick also had a speech impediment, so that he often involuntarily repeated words and sounds, with imprecise enunciation. He was the only brother to have smallpox so severe that it marked and pitted his entire face and body. The disease also damaged his eyeballs with white scars, which left his vision badly impaired. During adulthood, his body would flare up with boils and pimples, which he used to scratch frequently. And even though he tried various domestic medicines, ointments, and balms containing sulfur and other medicines, and consulted many sadhu and *hakeem* (medicine men), his skin never cleared up. It seemed like God wanted to test all the diseases and miseries on Nikk. For all these reasons Nikk was never married. My father, who had some knowledge of herbal and native medicines, would suggest to him: "Drink two glasses of cold water every morning on an empty stomach; then slowly your skin will become healthy and will clear up." And that simple suggestion would infuriate Nikk, who dismissed such advice as patronizing and grossly simple. Nikk never had much respect for his intelligent but tactless brother Naginder. My father would say, "*Ghar da yogi yogna, bahrla yogi sidh,*" which means roughly: "People ridicule a local yogi while they consider an outsider yogi as a *sidh* (ascended master with miraculous powers)."

Nikk was the only one among the brothers who did not follow the puritanical rules of all work and no play that the other brothers lived by. In the face of high resistance from his brothers, who preached about the futility of fun and the virtue of work, he insisted on going to fairs, shows, and circuses. When the circus would come to our village, we kids could only walk around the circus perimeter, looking through holes in the canvas walls to catch glimpses of the animals in the big cages. We were itching to see the elephants, tigers, horses, monkeys, bears, and the gymnastic feats of the circus, but like most children in our village, I was never allowed or given any money to go. That kind of expense was considered frivolous, and all entertainment was considered a bad thing anyway. Teenagers and independent-minded adults did go to the circus. Nobody could stop the grown-up and unmarried uncle Nikk from going. He could always convince my uncle Tiloka to give him the money for such purposes.

Nikk was always generous to his nephews and nieces. He would go to the fair with what little money he could get from his older brother Tiloka, and instead of spending it on himself, he would bring sweets for the children from the fair (something our own father would never do). Bringing *reori* (a kind of hard candy) from the fair was a tradition, and uncle Nikk avoided spending any money on himself in order to bring the reori for us. For the children, he would also bring *ber* (a wild fruit) from the fields. His primary job was to graze cattle, and he collected ber in the process, as cattle-grazing was a somewhat leisurely job.

During the thirties and forties, uncle Nikk had closely cropped hair and a trimmed beard, for ease of maintenance; but his turban covered whatever length of hair he had.

Trimming the beard was common among the younger men in the village, but cutting the hair on the head was considered unseemly and ugly for Sikh adults. Only the men who were ill, handicapped, incompetent or non-Sikh could have the hair cut. In our house, trimming the beard was also considered a vice. An educated Sikh would not trim his beard in those days; but most rural, uneducated, nominally Sikh young men (who were not *amritdhari*), trimmed their beards in the 1930s. They usually stopped trimming their beards and kept full-length beards after about the age of thirty or so.

At the age of about 46 or so, Nikk suffered what was probably a stroke. They called it *adhrang,* and it left one side of his body in a weaker state and his speech even more slurred and indistinct. He also had diminished control on one side of his face and mouth, which made eating and swallowing difficult. Thereafter he could not walk more than short distances. Although he lived with us or with uncle Mohinder, his brother Tiloka was the only one whom he trusted unconditionally.

In 1946, following the breakup of our joint family, my father's family moved to the old Inner House and left Nikk with his brother Mohinder in the Outer House. During the days of the religious massacres of 1947, when everyone was concerned about his own life and safety, Inder Singh died, younger than fifty, of weakness, neglect, and various diseases.

Mohinder Singh, the Fierce and Fiery Uncle

Uncle Mohinder had lost his father and mother when he was a toddler and had been raised by his sadhu uncle in Bhatinda, under hard discipline, lack of freedom, frequent physical punishment, and unpleasant circumstances. The British wrote the name of the town as Bhatinda, but every Punjabi pronounces it as Bathinda. And when Uncle Mohinder came back to Mehraj to live with his brothers, people called him Bathindya, which became a nickname for him. In about 1925, when he was in his twenties, he went to find a job in Hong Kong as many other Punjabis did. Hong Kong, like India, was a British colony and the British found it practical to have some policemen and guards who were non-Chinese (particularly Sikhs) in places like Hong Kong, Shanghai, and Singapore. (The Hong Kong police had identifications A, B and C classifying the English, the Sikhs, and the Chinese, respectively.) In the British mind, this minimized the possibility of any law enforcement personnel colluding with the local criminal elements.

Mohinder had attended school as a child in Bathinda probably for three or four grades, but he forgot much of what he had learnt. Then in Hong Kong, he taught himself enough English to read a newspaper and enough Chinese to read and converse in that language, in addition to reading the Punjabi language he already knew. All those who went abroad considered it a temporary absence and hoped to return to the ancestral home with money. Unlike some other people who were inclined to moonlight apart from their regular jobs to make extra money in Hong Kong, Mohinder did not accumulate any money. During the depression of the thirties, my older uncle Tiloka would dictate letters to my brother Kartar to be sent to Mohinder, urging him to come back to Punjab as "there was plenty at home and enough land to cultivate." I remember once Uncle Tiloka dictated a letter to be sent to Mohinder with threatening words: "If you don't come home now, we will have 'na mil vertan.'" Although this expression about breaking relationship was considered harsh, Uncle Tiloka thought this threat was the best device to motivate his younger brother to come home. After 12 years in Hong Kong, Mohinder came back to Mehraj in 1937, but he brought no money. The few things that he had to show were a pocket watch with a lid that opened when you pressed on its side, a timepiece whose hands and digits glowed in the dark, and his exercise equipment. He also brought a couple of suitcases of western style suits, ties, silk shirts, and other paraphernalia. Those fancy clothes provoked only ridicule from the villagers because there would be no occasions to wear them, and he, being the only one with such outfits, would look odd. But the clock with the glowing green hands and digits was very useful in the dark nights to determine the allotted watering time for the crops of different people according to their water rights. Otherwise, people had to build a fire to read an ordinary watch at night in the fields. Things like flashlights were not common in the villages, although my uncle brought a long one that took four D-size cells. Uncle Mohinder kept a sedate and expensive-looking brown sweater for himself, but another shiny, parrot-green sweater that he brought was given to Kartar. The parrot-green sweater was later passed on to me. After many years I donated the sweater to Sudhoo the Mirasi, who was forever after singing praises of my generosity and blessing the name of Brard *bans* (Brard dynasty) for that gift.

Within months of his arrival from Hong Kong, Mohinder's marriage was arranged in May 1938 to Nihalo, who was thirteen or fourteen years younger than he was. At first, as my mother and father arranged Nihalo's marriage to Mohinder, we felt awkward that Nihalo, the daughter of my maternal uncle, and therefore a cousin, would become my aunt by marriage to Mohinder. But it was not uncommon for a woman to bring her cousin or her niece in marriage to a brother or nephew of her husband. In time Nihalo and Mohinder had four sons, (Gurcharan, Kulwant, Ranjit and Harchet) and two daughters. The oldest daughter, was usually called Middi and the younger one was named Moorti. My cousin Middi had no formal schooling but was highly intelligent. She was taller than her father and was the best-looking girl on our side of the village. At the age of about twenty, Middi was married to a military education officer. Later, Moorti was also married, into a land-owning family. But Moorti died suddenly of brain hemorrhage or something similar soon after her marriage. The family grieved a lot at the loss of Moorti because they loved her so much and had made great efforts to see her settled. In later years, my cousin Kulwant came to be called Sarpanch (village head man) as he was elected the chief of our village repeatedly for many terms. His brother Ranjit, usually called Mithu, became a schoolteacher, while Gurcharan and Harchet worked the land in LaleAna, which their mother had inherited from her parents. So Mohinder and Nihalo's family was comparable to ours in size, only they were much younger.

Uncle Mohinder was a short man, about 5' 6," who had a handsome face, beautiful eyes, and big chest. He could carry a 250-pound load on his head for some distance, even after he returned from Hong Kong. He was tough and quarrelsome, but he was also socially adept and verbally skillful. Although he was clever enough to pick his conflicts carefully, he could be provoked easily. He was a fierce fighter, and sometimes his temper and anger could be out of control. I remember him beating many animals to control them or to punish them. Our Kala Untth (black camel) was afraid of no one except uncle Mohinder, because of the many beatings over time. Mohinder was the only one who could control that camel when it was in the masti (intoxicated) state. Several times he beat a cow, that refused to be milked, so severely that the cow collapsed. But even then Mohinder kept beating the fallen cow, hurling abuses, swearing, and declaring, "I am not going to the Ganga if you die." This refers to the old Indian practice of going to the holy Ganga River to wash off a really horrible sin. In theory all sins could be washed off in the Ganga water, although killing a cow was considered a worse sin than killing a man, because the cow had no ill will toward the killer.

In time, after Mohinder's marriage and the rapid production of children, there was developing a family to rival that of my father. Then the formerly loving and caring brothers evolved into hostile, belligerent adversaries and the separation of our joint family became inevitable. Only a few years earlier when Mohinder was in Hong Kong, his brothers missed him so much that they implored him to return home. Now they acted like enemies. Even after the separation, there were always issues that created occasional flare-ups between my father and uncle Mohinder. The last conflict was when my uncle Trilok Singh willed his Talwara land to my brother Kirpal according to the law. Uncle Mohinder felt that his sons should have gotten half of their uncle's Talwara land according to custom, as they got his Mehraj land. But this was not a simple case, as some of the Talwara land had been obtained with money and help from my brother Kartar; so Trilok Singh felt that Naginder Singh's sons deserved that land. Although there were no physical fights over the land, Mohinder Singh died in the late 1970s with some hostility in his heart toward my father. In later years, although he would speak politely to me, he would complain about the bad attitude of Kirpal and of my father. But uncle Mohinder always treated me well even during the times when he treated my father like an enemy.

Gulabo's Bad Kismet

Aunt Gulabo, formally named Gulab Kaur (rose princess), provides the example of a precious life wasted by tragic circumstances. She was one of the most beautiful women to live in our village. She was tall, thin, with exquisitely fine features and prominent, smiling eyes. Village women said "she can brighten up a house just by entering it." She had a kind, sympathetic nature and a tone-rich, pleasing voice. She was generous of nature and capable with her hands. Gulabo was the wife of my father's cousin, Channan Singh, who was nicknamed Viceroy. A generation earlier, that part of our family had built their house in the outer part of the village. As a child, whenever I was afraid of going to my own house because I had been bad, I would go to Aunt Gulabo's house and feel secure.

Once as a six-year-old, playing in the community courtyard of our Inner House, I was swinging an improvised hockey stick which hit Uncle Bhan Singh's aged mother on the side of her head. It was all due to my carelessness, as I really liked the old *amma* (respected old lady). Once she had given me a *paisa* (penny) after I took her buffalo to the water pond, and she said she would give me one penny every month if I took the buffalo every day to the pond regularly. A penny every month was significant money to me then.

The old lady was sitting in our common courtyard and spinning yarn nearby with the spinning wheel. I had swung the hockey stick to hit a rag ball, and on the back swing the stick hit her. The aged lady's head began to bleed, and I was panic stricken. The

46

adults had to put some rags on her bleeding temple and put her in bed before they had a chance to catch and punish me. Afraid of the punishment, I ran away from the courtyard.

When I tried to return home later and stepped into the common courtyard, my mother said "Come in; your horns are going to be petted!" This is a Punjabi sarcasm, meaning that severe punishment is going to be administered or you are going to get a fine beating. I immediately ran back and went to Aunt Gulabo's house. Aunt Gulabo listened, hugged me, and calmed me down, and then she brought me back to my house, pleading that "the little child should not be punished even though he was careless."

Any time when I wandered into Aunt Gulabo's house, I was treated to some sweet or delicacy. Since I never had a chance to be pampered by my maternal grandparents (*nanke*), who had died even before my mother grew up, Gulabo's treatment was the closest I came to being pampered by a sympathetic person who was not a parent. Whether it was a thorn in your foot or a sliver in your eye, Aunt Gulabo had the skillful and the soothing touch to extract it, and you could go to her to take care of such problems. Thorns pierced the feet of boys, and slivers of various materials or animal fodder got into people's eyes quite frequently. She would wrap the edge of her veil around her index finger and would lift your eyelid to remove any foreign matter in it with great skill and without causing pain or aggravation. And if you had a thorn in the foot, your foot would go on her knee as you would lean back, and her needle would take the thorn out. My mother used to say, "Everything about Gulabo is good, except her *kismet*," or "Gulabo is incredibly good but her *karma* is not good."

As luck would have it, Gulabo was from a poor farming family. She had the looks and bearing of an aristocrat but she was stuck in a life of poverty. Her husband-to-be, nicknamed 'Viceroy' by his expatriate friends when he was abroad, returned from Shanghai after many years of service and it was expected that he might have money. He was much older, but her people (maybe her parents were already dead and other relatives did this) married her off to the Shanghai-returned Viceroy, who actually was poor. It was rumored that Viceroy had to pay the bride price to her folks, as all the less desirable or older bridegrooms had to. After being married, Gulabo tried her best and worked very hard to make a good life for her husband and herself. The joke used to be that Gulabo had to power the fodder-cutting machine, because her husband was so weak that he could only put the fodder into it, but did not have the strength to turn the machine. And running the fodder machine was the men's job, not a woman's work. There were some other, rather indelicate things that this delicate and beautiful lady had to do because her husband was just not very capable. Their house, built by Viceroy's father, was just average for the village, but was better than our old house because they had the *chullahni* (separate kitchen) and *darwaza* (frontal building) which we did not have in our old Inner House.

Viceroy and Gulabo did not have much land; he did not have the strength to work hard and they had very little produce each year. Even a struggling farmer would have at least two oxen and a plough; but uncle Viceroy had only the one-horned ox whose other horn had been broken. The single ox with broken horn was a mark of poverty, because only the poorest of the farmers would have a defective-looking ox. In earlier years Viceroy had a broken-down camel which was not strong enough to pull the plough by itself. So he would yoke the camel and the one-horned ox together to pull the plough. In later years when he lost his camel, then Uncle Viceroy would combine the use of his ox with someone else's ox to make a pair to yoke and plow his field. Sometimes my father and uncles, who had a good farming operation, helped their cousin Viceroy with cultivation and harvesting.

It is ironic that Viceroy, having a better start in life, because his father was still alive when he became an adult, did not do as well as did my father and his brothers who started from nothing after becoming orphans. My father and his brothers were physically stronger, more ambitious and persevering; and in those days it was pretty hard to be a successful farmer without a brother or without physical strength, endurance, and good planning. A weak man was no better than a woman when it came to producing crops.

Gulabo had five daughters with Viceroy. In those days, the first-born daughter was accepted somewhat grudgingly, unless she was born after a son, in which case the parents felt better. The second daughter was considered an additional burden and any more than three daughters were considered a punishment from God. Daughters could not do farm work and were pure burden because the parents had the responsibility to feed, protect, and marry them off. It was believed that you raised a daughter only to give her away, while you kept a son for life. So the five daughters were a big load for Viceroy and Gulabo and made them even poorer. One of the daughters had only four toes on each foot, and people thought that was an unlucky omen and that she would bring more misfortune on them. The tall, skinny Viceroy was always sickly, weak, and unable to do much farm work successfully. Gulabo and Viceroy were always struggling, and those daughters were a big burden on their minds and on their meager resources.

Viceroy died in the prime of Gulabo's youth, when she was in her early thirties, leaving her with some surviving daughters. Uncle Mohinder felt that the beautiful Gulabo, being the wife of his cousin and thus a woman of his clan, should be kept and protected. Having a wife of your clan go to someone else was considered somewhat disgraceful, unless she went to her parent's house first, and anything about her future life happened later, out of sight of the deceased husband's clan. Mohinder had been in the habit of visiting and spending time in the home of Viceroy and Gulabo, even before Viceroy's death. It was common for people to go in the evenings and sit in the homes of the members of their clan or of friends spontaneously, without purpose, without invitation and without warning. Doors were usually open and one could enter any house, during the day or evening, and could just start talking casually. One would be offered food and drink even if one just came from next door. They could sit and talk about miscellaneous things if nothing important needed to be planned or discussed.

Even though Mohinder was married to Nihalo at the time and had growing children with her, he fell into a relationship with Gulabo after she became a widow. If he had not already been married, that would have been the perfectly proper and honorable thing to do, under the existing customs of the day. The wife of a brother or cousin was considered like a half-wife in the village culture. Even for a married man, it was not uncommon to take a second wife in those days, and a case like this would have been considered perfectly acceptable in our community. And the correct way would have been to bring Gulabo into his own house as a second wife, since visiting the house of an unmarried woman on a regular basis was not considered proper. But his wife Nihalo made a big stink about Mohinder having a relationship with Gulabo. And since Nihalo had her father's land as leverage, she was not powerless against her husband. So Gulabo could never move into Mohinder's house. In time, Gulabo had a son with Mohinder, but that baby did not live beyond a few months. Later still, they had a daughter named Seeto.

Gulabo herself died young, before the age of forty, of tuberculosis or something similar, as no one knew how to diagnose or cure diseases there in the 1940s. A sick person either recovered on her own or she died. All five of Viceroy and Gulabo's daughters died of some disease before growing up, and all except two of them died even before their mother did. The remaining pair of Viceroy's daughters were briefly under the care of Viceroy's older brother Amolak (who lived in our house most of his adult life, when he was not abroad) but those two girls also died within a couple of years of their mother's death. Seeto was the only daughter of Gulabo to survive, and she was too young to remember much about her mother or her death.

After Gulabo's death, Seeto grew up in harsh and hostile circumstances as a stepchild in the household of Nihalo, who considered her as the offspring of the enemy and an illegitimate child. Seeto spent many days crying, cringing at Nihalo's every harsh glance or cursing word. Seeto also felt mistreated by Nihalo's children and had to be content eating whatever they gave her. Mohinder Singh's children were not particularly mean, but they were young, and reflected the feelings of their mother. Seeto's status made her an easy victim. So she faced a lot of harsh words, rejection, and hostility. She came to our house next door to sit with my sisters and they showed great sympathy as she talked of the conditions of her life. They even tried to teach her how to cook things and to make simple things with her hands since proper girls were expected to be able to knit and embroider. Whatever happened to a girl, her honor or disgrace was shared by the whole clan to some extent; so our family also had an interest in Seeto's well-being. Little Seeto was secure and happiest when her father was around or if ever her father took her along to the farms, away from Nihalo and her children. But this was quite infrequent because it was not customary to take a little girl to the fields, while it would have been quite natural to take a little boy along.

But a girl was not as much of a threat as a boy would be to the stepmother, because she was going to be married off someday and was not going to inherit the land. In time, Seeto grew up to be a fine, graceful girl, with exemplary behavior, pleasing good looks, and she was well liked and respected by everyone. Even Nihalo's sons and daughters began to respect her when they grew up. They felt proud of her and they started treating her as one of their own. People remarked that she had some of the good looks of her mother, and certainly she had her mother's good nature.

Seeto was married into a fairly prosperous though uneducated farming family where she became highly respected. She had a family of her own and was a credit to her late mother Gulabo's name and her father Mohinder's upbringing and support.

Our Joint Family

The joint family of brothers, wives, children, uncles, and elders can form not by any design but automatically as boys grow up working together on their parents' land, getting married and having children of their own. There was certainly an economic advantage in staying together, with the oldest man as the nominal head. There was efficiency in the use of manpower and resources in the joint family system and there was at least the illusion of prosperity with the undivided assets. Everybody worked according to his or her ability and inclination; all their needs were provided for. Some individuals in the family could get by doing very little, enjoying more leisure and spending more resources. Separation from the family seemed unnatural, requiring change and upheaval, and sometimes involving horrendous fights and quarrels between married brothers and even between their wives.

Initially, as the unmarried brothers grow up in the parents' house, working together and fighting the adversaries of the family, it would appear unthinkable that they would ever become hostile to one another. Proper respect of the elder brothers by the younger ones was practiced according to custom. But time, marriages, wives, and children gradually change attitudes.

All the petty emotions, jealousies, and selfishness came into play when adult brothers and their wives interacted with each other from day to day and thought of their individual futures. The ultimate deciding factor, other than the temperaments of the individuals involved, were the feelings of "how much am I losing and others gaining in the joint setup, and how much better could I do after separation?" Then only if they were afraid that their circumstances would be worse after separating would people stay together as time passed. Some would say: "I would eat less but live independently, rather than live in this hell of togetherness." and they fought for separation. So the boy who would sacrifice anything and be prepared to give his life for "my brother" and "our family" in his younger days gradually changed his attitude as he formed his own family.

Any careless word said by one wife to another or to her child added to the animosity. Men might do the actual quarreling and fighting, but wives were frequently accused of poisoning the ears of the husbands against the rest of the family. There was always the perception and accusation that wives were the instigators and the poisoning agents behind the breakup of joint families. The truth is that if there were no wives, there would not be any families to break up. And even if the wives were angels of harmony, their very existence would ultimately cause the breakup. Unmarried men would not think of asking for separate property and having a separate farm operation. In fact, after the breakup of a joint family, an unmarried brother usually lived and worked in the house of a married brother who would control and use the unmarried brother's land and property.

If the parents were alive and able to keep the peace between the sons' families with their control over the land and resources, the joint family could last intact for a longer time. But separation was inevitable; it was only a matter of time. It was not socially acceptable, and in those days not even legally possible, for the parents to refuse to hand over the ancestral land and property to their sons who had decided to separate, even if they did not like them. Their choice was only about which son to live with after the sons were separated. Even after the family breakup, the elderly parents never lived separately from their sons; frequently they lived with the youngest son.

The division of property could be complicated and could lead to bitterness, physical fights, and even injuries, especially if the parents were no longer living. Who got what was not a cut and dried question. There could be considerations and quarrels about who contributed most to the family; whose wife's jewelry was sold to make payment on a common piece of land; who gave the family a good start by working hard in the early years; who had been a freeloader; whose daughter was married by using the family's common resources; whose children had been raised with common resources and whose wife is just starting to have babies with long responsibilities ahead; which two brothers would like to keep their resources together after separation from the others and who got the unmarried brother with assets but very little expenses; who got the shady side and who got the sunny side of the residential areas, and so on. Greed and differences of opinion were inevitable; the chances for conflict were many. And it was only by the compromising and gentle nature of the parties involved, or by the intervention of a strong and respected elder, that separation could occur without serious conflicts and violence.

The breakup process for our own joint family was prolonged and ugly; the serious quarrels started in 1943 and the family finally separated in 1945. There were many arguments and in the last year a few nasty physical fights, one of which almost resulted in a death, but for the narrow margin of escape. There were no planned assassinations, but while the conflicts raged and tempers flared, any sharp or heavy farm implement was a potential death weapon during an argument between the belligerent married brothers.

Eventually the house and the land of the four brothers were divided into two parts, with the land and property of one unmarried brother combined with that of each married brother. The unmarried brothers could not really oppose this arrangement, otherwise they would be considered bad people who did not want the next generation, the children of their brothers, to feed and flourish. They would be given daily meals and a bed, could get clothes made of the domestic *khadder* every six months; and there were no other necessary expenses. The bachelor would work for the brother's family according to his ability, but probably harder than everyone else, because he would have no distractions. Other people envied the families that had such bachelor brothers, because they was all benefit and no liability, all production and no dead load.

Our joint family was relatively large, with nearly twenty members in 1945. Uncle Tiloka was fifty plus, a widower without an heir but the head of our household; my father Naginder Singh and my mother Bhagi had four living sons and three grown daughters; Uncle Nikk never married, and Uncle Mohinder's family grew rapidly after his marriage to Nihalo; they had six children within seven or eight years. Add to this the farm workers and sharecroppers (*seeri*) who had to be fed daily. There was a big cooking operation at least twice a day.

It was hard sometimes to estimate who was breaking his back and who was a slacker. But in our joint family there were no conflicts over work, food, clothing, expenses, or about sharing things. All the conflicts were about the future. Uncle Tiloka used to say: "Stay together and you will be big *sardars*; you will have plenty of property and prestige;

your sons will ride horses and cars; your children can be educated and be married into good families; you will have every kind of *pedarath* (fabulous delicacy) to eat." My father was not keen on separation and he usually deferred to Uncle Tiloka on most issues. But Uncle Mohinder and his wife Nihalo felt that they were getting the short end of the stick. Uncle Mohinder's wife Nihalo was about to inherit all of the property of her father, as he had no son or other heir. With the expectation of that inheritance, Mohinder and Nihalo knew they could make it alone and therefore they had an additional incentive to separate.

My sister Maro had been married, and the other two sisters could have been married using joint family resources. I was learning English and was preparing for the matriculation examination; and the two younger brothers were all a load on the family. The fact that my brother Kartar graduated from college and became a military officer was a family asset. But Mohinder still felt that he was getting a raw deal and he wanted to be separated unless my education was stopped and I was put to work on the farms, and a few other of his demands were satisfied. He also wanted to know how much money Kartar was earning and he accused my father of keeping a joint account with Kartar in the Imperial Bank to which he himself had no access. He would say "Your daughter has been married off and one son is educated and others are in the process; but my children are all young and have required no expense from this house because their mother's folks give things to them; we are getting old and will be unfit to work in a few years; Gurnam is a boy who is thick of bone and ample of flesh and therefore very suitable to be a farmer. If you send him to school too, and don't put him to farm work to take the load off us, what has the joint family to offer me?"

I personally was quite pleased with Uncle Mohinder's argument. I always wanted to stay in the village, farm, and never wanted to go to school. I pictured myself at the head of an operation of several ploughs of oxen and camels, manned by workers and sharecroppers, sharing work with friends, owning high-quality camels, horses, and oxen, going to the fairs and performances with friends, racing camels and oxcarts, drinking with friends on the numerous occasions of festivals, weddings, singing circles and other celebrations. I had visualized only the unreal, romantic side; I had never experienced the harshness and desperation of the real farming life. No wonder I thought Uncle Mohinder had some good ideas about keeping me on the farm.

The joint family breakup was hard on Uncle Tiloka's spirit. It broke up the entire operation that was under him. Our house, powerful and prosperous by village standards at the time, disintegrated and the separated families felt poorer. Simultaneously we were losing a good part of the under mortgage land because of unforeseen economic changes. There was change in economic conditions from the Depression to World War II, resulting in inflating land and commodity prices. We lost some land that we held under the mortgage system, as described later. My father was in a more precarious state because of the major needs of his family, small prospect of any income, and his reluctance and inability to start a farming operation alone, since he had never been a plowman. The adults in our family felt some degree of depression and anxiety after the family breakup, and even the children felt sad. The feeling was not much different from that of a divorce in a family. We had never experienced such feelings and such alienation from those who were our family during all our lives. For some of us it was bewildering and depressing.

It felt as if those who were our family had become hostile adversaries forever. But such breakups were as inevitable as death; it was only a matter of when and how.

In most cases, conciliation started soon after the complete separation, as the separated families lived and worked in close proximity. Even though the adults stayed angry for some time, they treated each other's children in a civil manner. Nihalo and Uncle Mohinder were always nice to me. For most separated families there was usually no serious cause of contention after the property had been divided. The alienated families still got together for weddings, deaths, and other common needs. People used to say "One may refuse to go to a wedding, but one cannot fail to be present at a death," when talking about their obligations toward the alienated relatives. And when it came to community matters, it was always one's own clan against others, regardless of any internal resentment or quarrel.

CHAPTER 4

MY PRECIOUS SIBLINGS

My oldest sister, born in late 1920, was initially named Preetam Kaur, but she was always called Maro, which means thin or weak. This nickname was mildly derogatory in a culture where everyone wanted to be and look fat. Our family was glad that she inherited the looks of her father rather than her mother. When she was growing up, older women of the neighborhood would say that she looked just like Manno, my father's mother. Maro had the personal qualities that a parent could be proud of. For a girl in the village, this just meant being obedient, doing the housework fast and with finesse, and being conscientious. By the age of nine, Maro had the reputation of picking cotton faster than any of the adult workers. My father taught her to read *Gurmukhi* (Punjabi) at home, in spite of the crush of housework; and with some effort she learned to read the Sikh scriptures.

When Maro became a teenager, she developed a temper. When she was angry with me, she would make a gesture of biting her hand with her teeth and would say, "I will eat you raw if I catch you." To this I would say teasingly "Hey everybody, look how *Ladhu ka Jand* is throwing sparks." This was reference to a supposedly haunted *Jand* tree in the desert which was reputed to have fire burning on it at night, because *bhoot* (ghosts) were supposed to live in it. Girls in our society were very reluctant to pick fights with boys, but if we made Maro angry, it was not her style to let it go with a smile of frustration and helplessness, as my other sisters would; nor could she work things out by negotiation and tact. Before she was married she was in charge of keeping control of petty cash for the house and of any valuables that uncle Trilok Singh did not put in the family safe. After her marriage my younger sisters took over the cash responsibilities, because all my sisters were presumed to be smarter than their mother, who was never given any money to handle.

Maro was 21 years old, quite late for those times, when in February 1942 she was married off to Harnek Singh Dhillon from the village of Bhagwan Garh, about ten miles south of Bhatinda. His old-fashioned family called him Harnekm instead of Harnek, probably at the recommenda-tion of a sadhu, to make it sound like a Sanskrit-influenced name. One hundred and twenty-five people came with the groom's wedding party. My father was in favor of the simplest possible ceremony, with groom's party consisting of five people only, with minimum show and expense and no jewelry. But the groom's people would not agree to such simplicity, as they were obliged to bring their relatives and all the men of their Dhillon clan in the wedding party, according to their custom. Because of my father's opposition, Maro had not been allowed to pierce ears or nose, as my father felt that alterations to the body were a violation of God's creation. So Maro had no ear and nose ornaments, in stark contrast to the custom for new brides in those days. Our family did get the gold ornaments made for her head, as they did not require any body piercing. My father was against the saggi-phull ornaments for the head too, but in the rural environment of those days, a bride without saggi-phull on her head would surely look like a widow or an unmarried daughter of the village, and that would be a horrible image to start with at the in-law house. Ears and nose without any ornaments were also unacceptable for a married woman in that village, so later, at her in-laws' house, Maro's ears were pierced and she got a few other ornaments. My father, however, always thought that piercing ears and nose was an unworthy thing to do. The in-laws sometimes changed the names of brides, due to some conflict, preference, or superstition. After her marriage, her in-laws changed her formal name from Preetam Kaur to Kulwant Kaur, but she was always called Maro.

Maro's husband Harnek Singh was gentle, intelligent, and tolerant, with a great deal of common sense. He never drank alcohol, though he did use opium-like drugs; the use of opium was legal and was considered perfectly proper among men in those days. Maro herself was somewhat of a perfectionist. In her married life, her chief complaint against her husband, apart from the opium, was that he did not stand up to his parents. She felt that they did not respect him enough, and that consequently they also treated her as though she were insignificant. If she had been clever or manipulative, she might have dealt with her in-laws more effectively; by and large they were decent people. Whenever I went to visit there, I felt that they were superior, more affluent and cultured than our own family. But that might be because as a twelve-year-old I was easily impressed by the manners, appearance, and language of an unfamiliar family. Maro also had a touchy relationship with her two sisters-in-law. They were not really mean or vicious, but if the mother-in-law in an average house made a bride miserable, it was the duty of her daughters to do the same, if only by little innuendoes and subtle remarks. There was no physical viciousness in their house; it was just that sometimes even an apparently neutral remark could bite if you were the sensitive type. Maro never felt completely comfortable or in control of her life until some years later.

Maro's husband's younger brother Niranjan was the more favored son. Well into adulthood, he was away at boarding schools in Bhatinda and other places, frequently failing at most grade levels and not advancing to high school. He was a good hockey player and therefore was pampered by school authorities. Like many other sardar boys in boarding schools, he lorded it over the school servants and was respected by every body for being a sportsman. I always felt shy and intimidated whenever I met Niranjan, who was older than me in age but behind me in grades. He spoke with extra politeness and formality to me; in the villages such politeness could be a way to distance oneself. Those spoiled boys like Niranjan grew much older than other students in their grades as they usually had no academic inclination, kept failing, and going back to the same grade year after year. After Niranjan quit school, by recommendations, nepotism, and bribes he got a job as a *patwari*, a government official who keeps record of land transactions and ownership. But he could not, or did not bother to, do his job of maintaining the records. He was fond of drinking alcohol in excess, which used to be the stylish thing to do. So he would pay a little money privately to some unauthorized literate person to read and write for his job unofficially; such a person could not get the job for himself, since one needed influence and the ability to pay bribe to get a job like that. So Niranjan lived a life of leisure, with others his official work. Maro's husband Harnek Singh, on the other hand, was treated like an ordinary farm worker in the household, as his parents controlled all the land and property. This status never seemed to bother him, because that was the pattern of life in the villages, but Maro was more sensitive about his status and about her own.

Maro had to deal with a mother-in-law who in her own way was a memorable character. For the first few years Maro often complained that her mother-in-law was making her life miserable, though her mother-in-law was subtle rather than confrontational. They were gentle people; open quarrels were not the style of their house, unlike our own. Maro could grumble in their house, but she usually just dumped her frustrations and problems on us when she came to our village to visit, and this made us feel powerless and humiliated. In our culture, having your sister or daughter mistreated or unhappy and not being able to do anything about it robs you of all your pride. The happiness of a daughter or sister was a lifetime responsibility for a man in our society. A man would feel worthless and degraded if his sister or daughter was unhappy and he could do nothing about it. It would be rude for us to address her husband without proper respect. But sometimes when he came to visit us, my sisters called him on it and complained that he was not providing Maro with enough support against his own family. He usually tried to explain away the actual situation in his own gentle and conciliatory way. Her mother-in-law may never have intended any harm, but Maro felt oppressed by the unequal power relationship between them. With rare exceptions, such mother-in-law/daughter-in-law hostility was universal in our society in those days. In some families, though not in Maro's, this hostility could take the form of serious verbal abuse and even violence between mother-in-law and daughter-in-law.

I personally thought Maro's mother-in-law was a gracious woman. She was from a prosperous landowning family of Shameer village, had impeccable taste and manners, had patrician good looks, and usually communicated in calm, controlled ways. Her vocabulary was never belligerent, but sometimes, a few seconds after she said something you might realize that you didn't measure up, if she intended to have you feel that way. It was easy for her to say, "The wife of so and so in this brotherhood came loaded with ornaments, and her parents, the sardars of such and such place, gave her husband a horse and golden *kuntha* necklace when he went to visit this time. Those sardars have great style and class." But it could be interpreted as "What have you brought from your parents to our house?" Or she would say "All the women who looked at the bride's empty nose and ears without jewelry, were saying 'What happened here; where is the real bride?'" It must have been pretty hard for Maro as a bride to be without any earrings, nose rings and gold jewelry in a place where only the cursed widows and unmarried daughters were without such ornaments. Although Maro's mother-in-law did not harp on such issues frequently, she found subtle ways to indicate that her family's prestige had been lowered since the new bride had not brought enough jewelry and a big enough dowry. Every house wanted to be able to boast about the bride, the amount of dowry she brought, and the house that she came from.

Maro's father-in-law was a gentle and ethical man, and her mother-in-law was a gracious woman, with impressive presence and great dignity, but when it came to caste barriers, she was more exclusive than a Brahmin. She would never let any of her low caste farm workers come beyond a certain boundary in her courtyard. If she had to dole out food for them, the utensil which she used for doling the food into the worker's pot—without ever touching it—would not be placed among other utensils until after it had been given a special cleaning. When pouring liquid into the pot of a low caste worker, she would use a *parnali* (spout), pouring into it the liquid which would then flow into the worker's pot. This method increased the distance from her pitcher to the pot and thus ensured that no drop could bounce off the pot and on to her utensil or her clothing to defile her. A low caste person would not be allowed to touch her skin, and if one ever touched her clothing accidentally, that clothing had to be taken off and washed, and she would bathe herself before engaging in other tasks. She frowned upon the lax practices that she heard about in our parents' house, considering them as indirect violations of her own dharma. She believed that the failure in our house to maintain a strict distance from untouchable low castes would affect her indirectly; because if you touch someone from a low caste, you yourself become defiled and unfit to be touched by other high caste people until you have been cleansed and purified.

Maro's in-laws, the Dhillons, were the most powerful family in their village in the 1940s, although in Punjab at that time they would have been considered to be only of average means. They had some hereditary status, which my own family had none of; so I felt that they were in the category of real *sardars* while we were not. The fact that they had set up an oil-powered flour mill in the village in the 1940s indicated that they had assets other than land. Harnek's grandfather had been a *zaildar* (local supervisor of law and order in several villages), his uncle was a village *numberdar* (local revenue collector) and another uncle was a *safaid posh* (white wearer) with some government recognition or authority; no other family in their village had such standing. None of these positions had any direct authority to enforce laws, but the village people deferred to them. Such ranks did not have important authority in our village of Mehraj, but the situation was different in Dhillon's village, which was relatively behind the time. If outside officials came to their village, they would talk first to the Dhillons about the situation in the village to find out if anyone was misbehaving. In the absence of police officials, people sometimes brought complaints against others to the Dhillons' head of the family or elder. The elder could decide the matter and would sometimes prescribe some minor physical punishment (like a few lashes) for certain categories of people. On the local level their word was the law in those days.

There was some risk in handling people in this way as the Dhillons were not police officials or judges. In fact, during the 1940s some outlaws became angry with the Dhillons and publicly threatened to kill the Dhillon men. My brother-in-law had to watch his movements even during the daytime; he had to be careful, armed, and in the company of others while working in the fields. At night the clan houses were like fortresses with closed gates. This situation continued until the outlaws were killed by the police. After

World War II, the customs and patterns of life changed. Then the Dhillon family lost its clout, while some formerly poor farmers became more prosperous because of the economic changes.

Maro's life improved with time as her in-laws got older and her husband's sisters were married off. The prestige of our own family was raised relative to theirs when my brother Kartar became a commissioned officer, and that improved Maro's status. Powerful brothers usually improved a married woman's situation with her husband and her in-laws. Having the first son in the family, Shamsher, also gave Maro a sense of permanence and security. Later, Maro had sons Rajinder, Gurtej and Devinder. Her son Gurtej got mental disease in adulthood and died after suffering for many years. Both her daughters, Raj Preet and Manjit have their own families. Her son Shamsher practices medicine in Bhatinda, and sons Rajinder and Devinder are in the pharmacy business there. A generation earlier, going into any work other than farming or government service would have been unthinkable for a landowner's son. But with the scarcity of land and the new perspectives formed through education, *Jat* boys and girls are beginning to look for other opportunities. Maro and her husband, in their mid-80s, became pretty well respected in the village in their waning years. Harnek's younger brother Niranjan died many years ago, probably due to excessive drinking.

Recently, when I asked about his opium addiction, Harnek Singh said, "I still feel the need, but the wonderful days of good opium are gone, because opium is illegal now. Now we get only the leaves of the *post* (poppy) plant and grind them to get some mild effect of the drug. When the drug seller comes to the village, he sends a message to every addict to come and get some leaves. But this poppy leaf stuff is not very satisfying compared to the old *shahi nasha* (royal intoxicant) of real opium." In the village culture, people were usually not embarrassed to admit that they used drugs. Harnek Singh Dhillon remains in good health in his mid-eighties and still performs some farming tasks daily.

My Venerated Brother Kartar

My elder brother Kartar was born in November 1923, three years after my eldest sister Maro. From infancy, he was a child with a mind at peace. My mother said that as a baby Kartar never cried or complained, unlike most babies who had to be given opium to keep them in a good mood. For that reason women of the neighborhood called him Gugga Peer, the name for some Hindu holy entity who was famous for keeping quiet. Kartar grew up with a strong conscience, a kind nature, a sensitivity towards others and a compulsion to want to do everything ethically and according to the rules. Like our father, he had a great capacity to concentrate on whatever he needed to do. As a young student in a junior school in Mehraj, he was never late for school after he was punished once by my father for being late; in fact he would get there and wait outside, even before the sweeper/janitor opened the schoolroom doors. Since he was the first-born boy, our family had great expectations for Kartar. When he reached the fifth grade, they admitted him in the boarding school at Nathana, when I was still too young to know him. Kartar was the brightest child in his class, at first in Mehraj, and later in the Nathana boarding school. There he acquired a reputation for his intelligence and became a minor legend with the name Swalia, which I believe meant either a math wizard or a questioner. When he was in high school, his headmaster, Sirmukh Singh, admired Kartar and, having a son of the same age and believing that one becomes like the company one keeps, he encouraged his son to associate with Kartar. In fact the headmaster asked Kartar to live in a room in their house part of the time. Kartar would usually eat his meals in the boarding house as he was officially living there; but then he would study or sleep in the headmaster's house. In our culture it was quite common for individuals to live with friends or relatives for long periods, just like another member of the family.

At the age of about eleven, while he was in the boarding school at Nathana, Kartar heard stories of *bhagt* (in Sanskrit the word is *bhakta*) who devoted themselves to God or who even met God. Kartar became convinced that worldly pursuits were all false and that the true purpose of life was to find the all powerful God. Therefore he determined that he would renounce the world, become a bhagt or a *sadhu*, and would go in search of God in holy places. One day, without receiving permission from anyone, he left his boarding school in Nathana and headed for the Himalyan hills. He had planned this quest for God with another boy in the school, but the other boy backed out at the last minute. Kartar, however, was not going to be discouraged from pursuing what he thought was his true purpose in life.

It was a common belief that mountains were the abode of the gods; at higher altitudes one is closer to the heavens than are the people living in the plains. Therefore mountains were the preferred places for holy men aspiring to meet God. For the holy people, the mountains also provided peace and isolation from crowds, and some distance from worldly and sinful activities. Even the Hindu holy scriptures like the *Bhagwat Gita* mention that a bhagt should live far away from the distraction of the masses. For these reasons, serious ascetics and holy people set up their *dera* in the hills. Only a sadhu who did not have the awareness, or one who had some other over-riding reason like inheriting some large property from his *guru*, would settle for a river bank, a lake, or a forest. A mediocre sadhu would settle for any lowly tree by the village pond.

Anyway, after leaving his boarding school at Nathana, Kartar started walking along the banks of the Sirhind Canal, which goes by Nathana and also by our village Mehraj. He proceeded toward Ropar, which was about 70 miles away. He would go into villages at mealtime and would ask for *roti* (bread, food), which the village women usually are happy to give to bhagts. And begging for food was legitimate for a bhagt, as he was not supposed to own anything or to engage in earning a living. Kartar had only a bed sheet with him. But the weather was mild at that time of the year and he could just lean against a tree to sleep at night. A holy person might own a blanket but was not expected to live in comfort, as comfort was not considered good for the soul.

After traveling 70 miles to the vicinity of Ropar, Kartar headed toward Ambala, thinking that he would first go to the holy place of Hardwar on the Ganga river and then proceed to the higher mountains. He was not completely clear about his destination, although he had thought of going to a place like Rishi Kesh where the Sikh Guru, Gobind Singh is supposed to have sojourned at some time in his life.

This was not the age of rapid communication or of panic over missing children (except in the minds of parents), nor did the boarding school authorities feel any legal responsibility. Police would not attend to the matter of missing children in those days. Some days later, the school somehow informed my father that his son had disappeared.

The boy who had decided to back out of the plan of becoming a bhagt with Kartar gave a hint that Kartar was thinking of going to the mountains. My parents were shocked to hear of Kartar's disappearance, and my mother could not stop crying. Kartar, being the first son, was very precious to my parents; I was only four years old, and their third son, Gurdial, had not been born yet.

So my father went in search of Kartar and walked along the canal toward Ropar to trace him. He asked some cattle grazers, the canal maintenance laborers, and other people on the way if they had seen a lone boy a few days earlier. We used to follow the same procedure in finding our animals that had gotten lost, sometimes for several days, and more often than not we would find the lost animal that way. Some people confirmed seeing Kartar along the canal many days earlier, but he had already traveled beyond Ropar and was far beyond my father's area of search. So after searching unsuccessfully for a few days, my father returned home, dejected. My mother was in tears most of the time after learning of Kartar's disappearance. Many days later, about mid-morning, while my mother was quietly cooking *roti* and as I was playing nearby, watching the tears flowing continuously from her eyes, Kartar showed up in our front yard, all by himself. My mother burst into loud cries as she got up and ran to embrace him. My sad and quiet mother had been affecting me also with her tears and I was glad that the ordeal ended for my parents.

It so happened that in Ambala, Kartar had met some old gentleman who asked Kartar where he was from and where he was going. The man had been in service in Hong Kong and in those times had met some people from our village. The man told Kartar that he was too young and impressionable to become a bhagt. The man also told him that leaving his parents worried sick might not look good in the eyes of God. Somehow he convinced Kartar to return home. He put Kartar on the train back toward our village. I would have been beaten for such behavior on my return, but Kartar was too decent to deserve any punishment. In fact I never saw Kartar get a beating, although I heard that he was beaten once for being late to school when he was in the first grade. After this episode, Kartar got another nickname for a while. His friends called him Bhagt, a devotee of God, in addition to Swalia, the solver of questions.

To me and to all his siblings, Kartar was like a celebrity whenever he came home from the boarding school. This might have been because he did not live with us and had the reputation of being very intelligent; moreover, he was so kind and good-natured that conflict with him was unthinkable. Unlike a lot of boys who were violent towards their younger siblings, Kartar never mistreated anyone; our family just did not thrive on conflict but on compliance. Whereas in neighboring families even the girl children could not stand to be near each other, my mother would say, "I am lucky; even if I put all my kids in one bed, they still won't have conflicts or complaints. What would I do with that many children if they created trouble like other peoples' kids do!" Sibling rivalry was not very apparent in my family. Fights and violence among my siblings were rare and our quarrels were never vicious. Possibly it was the innate kind and humble nature of our mother that determined our behavior. Usually the younger ones obeyed the older ones and the older ones looked after the the younger ones. I may have been a bit hard on young Gurdial a few times, but Kartar was never harsh with me or with my other siblings. This trait of kindness and helpfulness in Kartar never diminished in spite of the many adverse experiences in his life. He was always helpful not just to his siblings but also to distant cousins and to his many friends in public life. Kartar never would do anything illegal or against social rules and ethics, although in later years he had no strong faith in any particular religion.

When I was of school age, Kartar would sometime wrestle with me without using his full strength and would let me win in order to encourage me. When during his school vacation he was sent to graze cattle, he would take me along, although we were 6 ½ years apart in age. At noon all the boys brought their cattle to water and sometimes the boys engaged in wrestling games, pushups and other competitive exercises. Kartar would set me to wrestle boys of similar age (or slightly older ones since I was strong for my age), and he felt extremely proud when I would win. He would encourage me to do pushups and other physical exercises to make me stronger. And he would tell our mother to feed me more *ghee* so I could become fatter and stronger. Since Kartar was learning English in boarding school, he would come home and teach English nursery rhymes and riddles to me when I was not even five years old. It all sounded like clever tongue twisting; I could speak the words but I had no idea what it was all about: "Twinkle Twinkle, Little Star...,"; "Every Lady in This Land..."; and "The more I looked at it, the less I liked it...."

Once when Kartar was about twelve years old, he came home from the boarding school. He had heard rumors that there were tribes of *bande khane* (people eaters) scouring the countryside, who supposedly killed people and ate their flesh. He expressed this concern to my father. My father tried to assure Kartar that there was no reason to fear, that there were no such people, and that the government would arrest them if there was any indication that they existed. Kartar insisted that those people were sneaky and clever like hunters and would not let the government find out when they took away, killed, and ate people. Kartar thought that he himself was safe and grown up; he was worried only about me, his five-year old little brother, when he himself would be away in the boarding school. Kartar gave me safety instructions to avoid being killed by the cannibals. He said, "Gurnam, don't go with any strange man anywhere. Don't let any man give you money or sweets; they might tempt you with more sweets and take you away and they could kill you and eat you." Even at that age Kartar was concerned about me.

Kartar's College Education & Military Career

I was never sent to a boarding school, but my brothers Kartar and Gurdial went to the one in Nathana village, six or seven miles away, and a dangerous three hour journey. The rural boarding schools of those times were not prestigious, expensive, or exclusive institutions. In the 19th century, even our village had a boarding school, although we had no road, no railroad station, and no electricity. Ours was only a primary school that had a building for the pupils from other villages to eat and sleep in. The very exclusive so-called "public schools" based on the English pattern were really private boarding schools in hill resort towns, in a world unknown to the rural people. These "public schools" were meant for the children of the British officials and for some aristocratic Indian children. The village boarding schools, like the one in Nathana, which my brothers attended, were established so that boys from faraway villages could go to school there. These schools had a dormitory-like arrangement. The parents supplied a *charpai* (bed) with the necessary

61

bedding, but usually a student had not even a trunk, because any additional shirt or shorts that the boy owned could be just hung on a peg, doorknob, or bedpost. Each boy did have a little canister to bring *ghee* from his home to add to his meals. The parents supplied the wheat flour for *roti* and *mung* beans for *daal*. The boarding house would have a *langri* (cook) who could buy fresh vegetables once in a while, and there was a teacher whose additional duty was to be cashier and supervisor for the boarding house. The school and the dormitory rooms, being government property, were free for the students. The cook's wage and incidental food expenses would be less than a couple of rupees a month for each student, as people could not afford to put much money into education in those days.

Kartar's arrival home from the boarding school in Nathana after every couple of weeks would be enthusiastically awaited by us children. His arrival time would be uncertain, as he had to walk the seven-mile distance home after attending school until noon on Saturday. We would gather the neighborhood kids like Kando, Nando, Seeto, Karo, and Gebo, and we would wait along the path from Nathana. We would stand on high ground and shout as we saw bodies approaching on the horizon from afar, "There, he is coming!... There! He is coming!... I see him!... no, that is somebody else...." There were not usually many people walking on any path in the countryside, so we could see individuals coming from half a mile away. Then we would shout again "There, he is coming..." and after much waiting, he would arrive with the empty ghee canister and a notebook, and every kid wanted to hold his hand as we walked home. To us, Kartar really was a celebrity.

After high school, it was a matter of great pride for my father, that Kartar was admitted to Khalsa College at Amritsar in 1939. This was the pre-eminent college of the Sikhs, located in their holy city. Boys of prominent Sikh families from all over the Punjab and some who had returned from foreign countries, would go to study there. Being the first boy from our village to go to Khalsa College was a very big step for Kartar. He won a merit scholarship and also the Nabha-Malwa scholarship, which was established by the Raja of Nabha for that college, to be given to the boy from the Malwa region (south of the Sutlej river) who had the highest score in the matriculation examination. Kartar even got a divinity scholarship since he was so conscientious and punctual about attending the Gurdwara religious service in those days. Kartar studied dutifully and avoided student politics according to my father's strict instructions. Student strikes were common in India even during the war. Once Kartar complained to my father, "I have to be careful about attending classes during the strikes; they call you a *toady* and *jholi chuk* if they catch you attending classes during a student strike." But our disciplinarian father always wanted him to tread on the straight and narrow and to avoid all radical student activities.

Kartar was built like our father, tall, thin and rather weak-looking when he was young, but after his teenage years he acquired a V-shaped body, with muscular legs and thin thighs like my father. I was built more like my mother's folks, not as tall and a little chunky. Kartar participated in the University Officer Training Corps, which was run by the British Indian Army on college campuses to train future officers. The Second World War was in full force at the time. And as soon as he graduated from college in 1943, Kartar was selected to become a King's Commissioned Officer in the British Indian Army. This gave a big boost to the family fortune and prestige.

The batch of cadets that included Kartar was run pretty fast through the Officer Training School, since the need for fighting manpower was at its peak in 1943. In the military, Kartar, who was brilliant, disciplined, conscientious, and without any bad social habits, was admired among the officers. In the latter part of the Second World War he saw some combat at the front in Burma, Malaya, and the Southeast Asia Theatre, where the British were fighting the Japanese. When the Japanese surrendered in 1945, he was sent to the Dutch East Indies (later to become Indonesia) where the British Indian forces were engaged in peacekeeping. Political activists there had acquired weapons at the time of Japanese surrender and wanted to expel their Dutch colonial rulers. In 1946, Kartar was sent back to India.

In 1947 India was being partitioned and was gaining Independence. All the British officers were going to leave India, following the Independence. Indian officers would then be occupying the high offices in the military, and therefore opportunities for advancement looked abundant. For a period of about a year in 1947-48, Kartar had a special civilian assignment in the interim emergency administration dealing with problems related to the Independence and Partition of India. During this assignment he had a magistrate's authority as an assistant commissioner. He could have transferred permanently into the civil service, as everyone in the village was urging to him to do. They argued that the civilian officers enjoyed great authority and power over the lives of the public and had unlimited opportunities to get rich. "The power itself is worth a lot even if you never accept a bribe directly, and you could help a lot of your own people with jobs and favoritism." the village people argued. But Kartar decided to return to the military life after his civilian assignment was over. He felt that it was easier to stay honest, and free of politics and corruption, in military life than in the civilian administration. By this time Kartar had become like the British in his attitudes. He was so straightforward, honest, and upright that he would never follow any unethical practice, and the civilian service was full of corruption even in those days. Besides, there was perceived to be a great deal of glamour and adventure in the military life compared to the civilian paper-pushing. Business careers had not yet acquired any degree of attractiveness among the educated people or the upper classes. After losing their own states, even the princes, the sons of erstwhile maharajas, would join the military rather than any business. In the process of returning to the military, Kartar switched to the Armed Corps, which had the highest prestige and best prospects for upward mobility in the Indian army. Kartar's regiment was called Deccan Horse; the tank regiments had retained their old names like Skinners Horse, Second Lancers, Third Cavalry, Hudsons Horse etc.

In December 1954, Kartar was married to Harjinder (Jeet) of the Randhawa family. Jeet's cousin Col G. S. Randhawa and his wife acted as matchmakers since they had known Karatar for about five years during their service together. They had invited him to meet Jeet once, some years before the actual marriage, when she was of high school age. In subsequent years Kartar and Jeet had four daughters, Kiran, Monica, Kavita (Vita) and Natasha. The youngest, Natasha, became a journalist and tragically died in a helicopter crash in Afghanistan in April 1993, while covering the political turmoil and civil war in that country after the Russian pullout. The family never got over the shock of her untimely death.

Kartar's rise in the service was pretty smooth; he had undergone the Staff College course and other assignments to prepare him for a high rank in the military. Subsequently he was picked by the Chief of the Army to command the latter's very own regiment, the 16th Cavalry. But his life as a lieutenant colonel commanding the tank regiment for some two or three years changed suddenly. Kartar was about to be assigned to his next post, but before he could be actually transferred, the 1965 war between India and Pakistan broke out. My two brothers Kartar and Gurdial were now fighting for India in two different tank regiments in that war. Kartar's regiment suffered heavy losses and he as the commander was blamed for those setbacks. At the conclusion of that war, Kartar saw no hope of a bright future for himself in the Indian army. The higher military officials tried to scapegoat all those commanders whose regiments they judged to have performed unsatisfactorily.

My then wife Gail, along with our young boys, Apar and Gyan, was visiting our family in India in 1966. She heard of Kartar's situation in the military and of the damage to his future career prospects. In her daring, damn-the-consequences style she said, "Quit your military job here; come to America; we will put you through school and you can have a second career in America." But when I was told of Kartar's intentions, I wrote back: "It is not good to get carried away by the rumors of riches and the good life in America. Most of the population here lives from paycheck to paycheck. Whereas in India you are a respected officer, here you will start life as a nobody. Here the future can be difficult and uncertain." Then Kartar wrote back to me: "I am a little hesitant to take such a drastic step myself, but my wife Jeet is 'mad keen' to come to America."

So in December 1967, after a 24-year military career, Kartar left the Indian Army to come to America.. He went to the University of California at Berkeley, earned his BA and MBA. degrees, and even made the Phi Beta Kappa society. Then he started a second career as a financial analyst for AT&T at the age of 47. He worked for that corporation and its successor for another 24 years or so.

Kartar had become the chief support of my father's household after our joint family was split up in 1945 and we separated from my uncles. The income from our share of the land was not adequate to support the family, as our fifty-ish father felt too old to work on the farm. The responsibilities of the family were considerable. Sister Maro had been married off in Feb 1942, but in that society the financial load of daughters on the parents never stopped altogether. After the parents paid for the daughter's marriage, they felt responsible for keeping her happy for the rest of her life. Two of my sisters still remained to be married and three of us brothers were to be educated. Kartar wanted to do the best for every one of his siblings, regardless of whatever sacrifices he had to make. Although my father did his share of worrying, it was Kartar who did most of the family's planning and financing. The village people expected such support from the eldest son, but some of the educated and fashionable boys who had started living in cities or who became big officials just avoided such responsibilities.

Kartar started a joint bank account with my father, into which Kartar's salary would go every month, so that my father would never need to ask for money. Kartar initiated the plan and started the construction of a new house for our family in 1948. He had the worry of further educating his youngest sister Chhoti and arranging for the marriage and settlement of his two younger sisters. He was also struggling to convince me, an intransigent teenager, to pursue a college education. With persistent effort and personal sacrifices, he funded and accomplished all of those goals with a remarkable degree of success. Things in families never go perfectly, but Kartar's consistent success in his goals for every member of the family was remarkable. In the later stages, his wife Jeet's positive attitude and generous nature also contributed to the success.

In 1952, my sister Karo was married; I was not asked to attend that marriage because I was in school in Ahmednagar, a thousand miles away. Sister Chhoti went to college and was married later in about 1960. I had a Master of Science degree in India, and the family helped me go to America to get a Ph. D. in Physics. Brother Gurdial went to college for a while, and then went on to the Indian Military Academy to become an officer; he would ultimately retire as a Major General. Our youngest brother, Kirpal, was educated, received a medical degree from Amritsar, and later became an orthopedic surgeon in the U.S.A.

Without Kartar's efforts and sacrifices, my siblings and I would have struggled like poor peasants in the village. Regardless of how the rest of his life turned out, Kartar had every reason to be satisfied with his accomplishments in raising his siblings from subsistence-level farmers to well-educated and well-established professionals. Kartar also tried to help any boys in neighboring families (distant cousins) who needed aid, guidance, and influence to obtain jobs. A few times Kartar even intervened with the police to release some of the village boys whom the police had arrested on frivolous charges to extract bribes. The boy's family would request Kartar to go to the police station and to put in a good word. In those days the prestige of the army was such that the word of an army officer was not ordinarily turned down; just his presence at the police station could make a difference to soften the attitude of the police. But of course Kartar would not intervene on behalf of any criminal, nor did we have contact with any real criminals.

Kartar used to grumble about having to visit our dirty village after living in high style as a class I officer "On His Majesty's Service" and later "On Indian Government Service." He would say, "Once I take the Bhatinda train, the degradation and dirt starts showing up." But he was also conscientious and dutiful, so he always came to stay with my parents and family during his vacation. In later years his wife also encouraged contact with my parents and our village. This was in contrast with the attitudes of some other educated boys from the villages, who after becoming officers and urban dwellers ignored their families, left their siblings to their own fates, and avoided contact with village life.

Kartar was not religious as an adult, but he was respected by the village people as an ethical man who had no black mark in his personal life. This was in a society where everyone minded your business and where people made sure they knew all your flaws. He avoided doing anything wrong or unlawful in a country where corruption was rampant. He was never known to cut corners. He never wanted to take away anyone's rights, never wanted to cause harm to anybody, and would never compromise his ethics. I can trust all my siblings in that they would never do anything wrong to me; but I can trust Kartar to never do anything wrong to anyone else either. As *Udhishter*, the quintessentially ethical man, was to the *Maha Bharat* epic, Kartar was to our family; but the former is a fairy tale, while Kartar had to live and function in the real world. I have not known any man as consistently honest, ethical, and compassionate as Kartar, and I know I can never repay the debt that I owe him personally.

My Sisters, Karo and Chhoti

Karo (name shortened from Kartaro), formally named Kartar Kaur, was born a couple of years before me. She was named after another sister who had died. Killing baby girls was unthinkable in modern times, but if one of them died naturally, people accepted that as God's will, although they were devastated if a boy died. The birth of each baby girl was considered a burden and a liability in those days and not something to be celebrated. But my father never resented having daughters, because he thought girls were as dear to God as boys were. He also said that girls were capable of doing more than they were allowed or trained to do. Karo seemed like an average healthy child with a gentle nature, high cheekbones, high set teeth and a nose that was too short to be considered attractive in Punjab. A long nose, a light complexion, and small teeth that did not show while smiling, were considered better; a short, flat or wide nose, a dark complexion, big teeth and thick lips were associated with the lower castes. My elder sister Maro was quick at work and did everything with skill and finesse and was therefore a difficult act to follow, but there were no particular expectations from Karo. At first my father thought that Karo appeared slow in thinking. He said that Karo probably had *motti matt* (a thick mind) like her mother, and education was unthinkable for her. So she was never sent to school as a child, which was typical of the village.

But later on Karo was found to be quite clever. During the important religious celebrations in the *gurdwara* (temple), they used to recite the entire holy *Granth* in 48 hours. Although it was considered beneficial to sit and listen to the holy words, ninety percent of the audience did not understand much of the recitation. For such special days, it was customary in the rural areas for some people, particularly women and children, to go to the gurdwara in the evening after dinner. Some took their winter quilts along and spent the night on the gurdwara floor while the recitation of the Granth was going on. Women and children would just fall asleep there on the temple carpet or lean against a wall or pillar. It was believed that being present at the time of recitation was good karma; and whether you understood anything or not, you were in God's presence. My mother was too busy to go to the temple, but the few-years-old Karo and other children could go there to spend the night during the recitation. My father would say it was improper to fall asleep in the presence of the Granth and that they were supposed to stay awake and listen to the recitation, but the little children could not really be expected to stay up all night. And the people who fell asleep on the temple carpet would wake up at the time of the Bhog ceremony of conclusion, early in the morning. Then they listened to the *shabad* (religious songs) and the preacher's interpretations and stories. The *ragi* (musicians) would sing the shabad, which were interspersed with additional stories and parables about ancient religious believers, God's devotees, miraculous happenings, virtuous people and wicked people, and so forth. These stories usually taught moral lessons and were intended to inspire and to teach virtuous behavior. The preacher/ lecturer would use humor to make the stories interesting, and the stories were the only things that the children remembered afterwards.

Karo would soak in every detail of the preacher's stories, because she listened more attentively than the other kids did. Then she would come home and be able to repeat every one of the stories in detail including all the humor, to the amazement of our parents. So they found out that she was not mentally dense after all. But since education for girls was not a priority, she just spun cotton, knitted, or crocheted and later on when she grew up she cooked great delicacies. Our father used to say that embroidery was a waste of time, did not make utilitarian clothes, and nobody needed those decorative clothes, so Karo did not do embroidery much then. She learned to read and write the Gurmukhi (Punjabi) alphabet at home, when she was not making useful things. As will be mentioned later, she also was educated by osmosis, without going to school and without much planning.

At the age of 24, Karo was married to Sucha Singh Sandhu, a school teacher, whose family had fled from what had become Pakistan four years earlier, during the Independence and Partition of India. In time Karo and Sucha Singh had three sons: Tejinder, an engineer; Khushwant, a merchant-ship captain; and Nav Parkash, a physician. Because of his profession, Khushwant was out of the country a lot, but his resourceful and imaginative wife Simi always livened up our family gatherings. Nav Parkash was at first trained as a surgeon in India; then he worked in Saudi Arabia for some time and later went to the U.S.A. In New York, Nav Parkash Sandhu became an anesthesiologist. He worked in a university hospital and also made some valuable inventions of medical procedures and devices.

My youngest sister Chhoti (which means small or young) was initially named Gurnam Kaur, with the same first name as mine. But after watching my behavior as a teenager, my parents changed her name to Gurdial Kaur, like the younger brother, thinking that the name Gurnam may have damaged the older son and that it was better to be safe about the daughter's name. Chhoti learned to read and write Punjabi, and for a time she attended the girls' school in the village. There was only one lady teacher for the girls' school, though in good years there might be an assistant teacher. Sometimes the teacher would hold the girls' classes in a room in the village *dharmsala* (community inn), since there was no girls' school building any more; sometimes she taught in her own house. And it was just a matter of walking along with other little girls to the teacher's house, which was about half a mile away on the other side of our village. Chhoti's presence at home was not important, with two older sisters handling the tasks, and the school was free. She probably learned the equivalent of two or three grades in this way and then stopped going to school.

After my brother Kartar graduated from college in 1943 and became an army officer during World War II, he insisted that at least the youngest sister should go to school, although it was too late for the older ones, Maro and Karo. But Chhoti was already past the age for the girls' elementary school by that time, so a little later she was encouraged to prepare privately for the middle school examination given by the State. There was an old schoolteacher named Moola Singh, a refugee from Pakistan, now teaching in the boys' school in our village. He would come to our house in the evenings to teach my sister. In those days people could just pass examinations and get certificates without seeing the inside of a school and could even matriculate without ever attending a school. A Brahman named Jai Gopal (for many years I thought his name was Jack Paul), who was an admirer of my father, would bring his sister to our house to study with Chhoti. He thought that his sister should learn more *Gurmukhi* and arithmetic, as she had also been in the elementary school with Chhoti. My sister Chhoti passed the eighth grade examination and that

Brahman girl also passed the eighth grade after a couple of attempts.

Sometimes my older sister Karo would sit nearby and listen when the teacher was teaching to Chhoti at our house. Karo thought that all the arithmetic stuff being taught to Chhoti was just common sense; and she already knew how to read Punjabi in Gurmukhi script. In fact, as my father had the habit of putting oral arithmetic questions to boys, especially to Gurdial, my sister Karo could sometimes figure out the answers which Gurdial could not, because he was 8 or 9 years younger than her. So she had learned some arithmetic just by handling everyday transactions. She was therefore sent along with Chhoti, without any schooling or expectations, to take the examination equivalent to the eighth grade. In that attempt, by sheer common sense, general knowledge, and personal abilities she passed in some subjects, though not all of them. On a second attempt, Karo passed the State's middle school examination in all the remaining subjects. With only that self-education at home, in 1952, after marrying Sucha Singh Sandhu, she started teaching at a school on a temporary basis. Later, she was admitted to a "normal school" for one year to get a teacher's certificate. Thereafter Karo taught in schools for nearly 35 years and even passed the Matriculation Examination, also privately and without going to a school. Karo would have been forced to retire early, but her date of birth had been changed by several years at the time of the middle school examination, to show her to be many years younger than she actually was; so according to the records, she was too young to retire. Official birth records were hard to find in those days and the headmaster of a school could certify any birth date according to his judgment and discretion. Karo, although older than me in age was actually certified by the headmaster to be even younger than Chhoti.

After passing the middle school examination, Chhoti was sent to a private girls' high school in Ferozepur for a while. She did not like that school much; so she returned home and after some efforts passed the Matriculation Examination. Then in about 1955 Chhoti was admitted to the Government College for Women in Ludhiana, which was well regarded in those days. After marrying a plant geneticist, Harjeet Singh Gill, Ph.D., who worked in the hills of Kulu, she did not live anywhere convenient to following a profession. She raised two sons, Harinder (Moti), a plant geneticist, and Jatinder (Bikka), who after medical school in India went to the U.S.A. and later became a staff physician at the Harvard Medical School. In 2005 Jatinder married Lisa Barna, herself a physician, and a vivacious, gregarious girl with joyful personality. Harinder had married a Danish girl, Lise Hansted, whom he had met while she was involved in research in India. Later on, they worked in Denmark during summers, and the rest of each year they worked in India.

Chhoti and her husband had planted an apple orchard in the Himalayan hills above Kulu Valley on the way to Manali, which became a second home to them as they lived in the small village of Katrain a few miles below the orchard. In later years her husband worked at the All India Agricultural Institute in Delhi. They retired in Chandigarh.

Not having been sent to any boarding school, I was frequently in the company of these two sisters in my early years before I went to college. In later years I felt that my life was vastly enriched by the personalities of these most affectionate, generously helpful, and eminently good-hearted girls. Whenever the three of us were together, laughter never stopped. Even as an adult, whenever I went back from America to visit India, it was always like the old times. The talk of all the incidents and memories of the times past started the laughter with each recall, and every evening with them was a verbal feast. Even after living abroad for many decades, whenever in the presence of these sisters I felt as if I had never left home and felt fortunate to have sisters with such wonderful caring, cheerful personalities.

I was close to and respected for both Karo and Chhoti. They were so competent and compared to me. When they were young they could do things with their hands so well. While boys could afford to be careless, the girls were always under pressure to prove their worth. It was so important to them that we should do well; they would do their best to take care of us and practically breathe for us. They would take care to get our clothes and other things ready, pack the suitcases and help us get ready to go places, whether it was to school or to an interview. Even before Chhoti was a teenager, although younger than me, she could milk a buffalo with great ease and speed. But whenever she tried to teach me, I would squeeze the buffalo's teat and the milk would go backward up into the buffalo's udder instead of squirting out. So I never milked anything bigger than somebody's goat, stealthily during my cattle-grazing days. Chhoti and Karo inherited the capability of doing things by hand that my father had. Chhoti also had such a good personality that no one ever derided her, and she never was mean toward anyone in her life. At her in-law's place, she was highly admired and respected. Her in-laws respected her ideas and every word she uttered, which was somewhat uncommon in our society. Now that my parents are gone, I get the most comfortable and secure feeling when I am in my sister Chhoti's house. Although all my siblings treat me well, my sisters Karo and Chhoti try the hardest to pamper and please me.

Did His Tenacity Make Gurdial a General?

My younger brother Gurdial was born in September 1936 when the family still lived in our old, Inner House. After two boys and three living girls (another sister younger than Chhoti had died in infancy), he was a welcome addition to the family. People used to think that the greater the number of sons, the more secure and powerful the family would be. Boys represented not just the ability to do difficult farm work; they also carried the potential to assert power in everyday conflicts which occurred frequently in the village. Boys provided security from physical danger, the importance of which people in law-and-order societies do not appreciate. In later years, our neighbor Bhan Singh had ten boys, and they were all valued and wanted. When a family had physical power, it did not usually need to use the power in any violent way; the mere presence of sons and men could achieve the desired objective.

When Gurdial was born, I went to our outer cattle corral and was proud to tell Uncle Tiloka about the birth of my new brother. *Neem* branches were tied with ceremonial *khumni* threads and were hung over the door as an announcement of the birth of a boy. As he was born on a Tuesday, he was named Mangl (Punjabi word for Tuesday) for the first few months. Later on, someone pointed out that there was a real loser with the same name in the village. So his name was changed from Mangl to Gurdial, because our family was afraid that people might call him by the unflattering name Mangli. Gurdial was a healthy, good-looking child; but at the age of about three years he had a bout of some

69

mysterious disease. That illness, including dysentery for many months, dried him like a prune, damaged his health, and changed his eyes, complexion, and appearance significantly and permanently. Although he recovered and lived, he never again looked the same as before.

The struggle against that disease may have left him with greater tenacity, drive and assertiveness. He became feisty, complaining, and assertive, with a need to do the best for himself. He was persistent and demanding as a child; when he wanted something, he would whine until he got it; and sometimes he got spanked for that behavior. He would present the best facets of his achievements in school and elsewhere when recounting his accomplishments to the family. If he performed barely average in a test, he would come home and say, *"Mein phukky uda ditti"*, meaning that he had blown it away. Or he would say, "I will surely get high marks," and the results later would come out barely acceptable. My older brother Kartar used to say: "Even if our Gurnam says that he did poorly in a test, you can expect good results; but even if this braggart Gurdial says he smashed the test, the results may be mediocre." Gurdial never failed to take initiative in talking up positively when it was advantageous to do so. He was unabashed in asserting his rights and talking about his abilities and exploits. He would say, "If you don't beat your own drum, who else will?" Like brother Kartar, he was sent to the boarding school at Nathana when he reached the fifth grade; there he was the smallest in size and hence called "Choocha". In high school his teacher ridiculed him when Gurdial said he wanted to become a military officer, saying: "You think your ugly mug is fit to become a lieutenant?" I would have been crushed by such an insult permanently, but Gurdial was not the one to lose self confidence just because a teacher ridiculed him; instead he became more determined than ever. And off course he was the best student in his class in that boarding school.

After the matriculation examination, in the summer of 1952, Gurdial was sent by himself to seek admission to Government College at Ludhiana, but he returned home unsuccessful. By that time I had come home after two years of college at Ahmednagar, in Bombay state, so I was then asked to take Gurdial to gain admission to some suitable college. We were planning to take the train to reach Mohindra College in Patiala, but an educated person on the way suggested a newer government college at Hoshiarpur that he thought might be better; so we took the train to Hoshiarpur. Unknown to us, Hoshiarpur was the college where the refugee University of Punjab had moved its teaching departments after being uprooted from Lahore, Pakistan, following the 1947 partition of India. Before that, Hoshiarpur was an unimportant town. But some local politician in Gandhi and Nehru's Congress Party used his influence to bring the University to this unlikely place, where many new buildings had to be quickly erected. And fatefully, Gurdial's admission made it practical for me also to seek admission there later, in the third year of college, although I was still unaware of the Punjab University system and the better opportunities there.

Gurdial did not enjoy the reputation for intellectual ability and perfect behavior in the family that our eldest brother Kartar did. But Gurdial had tenacity, enthusiasm, and activism going for him. In social graces he was better than all his siblings except perhaps my sister Chhoti, whose approach to family and social relations was always smooth.

Gurdial engaged in extracurricular activities in college and associated with the more aware, leftist, new-intellectual Jats (a real oxymoron!) and politically active students. I personally was of a politically conservative nature and never accepted the politics or association of those leftists, but Gurdial could readily work up enthusiasm for such activities and he was not shy about acting like a leader.

Gurdial was not exactly brilliant in his studies at the college level. My father would exhort him to work hard and be better than the competitors, especially if he expected to become a military officer. Father would say, "You should learn to speak English so that you will have a better chance of being selected as an officer candidate for the army. You should converse with other college boys in English only and not in Punjabi. Why do you have to be shy about speaking in English?" And Gurdial would protest that the boys might make fun of him by saying, "*Qui Angrais da putr banya hai!*" ("What an Englishman's son you have become!"), which would amount to real abuse. Then my father would demonstrate, with a threatening gesture, how Gurdial should respond to such boys: "*Keh de 'Aa, teri bhen di.......'*". Father would say, "While you can express your sentiments best in the mother tongue, nowadays you cannot rise in your career without mastery of the English language." Gurdial would whine and protest, but he continued to be bombarded with Father's advice to improve his fluency in English. Fortunately, after two years of college, Gurdial was selected for the officer candidate school of the Indian Military Academy at Dehra Doon, a great career path in those days. That path was something for which all four brothers were pushed to try, but only he and Kartar succeeded. Gurdial did well in the military academy, too. This was a great relief to my brother Kartar, who felt responsible for financing the education of all the younger siblings and who was the sole source of financial support for our entire family in those years.

Gurdial rose steadily in his military career. Later he married Sukhjinder (nicknamed Guddi), our brother Kartar's wife's sister. Over the years, Guddi and Gurdial had two sons, Sukhdial (Dinky) and Gurpal, both of whom would grow up to be military officers later. Guddi had great organizing ability and handled tough situations in sophisticated and courageous ways. She was an important factor in Gurdial's career in the Indian Armed Corps where your personal and social life affect your career. My nephews Sukhdial and Gurpal have both served with distinction in Kashmir, although both are in tank regiments, which do not normally operate in the mountains of Kashmir. Sukhdial was wounded there in combat a couple of times, once so seriously that he is still carrying the shrapnel that could not be removed from his body. That incident was a heart-stopper for his beautiful wife Gur Harjit (Tinky). Even though Sukhdial was promoted to lieutenant colonel in 2003, I don't think his bravery and performance have been fully rewarded yet. Sukhdial and Tinky have two brilliant daughters (Amanat and Natasha) who attend Sanawar, the same exclusive boarding school that their father had attended. Fortunately Gurpal was not yet married when he served around the Kargill glacier and dealt with the continuous attacks of the infiltrators from Pakistan. After returning from the front, Gurpal married Nimrit in 1999 and they had a daughter named Reet.

In the India-Pakistan war of 1965, my brothers Kartar and Gurdial were in two different tank regiments, fighting at the Indian border with Pakistan. During a daring night-time attempt to supply some trapped Indian troops, then-Captain Gurdial Singh was captured by the Pakistan military forces; he spent a few weeks as a prisoner of war before the armistice and exchange of prisoners ended that ordeal. Because of his traits and abilities, he rose to the rank of major general. This was not an easy accomplishment in the political climate that was so hostile to Sikhs in the 1984-1994 period following Indra Gandhi's invasion of the Golden Temple, her assassination, and the massacres of Sikhs all over India. One of the highlights of his career was to steer the development of Arjun, the newest battle tank of the Indian Armed Corps, when he was stationed in Delhi. After his retirement in 1994, he and his family moved to Chandigarh, where his wife Guddi had a house built without much help from him and where Karo and Chhoti had also built their houses in the adjacent town of Mohali.

Kirpal, My Favored Brother

My brother Kirpal was born in July 1941. My older brother Kartar felt embarrassed that his mother would have another baby while he himself was of college age. He called baby Kirpal by the name Faltu, which means surplus, unwanted, or useless. My mother would say to him, "Son, let's have the fear of God; please don't call him Faltu and unwanted; there are so many families who wish they could have one like this." Kirpal was a healthy, good-looking, and endearing baby and grew up to be a well-behaved child. He never seemed to have any conflicts, any rough edges, or any discipline issues. Being the youngest of the brothers, where age commanded respect, he could not very well be difficult; but it was also his innate nature to be unperturbed. He did all the things that normal boys do and was naturally popular with the children in our neighborhood. Cheeta, son of Bhag Singh, my uncle Mohinder's sons Gurcharan and Kulwant, and my brother Kirpal, were all born within months of each other, and the four of them went together everywhere as they played and explored, as they all lived within 50 yards of each other.

One of the remarkable things about Kirpal was that unlike Gurdial and me, he never required any correctional beatings to make him comply and behave properly. Usually, when a boy was beaten, the neighbors would hear his shrieks, as most of the activities of living were outdoors and within the hearing range of neighbors. The fact that Kirpal was rarely beaten appeared to be an oddity to our neighbor uncle Bhan, who told my mother, "Bhagi, I notice that you are not beating your boy Kirpal; you will ruin the boy and you will regret it someday when he turns out bad. We beat our boys as needed and you should beat yours too, so that he may behave better and have a better future." My mother told uncle Bhan: "But Kirpal does not do anything wrong; it is hard to beat a child when he does not do bad things." Uncle Bhan, the father of ten boys, who otherwise was known to be a balanced man, repeated, "Mark my words, you will regret it if you don't beat Kirpal, at least moderately, to put some fear in him." A little later my mother was sitting with Kirpal at home and said to him, "Kirpal, we should start beating you regularly; the neighbors say that you will get spoiled otherwise." And Kirpal, instead of being worried or anguished, just flashed his automatic smile.

His smile was continuous and automatic, because his teeth were set high and wide, and whenever he relaxed his mouth he appeared to be laughing. So smiling is what Kirpal appeared to be perpetually because his teeth were too big to be completely enclosed within his lips without some effort. The joke about Kirpal used to be that even if he said "mama" his lips did not touch. This was a take-off on the riddle: "What must touch if you say 'mama', but do not touch if you say 'chacha?'" The answer to the riddle is "lips". But Kirpal's lips did not touch regardless of whether he pronounced "chacha" or "mama". Later his lips caught up with his teeth to cover them with some effort, and that produced a rather attractive effect.

As a little boy, Kirpal was easy to like because his behavior was natural and frictionless and he was disarmingly innocent. An example of his innocence, when he was about four years old, comes to mind. Being without shoes frequently like me, he once stubbed his second toe, which got infected, festered and would hurt. But Kirpal did not complain much even when the toe was swollen and full of puss. So, in sympathy, I asked him one day, "Kirpal, does that toe hurt really badly?" And Kirpal replied, "It does not hurt all the time; but it hurts if someone hits it with a brick." He meant that it hurts only if you disturb it, but he had difficulty in expressing the thought exactly. How could one not like such innocence!

Kirpal was 4 years and 9 months old when he was admitted in school in the first grade, because our father did not want to wait for another year, until the following April, to admit him to school. So he was the youngest in his class and passed the matriculation examination before he was 15 years old. In fact all the boys in our family were small compared to their classmates and grew in height later; I myself grew in height up to the age of twenty. In time Kirpal grew to be about six feet tall, like Kartar and my father, and became taller than Gurdial and myself.

Kirpal was my favorite brother, mostly because he was 11 years younger than me, and because among the boys he was one step removed from me in age, with Gurdial in between us. Boys always worked off their aggression on the brother nearest in age and were protective of the brother who was much younger. Boys would not have any conflict with girls, because the girls were taught to be affectionate and compliant and not belligerent or antagonistic. I always wanted Kirpal to follow my footsteps. So in my teenage days when I was resisting the family's pressure to join college and was in favor of working on the land, I wanted one brother to be by my side to work on the farm. Gurdial had already been sent to the boarding school, so I would try to convince Kirpal to tell the family that he preferred farming instead of education, and we would work the fields together. Kirpal and I would carry on a conversation in the mock Pothohari language of the far west Punjab, mimicking the language of the refugee teachers who had arrived from the newly created Pakistan. I would train Kirpal to say that he preferred farming. In my presence, little Kirpal would say "Yes, I want to farm with brother Gurnam." But Kirpal would be afraid when my father was listening, and then he would say "Oh, I think I want to study in school." I felt a little betrayed by him as I was already short of any supporters in the family for my farming pursuits, and Kirpal was my last hope.

By the time Kirpal was in the fifth grade, about 1950, they had started teaching English in the local school in Mehraj, so there was no pressing reason to send him to a boarding school. But the local Mehraj school did not teach science, and our father thought that science was a necessary subject for any useful education. So when Kirpal passed the eighth grade, he was sent to the high school in Phul Mandi, a few miles away, and he went through the matriculation examination there. In 1956, he was admitted to Mahindra College, Patiala, before the age of 15, when he was still a small boy with a chirpy voice.

73

After Kirpal's admission to the college in Patiala, I got a job as lecturer in physics at Khalsa College, Amritsar; and then Kirpal transferred from Patiala to Amritsar to be near me. Later on, he was pushed by the family to try for selection into the military academy, but like myself he was unsuccessful during the military selection board interview. Then after two years at Khalsa College, he was admitted to the Medical College in Amritsar. After five years of medical training, he received the equivalent of an M.D. degree and did the necessary hospital internship. In 1966, he went to the United States to become an orthopedic surgeon.

In the U.S., Kirpal met his future wife GurSharan Kaur (Sharan), who was herself a physician. They decided to return to India in 1972 to practice medicine. Together they set up a medical practice in Bhatinda, about fifteen miles from our village. That made it easy for him to keep an eye on our aging parents in Mehraj. Kirpal established a reputation as a good orthopedic surgeon in the whole countryside around Bhatinda. He was well known in medical circles in Punjab for his competence and success in performing difficult and complicated operations. His wife Sharan handled patients with all other health problems in the clinic; so they handled cases with every kind of disease. They maintained their own version of a private hospital, with facilities for patients, and sometimes for the patients' relatives and caretakers as well, to stay on the premises for as many days as it took for recovery. Under relatively primitive conditions and without adequate equipment or supplies, Kirpal had to improvise and do his best for some quite complicated surgical operations; his wife Sharan had to be an anesthesiologist and an assistant surgeon as well.

But late in 1993, Kirpal and Sharan decided to return to work in the U.S.A., mainly because of the unsettled law and order situation in Punjab. The attack of the Indian military on the Golden Temple and other prominent gurdwaras in June 1984, the massacre of Sikhs in Amritsar, the assassination of Indra Gandhi, and subsequent massacres of Sikhs all over India, had created serious problems. Many common criminals pretended to become political activists and would use pressure tactics to extort money from prominent people for their cause of liberating Punjab from India. Kirpal thought it best to escape to the U.S.A., until the conditions in Punjab would improve.

Kirpal and Sharan's son Rupal, who had been born in the U.S. in 1972, attended the All India Institute of Medical Sciences in Delhi and became a doctor. Their younger son, Deepal, born in India, went to Maulana Azad Medical College in Delhi and he also became a doctor. Both sons followed the parents to work in the U.S.A., a couple of years later. In the year 2000, Deepal married Mamta Thukral, M.D., who had been his friend from their medical school days.

Siblings Who Died As Infants

In addition to the siblings described above, my sister, the first Kartaro, died in about 1926. I vaguely remember another sister who was born healthy in about 1935 but died within about three weeks, even before she was named. My sister Maro had taken the baby out of the house and into an old room to show off her 'pretty sister' to the neighbors. That room was the old house of some people who had died long ago and was now in Aunt Harnami's possession. My mother said that some evil spirit in that room caused the baby's death within hours. They might have been reluctant to let an infant boy be taken out so early in his life, but they thought nothing could happen to a baby girl. Another brother, Hardial, was born in late1938. He seemed robust, and healthy, but he died just before he was a year old. Then Kirpal was born in July, 1941, the tenth child and seventh survivor of our parents. There was even an eleventh, a stillborn baby girl, after Kirpal.

I sometimes wonder whether the children who died could have been saved with better medical care. I have been told that the ones who died were better looking than the ones who survived. The superstition used to be that the better-looking children are always more fragile and need more protection from harm, while the homely ones are more durable.

All seven of us who had survived beyond the age of one year had a reunion in Chandigarh, Punjab, in November 2003, to celebrate the eighty-three years of the life of my sister Maro, the 80 years of Kartar, and to give thanks to God for the fact that we were all in relatively good health. We again gathered there for a wedding in November 2005.

CHAPTER 5

My Early Days

I was born in the early hours of a warm day in late April, 1930, in the harvest season. My mother used to say I was born in *Baisakh*, the first month of the Indian year 1988 of the Bikrami calendar. (The Bikarmi calendar, according to which all our festivals and important days were listed, was used until the late 1940s, when people started going to government schools and started using the European calendar.) For the birth of her first child, a wife would go to her own parents' house, a couple of months before the birth, but not always so for later children. Since I was not my mother's first child, though, I was born at home. The house in Mehraj where I was born was probably the same house in which my father and grandfather before me had been born. My mother's first child, my sister Maro, was some 9½ years older than me, my brother Kartar, was 6½ years older, and my sister Kartaro (Karo) was about 2 years older; so my birth was not a major event for the family. But since I was a boy I was most welcome.

In the villages there would be a midwife, called *daaee*, assisting at births in most houses; a female relative and some female neighbor or two would also be present. The midwife was not a knowledgeable professional but someone of a lower caste, though not untouchable, who had watched and assisted in many births before. Such a midwife could not be too squeamish about dirty work like washing diapers, which was also the job of the *daaee* for the first couple of months in our houses.

It seems strange that in those days so little importance was attached to a woman's rights as a parent that my mother's name does not even appear on my birth records. Only my father's name was recorded, as was the name of the midwife present, Haati the Mehri (a Muslim water-carrier's woman), as a witness. It was as if in addition to his cattle and other assets, my father owned a wife and some children. Every man was listed as the son and grandson of so-and-so and possibly by his clan name and village; a woman was usually described as wife or daughter of some man. It did not matter how many wives a man had; all the children were registered as his, usually without naming their mothers. And if ever a wife left her husband—which rarely happened—the children stayed in the father's house if he wanted them.

My father was spending the night before my birth in the fields, since the harvest was still not secured. Someone had to keep watch over the harvested wheat in the fields during the night, because tribes of nomad *Ode* were passing through our territory that week. The Ode with their huge flocks of sheep and goats, their dogs, their donkeys, and their fierce and belligerent men and women, were considered a big menace. These nomads could stop two or three days at a place, cause damage by grazing their sheep in the crops at night, and possibly have fights with the local people and cause injuries before moving on. There was no law available in the countryside to protect against such peril. My father could have been putting his life in danger by chancing a confrontation with the Odes at night, but protecting the harvest was a matter of survival, and my father never shirked from putting his life in danger when necessary. Anger and excitement were not alien to him, but fear is something he never displayed. He would say "Without God's order, not even a leaf moves; so what is there to fear?" Fortunately there was no confrontation with any Odes that night.

My brother Kartar says that after my birth Aunt Harnami told him she had brought a baby boy to our house. That morning the six-year-old Kartar ran about two miles to bring the news of my birth to our father, who was still in the fields after the overnight watch. My father joined other family workers to start harvesting again when they arrived in the morning. According to Kartar, my father being a sentimental man, was very happy at this news, because a second son increased the safety of the first son; but there was no rush to go home till evening. It was expected that the attending women would do what was necessary to take care of the mother. Men were expected to keep out of the way in such matters concerning women.

For many days, neighbors and friends kept saying *wadhai* (blessing, congratulations, wishes for thriving and flourishing). According to custom, a string of little branches of the *neem* tree, about a dozen in number, each branch of the green leaves about a foot long, were tied with ceremonial *khumni* threads. These neem branches were usually hung in a row above and outside the door for all newborn boys, to inform everyone of the birth and to ward off any evil influence. The display of these branches was also meant to prevent any undesirable or cursed person from having a bad influence on the baby in its first days. At other times, walking informally in and out of each other's houses without invitation and without prior warning was common in the neighborhood. The neem branches were left hanging, sometimes even after they had dried and withered, unless the boy died before that. Baby girls were considered undesirable and therefore indestructible; so no neem leaves were tied at the door at their births. It is only after they started walking and talking that baby girls became more protected than boys.

I am told that I was born slightly premature and feeble but had my father's looks, so I received favorable attention from the women folks around. According to the custom, black marks were put on my forehead with eyeliner, to safeguard against the effect of *nazar* (evil eye) of strangers. It was a custom for women to apply *surma* (black kohl or antimony) to their eyes for decoration; even some fashionable men in the village would use black eyeliner. Some thought the black surma was to keep the eyes healthy, and I myself used it occasionally, until I left the village to go to college.

In the case of babies of light complexion, anything black, if applied carelessly to the face, was supposed to mar the good looks and therefore to render the baby less vulnerable to nazar. But if the child was already of dark complexion, he would not be considered too vulnerable to nazar, and then the black mark on the face might be unnecessary.

Women would say "Don't take the light-complexioned baby out anywhere without the black mark; someone's nazar might damage him."

Soon after a baby was born, some important woman gave the baby a mixture of ingredients including *gur* (solid brown sugar) or honey, and some other tasty but harmless ingredients. The superstition was that the ingredients of gurhti, and particularly the nature of the person administering the gurhti, would determine the character of the baby. So if a child turned out badly, the woman who administered the gurhti could be blamed, and if the child turned out to be good, the gurhti-giver got to boast about her gift and charm for the rest of her life. I was told that Aunt Harnami administered the gurhti to me.

It was not very common for men to be in contact with newborn babies, to fondle them or to play with them, until they were a bit less fragile. That was partly because they were working in the fields and usually not at home during the daylight hours. Male participation in child-rearing was minimal, especially in our rough, rural, macho culture. Women relatives were the ones who were home with the babies all the time. Every baby was breast fed for the first year of life and some women would continue breast-feeding for up to two years.

My early life was relatively uneventful. As a child I was slow in thinking, lethargic in movements, and unremarkable in speech until about the age of eight. Other boys of my age were clever, talkative, and adventurous like their own mothers. It was not my ability to think, but my lack of clever talk and general awareness that was noticed by my contemporaries. I have no memories of any event before the age of 4. At that age I vaguely remember being with my mother in a building which our family had bought from a man named Santokh, to shelter buffaloes. This Santokh-wala house was between our residence and our big, remote cattle yard. A vicious buffalo bull that had the habit of attacking people had entered the courtyard of our Santokh-wala house. To this day I remember the small white spot in the center of his head and a slight limp in one swollen leg, which some young men had tried to cut, out of spite for his mean nature. My helpless mother was scared of the bull and did not know what to do. I remember that I took a big stick that I could barely lift and went to hit the bull. Instead of charging at me, the buffalo bull decided to avoid being hit by ambling away. But to my mother I became a hero because I had driven the bull out of the yard. She said to her women friends: "I could not believe that my little son could chase away that mean bull; surely a girl could never do a thing like that even if she were a grown woman." But I neither felt the fear nor understood the risk; I chased away the bull as a part of my playing and because it was scaring my mother. That event built my confidence then, though in later years I developed various fears, even though I was told that it was shameful for a *Jat* Sikh boy to be fearful.

At the age of about 4, I also vaguely remember my older brother Kartar coming home from the boarding school at Nathana and reciting English nursery rhymes for me to repeat and memorize. At that time our whole family was camping all summer in our fields in a tent. That tent was made from *putti*, thick woven sheets of flax fibers or animal hair, about 12 ft by 6 ft each, which looked like large thick blankets. Such putti could also be used like carpet to seat any group; and putti covered with bed sheets could be used for seating and feeding a wedding party (*junj*). During the time we lived in the tent, I used to watch my mother cook and churn butter out of milk in makeshift arrangements, with the help of my oldest sister.

Except for some rain (and even that would be warm and welcome), living outdoors on the farms in the summer was easy, and the men did not need to travel back and forth from the fields to the house during the heavy work season. But in those days the custom of living on the farms regularly had not become common, and it was dangerous. Living outside the villages wasn't practical or safe unless there were many men in the family for defense. Besides, most people had small land holdings scattered about and separated by long distances, so living in one of those fields would not solve the travel problems. So people used to live in the villages and go to work daily to their different fields, just as urban people go to work in factories and offices.

The Sadhu and His Mango Plant

During that summer in the fields, I remember once walking behind my mother from our tent to fetch water from a well located near the Phulana water pond, about a quarter mile away. At the Phulana pond, under the *pipple* tree, there lived a *sadhu* with ash smeared on his naked body and also ashes in his dreadlock hair and beard. It was fashionable for such holy men to degrade their bodies by covering them with ashes. The sadhu lived in a straw shack and also had dug an underground *bhora* (burrow), with steps going down into it, for isolation, meditation, and *samadhi* (a state of deep concentration). As my mother was getting water from the well, I wandered away and saw a small plant with shiny, reddish-green leaves. I was fascinated by that beautiful plant. So I pulled it out of the ground, thinking it was just like many other weeds, only more interesting. Then I felt a little sorry and tried to put the plant back into the ground. But I could not fix the uprooted plant or make it stand in the ground; so I just left it there in frustration and walked back to my mother, feeling a bit guilty.

The Sadhu discovered the uprooted plant soon after my mother and I left, and he was furious. The next day, and every time thereafter when the sadhu came to beg for *roti* or buttermilk from our tent, he would complain to my mother, "Your *babrian wala* (scraggly-haired) kid uprooted my mango." I had had no idea that it was a mango plant, but there was no defense possible. People in those days did not think much of it if someone said insulting and harsh things to their kids. Children were meant to be rebuked and punished to keep them in line and to make them behave better. Even if the sadhu had caught and beaten me, no one would have objected to it.

I had experienced fear, and someone's anger, for the first time in my life, and from then on I always shied away from the sadhu's presence when he came daily to beg for food. Although I wished the grouchy sadhu could become nice and friendly, the holy man continued calling me insulting names and giving me harsh looks.

No Nickname Stuck

Most boys and girls in the village had nicknames; but my mother and father always called the boys by their formal names, usually using both the first and second name for each boy. My sisters were not always called by first and second names, and they all got nicknames, but somehow none of the boys did, apparently because of the importance attached to boys. A nickname was too informal and made the person unimportant and diminished in that culture. Neighbors and others did try to give me nicknames, but without the family confirming any of them with regular use, these nicknames did not stick. The neighbor Uncle Bhan used to call me by the name Jula (local word for Julius?). Karma of the Grevaal family (they were on their maternal grandparents' estate) distorted that name from Jula to Julma. To rural Punjabis this is the pronunciation for Zulma (one who commits *zulm* or cruelty), but the name Zulma was not considered derogatory in the village culture. Karma and a few others called me by the name Zulma for a few years, but without the family confirming it in the name did not really stick. Also I was in two different worlds: the world of school and the world of farming and cattle-grazing, which made it difficult for any nickname to stick.

In 1937, when in the third grade, I had my second toe cut when a boy named Durga, the son of a shopkeeper, accidentally dropped a steel bucket on my foot. This happened when we had been ordered by the teacher to draw water out of the well with the hand pump, in order to water the school flowers. I pumped water to fill the bucket while Durga was holding the bucket on the horizontal portion of the pump spout. When the bucket was full, I came to help Durga take the bucket down from the pump to carry to the flower bed. But Durga dropped the bucket accidentally as I got near him, and the heavy bucket fell on my bare toes. It cut the second toe of the left foot through bone and 90% of the way through, leaving the toe attached only by a little flesh.

My father knew how to prepare ointments for healing wounds. He washed it with the boiled neem-leaf water and put a bandage on my toe. But healing was not quick or easy. The toe was usually swollen and periodically full of pus. As a result of this accident, I walked with a limp for at least a year after the nearly-severed toe was joined. Without a shoe to protect it, the toe would get stubbed and would bleed again and again and stayed sore for more than a year. So the school boys called me by *Langa* (lame or limping) or *Dudda* (stubbed toe) for some time, even after the foot had healed and I was no longer limping. Still the name Langa did not stick, because my family called the sons by formal names and would never use the name Langa for their boy.

When I was about seven years old, we would play cops-and-robbers. It was easy to glamorize the robbers because everyone was afraid of them. At first I thought the scary mounted policemen were the robbers. They seemed powerful and important, and I thought that is what the robbers must be. So one day when Uncle Sirmukh asked me what I wanted to become after I became educated, I said I wanted to become a *Daku* (robber). He laughed, and then he and many others started calling me Daku. But my family was horrified when they heard the nickname Daku. Fortunately this name did not stick to me either, and I never got a permanent nickname.

Our Educational Environment

Hindus believe that their scriptures, *Ved*, *Puran*, *Upanishad* and others, were dictated by God and that some have existed from the beginning of the world, even before they were written, and therefore are holier than the books of any other religion. Buddhism and Jainism have different approaches to spirituality, but they do contain many traditional Indian concepts. The Sikh religion of Nanak (the Indian religious leader who founded

Sikhism) preached devotion to one non-living Creator, emphasized right actions and rejected superstitions in the prevailing practices of religions, without negating the basic teachings of any existing religion. But when the Muslim invaders arrived, their absolutist beliefs required the suppression not only of non-Muslim religions, but also of the native languages and cultural practices of India. Under Muslim rule, starting about the year 1000 and lasting until about the 1760s, most Hindu temples in North India were demolished. The existing system of education was rejected for being un-Islamic, and the use of the *Devnagri* script in which Sanskrit and the North Indian languages were written was suppressed. Persian became the official language, and the more Arabic words someone could add to it, the more prestige he enjoyed, since Arabic was the holy language of Muslims. Apparently similar things happened in northern Africa, in Morocco and wherever Islam spread. In prominent towns *madrasa* schools were started where boys could learn to read and write the Persian language. Then the North Indian languages began to be written in the Persian/Arabic script and the result was *Urdu*, the vernacular Indian language written in the Persian script. This language was introduced initially in the military forces, hence the name Urdu (army). Gradually Urdu became the language for common communication in North India, while Persian was for more advanced students. During the Muslim rule, people could learn Sanskrit or Hindi privately from some Hindu institution or teacher. When I was young, a good part of our Punjabi language was Persian, except the verbs, and the distinction between Urdu and Persian was also mostly in the verbs. After the partition of India, most Persian words in Punjabi were replaced by Sanskrit, at least in broadcasting and official communications. So whoever rules, makes the language.

The Sikh gurus developed the *Gurmukhi* script in early sixteenth century for the Punjabi language and for their holy scriptures. The Arabic script was foreign to their culture and the use of Sanskrit's Devnagri script had diminished in public life in Punjab by that time. Perhaps the Sikh Gurus just wanted to distance themselves from the old religions with this new script, although the Gurmukhi letters look much like simplified Sanskrit letters and follow the same pattern. But even during Ranjit Singh's rule at the beginning of the nineteenth century, the official language in the Sikh kingdom of Punjab was still Persian and not Punjabi. The Sikh rule did not last long enough to make language changes; and most officials and record keepers had been trained in the Persian language for centuries. Besides, a majority of the population under the Sikh rule was Muslim, for whom the Arabic script of the Persian language was more familiar.

After the British defeated the Sikhs in 1849, they set up formal schools, still called madrassa. Urdu continued to be the language for common written communication at lower levels, while English replaced Persian at the higher levels. When I was admitted to the first grade in our village madrassa in 1935, the first letters that my Brahman teacher taught me were not Gurmukhi or Sanskrit or Roman, but Urdu in the Persian script. Punjabi, Hindi, and Sanskrit were taught in some private schools or in the schools run by the princely states, such as the school in Bhatinda in the state of Patiala, where my father studied. In the fifth grade I started learning the Persian language, because Urdu and Persian used to be necessary for getting a government job. In general, the rural people spoke the Sanskrit-based Punjabi, while the educated people sprinkled more and more Persian and Arabic words in it. Persian was still taught in 1947 in our village school as the classical language, while Urdu was taught as the primary language; later they were replaced by Punjabi, Hindi and English.

Education Valued by Very Few

My father was a great believer in education and tried to educate his boys, against all odds. But common people in the village placed little value on education; in fact they usually made fun of literate people. Some villagers ridiculed the schoolboys, calling them softies, sissies, effeminate. The nasty extremists even made fun of the clothes and mannerisms of students and accused them of being the *londa* (homosexual, slave, subservient) of the teachers. The cattle-grazing Jat boys wore the *janghia*, a simple bikini-like loin cloth, while the school boys were required to wear the *kaccha*, which was like boxer underwear, as well as short pants. Some boys, usually the shopkeepers' sons, wore a pajama bottom to school. But to wear a pajama to school would give a Jat boy the image of a softy or female, and that would make him the object of ridicule and contempt in the eyes of the cattle-grazing boys who were the majority in the village. Any lower garment with a drawstring was considered effeminate in the rural eastern Punjab. So even wearing shorts was humiliating for the Jat schoolboys. Most Jat boys like me who were forced to go to school by their parents were embarrassed to be students; they wanted to graze cattle or persue other farm work rather than stay in school. Everything worked according to the example of others, and most people never knew any local person who benefited by education or who got an enviable job; so those people saw little value in literacy. Their role models were the people who were strong wrestlers, people who could bully others, or whose horse, camel, or oxcart could outrace the others. The jobs open to them in the military or the police, or even abroad in places like Singapore or Hong Kong, hardly required any education. So it seemed much better to send a little boy to graze cattle than to school. The village people believed that being a teacher or businessman was meant for non-Jat Hindus and that such easy work made people soft and effeminate. It was also widely believed that our Jat race did not have the aptitude for learning; the Brahmin and the shopkeeper castes were expected to be smart and literate. They argued that education ruins a Jat boy, who as a result of schooling becomes weak, unfit, and not a hardy farmer. They even made fun of some literate Hindu shopkeepers by saying *"Dekho Prabhu ke khel; parhay Farsi, bechay tel,"* i.e., "Behold Gods' play; after studying Persian, the fellow is just selling mustard oil!" What was the use of that lofty education when he was still doing mundane work!

The restrictions of caste and the "privilege" of land ownership also kept the Jat boys out of all occupations other than plowing the fields or soldiering. There was no chance of any Jat becoming a craftsman, engineer, carpenter, ironsmith, musician, entertainer, or trader or to undertake any profession that might lead to artistic skills and creative thinking. The Jats were encouraged to consider such occupations as degrading. Any innovation or creativity could hardly germinate out of their occupation of plowing the land. This is just the opposite of what happened to European Jews, who were sometimes forbidden from owning land and consequently went more often into education, crafts, trades, business, entertainment, and banking for generation after generation. The climate in Punjab was such that there was not much need to be indoors. An average farmer would spend most of his waking time outdoors, among trees, crops, and animals, and would wear out his body and dull his mind in the process. The unbearable heat could contribute to the lethargy of the body and mind. The village culture that denigrated and looked down upon the profession of selling in retail also hampered progress among the Jat farmers.

In the 1930s most small villages in our part of Punjab did not have even an elementary school, but Mehraj had one even in the nineteenth century. In most villages, no one could read or write, if they did not have a Brahman house or a shopkeeper there. Some people would go to a sadhu's dera (Hindu holy man's abode), usually a straw shack under a tree outside the village, to learn the letters of the Gurmukhi alphabet of Punjabi. In our villages there were many deras but very few Sikh Gurdwaras in the 1930s, although most of the people there were nominally Sikh. The boys who became sadhu (Hindu ascetic) did not come from Hindu families but were from among the nominally Sikh families, and the sadhu were usually supported not by the Hindus but by our Sikh people. Even a sadhu did not always know how to read or write. Pen, ink, and paper were inaccessible luxuries for most people in the village in those days. To instruct the pupil, the sadhu would spread a thin layer of ash on the ground and with his forefinger would trace letters of the alphabet in the ashes. The student, sitting beside the sadhu, would copy him and make letters with his finger on the ash-covered floor. Once you recognize the Gurmukhi alphabet and the vowel symbols, reading and writing is merely a matter of putting the letters together according to their sounds. Since all Punjabi and Sanskrit letters and symbols have unique sounds, no memorizing of spellings is needed. The actual names of the letters are their unique sounds, so there is no uncertainty about what letter to use for which sound. My Uncle Mohinder was able to teach me to read Punjabi at home in one week in 1937. Our school in the British territory used to teach only Urdu and some Persian and not our own Punjabi language.

Most people who went to the sadhu's dera just wanted to be able to read a *chittha*, the pamphlets of native poetry, or the romantic and heroic stories, in rhyme; very few learned to write. Gurmukhi (Punjabi script) was not used for official purposes; it would not enable a man to get a job, so it was not taught in the boys' schools. Although Punjabi was the mother tongue in every Punjabi home, only the Sikhs favored it. The Muslims felt that Urdu was their language because its script was Arabic, and the Punjabi Hindus declared that they wanted Hindi, the language of north central India, because its script was *Devnagri*, like the *Sanskrit* which was ancient and sacred. Since the official support of a language depended on the fraction of the population owning it, the script choice became a religious and political power play. Some Hindus said they were willing to accept Punjabi as their language only if it was written in the Devnagri script and not in Gurmukhi. Muslims said their language might be Punjabi, but it should be written in the Persian script. After the Partition of India, when Pakistan got the western half of Punjab, the Hindus of the remaining Punjab did not want to accept the Punjabi language with Gurmukhi script. So because of the language issue, in 1962 the remaining Indian half of the Punjab province was divided further into three parts: Punjab, Haryana, and Himachal Pardesh. Only the part where the Sikhs were a majority was thereafter called Punjab with Punjabi language and its own script.

Our School in Mehraj

In 1885 there was no high school anywhere in the entire Ferozepur district of the British territory. Mehraj, being one of the biggest villages with nearly 5,000 people in those days, had a vernacular middle school. When I started school in 1935, our school had an older building outside the village, made of mud bricks, plastered with mud on the outside and whitewashed on the inside. This building had six large classrooms with mud floors, and additional rooms for storage, a library and even a science laboratory. The students sat on the floor on hemp/flax mats or runners called *tupper*, each about a yard wide and running the length of the room. There might be two or three rows of students on tupper in each room, and the teacher sat on a wooden chair at one end. Sometimes in winter or early spring the teacher would ask the students to roll up the tupper and spread them outdoors so he could hold the classes outside in the sun or in the shade of a tree.

When my father was a little boy around the year 1900, the original school was located in Kotli Street in the center of the village. The mud-plastered building mentioned above was used as a hostel for the boys from other villages attending the school. Then around 1915 the old school in Kotli Street was abandoned, the mud-brick hostel became the classrooms for the lower grades, and a new brick building with two big rooms and a veranda was built for the upper grades. These new classrooms were very large, and they had windows and *roshndan* (light providers, above the windows), like the hospital building and unlike the farmers' homes of those days. The headmaster had a little desk and a couple of chairs in a tiny office at one end of the veranda. But he had the regular duties of a teacher as well, so he usually did not sit in his office.

In this location, a quarter mile from the village, the school shared a well with the hospital next door, as they were both government institutions. The doctor had more clout than the headmaster. So in the 1930s, the hospital had put in an ox-driven Persian wheel in the same well and they used the water to grow flowers, vegetables, and even some fruit trees on the hospital land. The hospital did not own any oxen, but the doctor could practically order any one in the village to bring his oxen to run the Persian wheel to draw water for irrigation for a while. The system of payments for such help was not common. Irrigating that soil created greenery and any greenery was a welcome sight in that arid environment. When the doctor was ambitious and activist, he would use the hospital laborers to put in a variety of plants and trees, even such things as bananas, *ber*, pomegranate and guavas. But when he was transferred and his successor did not care, the more delicate plants died out gradually and only the native, hardy, or ugly ones survived.

For our school, there was just a hand pump in one side of the same well to draw water. Student labor was used frequently to plant and water the flowers along the walkways and on all sides of a grassy square in the school grounds. Although the school peons were supposed to do such work, the students did a lot of gardening-digging, watering, and weeding. In the months of February and March, the rows and rows of flowers with intense colors looked spectacular, and the fragrance in the vicinity was enjoyable for the teachers and visitors. The headmaster received extra points for creating an attractive environment when the school inspector came to visit twice or thrice a year. In those days the surroundings of the school and hospital were made quite attractive and pleasant, because the villages were important places to live then. Now, seventy years later, that beauty and serenity is gone; the school and hospital surroundings look neglected, and the hospital is usually without a doctor. Teachers and doctors don't want to live in the villages anymore. Nowadays, some doctors and teachers do not show up for their jobs for weeks at a time, even though they are on the government payroll. Some live in cities and just pay bribes to their superiors to keep them happy and get paid without showing up for work. The village schools are inferior, and the competition for success in colleges and jobs is so severe that every parent and teacher wants to give his own children the edge by living in cities and educating them in the city schools. In the old days without electricity, telephones, or paved roads, life in the cities was not any better than in the villages, and people with talent and gifts were as likely to be found in villages as in the cities. But now, very few people of any capability, ambition or drive are left in the villages; such people move to the cities where opportunities are greater, while fewer children from the villages have any chance to excel.

My Initiation into School

In April 1935, a few days before I reached the age of 5 my father took me to the local school, to register me in the first grade. My first teacher was Ramji Das, an ill-tempered, gruff, barking and snarling Brahmin, not typical of the gentle Brahmin caste. He was always ready with a slap or other forms of punishment. Students called him *vadh khana* (bite taker), an appellation applied to vicious dogs and fierce animals. If a student was lucky he got into the class of Budh Ram, another Brahmin and a cheerful and usually praising rather than cursing teacher. But unfortunately for me this was not Budh Ram's year to teach my class.

In the second grade I was lucky to have Budh Ram as my teacher. I was lazy and tardy from an early age but Budh Ram did not want me to miss school. At first, he would come to our house in the morning to wake me up to bring me to school. In those days some teachers would go to students' houses to bring them to school so that they would have enough students in their class to teach. They would plead with the mothers to send the boys with them, so as to prevent the Jat students from getting into the habit of staying home and then dropping out. If the child's mother did not wake him up, the teacher would gently shake the child out of his sleep. For example my teacher Budh Ram would ask me to wake up with fondling, nonsensical, and pleasing words: "*utth meri giddero middero, tenu thandi kheer khuawa*". As I got out of bed, I would not need to change into any different clothes, but Budh Ram would ask my mother to wash my face, while he would flatter my mother. He would say "Oh Bhagwane (blessed one), send your boy to school with me and I will make you the mother of a deputy commissioner, or the mother of a tehsildar, or of a *thanedar*, at least the mother of a *patwari*"; all these words were the titles for government officials.

I thought I was slow and somewhat retarded in the first and second grades, although in a recent conversation my older brother Kartar said that this impression of mine is wrong. He said that my family was proud that in the second grade I had memorized the entire textbook and could recite it from memory. But since that book was only about 32 pages, this was not a good measure of ability. In the government schools, a child started with the *qaida* (basic primer; same word as in Al Qaida) in Urdu and with the letters Aleph, Be, Pe, Te... and sometimes Aleph, Be, Gim, Dal.... Then the students were required to have a *phutti*, a wooden board about two feet by one foot by a half inch, which was regularly coated with a thin layer of wet *gachni* (clay). When the clay dried, the student could draw lines on the phutti with a pencil or just write along imaginary lines with a *qalem* (reed pen). Before any reuse, the phutti had to be washed and new gachni applied to its surface; then you hoped for the sun to dry it. If on the previous day you had forgotten to prepare your phutti at home, you could try to wash it and apply gachni the next morning before school. But on a cloudy winter day, your phutti might still be wet, unfit to write on, and you could expect to be punished by the teacher. You would ask someone to carve your qalem at home with a *daat* (kitchen knife). This daat with its own pedestal was meant for cutting vegetables, and other food, but since pocketknives were not common and not readily available, the daat was used for many household cutting tasks. Sometimes a helpful teacher would carve the qalem from a thin reed, but the teachers did not usually own pocketknives either. The student dipped the reed qalem in a clay inkpot called a *dvaat*, which usually had a small rag in it to prevent complete spillage of the ink if it toppled over. The rag also kept the student from making a mess with too big a drop of ink while trying to write on the phutti. The inkpot looked like a miniature water pitcher with a pedestal; it could easily topple over and spill. When there was not much ink left in the dvaat, the student could just add water so as to be able to write with the ink remaining in the soaked rag, but the teacher would bark at him for having diluted, faded ink and illegible letters. The reed pen could break or deteriorate, and ink smudges were inevitable. So many things could go wrong, that the opportunities for the child to be beaten by the teacher were endless. Little boys who were not very clever, competent, and skillful, passed their existence in terror while in school, even if they were totally obedient.

In the third grade, students graduated to the use of a slate for working arithmetic sums. This slate was a thin sheet of stone with a wooden frame, about 12 by 9 inches. Some used sheets of metal painted black instead of the slate; the metal sheets had the advantage of not breaking, although they were not as good to write on as slate. A thin pencil, like chalk but harder, called a *slati* pencil, was used to write on the slate and solve arithmetic problems. One could erase the writing as necessary and reuse the slate for the next question. Even though smaller, the slate was more versatile and easily re-usable, while maintenance of the *phutti* was a nuisance and a great source of anxiety. Of course you could lose the *slati* pencil, or the grime on the slate could make the writing illegible, and therefore you were never totally free from punishment or anxiety in school.

It was only in the fifth grade that paper notebooks were provided for the students, but only a few pages a month, and usually only one small notebook for a whole year, so the use of the phutti and the slate also continued in the higher grades. To write on the paper, a pen with metal nib was obtained. It was also at that level that we got upgraded from clay to glass inkpots, some of them with threaded lids to prevent spillage. We also graduated to the commercial blue ink, which came in tablets to be dissolved in water, instead of the black ink in the clay inkpots used for writing on the phutti. In a household like ours, asking for money for something like ink was unthinkable for a fearful and non-assertive child like me. I was never given any money to purchase school supplies. My mother was sympathetic but she never had any money in her possession. My father bought and paid for my school book at the beginning of the year; the school itself did not provide anything for the use of students. Some kids used to try to make black ink at home by burning various reed-like materials, without much success. Most of the time I just borrowed ink from friends by begging them to pour a little of the liquid from their inkpots into mine, or I inherited some left-over ink from the older brother.

Every afternoon you would see little school boys traveling from the madrasa to their homes in the village, each walking with his *phutti* and *busta* on his head. The busta was a package containing books, slate, slati pencils, and reed pens with inkpot on the top, all bundled in a sheet of cloth. At the end of the school day each student carefully tied his busta in a square sheet of cloth. The phutti and busta were carried by each little boy on his head, much as a woman carried a pitcher of water. If a boy did not have a turban, the load of phutti and busta would be unstable, so he had to hold it on his head with both hands or carry it on one hip. Some boys would add old books from their houses to increase the size of their busta; the size of the busta had some show value and was a measure of how much a student had advanced.

Teacher's Rod and Other Abuses

My Brahmin teacher, the honey-tongued Budh Ram, was an exception to the harshness and cruelty of teachers in general. Punishments were not necessarily for bad behavior but even for such offenses as: not having a properly carved reed pen, or having a broken one, or not having any pen at all; not having ink in the inkpot, or having ink that was too faint and not black enough due to dilution; toppling an inkpot and spilling it; not having applied the clay to your personal phutti and drying it properly before bringing it to school; having bad handwriting, or not writing neatly or in straight lines; having ink smudges in your writing; having a slate that had accumulated grime that made the writing illegible, or having a slati pencil that was too small to hold; having unclean clothes; having slovenly appearance; answering questions incorrectly or scoring low marks; not saluting properly; being late to school; not having done the homework; writing with the left hand; and so on. The reasons for beating were plentiful, and if in doubt the teacher gave a slap or two anyway to demonstrate and assert his authority. I, being naturally left-handed, was slapped by RamJi Das until I learned to write with my right hand. But I have no bitter memories about it; there were too many beatings and punishments happening continuously in the early years to every boy. Beating was something that the boys expected from teachers, police, and elders at all times and in most situations; when it was happening to every body else around you, you did not feel so bad. Sometimes the boys could not write fast enough when the teacher was dictating the question, and they knew they would not have correct or complete answers to all the questions. There would be a pin-drop silence, except for the pupil's breaths and sighs, and many were sweating at the thought of the punishment and pain that was sure to follow. The teacher would sit in his chair holding the stick vertically between his feet and knees and say, "What is the stick saying? It says I am ready to sting any son of a pig who does not bring all correct answers." The trembling seven-year-olds would pile the slates with written answers in front of the teacher and await their individual fates.

We boys had not known any other life, so we took the beatings just the way you would take other unfortunate incidents like diseases, mosquito bites, stubbed toes or piercing thorns. The only thing we knew was that the cattle-grazing fellows had no teachers to beat them and had lots of freedom in the wilderness. Beatings were harshest when a child was small, because it was believed that creating fear and enforcing proper habits at a tender age by adequate beatings was the best policy. In my own case the beatings were minimal after I was nine years old in the fifth grade. Still, the best policy was to avoid the sight of teachers, fathers, or policemen, as you avoid going behind a horse whose nature it is to kick. As the rhyme said, "*Hakem de pichhe di, ghorey de muhr di; vatt jaiye passa, langh jaiye duor di*", which can be roughly translated as: "stay behind an official but in front of a horse; turn aside and pass safely far away."

Sometimes a teacher would get tired of slapping the boys. When it was too much trouble to beat and slap the kids himself, he would assign one of the older or smarter boys or the class monitor to beat the students. Slapping of the face was done by holding the victim's nose with one hand to position it properly for a slap, and then slapping the kid's face with the other hand. If the student assigned to slap a child tried to go easy on the targeted kid with a soft slap, the teacher might become annoyed and might ask the targeted kid to grab the nose of the chosen one and slap back to show how to slap properly. So the slapping kid had to be careful not to be too lenient or show favor while slapping, lest the tables be turned on him.

The other common form of punishment was *kann pakro* (ear catch). Boys were made to bend over in a half-crouching position, pass their arms under, inside and behind their legs and to catch their own ears while in that crouching position. It was very tiring to 'catch ears' for a long time, but any one crouching who lowered his back and was not high enough would get his rear hit with a stick or fist. Then either the teacher himself or the class monitor would hit the back of the crouching students with his fist, several times each. If the teacher walked out of the room, the tired crouching students in a row sometimes took a chance and lowered their backs for relief or loosened the grip on their ears a bit while still crouching. It was quite a strain to reach the ear with your fingers as your arms had to pass behind your legs first. But if you were caught lowering your back, you would be rebuked and told to raise your back higher, and you might get additional punishment. The punishment could also involve additional ear-catching time, with the back raised even higher. It is hard to imagine anyone wanting to be so cruel nowadays, but that was the mode of operation for the teachers then. Some teachers felt that their authority would be recognized better if they could induce fear, other thought they were only trying to make the students better, and some had naturally grouchy and sadistic personalities.

Some teachers carried a walking stick that had a hook at one end, called *khoondi*. The hook of the khoondi was useful for putting around a pupil's neck and pulling him closer for slapping or just for intimidating. The khoondi stick could also be used for hitting the palms of the students, and in some cases the backs of the hands. The teacher would tell a boy to extend his hand forward and would hit the palm with a hard stick, so that it would hurt enough to feel like a severe burn on the hand. And the boy would blow on his hand to relieve the pain before presenting it again to be hit. If the boy could not take any more hits on one hand, he would have to present the other hand to be hit until the teacher was satisfied that enough punishment had been administered. For hitting other parts of the body, the teacher had to use a flexible stick or a tree branch that could sting and even make blood ooze from the flesh, but not a hard stick that could break bones.

Up to the fourth grade I was slapped occasionally, although somewhat less than other boys. But in the sixth grade, when I turned ten, I would not tolerate any more physical punishment, except being beaten on the hand with a stick. I felt less humiliation in simply being hurt on the hands than I did being slapped on the face with the nose grabbed or being hit on other parts of the body. Once when I was ten and involved in some minor mischief in the school, the headmaster, who was passing by, saw me and slapped me on the shoulder twice. After that I refused to go to school. I told my Uncle Trilok Singh (nominal head of our household) that I would like to graze cattle and was big enough to do farm work. Uncle Tiloka was sympathetic, but he tried to persuade me to go back to school by saying, "Continue two more years, up to the 8th grade and you might qualify to become a *patwari* or possibly a *thanedar*." My uncle was always indulgent. I told him I never wanted to set foot in school again and that I would graze all the cows and buffaloes that we owned. I hated school anyway, and this was my big excuse to drop out. The headmaster, who actually was a relatively gentle Hindu, did apologize by saying, "I am sorry I did this. Gurnam is a good student, and I am not here to beat the child; but if I allow disorder, this place would have too much chaos." Uncle Tiloka was easy on me and let me stay home for a couple of days, while my father was not aware of the episode. But then came my father's growl, and he told me I must not stay away from school another day. I could not stand up to my father, nor could I negotiate anything with him as I tried to do with my uncle; so I went back to school the next day.

Unfortunately, the teachers were always male in those days, so there was little chance of compassion. Some teachers really were sadistic and would resort to obscene and filthy abuses, as if they were dealing with captured enemies or criminals. Certain children were the favorite targets of abuse, especially when the teacher did not fear any consequences. In such cases, it was just routine for some teachers to call the children donkey, son of pig, sister-fucker, monkey faced, son of owl, and other such names. I was never the object of the filthy verbal abuses that some boys got, partly because I was too fearful to do too many wrong things. I could take the beatings, but I would have quit school or run away if I had received any filthy abuses naming mother or sister. By the age of ten I was ready to die for the honor of a sister. But more importantly, my father was an educated man, and the teacher might suffer adverse consequences for any excesses against me. I could take the beatings, but I would never again have gone to school if the teacher had ever given me any abuse naming mother or sister as some other boys got.

Every time a new teacher came, the students would look at his face, dress, and mannerisms for harshness and estimate his potential for beatings and cruelty. The transfer of teachers was routine and unpredictable, at the whim of higher government officials; no teacher was allowed to serve at any school for too long unless he could bribe someone or had influence. We used to believe that Hindu teachers were going to be gentler because of their culture, Muslim teachers would be harsh and cruel, and Sikh teachers would be unduly strict. But these were nonsensical speculations and there were always exceptions and surprises. In the third grade I had a teacher named David (I heard that he was low caste, an untouchable, but had become a Christian). He had a mean temperament, but he was not hard on me as I was a good student. And I was scared of the Maulvi, with long beard, Turkish cap with a tassel, and Muslim dress. The styles and manners of dress varied, depending on the background, religious beliefs, and places of origin of the teachers. Some dress styles scared the boys because those teachers were from far away and spoke with different accents. Teachers were frequently known by euphemistic titles, such as *Maulvi* (for Muslims), *Munshi* (writer, literate), *Gyani* (enlightened one), *Ustad* (expert) or Master. The word Gyani implies enlightened or learned, and there really was a course of study in Punjabi with the diploma of Gyani. Sometimes we would describe the individual teachers by unflattering names that indicated their peculiarities, but such names were not to be repeated in the teacher's presence.

The fact that beatings and punishments occurred in other schools too, is verified by this little rhyme from the students in the boarding school at Nathana where my brother Gurdial studied in the 1940s: *Headmaster di Khoondi; Munshi Ji di Choondhi; Gyani Ji da Mukka; Drawing Master da Drawa Sukka*, which translates to, "The Headmaster's hooked stick; the pinch of the Munshi; the punch of Gyani; and the Drawing Master's empty threats," referring to the styles and brands of punishment for which the various teachers were famous in that school.

Drawing Seven Lines with Your Nose

If a boy violated a rule or committed a forbidden act, merely beating him was not felt to be a sufficient punishment. It was considered important to make sure he would never repeat it. So after the beating, he might be subjected to a ceremony of drawing lines on the ground with his nose. The boy would get on his knees and put his nose to the ground to touch the ground. Then he would be required to draw straight lines in the soft soil with the tip of his nose. Usually seven lines with the nose were considered the standard and a ceremonially important number, implying a pledge never to repeat the act for which the boy was being punished. Sometimes adults and petty criminals also were made to draw lines on the ground with their noses as repentance and a pledge never to repeat the same offence in the future. "Drawing seven lines with the nose" was an act of contrition and humiliation, an earnest pledge never again to do the forbidden act.

Our rural folks believed that if a child was not humiliated and he thought too highly of himself, he would be less likely to obey, would be rude instead of compliant, would be disrespectful instead of polite, and might not want to perform required educational tasks. So pampering of children was infrequent and was practiced only at *nanke* (mother's parents) houses. There was never any celebration of a child's birthday; only the birthdays of holy entities were celebrated. The notion of taking a family on vacation in that society did not arise; the wedding of a relative or going to a fair was the closest things to vacation. Tight control over the life of the village child, especially one in school, was considered the best approach. For the same reason continuous put-downs and humiliations of children were considered the best devices to make them perform better. The logic used to be that if a child were told that he is bad, incompetent, and worthless, he would make the effort to get better; but if the child is told that he is already good, why should he try to improve? Parents would say to a teacher, "I hope you are beating our son enough. We want you to straighten him out, make him obey, and teach him well." Parents thought that the hurt would last only during the beating but that any good habit, change in behavior, or knowledge acquired as a result of the beating would last for good, and therefore the net result of the beating would be positive. Praise was considered an absolute no-no and spoiler of children. Inducing fear and subjecting the student to a

90

maximum amount of humiliation were considered valuable methods. Unlike modern-day Western society, high self-esteem was considered dangerous for a village child as it could make him proud, arrogant, or disobedient with a swollen image of himself.

Next to physical beating, put-downs and cursing were considered the effective method to make the children behave and perform. It was common for a teacher to say, "You are the worst class I have encountered in my whole life. None of you has any worth. You are all going to fail and you deserve to fail. You are the most stupid children in the whole world, and your brains are full of straw and husk. Nobody would ever want you. You will never amount to anything. You are not good enough to be boys. You should have been girls; then at least you could produce babies, but now you are worthless. Every one of you is dull-witted and stupid. You are capable of doing nothing except turning food into shit. You are incapable of thinking correctly. So, this stick is waiting to do its job. My stick and I are going to make you miserable, and try to make men out of you." Of course all these things said by the teacher were false, because some boys from our school went into the police and other jobs, and some of them excelled academically. Those teachers had said the same things to their previous classes too. It was just the fashion for a teacher to say such things to assert his authority. The pupils just expected that it was his job to say the worst things; but they never really believed these things that he said.

Whenever a student saw a teacher, he was expected to stop on one side of the path, come to attention, salute, and stand there until the teacher had passed or until the teacher told him to be at ease. It was considered too casual and not respectful enough if the child just walked by as he saluted. Some teachers expected you or your parents to deliver fuel or other things to their homes. Cash was never the medium of bribe to teachers, but occasionally parents delivered vegetables, milk, other commodities, and fuel for the stove to the teacher's house. I myself sometimes provided fuel (dried cotton plants or cow dung patties) but never gave any grain to teachers over the years. The fuel was just carried by the school peon from our storage yard directly to the teacher's residence. My father was never the one to be a part of this practice of giving things to teachers; he wanted everyone to do his duty according to the rules. The teachers who wanted such bribes were not pleased with me, but they were not in a position to demand anything, as the police or other government officials could do. But a student always wished his parents would give something of value and importance to the teacher so that the teacher would look upon him with favor.

Another bad thing about school was that some teachers asked the students to come to their houses "to study more" after hours or on Sundays. That was a dreadful captivity in addition to the six days of school during the week. Most but not all teachers required this to varying degrees. Some teachers did it more for their own entertainment and pastime than for any real concern for teaching. Usually it also involved drawing water for the teacher's family and doing other household chores in addition to any study. Personally, I would rather have done the chores than study, but I was always the youngest and smallest in my class, and the bigger boys got to do the chores. I had to be content to sit with the books, sweating with unease in the teacher's presence and under continuous threat.

School Worse than Prison?

For some of the boys, all the punishments and humiliations went like water off a duck's back. When other boys got the same bad treatment, it seemed like a natural condition of life for everyone. But I was of a more sensitive nature, even though I suffered the least amount of punishment. My punishments usually came because I never had adequate or proper supplies for school or I did not complete homework. Anything that cost money was difficult to obtain. Most supplies like ink, reed pens, and slate pencils were hand-me-downs, borrowed, or makeshift replacements instead of good, functioning implements. Reed pens and slate pencils broke or got lost. I had a feeling of deprivation, fear, inadequacy and incompetence. I always felt that everything was my fault because I was lazy, stupid, clumsy, did not have proper things to write with, lost things easily, broke things easily, and got things dirty; and the teachers reinforced the feeling. In the early grades, I continuously felt that I was not able to do things right and continuously felt the threat of beatings, although the actual beatings were not frequent or severe in my case, compared to other boys. I considered the school to be an oppressive prison and wished all the teachers would just die and the schools would close forever. I hoped for too much rain or some other disaster to close the school. But school was there, six days a week, and then I might have to go to the teacher's house after school and even on Sunday. The teacher had nothing else to do and would be bored without something happening around him; in those days it was not customary for people to go away on vacation. Time passed very slowly in those societies. It was a blessing for us if some teacher's relative got sick or some other disaster happened so he would have to go away for a while—unless we got the mean, *Vadh Khana* teacher as his replacement.

I doubt if there were any clear-cut cases where such childhood abuse resulted in permanently ruined lives, but I am not sure about neurotic personalities in adulthood. Frequently, the children with harsh parents grew up to be calm, responsible, kind adults, and just as frequently the pampered, well-provided-for children grew up to be irresponsible misfits, underachievers, and a disgrace to their families. The effect of childhood treatment appeared less important than the traits in their own parents. But it is also true that the children who were beaten most frequently also told the most lies and committed the most antisocial acts.

The example of Sukhdev, the eldest son of Bhan Singh, comes to mind. He was nicknamed Flatu, the Persian or Arabic pronunciation of the name Plato, for being clever and talkative, and for bamboozling everybody else. Flatu's mother had died by falling off the roof of the house accidentally, while she was hanging clothes on the roof edge to dry. Flatu was then only about two years old and was sent to his mother's folks, as was the custom when a young child lost its mother. During his earliest years, therefore, he was raised in the *nanke* house, the house of his mother's brothers. In the maternal grandparents' or uncle's house, a child is always pampered and never punished. So the children who are raised in *nanke* are presumed to be spoiled. After a few years, when Flatu returned to live with his father and stepmother's family, he did not adjust very well to the stepmother. He was good-looking and healthy but erratic in his behavior, and he did not do well in school. He was known for small acts of mischief in the village, talking fast and loose, and he lived up to the Flatu name. People thought that Flatu was going to grow up to be a real terror. But as he grew into his teens, Flatu turned out to be one of the gentlest, kindest, hard-working, gracious, and socially responsible of boys, helpful to others in need. He turned out more like his mother and father than people had expected during his Flatu days and from the indulgent upbringing in his maternal grandparents' household. In spite of all the bad things that were said about him as a child, he became a very decent adult.

It is easy to see why there was a lot of fear in my early life. There was fear of my father, fear of the teachers, fear of failing in school tests, fear of not being as fast as other boys, fear of not having a usable reed pen or slate pencil to write and being beaten for that reason, fear of being asked to carry food to someone in our fields a couple of miles away at night, fear of admitting that I was afraid of *bhoot chrail* (ghosts) and wild animals at night in the wilderness, and similar fears. When I was found playing and rebuked for it, I also felt guilty for having been bad. I felt the same kind of guilt when the teacher condemned me for not having a good pen or having unclean clothes. The reasons for fear and guilt were endless, so that fear and worry became a habit that I carried to my later years. The only ones I was not afraid of were my mother, my siblings and my Uncle Tiloka to whom I could talk back without punishment. Even though I was the smallest of my classmates, I had no fear of any bullies in school or in the fields while grazing the cattle, because I was tenacious enough to defend myself. Of course most people liked a child who was full of fear as the fear made the child conform, obey, and perform better. That is why parents would ask the teachers to beat some fear into their boys, as they felt that a child without fear would be out of control and would not be a good student. And they felt that once the child was made obedient by the teacher, that habit of obedience would also be useful when the boy came home. I have often wondered if I would have been a better or a worse person, if all those fears had not been induced in me.

Attempted Run to Freedom

Once, three other boys and I aged 9 to 10, who all hated school, decided that we would just run away and never come back. We wanted to go to some territory far away where our families couldn't find us. We planned that we would first get a few goats, cows, and buffaloes and would become cattle grazers, which seemed like an easy way to start new lives away from our families. Sheep were considered dirty animals, so we did not want any sheep, but a goat was a cute animal and gave milk. We planned to start life with building a thorny bush fence as an animal corral and a straw shack to live in, in the manner of pioneers. There used to be plenty of empty, unused common land around the villages in those days; transients, nomads, and low-caste people often used the common village lands without having to get anyone's permission. And people used to graze their animals everywhere, in the wild lands or in other people's lands that did not have crops. Initially without money, we would slowly get rich with a lot of animals and we would have plenty of freedom. We expected to find some girl to be our wife and to cook our meals, and we would live together happily away from the tyranny of teachers and parents. We even discussed who was the oldest and was going to be the husband and who were going to be *deor* (younger brothers-in-law) of the wife, so that she would not need to cover her face from us. The four of us started mid-morning and went several miles, past the village of Baath to the vicinity of Bega Lehra. We ate *ber* (a wild fruit common in our area then) and made plans as we traveled. But toward the latter part of the day as the sun had gone down to three rope-lengths from the horizon, one of the boys started weakening and wanted to return home; then another wanted to follow him. Only Mukand and I still wanted to run away, while the other two started walking back. But then we realized we two could not go alone, as the others would tell our parents, who would then come after us. So the whole plan fizzled and to my disappointment we all came home before nightfall, ending our dreams of independence. My father found out about the incident the next day, as we had been absent from school; he wanted to beat me to a pulp. As he came toward me, I tried to take shelter behind my sisters. He caught me anyway, but after almost getting to the point of beating me, he was sentimental instead and told me how important and precious I was to the family. And he admonished me never to entertain such a foolish thought again or to endanger my life.

Having talked about the oppressive environment of school, I should say something about what we learned. We learned very few things compared to children of today. We had one small book for each year up to fifth grade, although the books became gradually bigger. But every little thing was imbedded in our brains by repetition. For example, each class was divided into two rows facing each other, and they would recite the multiplication table alternately, much like singing duets; one team would recite one product of the table and the opposite team would recite the next product and so on. Usually there would be one small book that the students would read over the entire year, and in higher grades a small book for each subject. By the eighth grade, we did learn some arithmetic and geometry, a limited amount of history and geography in Urdu, some Persian language, and a little bit of science. Our school was not approved for teaching English and English teachers were not as easy to find as Urdu and Persian teachers. In those days, even at the college level the intensity and quality of education was low, which left the students at a disadvantage when competing with those in other provinces.

Few But Unforgettable Beatings

The beatings from the teachers, although hated and feared, were not significant events, but beatings from father had an everlasting effect on me. Although my father had beaten me only two or three times in my life, unlike other boys in the village who got regular and frequent doses of it, I was affected strongly by those beatings. As a result I was extremely afraid of my father and always wanted to avoid his presence. And in later years, his rebuke was as effective as a beating; so I also dreaded his disapproval that could come at any time. Mother was the comfort zone for me, but she did not really have the power to stop any beating if my father intended it. My mother never hit any of the boys, partly because there was not much need for it, as we children were usually well behaved, but also because unlike other women, she did not have an irritable nature. The other powerful figure in our house, Uncle Tiloka, the head of our household, was usually gentle and persuasive, rather than harsh or oppressive. He ranked above my father for major decisions, but my father's authority would prevail in the matters of children.

Once at the age of five, when I was in first grade, I was trying to avoid school. On the way to school, I decided to hide in a large hole in the trunk of the big *Neem* tree by the pond. While trying to hide, I was spotted by Uncle Amolak, who was on his way to visit the hospital that day and who later reported to my father that he had seen me away from school. Absence from school would have been a serious offence by itself, even if I had just stayed home; Kartar was never allowed to stay home even when he was ill. But after being sent to school and then hiding somewhere on the way, my misbehavior called for major corrective action and a memorable lesson. That afternoon while I was walking behind my mother, going from our house to our cattle yard a quarter mile away, my father came from the other side in a rage, grabbed and started beating me. The beating may not have been hard, nor did it last very long, but it scared the wits out of me, since nothing like it had happened to me before. After that beating, I hardly ever missed school regardless of sickness, bad weather, or any other circumstance. For other boys it was a common practice to be absent from school with the slightest excuse; but in our house it was totally unacceptable to miss school.

Again, once when I was about the age of 7 in the third grade, my father was trying to teach arithmetic to me while sitting on a *charpai* in the community courtyard of our Inner House. He told me to continue doing the arithmetic assignment, but I wanted to run off and play. My friend Mukand wanted me to go killing lizards with him, and I had the urge to run away and join him. When I attempted running off, however, my father told me to get back to work. I just giggled as if he was not giving me a serious order, and I ran around in the courtyard. My father felt that I was ignoring his order and he chased after me. He caught me easily, put me between his knees, and slapped me mercilessly for a relatively long time. During the beating, I shrieked and looked toward a grown-up neighbor girl, Aunt Harnami's daughter Chand Kaur, who was watching the beating. I was hoping she would intervene. She later said that when I was looking hopefully at her while shrieking, she wanted to intervene by saying, "Uncle, have mercy; stop beating the child. Look at his tearful face...." But she said she was afraid that my father might shout and growl at her or worse, so she had no choice but to let the beating continue. People always intervened whenever they saw something unreasonable, even at some risk to themselves, but Chand Kaur sensed that she could make no difference as my father was furious. His philosophy was that if he allowed one misdeed, it would sow the seeds for other misdeeds; he felt that he was doing what was best for his child. He was saying, "A *bhoot* (evil spirit) has entered this boy and the bhoot needs to be removed." Sometimes people actually tried to beat the bhoot or shatan (devil) out of those whose behavior was abnormal.

My father felt no further need to beat me, because after that I would never disobey a direct order from him, even during my teenage years. Furthermore, he also did not need to beat me because unlike my younger brother Gurdial, I would not whine, demand, or insist on anything, as I was more afraid of disapproval than Gurdial was. Our Gurdial was not afraid of being rebuked or even spanked, but I was too sensitive to bear such treatment. As a result Gurdial seems to have learned to deal with people more effectively than I have. He takes the initiative without fear, while I am overly protective of myself. In my teen years I would displease my father more than any other of my siblings, who were quite compliant. But I would do this not by opposing him directly, but by avoiding him and by not doing what was expected of me. Even when I felt no need to obey, I would still not act defiantly, but I treated my father with respect, in the manner of our family culture.

Girls in our society were never hit by their fathers. Besides, they were usually compliant, and the activities of their lives were such that there was no need to punish them physically; a little yelling would make them cry and generally would accomplish what was needed. Married women were not always so lucky, and some married women were beaten by their husbands until they had grown sons to stop the practice; a few wives were beaten almost as frequently as the young sons were.

All Play is Waste and Mischief

In spite of all the demands of the teachers, there was still some free time. Father was not always around. My mother was more indulgent and would not prevent me from playing; and there was no serious consequence if I went against her wishes. But my father would not allow me to play outside with children of my own age if he saw me doing so. Play and pleasure were associated with waste and mischief in the old culture, especially in my family; each family seemed to have its own culture. Work, worship, and service to others were the virtuous behaviors one needed to practice in order to be approved. Other children did not have such strict fathers and could play day or night unless they were wanted home for dinner or to sleep. No one seemed worried about me if I did not come home until late at night, since nothing very useful could be done at nighttime. But if I was ever caught playing during the daytime, although I would not be beaten I would surely be scolded for wasting precious time. Then I would be sent to study, or more frequently I would be told to go and water or feed the cattle or do other chores, of which there were plenty in a farming family. Even Uncle Tiloka, who was never harsh, would say, "Moving the cattle from outdoors to indoors is as good as playing hide and seek, so why waste time in playing?" I did feel a slight sense of injustice due to this restriction; but it was like living with other realities of life, or with a handicap. Each child had some restrictions, and some would say, "No, I can't do such and such a thing because I will be beaten if I do that." But I felt that everything enjoyable was forbidden by my father. Rightly or wrongly, I felt that I was selectively prohibited from going to the weddings of relatives, which usually lasted for many days. My sisters could be sent, and they would later tell me how much fun they had had and counted all the cousins they had met. The names of those cousins sounded fascinating; like mythical beings; the cousins and other relatives sounded bigger than life to me as a young boy. The girls' tasks were not considered critically important and they did not have to attend school, so they could be sent to weddings. And little boys like Gurdial could be sent because his school work was not important enough yet, and he would also whine and whimper if he was not allowed to go. But I felt restricted and deprived of fun and pleasures. I felt underprivileged compared to the children who could go to the homes of their maternal grand parents (*nanke*), where they were pampered. My maternal grandparents were dead even before my mother was one year old. I never saw their village except once in 1938 when I went with Uncle Mohinders *junj* (bridegroom's party). Other than that event and going to sister Maro's house, I never went more than seven miles from our village until I was 16 years old.

Even those people who allowed their boys to play considered playing to be harmful. Just as some adults indulged in alcohol and opium and were difficult to restrain from other vices, children's play was treated like a vice. I don't remember ever receiving a toy or gift from anybody as a child, and I don't remember any of my siblings having one either. Some indulgent parents or grandparents did buy colored toys of wood or metal for their children, and some made toys with their own hands for their small children who were not big enough for any useful work yet. But they usually decried all play by growing boys as a waste, possibly addictive, and a distraction from the important tasks.

The Freedom and Adventure of Cattle Grazing

Given the harsh attitude of my elders toward play and the abusive treatment at the hands of teachers, it is not hard to imagine that I hated school. I hated the proverbs about the value of education and was glad to get away from school. The best days for me were the school holidays of four or five weeks a year. I was usually sent to graze cattle during the holidays. I could have avoided that by saying that I needed to do the schoolwork that the teacher had assigned for the holidays, but I loved the cattle-graze life. I rarely completed the school work assigned for the holidays; I procrastinated and avoided the homework until there was no time left to complete it. The dreaded day of return to school was doubly traumatic for me because the incomplete homework would be the perfect reason for the teacher to beat me. I remember the sinking feeling in my heart each time the holiday ended and school was to reopen. All the boys whose schoolwork was incomplete or unsatisfactory were beaten. Very few escaped the beating entirely.

But when I went to graze the cattle, I could forget all about school. There I could play with other boys without restrictions and could experience freedom from all oppression. The opportunities for fun were unlimited there. We would discover new grazing fields; after the farmers had harvested the crops, any remaining stubble and unwanted growth were good for the grazing cattle. We would find the burrows of wild animals and sometimes catch their young. We would bring the buffaloes and cows to water at noon and check out who had had brought what food along and possibly share it for lunch. Then we would climb trees by the bank of the canal and jump from the tree branches into the canal water. Sometimes we would jump from the bridge into the canal and be carried along by the current. We competed with other boys swimming against the current or back and forth across the canal. We competed in singing songs, sometimes the ones with filthy language. Some of us would climb to the tops of telegraph poles; at other times we would pull the telegraph wire down toward the ground. This could be done by throwing the end of a turban rope (two or three turbans tied end to end to achieve the needed length) with a weight at one end over the wire. The wire would sag as we pulled the rope down and then it could be caught by hand, although we were fearful of breaking it. Wire lines, with poles to support them every fifty yards or so, went along large irrigation canals and along railroads. We never quite understood their function and knew only that they were government property. We thought that something passed through the wire and that we could get into trouble if we broke it and spilled the contents in the wire. We would play cards and make the loser round up the straying cattle. We would hope to catch and kill a *goh* (big lizard) and have shoes made from its skin. I would put my ear at the mouth of a foxhole or some other large hole and listen for the sounds of wild animals inside. We would scare a herd of deer and watch them fly away in all directions. We would count the number of male and female *rojh* (a wild animal taller than a cow but swift as a deer) in herds. Sometimes we would catch some shepherd's goat and stealthily drink its milk directly from the goats' teats. We would climb trees and find bird's eggs or chicks in them, just for curiosity and to boast to everyone about it. A couple of times I caught a baby deer and wished to take it home but then had to release it, because the elders would disapprove; they would say that the village dogs would tear it to pieces. We would compose songs and rhymes about other people or events; we were proud to discover something nasty, something peculiar or even scandalous about someone and make a song about it. Boys took great pride boasting to their friends about such things as how strong their cousin was, how many people their camel could carry, how strong their ox was, or other similar claims. We played cops and robbers games; we discussed fairs, singing groups, wrestling matches, and the older boys would even discuss people's illicit affairs. In the late afternoon, boys would enjoy riding their buffaloes on the way back to the village and sometimes would race against other boys' buffaloes. A cow would not let any boy ride it, but a buffalo did not mind if the owner rode it. The enjoyable activities and opportunities for excitement were limitless when we were grazing cattle and not in school. I saw great adventure in the outdoor life and so I wanted to be put to farm work and grazing cattle.

The captivity of school was just the opposite of all those outdoor experiences grazing cattle, with no teacher, no beatings or scolding, and no restrictions! I never wanted to be in school; outdoor life is what I wanted, like other boys of our Jat caste. My eighth grade class had dwindled to two pupils, because all the Jat boys except me had dropped out earlier. I used to wish I could drop out, too. The only other boy remaining in my eighth grade class was Buggoo Ram, a shopkeeper's son, and not the company for a Jat boy to be proud of. In the culture of Jats, people who were not landowner farmers were considered weak, effeminate, devious, and cowardly; the shopkeepers in their own minds probably thought of the Jats as stupid, crude, and uncivilized. My longing for a life of grazing cattle and farming never truly died out, and it was to be a great source of pain to my parents in later years. My priorities at that age were to be physically strong and to stay on the land, but my family wanted me to be educated. Once I told my non-student Jat friends, "Next year I am going to be twelve, and big enough to tell my father that I don't want to go to school any more; next year I will quit school and join you in grazing cattle and farm work." The word about that conversation got back to my father and I was rebuked severely for such thoughts.

Getting Through Middle School

Being the youngest in each class, I was rather overwhelmed in the earlier grades; but I improved as I grew older. Once when an inspector came to test the students, my father came to school to watch how I would perform in the third grade examination. He was very pleased when a shopkeeper's boy named Parkash and I were the only ones to answer every question correctly. By the time I was eight years old, in the fourth grade, I was considered a good student. World War II had not started yet, but when in 1939 the rumors of tension between Hitler and the British were widespread, women of the village would say to me, "Gurnam, you are an educated boy; what do you read? Is a war going to start?" I had no clue; but as the number of airplanes flying in the sky had increased, so we thought something ominous was happening. When Hitler advanced on

Poland and the war started, Indians in the independence movement cheered, as they wanted the British to be defeated by Hitler. We rural Indians, specially the landowners, were generally pro-British, but the urban politicians were pro-Hitler, considering him an enemy of their enemy. There was a prominent leader named Subhash Chander Bose, disaffected with the passivity of Gandhi and Nehru's Congress Party, who went to Germany to convince Hitler to invade India. It is said that when Hitler spurned him, he later went to Japan. There he helped to form the Japanese-sponsored Indian National Army assembled from captured Indian prisoners of war, to fight against the Allies. He perished somewhere outside India during World War II.

As a nine-year-old in the fifth grade I became the best student in our class, because the shopkeeper's son Parkash had left to attend some better school. My class of about 30 from the first grade had dwindled to about 9 by the fifth grade. In each grade a portion of the total would drop out. For example, Ghoke the Mirassi had failed several grades, so boys from the lower grades would catch up with him and then pass him. At first he was two years ahead of me, then he was in my class, and then he flunked again and was left behind. My friend Mukand, although a Jat boy, was smart; but he was married off in the seventh grade at the age of thirteen and therefore he left school. There were only two of us left in the eighth grade, myself and Buggoo, son of Atoo (Atma Ram) the shopkeeper. Our class of only two students took the middle-school examination given by the State of Punjab in February 1943. Being the best student in that eighth grade class of two was not a major feat for me, even though the other boy was the son of a shopkeeper and was therefore expected to be smarter than the Jats.

The state of Punjab used to hold the middle-school (eighth grade) examination in February of each year; for this purpose the students had to go to some large town where the examination was held. In Karatr's days the nearest place to take the examination was Abohar, but by my time we could take the same test at a closer location, Rampura Phul. Our headmaster Ram Partap accompanied our class of two students like a chaperone for the few days that it took to complete the examination. Once that examination was over, I seemed destined for a life of cattle-grazing and farming, because I did not have the qualifications to enter a high school. One had to go to an English medium school in order to be able to go to high school. Most people who went to our vernacular middle school never went beyond the eighth grade, so everyone expected that I was going to be put to plough starting in February 1943.

I had not been considered important enough to be sent to a boarding school in Nathana where English could be taught; the first son of our family, Kartar had already had been educated there. My father did want me to be educated, but the youngest uncle, Mohinder, in our joint family, wanted at least one of us boys to work on the land. He wanted me to be productive for our household by engaging in farm work and not be a financial burden by being in a boarding school. My continuing in the local middle school and living at home amounted to a stand-off between my father and uncle. Whereas my being sent to a boarding school would have triggered the immediate breakup of our joint family, my father would not take me out of the local school altogether, because it cost nothing and was no burden on the joint family. Later on, my younger brother Gurdial was sent to boarding school, but by that time the joint family had already broken up. I hated school anyway, and I thought that Uncle Mohinder had the right idea about keeping me on the farm. So I was glad when I passed out of the local middle school and that seemed like the end road of education for me.

My childhood had been marked by a feeling of imprisonment in school. I had a strong desire to be out in the fields, to associate with the cattle grazers, to do things with my hands, and to become good at performing the farm tasks. Work in the fields felt more like play to me, although I was not capable of serious farm work yet. My family's workers and sharecroppers would tell me, "Stay away from farm work; this is for ignorant savages like us." But at that age I wanted to be tough like a savage and then be able to boast to my Jat friends. My Uncle Tiloka usually assigned my father to the miscellaneous tasks, but he never put my father to the plough. Usually our sharecroppers were put to the plough. There is no flexibility in that work; it is the same drudgery every day and ages the ploughman before his time. If a boy did not gain much in height after puberty, people in the village would say, "That boy was put to the plough when he was still too young; that is why he got worn down and did not grow in height; he should not have been put to the plough at such a tender age." But plowing was also the fundamental and defining task of farming, so I wanted to practice plowing with our oxen. I always wished that my family's workers would let me hold the plough behind the oxen, even for a short while, to make a furrow. But they would say, "No, no, you will stab the foot of the ox with the plowshare from behind; and when you are old enough to do it right, you will not want even to come near the plough; plowing is the fate of uneducated savages like us." They might have been right, but I wanted to have the feeling of doing something grownup, doing it right and then boasting to my friends about it. My friend Mukand, who was about a year and a half older than me, used to say, "I was able to steer the plough straight for 20 yards today!" or "I sowed a fist-ful of wheat through the *pour* that was mounted behind the plough." I wanted to be able to boast like Mukand.

My Life as a Lonely Herdsman

Our people used to talk about the year 1990 of the Bikermi calendar, 1932-33CE, as the year of great rains and bumper crops; but the year 1942-43CE turned out to be almost as good. In early 1942, cattle prices had been depressed because of the drought and near-famine conditions in the prior year; so my Uncle Tiloka bought many new buffaloes and other animals with the hope of a better 1942-43. He would go to cattle fairs and buy buffaloes that were not then giving milk and therefore were unwanted and were sold cheap. He even bought a young camel or two with the hope of having them grow in size and price. He did not buy any oxen because he did not want to plow more land and had in fact cut down the operation by selling our *Gora* (blondish) ox after the frustrating years of drought and depression. The large herd of buffaloes that he thus accumulated could not be driven to the village daily after grazing, as we had no yard exclusively for them any more. Our family was now living in the house built in the former corral, so the buffaloes had to be kept in the wilderness at night, after grazing during the day. During the summer, they were kept in our field, but when the fields were sown with wheat in the autumn, some other venue had to be found. On autumn nights we started to keep them under some *tahli* trees in the government reserve land along the Sirhind Canal about two miles from our house. It took two people to control and watch the herd at night, and someone had to carry food from the village to the herdsman. There was not another soul in that vicinity at night. It was a lonely and risky life, and it would have been easy for some deranged outlaw to kill you there. When a job was so unpleasant and dangerous that no one else in the family wanted to do it, my father was made responsible for it. So he had to take the herdsman's meals and watch the herd at night, although his work was too important to send him to graze cattle during the day. In fact my father had a close brush with *daku* outlaws. One night they had threatened to kill him there. So later in the month of November 1942, the family built a corral with a *barr* (thorny fence) under the canopy of a large *beri* tree. We had some partial thatch cover against rain over a small portion of the corral, and this provided partial protection from wind and rain. For the herdsman, a tiny straw shack was built just at the gate of the corral which could barely accommodate two thirty-inch by six-foot beds with no additional room for a step. The straw hut and the corral had gates made of thorny bush and straw as partial barrier against cold wind. There was some psychological security in being in your own field instead of being in the forest, but the fact of being very far away from any other human at night with no possibility of help in case of danger used to make me uneasy. As a twelve-year-old, I frequently had the duty of either taking food for the herdsman at night or being there alone as a guard at night and then returning to the village in the morning to attend school.

In February 1943 when I had taken the middle school examination, herding buffaloes became my full-time job, even before I was thirteen years old. So I got what I used to wish for; but that lonely life was not what I was expecting. Uncle Nikk was sick of the herdsman's life under those circumstances and preferred to do some other farm work; in fact so did I, because the harvesting and other farm work was done in the company of coworkers. But twelve-year-old Gurnam did not have the choice, so I was ordered to be the herdsman during the day and guard of the corral at night. These herding conditions were not like the cattle-grazing camaraderie of my earlier days when we took the cattle from the village in the company of other boys, played games with friends during the day, and all came home together in the evening. Now I had to stay alone in the wilderness overnight. And because of the large size of my herd, our cattle could not graze with others and I had to be alone all day. Other cattle-grazers resented our big herd and would avoid me, as my large herd could quickly use up the grazing resources that others wanted undamaged for their own cattle. All grazing in those days was in other peoples' fields after they had been harvested, and sometimes in the uncultivated common lands which were left wild. Nobody would forbid you to graze on his lands according to tradition and by the generally recognized need of the animals to feed, but sour looks were not uncommon.

With the new duties, even before I was thirteen years old I was saddled with this lonely and unpleasant work. I could come home only once or twice a month for part of a day, to have to wash my hair and for a change of clothes. Food was delivered to me during the day at uncertain times and places, since the person who brought the food had to just guess my location according to indirect messages or inquire from other cattle grazers. Being hungry and thirsty was a fact of life, so I developed the habit of eating as much as I could when the food was brought to me. My body also learned to do without food and drink for long periods without fading and without feeling faint. When the canal stopped flowing, water to drink was not always easy to find, and even if you could find some stagnant water, it was really unappealing. I was very averse to carrying water with me. Carrying water in a heavy *lote (clay pitcher)* was difficult when you had to run to round up a willful cow or buffalo. Carrying the water lote was for old and slow people. So I could not carry any water with me; I just had to depend on finding a source of stagnant water somewhere along the way unless the relatively safer canal water was running. In a state of extreme thirst, I would have to put my mouth to any puddle or pond I was lucky enough to find, before it was muddied up again by the buffaloes walking through it and urinating in it; unfortunately, a buffalo has the urge to urinate whenever it steps into water.

The time when the canal was closed so as to divert water to other regions of the country, were extremely stressful for my cattle and me in that warm climate of infrequent rains and scarce water. Sometimes, in desperation the cattle and I would put our mouths to any little puddle or pond where water had not dried up yet, even when I saw little worms crawling in the water. To prevent those critters from entering my mouth while I was drinking from the puddle, I would use the end of my turban cloth as a filter in front of my mouth and let the water be sifted through the turban cloth. When water could not be found, the cattle would get to the verge of madness with thirst and I would feel weak, too, so we could not be very choosy about the cleanliness of water. Sometimes I would have to drive the cattle to some pond far away, around of other peoples crops. When I got there the pond water might be dirty, or the pond might be completely dry. Even if I found some water and the cattle got a drink, by the time I returned with the cattle to the corral, they could be thirsty again, and they would have to survive all night and some part of the next day before their next opportunity to drink. When the canal water came again after many days' closure, it could be muddy or relatively clear, depending on the season. But muddy or dirty, if it was running water, it was considered safer to drink than any stagnant water. It was the water standing in ponds, or residual in some puddles in the irrigation ditches, that was really unclean, and it might be mixed with mud or contain buffalo urine and worms. When it held crawling, wiggling, struggling bugs and creatures that had not yet died, one hoped that since the worms had not died, the water would not be poisonous. My only defense was to use an end of my turban cloth as a filter over my mouth. In those days I never fell ill due to the contaminated water.

One of the ways that people tried to make the muddy water acceptable to drink was to dissolve a little of what we called *phatkri* (alum, aluminum sulfate?) salt in the water. The phatkri had the property of curdling the dirt and slime from water, like split milk; a short time after it had been dissolved in a small pit of water, the slime from the curdled water would start settling slowly to the bottom. After a half-hour, one could drink that water and would even hope the phatkri had killed any disease-causing organisms in the puddle. The phatkri used to be given to camels to prevent disease; it certainly was extremely harsh and sour and thought to be curative.

Sometimes my six-year-old brother Gurdial would be required to bring food for me to the cattle corral in the wilderness at night. Little Gurdial would whine to my mother to get the roti ready quickly so he could travel some distance before it was too dark. He had developed a method of countering the fears as he passed through the bushes and tall crops in the dark. From a distance of many fields, before the fearful Gurdial reached me, he would start shouting my name, "Oh brother Gurnam, I am coming!" This was to announce to any potential threat in the surroundings that he had a source of support. He would keep shouting my name so that nothing would hurt him, or so that I would know of his arrival and would save him. People returning from the fields in the evening who saw little Gurdial going to the fields in the dark would jokingly say "This can't be a human child walking toward the wilderness in the night; it must be a baby *bhoot* (ghost)." So some people gave little Gurdial the nickname of Bhoot. Compounding his fear was the fact that this corral with the fence of thorny bush was on land that were not irrigated; the bhoot were supposed to thrive in un-irrigated lands and to avoid water. Moreover, that had been a year of bumper crops, when the millet had grown up to seven feet high and was so abundant that farmers just removed the kernels from the top and left the drying plants standing for the rest of the year. There was too much plant matter to cut the crops down near the roots, so the standing plants created a jungle-like effect where visibility was poor. Being alone in the wilderness every night, barely thirteen years old, I myself was not completely free from the fear of bhoot and of wild animals. But admitting such a fact would have been considered cowardly and disgraceful for a Jat Sikh. If it was not too dark, Gurdial would return immediately after delivering the food to me, but sometimes he would stay overnight with me and return in the morning to attend school.

What made it more unpleasant was the fact that this was not the pattern of life for anyone else in the village. All farmers lived in the village and came home at night; nobody remained in the un-irrigated regions. But my uncle and family were determined to go to extremes in order to make a better future. They wanted to work a little harder than the others, suffer if necessary, and do the unpleasant things that the comfort-loving village people would not do. No physical hardships or privations were too extreme for my family if they could promote their goal of some prosperity, as they were orphans who had started with meager resources. They used to talk about people who refused to face difficulties and drifted into poverty. For example, some people, instead of working hard to improve their lot, would mortgage their land in order to live. But my Uncle Tiloka set the pace for the rest of the family by insisting on "hard work and no waste," and the whole family revered and followed him. He was really doing it for us, as he had no wife or children of his own.

Turning Point in Kotli Street

After the harvest in May 1943, our cattle were moved again to our fields in the irrigated areas, where other people could be found more often. Uncle Nick was more willing to be with the cattle in that more comfortable environment, and I got more chances to go home to the village for part of a day. One day when I was allowed to go home, my father took me to the shoemaker to have my feet measured for shoes. The only shoemaker on our side of the village, Qamri the Mochi, was not making or repairing shoes any more as he had started working as a watchman. But there were some shoemakers on the other side of our village, so my father and I walked toward the shoemakers' house through Kotli, the bazaar street of our village.

In Kotli, we started talking to an old Muslim acquaintance of my father, Mr. Ahluwalia. Some Sikhs from the Klal caste had adopted the family name of Jassa Singh, the great Sikh general who was called Ahluwalia because of his ancestral village. That name had become so prestigious that even the Muslim Klals in our village took it as their family name, thinking that the name Ahluwalia meant the Klal caste. This Mr. Ahluwalia of our village was a retired liquor seller, which had been his hereditary profession. In old age he usually sat on a *charpai* in the street, in the sun during winter and in the shade during summer. People would greet the old man as they walked by and sometimes stopped or sat down on his charpai to talk. It was customary for older men to ask the children some questions. Ahluwalia (he was called by his last name only.), the only literate man in his local clan of about twenty Muslim adults, asked me several questions about geography and arithmetic, which I had no trouble in answering. Ahluwalia was impressed and said to my father, "Naginder Singh, your boy is bright; you must educate him further."

Ahluwalia's words were not lost on my father; they just reaffirmed his own inclination to educate me. But I could not be admitted to any high school because I had not gone to any English medium school. In our joint family system, my younger uncle, Mohinder Singh, had argued that "Gurnam's thick limbs and chunky body were suitable for farming. He must not be sent away to school." On that day after Ahluwalia's comments, my father told me, "You should learn English, even if it leads to the family breakup; but realistically there is no school that can admit you." Ahluwalia told my father about a private teacher named Kesho Ram in Rampura Phul, who handled difficult and unusual cases. So it seemed worthwhile to talk to Kesho Ram about my studying English privately under his guidance and possibly continue there to study privately for matriculation examination. This arrangement appeared workable because I could still live at home and would not have to be sent away to any boarding school.

Pivotal Meeting with Kesho Ram

In October 1943, after I had grazed cattle for more than six months, my father took me to Kesho Ram, who used to hold classes in a portion of his small rented house in Rampura Phul, a few miles away from our village. He seated the ninth grade class in one room and the tenth grade in the veranda of his flat. Then he would switch from one class to the other all day, giving an assignment to one class to be done while he faced the other class. He alone taught all the subjects to both classes. He was reluctant to take a single student like me when he could be teaching a whole class in the same amount of time. I also was reluctant to travel more than four miles each way, six days a week, but disobedience or defiance of my father's wishes was not yet a part of my habits. Besides, I had had a taste of the lonely and harsh life of cattle grazing and was not enamored of that life any longer.

The meeting with Kesho Ram was one of the decisive points in my life. He was noncommittal about how well he could teach me the English language or prepare me to study for the matriculation examination. If he did so he would be taking time away from classes, which paid him per student, whereas my father would pay just the few rupees per month that every other student paid. Kesho Ram thought I might not learn anything sitting alone while he would be busy teaching his regular classes. But in that culture people used to try to accommodate the needs and requests of others, if the request was urgent. My father felt that sitting in an environment where there were other students would be a good influence on me regardless of how much I learned. My time was not worth much. I would eat and sleep at home and slowly walk through the sandy paths from Mehraj to Rampura Phul every day, picking and eating *ber* or *pinjhu* or *peelu* from the bushes and trees along the way, and would get to Kesho Ram's place at a leisurely pace in a couple of hours. No one was recording my attendance; I had no classmates, and with a private teacher there was no chance of physical punishment. Only the government school teachers felt that they had the authority to beat students.

After some persuasion Kesho Ram agreed to teach me and allow me to come and sit in the veranda outside; his reward for accepting me as a student would be that some day, if I learned English adequately, he would have one more student later for his ninth grade class. He used to prescribe a lesson for me daily, and before I departed for home he would ask how I was progressing and would check anything I had written before letting me go. As time went by, he would also let me watch the ninth grade English class sometimes, to provide relief from complete isolation. At first it was strange for me to watch the movement of the lips of the older boys in the ninth grade speaking a foreign language. What interested me most were the stories that Kesho Ram told as he was teaching, to go with every explanation. He was a great story-teller and a humorist, characteristics I had not expected from teachers, as the ones I had known were mostly officious, dour, cruel, irritated, and threatening.

Gradually, over a period of about a month I learned to read and write the English alphabet, and in three or four months I could understand simple short sentences. After six months had passed, Kesho Ram decided to ask me to leave. It would still have taken me two additional years of English instruction in the junior-senior program to qualify for the ninth grade if I could get admission somewhere. A regular government high school could not accept a student like me without two additional years of English instruction and a certificate. That informal learning from Kesho Ram for six months did not count.

I had not learned enough English to read well yet, but at the insistence of my father, Kesho Ram agreed to let me just sit in his ninth grade class and see what happened. So I could either progress with the ninth grade or quit. My adjustment was better than expected. I started to learn as well as the other students, most of whom either had been rejected by other schools, or had failed in school, or did not qualify to enter any school. After a couple of months, I was as good as any other student in the ninth class. Kesho Ram moved the classes to an abandoned *gurdwara* building in the farms on the Rampura side of the railroad tracks. This increased the walking distance for me, to nearly five miles each way.

Father Nixes My Illegal Plan

While still in the ninth class, one winter I shared a room with Gogan (not his real name) in Rampura Phul instead of traveling the 5 miles each way from Mehraj to the class. Gogan was five or six years older than me and was the son of the sardars of Dyalpura. He was closely related to the Phulkian princes, and once he had even put a claim to the throne of the State of Jind when the old *raja* died without leaving an heir. But Gogan's claim to become a *raja* was not honored by the British, who had the decisive power in disputes over succession. Unfortunately Gogan's mind could not relate to anything

105

academic. He had tried in other places to pass the matriculation examination but had failed badly. I heard that he had had some interaction even with my brother Kartar when they were in the same boarding school at Nathana, many years earlier. As with many such misfits, he had been sent to the teacher Kesho Ram as a last resort. He had been promised by an aide of a *maharaja* that he could have a job of his choice, but only if he could get a high school certificate. Kesho Ram tried his best to teach Gogan privately for an extra fee. I could learn things more quickly than him, as I was usually listening in the same room when Kesho Ram came to teach him. But geometry and algebra found no place in Gogan's brain. Then Gogan had a suggestion for me: "I know you are only fourteen years old and in the ninth grade; but in a few months you could learn all it takes to pass the matriculation examination. Why don't *you* take the examination in my name and I will get the certificate?" I foolishly thought it might be great fun to play such a clever trick. After all, Gogan was the son of a *sardar* family, and he would be an even better friend if I helped him. For that plan to work, however, it would be necessary to identify me by the name Gogan officially and legally (rather, illegally). But Gogan had the influence to arrange that.

So one day Gogan and I traveled by train to Kot Kapura where a magistrate was a friend of Gogan's family. Gogan and I appeared in the court before the magistrate, and Gogan gave the magistrate some papers containing the application forms for the matriculation examination, along with three copies of my photograph. The magistrate certified, with the seal of the court on my pictures, that the person in the picture (me, Gurnam) was Gogan Singh, belonged to village Dyalpura, and had been born in the year 1924. The copies of my picture certified by the magistrate were attached to Gogan Singh's application for the matriculation examination in triplicate. I would walk into the examination hall where my name would be Gogan and my face would be matched by the examination supervisor with the picture and the roll number pasted on the desk. It would be all straightforward, since the magistrate had certified the name Gogan on my picture and on the application. The examination for the different subjects would take nearly a week. There was a small possibility of being discovered, but who was to question me when a court had certified my identity as Gogan Singh.

I happened to boast about this plan when I went home. But when my father and Uncle Trilok Singh heard about it, they were horrified. They were extremely angry and disapproving, and scotched the plan, saying it was a fraud and a crime. They smashed the whole scheme instantly, with a severe warning to me against such ideas in the future. My father emphasized that one should not do such unethical things; my uncle said that small crimes at my young age would lay the foundation for even more corrupt ways later. My mother also said, "Son, have you ever seen any big mansions built by robbers and criminals? They all die with ruined lives. An honest law abiding life is the best." I was surprised at the reaction of my family, because I was just trying to help a friend. The magistrate surely did not have any compunction about certifying falsely to aid the process, even knowing fully well that I was not Gogan Singh but his friend! Anyway, I had to refuse to take the test for him. Gogan was quite disappointed in me, but I had no choice but to dissociate myself from his scheme.

Kesho Ram, the Most Memorable Teacher

One of the most memorable people in my life was the teacher Kesho Ram. He was moderately tall, thin of limb, fair of complexion, with an oval face bearing many pockmarks, an impressive hairline, straight black hair, straight nose, and smiling eyes. His slightly protruding front teeth gave the impression that he was always smiling, and smiling is how he lived most of his life. He might have been about thirty but every adult appeared older to me when I was thirteen years old. By that age I had become sufficiently arrogant to not respect any town-dwelling Hindu teacher, since village farmers thought of townspeople as soft, effeminate, weak, and not manly. We expected them to be merely clever and tricky. But Kesho Ram had a most remarkable mind and a very likeable personality, in contrast to the teachers I had met before. He had my unreserved admiration for his personality, his humor, and his integrity. His intelligence and gifts were not due to his being a Brahmin, as his father was a man of little learning. His younger brother, Bhag Chand, though very good looking, was of average intelligence, and his bright young son Kul Bhushan did not really have the same spark as Kesho Ram himself did, in spite of all the guidance and advantage provided to him. Only a high school graduate himself, Kesho Ram had acquired a vast amount of knowledge about nearly every subject in the world, from history to science, from geography to mythology, from psychology to commerce, from Urdu, Persian and English to Punjabi, Hindi and Sanskrit, from art and music to theater and drama, from the contents of scriptures to the requirements for military leadership; his mind spanned everything. He would say, "You are not getting a complete education here because we lack facilities for sports and for teaching science. But unfortunately those students in the government schools are not much better off, in spite of the resources of their schools." He tried to produce bold, ethical thinkers from his motley crowd of mediocre pupils; he thought they should be ready to tackle any matter in life and not merely pass a test.

Being in Kesho Ram's class was more like being in a comedy theater than in a disciplined environment. Every point he made was illustrated by a humorous example or story. He could make any dull subject interesting. It was by illustration, animation, and dramatization of the ideas that he was so effective as a teacher. And he somehow managed to find a funny story or anecdote to go with every topic for the purpose of illustrating his point. You would think he was wasting too much time every day on irrelevant stories and humorous topics, exploding myths, blasting superstitions, talking about politics and economics, about ethics, about other societies, ancient heroes and modern day politicians, human ingenuity and wonders of nature, philosophy and mechanics, table manners and personality disorders, and so on and so on. How could he get any teaching done in the two classes that he was responsible for! He had a moderate respect for *Vedic* knowledge and ancient wisdom but had no patience with the exploitation of ignorant, religious, and superstitious people by the Brahmins and other deceptive practitioners of religion. He himself was from a Brahmin family, but he believed in truth and ethics rather than in any religious dogma. Some people called him an atheist, but in reality he just refused to compromise with falsehoods. In practice he was one of the most ethical and truthful people I have ever met, a noble soul in spite of the cultural pressures to compromise.

Most of Kesho Ram's students were from the bottom of the barrel; they had little hope of getting an education in any government-approved school. Most were the rejects from elsewhere and had either failed or could find no place where they would be accepted for admission as students, because of special circumstances like my own. That is why they came to Kesho Ram for help. Some of them had only a minimal ability to absorb facts; they just wanted to get the matriculation certificate somehow. Some would say, "My brain is full of straw; nothing useful can be stored there" or, "Things can go into my ear but they don't stay in my head." From such misfits and underachievers, Kesho Ram sometimes obtained performances that were better than those of the shining students in the better-equipped government schools.

Unlike the government school teachers, Kesho Ram treated every student like a friend, although proper decorum and humility before a teacher were automatic in students in that culture. In spite of the leniency and informality, he still never had a discipline problem or disorder in his classes. With humor he could accomplish more to convey his message than anyone could by badgering, by humiliating, or by insulting the students as government schoolteachers usually did. The worst things that any student in his class did was to be absent or tardy, faults which if repeated in a regular school could result in expulsion. But one could walk into Kesho Ram's class at any time of the day, even after an absence of many days. A typical conversation with a frequently absent student would go like this: "Budhu Ram, did you come to the class yesterday?" Budhu Ram: "No, sir." Kesho Ram: "Did you come the day before?" Budhu Ram: "Yes, sir." Teacher: "And the day before?" Budhu: "No, sir." Finally Kesho Ram would say: "So, Budhu Ram, you have adopted the *langa dang* pattern?" That is the pattern a buffalo follows when it wants to skip every fourth milking time. But only a rural Punjabi who has milked reluctant and errant buffaloes can appreciate the fit and humor of this analogy.

Early in the 10th grade, I did not go to school for about two months as I had a bone infection, swelling, and an eruption in my left leg. I recovered from the illness after a few weeks, except for the fluid oozing from the infected leg bone, but then I fell back into my old thought pattern and got so used to being in the village, that I did not want to go to school any more. When Kesho Ram took the unprecedented step of coming from Rampura Phul to visit me in our house in the village of Mehraj, an undertaking that no one would have expected from a city teacher, I told him I had quit my studies and never wanted to go to school again. Kesho Ram seemed very disappointed. Although I liked him, my love of village life had not diminished. Some time later, however, I was forced by my father to rejoin Kesho Ram's class, so I did go back after a couple of months.

By then Kesho Ram had announced to the whole class that I had dashed his faith, hopes, and plans by dropping out and that he was very disappointed in me. He said he had lost the opportunity to show people in the surrounding area what results his teaching ability could produce. He had expected to give special coaching to me for a couple of months before the final examination, but now he was turned off by my attitude, and he had dropped all such thoughts of high achievement. I had missed many lessons during the couple of months' absence and had much catching up to do. Some of the words in math class, like componendo, dividendo, invertendo, and alternendo that the other students had learned in my absence, sounded totally strange and intimidating to me. It was not clear how I would catch up and how I would perform in the Punjab State Matriculation

Examination. But when it came to the examination a few months later, that absence from school did not seem to have been too damaging for my final results. I still scored higher than the doctor's son Mohammed Balal and the shopkeeper's son Hari Ram. I not only scored higher than all of Kesho Ram's other students but also beat the highest score of any student in the government high school of that town. Kesho Ram was so pleased with my results that he led a procession through the town of Rampura Phul in celebration. He declared that his one-man school had beaten the Government High School with its impressive buildings, many teachers, and better facilities. I was in the village and did not show up at Rampura Phul for the procession. I would have been embarrassed to be in a procession like that.

Matriculation and Other Examinations

About the last week of February 1946, we had to take the matriculation test. The Punjab State Examinations used to be given once yearly to students at all levels, i.e., middle school, high school, F.A. (Intermediate College), B.A., and M.A. You could choose any big city in which to take the examination by specifying it in your application form. But the date and sites were fixed for the test in each subject in the whole state, and the test questions given for each specified subject were the same everywhere. The completed examination papers from each site used to be shipped to an examiner whose identity was kept confidential. This is the only system in India where there was seldom any corruption, although attempts and scandals could still be heard of. It could take about a week to complete the tests for all the subjects and then some additional weeks to get the results from the examiner to the government offices. When the State of Punjab published the results of various examinations in the newspapers, the students and their parents searched for their own roll numbers and results with great anxiety. Anyone who failed would have to wait a whole year to try again the following year; even worse was the situation when you passed but achieved a very bad score, which could ruin your prospects for job or admission to higher education. That is why the annual tests were such a dreaded thing. A misunderstanding, a few errors, any minor illness or an accident or delay, might result in a poor performance in any subject and might waste a year of your life, or worse.

For the matriculation examination, my class had chosen the town of Bhatinda; in my brother Kartar's time such a convenient location was not available. Students from many other schools would also come there for the same purpose at the same time. When the time came, our teacher/advisor/chaperone made arrangements for meals and lodging in Bhatinda for all of us, for the duration of the examination. We took our own bedding, provisions, cooking utensils, and a cook along. It was not a complicated undertaking and was advantageous as expense was a big consideration. Village people were not in the habit of eating anywhere except at home or with relatives. In the larger towns there were some *tandoor* (ovens) or *dhaba* (eateries) for the purpose of providing inexpensive meals to people who went for court dates and to other travelers, but few people would spend money to eat at such places. So when Kesho Ram took his class for the matriculation examination to Bhatinda in 1946, we stayed in a *serai* (free inn), called *dharmsala*, that had been built by a wealthy person as an act of charity. That dharmsala provided a place to stay and cooking facilities without charge; such free dharmsala were available in all towns and cities in those days. The cook that our group had taken along, provided all the meals for us every day.

Kesho Ram did not believe in studying hard on the days of the examination. While the students of other schools, in panic mode, dug into their books on the evening before an examination, Kesho Ram took his students for walks in the countryside in the afternoons. After each day's test, he wanted to help us refresh our minds and to make us feel relaxed and confident. In those days one could walk from the center of the city of Bathinda to the fields, crops, or sand dunes in ten minutes, whereas now it could take more than an hour to do the same. A part of Bhatinda was still like a village then. In the 1940s the farmers of the town kept their cows, buffaloes, oxen and camels in their houses in the city, just as they would do in any village. Bhatinda women still fetched pitchers of water from the community well. In the 1940s, I saw many farmers taking their ploughs and oxen from their homes in the city out to their farms in the morning, just as they did in all the villages. It was only in the 1950s that the government acquired the land up to many miles from the city and ended that way of life for the Bhatinda farmers. Anyway, in 1946 my classmates and I had the opportunity to roam in and around the town of Bhatinda during the week of our matriculation examination. For me it felt more like a holiday than like the stressful time of examinations.

On the last day after the examinations, three of my friends and I contracted to eat at an all-you-can-eat, fixed-price *dhaba*. In those days, the restaurants used to charge one *anna (1/16 of a rupee)* per *roti* (unleavened bread), but the spicy daal and vegetables eaten with the roti were given free of cost if you paid for the roti. All four of us sat to eat at the table of this dhaba and started eating together. We ate the thin roti faster than the cook could prepare it, and it appeared that we could keep eating like that for a good part of the day. The dhaba owner was getting anxious and frustrated as my friends and I were not anywhere near full and were consuming the food as fast as the cook could cook the roti. Other paying customers were waiting, but any diversion of the limited supply to them would only have given our group the time to digest and become hungrier. After an hour of this, the owner said to us with folded hands, "Please have mercy on me. I won't charge you anything if you will stop now and walk away; because otherwise you might not stop all day and I would lose other customers who pay per roti. I made a mistake with the fixed-price offer." We agreed to leave his restaurant under those terms.

The next day, on 1 March 1946, I went with my three friends, Harnek and Sodagar of Mehraj and Amar Nath of Phul, to a photography studio in Bhatinda to get a group picture to memorialize our taking the matriculation examination. That became the earliest photograph in my possession, as I had lost the picture of me taken by the fashionable Hari of Sadhan Ka in our village in 1937. Of the four friends in that picture, Harnek died young in his early thirties and Sodagar died in his forties. They were both healthier, taller, stronger and better looking than me in 1946, but life in the village could bring any disease to you and cures were uncertain. I lost track of Amar Nath, who was a Hindu from the town of Phul and thus not from our landowner community. Amar Nath was quite stylish and more sophisticated than an average town Hindu. He just wanted to associate with us because he pretended to be daring like a Jat, and he wanted to have some Jat friends.

110

Malaria and Exotic Diseases

It is incredible to me that both my friends, Harnek and Sodagar, who used to be stronger than me, died so young. I reflect with great nostalgia on the times we spent in their houses, the long nights of conversation on exciting local topics and the joys of discovering and sharing various secrets. I really had great affection for Harnek and his family and we had spent many days and nights in his house during the mid forties. At least my best friend and old classmate Mukand lived to be nearly seventy. But disease was a common experience for the village people and I experienced much of it.

The illness that had caused me to be absent from Kesho Ram's classes for two months in 1945 was preceded by a high fever overnight and extreme pain in the left leg. Such violent physical flare-ups have occurred to me usually during the nights, and on those occasions I have awakened with unforgettable illnesses. A malady in 1956 also happened overnight and left lingering effects for decades. In 1999 I woke up with a stabbing eye pain at night, which was later determined to be due to a tumor behind one eyeball which turned out to be benign but was not removable or curable.

For that fever and swelling in the leg in 1945, I was taken to a licensed but not particularly qualified private practitioner, Dr. Dhillon. Such doctors handled patients with every malady, whether it was heart disease, cancer, broken leg, sore eye, high fever or persistent cough. They usually prescribed medicines by guesswork after superficial examination. The "doctor" did not understand anything about my fever or about the swollen leg that was about to burst open. But with an air of authority he gave me some pills anyway. He also gave me some ointment to apply on the leg and sent us home to the village. After several more days of fever and severe pain, my leg kept swelling to such a point that ultimately the infection and puss weakened the skin. Then the fluids in the swollen leg burst through the skin and started oozing slowly from a couple of openings That sore leg drained puss and fluids for about three years, in spite of the various ointments and remedies that doctors and healers gave me to apply. But after the fever was gone, the sore on my leg did not slow me down in any way. Elders of the village would say, "Young man, avoid walking on this leg with the open sore; avoid letting any dirty things touch your leg; you will get *pulm daur* (gangrene); you are a strong fellow; it will be a shame to have that leg amputated." But nothing seemed to work to heal it. It would appear to heal on the surface and the holes closed briefly, but a day or two later it would burst open and start oozing again. In retrospect my physician brother Kirpal says that the leg bone was probably infected deep underneath and that the infection just might have healed by itself slowly. In 1948, when my mother went to visit her sisters in TaruAna she mentioned that she was worried about the condition of my leg. They took her to a wise man named Balak Ram to whom she described the sore on my leg. Balak Ram gave her a reddish ointment (it could have been a mercury or lead compound) to apply to the wound. I had no hope that such a concoction from a quack would heal my leg, but within two weeks of starting the application of that red ointment, the wounds in the leg closed for good, although the indentations and scars on the leg have remained ever since. It appears that by a coincidence the infection in the bone was healed at the same time as the wounds were closing on the surface. I was fearful that the leg would swell and burst open again as it had done several times before; but it never gave me any trouble thereafter.

I used to suffer from malaria seasonally, more often than many other people in the village did. It used to be just very high fever for some days, aches in the head and body, severe trembling due to feeling cold in spite of the summer heat, and weakness for a few days after I recovered. Sometimes I would fall unconscious due to the high malaria fever and hallucinations would set in when I was in the half-asleep state. In semi-awake nightmares I would feel as though I was being thrown in a well of pointed spears held in the hands of weird creatures, like some demons from mythology. I would have the feeling of being thrown into fire and being torn apart by hideous beasts and wild creatures. Unpleasant scary feelings came while I was in the semiconscious state during the fever for a good part of each day. When the fever abated, the debilitation was nearly total and the experience would be repeated the next day.

In the days before World War II, no medicines were available in the villages, and people with malaria just took some tea or herb or they had a "wise man" perform Toona (magic gestures and words). Getting warm and sweating under the covers seemed to be the most effective remedy, but you could not feel warm easily until the fever left you. Sometimes the fever would come on alternate days. Then it was termed Teja or Teya, meaning every "third day," and it would strike with vengeance, as if it had had a chance to recover its power during the day when it was not attacking. Sometimes a wise man would be brought to heal you by telling the story of the evil creature called Teja. A few times I was told this story, about how Teja came and drained a bowl of blood out of the youth's body, drank the blood, and left the youth nearly lifeless. Then one day, a brave warrior came to help. He cut off the head of Teja so that it could no longer drink blood, and there was no fever after that. People would get better with such stories about as fast as without the stories. I personally never knew anyone who died of malaria, but the disease was so bad that it formed one of the curses and abuses that women uttered: "May the Teja fever rise in you," which was like cursing someone by saying, "May the plague break out in you."

During World War II, quinine became available to those who were aware and resourceful, but that was not an instant cure. Some people lost thirty percent or more of their body weight during a bout of malaria. Like most people, I recovered my strength pretty quickly after the disease that could last a couple of weeks. My friend Nawab Din the Araeen even thought that one emerges stronger than before after each bout with malaria. He had watched his younger brother Jalal Din rebound and become stronger each time after the disease. But I doubt if there was any truth in that statement; his brother was just getting stronger because he was still growing. The worst season for malaria was July to October, also called the *kacchi rut* or *kaccha mausam* (raw season).

But malaria was no big calamity for me. Unlike the previously mentioned disease, which could have caused the loss of my leg, malaria just caused lost time and some suffering and annoyance. As the years went by, I had malaria less and less frequently, the worst period being between the ages of nine and seventeen. In my college days I never again got any malaria, because my environment and my way of life had changed. I also suffered from something like pneumonia or typhoid once in my teen years. The doctor could not really tell what the disease was; he gave me antibiotics like he was giving to many ill people at the time.

Sore eyes were a common ailment, especially among children, some of whom would

112

have their eyes so swollen that they were completely shut for days, until the natural healing process brought the swelling down. It was common to have mucous ooze out of the sore and swollen eyes. Overnight the mucous could harden, so that by morning the child could not open his eyes, even when they were not completely swollen. Parents would try to soak these shut eyes with warm salted water to open them. I had such problems with my eyes when I was young but not after the age of twelve. These afflictions may have been just simple infections. For serious eye diseases like trachoma, one just depended on God's help. Eyes were considered the most precious part of the body. There used to be a joke about the news of a fellow falling off a roof, where the listener asked, "Is his eye safe?"

Unlike other rural villages, our village had a government hospital and a doctor, and hospital visits and medicines were free of charge during the British rule. Although the government policy might say that it was a free hospital, in any free hospital you usually could not get treatment for a serious ailment without personal influence or payment to the doctor. And the doctor did not usually have the free medicines, except for ordinary things, like Vaseline for a wound, a solution for sore eyes, or a liquid for a stomachache. The doctors did not have good diagnostic facilities, knowledge, or ability and mostly gave the well-known medicines by common sense and guess work. It was also possible for any unqualified person in town to practice medicine and sell medicines without any medical degree or license. If they became familiar with the names of famous medicines while working for a doctor, such untrained people could open their own shops and give the patients the same medicines as the doctor did by similar guesswork. In fact they could make more money than some doctors, because many people felt more comfortable going to these village medicine providers rather than to a doctor. Generally people were cured more by time and by innate immunities than by medical help. And if they died as a result of any wrong medicine, there was no bad consequence to the practitioner, as nobody was going to sue him. Most people accepted death as God's will.

In addition to the allopathic system, we used to hear of the AyurVedic system, the Homeopathic system, and the Yunani (Greek) system. There were also advertisements from various healers who claimed to have developed special cures for specific diseases. And there were others who cured by *hathaula* (cure by hand waving) and *toona* (magical or sacred words). For ordinary ailments, people tried self-medication, such as pouring heated oil in the ear for earaches, chewing cloves for a stomach ache, gargling with salt water for a sore throat, drinking hot tea and trying to work up a sweat in bed for a fever or headache, washing a wound in water boiled with *neem* leaves to keep away infection, applying a paste of ground mustard or powdered herbs to a body part that hurts, and drinking concoctions of various herbs, dried fruits, barks of some trees and well-known salts and chemicals for various ailments.

Roadside Dentists and Wandering Healers

The village people did not appreciate the value of healthy teeth and ignored their teeth until they started hurting. A dentist could hardly thrive there, when killer diseases were the main concern. I never went to a dentist in my entire life in India. But I left India at the age of 27, somewhat before the age at which people used to start losing their teeth, so I escaped that fate by just a few years. In America I was told at the age of thirty that I was about to lose a tooth unless I had preventive work done. Fashionable rural people in Punjab would brush their teeth with a fresh twig cut from a *kikker* tree. The bark of the kikker tree is spicy and creates a nice fresh taste in the mouth. First, one chews on the end of the kikker twig; then the resulting bristles do a pretty good job of cleaning the teeth. But most men were not motivated to bother with brushing teeth. Women from middle-class families were more conscientious about such matters and would ask the men to bring a *danten* (tooth brush) of the kikker tree from the fields. Men could have loose or hurting teeth by the age of thirty, and teeth falling out by age forty, even when they did not have any cavities in them. They would just throw away each tooth as it came off.

There were traveling "dentists" who could relieve you of any loose or hurting tooth. Such a dentist could be sitting on a mat on the ground by the roadside. He would have a display of previously extracted teeth on the mat as a form of advertisement. Some would claim to guarantee instant extraction without pain, as long as the tooth was somewhat loose. Such dentists took pride in removing a tooth magically with their thumb and forefinger, without using any instrument. Some traveled on the trains and hawked their skills as they went from one train compartment to another. Anyone who suspected a hurting or shaky tooth could raise his hand, pay a few pennies, and the "dentist" would use only his thumb and index finger to take out the tooth. The remarkable thing was that unlike the city dentists, the hawkers never used any instrument to pull the teeth and the process was usually painless and instantaneous. The owner of the tooth always felt better after the tooth was removed and put into his palm. But he would have to spit the blood out of his mouth somewhere nearby.

Quacks thrived in that environment. Apart from the door-to-door healers with suction horns and jars of leaches described elsewhere, there were various kinds of traveling medicine sellers. They could be traveling in trains or sitting by the roadside. The village crowd would gather to listen to their pitches at the fair. The medicine seller would put a little chemical in a bottle of clear liquid and make the liquid turn red, to demonstrate what happens to an eye when infection or foreign matter enters it. Then he would put another little medicine into the bottle to turn the red liquid back into clear liquid. And with that demonstration he would claim that your sore or red eye would become clear if you buy his medicine and put it into your eye. He would also claim that anyone with poor eyesight would see better after the use of that medicine. Since eyes were so precious to people, it was not hard to find buyers for his product regardless of its usefulness.

Since their audience was exclusively male, some roadside healers sitting on their mats would make a pitch to the men who were experiencing sexual difficulties. The well-known pitch would go like this: "There is some guy whose wife has a sour expression on her face; she barks at the children and shouts obscenities at the dog. She says she never felt any happiness after coming into that house. If her husband asks for food, she snaps at him; if he asks a question, she is grouchy and does not reply. Now, if the husband takes these pills of mine for a few days, his organ will increase one inch in one day, two inches in two days and three inches in three days. His organ will become hard as an electrical pole of steel; it will do various errands for him and will perform many miracles. The next day his wife will be smiling; she will be singing while working; she will cook the best delicacies with pleasure; she will serve her husband willingly and will treat him like lord and master." On hearing such ridiculous claims many people would assume that the healer was a fraud, but it was not hard to find suckers who would buy his pills and powders. Other quacks would sell powders for your stomach to relieve pain or constipation and some would sell tonics for your joints and for other enhanced powers.

It was not uncommon to have a cut or an injury while working in the farms. Some fellow would accidentally slash his finger with a sickle while harvesting and the finger would bleed profusely. I myself slashed the last two fingers of my left hand with a sickle several times during the harvest seasons; one sickle cut was so severe that it left a lasting scar and a permanent change in the shape of my little finger and its nail. The village people used to believe that urine heals any cuts. So one would ask one's companion to piss on the cut finger, as there was nothing guaranteed to be more sterile than the urine available on the spot. Then one would tear a little strip of cloth from the turban to put a bandage on the cut finger. Donating a little urine for someone's cut was considered a helpful act. I have heard even some women using the expression "She is so selfish that she won't even piss on your cut finger" while describing personality flaws.

The Goddess of Small Pox

In the generations born before me, smallpox was quite common. In the 1930s, some boys in our school used to have faces pockmarked in varying degrees of severity, and some friends and classmates of my younger brother Gurdial had smallpox in the early 1940s. The pockmarks were not always like freckles on a European skin; they could be like shallow pits on the face. Some people had just a few scattered marks; others might have a spot or two and may not even have known that they had been exposed to smallpox. But some people could have many such marks or a completely pitted face. There was not much of a stigma in having them and sometimes the pockmarks were an identifying feature of a person, as they would last for life. Some people thought the smallpox marks looked interesting and even attractive on people who were already good looking. But in rare cases the disease was so severe that the facial skin would be completely covered with pits and even the eyes could have scars, resulting in partial or total blindness. Although I did not personally know of anyone dying, I heard that some people could die of the pox. So it was not just for cosmetic reasons that people were fearful of smallpox.

Some people believed that the disease was caused by the wrath of the goddess Mata Rani and in fact the disease was named after the goddess and called mata. They would invoke *Mata Rani* or *Mata Devi* (the goddess of smallpox) to be gentle with their children even if they were to get the pox. Some people would take their children who had contracted smallpox, to a small mud structure constructed in honor of the goddess. There the children were required to bow to a donkey and say, "O donkey of Mata Rani, please heal me." People who believed in the goddess did not want to be vaccinated, because they thought it might make the goddess angry and also the vaccination needle would hurt. My father made sure that all his children were vaccinated against smallpox, so none of my siblings were ever infected, but many women would hide along with their children when they heard someone say, "The needle-piercing people have come!" Once I accompanied three neighboring women and several children to hide behind an upper story structure, to avoid being caught by the "needle people" sent by the government. Although I already had my vaccination, there was a fear that the sadistic needle people might vaccinate me

115

again by force. Sometimes the vaccinated spots would flare up and would be infected with puss. The vaccination program must have been started in our area by the beginning of the twentieth century, because I saw the vaccination marks on the arms of my father, born in 1896, and of Uncle Tiloka who was born about 1894. After the 1940s, no fresh cases of smallpox seem to have appeared in our village.

As a young child I was not afraid of dying because I thought death was for other people; I did not think it was possible for me to die. When I was five, I asked my mother why Bhan Singh's father had died. She told me that God sends people to live on earth according to His will, and when He decides it is their time to return, he takes people away. I said, "Why don't they run away or just hide?" Then I was told that their bodies remain, but life is taken out of them by God, so that they cannot move and death takes away their breath. "Can't they just live without breathing? I am never going to die. I will just run away if I feel that I am dying. I could die only if someone cuts off my head from the body and throws it away." To quiet me down, my mother told me it was not nice to talk about death. But after some of those illnesses as a growing boy, when I became unconscious in bed, I began to believe that it was possible that I could become unconscious forever. The concept of invincibility was washed from my mind by the age of seven or eight, when I realized that no parent could help if I became permanently unconscious.

Helping Uncle Tiloka in Talwara

Soon after I completed the matriculation examination in March 1946 it was decided that I should go to help uncle Trilok Singh with harvest work in Talwara, Rajputana, where he had moved after the breakup of our joint family. We still had a lot of respect for him, although we were now separated. After 1945 Uncle Tiloka reclaimed some of our family land in the flood plain of the Ghagger River around Talwara by cutting trees and clearing wild bushes and grass. That was the first year he sowed mustard in the wild land that had never been cultivated and it was a pretty good crop. Trilok Singh and his brothers had tried to clear and farm their land in Talwara about three decades earlier when they were inexperienced young boys. At that time the family had a *biswah* (one twentieth of the entire village) of land amounting to hundreds of acres. But inadequate rains, poor crops, and the prevalence of mosquitoes and the consequent malaria in that area drove the inexperienced young brothers to abandon the wilderness and move back to the ancestral Mehraj.

But returning to the Talwara land and adding to it to make the family's holdings large again remained a dream of Trilok Singh. That thought had prevented him from buying land in Mehraj outright; instead he controlled and used the land under the mortgage system, which turned out to be a very bad strategy. My uncle always said, "We don't want to purchase any land in Mehraj because that will distract us from our goal of moving to Talwara where the same amount of money would buy many times greater acreage." In earlier times, land in that Rajputana area had very little value, and a Hindu Jat friend of my uncle, Shiv Karan of the Jandu clan, had created a considerable estate in his lifetime after starting life as a cattle herder. Uncle Tiloka used to tell stories of how Shiv Karan and some of his contemporaries had accumulated large tracts of land and had become prominent in the area; he wanted to do the same for his family of nephews and nieces. He, of course, had no living wife or children after he lost his wife and infant son when in his early twenties.

In 1946, when I went to help my uncle Trilok Singh gather the harvest, we lived in a temporary straw hut that he had built in the fields about four miles from our modest house in Talwara village. The daily commute from the house by foot through the jungle of Talwara Jhil (lake bed) would have been wasteful. Harvest work was hard and life was lonely, but it was temporary. I had the experience of meeting a variety of colorful farmers and herdsmen with their strange language and accents. Uncle Tiloka and I worked long hours, prepared our own food mornings and evenings, and secured the harvest in a few days. I was impressed with my old uncle's ability to organize everything single-handed and to get good results; he also had to be able to tolerate the lonely life in a land of strangers. He was just over fifty then, but to me he was as old as Adam. When the grain was secured, my uncle and I moved to our Talwara house. The Talwara area was more primitive than our Mehraj village. There I saw strange wells whose walls were lined with reeds and straw rather than with bricks as one saw in Punjab. Women with strange clothes and languages were the nearest neighbors, and also nearby were some Majha (mid-Punjab) Jats, with strange accents and turbans, who had migrated recently. Pretty soon it was time for me to return to Punjab as the crop had been taken care of.

Reluctant Collegiate in 1946

The month of May was the time for college admissions, but I did not wish to go to college. Brother Kartar was posted at some far away military station. In his letters to my father he had been very forceful insisting that I be sent to college. Finally Uncle Trilok Singh, instead of my father, was sent along with me because I was more comfortable with my uncle. He took me by train to Amritsar in May 1946, and I was admitted to Khalsa College there. Surprisingly I qualified for the Nabha-Malwa Scholarship, which was established by the Raja of Nabha, for any boy from south of the Sutlej River who had the highest score in the matriculation examination. Kartar had qualified for the same scholarship a few years earlier when he studied there. The scholarship was only six rupees per month, but not an insignificant amount in the days when a laborer earned that much in a month.

The glorious days of Khalsa College were not over yet in 1946, because the partition of Punjab and its disastrous consequences were still in the future. Khalsa College had been established about the end of nineteenth century on the Grand Trunk Road to Lahore, some miles away from Amritsar, the holy city of Sikhs. But even by the 1940s the city had extended with commercial development along the Grand Trunk Road up to Khalsa College. The Grand Trunk Road ran from Delhi through the cities of Panipat, Karnal, Ambala, Sirhind, Ludhiana, Jullundur, Amritsar, and Lahore, and from there it went to Peshawar at the mouth of the Khyber Pass. It was a busy highway even in those days. *Tonga, Rickshaw* and other transport were readily available to go from the College to the city or to the railway station; there were few trucks and buses. On the college campus, athletic facilities, swimming pools, numerous sports grounds, grassy fields, recreation areas, student hostels, professors' residences, and even an agricultural farm made the campus the size of a small town. The hustle and bustle of the place was its great asset, and although many students were serious, some rich boys stayed in college just for the good life. Some of them just kept repeating year after year if they could not pass the examinations. They dressed in the best clothes, had plenty of spending money, were supplied with all the necessities by their parents, and enjoyed life with friends in the college. Khalsa College had pretty good academic standards, and its athletes and sports teams were respectable. Boys from Sikh families from all over the Punjab and from the Frontier Province, and some from expatriate families outside Punjab, were selected for admission.

Khalsa College had several different hostels for students, named after the princely states that might have funded their construction. The main building of the College was in the architectural style of North Indian forts and Mughal palaces, and so was the Patiala Hostel. The Nabha Hostel was less impressive, and that is where most of the freshmen ended up sharing rooms. Some special students were given individual rooms in the "cubicles building." Each hostel had its own cooks and servants. Most boys were from rich families and were used to having servants; they continued the same style when they were in college. The hostel servants would take *ghee* from the rooms of students and re-fry their food with spices and onions according to individual tastes. They would make your bed in the morning and would fetch things for you from the stores outside the College gates, if you were one of the influential boys and you tipped them once a month. They would call your friends to join you if you wanted to make dinner time a real party. Friends would always share the goodies that their parents had given them to take along, such as *khoa, pinni, punjiri and laddu jalebi.* Poor people would seldom go to college in those days, and the families of most students in Khalsa College were more prosperous than my own; so I had to avoid some of the activities which the rich boys took for granted. Unlike the informality of modern days, college students in those days were usually dressed in expensive clothes to set themselves apart from common people. Some families, whose sons were treated like princes, would send their servants to bring special treats to the College if too many days had passed between visits home by their sons. It was for most students a life of relative leisure, luxury, great camaraderie and optimism about the future. The students made lifetime friendships during their days in Khalsa College. None of the students had to work during the school breaks to earn money. During the college vacations, some boys would be invited to spend time, maybe even weeks, at the homes of their friends just as though they were relatives, since the depth of friendship in that culture was different from the superficial attitudes of today's urban life.

To get acquainted with all the possibilities in Khalsa College took a while for a new student like me. I started going with my older friends to movies, to stroll on the Mall Road and in the Company Bagh area in the late afternoons and early evenings. Visits to the Hall Bazar shopping area and to the holy Golden Temple in the city of Amritsar were a part of our recreation. People who were athletically inclined had extensive facilities available in the College. Since I was not athletic or trained in sports, I just went swimming in the pools that the College maintained, as all the activities were free but optional. We would go swimming and in the late afternoon go to walk on the *Thandi Sarak* (Cool Road) in the *Company Bagh* area. Once we even went to Lahore, the capital of Punjab, to see a hockey match between the team from Khalsa College and that of Government College, Lahore, and we returned home by evening.

In retrospect it is hard to imagine that I did not fall in love with that Khalsa College lifestyle, especially when the family was willing to supply me all the money I needed. But my heart was not in academics; I wanted to be back in the village. I had an ingrained distaste and discomfort when it came to student life and city life. With no intention of continuing studies in College, I just signed up for some arts subjects. The students used to call such courses "the royal road," meaning that they were leisurely and comfortable, as opposed to the difficult subjects like mathematics and sciences. But even then I attended very few classes; I slept late and never got into the College student routines. Then I felt guilty as I thought it was immoral to betray the parents' trust, but I justified my behavior to myself by thinking that they were making me do things against my wishes. I renewed acquaintance with two boys from Rampura Phul and who had been one year ahead of me in Kesho Ram's classes. Although I was fascinated by the style of speech of the boys from other regions of Punjab, and in time I might have developed friendship with such boys, those from our Malwa region automatically considered me as one of their own. The Majha-Malwa rivalry, sometimes bordering on hate and resulting in violence, was prevalent among the Sikh students also, although it was much worse among our rural population. It was common to deride, ridicule, and talk hatefully about people from the wrong side of the river in their absence, and they did the same. Such rivalry ceased to exist after the partition of Punjab, as there was then not much of the Majha region left when a good part of it went to Pakistan.

Pretty soon I came home, as the College closed for the summer break. Summer jobs were unknown and unavailable in those days, so the college boys had real vacations. Many families treated their college boys like royalty and usually they were not put to any farm work. My father had stopped farming, so there was no farm work for our house anyway. After the summer break, I did not expect to return to college, but since I could not disobey a direct order, I was escorted back to the college by my father. He thought he would also use that trip for a pilgrimage to the Golden Temple. Every Sikh wished to see the holy city and dip in the holy pool of the Golden Temple. Then my father left me at Khalsa College and went home. But as soon as he returned to Mehraj by train through Ludhiana, I decided to depart from College too and took a different train route, through TarnTaran, Kasoor and Ferozepur. On the way I stopped off in FaridKot, where the *dassehra* festival and fair were in progress. I spent the day enjoying the *dassehra* festival and then instead of going home, I took the night train through Bhatinda to visit my married sister Maro's village. I stayed at my sister's house for many days. There, my brother-in-law would take me to meet the local people; he would take me arouns his fields or take me on his camel to other villages to meet his relatives; they would feed me their best, and I had no responsibilities.

Being a guest at a relative's house used to be a great privilege in our society. Everyone treated a guest very hospitably. People genuinely enjoyed a relative's visit, as it created excitement in their own simple lives. It was also a part of the old religion to treat a guest with utmost generosity and devotion. They fed him the best and provided all the local comforts. And when the guest wanted to leave, it was a custom to insist that he stay longer. The time I spent with relatives have been so memorable and the feelings of pleasure have been so positive that no vacation as an adult has ever given me such good feelings again. From my sister's house, after a few days I traveled to the homes of my mother's three sisters, all of whose families were in the village of Taru Ana. I had never seen that village before because I had never been allowed to go to weddings. But I had heard all the names. With so many cousins there, it was an exciting visit for me. I spent some memorable days in Taru Ana.

Bad Karma, Bad Kismet

Ultimately I had to go home to a disappointed and unhappy father. He did not curse me openly, but he showed his disapproval at every opportunity. My mother would say, "Son, it seems that you do not want to do the right thing nowadays. When your *karma* is bad, you want to do only what is bad for you, so that your misery will be assured. But those who hurt their elders surely come to grief later. And whether we live to see it or not, you will suffer much. The sayings of elders never fail to have their effect; and then your repenting will do no good. Mark my words, a great deal of suffering is coming your way." I would retort, "Mother, you are not a saint; how can your words cause any suffering to happen for me!" Then my mother would again say, "Son, we want only the best for you; but if you torture us mentally and we say something spontaneously or in anger, our words will not go without effect. For God's sake, don't make us utter any such words. Many years ago, young Dubboo, whose parents were dead, used to act troublesome and arrogant and torture his uncle Fattah, who was his guardian. And Fattah used to say, "Dubboo, misery will come your way, although I may not live to see that day," and surely a hundred misfortunes of every kind have befallen Dubboo. Words of elders never go blank. Bad *kismet* is created; it is not automatic."

I would argue that it was useless to get any education, that I did not want to be among city people and that life in the village was more exciting. She would say, "You are young now, but think about your future. Here you might become a struggling farmer, probably in poverty, with a wife in rags and a bunch of runny-nosed kids whose needs you might not be able to fulfill. You have a good mind for education and could have a bright future if you follow the right path." To this I would reply, "I don't give a damn about education or my future. In India the life expectancy is 32 years (this was true before World War II.) and I am already sixteen years old, so I have already lived half of my life. Only the second half remains; it will pass quickly, too, and I want to live it right here in my own village. I will be dead in about 1962 according to the life expectancy in India, give or take a year. Life is too short to waste on studies." I was just using the statistical life expectancy in India in a twisted way to argue my position.

It was getting to be the end of the year 1946 and my brother Kartar came home on leave. He was shocked and annoyed that I was not in college, but instead of being angry, he tried to use persuasion to change my mind. Kartar tried to get me to wear the clothes of an educated man: a pantaloon, a coat, and a *Patiala Shahi* turban such as the high-class people wore then. Kartar would say, "You look like a young Maharaja in those clothes." But I would feel extremely embarrassed in a pantaloon in the village, although I did not mind such an outfit while in college. The Jats in the village considered the wearing of pantaloons to be effeminate, perhaps acceptable for city Hindus and foreigners but not fit for the manly Jats. Kartar argued, persuaded, and painted pictures and scenarios of my future, but I would not be convinced to leave the village. Money had already been wasted on me, and my family had not expected that I would simply quit after all the college fees and expense had been paid. In order to raise the stakes, Kartar asked me to sign a statement saying that I would relinquish all my rights to inherit the family property if after money was spent on me for studies, I deserted college and thus wasted the money. I signed the statement defiantly and mindlessly.

But after many arguments, persuasions, and manipulations, Kartar did force me to go with him to Khalsa College. There we met the principal of the College, the venerable Jodh Singh, who was one of the leading lights of the Sikhs at the time. The principal agreed to readmit me into college. Kartar paid all the fees in arrears and restored my status as a student. But I was just itching to disappear as soon as Kartar left. And he hung around Amritsar for a while in spite of his other commitments, because he wanted me to stick to the place. As soon as Kartar departed and it appeared safe, however, I went to see Principal Jodh Singh and asked him to have my fees refunded. I said I did not want to study any more and needed my money back. Jodh Singh growled at me, "Your family sent you here to get an education and you just want to go to the village and become a *badmash* (bad character)! But I can't keep you against your will; you are free to go. According to the College rules, I can't refund your tuition fees; I will release only your hostel fees!" As I left Amritsar this time, again I did not go home but rode the train through Ferozepur and Bhatinda toward Sirsa, got off at the KalianWali train station, and then walked to Taru Ana. There I stayed for weeks again with my mother's three sisters and their families.

Taru Ana was in the sandy desert without any irrigation. Drinking water was not always readily available in that region. Wells with potable water were few and far between. Water was found only at great depths in that area and most wells there had sour or bitter water. People drank water from the ponds in the years when there was some rain. There was an understanding within the community not to take the buffaloes to a designated pond to keep its water clean for human consumption. When the pond dried up, their men had to transport drinking water from other areas in clay pitchers fitted on the saddles of their camels. Even those sources from which they got water were sometimes many miles away. Thus women spent most of the time during drought years in hauling water. There was a well in the village, but the water from it was so bad and bitter that even the cattle would not drink it. They could use the well water only to bathe and to wash clothes. In the years when it rained, women would bring water from the village pond in pitchers on their heads. In such years the crops would be plenty; so life felt secure. But during drought, life would be precarious and summers would be unbearable. Sometimes they would have to send their animals to relatives, or send the men away for months to graze the animals in irrigated regions. My mother would say sadly, "There is drought and famine in TaruAna this year; the conditions at my sisters' houses are very bad. They are sending their animals to my brothers' village." LaleAna was our maternal grandparents' village, and it was closer to TaruAna than to us. In one year of serious drought, my maternal cousins had driven their animals to our region also, although we were two days journey from their area.

But when I was visiting, it was a good year in that region. The ponds were full of water, their granaries were full, the people were happy, and I was glad to be there. In the Punjabi culture, a mother's sister is like your half-mother and she usually treats you even more affectionately than your own mother would. My boy and girl cousins treated me with great affection too. With three of my mother's sisters and with the additional friendly families of their clan, I could just choose informally to go to dinner in any house I wanted, as everyone treated me like a guest. They all lived within a hundred yards of each other, and each house would urge me to come for dinner. Even their neighbors who were not directly related to my mother would say, "Oh MehrajKa (of Mehraj), come, eat with us today." It might not be any grand feast; it could be just *daal, roti or sabzi* and possibly some *kheer* or desert. In the villages it was a custom to ask friends to sit for dinner if they were near your home at mealtime. All those TaruAna people were affectionate and hospitable to me.

My cousins would ride their camels with me to the fields and we would inspect the different crops. Sometimes we would share whiskey in the evenings and play the hand-cranked gramophone with the big horn, for music and comical songs. During the day we would sit at the crossing and watch women fetch water from the well or the pond; we would trade stories about weddings, fairs, and *gidhha* performances. All those cousins and the hustle and bustle of the wedding season in their village made me want to stay there. Gradually, however, my conscience bothered me, and that hollow feeling told me I could not continue that pattern forever. With some trepidation about facing my family after my atrocious behavior, I took the train home.

After those many attempts, the family gave up trying to force me to go to college, although their nagging continued. When a child or spouse decides to drag a family through the dirt, there are no easy cures. I was causing them real pain and anguish, and they had run out of options. After many frustrations, my father developed an attitude of non-cooperation and contempt toward all of my activities, to show his displeasure. He would still talk to me, but he showed his disapproval when it came to the matters of my attitude and daily activities.

Early Drinking and Other Activities

My drinking with friends in the early years is something that my father did not approve of. One day in 1946 I was sent to sell a couple of useless buffaloes at the annual cattle market in Rampura Phul. Even the mere appearance of clouds could change cattle prices. Fortunately there was a little drizzle that day, which meant abundant feed and an optimistic outlook. Therefore I was able to sell the buffaloes at prices above my minimum target. I wanted to celebrate after this accomplishment. I deposited the proceeds of the sale with our family's *ahrtia* (broker of commodities; banker) in that market town and kept a small amount of money for myself. Then I went to the government-licensed liquor shop and bought a bottle of whiskey. I was only sixteen years old but there was essentially no age limit for buying liquor or opium. I started walking home the distance of five miles from Rampura Phul to Mehraj. On the way I opened the whiskey bottle, got a little water from the irrigation canal, and started drinking the whiskey. Not being an experienced drinker and having low tolerance for alcohol, I became intoxicated pretty quickly and was staggering as I walked toward the village. I could not very well go home in that condition; so I headed to the house of an older bachelor friend named Bachan, son of Munshi. Young guys occasionally got together to drink and to cook meat at Bachan's wife-less house, since women in some families would not allow meat in their kitchens.

122

A neighbor of ours named Harditta had seen me walking under the influence of alcohol. He reported that condition to my father, saying, "I saw your young boy staggering drunk and going to Munshis house; that boy is too tender to drink whiskey at this age; it will burn the lotus of his liver; liquor will destroy his body at this tender age." People in the village knew the words but they did not know much about the functions of heart, liver, and stomach. They thought that the heart feels, the stomach thinks, and the liver is the critical tender spot where food and drink goes, and that it can be burned by eating bad things. Women would say, "The heavy meal from this morning is stick on my liver and I don't feel good"; or, "I ate this spicy food and my liver is burning"; or, "You stupid girl; don't you have any intelligence in your tummy?" Anyway, my father was furious on hearing Harditta's words about my intoxicated state and the possible damage to my body. He also thought that I might have blown away money from the sale of the buffaloes. It was night, but he traced me to Munshi's house and at the door he shouted for me to come out. Still under the influence of alcohol, I staggered out and my father hit me from behind as if spanking a child. This I could not tolerate, and in my intoxicated state I reacted violently and confronted my father. But deep down, I was afraid of my father. So I quickly disengaged and just went away. I spent the night at uncle Mohinder's place in our Outer House area, from which my father's family had moved back to the Inner House following the breakup of the joint family in 1945. I avoided my father for a few more days until he calmed down. I was the only one of the children in my family to confront my father in this way and I felt very ashamed. I believed that being disrespectful to parents was dishonorable and a big sin, and I never did such a thing again. Uncle Bhan told my father that he should learn to handle matters with discretion and recognize that he could no longer treat a grown boy like a child. I was not in the habit of drinking frequently, and drinking was never a big issue thereafter.

The main issue now was that the family wanted me to go to college and I did not want to leave the village life. They recounted the benefits of education and the misery and drawbacks of farming life. They pointed out that my infected leg would get worse in the dirt of the farm environment and might even get gangrene and need to be amputated. Father even opined that "The reason Gurnam is shorter than Kartar was at the same age is that Gurnam did not go to college. If he had stayed in college, he would be three inches taller by now because he would not have been carrying loads on his head to crush his spine, and gymnastics on the parallel bars at college would have stretched his spine to make him taller." They had seen the skinny Kartar dangling from the rungs of a ladder when he was back home from college as he used to believe that dangling from the rungs of a ladder would make him taller.

In reality my mental makeup was like that of chained men in 'Platos Allegory of the Dark Cave'. Those men had never seen anything outside the cave and could look only at a wall on which shadows of moving people were falling because of a fine burning behind the moving figures. The chained men did not want to, and could not cope with the sights outside the cave. They were comfortable only in the dark cave where they had lived all their lives.

Too Much Blood or a Bad Case of Nazar?

My family was puzzled and expressed their frustration: What could be the cause of

Gurnam's unthinking stubbornness? Why does he not follow the right path to education like his brother? Why does he want to mess with dirt farming in the village? The family looked for possible causes. Could it be some evil influence? Was I interested in or involved with some woman? Was it simply bad *kismet*? Was I suffering from a case of *nazar* (an evil eye or a bad spell)? Why is the boy so determined to ruin his life? My sister's husband, Harnek Singh Dhillon, thought that a *taveez* (talisman) from the holy sadhu in his village would help if I wore it around my neck. In fact he had a taveez prescribed and made for me by the sadhu in his village, but I would not wear it, as I always ridiculed such devices and superstitions. Uncle Trilok Singh said I suffered from too much energy and too much blood. He observed that "After that strenuous workout running the fodder-cutting machine the other day, Gurnam was jumping into the air instead of collapsing. He seems to have too much energy and too much blood. Maybe we should have some of his blood taken out and then his energy level will be normal and it will not block his senses." But I would not agree to any bloodletting either. I thought they were all wrong, kill-joys, old people who wanted to take the fun out of my life. My mother and sisters thought it was better to have a strong boy around the house than to do anything drastic to his body by bloodletting. Mother would just say with resignation, "When your kismet is bad, it takes you away from the good and steers you to the bad, so that your suffering may be assured."

Maybe my uncle had a point about excessive blood or energy blocking good sense. Although I was quite conscientious and did not do anything unethical, as some other teenage males did, I had a feeling of invincibility in those days. Some of the healthy and energetic teenagers used to feel fearless and indestructible; some would fight others to assert their power, and others would take risks. They had a tendency to attack others or even to destroy things, especially when they were under the influence of alcohol. Their hormones or their energy made them act haughty and feel invincible. For a few years, such teenagers had little fear of any consequences or even death and were feared by their enemies until they passed the teenage years and became more responsible. I never did anything destructive or antisocial; I just did not want to go to college.

However much the family tried, nothing worked to change my mind toward education. I was stuck in a narrow frame of mind in which my friends and the village meant everything to me. The only motivation I might have had to go far away would be if I had no way to make a living and was afraid of starving. In the old days men were not so willing to leave their homes and go to other countries. Even when they did go, they considered it temporary, like an exile. They never wanted to go anywhere permanently but just to earn some money so that they could come back to their village and live comfortably afterwards. Almost everyone who went to Hong Kong or Calcutta came back to retire in the village. Even Uncle Tope Wala, who had gone to America about the year 1902, came back to live in the village after 1946.

My Risky Teenage Years in the Village

It was already 1947. I was at home doing nothing useful and being a source of pain to my parents. Drinking with friends during fairs, festivals, music performances and other occasions was to be expected, but my mother feared that I would get into a fight with someone and drag the family into serious problems. The family knew that young boys got drunk and tried to prove their fearlessness and readiness for a fight. They asserted their manhood by proving that nobody could stand up to them. Predictably, other young men might have similar ideas, and conflicts could arise easily. People depended on their friends to back them up in a fight. There were occasions when a person got seriously hurt or even killed. Who got arrested for the crime, who got tried, and who got punished ultimately, were the result of complicated dynamics and the person punished was not always the person who had committed the act. It could depend upon whom the police could arrest easily, against whom it was easiest to get witnesses (true or false), whose family would care enough to pay bribes, and other factors. My family thought that some of my associates might kill or injure somebody in a fight, and then our family would be a juicy target for all the bribe-seekers and the exploiters who might become false witnesses.

The fears of my family about possible violence were not entirely unfounded. One day while I was absent from the village, my father put some laborers to work making bricks from clay by digging the clay from a quarry. The men of Bukken clan became angry with him and said that the clay quarry pit was on their land, although other people quarried small amounts of clay there off and on. The Bukken family claim to this *shamlot* (common land) did not have any clear basis. Such claims of ownership were initially asserted by frequent casual usage, then by exclusive usage, and finally by putting up a fence. There was always the temptation for people to claim, use, or occupy a piece of common land so that after some time they could establish a claim to it. If you had the force of one or two strong brothers behind you, the chances were good that no one would challenge your control of the land. You could erect a fence of thorny hedge, and if no one objected, you would become the de facto owner of the property. The Bukken Ke family had started claiming ownership of that tract of the clay quarry but they did not have any established right.

Anyway, when I returned to the village from my trip to the relatives, I was told by other people that there had been a heated exchange of words between my father and the Bukken clan. I felt this was a violation of my family's honor, and I could not "keep my mustache intact" if anybody spoke rudely to my father (I did not really have a mustache or beard yet.) That evening I went to the Bukken family homes with the side-by-side courtyard doors. I shouted abuses and challenged them to come out and fight. Then I struck my sword against their wooden doors. In that society even the act of clearing your throat in front of someone's house could be taken as a provocation, if any tensions existed previously. There had been cases of serious violence just because someone had made the sound of clearing his throat by fake coughing, which was taken as a challenge by the other party, who retaliated and the situation escalated into a violent fight. Striking a sword against someone's house was likely to be a precursor of major trouble. The men of BukkenKe family came out of their quarters into their common courtyard but remained behind the wooden doors. They shouted back and threatened to kill me. But their women started crying and grabbing the men and would not let them open the door to get out to fight. It was nighttime and they did not really know what would confront them outside. They might have assumed that I had supporters with me or that I had a dangerous weapon. Although I was still young, I had developed a minor reputation for drinking with some tough guys; and that was probably on their minds. None of the BukkenKe men came out, as their women were clinging to them. I struck my sword at the door again, abused them some more, and walked away to join my friend, Mukand, SobheKa, who was waiting at the well, just fifty yards away.

Thinking back, the four Bukken family men could have beaten me to pulp. They would have been justified since I was attacking their house. I had no dangerous weapon with me, but they overestimated the threat. My threatening voice in the darkness of the night had created fear and uncertainty, and their women knew that such conflicts could lead to horrible results later. Feuds could escalate and go on for generations. My friend Mukand did not want to join me in that attack as he had to pass near the BukkenKe house every day, and he did not want to have enmity with them. Moreover, Mukand's family was closer to BukkenKe than to us, through ancestral links. Later that night, Mukand and I walked to the train station as we already had travel plans. We went to visit my Sister Maro' village. Thereafter we spent a few days of leisure at Mukand's in-laws' house in Chor Mar village further in the desert.

The house that I attacked did not ignore the incident. On my return after some days I learned that the BukkenKe family went to the police in Nathana the next day and had reported the attack on their house. Since I had gone away and was not available to be arrested, my father was taken by the police for "questioning." Possibly some bribe was paid. In any case the police ignored the case. I did not gain much of a reputation in the village after this incident, because I had not caused any injury or gone to jail. It was a common practice for the police to arrest other family members if an accused person could not be found or did not surrender to police. I was ashamed and troubled to learn about the difficulties I had caused to my father. Uncharacteristically, he never complained to me about what had happened and never even mentioned any problems with the police caused by that episode.

Everyone expected that any trouble created by me would affect my family. That was a source of great concern to my parents. It was also well known that my mother's brother Sohna had been sentenced to twenty years in prison for murder, although he claimed that he had not even seen the murder happen. It is said that some enemy had put the victim's blood-drenched clothes in the *tandoor* of Sohna's house and had led the police there to "discover the evidence." This all happened in the princely state of Patiala where the system of justice was worse than in our English territory. Sohna's family had to sell some land to bribe police officials, but nevertheless he still was sentenced to twenty years in prison, of which he served fourteen years. I was frequently accused by my father of having habits like my maternal uncle Sohna, as fathers like to attribute any bad traits in their children to inheritance from their wives' folks. He would point out how wild and reckless Sohna had been in his youth.

My mother used to tell of an incident about her brother Sohna. In his youth he was quite wild. Once as a teenager when he was drunk and stumbling around the house late at night, in a semiconscious state looking for more liquor to drink, he came across a bottle of kerosene which was meant for lanterns. Sohna being in the drunken state and in the dark, could not really see much. Like any tough guy (only softies and sissies need mixers and diluters) he put his mouth directly to the kerosene bottle, thinking it was whiskey. The already drunk Sohna swallowed some kerosene before he realized that what he had swallowed was not whiskey. They say that he was screaming, shouting, and shrieking as his body burned inside from the kerosene. There were no hospitals or facilities to help in those areas, and he was feeling hotter than hell on a summer day. He ran to the buffalo pond to cool off by immersing his body under water to get some relief from the burning sensation in his body. It was a long time before the effect of the kerosene diminished and he could come out of the buffalo pond. And that was not the only wild thing Sohna ever did.

My mother also used to tell stories of how her brothers, when they were young men, would get drunk uncontrollably and would fight with each other. They did not have any living parent to stop them, and when drunk they would want to tear each other apart, pull each other's hair, and wrestle with all force. They were both strong and it would be necessary to have a couple of men break them apart, while the sisters and wives were completely helpless. The next day when they sobered up, they would have no recollection of the fight and would talk respectfully and cordially to one another. My mother told us many stories of their excesses, their drinking, their hunting dogs, their physical prowess, and their lack of attention to the farm work. Their farm work was usually done by sharecroppers as the family did have a fair amount of land.

But I had no thoughts and worries about being framed for any crime of violence. I had never been arrested or even seen the inside of a police station. Fortunately my involvement in any other incidents never went beyond posturing, except once when I threatned to kill my younger uncle with my spear, as he had spoken rudely to my mother. My uncle's wife prevented our fight when I went to attaack him. I was never totally reckless and was relatively well behaved for my age. The fear in my mind, cultivated in the early years by my father and my teachers, may have been one reason why I never did anything that I would consider seriously wrong or dishonorable. Accidents, mistakes, and poor judgment were of course unavoidable. But the family was worried about the parallels between my behavior and Uncle Sohna's, and they expected the worst.

Our Land Dispute with Two Families

The opportunities for conflict in that society could arise easily. After the dissolution of our joint family in 1945, we had moved from the Outer House back to our old Inner House, which was at the end of a dead-end street. To get there we had to pass by the house of Bachan, son of Bhakku, with whom we had a land dispute. Bachan and Gurditta the Numberdar (revenue collector) had joined in an effort to wrest control of some land that was in our possession under the mortgage system. In the spring of 1946 we had a confrontation when Bachan and others, along with government officials including a *patwari* and a *tehsildar* on horses, and a couple of *chowkidars*, came to assert the occupation of the disputed land by running a plough through it. We had decided to oppose this claim of possession. Our plan was to attack them, not with cutting weapons but with sticks, which would be a lesser offense legally but would still thwart the occupation. We had expected only two or three people, but now there were many opponents including government officials; and it looked bad for us. We were already there and it was hard to let the land be taken away from us. So we attacked even without much hope of success. I was sixteen years old and energetic; so I was in front while my two uncles were behind me. My father and the disabled uncle Nikk were not with us. Bachan of the opposing party was at the plough. One of the minor officials from their party, a tall Muslim and retired military sergeant, came to attack me. I swung to hit him but he was able to avoid being hurt. The others in their party also started advancing to attack us. Seeing the situation unfavorable, uncle Tiloka shouted for me to retreat and we went away toward our Phulana field where my father and the invalid uncle Nikk were resting. Although Bachan was a big tall fellow and had the reputation of being a vicious fighter, he had apparently been instructed by the officials to keep a low profile; so he never came to attack me. To make even one furrow with the plough in front of witnesses was a symbolic act that demonstrated the effective control of the land by the other party.

Subsequently the officials also filed a charge of criminal violence, injuries, and riot against every male in our family except Kartar, who was in the military. Although only three of us were present at that confrontation and there were no injuries, the case would have been weak without including at least five people; and it was easy to get a doctor's certificate to prove injuries to anybody. For example in another case my uncle Mohinder wanted to file a case of violence against another party. Mohinder took me to the government doctor in order to obtain a certificate as the proof of injuries to his body. After a small bribe, the doctor gave me a rod and told me to hit my uncle on the back several times. Then the doctor took measurements of the marks from my uncle's back and gave him a certificate so that he could file charges of assault against his opponent. A bribe to government officials could create a false case against anyone.

To avoid my being entangled in that violence case, my family asked me to go to college in Amritsar and avoid arrest. My uncle had paid some bribe so that I was never arrested, but my name was included as a defendant in the case. We had to go to the courts frequently for about a year, to towns like Ferozepur, GidderBaha, Malote and Bhuccho, as a result of that incident. We paid bribe to officials, but even so the officials did not want the judge to drop the case against us. We traveled to the courts of whichever judge was in charge on the set date, although no actions were taken by the court, except postponement. No progress was made in that case for a whole year.

In the process, we met many other famous and infamous accused people from different villages involved in their own cases. Gurdev Meany ka, and Ghoke Mirasi used to appear on the charge of kidnapping the daughter of a *numberdar*, although the girl was their friend and went with them willingly in order to escape from her old husband, to whom she was married against her will. Ghoke, who had once been my classmate, told me the girl had an affair with him. She wanted to escape her situation and came to his house first. And before being taken away by Gurdev, she offered to leave all her golden jewelry with Ghoke, because she was not sure where she would end up. Ghoke said something like "*Jidher gya bania, odher gya bazar.*" which implied that if he was losing her, he would not want the jewelry. Another fellow named Sher Singh of Gidder village (it's funny that his name means tiger lion although he was from the village named coward jackal) used to appear on charges of violence involving irrigation water dispute. In India, the harassment and expense of a case is worse than the final punishment, because nine out of ten appearances just result in the change of court date to a later time.

Then it got to be the spring of 1947, and the violence due to the impending Partition of India intensified. I remember the Sikh judge presiding in the Ferozepur court who examined the case and said, "There is no substance to this case. These people have been dragged through the courts for a year. The violence and disturbances in the country are getting worse every day and it is getting dangerous to move about. I want to dismiss this case." The prosecuting officials objected, but the judge said, "Why are you officials not arresting those real criminals who are perpetrating political violence all around you?" The judge dismissed the case against us over the objections of the officials.

Drunken and Armed Bachan

Even after these events, Bachan, son of Bhakku, told my father that they wanted only a "paper fight," that is, only a legal recourse and not any violence over the land. In fact their legal position in that land dispute was more justifiable than ours, and our family was being unreasonable. We had had possession of the land under the mortgage system for nearly fifteen years. The owner wanted to sell it to someone else, and my family did not want to relinquish possession. Other village people were reluctant to challenge our control over that land, but Bachan had a reputation as a fierce fighter and the family of Gurditta the Numberdar, joined him. It was the arrogance of our family in not negotiating with but actually insulting the owner that had led to the land dispute in the first place. Ultimately a compromise was worked out because Gurditta, being a gentler man, decided that if someone died in the dispute, the land would not be worth it. We retained a better portion of the land in the compromise.

However, one evening as I was returning home, Bachan who lived on the way to our house, came staggering out of his house, blind drunk and out of control, with a spear in his hand. As I stopped to look at him, he put the tip of his spear against my chest and said, "If I wanted to, I could push this spear right through your chest, but I have told your father we will have only a court fight." I stood my ground; showing fear would have been worse as I had to pass by his house everyday. I thought that he would not dare to hurt me. Although I was vulnerable at that moment, he knew that I was not the only son of our house and that our men would surely take revenge if he killed me. An only son of a house had more fear of being killed than a boy with brothers; if an only son was killed, the next of kin could inherit his family's land even if he had living sisters. I did not really want to pick a fight with Bachan either, as the land dispute and the court case accusing us of violence were already going against us. Bachan started to say something nonsensical and then staggered out of control, and fell down intoxicated. Incidents like that provided plenty of chances of conflict in the village.

A few days later the same Bachan son of Bhakku, was at the Selbrah fair a few miles north of our village. I saw him drunk near the wrestling arena where people were starting to assemble in the later part of the day before the matches. Being drunk and acting recklessly was a way to intimidate other people. There, under the influence of alcohol, Bachan happened to confront Shamsher, son of Amla Singh, with some harsh words. The dashing sons of Amla Singh used to think that they too were pretty special. Shamsher would not tolerate any insolence from Bachan, whom he considered a low-caliber lout compared to his own patrician family. So Shamsher hit Bachan with a bottle full of liquor, the only thing handy, on the side of the neck near the jaw and just below the ear. I happened to be right there and watched the whole incident from a close distance. The glass of the breaking bottle cut Bachan pretty badly and his neck and jaw were bleeding profusely. Any kind of disturbance could be expected from people gathered near the athletic arena, so there were plenty of police in the area; they rushed toward the scene of this conflict. Shamsher did not want to be arrested by the police of the princely state; so he got on his horse and tried to race away. But all those policemen fired their rifles toward him at close range, killing the horse on the spot and felling Shamsher to the ground. As I watched this drama, I thought Shamsher was surely dead. But he was still alive although one of his legs which had taken many bullets was completely smashed. The other leg survived only because the body of the horse stopped the bullets from reaching it. That strong and handsome son of Amla Singh took more than a year to heal, and even then he walked with a severe limp in his distorted leg. Besides, he was prosecuted for the violent offense, while Bachan became the state's witness against him. My family did not want my life to go like the lives of Shamsher of Amla Singh and Bachan of Bhakku.

Getting My Feet into the Dirt

Finally my parents became resigned to the idea of allowing me to work on the family land. Nearly seventeen years old and a deserter from college, I was itching to run a farming operation. My father had quit farming in the year 1946, so some equipment and necessities of farming from our joint family breakup had come into the hands of my younger uncle, Mohinder. Mostly, though, Mohinder had acquired new equipment, including a new oxcart which took several months for two artisans to build with wood, steel, brass decorations, etc., as he believed in good quality things not merely in getting by. The oxcart was a major investment, a show piece costing more than a cheap house in those days, and meant to last more than a generation. In 1946, I would gladly volunteer to help friends in farm work; but mostly I volunteered to help in Uncle Mohinder's farm operation and sometimes I ate at his house, too. My family did not approve of this behavior, but it was common for unfocussed individuals to work in the houses of their kin without any compensation. In fact, getting paid by working for any individual was considered demeaning in the Jat culture. My father was also unhappy since the enmity from the acrimonious breakup of our joint family was still fresh between my father and uncle. I personally did not feel antagonistic toward Mohinder because he was the uncle who used to argue to keep me on the farm, and I thought he had the right ideas. Uncle Mohinder also liked the comfortable feeling and the public perception of a tough young man of the family being present in his fields. In that context, blood really is thicker than water; but unfortunately, one is also most likely to have conflicts with those with whom one has the most dealings.

Although it was not really in Uncle Mohinder's own interest, he agreed to make me an equal partner in our farm operation. We already had equal amounts of land, as the land of the family had been divided into two parts just in the previous year. For a nominal amount of money he transferred the ownership of our old black camel to me. He kept his two oxen. Being the owner of the legendary black camel was a matter of great pride for me. I also got the use of the equipment, which had come into his possession following breakup of the joint family. We hired two sharecroppers, one for each partner. Thus, I was a full-fledged farmer in 1947, just as I attained the age of 17. My sharecropper was Mukhtar, a young man from the Chuhra caste, not much older than me. Ironically, with the changes made in the laws after Independence, due to affirmative action the same Mukhtar was made the head councilman of our village in the year 2000. In our district, the law reserves political offices for the low-caste people although it is illegal to call them low caste now. My uncle's sharecropper was the trustworthy and hard working Santu, who had worked for our family for many years before. Our farming partnership was working pretty well as these things go. Uncle Mohinder and I never had any serious disagreements; and although well known for his temper, he always avoided any conflict with me. If he was unhappy about some issue, he would express it to me, but he was never belligerent or combative in our relationship.

In 1947, most crops, especially cotton, were disappointing. In fact that was the year of the end of the British Raj, the Partition and the beginning of Independence for India. There were religious and political massacres in our province of Punjab.

 ̄Disenchantment can set in the working of any partnership. Gradually my uncle began to think that I was not contributing anything critically important to his farming operation; he thought he could do just as well alone. He was also mildly hostile to the rest of my family. My father never participated, helped or advised in the farm work and made no secret of his dislike of my work. Anyway, after one year's partnership, Uncle Mohinder and I separated amicably. I had the black camel and some farm equipment. For the year 1948, I hired another sharecropper named Thanedar. Then I ran my own farm operation independent of my uncle, and we both had pretty good crops in 1948. My father had bought a 35-acre plot of sandy and poor quality land under the mortgage system, not far from our house, and even that land became productive. My father did not want to buy that land outright because he thought the land might keep me permanently in the village.

My farming venture was a limited success. The land was our own, so my success or failure was only a matter of degree, not of survival. The home and land were ancestral rights; a son could not be deprived of the family land, even if the parents did not like him. That is also why there was never a Jat beggar; a Jat could be poor but he always had a patch of land. My family had let me try my hand at farming with the hope that hard work would keep me out of other mischief. They even hoped it might make me hate the dirty drudgery and unbearable climate and might make me wish I was in college. But in my mind the charm of that life never died completely. For one thing, there were no serious consequences, except losing face, if things did not go right. My hardy nature made it easy for me to live with the usual and expected difficulties. I even enjoyed the farm work; in my spare time I had fun with friends. My mother and sisters thought I had a lucky hand; they thought that anything I sowed grew really well. My father, on the other hand, disapproved of my choice and was unwilling to praise me for anything related to farming. Once my sister Karo said, "Father was proud that you handled the big loads without flinching yesterday, but he won't tell you this to your face because he still wishes you went to college instead of doing this kind of work." For me the main purpose of farming was to provide camaraderie with my friends and to feed my addiction to the village life.

1947, the Year of Massacres

To the urban, educated Indians, 1947 might be the Year of Independence, when the British gave up India and divided the country into three parts: East Pakistan which became Bangla Desh later, West Pakistan which is now the only Pakistan, and the remaining India. But to the rural Punjabi people it was known as the Year of the Massacres (Vadh Tukk), or sometimes understated as the Time of Disturbances. Rural people were not literate so most of the news about what was happening, came by word of mouth. Late in 1946 we had started seeing Sikh refugees in market towns, with strange turbans and speech, who had arrived from the Muslim-dominated areas of western Punjab and from the Frontier Province bordering Afghanistan. Some of them had escaped after their properties had been looted and their relatives murdered. Activists of the Muslim League party decided that the fastest way to create Pakistan was by eliminating any non-Muslim people from their region of the country. When the British Indian government showed reluctance to divide India on religious lines, the leader of the Muslim League, Muhammed Ali Jinnah, threatened that the Muslims would take *"Direct Action"* if their demand for a separate country for Muslims was not met. Volunteers of the Muslim League then went on a killing rampage to drive out non-Muslims, to demonstrate that the different religions could not coexist and thus to break down the resistance of Indian politicians to the idea of partition. Those refugees who escaped death came to our part of Punjab and to Delhi, which was then at the eastern border of Punjab, and they related their horror stories. There was a lot of tension in our population, and there were cries by the refugees and by sympathizing religious people for revenge against Muslims.

The actual day of the Partition of India was 15 August 1947, but killings in the Muslim-dominated areas had started nearly a year before that. At the time of partition, whole villages of Sikh farmers from western Punjab had to abandon their lands and homes to escape from being killed in what was becoming Pakistan. People started coming to eastern Punjab in caravans of ox carts. If the people in the caravan were not massacred before crossing the new partition line into India, they had to find a way to make a living as refugees. Then in the summer of 1947 the same thing started to happen to Muslims in eastern Punjab. Groups of political activists, criminals, and fanatics full of hate for the Muslims found this to be a great opportunity for revenge, killing, and looting. On both sides of the border, the refugees were trying to escape from areas where they were a religious minority. If they were well defended or escaped notice, they made it across to the safe side; but government or military authority was not usually available nor particularly effective in protecting the refugees. In the later stages, looting of property became as much of a motive as eliminating people of the wrong religion. My father used to say that the partition line should be the Chenab River to be fair to the Sikhs. But the India-Pakistan boundary was set east of the Ravi River, because the Sikhs being a religious minority had no political power to have a voice in the decision. Approximately 80% of the landed property of the Sikhs was located in what later became Pakistan and about 50% of the Sikh population was there. Every Sikh and Hindu had to leave western Punjab, so the land could be *pak* (Pakistan means cleansed land or pure land) and could be cleared of any non-Muslims population. In the cities, the people were more aware, more mobile, and more resourceful, and not tied to the land; so fewer of the urban Hindus may have been killed. But stories of massacres and the abduction of women, who were never recovered but were left behind in Pakistan forever, were heard from the city people as well. The Jat Sikhs suffered the biggest losses, because their land and homes were not portable, while Hindus and urban Sikhs in the western Punjab were generally not the cultivators of land and therefore could move some of their belongings more easily. Being more educated and aware, they could decide to travel more quickly.

In the early 1950s I had a friend in Physics Honors School in Punjab University whose name was Faqir Chand Khanna, a Kshatri Hindu. He was a survivor at the age of about twelve, when his family was massacred by Muslim volunteers before the family could attempt an escape from western Punjab, which was becoming Pakistan. All his relatives present with him were killed, and he himself was left for dead and bleeding heavily among the multitude of other corpses. There were sword wounds on his neck, the side of his head, his leg, arm, hand and hip. The slayers had no indication that the blood-soaked Khanna boy lying among the corpses was alive or breathing. Later on, while removing the corpses for mass burial, a kind-hearted Muslim family found him breathing among the corpses and took him to their home to nurse him back to life. After some weeks they sent Faqir Chand Khanna to India, since, being a Hindu, he could not remain in Pakistan. His married sister, who had lived in a different city and had escaped to India, traced him and helped him to survive in India. Khanna never discussed those tragic events, nor did he ever complain in my presence about his fate. Whereas it was customary for most Indians to tell their tales of woe at the slightest opportunity, even to strangers, Khanna was a naturally upbeat fellow who had learned to accept his past. He walked with a severe limp because of the wounds to his hip and leg, and he had a badly atrophied and injured arm that lacked mobility. His writing hand, distorted with a huge scar, had difficulty in holding a pen. There was a big scar from a sword cut on the side of his neck, behind his ear. In spite of our fairly cordial association, I heard only a bare fragment of his violent story. Faqir Chand Khanna was a brilliant student. He was also one of the most popular and good-natured fellows on campus. He was big-hearted, generous, and a regular guy who never wallowed in self-pity and never talked about the massacre of his parents or of his misfortunes in the past.

A Jat Sikh born in a village of the District of Lahore told me recently what happened to his people. His family did not want to abandon their home, farms, animals nad other property. But then the Muslim police officials there called a meeting of all the Sikh dignitaries, like the *zaildar* and *numberdar*, to "plan for the pacification of the area." When all the prominent Sikhs were gathered in the meeting, the police gunned down every one of them. After that massacre by the officials, ordinary Sikhs hurried to escape to the Indian side of Punjab. The man told me that his family abandoned their house and land to join a caravan to go to eastern Punjab when it became clear that existence in their home was perilous. They left him alone in the house to keep watch, with the hope that they might be able to return if conditions improved and peace prevailed. Obviously the village people were not clear about the reality of partition and about what the future was going to be like. Many felt this was a temporary disturbance due to the continuing hostility of the religions, as had been the pattern in the distant past. Reality was much uglier than that. His parents and other members of his family who were with the caravan traveling to reach the newly created border were all killed before they could cross into the Indian part of Punjab. When he found out about that massacre, he got together with a Sikh carpenter's son and together they rode their horses through the night to cross the border into India. Unlike many other people, they came from a village relatively close to the newly created border and therefore easier to escape from. But most rural people did not have any concept of the Partition, the creation of a new border, or the new country Pakistan. They expected that they would return to their homes and lands after the disturbances were over.

At the time of Independence, all government agencies, including the police, were in non-functioning condition. The police did not function for the duration of the violence in rural Punjab. The personnel of the Punjab police and the military forces had to be divided along religious lines. If they were Muslim, they were sent to Pakistan to avoid being killed; they were ineffective in the meantime. In fact I personally saw several Muslim policemen who had been killed by Sikh fanatics, lying right outside the police station in the town of Phul, when I went there to watch the 'disturbances'. From a single British government, two separate governments of India and Pakistan had to emerge. On the Indian side of the dividing line, the new government was preoccupied with a multitude of problems and changes. At the village level, people were on their own; law enforcement was sporadic in cities and non-existent in rural areas. Surprisingly, there were very few intra-community murders or other crimes during this period of disturbance, because people had no idea whether they were going to be alive or dead the next day and the intra-community enmities were forgotten. Violence then was Muslim vs. non-Muslim and vice versa. The authorities who enforced local laws were not willing or able to prevent the local political firebrands from preaching or committing violence. Volunteers of the Muslim League targeted non-Muslims in the areas where they were dominant; conversely, similar violence against Muslims occurred in the eastern Punjab. Both sides felt that the violence was a necessary step in order to cleanse their regions of the wrong religions.

Recruiting Volunteers for Violence

One eyewitness told me of the scene at a railway station in the Muslim-dominated area of the new Pakistan from which he was trying to escape. He was a stranger to me, but we were both riding our camels along the same route toward TaruAna when he told me this story, as the violence was still fresh in his mind. He related that he saw a group of Muslim actors staging a skit at a train station where many others were gathered around them to see the "show." In the play, an old woman inquired of a young man, "Oh, Abdul, what happened to my son Mohammed Hussein?" Abdul replied, "Dear lady, your Mohammed Hussein has been slaughtered by the Sikhs." She started beating her thighs pretending to do *siapa* (mourning by physical expression) as she shouted and cried, repeating the following curse against the Sikhs: "*Hai, Vey Sikho, Tuhanu Maut; Hai Vey Sikho, Hai Vey Sikho...*," which means, "Woe, oh Sikhs, death to you!" Then she would ask, "And what happened to my daughter Kareema?" Abdul would reply, "Respected lady, the Sikhs have carried away your daughter Kareema." Again the lady would burst into cries and start slapping her thighs in mourning and repeating the same curse over and over: "*Hai, Vey Sikho, Tuhanu Maut;....*" Then another fellow in the drama troupe would say, " I will go to kill the Sikhs; I will avenge the death of your son and the rape of your daughter." Many other Muslims in the mob were inflamed by that presentation by the group and were ready to take revenge against the Sikhs for these supposed atrocities. This witness described the whole act to me with the actual West Punjab accents, so I believed that he was telling the truth. Such methods were used to inflame and motivate the population to kill the non-Muslims in Pakistan; Sikhs in the India inflamed the feelings of others in their own ways.

Then the Sikhs were bent on revenge in the Indian part of Punjab. The tensions were high due to false rumors. Someone in our village *satth* (plaza) said, "Hordes of Muslims are coming from Kasoor. They have crossed the Sutlej River and are advancing rapidly, killing every Sikh they can find." The refugee Sikhs would say, "The Muslims have killed our people; they have cut the breasts of girls in trains before allowing them to cross into India; they have taken away our property and women; why are not you people doing anything? Where is your rage and sense of justice!" We also started hearing other stories: "The Muslims of Burbur and Boha Bulhada are defiantly holding off all opponents with their armaments; they want to kill as many Sikhs as they can, before they have to abandon India to go to West Punjab," and, "The Nawab of Mamdot has collected a huge force and armaments to kill the Sikhs; we are all going to be killed by the Muslims unless we find a way to defend ourselves."

The Hindus of Punjab and the urban Kshatri Sikhs did not have a tradition of violence in those days; they were gentle, more civilized, or just interested in surviving. But the rural Jat Sikhs had a culture of killing each other violently and taking revenge. During this time of tension, many of the Jat Sikhs adopted the *Nihang* blue dress and steel arms (*buster* and *shuster*) which in the olden times were part of the Nihang warrior's traditional daily wear. The criminal elements joined these temporary Nihangs for the purpose of killing and looting, and the process appeared unstoppable. Some religious fanatics, some criminal elements, and a lot of the rabble with the motive of looting, all combined to start killing the poor Muslims on the Indian side of Punjab. They would decide which village they would attack the next day and would kill those Muslims who could not escape or hide or who were not sheltered by Sikh friends. They issued proclamations that they were going to burn down the house of any Sikh where any sheltered Muslims were found; but no Sikh houses were actually burned in our village.

The Muslims in our villages were no threat; they were generally hard-working people in low-paying occupations or were sheep-herding Sheikhs. Some were sharecroppers who were highly valued as honest, dependable, and hard-working hands; our people did not want to lose them. Although our people might be antagonistic toward the Muslim religion because of the cruelties during the invasions, in everyday matters they preferred to deal with the Muslim people. When we could get a Muslim sharecropper, we would not hire the low caste Hindus, because the Muslims were considered more capable, honest and dependable. I used to believe that Muslims were more trustworthy than others and my closest friend in the village was a Muslim. Before the political disturbances, our people valued our Muslim population. The name of Waris Shah, a Punjabi poet, was beloved among the Jat Sikhs and among other Punjabis; some of Sheikh Fareed's poetry was included in our Sikh scriptures; and some Sufi Muslims were well revered by our people. So, many thoughtful Sikh people tried to protect the Muslims.

It was unthinkable for a Muslim family to just depart from the house where they had lived for generations. Our local Sikh people did not want to allow any killing of their Muslim neighbors. My father went to the village *satth* to argue that we should not allow any outsiders and criminals to kill our Muslims and we should protect them. But the whispers were going around that it might be impossible to stop the killing when the armed killers arrived, and that anyone who gave shelter to the Muslims would have his house burned down. Then someone suggested, "What if we say that there are no Muslims in our village, and to make it right we make every Muslim into a Sikh tomorrow morning, and then those outsiders won't kill these "new Sikhs." I asked my friend Nawab Din how he felt about the planned conversion. He told me that some Muslims were reluctant to convert, but many of them were willing, saying "Oh yes, our ancestors were forcibly converted to Islam in the time of Naranga (Muslim Emperor Aurangzeb). We will only be going back to our original roots if we revert back from Islam to become Sikh." The Muslim elders of the village agreed to assemble the next day in the local *gurdwara* for the *amrit* ceremony to convert and become Sikhs. Some Muslims were suspicious of the scheme, because they thought it might be just a plot to kill all the assembled Muslims in the gurdwara, at one place in a short time. The Sikhs were sincere, though, and would never have desecrated their temple.

But early the next day, before anyone showed up at the Gurdwara, other things started happening. That was the day that the organized killers had planned to launch the attack on Mehraj. Instead of the opportunity to go to gurdwara to convert, the Muslims were faced with killers going from house to house to find people to slaughter. I was working in the fields that day, along with my sharecroppers. We did not expect any disturbance to happen in the village that day and the farm work had to continue. Our field was on the *Tedha Rah* (transverse way), and I saw a couple of tough-looking guys riding with veiled women (obviously abducted) on their camels. They told me that they had captured those Muslim women during an attack on another village. They said that there was also an attack happening on Mehraj. On hearing this man, I rushed from the fields to go to the village immediately, leaving our sharecroppers to continue the work. On the way I saw a Muslim acquaintance named Firu (a contraction of the name from Faqir Mohammed to Faqiru to Firu) running away from the village. I tried to stop him to talk, but as he ran he just gasped, "Don't ask me; horrible things are happening!" He was out of breath and had no time to stop and talk. I encountered a few others also trying to escape the danger. I quickly went to our side of the village to find my Muslim friend Nawab Din, in order to protect him. Nawab Din told me: "Gurnam, no one should be able to harm me since I have many friends around here; but can you do me a favor? Go back to the fields and protect my father and brother; there is little danger to you in going back to the fields." So I ran back to the fields to find my friend Nawab's relatives and to protect them. I went to the field where I expected to find them and shouted their names, but no one was there. They had run away in fear or were hiding somewhere else with others. I returned to the village just before dark, disappointed and dejected for not having saved anybody. On return I was told that Nawab Din and the other men of his family had fled, their women and children were sheltered in someone's house, and his mother was killed when she came out cursing the killers. As it was getting dark, I went toward Nawab's house and saw the dead body of his mother on the street near their house. That scene was hard for me to bear; this was the mother of my friend now lying dead in the street in the most undignified state. On seeing her body I felt great revulsion and a horrible taste in my mouth. Many other people had also been killed and their bodies were lying in the streets. I was standing on a roof edge when the killers were dragging the son of the potter Abdullah from his house. There were rarely any guns; the weapons were swords, axes and spears. A killer suffered no consequences for his crime at that time; there was no law and no protection except by your own sword and manpower. Subsequently, there was never a trace of Nawab Din or his brothers, Ibrahim, Bhag Din, and Jalal Din or of their father Imam Din, even though they were in separate locations before they disappeared.

For me the major change was the loss of my trusted friend Nawab Din. Only four months earlier, on April 13, 1947, the Indian New Year's Day, Nawab and I had gone with five other friends walking overnight to the Baisakhi fair in Talwandi Sabo, twenty five miles away from our village. This was an all-night walk. We were aided by strong tea from the free food stalls hosted by the villages along the way, and by a pinch of opium for those who needed it. By morning all seven of us had reached the house of the married sister of our friend Chand SobheKa, in the village of Bhagi Bander, a couple of miles from the fair, and Chand himself was traveling with us. We rested for an hour or so, washed up, and had breakfast before starting for the fair.

The Baisakhi fair was really a Sikh religious celebration of the birth of the Khalsa on the Indian New Year day. And that shrine at Talwandi Sabo, fifteen miles south of Bhatinda, is called DamDama Sahib because Guru Gobind Singh had rested in this relatively remote location after some difficult battles and bad losses, to reflect and to compile some sacred writings. Talwandi Sabo therefore was the stronghold of Nihangs with their blue uniforms and shiny steel weapons, living in the past and not always in touch with their mental faculties. In the *divan* location of the fair, there were some anti-Muslim speeches, since disturbances had started a few months earlier in West Punjab and refugees had started arriving with their tales of woe. Tensions were high during that fair. Nawab Din, a Muslim in appearance and in the middle of a Sikh festival, must have been uneasy, because those reckless and unpredictable Nihangs could run their weapon through someone mindlessly. Initially we never thought much about the religious aspects of it; we were at the fair for adventure and to have a good time. Even though Nawab Din was surrounded by friends during those two days of the Besakhi fair, we all started to become uneasy out of fear for his safety. Four months later, Pakistan had been created and Nawab Din was dead.

Mutual Trust Amidst Hatred

I could not believe that conditions could change so quickly and so totally. What happened to all the friendships, the trust, and the relationships that had existed between people of different religions? About two weeks before the killings in our village, Nawab Din, his father Imam Din and I had slept in our cornfield overnight. In the summer it was quite common for some men to sleep in the fields, as it was cooler there at night. We could start work in the field early in the morning instead of spending the cool morning hour in traveling from home. Nawab and I climbed up to sleep on a *mannah*. The mannah was a platform made of tree branches and straw, supported on four wooden posts fixed in the ground. Nawab's father slept on a charpai, just close by. Nawab and I behaved like brothers to each other; so there was not any serious issue in sleeping on the same platform, in spite of the caste and religious differences. As we were asleep, a very strong wind suddenly toppled our mannah platform, because its posts were set in ground that had been softened by standing rain water. We fell into the muddy cornfield and were awakened in a state of shock and panic in the dark night. It felt like a nightmare. Before we came to ourselves, I was afraid that we were being attacked by someone due to religious hatred. Our nerves were really raw because hostilities and violence were flaring up in other areas and people of opposing religions were killing each other. As Nawab Din was wiping the mud off his body, he said to me, "Gurnam, I admire your courage and trust. Even when Muslims and Sikhs are killing each other, here you are sleeping in the midst of two Muslim men in the wilderness." But I totally trusted my friend, and we still considered the Muslims of our village as our own people. Two weeks later everything had changed.

Following the day of those killings in our village, I and our neighbor Uncle Bhan Singh would go to the fields every day with food. We would shout the names of Nawab's brothers and of other Muslims who might be hiding in the crops, to come and get food. Some Muslims including Firu, whom I had seen running away on the day of the Mehraj massacre and who was hiding in the fields, came and got food; but nobody from Nawab's family ever showed up. People in the village would ask me, "Nawab Din was your close friend; did he contact you yet? Surely he will send a letter to you if he went to Pakistan. He was too smart and strong to be killed so easily; he must have escaped to Pakistan."

The only adult male of Nawab's family to survive was his brother Shahab Din (Shahbu), who was in the Indian military. He was sent to Pakistan when the Indian army was divided according to religions and all Punjabi Muslims were sent to Pakistan. I remember the day in about 1940 when Shahab Din and his younger brother Nawab Din (later to be my friend) had together appeared as teenagers in front of a recruiting officer in the compound of our school. They were both coerced to volunteer for the army, as the British Indian government needed soldiers during WWII. I remember seeing the naked chests of both brothers marked by the recruiting officer with pen, as we watched all the recruit candidates in the school yard curiously from a short distance. On their chests were written the measurements of height, weight, chest, waist size, age and other comments by the recruiting staff. They did not bother to use any paper and instead wrote all the data about a recruit on his body and all the decisions were made on the spot. The older one, Shahbu, was recruited and sent into the army, which saved his life later. Nawab Din, the younger one, still in his mid teens, was too young and physically immature to make the minimum grade for recruitment. That was a few years earlier, and now he and all adult males of his family, except Shahbu in the army, were dead. A young son of their brother Ibrahim survived with the women; the family had no other male children.

Some weeks after the Partition, when things calmed down, our people became remorseful for allowing the massacres to happen and for not doing enough to save the Muslims. I myself wished I had had the foresight to anticipate what could happen, and I wished I had hidden my friend Nawab Din somewhere. Everyone blamed the outsiders for the massacres. Our people felt that what had happened was most tragic and unfair; they felt a great sense of loss. Muslims who had escaped to hide or had been sheltered by friends were able to come out of hiding and were starting to plan to return to their old homes. Most of the surviving Muslims were still staying with Sikh friends. But after a few weeks they were rounded up by the police and according to the policy of the government were taken to refugee camps and then transferred to Pakistan.

Some months later, Nawab's brother Shahbu came from Pakistan to our village Mehraj, to find any property the family might have left with friends, and to investigate what had happened to his brothers. In anticipation of the danger and to avoid any looting, his family had placed their belongings and animals with friends, thinking that there would be no danger if there were no assets to loot. When Shahbu came from Pakistan, everybody was helpful and hospitable to him and we all grieved for his family. He stayed and ate with our families in the village for a couple of weeks. I gave him the two boxes that Nawab Din had stored in our house. I also collected additional money and clothing to give to Shahbu, as the latter said they were totally indigent, without resources in a refugee camp in their newly created country. Then I borrowed additional money from Aunt Harnami to give to Shahbu. When my father had to pay back that debt, he grumbled about my going into debt without asking him.

Those of us who lost Muslim friends felt devastated for a while. But death was everywhere and your own death could come at any time at the hands of Muslims; so to some extent we had become callous about death. The continuous talk about the Muslim threat had also reduced sympathy toward all Muslims. People like me were in a confused state of mind because of the loss of Muslim friends on the one hand and the fear of being killed by Muslims on the other. Some days after the attack on Mehraj, a couple of friends and I went to Phul, because there was a rumor of an imminent attack on Phul. No neighbor would ever kill a Muslim; the killers were organized gangs that would decide which village to attack next; so each event was like a battle front. The town of Phul had a strong settlement of Muslims in the Lohar Bazaar (Blacksmith Street) where some people from Mehraj used to go to get simple steel implements and weapons made. It was expected that the battle action might be worth watching there. In that culture, people always gathered to watch, whether it was a verbal quarrel, a roaring fire, an accident, or a furious battle. We were late in reaching Phul, but as we were walking through the streets, skirmishes were still going on. A large number of people had already been killed. Some were lying unconscious with severe wounds but their bodies were still wiggling and moving. There were some dead Sikhs lying in one area and their friends were calling them heroes and martyrs. By the Phul police station, the slashed bodies of several Muslim policemen in uniform were scattered about in the street. But the biggest massacre was in the Lohar Bazaar. Every Muslim there who could not hide or run away died fighting, and some women were taken away by force. My friends and I never came in the line of attack as we were somewhat late. We returned to tell the tales of horror to the people in the Sutth; but the village people had heard so many such stories and had seen so many dead bodies, that nothing shocked them anymore. After all, everyone had seen the low caste Chuhras removing dead bodies from the streets by cart-loads and dumping them into the well in the Muslim graveyard located on the old way to Sidhana. So the death of my friend, that would have been a devastating event in normal times, was overshadowed by the impact of the many other deaths and conflicting emotions that had made me numb.

War Mentality in Our Village

Even after the killings stopped, ignorance, uncertainty, anxiety, and rumors were widespread. Someone would say, "the Muslims of Kasoor have crossed the river Sutlej and may be getting here in two days; be prepared to fight and die." The village carpenter/ blacksmith was making spears, axes, and other weapons for all the men, free of charge if you could provide the steel to make them with. We all felt that we couldn't be sure whether we were going to live or not, so we didn't think about anything except defense.

The blacksmith was doing his part working long hours, and nobody was expected to pay him anything for the extra work. The thought was that if the enemy killed all the men and your women were at their mercy, what good would money do? Your choice was to kill or die. Every teenager had a spear mounted on a seven-foot-long bamboo stick, ready to do battle. I too had a special steel bar in the house that I gave to the ironsmith to get my spear made. I was seventeen years old and took the defense of the community seriously.

Young volunteers were assigned duties by the elders. We would stand guard all night at the street entrances to the village. I and a companion took our turn as guards at a post with our spears. Actually, at night we stood on the rooftop of the house of Gujjer at the west entrance of the village. Every twenty minutes or so, we would shout warnings to the guards at other street entrances, according to the instructions of the village elders, to keep everyone awake. At times like this we wished we had a walled town like Phul so that we would need to guard only the entry gates. Mehraj was bigger in population than Phul, but being in the British territory it was not important enough to have a wall, whereas Phul was in the domain of the Phulkian Prince of Nabha, whose ancestors had built the wall all around the town.

Once, in the middle of the day someone came into the sutth (plaza) and reported, "The Muslims have reached Kalyan, only six miles away; all those who are willing to die to stop the Muslims there, come with me unless you want to wait until they are in your streets and homes!" Many of the young men ran to get their steel weapons and assembled in the Sutth (plaza). Then another older, wiser man named Kartara said, "Hey fellows, wait and think; none of you has seen the Muslims with your own eyes. If you go to find them six miles away and they come from another direction in your absence and ravage your households, what good will your bravery do? Better to make a stand here, be here united, and be prepared to fight and die." So the plan of going to fight the "approaching Muslims" at some front many miles away was dropped and the vigilance at night was strengthened. Although there was a concentration of Afghan Muslims living in Kasoor, no Muslim hordes showed up in Mehraj. But the stories of massacres on trains and in ox-cart caravans kept circulating and nerves were raw during those weeks.

During all this period one never saw a policeman or a military man who could provide assurance. The new government of Nehru and Gandhi's Congress Party was not fully organized yet, and the forces were being divided according to religion. The movies that are made nowadays show the military protecting the refugees and helping them find their lost relatives. That is mostly false propaganda to give the military a good image. In reality, in the rural areas there was rarely any help from the military, police or other authorities until long after the actual partition, and until after most of the massacres had taken place. In fact rumors used to circulate to the effect that the military and police in Muslim majority areas took every opportunity to kill the fleeing Sikh refugees.

Verification by Genital Inspection

During the time of partition, it was dangerous to look like a Muslim in the Indian part of Punjab, just as it could be fatal to be a non-Muslim in the Pakistan portion. Muslims who were hiding from violent people tried to dress like Hindus or Sikhs, while some Sikhs in western Punjab might have tried to trim their mustaches and alter their turbans to look like Muslims. It was hard to fake being a Sikh because you could not grow a

140

beard and mustache instantly. But a Sikh could change instantly to Hindu if he cut his hair and beard. Even some Hindus could be stopped by the murderous gangs of Sikhs, with the suspicion that they were Muslims. In order to verify that they were Hindu, they were usually ordered to drop their *dhoti*, pajamas, or pants, so that their genitals could be inspected. If they were circumcised, their heads could be cut off. If the foreskin on the penis was intact, they would be allowed to go free. Circumcision was the indisputable proof when there was some suspicion about a man's religion being Muslim. On the Pakistan side, a man could lose his life following the genital inspection if his foreskin was not cut off.

During those days, people working in the fields stayed in groups for safety. One night I and my young sharecropper Mukhtar had our turn to water the cotton field. It was a dark night and we were watering the different sections of the field when we heard a rustling noise in the cotton plants. All of a sudden three Muslim men came out of hiding. They said they only wanted food, as they had not eaten for some time. Although suspicious and fearful, with a grip on my spear and a careful eye I gave the Muslims all the food I had, and they were thankful. The fellows again disappeared into the dark night. If they had been vicious, the Muslims could have attacked when we were unaware or possibly killed my sharecropper and me. But then their chance of survival would have been lessened. Whereas most people were helpful to the hiding Muslims; if they had killed us then the village people would have hunted them down. If they were not caught, they would have died of hunger, as the rumors of "killer Muslims in the fields" would spread rapidly. Besides, like many Muslims of Mehraj, these escapees were gentle and humble people. No hiding Muslims killed anyone in our village; the killer Muslims were only in the areas where they were the majority power.

There was a mood of real sorrow and repentance in the countryside as people started recalling how "our Muslims" never did anything wrong and how those outsiders, criminals and looters, caused all the killings. People thought all this was due to some curse on the land and that the souls of all those innocents killed were going to haunt us and bring more calamities on the land. After very dry months, rains came with a vengeance. Some people feared that God was going to punish the land by flooding and drowning us for the sin of all those killings. Some fanatics said God was happy at the elimination of the followers of Mohammed, and that God was just cleansing away all the spilled blood with the rains. Hopes were few; fear and uncertainty was everywhere. The village people did not really have a clear concept of the implications of the political division of the country. To them this disturbance was a continuation of the historical enmity of religions; the massacres and the revenge were similar to the historical events of which we had heard stories all through our lives. We had seen cartoons showing big, ugly, demonic looking Muslims executing innocent "Sikh martyrs." We had heard that the Muslims were cruel people, had strange customs, worshipped in strange ways, and came from other countries to kill our people, and that killing non-Muslims was a part of Mohammed's faith. But in reality the Muslims were not any worse than our own people. They naturally felt that India was their land, as their ancestors had lived there for generations. The Punjabi Muslims were a diversity of native Indian converts, and Afghan, Persian, or Turkic/Mughal invaders; and the ratio of the foreign races increased as one went west toward the Khyber Pass.

141

Even if a person did not see the actual massacres, the signs of them were abundant in those days. Oxcarts full of dead bodies were taken from the streets and dumped into unfinished wells. As the boys grazed cattle by the banks of the canal, they could count the number of dead bodies floating downstream in the canal, hour by hour. Those bodies that came from long distances upstream were swollen and discolored to varying degrees. The crows feeding on the floating swollen bodies presented a macabre sight. Most people had become jaded, and no one was shocked any more by seeing the stream of dead bodies. But now we could not put our mouths down and drink water from the canal. If the number of dead bodies floating per hour was increasing, the conflict must be intensifying upstream. As the summer heat subsided, in September 1947 the dead bodies stopped floating down the canals.

Gradually both new countries started policing their respective territories and settling the refugees. The government ordered that all surviving Muslims in Punjab must be brought to refugee camps for transfer to Pakistan. My uncle Mohinder had kept two small Muslim boys in his house and had fed them for a few months, and many others were looked after by the Sikhs in our village. But the government would not allow them to stay. If some Sikh had a Muslim woman, there was no choice for her to stay in India even if she had lived with him for a long time; she would be forced by the police to leave for Pakistan. Sometimes the children were hidden by the fathers, but most were sent to Pakistan along with their mothers. Police threatened severe penalties against anyone who assisted a Muslim in avoiding deportation to Pakistan. But I doubt if anyone was actually punished. The Mirassi caste, and those in the domain of the Muslim ruler of Maler Kotla, were not deported because they enjoyed the favor of Sikhs for historical reasons. Most other Muslims were removed by police from the Indian Punjab, just as all Sikhs and Hindus were eliminated from Pakistani. But in recent years numerous Muslims have been migrating to and settling in the Indian Punjab and they are living peacefully.

Indian Tendency to Blame the British

Regardless of what the urban, educated Indians might say about the "British strategy of divide and rule," the British cannot be blamed for the Partition of India. It was a result of the mutual hatred of religions for centuries that had expressed itself at every opportunity and did so again in 1947. The British just kept the country together to rule as long as they could. Fanatics were not hard to find in any community, although the Hindus were not as violent and aggressive then as they became after they achieved dominance as rulers of India in 1947. The British can be blamed for conquering India, but they were not any worse than previous conquerors had been in history; the strong were just expected to conquer, enslave, and rule over the weak in those times. The British were pretty nasty and cruel while conquering, though, and they did treat the Indians with contempt generally. Even later on, some officials could be quite ruthless if they felt that an activity was a threat to their Empire. For example in 1918 a British general named Dyer ordered the massacre of everyone gathered in the Jallian Wala park in Amritsar during a holiday and killed about two thousand people in a few minutes. He later said that he was just doing his duty.

During their rule subsequent to the conquest, however, the British were perceived as competent administrators, although they treated most Indians as inferiors. They started conquering India in the eighteenth century, and it took them another century to extend their rule into Punjab by 1849. After they established order they started the projects that changed the face of Punjab and brought unprecedented prosperity to the rural areas. The rural people in Punjab had much to say in favor of the British and very little in favor of freedom fighters like Nehru and Gandhi, who they thought had never done them any good or ever built anything. Rural Indians also had bad memories of the harsh pre-British, Indian rulers, and they disliked the petty Indian officials, who were corrupt, unjust, cruel and oppressive. They thought the British were good administrators and just rulers. Many rural Punjabis and big landowners did not want the British to leave or the Indians to be in power again. But of course most of us rarely saw an Englishmen. The British officials, if they ever came to the village, would say nice and polite words to the village people. Even when they mispronounced the Punjabi language like, *"Ham tum log ka bahut dhanbad karta hai...."* the village people thought that they were polite and making the effort. The words mean 'I thank you people very much.', but the pronunciation was the funny part, because their sounds of English 'd' and 't' were so different from the Indian pronunciation. The villagers thought the English not only were gifted with intelligence ("He has English-like intelligence") but also were very polite and kind, whereas the Indian officials were known only for their rudeness, cruelty, and corruption. The railways, an efficient administration, a fair justice system, irrigation projects, and some impressive buildings made the British highly esteemed in the eyes of ordinary people. The Indian rulers of earlier times erected monuments only to glorify or please themselves and not for the public good. The British civil servants dedicated their lives like missionaries to improving the lives of their subjects and to serving their King or Queen honestly. No wonder that the rural people praised the English rule. In fact, one of the questions in our classes used to be to enumerate the "Blessings of the British Rule." The big landowners and the titled families were strong supporters of the British rule, because their privileges were protected by the British. Even my father thought that the English should not leave India, because they were good rulers. Many conservative people used to say that the *Dhoti-Topi* (garb of the Congress Party) politicians of India would mess up the country. The village people were not politically aware, and for them it made no difference who was sitting as the ruler in Delhi. They only saw the officials, and they knew that the native variety of official was worse than the English. It was the politically aware, educated, and urban people who hoped to acquire power, and some who felt mistreated as the subjects of an enslaved country, that resented the English rule.

On 15 August 1947, India became independent of the British. Pakistan was formed as two Muslim-dominated territories, East Pakistan in the eastern part of Bengal, and West Pakistan, formed from the western part of Punjab, The Frontier Province, Sindh, and Baluchestan. Life in Punjab was never the same after partition. First, there were shortages of some necessities of life because of the disruption in most economic activities. Certain occupations had been exclusive to Muslims by caste, religion, or tradition because religious conversions took place by whole castes, clans, or occupations at a time. The specifically Muslim castes and occupations, except the Mirasi, disappeared from the Indian Punjab as a result of the migration. In our village Mehraj, all of a sudden there were no cloth-weavers, oil extractors, cotton ginners, potters, water-carriers or grain-roasters left. No workmen among the arriving refugees had the same occupations as the departed Muslims did. So instead of local hand-made things, the public had to get used to shortages and gradually to factory-made things purchased from the market. This provided stimulus to cloth mills, metal pot makers and other replacement goods industries. The Muslims in our area were land-less workers and artisans, although the Muslims near the border areas and in certain other regions were big landowners. In their place came Sikh refugees who could not do artisan work. The Jat Sikhs had to leave all their lands in Pakistan, but there was not as much land for them in Punjab left by the Muslims. In towns, the *Kanjri* prostitutes and women singers whom one saw with fancy clothes, red lips, and provocative make-up, riding horse-drawn carriages, all left for Pakistan since they were Muslim. Spinning and homemade cotton cloth became impractical without the weavers. With no need for spinning yarn, young girls could think of school. People became more accustomed to strange accents and new words in our Punjabi language. Rural people started marrying other Punjabi people born in distant regions, whereas in earlier times relations were limited to a distance of one day's oxcart ride. My eldest sister was married in 1942, before the Partition, to a man only twenty miles away; but after 1947 all of my other siblings were married to those who were born or raised outside the boundary of modern India.

With Partition and Independence, millions of people lost relatives and property, even if they themselves were successful in fleeing. After reaching India they grieved for their massacred and lost relatives. Others grieved for the loss of their ancestral homes and properties, the likes of which they could not get in the new land. Some people bribed or influenced the officials to take possession of good houses abandoned by Muslims, while others settled wherever they could. The formerly prosperous and proud farming families, nearly all of them Sikhs, recalled their fertile lands in LylePur, Montgomery, and other districts, which had been settled only about fifty years earlier, after the construction of irrigation canals. They talked about their fields, orchards, big houses and the good life lost to them forever. In India they were lucky to be allotted a fraction of the lost land in strange locations and of uncertain productive capacity.

Many of the urban Punjabis came over and settled in the cities of Punjab and adjoining Delhi, but others chose to go to cities all over India, like Bombay, Poona, Calcutta. The Indian cities became more crowded, since the Muslim population was not required to leave any part of India except Punjab, but almost every Sikh or Hindu had to leave Pakistan. Delhi used to be a small town compared to Lahore, the pride of old Punjab and its capital; but after the 1947 partition, the population of Delhi proliferated with refugees. The Punjabi refugees were an enterprising lot, and within a few years, after starting as petty traders many of them became prosperous. The success and prosperity of the Punjabi refugees was held up as an example by journalists, politicians, and speechmakers for the rest of the poor Indians to emulate.

CHAPTER 6

OUR ENVIRONMENT IN THE VILLAGE

The southern portion of Punjab was characterized by sun and sand. The months of May and June, preceding the monsoons, would be marked by scorching sun, high temperatures, and dust-loaded hot winds. You could sit in the shade but the hot wind, called *loo*, was so fierce in the month of June that it could scorch a tender complexion, even without the sun. The best protection was a mud-brick house, low into the ground, with thick earthen walls, facing north or northeast, with only one door and no windows, to minimize the exchange of air with the outside. Rich people in the cities tried window screens made from fragrant grasses and moistened them with sprinkled water continuously to keep cool. But loo was the enemy of the rural people. It dried or burned plants and crops quickly if they were not watered. It put stress on animals and they lost weight; many were hyperventilating even while standing still in the shade. The only trees that thrived in our area were those natural to the desert. The loo dried all water in most ponds by that time of the year, marking the clay at the bottom with patterns of huge cracks. The complexion of those working outdoors turned much darker and would remain that way until about November when the sun became less fierce.

If the hot loo was oppressive, the dust storm called *kali boli* (black hurricane?) was scary, as it created a dark world for the duration. One would see the wall of dust approaching as a wide front over the entire horizon, usually from the west or south. Its color could be black, gray, brown, gold, or even red, depending on its origin and the nature of the particulate matter. It could have originated in the Rajputana desert, the Arabian desert, or even the Sahara. Black and red were the scariest of *kali boli* hurricanes; in their midst, one could not see anything even a few feet away. But the color was not always a good indicator of the ferocity of the dust storm or of its duration. Those dust storms were scary, and unpleasant, but they were seldom deadly. After the initial forceful hurricane and possibly the breaking of trees and loose structures, the wind could keep blowing with lower velocity for several more days. After it passed, there would be much sand where you did not want it. Your eyebrows, ears, nose, beard, and clothes would be full of sand, which was an unpleasant feeling. A turban was really helpful to keep the sand out of the hair, as an end of the turban could be used to cover face, nose, ears, and beard; a hat would be useless in such wind. In the sandy areas, old sand dunes sometimes shifted locations, and new dunes could appear near any collection of bushes or obstacles that created eddies in the wind.

In the dry heat of early summer, there would be tornado-like, but not deadly, twisters called *barola* that circled furiously but traveled slowly, dragging a lot of dust and debris with them. They were never as powerful as the tornadoes of the American South and Midwest. Even our dust storms, although scary, were never as ferocious as the Caribbean hurricanes; our environment was more like non-coastal, Southern California, but sandy and dusty, not rocky. Later in the season, the chance of having rain increased, and the chances of the barola twisters decreased. The arrival of monsoons after mid-July raised the hope of rain, ended the season of barola, kali boli, and loo winds and was another reason to rejoice.

One of the benefits of the sandstorms was that they filled the furrows of the plowed fields with new soil. Since the soil had been depleted after centuries of cultivation, the addition of any new soil was beneficial. In the irrigated lands, fertilizers were used; and any deposits from the canal water would also enrich the soil. But there was no fertilizer or manure used in the non-irrigated lands. The farmers just tilled their fields before the sand-blowing season started; then the winds would deposit new soil into the furrows when sandstorms blew in.

After excessive rains during the 1950s, the ground-water table rose, and there was occasional flooding. As irrigation became widespread, there was increased greenery. Consequently, the dust storms became much less significant and the sand dunes that had dominated the landscape in some Mehraj territories up to the 1950s gradually vanished. Sandstorms seem to have become less frequent and less severe. But sand is still present under the houses, structures, and roads that were built on top of the sand dunes originally. In places like Bhatinda, whenever the workers dig up any road, they find the sand dunes underneath.

Once in the early summer of 1942 there was a severe dust storm followed by some rain. The upper story of our Outer House used to have a galvanized steel awning-like structure, but during this storm the wind was so strong that the structure was torn off from the house and from the supporting pillars, and parts of it were found about two hundred yards away outside the village. If the flying sheets had hit a human, it would have meant instant death. My father and Uncle Nick were out in the fields that night, and the family worried about their safety as many trees were broken and branches were flying about. Fortunately they took shelter behind the trunk of a tree that proved to be strong, and they survived without injuries. But storms in Punjab were seldom so severe.

Our area of Punjab was mostly flat and usually dry, with inadequate, seasonal rain and a hot climate. The mountains were a hundred miles north of us. But the songs about "our beautiful Punjab" were still plenty. The weather did change from month to month. January was cold enough to get below freezing on some nights, and water puddles sometimes froze in a few places, although rarely in the plains. In general the daytime temperatures in winter would be mild. By the month of February the crops could be dense and lush; the mustard flowers and greenery of wheat fields made the irrigated areas quite pleasant and inviting. March was when kernels or pods of grain formed in the winter crops; and the weather was warm and perfect for roaming outdoors. While wandering through the fields you could eat the *ber* fruit which were abundant in my days

146

or the raw chickpeas, which tasted like sweet peas. We even enjoyed eating the Punjabi mustard stems. Chickpea plants could be pulled out and put on a burning brush pile, to roast their pods to make *holaan* (roasted chickpea pods), a delicacy. You did not really have to go home to eat a regular lunch at that time of the year. In mid-April, the Indian New Year started with the month of Baisakh. By then it was hot, every crop ripened, and the harvest was in full swing. Some people were able to finish their harvest in April. Those who were slow could still be thrashing and crushing the harvest in the *pirr* grounds until May.

About the time when the harvest was completed, the farmers made new sharecropper agreements for the next year. We as children would anticipate our family's choices as they hired sharecroppers for the next year. We listened for the speech peculiarities of the new ones, and we would watch how they worked around the courtyard, taking care of our animals. And although we might have liked the last ones, there was some excitement about getting a new one; it felt like getting a new horse, or pet. I still remember the twenty or thirty sharecroppers we had during my young years. In fact we used to count or remember the years according to who our sharecropper was then.

In mid-May, the heat became unbearable, hot winds started blowing hot sands, and fields were bare with little vegetation. In the areas without irrigation, there was not much activity in the fields except some plowing in the early hours of the day. But in the canal areas, people would start to irrigate their fields in order to plant cotton. By June the cotton had been planted, but the heat was so severe that the plants could die without frequent watering as the *loo* (hot wind) became unbearable. You could get out of the sun, but it was not easy to escape the loo in the countryside. Sun and sand made life quite miserable, but the rural people had to accept it as the way of nature. Clouds started appearing in mid-July, but not very regularly. When the rains started in the month of *Sawan*, after mid-July, they created a lot of joy in the villages; the village girls started celebrating the Teejan season then. Summer crops like beans, millet, and corn could be planted then, but in the un-irrigated lands the crops were always in a precarious state, at the mercy of additional rain. In good years it would be a pleasure to look over the full fields, the ponds could be full of water and the animals would look healthy. Young boys played in the warm rain; they would even stand under the waterspouts to feel the warm water flowing from the roof and hitting their heads and bodies. Crops like corn could be ready in late August, and the summer crops like cotton, millet, and beans would start maturing in September. Breaking the ears of corn and roasting them on a burning dry brush pile, could provide a farmer's lunch. In October and November the sowing of wheat, chickpeas, and other winter crops continued, and at the same time the cotton was ready to be picked. December was cool, with some green color when the winter crops began to spread and fill the fields.

Crowing Rooster and the Modern *Ghari*

No precision in measuring time was really required until the days of irrigation canals, when it became necessary to measure allotted watering time according to land rights. Before that the farmers knew all they needed about time just by the position of the sun or the stars. We did not know the difference between planets and stars, but we could tell the approximate time at night by the position of some planet or star, although the positions could vary gradually from season to season. For example a fellow would say: "I went to the fields when the star was two ropes high and I reached there before sunrise." So 'rope lengths above the horizon' was as precise as they needed to be. If you were not sufficiently motivated to get up any earlier, then the rooster's crow (*kukker di bang*) could wake you up, as the roosters started anticipating the arrival of the day before morning light. In the quiet of the village morning, the rooster's crow could be heard a quarter mile away, so even people who did not own any chickens would hear them. Before twilight it appeared that the roosters from different neighborhoods were competing in announcing the arrival of day. After daylight the roosters quietened down and housewives woke up to start their chores.

Before the 20th century, time was measured in terms of *paher* (watch period, equivalent to 3 hours) in the military, police, or private service, so a day and night together were worth eight paher. Time among the village people was defined according to activities or according to natural occurrences, such as *paher da tarka* (one watch before sunrise), which was considered the ideal time to wake up for a farmer or a religious man. Similarly *peh phati* (morning light break), sunrise, *lassi vela* or *sheh vela* (buttermilk time or breakfast time), *dupehra* (second watch, noon), *teeja paher* (third watch), *aathen vela* (afternoon time), *vugg vela* (cow herd time), sunset, midnight, and so forth, defined the time periods. There was no need for precision.

By my time, some fashionable, affluent people and those returned from service in Hong Kong or Calcutta owned *ghari*, (watches). The only farmer who had to own a watch in the village was the *ghari-baz* (watch-keeper) who had to keep track of the time for providing irrigation water to the different farmers' lands. Ghari-baz was a voluntary position that was assigned by informal voting, with compensation of one extra hour of canal water to the watch-keeper. The landowner next in line would be waiting for the approval of the ghari-baz to go and divert the irrigation ditch water from the fields of the previous irrigator to his own land. At the signal of the ghari baz, he would run as fast as he could to get to his field, so as to not lose any time, and he would divert the water from the previous farmer's land to his own. Disputes could arise at times, because some arrogant Jat might just say, "I don't care if the ghari baz has sent you; I won't let you cut off the water from my land until all my withering crop is watered." Murders over watering the land were common in Punjab and were a great source of bribes for the police. That is one reason why it was good to have brothers for protection, so that no one would intimidate you or take away your water rights.

The word *ghari* is used for watch, and it also used to be a unit of time (something like 60 ghari in a day), but this unit of time is used less and less in the current Punjabi vocabulary, except by old people and in old songs. Ghari means a small clay pitcher, and the definition of ghari as a unit of time was based on how long it took a standard empty clay pitcher with a standard hole in the bottom, when placed in water, to fill and sink. It was like the emptying time of the sand in an hourglass, used in the western world, but the latter is a more convenient device. Village people like my mother used to say, "You should rest for a couple of ghari before you start work again." Another word from the old timing system was *pal or pul*, which is the duration of a pulse or heartbeat, approximately a second. Nowadays the same word ghari (which used to mean small pitcher) is also used for the spring-loaded and electronic devices that measure time. And hardly anybody knows where the words, *paher*, *ghari*, and *pul* came from. Paher is three hours, not a conventional time unit as hour is, and even the clay pitchers have largely disappeared from modern life; only pul remains, approximating the duration of a pulse.

Plowmen's Songs

As mentioned elsewhere, we farmers lived in villages and not in our farms; we went to work in the fields just as urban people go to work in factories and offices. Thus we were able to participate in the social life of the village regularly and interacted with our neighbors on daily basis. But in the busy season, a farmer had to get up one paher (three hours) before sunrise to be considered serious about his work. It could take a good part of an hour to get ready, gather equipment and supplies, yoke the oxen, and tie the plough to the yoke to drag it to the fields. Sometimes the plough was in the house because it had been brought back from another field; so it would be tied to the yoke of the oxen and dragged to the new field. It could take up to one hour to walk to a field. A farmer would be ashamed of himself if he could not start work before the break of dawn; other people would joke about him if he were habitually late. There used to be jokes about the crab grass laughing at a fellow named Mohinder, one of my contemporaries who was fashionable, habitually late, and not serious about work. Two crabgrass plants are talking: "Here comes Mohinder: he might uproot us." The other crabgrass plant laughs confidently when Mohinder comes to uproot it with his plough, because it thinks that a fashionable guy could never eliminate it: "Here comes Mohinder, but no worry; a softy like him can't uproot me completely..Mohinder, Ha, Ha, Ha, Ha..."

Walking in the cool mornings in the generally warm climate and reaching the fields before daybreak has an uplifting effect. The breeze is usually light before mid-day. During summer after the rainy season, crickets would still be chirping and the bushes might be buzzing with fireflies. These fireflies would appear like a flurry of shooting stars in the dark of the early morning, although the fireflies were not abundant every year and were seen mostly in the areas of good vegetation. Most land plots were small and neighbors worked within hearing distances of each other. You could recognize the familiar voices as the different plowmen started their songs while it was still dark. If you were a ditch-digger or were harvesting something, the work was too strenuous to allow any singing. But an experienced plowman merely had to walk behind the oxen while holding the plow steady, which allowed plenty of attention and energy for singing. In fact singing was practically a necessity for the plowman in order to keep his sanity, since his work was monotonous. Although almost everyone knew the words, only the best could sing with effect, and they were highly admired. From the songs you could tell which plowman was tilling which field. This went on only until mid-morning, because after that the sound did not carry to long distances very well, as it did in the calm early mornings. Also, one did not have to watch one's language carefully during the early hours. But mid-morning was the time when the women-folks would bring the *roti* (meals) for the ploughmen; and it would be disrespectful to the women if they heard your off-color songs.

Singing was a frequent activity for many other people, too. Apart from the ploughman, the fellow driving his oxcart had nothing else to occupy him when he sat on the cart in the middle of his two oxen. Singing was automatic for the waterman as he waited for the leather water bag to come up from the bottom of the well. His voice, echoed by the well, sounded really pleasant and haunting; from far away it sounded like the *azzan* of the mosque. Some boys staying in their fields at night had nothing else to do except sing until they wanted to fall asleep. The herders and cattle grazers had their own songs. In fact, singing became a habit for most rural people as they worked or walked, and that habit could be awkward in urban environment. I myself had memorized hundreds of songs and couplets, but when I reached America, my friend Yoginder, who had come there a year earlier; said to me, "Gurnam, don't go around singing songs when you are in this country; they will think you are fit for mental asylum."

Hellish Life of a Farmer in Punjab

My father used to say to me "Gurnam, you know what they say about *churasi*, the torturous cycle of eighty-four *lakh* (8.4 million) births and deaths, that a soul may go through during its cycle of transmigration. That *torture of churasi* is right here in the life of a farmer; so get out of this cycle of churasi and get nirvana through education." From my point of view, the village life was exciting. But my father was right about the harshness of the farmers' lives in those days. Of course now the conditions have become quite comfortable, with the mechanization of most farming tasks.

I have already described the harshness of the Punjab climate. The harvest season for wheat, barley, and chickpeas came in April when it was already hot in North India. A worker had to remain in a squatting, crouching position all day as he cut a swath through the standing wheat crop and formed it into sheaves. The scorching heat and the stinging dust of the dried plants would cause a burning sensation on his skin and heat his body to an unbearable level. The chickpea crop was not as tall and suffocating as wheat, but the sting of its dust was harsher. Each man moving in the squatting position would be cutting and gathering five to six rows of the crop. He would hold the sickle in his right hand and a bunch of plants in his left hand as he cut, gathered, and piled the harvest and proceeded along the furrows. Usually he was in competition with others, who had their own rows to cut and gather. A few minutes of moving in the crouching position would be hard enough; but to do this all day in the intense heat and in the stinging crop dust, required great endurance. The low caste Chuhra with black complexion and hardened skin could tolerate those conditions. The Brahman, shopkeeper and Kariger castes could never endure such heat, and they never had to do so, as their occupations required indoor work only. After cutting and gathering, the workers gathered the small sheaves of the crop to form larger sheaves and then piled them in the form of a *mandli*, a rectangular pile of the harvested crop, in the field.

The process of hauling all the mandli piles from different fields to one location was also laborious. But the piles from the various fields had to be brought to one location near the village by oxcart, a process that could take a good part of a month if the harvest was abundant. The hard and sand-free patches of ground where everyone brought and piled his harvest were called *pirr* (or p*ird*). Each family would have their traditional and recognized, but not owned, pirr location on the periphery of the village, although anyone else could use that land when it was not needed for harvest processing. When I was a young boy, there was so much unused, common village land that a family could just move to a farther location for their pirr if they needed more space for their harvest. But by the 1950s, free village land had become scarce as most common land had been claimed by someone or another.

In the pirr grounds, the farmers worked side by side, each to extract the grain from his harvest. This was the only time when most farmers were working at locations near the village; anyone who was weak or old was relegated to grazing cattle. There was some cooperation, much socializing, and lots of banter, jokes, and stories exchanged among the men working in the pirr. Usually other people would come to assist a fellow in a difficult task that needed to be finished quickly to proceed to the next stage, such as turning over the half-crushed wheat harvest. Such assistance was unsolicited, spontaneous, and usually reciprocated.

The process of extracting the grain from the wheat harvest was crude, slow, and laborious, and the heat became even more intense in late April. For the harvested wheat the crushing device was a load of tree branches, thorny bushes and dried plant matter assembled together, called a *phallah*. The phallah was dragged by two oxen, or sometimes by a single camel, all day over the wheat harvest, which would be spread in a circular or doughnut pattern on the ground. To crush the harvest properly, the phallah had to be dragged over the spread harvest in a circular pattern for several days. The farmers hoped for high heat and a lack of wind or humidity to speed the crushing process with the phallah, the very conditions which made them and their oxen uncomfortable, exhausted and sometimes ill. In rare cases, a man or an ox collapsed from the heat; and all the farmers' boys in the neighboring pirr would ridicule such weaklings, calling them sissy, fair-faced, softy, and other names that attacked their masculinity.

After harvested wheat was thus crushed to fine chaff called *toori*, it was ready for winnowing in a good wind. The winnowing process involved throwing up a fork full of the crushed harvest so that the heavier grain would fall nearly straight down and the lighter chaff would fall some distance away in a separate pile. The farmer hoped for a light wind to separate the lighter chaff from the heavier grain when it was thrown up into the air by the fork, before the grain fell back down. But if the wind were too strong it could carry away the precious chaff, which had to be gathered separately from the grain and without which the cattle would starve later. The proper wind speed was moderate enough so that the chaff would not fly away, yet strong enough so that it would be separated from the grain. Sometimes, additional crushing by the feet of the oxen going in circles was necessary if the first process with the phallah had not done a good job of crushing to extract grain from the kernels. A second winnowing with a *chhajli* (flat bottomed, rectangular basket, open on one side) then separated the wheat from any remaining chaff. The grain was thus made into a long pile called *bohl* for the purpose of weighing it and putting it into sacks. The weighing was required not just for the owner's knowledge, but also because a portion of the grain had to be given to the *seeri* sharecropper as his wages for the year. Usually the sharecropper was given the cash price of about 1/5 or 1/6 of the harvest and not the actual grain. The chickpea thrashing and crushing was a little bit faster and could be done without the phallah device, but the sting of its dust was nastier. In the processes mentioned above, some ox dung and urine were inevitably mixed with the grain during the month of crushing. For those who did not see it and would eat it later, such impurities might not make any difference; the ox dung and urine could not be any more harmful than what goes on in some modern-day restaurants.

151

When the wheat harvest season was over, there was possibility of respite from drudgery, at least in the lands that were not irrigated. Without irrigation, farmers merely had to plow their fields before the hurricane and rainy season, so that the land would soften a bit and any weeds would be destroyed. When the rainy season started in July, they would sow the summer crops of millet and beans and hope that the crops would not die for lack of additional rains. After the rainy season ended in September, they had to plough again in order to break the soil, because the moisture is easily sucked out of the unbroken compacted soil by the scorching sun. Without adequate moisture in the soil there would be no hope of planting the winter crops. In the desert regions with no irrigation, they depended entirely on the rain for their livelihood. If there was no rain, there would be little work.

In our region, roughly half the land was accessible to irrigation water, and life was much harder for the farmer. Cotton had become an important cash crop after the irrigation canals were created. Preparing the fields and planting cotton was not a difficult task, but a couple of months later, sitting in the tall cotton, weeding and hoeing in the unbearable heat with high humidity and little wind, could be the most miserable task. Work like that was necessary if you did not want the cotton to be choked with weeds and did not want nutrition to be sucked out of the field. The farmers also used to spread manure in the fields by the basketful, usually in the unbearable heat; that was about the most unpleasant activity. Whether it was digging an irrigation ditch, carrying animal fodder on the head and then operating the fodder cutting machine to make it edible by the animals, or weeding a cotton field in the heat and humidity, it was torturous and back-breaking work. There were countless tasks of unbearable difficulty and discomfort in the oppressive climate; if a farmer was weak, squeamish or comfort-loving, he could not make a living.

In the lands north and east of us, the ground water table was higher, and they had wells for irrigation. Ox power was used there to draw water from the wells for irrigating the lands. But making a living by well irrigation was not lucrative or easy. My father used to say "Earnings of a well are eaten by the well." The care and feeding of the oxen to run the well, maintenance, repair of broken parts, and other incidental expenses could consume a good part of the farm income. There was no rest period for the farmers in the irrigated areas. They had to start irrigating and plowing the land immediately after the wheat harvest in order to plant cotton, animal feed, and other summer crops. All work was continuous, hard, and in vicious hot weather. In the winter there were other difficult and unpleasant farming tasks, like walking in the freezing irrigation water. My uncle used to say: "If you want to take life easy, wear clean clothes, or live fashionably, then you can't make a living as a small farmer."

Sharecroppers and Farm Labor

Our sharecroppers, called *seeri* (one who shares), were the farm workers who were hired by the farmer with agreements lasting one year at a time. Their wage was a share of the crop instead of cash, and they surely made the farmer's life easier. They were different from the independent sharecroppers who had their own farming operations and equipment and who cultivated the landowner's land and gave him a part of the harvest for use of his land. There also used to be a special category of permanent sharecroppers. Big landowners who never worked with their own hands had such permanent sharecroppers, called maroosh, whose sons would inherit the right to cultivate the land, generation after generation. If the maroosh had no sons, however, that right reverted back to the landowner. The lands of our ancestors were once cultivated by maroosh, but over time much of the land reverted to our clan. Although our people were no longer big landowners, our family still used to get a share of the crops from the maroosh who farmed some of our family's land until about 1950, when the Indian government abolished the rights of landlords by law.

But the hired seeri sharecroppers were more like servants who did farm work and got paid a share of the cash crop at harvest time. They also took care of the farmer's milk animals and the cutting, transporting, chopping, and feeding of the fodder crops to all the animals. Growing animal feed crops and taking care of the animals frequently turned out to be a big portion of their job, for which they got no compensation. Any cattle raised and sold, and any milk products used or sold by the owner, did not benefit the seeri at all. Since that was the custom, the seeri did not complain about the fact that they were not deriving any benefit from animal products or animal sales. The seeri would also do any odd jobs and difficult tasks around the house, such as carrying wheat to be ground at the flour mill, transporting anything heavy from one place to another, and miscellaneous and incidental errands. When his meals were provided by the landowner, the seeri received 1/6 of the harvest of grains and cotton produced by one plough; if he was not given food, he got 1/5. And if the landowner ran two ploughs, then the seeri would get 1/12 or 1/10 of the total crop. If the seeri was unmarried, he usually slept in the owner's animal area, for the sake of convenience and security; but most of those workers were usually married in their teens. Since they did not practice female infanticide, they could all get wives, and they had more children than the landowners did. Usually 20 to 100 rupees were loaned to the seeri at the beginning of the year, to pay off his existing debts and obligations; but that money had to be returned to the landowner at the time of harvest. The landowner would deduct the amount of that debt from the seeri's share of the crop. In bad years when his share of the crop might be less than the debt, the seeri would still owe money and had to go into the same bondage for another year to the same or to another farmer. To be hired as a sharecropper was generally better than looking for farm work for daily wages. Only the best workers were in demand as seeri; the weak, and unreliable or unstable workers would just scrape by on seasonal farm labor, which was scarce during the thirties. Once hired, the seeri became a part of the farmer's household for practical purposes, just like the oxen and camels were, for at least one year. The sharecroppers' year ended when the grain harvest was taken care of, about early May, but the date of the change-over for the seeri was somewhat flexible. Though the seeri made the Jat farmer's life somewhat easier, his own life was a couple of notches harder.

My family used to have two seeri for each year. We used to remember the years and times according to who our seeri were in those years. Usually our two seeri would run the two ploughs. If uncle Tiloka ordered one of them to a more difficult task, he took over his plough for the day. Most of the seeri were from the Chuhra caste, but the Muslim castes who worked as seeri were preferred since they were better workers and more reliable. In our village even a Hindu shopkeeper had hired out as Uncle Bhan's seeri in tough times, and Freedu from the Ahluwalia Muslim caste was Uncle Bhan's seeri for a few years.

Shahbu, Our Seeri in Training

The year 1941-42 had been bad for crops; and after being discouraged by a couple of dry years, our house decided that they would not hire a seeri for the next year. Discouraged by the long draught, our family had scaled back on farming. That is the year they sold the Gora ox to a *GadianWale* nomad and parceled out any surplus land to independent sharecroppers. There were four men (my father and brothers) and some children to help; and if there were no rains, as in the previous year, there would not be as much work for the seeri to do. So they thought they would do without a sharecropper in 1942-43. For that year they just hired a young boy of 13, named Shahab Din (Shahbu), the middle son of Tahri Khan. The barely teenaged Shahbu was too young to qualify as a seeri, as he had not done any recognizable work up to that time and would need a little training to man the plough. Instead of any share of the crop, Shahbu's compensation for the entire year 1942-43 was 24 rupees, equivalent to about five dollars, and he would eat his roti (meals) from our house. In addition we promised him *panjseri* (10 pounds) of ghee to make him stronger and hopefully fatter; as he weighed so little then, any increase in weight would also increase his market value for the future. And Shahbu rarely visited his own house; he would sleep in our cattle area or in the fields for the night. He would work every day of the year from morning to late night, first in the fields and then feeding the animals. According to the plan, Shahbu would be in charge of the ox plough and Uncle Mohinder could man the second plough with the camel if there were any rains. In the year 1942 Uncle Tiloka also bought a large number of new buffaloes and animals to raise for profit, and that created a lot of extra work for the family. Cattle prices had been depressed due to drought, so the animals were cheap to buy; and Uncle Tiloka thought there might be more profit in cattle than in the crops. But the family was faced with a lot more work as a result of the additional animals.

Unexpectedly, 1942-43 turned out to be the year of good rains and the biggest crops our family ever had, and therefore the amount of work increased several-fold from the previous year. We were not the most affluent family in the village, nor did we have as much land as the top families. But in that year we had the biggest grain pile in the pirr compared to other families. Shahbu had to do the work of two men for the meagerly 24 rupees for the whole year. In the harvest season that year, he could have earned more than his year's wage in less than a week, if he were free. But people did not violate agreements in those days, and Shahbu's father, Tahri Khan was a simple man known for his honesty and word of honor. Everyone in our family was swamped with work that year, and even I as a twelve-year-old had to be pressed into service for grazing the cattle and other tasks whenever I was free from school.

Uncle Karma and the LaleAna Ox

With no adult seeri and the big harvest that year, we needed many additional workers. We could hire temporary laborers for harvesting; but transporting the harvest from the different fields and collecting it all at the pirr grounds for thrashing and crushing was a major project. My maternal uncle Amar Singh from LaleAna, hearing of the needs of his sister's (my mother's) family, sent his strongest ox and an energetic worker named Karma for the harvest season. In situations of need, a sister was usually given priority over one's own interests, and that is what my maternal uncle did by sending his best ox and a reliable worker. Karma had to walk the distance of 25 miles from LaleAna with my uncle's ox to our village. There is no way we could have transported the harvest without our extraordinary black camel and the LaleAna ox, since our own *chappa* ox (an ox with backward horns) had disgracefully bad habits and was totally dysfunctional. Our home-grown oxen used to be as good as any, but they had all died of old age. The last one had died just before the harvest. Someone had sold us this chappa ox that had no sense of pride. The chappa ox never wanted to pull his share and would usually drag backward when our camel and the Laleana ox were pulling the oxcart forward.

The frustration of owning a bad ox is hard to bear. A normal ox gives his all when spurred and applies all his strength to pulling, as a matter of habit and loyalty. But if you don't use extreme caution when buying an ox, someone could sell you one with a bad character, just as someone could pass a base coin on to you. If you hit or spur it, the bad ox goes into the cringing mode; he can drag backward or might even sit down instead of pulling and may just stick his tongue out in the cringing mode if you hit him. There was some risk in buying any animal, but buying a bad ox was a continuing source of frustration and pain. Our chappa ox was an example of such pain. Fortunately, my maternal uncle from Laleana sent his strongest ox to rescue us that year.

Uncle Karma, who had been sent by my maternal uncle to help us, was not any ordinary laborer but a man from my mother's village clan. It would be an insult if you offered to pay cash for his services for a few weeks, but a new shirt and turban as a gift at his departure were appropriate. It was common for men to go and assist in a sister's household, even when she had been married for 25 years, as my mother had been. But it would be unthinkable for any man from the husband's side to work at his in-laws' house, as traditionally the husband's household had the superior status. A family felt responsible for seeing a daughter prosper, and the men felt good about helping in the house of a married sister or a paternal aunt. A maternal aunt was a mere equal and had no privileged status, but a paternal aunt, being a daughter of one's clan, was like a sacred person.

Karma was an enthusiastic worker who mobilized all our hired laborers and encouraged everyone else around him to be equally energetic by example. The engine behind his energy was strong tea and some opium. He would make tea for every body in the harvest field, and we would give a pinch of opium to each worker. After that strong tea and opium, they all picked up speed and feelings of pain or fatigue were forgotten. That was the beginning of the habit of drinking tea for my father and his brothers. In earlier times they used to condemn tea and all other stimulants as evils to be avoided, saying, "Tea is bad, tea is the lowliest of low; avoid tea as you would avoid contact with any *chuhri* or *chumar.i*" the last two being the words for untouchable caste women. Opium was always discontinued after the harvest, but tea became more of a custom in subsequent years in our household as in many others in rural Punjab. Anyway, that year our family owed a lot to the help of our worker Shahbu, to Uncle Karma, and to the LaleAna ox, whom Karma took back with him after the harvest.

Land Mortgages and Economic Lessons

During the Great Depression, prices of grain and other commodities did not change much, and in fact sometimes prices went down and stayed down. Then it was advantageous to control land through a mortgage rather than by buying it outright. Under the mortgage system in Punjab, instead of interest on the mortgage amount, the lender got possession and use of the land for the duration of the mortgage. He could get more acreage that way, since the cost per acre would be lower under the mortgage arrangement than the cost of buying the land outright. The owner/mortgager could pay off the loan in any year and regain control of his land after the harvest in the spring. During the depression of the 1930s, however, if someone mortgaged his land, it was not probable that he would be able to buy it back in any short time. Money was scarce, and although the lender would be perfectly happy to get his cash back and release the land, sometimes he would get attached to the land. Many lenders expected to become permanent owners of the land, sometimes by lending additional money against the already encumbered parcel. In the unlikely event that the mortgager could pay off his loan and get his land back, the money returned to the lender could always buy a comparable piece of land to replace it. So it was advantageous to acquire land under the mortgage arrangement, as money was hard to get, land prices were not changing much, and there was no inflation.

Trilok Singh, the head of our family, had acquired enough land under the mortgage system for our own farming operation and even some more to be worked by independent sharecroppers. Because of his good reputation and reliability, he could borrow money from moneylenders to acquire land. Then came World War II, and prices of most commodities, and consequently of land as well, that had been depressed for years, went up gradually at first and then rapidly after1943. Land that had formerly been available for 250 rupees an acre suddenly became worth 1,000 an acre, and even more later. The mortgager could put all his debt against one quarter of his formerly encumbered lands and could get back control of all the rest without having to provide any cash. And the cheaper rupees that the lender got back now could only buy a much smaller amount of land, which could change his condition from prosperity to adversity fairly suddenly. Our family had considered the mortgage lands under our control as if they were going to be ours forever. But by 1945 we experienced a fairly sudden and shocking change in prosperity as a result of losing the mortgage lands; and the devalued rupees we received had very little purchasing power. We had paid silver rupees to acquire the lands but we were getting back paper currency which became common during the war. Because of inflation, the paper rupee became worth much less than a silver rupee. Not only did the silver rupees become unavailable during the inflation, the merchants started charging 25% to provide the change of coins for a paper rupee. During the war you could not get change for a paper rupee until the government changed the content of coins to base metals. About the same time our joint family started breaking up, and my father felt that he would not be successful in continuing the farm work alone. He was never a ploughman anyway, and although he could perform the hard tasks when necessary, he was really a scholar at heart. With the loss of mortgage lands, the breakup of the joint family, and the reduction in income after we quit farm work, our family felt an economic squeeze. Fortunately, my brother Kartar had become a military officer and subsequently became the family's main support for many years afterwards. Kartar opened a joint checking account with my father who then got continuous access to all his money.

The rampant inflation saw a reversal of fortune for a lot of other families, too. People who had squandered and mortgaged their inheritances with lives of leisure and spendthrift habits, and had become paupers in earlier years, got an opportunity to get their lands back without any effort; and they became prosperous again. And those who had worked hard and been frugal enough to accumulate money to obtain lands under the mortgage arrangements got nearly wiped out by the inflation when they received the cheap paper rupees back. Although all transactions in the 1930s were paid with real silver rupees, during World War II the paper currency drove all silver coins underground and made them unavailable.

Some decades later I had that lesson of inflation in mind when in the 1970s in California I purchased a large property in a highly leveraged debt arrangement. Later I saw its price rise by several million dollars compared to the amount of debt on that property, and forty times my original down payment. In that case I used every possible technique to get on the favorable side of the inflation equation. When inflation is high, you are lucky to have land, real estate, and non-perishable commodities, preferably bought with fixed interest-rate debt and very little of your own money. If you are holding currency or have loaned money at a fixed interest rate for a long period, high inflation would eat your assets every day. In the days of the Great Depression, it was possible for prices to go up as well as down for prolonged periods. But in the modern democratic and capitalist system, governments and corporations cannot allow deflation. Social and economic systems are designed so that only inflation and not deflation is acceptable and some inflation is now guaranteed. The decision-makers in government and in corporations have become aware that if wages and prices don't rise and if inflation is not promoted, they will face unhappy employees, stockholders and voters.

CHAPTER 7

RELUCTANT BREAK FROM VILLAGE

For many reasons, everyday life in the village was a pleasurable adventure for me. I did not mind the heat, the dirt, and the harsh life of the farmer; I never wanted to leave that life. But gradually there were setbacks and difficulties, like the death of my friend Nawab, my family's severe opposition to my choice of lifestyle, brother Kartar's insistence that I change my ways and get an education, and the regular bouts of malaria each summer.

The turning point in my thinking came in 1949 when I suffered something akin to a complication of pneumonia (who knows; it could have been typhoid or even something else), which cost me more than a third of my body weight and all my strength. After I had been ill for some days, my family tried to take me to the local hospital on horseback, on the horse belonging to Chand, son of Harnami. But I had neither the consciousness nor the strength to ride the horse. So they had to carry me on a *charpai* (string bed) on the shoulders of four people, like pall bearers carrying a dead body. The local doctor had no real diagnostic capabilities and had to guess what the disease was. He gave me a medicine he thought might work, probably an antibiotic left over from the treatment of another patient. It was for the peace of mind of the parents and relatives that I was taken to the doctor, but even there I did not recover for many more days. In that sickness, lasting more than a month, most of my flesh disappeared. My knees and ankles looked much bigger than my thighs and calves did; my waist had wasted and my cheeks, temples, and eye sockets were sunken and hollow. My mother and sisters were deeply worried. But I recovered after a few more days.

For me that pneumonia/typhoid complication, or whatever it was, about the age of nineteen, began to change my attitude; at least it moderated the intensity of my love for village life. I began to feel that maybe the village life was not completely blissful after all. I could easily have died of the disease in the village. On the other hand, even if I had been a lowly soldier in the army, the military doctors and nurses would have had a real interest in saving me from disease and might have had the knowledge and experience to do so. The army would have considered my body to be more useful for cooling an enemy bullet than as a feast for germs. I started thinking that perhaps I should place myself in better circumstances. However, I still could not bear the thought of leaving the

158

village to be in some city full of strangers whom I never considered with much favor or envy.

Later in summer 1949 my brother Kartar again visited Mehraj on vacation. I seemed destined to be a farmer for life. In spite of all the previous disappointments, Kartar never gave up on me. This time he did not put undue pressure but just invited me in a congenial way to come for a visit to Ahmednagar where he was stationed. Some village people did go to visit relatives who were in government service. There used to be humorous stories of how the cultural klutzes of the village handled themselves when they went to visit their up-to-date, modernized relatives. And there were other stories of characters similar to "Crocodile Dundee" with their folksy common sense making fools of the phony and pretentious urban people. Whenever Kartar came to the village, he would tell interesting stories of other officers, their wives, and his friends. I thought I should see those ways of the anglicized officers and their wives and could then come back to the village to talk about them. And I thought that if I visited Kartar in the military cantonment, I might have a chance to shoot guns at a firing range. Guns were of great interest to me at that age. Once, Kartar had brought his army revolver to the village, and it was a thrill for me to be able to touch it. I even had sneaked the army revolver out of the house to show off to a friend, an act considered highly illegal in those days because only a licensed person could touch a weapon. One day my sister Chhoti was playing with that revolver and pulling the trigger at random. She did not realize that one of the chambers still had a bullet in it and she almost put the bullet through my chest, before I grabbed it to take my turn and examined it. The idea of shooting a gun was exciting to me and provided additional motivation for me to visit my brother at his military station.

Although India had gained independence in 1947, it was still a part of the British Commonwealth, and in 1949 when I went to visit Karatar, his official correspondence still said "On His Majesty's Service", as George VI was nominally still the Emperor of India. The British officers were being replaced rapidly, but some of them were still trying to decide whether to go to England or to some other Commonwealth country like Australia or Canada. It was in January 1950 that India became a republic and words like "Royal Regiment", "King's Commission," and "On His Majesty's Service" were no longer used.

Anyway, I finally agreed to visit Kartar in Ahmednagar. My sharecropper, Thanedar, would continue to handle my farm work in my absence. After I had made the promise to go for a visit, however, I began to have second thoughts. Ahmednagar, where Kartar was posted, was a thousand miles away, with strange people speaking different languages and dressed in different clothes. But in my circles a man did not break his word, and I could not back out of my promise; besides, this was only to be a visit, and I would be coming back anyway.

So in September 1949, I took the train from Rampura Phul station. At Bhatinda Junction I changed from the regional train to the long-distance train called the Bombay Mail; the word 'mail' for a train implied 'special and fast'. Long-distance trains had names like Frontier Mail, Punjab Mail, Calcutta Mail, Simla Mail, and so on. They carried mail and were faster and better equipped than the regional trains and stopped at fewer stations. The Bombay Mail passed through famous cities like Delhi, Agra, Jhansi, Gwaliar, and Bhopal. It took three days to reach Bombay from Bhatinda. The rail journey through the country, the sight of strange geographical features and rocky land, the appearance of animals with unfamiliar characteristics like oxen with long backward horns, and the sounds of beggars singing in mellow, haunting tones were all new experiences for a boy from rural Punjab. After two days of the rail journey, I had to change from the Bombay Mail to a regional train at a place called Manmad, about hundred and fifty miles short of Bombay. From the railway junction of Manmad to Ahmednagar it took three or four hours to travel by the slow train.

Coping with Cultural Transition

It was late afternoon when Kartar met me at the Ahmednagar railway station. According to his expectations, I had put on a pantaloon instead of the village clothes, but the first thing he said to me at the station was, "Put your shirt inside your pants; otherwise people will think you are some uneducated, village rustic." Kartar had brought an army vehicle with a driver. It was fashionable in those days for officers to drive and have the army driver ride in the back, because officers almost never liked to be passengers in the army vehicles. When two or more officers were in a vehicle, the senior-most officer usually drove while the subordinates and the driver on duty rode along. I had expected that Kartar would drive me to his living quarters, but since he was still a bachelor in those days, he lived in the officers' mess barracks and not in a house. Consequently, it was not possible for me to stay with him.

Kartar had arranged for me to stay temporarily in the house of an officer with family quarters, Captain Bahal Singh. The captain had come through the lower ranks. He was therefore less pretentious than an average officer, and he had a traditional Punjabi wife and five young daughters. Karter had arranged this accommodation with a traditional Punjabi family rather than with his fashionable friends to avoid embarrassment to himself. He knew I would inevitably show my village manners and language, and any interaction with the westernized wives could result in ridicule and might ruin Karatr's image. Everyone in those circles was highly image-conscious and judgmental. Furthermore, Kartar also thought I would suffer less of a transition shock with that family than with the ultra-sophisticated wives of some of the other military officers. Those officers' wives had to be able to fit in with the club life and to interact with the British officer's wives. But the Indian officers' wives usually over-compensated when it came to social behavior and creating and maintaining an image. Affected speech, artificial manners, banter, and purposely mispronounced and ungrammatical ways of speaking any vernacular language, just as an Englishman would do, were the hallmarks of such educated Indians. These Indians tried to set themselves apart from other natives by purposely speaking the native language incorrectly like foreigners. I could not speak the English language in those days, and Captain Bahal Singh's wife was one of the few wives who did not speak English. Once, in the process of answering a question, I erroneously described her as "She Bahal Singh" instead of "Mrs. Bahal Singh," and that usage became a big joke among Kartar's friends. In that house I was less stressed about table manners, topics of conversation, and unfashionable language than I would have been in the homes of some of the other officers.

Once while I was still new to this scene, Kartar took me to a party of his close friends; they were all Jat Sikh officers from Punjab and therefore considered relatively safe for me if I made a faux pas or spoke in the village style. The party was in the house of one

160

Major Naginder Singh, a handsome, towering officer from the Patiala Lancers, with a charming, sophisticated wife who came from an aristocratic family of the State of Patiala. When the forces of the State of Patiala were dissolved after Independence, the Patiala Lancers regiment, whose officers were mostly Sikh, became one of the Indian Armed Corps regiments. To me, the house, the furnishings, the women, their clothes, the servants' livery and manners, and everything else looked overwhelmingly impressive and opulent. I had not been in the midst of such glamour and luxury before. Most of these officers and their wives came from privileged, rich families, the likes of which I had never encountered before. I was the subject of curiosity. It was not very long before one of the women patronizingly asked me some mundane question. I started to answer the question in the language and vocabulary of the village. There was some mischievous laughter from the listening women as I used village words like *'juak'* for children and *'leeray'* for clothes, because they thought it so quaint and rural. Now, the village word juak is just an inexact pronunciation of the Sanskrit word *juvak or yuvak* for youngster or youth. A word like juak sounded crude and rough to the women, although if I had said it with proper tone and polish it would have passed. Such a reaction made me even more self-conscious. Later on, Kartar got teased about those uncultured words of his "village brother." For such reasons Kartar was careful not to invite me to many of the truly fabulous parties that were a part of the Armed Corps Center's tradition at Ahmednagar in those days and about which I only heard conversations between Kartar and his bachelor friends. At another party one of the women remarked that "Gurnam is rather short," and she joined her friends in teasing Kartar by saying "You brothers are both imperfect; one of you is too short and one of you is too dark." I think I was still growing then, and my height increased by nearly two inches after the age of nineteen, so later I became approximately 5 feet 10 inches tall.

I did not realize at first that I could not stay at Captain Bahal Singh's house for more than a week. It was not like the village, where hospitality was unlimited and a visit with friends and relatives could last weeks and months if one so wished. My returning to the village would not be acceptable to Kartar and was something I did not have the courage to demand. So Kartar arranged with the principal of the local college for me to stay in their student dormitory even though I was not a student. He was able to make this arrangement because Ahmednagar College was a new and private college and its principal, Dr. Havale, wanted to be courteous to an army officer. This college had been started under the auspices of an American Christian Mission, but a majority of the students were local Hindus. Like me, most of the Christian students felt like a minority there, and I found the atmosphere relatively friendly.

As an indication of how small and cozy the college was, I learned that a professor of chemistry, Thomas Barnabas, had married the principal's daughter and thereby had become the vice-principal of the college. His brother, Joseph Barnabas, a bachelor, was a professor of physics, the warden of the student dormitory, and the person in charge of funding for sports and facilities, among his other duties. Another brother, Philip Barnabas, was a student at my class level, a gentle, good-looking fellow who lived in our hostel. Unlike the more recent low-caste Hindu converts, the Barnabas family was from the southwest coast of India, where many Indians had been introduced to Christianity probably even before the Romans and other Europeans were converted. I really enjoyed the friendly attitude of the Barnabas brothers, as they were genuinely kind and generous in a society where people in positions of power and authority were often snobbish and standoffish, so as to put you in your place. I was one of the select few who were occasionally invited for special Saturday night co-ed parties at the principal's house. I think they did this because they thought of me as a foreigner and also as being of a different class from that of the local people. Coming from a society where talking to women who were not relatives was unusual and uncomfortable, I was put at ease by these assertive Christian girls, who included the principal's daughters and some girls from the college hostel who could talk with poise, grace, and friendliness to strangers. To some extent, these interactions gradually prepared me to deal with the military wives of Kartar's friends without feeling unduly awkward.

One cosmopolitan friend of mine in the hostel was Prahlad Ahuja, a refugee from the Frontier Province of the newly created Pakistan. He told me that most Hindus from his area near Afghanistan used to believe in Sikh scriptures and worshipped according to the Sikh tradition, but unlike our people they did not keep uncut beard and hair. Another frequent companion of ours was Baladhar Gangadhar Tilak, an extremely witty, talkative, spoiled, nonconformist son of a Brahmin attorney from Bombay. Both of these fellows had more in common with me than with the local people. My roommate was a local Muslim who was gentle, quiet, cultured and quite unlike the Muslims in our village. He was somewhat formal with me whereas a Punjabi Muslim would be totally open and friendly. In recent years while traveling in European countries, I have met Punjabi Muslims from Pakistan, and every one of those fellows has treated me enthusiastically like a brother. So the Punjabi culture and language seemed more important for friendship than religion.

Other students in the college were not as outgoing and gregarious as students I would have found in a college in Punjab. But on one occasion two or three of the college boys, who were farmers' sons, invited me to visit their village. I had told them I was a farmer's son and this encouraged them to invite me. We went to their village by train, to return the same day. When I thought of farmers, I expected that they would be like the prosperous people in our villages, who sent their sons to college. The parents of these boys had some land, but their standard of living was lower than that of our low-caste laborers in Punjab. Their food was poor and unappealing. Their houses were tiny, shabby shacks and not particularly clean, and they all had to sleep on the floor. In fact, when in the college dormitory their boys were afraid to sleep on the *charpai* beds, because they were afraid they would fall off while asleep, since they were not used to sleeping on beds. This was a far cry from Punjab where the college boys of those days acted like aristocrats. Unlike in Punjab where family names were seldom used, here in Maharashtra it was customary to call everyone by their last names only.

I got used to the life in Ahmednagar pretty quickly. There were new friends, gracious authorities on campus, and enough college activities to make life interesting. The climate was milder than in Punjab. I started liking college life and was not nostalgic for the life of the village in any serious way. I had to speak English to everyone in college, as the local Marathi language was unfamiliar. In the hostel the crowd was heterogeneous, but I hung out with my cosmopolitan friends Ahuja and Tilak, and not with the Marathi speakers. Of course I had frequent interaction with military families and sometimes visited their homes with Kartar.

Brother Kartar provided for my living expenses. Whatever Kartar's other financial responsibilities were, he never let me feel as though there was any shortage of money. He took pride in making sure I had good clothes. He had a tailor to make me a white summer suit and a couple of formal woolen suits, so that I often felt overdressed compared to other college students. I would visit Kartar in the officers' mess on some days. It was a three-mile bicycle ride, and slightly uphill, but I also walked many times.

Sometimes I was invited to a party in the cantonment area. The officers' parties were quite impressive because they were recreating what the British officers had been doing. I would watch with curiosity and awe the people and their mannerisms, the ladies' expensive clothes and jewelry, the fabulous food, the butlers so eager to please, the party games as they were in English society, the teasing of bachelor officers by the married women, and the general humor and banter between men and women. They were a select and disciplined group of upper-class people who conducted themselves with all the social graces, although occasionally excessive drinking or a minor scandal did occur.

Kartar wanted me to acquire better manners and polish so that I could be selected for the Indian military academy to become an officer. He introduced me gradually to the wives in some families and encouraged me to pay occasional social visits to them. He would say, "Don't go to any Punjabi-speaking family. You can visit Das Gupta's wife, as she is newly married and has time to spare. Speak carefully and practice proper manners when you meet Doctor Wadhwa's daughter. You will benefit by learning how to conduct yourself in society." As in English society before the advent of automobiles and telephones, it was a custom among the young officers to go calling on their friends or superiors between certain hours, without prior announcement and without waiting for an invitation. If the host was not at home, they would just leave their calling card or a note. For me it was a whole new system of manners, as I came from a culture where customs were simple and informal. Boys who had grown up in affluent urban society automatically learned customs like how to introduce yourself or someone else to another; how to accept an offer of a drink and how to decline an offer; how to conduct oneself at a dinner table; how to handle a table napkin, knife, fork, and the different spoons; when to begin eating; how it was discourteous to ignore a person sitting next to you and how much to talk to a person sitting on either side of you at the dinner table; and how to take leave or say thanks. For me all that was new, and I had little self-confidence. A villager from Punjab would have been able to function better in the informal American West, but the situation of a military officer's life in Ahmednagar in 1949 was close to that in upper-crust nineteenth century England. At that time some English officers still remained in India who probably had been born in England in the time of Queen Victoria, and every Indian officer wanted to act like them.

Grooming for the Military

Although I was not a student, I lived on the college campus in Ahmednagar while waiting for the next academic year to begin. Meanwhile, in late 1949 I took the two-day written examination for entry into the Indian Military Academy. Although I had forgotten some of what I had learned from my teacher Kesho Ram and I had never opened a book while living in the village between 1946 and 1949, I still passed the written examination on the first attempt. This success gave Kartar the confidence that any effort and expense to reform me were justified.

To help prepare me for life in the military, Kartar took me to Bombay and showed me the Gateway of India, the Marine Drive, the Victoria Terminus railway station, and other sights. He also took me for tea to the Taj Mahal Hotel whose luxurious carpets and elegant appointments were overwhelmingly opulent for a person of my class. Kartar wanted to familiarize me with the ways of the upper class.

But I still lacked the polish, the confidence, and the facility in speaking English that were necessary to get selected by the interviewing officers of the military selection board. Boys from the public schools (which really means private, exclusive, English medium schools), who spoke English and had confidence and polish, were invariably selected by the board, if they managed to get through the written test. After I qualified in the written test, I was invited for an interview by the Military Selection Board at Bangalore. At that time, however, that process was totally beyond my village experiences, and I was not selected. This was discouraging, but there was a second chance. Early in 1950 I again took and passed the written test. This time I could communicate a little more confidently in English. Kartar prepared me for the military interview; he even tied a starched turban on his own head and transferred it to my head when it dried. I took that pre-tied turban with me to wear at the interview instead of my own sloppy turban. It was common for a man to get some skillful person to tie a turban for a special occasion like a wedding, to make a good impression. The turban style can change one's appearance drastically, and sometimes can tip the balance in one's favor when other things are marginal. Kartar's turban was a little bit big for my head, but with a little paper shim it served the purpose. This time I did qualify at the Selection Board interview as well, and consequently was tested for medical fitness, which test I also passed. So the turban tied by Kartar for my head might have made a difference in my selection.

In the summer of 1950, it appeared that I was headed for a career as an officer in the military, and Kartar's efforts were coming to fruition. In the meantime, I had become a student at Ahmednagar College where I was living. I took courses in Ancient Indian History and Culture, Political Science, and other subjects. Our family considered these to be useless subjects, but they were intended merely to legitimize me as a student so that I could continue to stay in the college hostel. I was not planning to stay at the college for long, since I thought that I would be going to the Indian Military Academy in Dehra Doon. Therefore, it did not matter what academic subjects I registered for; often I did not even attend classes. Following my apparent success, I started walking and talking with a different air, as I assumed I was soon going to be at the level of those Class-1 officers of the Government of India, and I thought I had made a quantum jump in status. Kartar remarked about a change in my confidence level and about my new brash speech.

But my brash speech and confident manners were short lived. It turned out that there were only twelve open positions at the Indian Military Academy for that batch of candidates. Although that number was increased to thirty later on, I was not high enough on the "merit list" for admission to the Academy. Moreover, I could not compete for the next batch for admission to the Academy as by that time I would be over-age, since 21 was the age limit at the time of entry. So I was shut out of the military academy. That was a big disappointment for everybody in my family and a disaster for me.

To appreciate the gravity of the situation, one must look at the possibilities in those days. To pay for many additional years of schooling seemed unrealistic, and in any case I was too old for admission to any technical or professional school. All engineering or professional colleges and government jobs had relatively low age limits for entry. In those days, even after years of non-technical college education, there would have been nothing for me but some mediocre clerical job in India, unless I were exceptionally capable, and that was not expected of a boy from a village like Mehraj. Military officers held the most desirable and glamorous jobs in those days. To be shut out of the military academy was like being doomed to a life of mediocrity. Life in India was not like life in America, where even poor people are treated with dignity and can feel equal to others and where there are no barriers to advancement if you have the ability. In India your life was determined by your class level, and people of higher levels treated you as if you were some inferior animal. Even your relatives could treat you like a servant or an inferior if you did not match their status. Some might discriminate against you in subtle ways, and you could be excluded in other situations where they felt you would not fit in. So the failure to make the grade in the military selection process seemed to be the end of my new ambitions.

Alternatives to Military Life

Back down to earth and reality! The first thing I did was to switch from liberal arts to science subjects in the college. I had a lot of catching up to do after being registered for half the academic year in the arts classes and having attended even those classes only sporadically, while the rest of the class had been learning the science subjects for several months. To relieve the financial burden, Kartar tried to persuade me to quit my studies and join the military as a common soldier with some hope that some day I might become an officer. Cases where troopers became officers were rare in peacetime, but it could happen if one were exceptionally capable and lucky. Kartar himself had commented one day that the Indian army treats soldiers like well-controlled animals, so that they will obey and be useful when needed. "They can't be allowed much freedom of movement or liberty of thought if you expect them to obey without question," they used to say. The non-commissioned soldiers, below the rank of lieutenant, were restricted in their movements and activities. They were forbidden from visiting the officers colony in civilian clothes. Even if such a soldier had family relationship with an officer, it would be unlawful for him to visit the officer's residence. An officer could be called for questioning by his commandant if it was discovered that a soldier of low rank had visited the house of the officer, socially and not in the line of duty. Mixing with low ranks, even in civilian clothes or in off-duty hours, was "just not done." The officers and the non-commissioned soldiers were just like different castes; they were allowed to interact only in the line of duty. So it is easy to understand why I was reluctant to enlist as a soldier and be treated like an animal or a low caste.

I was ambivalent about joining at the bottom rank of the military. On the one hand, I would feel guilty of being a financial burden if I continued college, and on the other hand I feared being treated like a subhuman if I became a foot soldier. The person who strengthened my resolve was my college friend Prahlad Ahuja, who said forcefully:

"Gurnam, don't ever join as a sepahi! As a lowly soldier you will be treated like a donkey by the sergeants and commanders. All intelligence and ambition will be hammered out of you. You will be in the company of ignorant people and you will become a low-class person trained to be nervous in the company of officers. You will acquire the mentality of an obedient servant, which will leave you fit for nothing better than service as a lowly soldier who at best could clean his rifle, polish his shoes, and salute smartly. You will never have any rights. You will be lucky to go on leave for four weeks a year; the rest of the time it will be like jail. Military officers themselves say, 'We have to treat the soldiers like trained cattle; any freedom to roam or initiative to think will ruin them.' I am convinced that you should be college-educated; you are too intelligent to join as an ordinary soldier."

Brother Kartar was willing to listen to my suggestion of further education instead of my immediate induction as a soldier. But he had to think of his responsibilities to the rest of the family. He could not deprive them to put all his resources into me. And he had to think of his own marriage too, as all his friends were in the process of selecting wives. The military wives were always making suggestions to the bachelors about possible matrimonial matches with their nieces and relatives. So I made a promise to look for a suitable job, if Kartar would let me complete two years of college there, as one year was nearly over already. Kartar agreed to let me continue in Ahmednagar College; he himself was soon transferred to northern India. I spent the next year in Ahmednagar College, still maintaining contacts with some military families. In April 1952, I completed two years of college, got the Intermediate Science certificate, and then returned home to our village. Regardless of where one went, there was always the precious ancestral land and the village home in Punjab to come to. There was always the comfort of the extended family and the community, which gave the feeling of belonging.

At one time my family had been willing to do anything to educate me, but I had rejected all the help then. Now other needs were pressing on the family, and I did not deserve support if Kartar had to sacrifice his own future and ignore the fates of our other siblings. By that time I had come to expect that because of my bad behavior in the past, I was not entitled to much. Gurdial was ready to be admitted to college and two sisters were of marriageable age. In spite of all this, Kartar told me that I could enroll for the third year of college, but I must keep looking actively for a job at the same time. It was agreed that the purpose of going to college was merely to increase my chances of getting a job. It was thought that an employer would consider hiring a college student before he would employ a sit-at-home do-nothing fellow from the village. Besides, college would keep me out of the village, where it was possible to "get absorbed into the dirt." It was a common experience that people who had come from government service or returned from abroad with fashionable clothes and bright ideas would criticize the village people for their sloppy thinking and outmoded ways of doing things. But after living in the village for some time these forward-thinking people themselves fell into the same way of life as the village people had. These formerly fashionable people would become the butt of jokes for their fancy talk of the earlier times and their later deterioration, dirty clothes, sloppy ways, inefficient work, and stupid mistakes. With these considerations, I was encouraged to join the third year class at Punjab University College in Hoshiarpur, where my younger brother Gurdial had already been admitted earlier in 1952.

Aiming High in Hoshiarpur

To fulfill the agreement with Kartar, I half-heartedly applied for a job as a forest ranger, for which Kartar had seen a newspaper advertisement; I also applied for the job of police assistant-sub-inspector (ASI). Now, ASI might not be a class-1 job, but a college degree and a lot of powerful "pull" was still usually required to get the ASI job. Very few of the applicants were selected and some college graduates would use influence through cabinet ministers to land the ASI job. As an ASI, one would have the authority to terrorize the poor, ignorant, rural people, and could extract a lot of bribes from murder cases or from smugglers and other law violators. Many ASI would become rich in a few years, acquire big properties and their wives would display wealth in various ways. I kept corresponding with the forest service and even got called for an interview, but my heart was not in forestry, and therefore I never went for the interview. The ASI job had more of a power and money lure, but by the time the ASI application response came, and the call for an interview was received, I was in the fourth year of college and had been exposed to new ideas, new people, and new experiences. By that time the ASI job also did not have much appeal for me. My sights had been raised by the company of fellow students from good families, and by acquaintances who were pursuing higher goals. I did not want to settle for any low prestige job.

The Punjab University College at Hoshiarpur in those days was the perfect place to raise your sights and aims. The elite of Punjab studied in that College in the 1950s. Both sons of the Chief Minister of Punjab, the venerable Partap Singh Kairon, were students there in my days. Some of my acquaintances there were selected to the Indian Foreign Service, the Indian Administrative Service, the Indian Police Service and other "class-1" jobs. Those were the boys who were going to run the country. Some of my friends and acquaintances were going to medical school to become doctors; other friends and acquaintances were going abroad to England and America for higher education. My very close friend Gurpreet was the son of the minister of education from Patiala. When I had gone to stay in his house for a few days, the police ASI, would be like attendants and doorkeepers in the house of my friend. Interactions with students from such families and with those of high abilities changed my attitude so much that the job of a police ASI seemed unappealing to me, although I did not always feel that I was of the caliber of the people I was associating with. I never disclosed to Kartar that I was ignoring the job searches and interviews, so I felt a bit guilty.

Without telling Kartar about my reluctance to pursue the ASI job, and ignoring the interview call, I asked him if I could continue in college a little bit longer, as I would have a B.A. degree pretty soon. Kartar's reply was memorable for his generosity and willingness to sacrifice. Although I cannot recall his exact words, the gist was this: He had the responsibilities to educate and marry off the remaining sister Chhoti into a good family, to educate the three brothers, and to improve the family circumstances. He was thirty years old and all his friends were married. If he were to marry then, his wife might not allow any further expense to improve the family's circumstances, particularly if she were of the stylish variety. If he married a village wife from a traditional family, it might be possible to help, but it would still be difficult. Many officers, those from rich families, could not live on their own salaries and had to get money from their parents for special purchases. He was contemplating all those things. But he said he was not going to let me down, and I could continue studies while looking for a possible job. And, he said, "By the way, do dress well and live respectably; it makes a difference." I said to myself: "What a brother I have! What a man!" I felt elated but also guilt, since I had wasted precious years in the late forties, which could have been used to become employable and to assist my older brother. I am a bit embarrassed to recall that about fourteen years later when Kartar came to stay with me and went to the University of California at Berkeley, I provided for just the minimum necessities to him, while he had been positively generous to me. Apart from the money, he guided me until I earned the Ph.D. degree.

Burdened with guilt about being dependent on my older brother, I became extremely careful about spending money. I avoided going on educational trips and class excursions to Kashmir and other places, as the excursions, though recommended, were optional. I would have liked to go but I did not feel entitled. I arranged my life so that money considerations entered every one of my plans and activities. I even avoided going to the college coffee shop where a lot of socializing took place. My clothes were better than most, because Kartar had them made by tailors under his own supervision when he was trying to make a military officer out of me. Those formal-looking clothes with empty pockets did not give me a good feeling; I would have preferred to wear understated clothes and to have no concerns about money to spend. It was common for friends to treat other friends to various things, but I did not always want to be the recipient. What made it awkward was that my associations were mostly with rich boys from prominent families, and they were more generous to me than I was to them.

I scored First Division in the B.A. examination, good enough to qualify me for admission to the Physics Honors School of the Punjab University. That admission would get me a Master of Science degree after two years and qualify me to teach in college in India. This would not be prestigious, but it would still be a moderately respectable track to get on. In those days the top status belonged to the military or other class-1 government officers, engineers, and doctors, in that order. College teaching would not be as lucrative as the police ASI job, and in the eyes of street people a police officer enjoyed better status than a professor. It was unthinkable for me to try for the class-1 jobs, because I was beyond the age limit for any Indian Administrative or Foreign Service post or for admission to any engineering or professional college. My family would not even consider something like the study of law. We considered law to be a parasitic occupation requiring cunning and dishonest behavior, although I don't think that way now. Being four years older than all my classmates (thanks to the four years of my errant ways in the village), I had missed all the good opportunities. But admission to Physics Honours School now would mean two more years of sacrifice for Kartar, who had to supply the support. He decided that I should get the M.Sc. degree regardless of the difficulties. This plan would keep me in the University College at Hoshiarpur for two more years, up to June 1956.

The two years at Ahmednagar, although they had been a necessary step, were not as rewarding as they would have been if I could have spent them at a college in Punjab. The first two years of college are when close, lifetime friendships are formed as boys participate in social, athletic, and entertainment activities together. I had spent those two precious years in Ahmednagar, the land of strangers whom I would never meet again during my entire life. For a time, a letter came every few months from Parlahd Ahuja in Bombay, then less frequently, and then all was forgotten. On the other hand, friendships formed with college boys in Punjab would last a lifetime. My college in Hoshiarpur was a much better place to be. It had become an "instant university" when the refugee teaching faculty, who had to leave the University of Punjab at Lahore when that city became part of Pakistan in 1947, regrouped after being displaced. The administrative offices of the University were located at Solan in the Simla Hills, the Botany department was at Khalsa College in Amritsar, the law college was in Jullunder, and so on. Hoshiarpur was a town of no importance, the last stop on a railway line. The only reason the remainder of the refugee university ended up there was that a local politician high up in India's ruling Congress Party used his influence to start Punjab University teaching departments there. They quickly built new buildings and started new departments in them. Later, in about 1960, the university was moved to the newly built capital of the Indian part of Punjab, in Chandigarh.

But the 1950s were the glorious days for our college and for the town of Hoshiarpur. Two sons of the chief minister of Punjab were studying there. Manmohan Singh, a student of economics in those days, with whom I ate lunch sometimes in the student hostel, later went on to Oxford University in England. Much later, he became the finance minister of India and the architect of India's post-socialist economic reforms. Still later, in 2004 he ended up being the prime minister of India. There were some visiting professors from foreign universities, and many foreign students from third world countries. The American Embassy in Delhi frequently sent a staff member, like the charming Mr. Sethi, to our campus. He would show old American movies and documentaries once or twice a month in the open-air theatre "to improve the understanding between our two countries." There were many academic seminars, debates, theatrical plays, and social clubs, like the TKT (talk over a cup of tea, headed by Miss Stock of the English department). Sports and athletic events, drama and comedy nights, and numerous other activities were available to participate in. I was foolish enough to join the National Cadet Corps, a military training corps for college students, with some hope of becoming a military officer through an alternate route. In retrospect this was one of the mistakes of my life and a real robber of opportunity. It took most of my spare time and kept me out of some wonderful and rewarding social and creative opportunities on campus. But I still had a good time. My professors always treated me with high regard; some of them mentioned my name when they wanted to give the example of someone notable or exemplary. Some would just say, "Oh, Gurnam has arrived; now let us begin."

The undergraduate men's hostel where I initially took up residence, half a mile away from campus, was an abandoned Islamia High school converted to a hostel after the Muslims had left for Pakistan. The rooms in this hostel, being really the classrooms of the old Islamia School, were unusually large for a hostel. I shared a room with Naginder Singh, a good-hearted Rajput from the mountain region, and with Baldev Sahai, a shopkeeper's son who was good at mathematics. For the upper-level graduate students, the university took over a portion of the newly constructed "Model Town" still farther away toward the *Cho* (seasonal river). The Model Town hostel was really a complex of homes, built as civilian residences scattered over a large area. But due to the needs of our 'instant university' it was acquired to make a hostel. The only student activity common to all students there was at the dining facility. In theory the senior students did not require much supervision. But there were always rumors flying about some hanky-panky going on in the unsupervised Model Town hostel units where the chief minister's son and other big-wig students lived. I had the opportunity to live in the Model Town hostel one summer. Mango orchards were nearby and walks with friends to the sandy banks of the seasonal river were a source of joy. In the older part of the Model Town, middle class families and some professors lived.

But I preferred living in the undergraduate hostel which was closer to the college and a shorter walk. There was hustle and bustle in the central courtyard and in the dining hall. The kitchen servants attended to our needs. We chatted with friends, told jokes, and shared stories of the day at mealtimes and planned activities for the evenings. Frequently, we walked to the "city" to look around and explored its bazaars. Hoshiarpur was compact enough to not be overwhelming but old and complex enough, with small industries and handicrafts, to be interesting. At other times we walked toward the Model Town and observed the civilian population between the two hostels. There was always some interesting activity or function in the college campus after dinner. We were in the company of friends, the homework was negligible, and the pressure of examinations came only once a year. For me, every day in this college was a delight, except for the nagging guilt of being a burden on my family.

Segregation of the Sexes

The system of co-education had been adopted at the college level, but girls in the University College made up only about ten percent of the student population. This was not only because fewer girls were sent to schools then, but also because there were colleges exclusively for girls in other towns, where the parents felt their daughters were "safer." In our English class there would be four or five girls in a class of about fifty students. The professor would make sure the girls sat in front and were separated from the boys, and he kept alert to make sure that boys were not up to any mischief where the girs were concerned. It was uncommon for boys and girls to socialize together or talk casually. There was a hostel for women about 100 yards from the campus; the boys' hostels were much farther away and in a different direction.

In earlier times, it was not acceptable for unrelated men and women to spend time together; but customs were being relaxed and changing fast in the 1950s. Most of the boys wanted to develop a cordial relationship with some one of the small number of girls on campus, but only a few were ever successful. City boys were smoother and some of them were friendly with girls, but the rural boys would consider it a scandal if a boy walked a girl to her hostel, or rode his bicycle along with hers toward her house.

Those who were shy, unsophisticated, and not outstanding in any activity had little chance of interaction with girls, although they all wanted to. If a girl had to initiate a conversation, she would pick some talented or outstanding boy, not some mediocre slob. Those who were in drama, debating clubs, TKT, the student magazine, or some special activity club could find an excuse and a reason to talk to girls. For most of the boys with village backgrounds, who had always been forbidden to talk to women not related to them, talking to a girl felt like crossing a barrier. The first efforts of the boys from villages to speak with girls were frequently accompanied by extreme nervousness and excitement. For them, talking to a girl who was not a relative was the equivalent of "scoring". As time went by, some of the boys got used to the experience, but many never talked to a college girl during their entire four-year stay at college. The only boys with village backgrounds who had contact with girls were the communists, as the communist girls were rarely shy or timid.

I was one of those shy village boys. I had a strong crush on a girl named Diljit Kaur, who used to attend our English class. She may have been preparing for some special examination, as she did not attend any other classes. From her regal face, impeccable composure, and sophistication it appeared that she was highly intelligent. Diljit was professor's sister there, who was able to use his influence to arrange for her to attend the English class only without being a regular college student. The professor was a tall, good-looking man, and if he had not had the turban and beard, you might have thought he was an Englishman. (The awkward shape of his turban indicated that he was not a Jat and obviously was not from south of the Sutlej. In those days, turban styles used to be peculiar to individual castes and regions, although homogenization was starting to set in.) I had learned that Diljit was from a famous Ahluwalia family of Kapurthala. Whatever her caste or religion, she was like a princess to me. Her family now lived in the Model Town area of Hoshiarpur. She had a younger sister who was equally pretty but was more ample in build and had lighter complexion. As was the custom in those days, the family or a part of it would go for a walk around the Model Town neighborhoods before twilight. My friends and I would.walk at the same time in order to steal a glance at Diljit

All my friends thought Diljit was exceptionally beautiful. They would say, "God has crafted her carefully in his leisure time while most of us were just made in a hurry; and some of us even look as if we had been manufactured on contract." She was tall, with perfect body architecture. She had patrician facial bones, with sharp small nose, medium high cheekbones and a dimple on the chin that made a knockout impression. Her features included the most perfect set of teeth and large, limpid and expressive eyes. She had an impressive walking style. People in our villages really admired a good walking style. A woman's legs were not open to scrutiny and a married woman's face would be covered too; but walking style is something that could not be hidden. Diljit was always elegantly and properly dressed and had a great dignity about her. Her hair was done in the most alluring styles; sometimes her hairstyle was an imitation of some historical figure or some movie star. Sometimes there were four or five rolling curls dangling on each side of Diljit's face, sometimes there were simple braids, and sometimes she wore a chignon on the back of her head, which made her look extra sophisticated. When I felt the teacher was just talking about ordinary, familiar stuff, I would draw Diljit's pretty face on paper instead of listening to the lecture.

I wanted to talk to Diljit and develop a friendship, but I was intimidated by her elegance, and that made it hard for me to initiate a conversation. She might look at me briefly but would immediately lower or divert her gaze, so as to not seem immodest. She would not smile at me because that would be like inviting attention, but whenever she smiled while talking to other girls, her beautiful teeth and expressive face made a dramatic impression on me. In my mind she became more and more beautiful and more and more unapproachable as time went on. One day she came to our English class with glasses. She was not any less beautiful, but I felt as if the glasses were like a blemish on perfection. Even when the English class was divided in two sections and Diljit was assigned to the other section, I did not give up the hope of talking to her. Finally there came the news that Diljit was engaged to be married to a military officer. Although I had never even talked to her, I took the news of her engagement as a big personal loss. But soon it was springtime and the end of the academic year. This provided a fortunate transition period for me, as I had to go home to our village for the spring holidays. Gradually I recovered from this imaginary loss, but my longing for Diljit always left an empty place in my heart.

I had been smitten this way before once or twice; but I had never developed the courage or skill to speak to girls even when I was of college age. I think this was partly due to the fact that it was continuously pounded into us that making contact with a girl was wrong unless she was already a relative or the situation required one to speak with her. "Nice girls" were trained to not look or smile at strangers, and I could never approach a girl unless she indicated interest by a smile, a gaze, or body language. Even after I experienced the freedom of America, I waited for girls to indicate interest by a look or smile or even by initiating conversation.

Physics Honors School and My First Paying Job

In the B.A. examination, I had scored high enough marks to qualify for admission to the *third* year of Physics Honors School, but my admission depended on my passing an additional examination in mathematics. Students already in the Honors School had taken those math courses over the two prior years. For most students the first year of Physics Honors School began after attending two years of regular college; so the alternate route of passing the B.A. examination and entering the third year of the Honors School was like starting the fifth year of college. Anyway, I prepared for the required math test on my own for a couple of months during the summer break, and I barely squeaked through that examination. As a result, my admission to the third year of Physics Honors School was confirmed. That situation was like a professional school. Once a student got into Physics Honors School, he expected smooth sailing until graduation with an M.Sc. degree, unless something went wrong.

So a year later, I received the B.Sc. degree in the first division from the Physics Honors School. Second division was considered mediocre and third division barely fulfilled the requirements for passing. After one more year, I expected to get the M.Sc. Degree and again hoped to place in the first division. But a couple of days before the M.Sc. written examination, I came down with a serious illness; I could not even get out of bed, much less appear for the written test. The doctors who came to my hostel room to attend on me never understood the nature of the malady. That illness was very nasty and totally debilitating. The effects of that illness stayed with me for a couple of decades and some were even permanent. It could have been caused by the pickled pork that my roommate Naginder had brought from his home in the mountains. I had never eaten anything like that before but I expected that it would give me strength. A couple of my professors from the Honor School came to my sickbed in the hostel and sympathized about my being ill and being unable to take the M.Sc. examination. According to the regulations, the examination could be taken only once a year. Instead of requiring me to take another examination the next year, however, the authorities gave me a pass without having to take the written test, just based on my work during the year. But without the examination, they placed me in the second division, which was a lower score than I aspired to. This diminished my chance of being competitive in getting a good teaching or research job.

For example, when I applied for a lecturer's position at Government College, Ludhiana, I was not accepted; another candidate who had scored in the first division got that job. A couple of weeks later in August 1956 I did get a similar job as a lecturer in physics at Government College in Gurdaspur, a less desirable location. Before that I had never had any kind of paying job; I had done only the farm work on our own land. In our society, getting paid for labor, whether from an individual or a house, was considered menial. People worked for friends and relatives without pay, whether such work was temporary or went on for years. Our Jat people would work only for the government or for a corporation in a city unless they could go abroad, where they would do any kind of work.

This job as a lecturer in physics was not a bad start for me. It involved supervising and demonstrating the laboratory experiments and occasionally filling in as a class lecturer. I knew some other graduates from the Punjab University who were working there in other departments about the same time. In Gurdaspur I lived in a rented house that I shared with other "professors." Like other bachelor lecturers, I ate all my meals at a Punjabi style *dhaba* (restaurant), according to a monthly contract, as was the custom in those days. One paid the agreed amount per month and one was served the going fare for lunch and dinner every day.

But Gurdaspur was a small town and a dull place. My associates, particularly a young Hindu lecturer in chemistry, would say to me, "Gurnam, we don't have much of a choice and have to rot in this nowhere town Gurdaspur. You, on the other hand, could go to some place like Khalsa College, Amritsar, and could have an exciting life there. Do yourself a favor and escape this dead town." I was inclined to think the same way. So it was after only a few weeks in Gurdaspur that I arranged for an interview with the authorities in Khalsa College, Amritsar. I already knew some people in that city and had spent the Diwali festival there with the many relatives of Kartar's wife. I had gone in a truck with boys and girls of those relatives to the Golden Temple, on Diwali evening in late October 1956. They were a lively and cheerful bunch and I had already become friendly with some of them. So the thought of living in Amritsar was quite appealing to me; a job in Khalsa College, Amritsar, would be much better for my future, I thought.

Lecturer in Khalsa College, Amritsar

Very quickly after I applied for the job, I was called for an interview at Khalsa College. The interviewing committee included the Principal of the college, the head of the physics department, a trustee of the governing board of the college, and a couple of other people. The head of the physics department, Prof. Bali, a clean-shaved Brahmin who wore a turban, had retired, leaving a vacancy. Being a well-turned out Sikh with beard and turban helped me in getting the job at Khalsa College. My interview went quite well and they invited me to join the staff of the physics department as soon as possible. Since the job in Gurdaspur was temporary, I resigned there immediately and joined Khalsa College at Amritsar as a lecturer in physics in November 1956.

My days in Amritsar were also some of the most exciting times of my life, although a bit hectic near the end, when I was preparing to depart for the United States. The college maintained residences only for the principal and some senior faculty members, so I lived in a building on the College campus called the Patiala Hostel. In the heyday of the institution, the Patiala Hostel accommodated the senior students, but the prestige and enrollment of the college had declined after the Partition of India. There were no longer any Sikh students from far-away places like the North West Frontier Province. More students were local and fewer needed to live in the hostel. So now a part of this hostel was allotted as residences to a few junior faculty members who were bachelors. We young "professors" had common dining facilities and a cook; there was great camaraderie, intellectual stimulation, and discussions on various subjects at dinner times. Discussions ranged over many topics, such as national politics, the value of socialism to thwart communism in the developing India, Shakespeare's plays, the benefits of eating raw, hot green peppers, and so forth, as the young professors had expertise in diverse fields.

My job at Khalsa College in the physics department required more teaching than the previous one at Gurdaspur did. I was a bit raw and inexperienced at this and controlling the huge class of high-energy freshmen from various backgrounds. Some of the students would test a new teacher to see what mischief they could get away with in class, and some would even make funny noises like grade school kids. Khalsa College students did have the reputation of being tough and physical, but I did not expect them to be childish. A lecturer had to be tactful about class control; he taught the students but he had no authority to give them scores or grades, so he had the responsibility but no power. Since the college examination was only given once a year and the all-important university examination was given only every two years, most freshman students were not terribly concerned about studies yet. With some tips from the experienced professors like Khanna and Bedi, and by developing familiarity with the students, it took me a couple of weeks to make the lecture room orderly. After that I settled into the teaching routines quite well. My time in Amritsar was highly enjoyable but it passed too quickly; the academic year ended about mid-June 1957. I was not going to lecture there the next year as I was preparing to go to America, so even my Khalsa College experience was brief.

Communists on Campus and in Society

Leftist politics were very much a part of campus life in the 1950s. Even in the Punjab University College at Hoshiarpur, some of the best and the brightest student leaders advocated communism. College campuses and labor unions were hotbeds of communism, although this was not true of society in general. Bright young students and most professors of economics saw communism as the answer to all the ills of humanity. They thought communism was about equality, brotherhood, and fairness, where the existing wealth and property would belong to everybody in the nation, not just to the elite and the exploiting and bloodsucking capitalists who happened to possess it then. They also said that inequality of wealth meant an unjust society. The professors of economics even believed that the capitalist system was too wasteful and not efficient for the production of things that humanity needed. They believed that a cooperative farm was more efficient for production and for the use of labor than individual farmers running separate operations. So they tried to bring about communism with missionary zeal and were frequently inspired and aided by communist countries like Russia.

At first the ruling Congress Party of Nehru was favorably inclined toward the communists; they had been struggling against the "British Imperialists" up to 1947 and considered the communists as their natural, anti-imperialist allies. But soon after the

Independence of India, the objective of the communists became not democratic socialism but grabbing power for their own party, which they thought could be done only by sabotaging the existing democratic institutions. They started derailing trains, bombing industrial facilities, and terrorizing landowners, with the purpose of creating anarchy. They hoped that the Communist Party would take over if they could just destabilize the country enough, as the Russian communists had done after World War I and the Chinese communists had done after World War II. Soon the new Indian government started cracking down on these terrorists and looked at communists with suspicion. The Indian government itself was socialist and anti-capitalist, so they were not really suppressing the peaceful communists. Just as religious fanatics cannot accept co-existence with other religions, the communists were impatient for their own party rule. They did not want to wait to win through the ballot, although in the provinces of Kerala and Bengal they did control the elected provincial governments, off and on. The communists said that their chance of winning through the ballot was not good, because "the imperialists use unfair methods to win over the ignorant masses." So the communists saw their best hope in violence, terror, and anarchy, until the laborers and peasants were "awakened."

Most professors of economics in India would say: "Social justice is not possible without the government's control of the means of production and without equitable distribution of wealth." In 1956, a great cheer went up among campus communists in India when Russians cracked down on the freedom fighters in Hungary and suppressed the anti-Communist revolt. They said, "We must crush those reactionaries like Imry Nagy everywhere to create the workers' paradise under communism on this earth." The Indian government was pro-Russia and may have condoned the suppression in Hungary, but they did not want to encourage the communists in India. To its believers, communism was like a religion. Not only did they want to overthrow the present rulers and control the government in their own country; they felt that until the entire world was under communist rule, there would remain a threat of capitalism. It was like the Wahabi Muslims, who believe that any *kafir* (non-Muslim) alive is a threat to Islam. The communists felt the same way as the zealots in every religion feel about dominating the world with their belief. They said that reactionaries who arose against communism should be dealt with the same way Christians used to deal with devil worshippers. Their view was that communism could be in danger as long as the "evil of capitalism" existed anywhere in the world.

The Communists were skillful at writing stirring songs and slogans to arouse the laborer and the peasant and to inspire missionary zeal in the intellectual. The Russian embassy would mail to anyone of influence, the magazines in English such as *Soviet Life*. Those magazines presented grandiose pictures and impressive images of the wonderful life and prosperity under communism. Pictures of tractors operating on cooperative farms, of large factories, of the visiting communist party leader cheering their patriotic work, of marching groups of healthy, uniformed school children, and of the development of large technical and industrial projects were all designed to display the virtues of vibrant and benevolent communism as an alternative to the decaying and pernicious capitalism.

The young communist students argued that all the progress and prosperity in Russia and China, as presented in the magazines, was due to communism. "Where there are no capitalist blood suckers to drain away the wealth, society prospers automatically. Look at those pictures of fat and healthy Russian and Chinese children in the magazines and compare them with the scrawny Indian children! The capitalists have put chains on women also. Whereas in the Soviet Union women are free and prominent in every walk of life and there is equality of sexes, Indian women are held back by the exploiting capitalist system," they would assert. As one would expect, the women in India who were active in communist propaganda were more educated, assertive, outgoing and articulate than the average woman. In some people's minds and according to some campus gossip, the communist girls were ladies of easy virtue; people who spread such rumors said that the communists did not believe in God and had no morals. But these gossip mongers were confusing assertiveness with loose behavior.

Whenever people were frustrated with social problems or with government incompetence and inefficiency, it was common for people to suggest remedies without much thought and based purely on their personal prejudices. The conservative or right-wing thinkers would say: "What this country needs is a dictatorship; a tough dictator could beat the stupidity and corruption out of this country." On the other hand a left-leaning person in India would say: "Communism is the only answer to all that corruption and lack of discipline; those communists know how to organize and run things; they can improve and make progress in any society." Once my wife went to visit India in the 1960s, where she experienced a lot of inefficiency and disorder in the working of everything. And her remark was: "This society is so hopeless; even communism will fail if it comes to India." This remark was indicative of the popular belief still prevalent in those days that communists could fix anything and could make any society function efficiently and smoothly.

My father was very much against the communist politicians as they sang their songs about redistribution of wealth and land. He would say, "The communists don't believe in God; they are immoral and want to break the social order; they want to take away the lands that our ancestors acquired with great struggle and want to give our property away to the landless low castes. Where is the justice in taking away what is rightfully mine! Let these people go somewhere to acquire property as our ancestors did long time ago. Hard work and initiative is necessary, and not robbing people of their property."

In the University College at Hoshiarpur the communists operated through the leftist party on campus, called The Student Front; even the principal of the college was afraid of confrontation with leaders of The Student Front. In Amritsar, around Khalsa College and particularly in the Medical College, the most articulate and influential groups of students were the communists. To be a communist was to be a fair-minded intellectual; otherwise you were in favor of the bloodsucking capitalists and the selfish, backward-thinking landowners. Some of those medical college students regularly visited the residence of a relative of my brother, Dr. Surat Singh Sarkaria, near Khalsa College. The respected doctor had sympathies with these student communists; he provided support and facilities for their meetings. So there gathered a social circle of singers, poets, skit performers, speech makers, party workers and fun loving people around his residence. You did not really have to be a party member to join the fun. Young communist girls were as active, articulate and ideological as the boys were. I was used to the ways of village women who were trained to be inhibited and who were expected to avoid conversation with strange men to whom they were not related. But the girls who associated with communist student leaders on campus were usually bold and assertive; they never acted shy and coy. The communists seemed to have brought some verbal equality, frankness, and courage to girls in India. But perhaps this change was just due to the upbringing of those educated girls, who were a couple of decades ahead of the villages in advancement, and not due to the communist ideology specifically. In any case, social changes were taking place rapidly among women about that time because of education.

Once I was invited by a group of mostly communist boys and girls to go on a bike ride and picnic. We rode our bikes to the picnic site on the banks of a canal a few miles from Amritsar. The games, the songs, the poems, the skits, and the entertainment by the communist volunteers were quite enjoyable, sometimes moving. The songs expressed optimism about the uplifting of downtrodden people, the virtues of communist ideology, patriotism, and paths to progress. In this picnic they all acted like sincere friends and likeable individuals. They were local boys and girls and not some threatening strangers or crooked politicians, so they all trusted each other. There was no excess or slickness, but sincere interest in improving the condition of people and of the nation, and in eliminating injustice. They were young idealists and not the hated terrorists who bombed buildings, derailed trains, or killed landowners, as the regular communists were reported to be doing in those days. I liked the whole experience and became a close acquaintance of some of them. But as in my Hoshiarpur days, I could never overcome my conservative Jat landowner mentality to embrace communism.

Since most of the communist students were pretty bright and articulate, many of them got the top administrative and police jobs in the Indian government through competitive examinations. Nearly all of them were altered by the experience of power, privilege, and responsibility. These former communists, now in positions of authority, gradually started arresting, prosecuting, and punishing other communist and leftist lawbreakers. Protecting society from terrorist and other violent activities of the communists became part of the job for these former communists. Some of the former communist students traveled to capitalist countries like Australia, Canada, and England as they did not have any record of being criminals. In their new countries they soon forgot about communism and started accumulating wealth to become full-fledged capitalists.

Not an April Fool

After World War II, there seemed to be a wave of liberal thought, optimism, and generosity among U.S. policy makers toward the outside world. Americans wanted justice and prosperity in the whole world and they wanted to help create it. The hardships of the Great Depression and World War II had passed; unemployment was low, and America felt prosperous and optimistic. The professors in universities wanted to do their part to educate foreign students. Even some conservative policy makers felt that these U.S.-educated foreign students would create goodwill for America when they returned to their own countries and therefore would be worth the investment. Among these foreign students, some from India were also admitted to American universities.

When I was in Amritsar, I had started applying to universities in the United States to obtain admission to a graduate school in physics, with the hope of working for a Ph.D. If I had not fallen ill and had been able to take the M.Sc. examination, I could have obtained a first division (top grade) M.Sc. degree at Punjab University. Then my chances in India would have been better. But under the circumstances, it made sense to try to go abroad for higher education. By that time, I knew the big university names like Berkeley, Harvard, MIT, Stanford, UCLA, Columbia, Princeton, Cal Tech., and so on. I applied for admission to a few of these famous universities. Most of them responded positively but they did not promise any financial assistance.

Then one day in early 1957, when I was back in Hoshiarpur to visit some college friends, my former classmate, Faqir Chand Khanna, who had become a research fellow after getting the M.Sc. degree there, said to me, "Gurnam, I have this application blank from the University of Washington, which is in Seattle on the west coast of the U.S. and not to be confused with Washington, D.C. I personally have no plan to go anywhere this year since I have a fellowship in this university. Why don't you take this application blank and apply for admission to their Ph.D. program?" I brought the application back with me to Amritsar and requested two professors in Hoshiarpur to write letters of recommendation directly to the University of Washington, as required by the rules of the application. Then I sent my completed application to Seattle. I did not really expect much of a response; in India such applications were usually thrown in the waste basket. My application was apparently a bit late also, and the University had to decide quickly.

To my surprise and delight, not many days had passed before I received a telegram from the University of Washington saying, "We offer you an assistant-ship for the 1957-58 academic year, Stipend 175 dollars per month for Nine Months. University fees exempt. Early decision appreciated. Letter of confirmation follows." In fact the telegram reached my village on 4-4-1957, because that was the home address I had given; I think my father mailed the telegram to me then. The letter of confirmation written on April 3, arrived the next day. I mentioned to a friend in Amritsar that I had an offer of admission in the U.S. and possibly a teaching fellowship to go with it. His reaction was "Have you looked at the calendar? It is April Fool time! Some body is surely making an April Fool out of you." My brother Kartar was visiting his in-laws in Amritsar at that time to attend their relative's wedding. He said to me, "Gurnam, let me take a look at the letter you received from America." He read the letter and then said, "This looks real!" Then he held the paper against the sun in front of his eyes. The watermark, stamped in the paper in a circular pattern, said "University of Washington. 1861." Kartar remarked, *Shaid teri kismet badl gai*," i.e., "perhaps your fortune has taken a turn." It was only after this event that I told Kartar that two years earlier I had purposely skipped the interviews for the forestry job and for the ASI job. Kartar said, "That was a very bad thing you did; how did you know or expect that you would get this opportunity?" But I was happy not to have taken the lower road, and Kartar was happy for me.

One never knows what step will lead to what end, or which fork in the road will turn out to be the more beneficial. If I had gotten the forestry job or the police job, or even the military job, my life might have been entirely different. If I had been lucky and had not been ill at the time of my M.Sc. examination, I would have gotten better grades and my employment prospects in India would have been a bit better. Then I would never have come to America. I would have retired in India at 55 as an old man. And if I had had any success with some of those girls that I was fascinated with, I would not have tried to go to America. Now I am questioning if getting the education and going to

America really provided a happier life than I might have had as an uneducated landowner, grand old patriarch in the village, commanding obedience from my sons and their families and respect from everyone in the village brotherhood. In old age, riches in America cannot make up for the loss of separation from the extended family and break from the ancestral village land.

On the 14th of August in 1957, I said farewell to my mother and sisters. My cousin Sarwan walked some distance with us and said goodbye. Then my father, brother Kirpal and I rode our camel to Rampura Phul where they put me on the train. I had to travel to Delhi first to pick up my travel papers. As the lights of Indian Independence Day on August 15, 1957, were shining bright there, I departed from Delhi alone for America. Actually I took the train on August 15, from Delhi to Calcutta in order to catch the Thailand Airways flight from Calcutta to Hong Kong. I did this to save about five dollars in airfare compared to the Delhi-Hong Kong flight, as I had borrowed the travel money from Kartar and felt awful about putting additional demand on him.

Going to America used to be a big deal, with dozens of people giving the traveler a grand sendoff. In 1955 when my friend Gurpreet went to study in America, two buses full of people and many of us in several cars traveled from Patiala in Punjab for a three day trip to say farewell to him at the airport in Delhi. For the duration, his family arranged for all of us to stay in Delhi. We all had a big party in Delhi, like it was a wedding. By contrast, my departure in 1957 was a lonely affair, with only my father and brother Kirpal at the train station. And I was also willing to suffer the two day Indian train journey from Delhi to Calcutta, just to save a little on airfare.

CHAPTER 8

RELIGION IN OUR SOCIETY

I am a Sikh by heritage and culture but I was never very religious. I am writing this because religion permeated every aspect of our rural life. It was common and not impolite to ask a stranger, "What are you?" That was a question about his inherited religion and caste, and then people treated him according to his answer. Whether you were a believer or not, the prevalence of religion in society always affected your life, and in some circumstances you could even be victimized because of your religion. What follows is based on my personal perceptions rather than on any authoritative religious knowledge. In keeping with common English usage, I sometimes omit embellishments like Sri, Guru, Sahib, Ji, etc., that are commonly employed with the names of sacred persons and entities in Punjabi usage, but such omissions should not be interpreted as diminished reverence for those entities on my part.

Sikhism evolved from the teachings of Guru Nanak, who was born in Punjab in 1469. Nanak did not try to start a new religion and never said that the old religions were false, but he decried the frequent perversion of religions that, he believed, were not being practiced truthfully by many of their followers. He also rejected the irrational superstitions, meaningless rituals, caste systems, fake piousness, and hatred of other faiths that were being practiced in the name of religion. He spoke against inconsistencies between professed beliefs and actual deeds. Nanak also decried the prevalent attitudes toward women, saying something like this: "You are born of a woman; you marry a woman; no one would exist without a woman; how can you call her bad or inferior, the one to whom kings are born!" He conveyed his famous message to Muslim and Hindu religious figures in terms like this: "Let compassion be thy mosque, let faith be thy prayer mat.... Let truth be thy prophet, good deeds be thy prayer, let honest living be thy Quran...." He wanted people to practice devotion to God, truth, honest deeds, humility, compassion and service to others; and not just depend on outward symbols of piety.

The mystical experiences of Nanak and of his successors were written in the form of poetry and became our scriptures. Ironically, his teachings and the work of his successor gurus, evolved into another religion. His disciples were called Sikh, a Punjabi pronunciation of the Sanskrit word *siksh*, meaning learner, disciple, or seeker. The basics of Nanak's teachings start with the *Mool Mantra* (root mantra, essential word, basic belief) in the beginning of the Sikh holy book called *Granth*, and are stated thus: Ik *Ongkar, Sat Naam, Karta Purkh, NirBhau, NirVer, Akal Moort, Ajuni, Se Bhang, Gur Parsad*...This can be translated as: One God Who is All Pervasive, Eternal Truth is Its Essence, Creator Being, Without Fear, Without Enmity, Timeless Entity, Not a Life Form, Self-Existing, By the Guru's Grace.... The word *naam* can mean "name" or "identity," but in Sikh scriptures it is given the transcendental meaning of "God's Essence." The word *guru* means a revered teacher or spiritual master; but in the Sikh scriptures the words *Guru, Waheguru* and *Satguru* are used to describe God because He is the Teacher, Wonderful Master and True Enlightener. Nanak expected that his Sikhs would be familiar with traditional Indian concepts like *karma* (deeds whose consequences the soul reaps later), *dharma* (divine law on which the order of the world rests; sacred duty), *punn* (pious deed), *paap* (harmful deed), *atma* (immortal soul) whose aim was to merge with *Parmatma* (highest soul, God), the suffering of atma in the material world, and *mukti* (nirvana) achieved when the soul is released from the cycle of *transmigration,* to merge with Parmatma. These concepts were a part of our ancient beliefs, culture and vocabulary.

Nanak did not repudiate all Hindu traditions but did speak against superstitious practices, corrupted ways, and the caste system which had become imbedded in our culture. He did not reject the Muslim beliefs either, but he did disapprove when he saw discrepancies between the professed beliefs and the actual actions, in particular the discrepancy between a religion of peace, and the violent, intolerant, hateful actions of some of its followers. He referred to God with Hindu names like Har, Ram, Gopal, Gobind, Prabh, Brahm, as well as the Muslim names Allah, Maalik, and Rabb, etc. According to Sikhism it is wrong to separate people on the basis of religion. Nanak said, "There is no Hindu; there is no Muslim" and that all people are from the same *Nature* and created of the same *Light*. He also said that pilgrimages, penance, and rituals were not as beneficial as ethical living, compassion, and service to others.

Guru Nanak was succeeded by nine other human gurus whose teachings and writings followed the same spirit. The second guru, Angad, perfected the Gurmukhi script for the Punjabi language. The third guru, Amar Das, added to the scriptures and organized the Sikh community. The fourth guru, Ram Das, founded the city of Amritsar, including the sacred pool and temple. The fifth guru, Arjan Dev, compiled the teachings of Nanak and the other gurus into the book which became the holy Granth of the Sikhs, including in it also the poetry of Indian sages like Kabir, Farid, Namdev, Ravi Das, and others whose writings were consistent with the Sikh principles. When the scholarly Guru Arjun Dev, was martyred at the hands of the rulers of India, his successor Guru Hargobind decided that it would be necessary to defend the faith by the sword; that event shifted the thinking of the Sikhs. The seventh guru, Har Rai, taught while traveling all over Punjab, including to our village. The eighth guru, Har Krishn, died at a young age. When the ninth guru, Teg Bahadur, was beheaded by the Emperor of Delhi for preaching non-Islamic doctrines and defending non-Islamic people, his successor, Guru Gobind Singh, realized the importance of defending one's beliefs by the sword. The peace-loving, spiritual seekers then had to learn to defend themselves.

Nanak did not intend to start a new religion, but with the new name Waheguru for God, with its own holy book, Granth, with the new script for the Punjabi language (although Guru Nanak used neither the script nor the modern Punjabi language exclusively),

181

and with the symbols and rules introduced by Guru Gobind Singh, Sikhism did nevertheless evolve into a religion.

Guru Gobind Singh had the miraculous ability to inspire others and also to draw inspiration from higher sources. He invoked Waheguru, although he could call it Shiva or a goddess like Chandi because many such names were used to address God, to empower him. At the *Baisakhi* celebration on the Indian new-year's day in 1699, he invited any Sikh who would be willing to make the necessary sacrifices to volunteer for a special cadre dedicated to defending the faith. For the first five volunteers, called *Panj Piaray* (the five beloved), he conducted a special initiation, the a*mrit* (nectar of immortality) ceremony, after which they were designated "saint soldiers" or *khalsa*, whose uniform was to consist of five symbols: uncut hair, a special comb, a steel bracelet, knickers to the knee, and a sword. He added the word "Singh" (lion) to their first names and to his own name, and he dropped their family names to discourage caste identification. People attribute various meanings to the symbols. The most common I have heard are: Uncut Hair is for natural and simple appearance as spiritual people; Comb is just to keep the hair in order; Steel Bracelet is to remind you to do only what is right; the regulation size Knickers are to avoid unchaste activity and the Sword is to use for the righteous defense. All the Sikhs who were thus initiated with the amrit and who wore the five symbols, were known as a*mrit dhari* or *khalsa*; the remainder who adopted the basic Sikh teachings but who did not wish to keep these symbols were called *sahej dhari*, the easy going ones. Over time, the sahej dhari voice diminished among the Sikhs, because the amrit dhari or *kesh dhari* (hair keepers) began to consider those without the symbols as lesser Sikhs. Some of the sahej dhari Sikhs fell back into the Hindu fold, depending on their clan affiliations and circumstances. Only the Punjabi-speaking Jat did not fell back into Hinduism, although many continued some traditional Hindu practices.

During his lifetime, Guru Gobind Singh declared that there would be no more human gurus, because followers tend to worship a human guru like a god. He ordered that henceforth the *word* in the holy Granth should be treated as the guru and guide. He said, "Those who call me God, will die in the pit of hell; I am a servant of the almighty God and just came to see the play of this world." Even in the seventeenth century, he wanted to give power to the downtrodden. After counting the names of some underprivileged castes, he declared, "…To these humble people, I want to give the kingdom." Although Sikhs were expected to follow the ways prescribed by the tenth guru, there were no special restrictions on food or personal activities. In fact the Sikh teachings were not about the issues of food, dress, and rituals; they were about truth, deeds, and man's relationship with God. The Sikh community did formalize some rules, such as: do not cut the hair; do not smoke tobacco; do not commit adultery or take a Muslim woman as wife (to prevent abuses during wars); and do not eat *helal* (Muslim kosher) meat. Muslims were required by their faith to kill an animal slowly while reciting the *Qalima* over it (to make it kosher or legitimate), but Sikhs said the slow method of slaughter was unnecessarily cruel and that any killing should be by *jhatka* (with a quick jerk; with one cut). Nowadays, though, the only one of these rules that ordinary Sikhs follow strictly is the "no smoking" rule; violations of the other rules are generally tolerated or ignored. *Reciting God's Name, preparing ethical deeds, telling the truth, living in humility, acting with compassion, earning an honest livelihood, and sharing with others* are the essentials.

182

A practicing Sikh recites selected portions from *gurbani* (Guru's holy word), such as *Japji, Jaap, Svayye, anand,* usually after a bath before sunrise; some recite evening and bedtime prayers also. Other selections like *Asa di Vaar* and *Sukhmani* may be recited by more devoted people or on special occasions. A *granthi* (priest) in the *gurdwara* (guru's door, Sikh temple), reads appropriate portions of the holy Granth for each occasion. For important occasions, the entire Granth is recited, sometimes without interruption (*akhand paath*). After *bhog* (completion) of any recitation, they recite *anand* verses and the final *ardas* (prayer or invocation) is spoken. The ardas is followed by distribution of *parsad* (consecrated food, usually made from flour, sugar and *ghee*); afterwards, everyone is expected to share the common *langer* (free food) in the *gurdwara*.

After Guru Gobind Singh ended the tradition of human gurus, Sikhism was left without any recognized leader. The organizations that evolved to manage the affairs of the Sikh community were not as effective as a single recognized head would have been. After a long struggle, in the 1920s the Singh Sabha movement had the Gurdwara Act passed. That law established the S.G.P.C., an organization to manage the gurdwaras in Punjab. Nowadays, however, some of the energy of the S.G.P.C. is devoted to politics and the acquisition of political power. In the village gurdwaras no qualifications were required for priests who recited the holy Granth. Anyone who could read the Gurmukhi script could serve as acting priest for the day. It could be an old farmer, a young housewife, or even some unemployable drifter who had learned the Gurmukhi letters. I hear that in some gurdwaras, ritualistic practices are observed, of the type that Guru Nanak considered useless superstitions.

Understandably, members of the Brahmin caste, who were pillars of the old Hindu religion, rarely became Sikhs. The *Kshatri* were the first Sikhs; they were more aware and more learned than people of the lower castes, and the Sikh gurus themselves were Kshatri. But gradually other non-Muslim people, notably the Punjabi *Jat*, became followers of the Sikh gurus. They did not consider this a change of religion but just additional spiritual practice with the benefit of the blessings of a holy guru. Some Muslims also became admirers of the fifth guru, Guru Arjan Dev, but when Emperor Jahangir heard about it, he took measures to forbid any Muslims from becoming Sikhs. It was dangerous for a Muslim in India to follow any practice other than Islam, because after a fatwa, such a convert could be killed by other Muslims for committing such insult to Mohammed. There were no significant instances of Muslims abandoning Islam; their leaders would never allow such a convert to live as an example for others. The only choices for a Muslim were to believe, to pay lip service to Islam, to keep quiet, or to die.

Spiritual and Worldly Swords

A religious institution could enrich its leaders with offerings and donations from worshippers. The successors of Guru Nanak began to acquire wealth, power, and prominence. For hundreds of years the Muslim rulers of Punjab had humiliated their Hindu subjects, so they could not tolerate the Sikhs and their upstart religion. Besides, the Muslims believed that anything non-Islamic was a curse on the earth and an insult to Mohammed. The prominence of the Sikh gurus drew the attention of the rulers. The death of the scholarly Guru Arjun at the hands of the rulers of India turned the Sikhs into a militant defense group. Starting with the sixth guru, the Sikh gurus were expected to be both spiritual guides and worldly kings, capable of self-defense and having steady sources of income. And after the tenth guru, Gobind Singh, the Sikhs got a reputation for being fierce warriors, not just spiritual seekers. Attempts by the rulers to suppress and eliminate the Sikhs were continuous. Guru Gobind Singh's father was executed by the Mughal emperor, and the Guru also lost all of his four sons and many of his followers in the conflicts and battles with the rulers, their provincial heads, and their allies.

Guru Gobind Singh died in central India in 1708 after being stabbed by two of his Pathan Muslim retainers. Then his disciple Banda, who had been a *sadhu* (Hindu ascetic) before meeting the Guru, came to Punjab with the Guru's arrows. He gathered the Sikhs in 1710 to conquer the provincial stronghold of Sirhind, and the Sikhs occupied an area of Punjab between the Sutlej and Jumna rivers for a time. But in December 1715, after a long siege and much loss of life the emperor's forces finally defeated and captured Banda, his family, and several hundred of his surviving supporters. They were taken in chains to the emperor in Delhi, and a few of them were cut daily in public. The executioners would saw off a head slowly, or cut one limb, or remove one eye at a time to prolong the suffering and for a public spectacle, until all, including the children, were killed. But the Ardas mentions this every time; why should this be deleted?

Sikh Heads as Trophies

For several decades there was a general proclamation to kill any Sikh that could be found; and a price was paid for each head of a Sikh brought to the government officials. All Hindus were ordered to cut off their beards, because before that time there was little distinction between ordinary Sikhs and Punjabi Hindus. They say that bounty hunters would sometimes cut off the head of a woman for the reward and would claim that the head belonged to a teenage Sikh who did not yet have a beard. During those times, long hair and a beard, except in the Muslim style, became a fatal liability. This system of rewards for Sikh heads was in effect periodically during the first half of the 18th century. To survive, the Sikh warriors hid in the mountains or jungles and made occasional raids into the plains to replenish their supplies.

Zakaria Khan, who succeeded his father as the governor of Lahore and ruled from 1726 to 1745, appealed to the Muslim population of Punjab to annihilate all surviving Sikhs. According to written records, several *lakh* (hundred thousand) Muslims volunteered for the holy war. "Bilochi, Sayyid, Mughal, Pathan, Gujjar, Teli, Mochi, Doom and other Muslim tribes and castes gathered under the Haidri Flag, and under the command of Mir Innayat Ullah, to eliminate the last remaining Sikh." The *ghazi* (volunteers in a holy war) killed as many Sikhs as they could find, but they did not have much success against the scattered bands who did not have any specific stronghold. Subsequently the scattered Sikh bands were emboldened to form *missls* (armed militia). These Sikh missls eventually established Sikh dominance in Punjab as the Mughal Empire fell into decay. The missl of Ranjit Singh consolidated their powers to rule over Punjab, starting at the end of eighteenth century. Only the Phulkian Missl and some minor rulers south of the Sutlej River remained independent of Ranjit Singh, who became the King of Punjab north of the Sutlej River and all the way to the Khyber Pass. After he conquered Multan and Kashmir, he was considered a significant opponent by the British, who ruled the rest of India by then.

Ranjit Singh was a powerful monarch and a skillful administrator, but after his death palace intrigues and internecine strife began, as different families and power blocks tried to place their sons or favorites on the throne. Some who aspired to or succeeded to the throne were murdered; many thousands of soldiers and others also died in those conflicts. Finally a small child named Dalip Singh came to the throne, with his mother Jindan acting as regent. The British were determined to conquer Punjab in order to complete their control over India. The English could muster the power of all India and the military superiority of the British Empire against the rulers of Punjab; the Sikh government was in disarray after the death of Ranjit Singh; and the morale of the Sikh army under generals with questionable loyalties was low. These causes led to the Sikh defeat in the first Anglo-Sikh War of 1846. The British subsequently defeated the remaining resisters decisively in the second Anglo-Sikh war in 1849 and annexed the Punjab, thus completing their conquest of India. Being a small religious minority amounting to less than 10 percent of the population in their own kingdom, the Sikhs could only have continued to rule by proper strategies. In the unstable environment after the death of Ranjit Singh, the British drive for conquest left little hope for the Sikh kingdom.

In 1857 there was a mutiny in India against the British but the Sikhs refused to join the mutiny, because merely eight years earlier the rest of the Indians were allied with the British in conquering the Sikhs. Moreover, though doubtlessly some joined the mutiny because of their outrage against the British rule, others just wanted to bring back the old Mughal Empire, and the Sikhs did not want Mughal rulers ever again. The Sikh community and the British had good relations thereafter, and the British came to prefer the formerly refractory Sikhs as reliable soldiers.

The Nihang Singhs of Boodha Dal

The Nihang were the "Guru's Warriors," still clinging to their anachronistic ways from the eighteenth century. Boodha Dal (the elders' army) and Taruna Dal (the youngsters' army) were the actual names of groups of Sikhs fighting against the oppressive rulers of Punjab in the eighteenth century, and later they were a part of Ranjit Singh's forces. They were supposed to be religious and god-fearing, but being ready for war was their full time occupation. They would leave their families and occupations to devote their lives to this pursuit, just as Hindu men with spiritual inclinations used to renounce the world to become sadhu ascetics. The importance and prestige of the Nihang dimished after the British victory in the second Anglo-Sikh War of 1849. In my day they had become a caricature of their former glory. They had weapons of steel only but no firearms, and they had not fought in any war for nearly a century. Their garb was that prescribed by Guru Gobind Singh for the Khalsa, mostly blue with gold or white accents, and they wore various steel weapons at all times. Some of them exaggerated their turbans by tying steel ring weapons and even small daggers into the turbans. Many of the Nihang were skilled swordsmen and were good at the use of other steel weapons, but some of them were no more than dysfunctional fellows who dropped out of society and joined the group, just as some men became sadhu to escape work.

The Nihang had a colorful vocabulary full of euphemistic words for everything, because *chardhi kalaa* (an upbeat spirit) was their motto and mode of behavior. Thus when all had died in battle and only one remained, they would use the words "*sawa lakh*" (a hundred thousand plus a quarter) to describe the single survivor, as if there were still plenty left. When food ran out, it was called *swaii* (in excess). The lowly roasted chickpeas were called almonds, and so on. They had grandiose or colorful words for most objects and actions, such as for sleeping, for red pepper, for lice, and for body functions.

Until the middle of the 1940s, the remnants of the Boodha Dal still toured around the villages. In the 1930s, they would arrive in our village, 100 to 150 in number, with all pomp and show. Their horses were beautiful and huge in size compared to the ponies of ordinary Indians. A couple of lead horses with double drums mounted on each horse would announce their arrival. And they would descend on a village like a royal army, with the *jathedar* (general) on a prancing horse in front and his deputy and assistants behind. They would set up camp in the grove of *pipple, bohar,* and *neem* trees. The village elders would provide fodder for the horses and provisions for the men, as people thought this was a worthwhile charity to the *Guru's Own Army*. It was fascinating for young boys to see their horses, tents, uniforms, and weapons, and even the huge steel vessels for cooking and feeding on a large scale. Steel was like a holy metal to them; they used steel for every purpose and would not touch a brass utensil. The Nihang did everything with great flair and their language was impressive to match.

They would hold a tournament of war games in the fields and grounds near the village. The public attended it with great enthusiasm, as there was no restriction, nor any charge. There would be horse races, tent-pegging in which a lancer on a galloping horse pierced a target, swordplay, fencing, throwing steel rings to cut targets at long distances, archery, javelin–throwing, and so on. One very agile Nihang named Bali Singh was particularly good with sword and shield. Bali Singh would come to our school and invite all the boys to throw stones at him to demonstrate that he could defend himself with a shield under all circumstances. Even when the Nihang were not doing anything special, boys were fascinated by their outfits, horses, war drums, tents, weapons, cooking utensils, and steel bowls. We wanted to hear their colorful vocabulary and watched them curiously as they took their horses to water at the pond. The village boys never wanted the Nihang to leave, but the Nihang had to be on the move and not get used to easy living.

Religious Practices in Our Village

Our entire clan of Mehraj in the 22 villages, and in fact most landowning *Jats* in the region, had started following the teachings of the Sikh gurus in the early days of the seventeenth century, but the transition from Hindu to Sikh was not a religious conversion. Most people just combined their old cultural practices with reverence for the Sikh gurus and scriptures. Even during my childhood in the 1930s, only a few of the nominally Sikh villagers *actually* followed the Sikh religion, and they were the *amritdhari* (formally initiated) Sikhs. Some of our families still gave charity to Brahmins on the occasion of *sraadh* days, kept the *karwa* fast, fed the *dhiani* (maidens), kept images of Hindu gods in their homes, burned incense, celebrated Hindu festivals, and followed other Hindu customs. Others followed some *sadhu* (Hindu mystic), and some worshipped at the *mutti* (tombs) of dead ancestors. Still, all those of the Jat caste in our area called themselves Sikh. But the customs were changing gradually as old grandmothers from the nineteenth century died out. There was some resistance to the Sikh ways among the older people, as they wanted to continue the traditional customs; some men of the older generation would recite derisive couplets against the Singh Sabha and the Akali movement. But gradually the younger generation started abandoning the Brahmanical customs, and after passage of the Gurdwara Act in the mid-1920s, many *dera* (holy man's abode) of Hindu tradition were legally changed to *gurdwaras* (Sikh temples). Some of the dera were able to resist the change to gurdwaras by removing the holy Granth from their dera and declaring that they were not Sikhs but traditional Hindus.

The split of Sikhs from Hindus was accelerated by a movement called Arya Samaj starting late in the nineteenth century. Dyanand Saraswati, the leader of Arya Samaj, preached that there was only one god, and that god had nothing to do with a caste system. The Sikhs thought that this was a good message and was much like their own beliefs; so they invited him to expound his thoughts. But when he spoke in Punjab, instead of preaching conciliation and cooperation, he started deriding the Sikh gurus and their teachings. He said Nanak was a semi-literate preacher; that the Sikh scriptures did not teach anything important, and that it would be better for the Sikhs to follow the Arya Samaj and the Hindu scriptures. The Sikhs recoiled from his attitude, and this insult by the Arya Samaj leader motivated the Sikhs to distinguish themselves from Hindus. The Singh Sabha movement then tried to awaken the Sikhs to assert their identity separate from Hindus. Later the rift between Hindus and Sikhs got wider and wider.

The head of our household, Uncle Tiloka, never went to a *gurdwara*, nor did Uncle Nikk. But my father had himself formally initiated as an amritdhari Sikh early in the 1920s. He practiced the Sikh religion by reciting the appropriate portions of the scriptures, early in the morning after taking a bath, and of course by keeping his hair uncut and wearing the symbolic Sikh garb and accoutrements. During my childhood, some Sikhs in the village went to the gurdwara on Guru Nanak's and Guru Gobind Singh's birthdays or on *Sangrand*, the first day of the Indian month; but more of our Sikhs still followed the Hindu sadhus. My father taught us informally about the lives and teachings of the Sikh gurus, and we learned continuously by osmosis and by his example. My siblings learned portions of the scriptures by heart and could chant some *shabads* (religious songs). We believed that God had made us Sikh and that it was our duty to recite *gurbani* (God's word). In my younger days, my concept of religion was more like that of a tribe, race, or nation, and we believed that our gurus were like gods. As children we performed the ritual of *matha tekna* (touching forehead to the ground) in front of the holy Granth in the gurdwara, and that was considered adequate practice for ordinary Sikhs. We went to the gurdwara at least twice a year, on the birthdays of Guru Nanak and Guru Gobind Singh. Many village families would pledge or donate a *degh* (dish of consecrated food) to the gurdwara with the hope of having their wishes fulfilled.

When I was a little boy, there was a Hindu temple, called shivdwara, near the center of our village but no gurdwara because in the old days, our people were Hindus. There were also numerous dera (abodes, institutions) of Hindu sadhus, whose followers were nominally Sikh. But the nearest gurdwara, called Chhota Gurusar, a mile away behind the sand dunes, was more like a shrine. The second gurdwara, also called Gurusar, where Guru Hargobind had fought a battle in 1631, was three miles away in the wilderness and not a place of regular worship either. By 1930, a few years after the Gurdwara Act was passed, most Hindu deras were being converted to Sikh gurdwaras, and that is when the dera of Sidh (ascended master) Tilak Rai, closer to our village, was turned into a gurdwara.

Village people were never married in a gurdwara; apart from some brief religious rituals, weddings primarily were community celebrations and took place at brides' homes. In addition to gurbani recitation, the gurdwara was a place where anyone could go to seek shelter and eat. The only restriction was that the person would not be allowed to smoke tobacco or engage in anti-social behavior. And the food could be a mixed bag, either something that the *bhai* (brother, the resident Sikh) could collect from the village or what someone could prepare from the simple provisions. Most of the time, the gurdwara food consisted of just roti (unleavened flat bread) and daal (lentil soup with spices). Any traveler could go to a gurdwara for food and bed. I remember that one day my friends and I cooked Aloe Vera vegetable in our Gurdwara, because lot of Aloe Vera was growing there. Even I stayed one night in the Hong Kong gurdwara in 1957 when I was on my way to study in the U.S.A. people could live in a village gurdwara all their lives, but it was not an exciting life. Some older fellows, tired of nagging from their families, would threaten them by saying, "If there is one more day of treatment like this, I am going to leave home and sit in the gurdwara," but such threats were seldom carried out. Idle men sometimes wandered into the gurdwara premises without purpose and slept there under the trees during the daytime. There were no idle, useless, or surplus women of any age. If nothing else, an old woman could always spin yarn or watch a child; but sometimes old men in the village were worthless, demanding food and doing nothing useful.

We considered the Hindu deities as part of ancient mythology. We talked of them with respect, just as Muslims talk about Abraham, Moses and Jesus, or the way the Semitic religions regard angels, but we were not expected to worship them. Their names were part of our folklore, but our Waheguru was held to include the powers and functions of all the gods and goddesses. Guru Nanak frequently expressed his thoughts in his writings by referring to Hindu deities and to the ancient Hindu scriptures; he said The Great Creator installed those gods and goddesses, like Ishwer (Shiv), Gorakh (Vishnu), Brahma, Parvati, Lakshmi, Saraswati, Inder, and others, as functionaries for running various aspects of the universe. Nanak expected us to be aware of Hindu thought and beliefs, but he did not want the Brahmin system of castes and superstitions to misguide us.

My mother almost never went to Gurdwara until she was old; she did nothing specifically religious but she would repeat God's name before beginning every significant task, especially if she was concerned about the results. She believed that God does what He decides is right; and if what happens is bad for us, then that is His will. Of the boys, my brother Gurdial is the only one who has a mind-set like my father's. The rest of my brothers are more or less free-thinking, but we all consider ourselves Sikh by heritage.

The Evolution of My Personal Belief

As a child I believed that the Sikh gurus were like Gods and that sincere prayer to them could help me if I were in trouble. If some of my cattle were lost and I needed to find them urgently, I would pray to every source, in order to get out of trouble. In addition to Guru Nanak and Guru Gobind Singh, I would even bring to mind *avatars* like Ram, Krishna, or Budha, as it did not hurt to ask for additional help. For other times, when I was alone in the wilderness at night with no humans within a mile and feared for my life, I had memorized some phrases and sentences from *gurbani* scriptures and from other sources to help me cope with my fears. These sentences could be translated like this: "Oh

God, there is nothing in me that is mine; my life is all yours; why should I begrudge returning to you what is yours? Without God's order, not even a leaf can move; so why should I fear? There may be thunder or lightning, it may be moonlight or pitch dark, but I will not fear because my God is with me," and similar thoughts. Like my siblings I had learned to read the Gurmukhi script at home. I had also memorized the entire *JapJi*, the first portion of the holy Granth, and some of us chanted a *shabad* or two.

After I became a teenager, I usually ignored religious activities and thought that religions were like superstitions which affect only religious-minded people. But I automatically considered myself to be a Sikh; I thought it would be degrading to be anything else. The Sikh religion required a person only to keep God in mind, to act ethically, and to share with others; so being a Sikh was easy. For social conformity, I did join a prayer on special occasions and bowed in front of the holy book, and that was considered adequate devotion for normal people.

As an adult, my thoughts have been affected by my commitment to reject any beliefs and myths that seem obviously false. Rejecting falsehoods and claiming to understand God's will, involves judgment on my part; and setting myself up as a *manmukh* (self-appointed judge) in such matters may be against the Sikh teachings. But how can I determine what is true, without thinking and judging? Judgment is unavoidable if one is committed to truth and not to blind faith. I think my actions should be in harmony with God's creation, and not those actions which cause destruction, pain, or waste.

I believe in God as the power that created the universe and according to whose laws everything operates. I believe that to every atom and molecule, God has given attributes, and to every cell and organism God has given an urge for self-promotion that determines their course. Those laws and attributes create not just grandeur, beauty, and amazing functions, but also create *defects*, disasters, accidents, disease, diversity, selfishness, anger, greed, hatred, violence, and crime. I think God pays no attention to individuals, their sufferings, or their prayers; His rules run the universe automatically. The Sikh concept of "the timeless and formless creator, without enmity or fear, unborn and self-existing," still gets my vote. If God has no enemy, that implies He also favors no one; all our gifts, disadvantages, and differences are a matter of *chance* according to His laws. God is not merciful, kind or forgiving, because that would violate His law of cause and effect. I think that reciting God's name, prayers, meditation, chanting, and similar activities are all beneficial for humans, even though God does not care about or automatically reward such activities. Like my mother, although only as a matter of habit and without much conviction, I still recite the name of Waheguru whenever I begin any important task.

I believe that God does not listen to or act on prayers, not even from any prophet or messiah. Even Jesus is reported to have said, "My God, My God, why have you forsaken me?" God does not change the course of events to benefit his devotees. But I believe that prayer or meditation can still be beneficial. When a human recites *gurbani* (God's word) sincerely and with devotion, his behavior begins to change, and this change benefits himself as well as society. According to Sikh belief, from being *manmukh* (self-willed), he can change gradually to become *gurmukh* (living in accordance with God's will) if he follows the spiritual practice. In gradual stages he can ascend to *Satch Khand*, (supposedly where God is), and his soul is liberated from the *cycle of transmigration*. According to Sikh teachings, *karm* (deeds), *dharm* (the spiritual path), *gyan* (enlightenment) and *satch khand* (the region of Truth) are the ascending stages of spiritual development. I personally have not followed any spiritual practice to enlightenment, but I do believe that chanting, meditation, and prayers can benefit the individual, even if God does not listen.

It seems to me that all creatures are designed with selfish traits; so anger, greed, attachment, pride, and the lust for reproduction, for power, love and glory, come automatically to humans. Subject to such urges, violence, destruction, and pain can result from the unreformed mind. But it is possible to train the mind to be compassionate, ethical, and harmonious with God's creation. Prayer, meditation, reflection, and devotional practices can steer a human toward such harmony and turn one into an enlightened soul (gurmukh). As our thoughts affect our body's hormones and vice versa, so can spiritual practices and meditation affect our minds to create peace, harmony and health. Any religious practice followed with devotion can be beneficial, as long as it does not become a vehicle of hate for other religions. Some day, if I find the motivation to follow a spiritual practice, it will be similar to the recitations of the Sikh scriptures that my father performed every morning. Because of my cultural background, it would be hard for me to achieve the same degree of serenity by any other practice. I also believe that Christians, Muslims, Hindus, and Budhists would benefit by following their own respective paths, without thinking that practitioners of other faiths are insulting their prophets and without trying to kill or convert others.

Non-Sikhs Around Our Community

According to the Vedas, gods are pleased by man's rituals and offerings; when the gods are pleased, they supply abundance of blessings, and one is purified from the effect of any impious activities. Although our people were not supposed to follow Hindu traditions, they still used to perform the *yugg* (an unlimited feast) under the direction of a sadhu in the name of the god Inder, in hopes of rain; a great many children in Punjab have the word Inder incorporated in their first names.

Hindu religion is the accumulated wisdom recorded in the Vedas and Upanishads, with the addition of the Mannu Simriti and the epics of Ramayan and Mahabharat, the last one including the Bhagwat Geeta. Mannu was the one who formalized the customs, rituals, social rules, and the caste system, and his book Mannu Simriti became one of the sacred texts.

The hereditary occupation of the entire Brahmin caste was religious and scholarly study that provided continuity from one generation to the next. Hindus had a *jujman-prohit* (client-professional) relationship with their Brahmin. The Brahmin performed the rituals as prescribed in the Veda (holy books) at the time of naming the child, at the first haircut for a boy, at the sacred thread ceremony for a boy, and at weddings, deaths, and other occasions. He also guided people in matters of caste, various rituals, and social rules, according to the Vedas and the Mannu Simriti. Hindus believed in gods of different categories, with supplementary gods and goddesses to run different functions in the universe. Beliefs and practices varied greatly from one region to another, from one sect to another, and from one family to another. A Hindu might be a strict vegetarian and consider the killing of any animal a sin, or he might be a hunter and meat eater. He might think that killing anything is a sin; but another might think killing is necessary, since in

190

the Bhagwat Gita, god Krishna convinces Arjan that killing his opposing relatives was his sacred duty. The holy Bhagwat Gita is really a sermon by Krishna to persuade Arjan to act without thinking of the result, to kill dispassionately and to detach himself from result and the fact that the opponents are his kin. A Hindu might be a reformist *Arya Samaji* or he might follow the traditional *Sanatan Dharma*. His gods and goddesses in South India might be drastically different from those in the North, and his customs of worship would seem strange to a Brahman from the North. For example, I read in the newspaper *The Tribune* in Chandigarh on 18 April 2000 that "Idols of god Venkateshwara and his two wives had been flown from Tirupati in South India and would be installed tomorrow in their new temple built by the many people from the South who are now in the government service in Punjab..." In all of the above cases the people involved were Hindu, regardless of whom and how they worshipped. Remarkably, one never heard of any conflict or violence among such a diversity of beliefs; the only conflicts the Hindus had were with the Muslims, and after Independence also with Christians or Sikhs. They did not consider anyone else's belief to be a threat; it was the potential political power of followers of a hostile religion that was perceived as a problem. In the old days the Hindus had no desire to convert anyone to their religion; how would they decide the caste of a convert, as only God could assign a person's caste!

In the days before the Singh Sabha movement started severing the links to their Hindu past, Sikh families in Punjab participated in the traditional Indian festivals such as *Diwali, Lohri, Holi, Besakhi, Dussehra, Saraadh*, and *Karwa*. Some village people, like Aunt Harnami, fed the sadhus, Brahmins, and virgins, and gave them *daan* (donations) as acts of *punn* on certain days or after fasting. Some village families constructed tombs called *mutti* or *marhi* in the names of specific dead ancestors whose souls they believed were wandering around. They felt it was their duty to see the dead ancestor settled in a new and better life; so they made offerings to God on behalf of the dead ancestor. They believed that if the dead ancestor were not assigned to a new life but was angry, he might cause sickness, he might cause an ox to die or buffalo milk to dry up, or he might send some other calamity. I once heard neighbor Aunt Harnami complain that her buffalo, though well fed and full of milk, would not let any one milk it. "Surely the old Baba Jwala Singh must have entered the buffalo and is teaching us a lesson for not honoring him," she thought. Jwala Singh was a soldier in the army of Ranjit Singh at Lahore in the early nineteenth century. He was said to have drowned while crossing the Sutlej River on a trip home. Sometimes Aunt Harnami would select a man who was considered innocent, without sin or guile, as a surrogate for the Baba. She would propitiate the dead ancestor by providing this surrogate a feast and then donating a turban. The surrogate had to be unmarried, which in those days was synonymous with being a virgin; a married householder was never considered a sinless person. Uncle Nikk qualified for the feast and favors, since he was never married. My father always spoke against such old beliefs and ridiculed superstitious practices like the feeding of virgins, bathing in the holy Ganges, propitiating the goddess of small pox, or fearing the power of curses or blessings.

There were no Budhists or Jains in our area. The founder of the Jain religion was as profound a thinker as Budha was and he lived just before Budha did, but since not many kings or empires promoted Jainism, this religion did not become prominent.

The Muslims in our village were insignificant in number and status. The religious

Muslims were perceived as rather severe, sulky and forbidding, but the non-religious Muslims were fun loving and trustworthy. Many of them were gifted poets and performers. We felt that all those Muslims praying five times a day must be honest, and truthful.

Religious Chauvinism and Religious Hatred

The village people considered religion not just something to live by; they used it to differentiate themselves from others. We felt grateful that God chose to make us Sikh and not members of any other religion. In the ordinary villager's conception, religion was somewhat like tribe, caste, race, or nationality. Our gurus had told us not to discriminate on the basis of religion or caste—"*Mannus ki zaat sabh ek hee pahchnbo*" (Man's entire race, recognize it as one)—but in practice, people often derided other religions. Muslims may have the greater religious zeal to kill or convert the kafirs in order to please Allah, but most religious people hated other religions, at least secretly. They wished the rival religions would just vanish somehow and their own religion would prevail. Promoting one's own religion was as important as cheering one's team, hoping one's political party to win, or having your country defeat a rival country. At the same time, elders pointed out how seriously the people of other religions practiced their faith and decried what backsliders our own people were.

Because of the patterns of prejudice and the historical oppression by Muslim invaders, many people in our village considered Allah, Mohammed and Sunnet (circumcision) as things foreign and therefore. They believed that it was the religious duty of a Muslim to kill a *kafir* (non-Muslim). It was a common belief that a Muslim who dies in the attempt to kill a non-believer goes straight to Allah; so why should he linger on earth? The ignorant people believed that Islam was about cruelty and killing other people. When I went to college in 1946, I was told never to go into Muslim neighborhoods, because "they stab and kill any non-Muslim whom they can corner." Such beliefs about their fanaticism and cruelty were reinforced by oral stories and even by written ones, such as the autobiography of Babar. About one day's activity the conqueror Babar wrote something like this: 'After we finished our afternoon prayers, we cut off the heads of all the prisoners we had captured that day and built a large pyramid of their heads, according to our custom.' The perception about Muslim cruelty in our minds was reinforced by the plight of Sikhs mentioned in prayers, such as "Reflect on the deeds and sacrifices for dharma by those who gave their heads, had their limbs chopped bit by bit, had their skulls removed, were sawn into parts, were boiled in hot cauldrons, were put on hot griddles; think about Sikh women who were forced to wear necklaces of the chopped limbs of their babies...., but did not give up their faith."

But perhaps such hatred and cruelty were more of an old Mongol or Turkic, and not really Muslim, customs in those ancient days. I personally did not think that it was the duty of every Muslim to kill an infidel, because my best friend in the village was a Muslim, and he was a very sincere, trustworthy and rational-minded guy. When I was growing up, all the romantic couples like Heer-Ranjha, Leila-Majnoon, Sohni-Mahiwal, and most of the popular Punjabi and Urdu poets, song writers describing romantic stories and pleasures of wine, musicians and even prostitute entertainers in Punjab, were Muslim and not Sikh or Hindu. I thought that compared to the pleasure loving Muslims, our culture was boring and puritanical. But apparently now the Muslim culture has become rigid and repressive after the creation of Pakistan.

I also thought that the melodious *azzan* (call to prayer) by their *muezzin* from the mosque created a rather pleasant effect. But some Jats felt the loud azzan was an ominous threat. It was perceived like a war cry, because the expression "Allah hu akbar" (which possibly means "Allah is great" but was interpreted by some as "Allah be dominant over others"), often repeated by Muslims, is also spoken as a war cry when they attack to kill their enemies. My mother, like other simple people, would say, "The sound of azzan is very bad, because on hearing it, even the cows feel pain and fear; the cows feel the fear of being killed and eaten by the Muslims."

One source of contention between the Muslims and others was that Muslims could butcher a cow, but the Hindus believed cows were holy and felt it was their duty to defend them. Conversely, the Muslims hated anyone who kept or ate a pig, because the consumption of pork was forbidden by Mohammed. Muslim policemen would threaten and warn low-caste people in our village to stop keeping pigs. During my childhood, the village Sikhs felt the same way about cows as the Hindus did, but after Independence, the Sikh farmers resented the stray cows and tried to push them across the border to Pakistan.

The religiously strict Muslims had to trim their mustaches and grow their beards as required by Mohammed, so any man without a mustache but with a long beard seemed threatening to us. But if a man were clean shaved then he was not perceived as a threat. Another practice that really set the Muslims apart was that their boys had the foreskin of the penis cut off; our people thought this custom was extremely weird. In some families their boys had the foreskin cut at the age of ten or eleven. The consequences of circumcision were not merely a personal and private affair. While grazing cattle with us and away from women, some of these Muslim boys had to dangle their penises uncovered for some days until they healed, because the touch of cloth would hurt the freshly cut flesh. Sometimes they used a spacer to avoid contact with cloth. Their prayers were not of concern to us, but their men were forever estranged from us by the practice of circumcision. Of course the Muslims might have felt the same way about the Sikh hair and garb. Hindus were the most innocuous people in our village, because they were not considered capable of committing any violence, until after the Independence of India when they became politically dominant. Hindu fanatic organizations were more active in other states.

Some Indian Muslims in larger towns made obvious efforts to separate themselves from the country of India. Their songs suggested that they were stuck in India physically but their hearts were in Arabia. Some of them would claim, "We are not to be equated to the Indians, because we came here as conquerors and rulers." To every important thing they wanted to give an Arabic name, so the leader of the Muslim League, a party that demanded a separate country for Muslims, was called Qaid-i-Azam (Qaid is the same Arabic word from which Al Qaida is made). It was considered sinful for a Muslim in our area to learn any script other than the Arabic/Persian. English was not yet common in the rural areas, but if a Muslim in our area tried to learn the Punjabi language with the Gurmukhi script, he was condemned by other Muslims for committing a serious violation. The religious extremists had no regard for India as a country. They would say that wherever Muslims exist, they should either rule that country or break away from it, and that Muslims from all over the world should form one nation. They did not want to live in a country polluted by other religions, and in that spirit they demanded a separate Pakistan (cleansed land). Separatist Muslim factions with the same ideology exist even nowadays in Kashmir, Chechnya, and other places. If an unfavorable event occurred even as far away as Turkey, the fanatics would cry out, "*Islam khatre mein hai!*," which means, "Islam is in danger." By this they did not mean that there is any danger to freedom of Muslims or their prayers. They meant that their goal of world domination by Islam may be delayed although. They believed that Islamic domination of the world was inevitable. Such ideologies drove additional wedges between religions and made the break-up of India to create Pakistan unavoidable.

Although majority of the Muslims in our village were peace-loving people, they were helpless before the tide of religious fanatics who brought about the partition of India. The voices of many thoughtful, progressive, and scholarly Muslims in India, who never wanted the country to be divided, were drowned out by the separatists. Muslims from India did not migrate to Pakistan, except from the Punjab (and perhaps Bengal) portion of India. Many of them, being gifted writers, singers, performers, and craftsmen are an asset to India. There is no doubt that during some periods the Muslims were hated by the Sikhs, because of the inevitable cruelty during the early invasions, wars and rule. But after the Sikhs established their rule over Punjab, Muslims were the most trusted ministers and advisors in the Sikh kingdom of Ranjit Singh. Those Muslims were not only wise and cultured, they never betrayed the trust as others did. In my early youth, the most admired Urdu poets in Punjab were also Muslim.

In my travels through Europe and the United States, whenever I meet Punjabi Muslims from Pakistan, they treat me like a brother, with genuine affection, and they insist on speaking to me in our common language, Punjabi. Then I say to myself, "What a loss we have suffered by dividing the country, because of the curse of religions!" I understand that Islam was not always hostile to others. In some periods, as when a ruler like Akbar emphasized tolerance of alternative paths to God, Muslims were accepting of others. I have heard that the Moors who ruled Spain and Portugal were also quite tolerant. But whenever the religion was injected with hatred and intolerance, as in the days of the emperor Aurangzeb, and in modern times with the Wahabi and Salafi movements, their aim became to eradicate other religions from the earth. Like Christianity, Mohammed's religion may state that people of other religions are unacceptable to God, but most educated Christians have become tolerant over the last few centuries; so it is to be hoped that Islam can also learn to tolerate non-Muslims.

In some contexts rural Punjabis respected any holy man, even if they did not follow his religion. They might go to pay respect at the tomb of a Muslim *Pir*, visit a Sikh shrine, or feed a Hindu sadhu to get his blessings. They had the feeling that God favors all holy people, and that one would benefit by receiving their blessings. Unlike the Semitic religions, whose adherents believe that followers of any religion other than their own are doomed to a life of damnation, rural Indians believe that God listens to all people who do good deeds and that there are many different paths to God.

From Sat-Yug to Kal-Yug

Our elders used to talk about the four ages through which the human race has lived.

Those ages were called *Sat Yug, Treta Yug, Duaper Yug and Kal Yug*. The mythical Sat Yug (Age of Truth) was the ideal age of truth, honesty, integrity, justice, fairness, beauty, innocence and all good things. In Sat Yug there was no crime and gods worked among the humans. The birds and other animals could speak the human language in the fairy tales of Sat Yug. The doors of houses did not need to be locked; people could leave their gold and wealth in the open and no one would steal it. There was abundance, but there was no greed, as people felt contented and blessed. And of course no one would cheat, rob, or kill others in the Sat Yug age.

The mythical ages Duaper Yug and Treta Yug, although not totally blissful, were supposed to be full of action, heroic people, and miraculous happenings; but you could expect problems and conflicts during these two ages. During these two ages some avatars (gods incarnated as humans) appeared on earth in order to steer humanity to the right path. God/Prince Ram ruled during these ages as described in the epic of Ramayan; and the great conflict of the warring princes, including Lord Krishn who is described in the epic of the Maha Bharat, occurred during these ages. The Bhagvat Gita, the holy text that Krishn gave to the warrior Arjun to instruct him about the soul, its imperishable nature, and his duty according to dharma that required detached conduct without concern for the fruits of his effort, is a part of the Maha Bharat epic. There is some account of the struggle between good and evil in the Ramayan also, but the gut-wrenching events in the Maha Bharat; the eternal political, social and moral issues of greed and conflict; the interplay of truth, duty, morality, deceit, cunning, bravery, honor, good and evil, dharma, unscrupulous tactics and the resulting destruction, all combine to make the Maha Bharat one of the most powerful epics of mankind.

But all modern and real history (as distinct from mythology) has occurred in Kal Yug (the Black Age), the present age, full of dishonest people, a multitude of sins, deceptive schemes, clever thoughts, bad intentions, immoral acts, other unethical behavior and violence. Kal Yug became just the exact opposite of Sat Yug, which was the age of truth and righteousness. So when Kal Yug arrived, people tended to lie and became crafty, selfish, clever, perverted and mean-spirited. Evil became predominant, and it became harder to stay honest. My mother used to say, "These days children are so talkative and clever; they can 'clip the ears' of their elders; they know all the tricks and say things we would never even have thought about; all these clever minds are due to Kal Yug." In the villages there were songs decrying the deterioration of society due to Kal Yug. I still remember a Punjabi song from a hand-cranked record player: "Dekho Raj Kalu da Aya; Chober Nauker Naran de...", which can be translated as, "Behold, the reign of Kal Yug has arrived; that is why young men have become subservient to women..." In the culture where women were expected to serve and please their husbands, putting women ahead of men and having men conform to the wishes of women was considered a perversion of the natural order. Most evils were attributed to the effects of Kal Yug. Older people used to say, "If all sin is washed off the land, Kal Yug will pass; Sat Yug will dawn again some day, and then it will be all truth, innocence, honesty and justice."

Yum Raj and Dharm Raj

Our people used to say that when it is decided that your assignment on earth is complete and it is time for your soul to take a new body, *Yum Raj* (Yum the Enforcer) comes to get you. This entity, roughly the equivalent of the Grim Reaper in the West, takes your soul to the court of *Dharm Raj* (The Enforcer of Dharma), who takes account of your karma—that is, your actions during life—passes judgment on your soul according to the rules and rewards you appropriately according to your deeds. Your acts of *punn* (piety, charity) and your debts of *paap* (sin, harmful deeds) such as dishonesty, cheating, infidelity, greed, cruelty, lying, or killing are weighed by Dharm Raj, who also considers the longings and attachments of your soul to things in worldly life. The souls that are obviously good are sent to wait in *swarg* (heaven); the ones that are obviously bad, wait in *nerk* (hell). Pure and god-like souls achieve nirvana or mukti, to be merged with God and be liberated from the torturous cycle of transmigration by births and deaths.

The next best souls are sent back to take a human form, according to merit, such as a Brahman scholar/teacher/preacher, or a Kshatri prince/warrior, or a Vesh farmer/artisan/trader, or a Shuder low caste or untouchable, in descending order. If the grade of the soul is too low to come back as a human, it might return as an ox, a snake, a pig, a cat, an ant or any living thing, all according to one's karma and the mentality that the soul had been cultivating. Only the soul of a human being can progress, through right living, toward nirvana. If the quality of a soul is below the human, it cannot hope for nirvana but must wait until it can be reincarnated as a human to get the opportunity to liberate itself. You can be a good ox, but until you can be reincarnated as a human, you cannot even work for nirvana. And until the soul achieves nirvana, it has to find its next assignment. Instead of a permanent hell, the low grade soul is made to suffer through the torturous cycle of *Transmigration* through *chaurasi lakh* (84 hundred thousand) possibilities of different kinds of lives, unless and until it can be incarnated as a human; and then the soul gets another opportunity to become fit to achieve nirvana. Our village people talked of this "chaurasi" as the ultimate torture. My father would say to me: "Gurnam, get out of this chaurasi of farming; go to college and make a better life for yourself."

Sadhu, Sant and Bhagt

A *sadhu* is a Hindu ascetic who practices *sadhna* (holy discipline) by renouncing worldly life, to devote himself to God. Celibacy, poverty, humility, detachment, and the discipline of mind and body are the essentials for a sadhu. The respectful address *'sant'* is roughly equivalent to the English word saint, but since titles were commonly inflated in India, any sadhu could be called sant. The word *bhagt* is the same as *bhakta* in Sanskrit and means a devotee of God who keeps God in mind, sings His praises, and meditates on His name. Hatred, lust, anger, greed, attachment and pride were considered barriers to holiness. Celibacy was the essential requirement as one had to be a virgin to be considered sinless. Poverty was a way to detach from the world of material desires. As long as a soul longed for fame, love, power, material things and comforts of the body, it had no chance to be liberated from the world. A sadhu had to become indifferent to friends or enemies, gold or stone, pleasure or pain. To attach to God, he had to avoid worldly distractions and live in a solitary place away from the masses, where he could acquire enlightenment and ascend spiritually to become a *sidh* (a master, with supernatural powers), achieve nirvana, and become one with God.

When I was young, there were many *deras* (abodes) of sadhu around our village, and our nominally Sikh people provided continuous support to these Hindu holy men. The sadhus were working for their own salvation, but they were generous with their blessings and advice and even taught whatever they knew. They provided solace and comfort to anyone who came to them. Many of them did not wear any clothes except a little string around the waist and a loin strap to cover the genitals. They lived away from population, under trees, in temporary straw shacks, or in underground burrows. They tortured their bodies, as they believed that involvement in the comforts and pleasures of the body impedes the liberation of the soul; they did not want their soul to be subject to the obstacles of flesh. Renouncing the use of clothing was a part of this degradation of the flesh. To torture their bodies, a few sat in cold water in the winter, but most sat in the center of a circle of several fires, sometimes four, five, or even seven, during the hot summer, although a single fire could also serve the purpose of *tapp* (body roasting, penance).

As a school-age boy on my way to Rampura Phul, I used to pass by the Diggi pond where there was also a well for travelers to drink from. There on an earthen platform a sadhu used to sit with closed eyes at the center of a circle of smoldering fires of dried cow dung patties, in the scorching sun on hot summer afternoons. The patties were donated by devoted Sikh families who hoped to get his blessing. Hindus would not travel that far to the wilderness to aid the Hindu holy man, as they were either shopkeepers or Brahman and would not have much reason to leave the village; the sadhu's supporters were the Sikhs whose farms were in the vicinity. When he was not torturing his body with the smoldering fires, the sadhu would talk to people, but I was too shy and young to ask him any questions; I would merely greet him as I went by to drink water there. Another naked sadhu at the Phulana pond near our fields practiced similar body roasting. Some cynical people used to whisper that this fellow was just a low caste Chuhra from Bhagi Bander village, who got tired of plowing fields in the service of Jats. The joke used to be that the scorching sun of the month of Bhadon (August) turns many a farm worker into a sadhu.

Most sadhus owned a blanket for cold winter nights, because killing the body would deprive their soul of the opportunity for liberation. The purpose was to degrade the flesh, to become indifferent to suffering, but not to end life. The sadhus smeared their hair, beard and body in ashes and had elaborate dreadlocks; they could form the dreadlocks into huge topknots or just let them hang loose. Sadhus of one order pledged to stand on one leg only, but they were usually supported by a sling from a tree.

Many sadhus did not totally disengage from worldly affairs. Some were teachers and preachers. "Sants" from some orders wore clothes and lived in impressive buildings called dera or ashrams, with land and other property donated by worshippers over time. My grandfather's younger brother, Bhagt Singh, had become a Hindu sadhu, because my great grandmother had pledged to donate him to God if he survived the severe smallpox when he was a little boy. As he survived the smallpox and became a teenager, he went to check out a party of visiting sadhus near the village, and offered himself, just as one enlists in the army. His guru gave him the name Brahm Jot (God's light) when he was initiated as a disciple. Later he controlled a good deal of wealth even when he professed to live in simplicity.

Some varieties of sadhu wore ochre-colored clothing and shaved the head and face, but most sadhu never cut their hair or beard. Some meditated and others practiced yoga;

197

some would go into a state of samadhi (concentration leading to a trance in which the sadhu would detach from his surroundings). Some sadhu wore around their necks a *mala* (rosary) of large beads that was used as an aid to meditation. Many ordinary old people in the village also kept a mala and passed one bead at a time through their fingertips. No one in my family had a mala, so the mala was something mysterious for me. Some sadhu studied scriptures and chanted m*antras*; others were totally illiterate and ignorant of all *mantra, yantra,* or *tantra*. Some ancient scholarly and famous sadhus were called *rishi* (sage) or *moni* (non-speaking holy man).

Since the sadhu preferred to live close to nature and away from other humans, the mountains, lakes, forests and river-banks were their preferred abodes. Even so, the average sadhu just lived wherever some guru would accept him as a *chela* (disciple). If he decided to live on his own, he could just find a tree by the pond in a suitable situation near a village and make it his dera. Since owning anything was a barrier to godliness, they lived by begging or on food brought to them. Although our family did not believe in this practice, we gave them food whenever a sadhu came to our door. Some pretended to have supernatural powers and to perform miracles; others prescribed cures for various diseases, and some gave *talismans, taveez* or amulets to wear around the neck to ward off disease and bad influences. Some would give you a talisman to bring good fortune and even love. Some healed by touch while others just did *hathola* (a cure by waving the hand), mumbled some Sanskrit words, and verbally assured people that they would get better. Some sadhus, like my father's uncle, learned the power of herbs and were able to cure serious diseases by preparing effective medicines. Our neighbor, Aunt Harnami, used to feed the sadhu occasionally. Once, half a dozen of them came to her house, marching to the sounds of conch shells and droning brass horns. While they ate their meals and blessed her house, they were an awe-inspiring sight for me, as I was about five years old then.

My Fruitless Association with a Sadhu

Once my older brother Kartar had attempted to become a bhagt at the age of about eleven. He left his boarding school to travel toward the Himalayan mountains in search of God. I have always been too materialistic to become a sadhu, but I wanted very much to acquire some of the powers that the sadhus were reputed to have. One day at the age of fourteen, as I was walking to Rampura Phul to go to my teacher, I met a sadhu traveling the same way. He was probably in his early thirties, but with long hair and a beard the sadhus tended to look older and more formidable. This sadhu wore ochre-colored clothing appropriate to his sect; he seemed fairly impressive in his talk and acted quite friendly. I asked him if he could teach me how to perform miracles. I thought that it would be impressive to be able to fill a glass with water out of nothing; but turning dirt into laddu (sweets) would be even better. My brother-in-law Harnek Singh Dhillon had told me that the sadhu in his village could produce a platter of laddu out of nothing, and the sadhu actually fed such laddu to the visitors once. Anyway, this sadhu traveling with me said that he was willing to give me some powers, but I would need to learn some new things and new attitudes. He encouraged me to continue to walk along the irrigation canal with him.

After we reached the twin bridges at the Rampura Phul falls, where the canal splits into two, the sadhu turned along the canal branch going south. Although I needed to go east, I kept going along with him with the hope of acquiring miraculous powers. He said I should first learn some mantras, and he asked me to repeat some strange Sanskrit words after him. I still remember some of those meaningless words: "Oang, Sohang, Sri Ram, Oang, Sohang, Sat Nam,...Narsingh, Bhishnam, Bhadrung, Mittrung, ...Ahung...and so forth." I learned the phrases quickly; but I still had no special powers. We had already traveled nearly two miles away from the direction of my school, and it was getting late. I told the sadhu to hurry up and give me some powers, as I had to go to school. The sadhu started getting annoyed with me for not having the patience to learn. Then he said that there was no way I was going to get any powers instantly and that it would take a long time to cultivate any real power. He urged me to continue to travel with him, but I was not willing to go any further. He probably needed a disciple to serve him, because a sadhu with a disciple would have enhanced prestige. Developing doubts about the possibility of acquiring any powers, I separated from the sadhu and walked back toward my school. I was nearly two hours late for school because of my false hope of acquiring powers, but in the my teacher Kesho Ram's class no one feared punishment for being late. Anyway, my effort to acquire miraculous powers ended fruitlessly. The Bhagwat Geeta says: 'Perform your duty, without anxiety about the fruit of your work.' But I was thinking in a totally selfish way to acquire powers instantly and wanted the fruits without the slow process of discipline.

As the influence of Singh Sabha rose in the 1930s, the number of Sikh boys who used to become sadhu to follow the old Hindu practices started declining. Before 1925 some of the aspiring sadhu would even adopt Sikh garb and were still worshipped as holy men. Such aspirants in rural Punjab ran private deras. Some sophisticated sants associated with powerful politicians. The recently prominent ones like BhindranWala and Virsa Singh commanded great respect. Some holy men started meddling in politics. Even nowadays, powerful politicians and government ministers court the support of holy men. Some articulate and charismatic sants became heads of cults. A flowery, esoteric, euphemistic and flattering language was always an asset for a sant's success, reputation, and fame. In that culture the distinction between gods and holy men was only a matter of degree. For example, Atma, Mahatma, and Parmatma mean soul, great soul, and the highest soul (God), respectively. So it was easy to blur the difference between good men, holy men and gods. The classical variety of sadhu are found mostly outside Punjab now.

There were no female sadhu in Punjab, but in the southern parts of Hindu India there were female temple worshippers and dancers called *devadasi* (God's servants). These girls were thought to have been donated by their parents to the temples as an act of charity (punn). They lived in the temples, danced in the service of the gods, and performed service to others for the rest of their lives. But I have heard that the status of a devadasi was by no means equivalent to that of a Christian or Budhist nun.

The Hair Struggle

In my time, men of various religions could be identified by their clothing, headgear, or hairstyle. As the twentieth century progressed, however, more and more men of other religions in Punjab gradually stopped wearing turbans and some adopted Western haircuts.

Then the Sikhs, with their uncut hair, beard, and turban, became totally distinct from other Punjabis. Maintenance of the uncut hair was always a problem for little boys. Although I was not a particularly neglected child, I had a mother who "did not even have the time to scratch her head," as the Punjabi saying went. Taking care of children's hair had to wait when other tasks kept her occupied. My mother's day included many trips to haul water from the village well for the family, cleaning house, churning milk, cooking food for the entire family, delivering morning meals to our workers in the fields, preparing the evening meals for everyone, and numerous other chores incidental to the farming operation. Under these circumstances, keeping children's uncut hair clean and arranged at all times was unthinkable. I also had a lot of hair, and that made the upkeep harder. I remember I used to wish that I had no hair on my head, but my mother said that hair was a gift from God and not to be spurned. She used to say, "Look at unfortunate old Uncle Hazoora; he lost his hair, and now he can't make even a miniature *joora* on top of his head."

My mother once told me that when I was only a few months old and not yet able to crawl, she used to put me to sleep on a *charpai* in the verandah and go to deliver lunch to the workers in the field a couple of miles away. It was not uncommon to leave babies unattended outdoors, as there was little fear that anyone would steal or hurt an unimportant baby; only the babies of wealthy families had to be guarded and protected. Besides, our house was on a shared courtyard at the end of the street and therefore relatively safe, although there was no barrier from the street. She usually had so much to carry to the field that she could not take me along. It took her as much as two hours to return from the fields, and in the meantime I sometimes woke up and started crying. A murderer and fugitive named Channon the Daku, of Khote village, occasionally visited next door and stayed in the house of Aunt Harnami, as he was a cousin of her husband Buggoo. Such murderers were not any threat to neighbors; they were not common criminals but had become fugitives after murdering their enemies to settle some scores; most of them committed armed robberies after they became fugitives. Having a yard common to all our houses meant that everyone was subjected to whatever was happening. The outlaw Channon would say to my mother: "Bhagi, please don't leave your Akali (his name for me, since my father had become an amritdhari) behind, because he cries a lot in your absence. Please take the poor infant with you in the future." But taking a baby along with the rest of the load was impractical. Neglect of children was inevitable in that environment; and keeping the hair clean and arranged was secondary or tertiary in priority.

Father Boycotts Home; Gurdwara the Last Resort

My father had become initiated as an *amritdhari* Sikh in the 1920s. That initiation is more exclusive and demanding than a Christian baptism; it is voluntary, and not every Sikh is initiated with the amrit. The primary requirement for an amritdhari Sikh was not to cut hair from any part of his body. Some people called these initiates Akali (belonging to the Timeless God), and they were usually identified politically with the Akali Party. Being an amritdhari, my father had become very strict about keeping his children's hair uncut, although most of the nominally Sikh boys in our village, and most cattle grazers, would have their hair cut in those days.

200

Once Uncle Tiloka, seeing that his young nephew Kartar had such struggle with his hair, cut the hair of my brother Kartar to the scalp. Tiloka thought that was the best way to make life easy and to prevent head lice. When my father came home and saw his son with cut hair, he flew into a rage at this desecration, protesting that "someone had murdered the hair of his son!" After thus expressing his extreme displeasure, but not wishing to fight his respected older brother, my father said he could not bear to see his son with cut hair or even to live in the same house. But the damage could not be undone. So my father left the house as a protest and went to live in the gurdwara (Sikh temple). If a man were angry with his family, it was not unusual, and could even be respectable, for a man to live for a while in the gurdwara. A place to sleep and food to eat were always available free to anyone in a gurdwara. Some men who got into fights with their families would threaten to "go and sit in the gurdwara," although they rarely carried out the threat. My father, however, actually left home and started living in the local gurdwara. He would go to work from the gurdwara to our fields every day, but he would not come home. His self-exile continued until Kartar's hair grew long enough to gather into a topknot. They tied a small turban on Kartar's head and told my father that he should come home because the boy looked like a Sikh again. After that there was never a question of cutting any child's hair in our house.

Shaving or Cutting Hair Makes Ugly Man!

People get so used to what they perceive as normal and good-looking that they considered any deviations from it as abnormal, unbecoming or ugly. Among the Mehraj Jat families, once a boy became a teenager it was considered unfortunate and not respectable for him to have his hair cut and not to wear a turban. But when boys were younger, maintaining their hair uncut was inconvenient, so although nominally Sikh, the village Jat parents sometimes cut their young boys' hair. Some relatively grown-up nonconformist teenagers with independent streaks tried various alternatives. Chand, the son of Aunt Harnami, used to cut his hair secretly and then tie a turban to hide the fact. But close attention would reveal that he had no hair under the turban and no tell-tale joora (topknot) of hair bulging out. Then he started putting an onion on top of his head under the turban to make it appear that he had a joora, because a joora would be the same shape and size as an onion. After a while, though, the secret of his fake onion joora would be discovered. Then the family would insist that being a grownup he must look respectable, and that he had to stop defacing (*verg mara*) himself by cutting hair. They would say: "With that cut hair you look like an unfortunate bum; who will betroth his daughter to you to marry?" Then Chand would let his hair grow long, but to reduce the volume of hair, he would shave the hair from the center and make a joora with the hair that still remained on the periphery of his head. When people discovered this, they used to tease Chand by saying, "Gurdwara on the periphery, but mosque in the center", that is, long hair like a Sikh around the edges but cut hair like a Muslim in the center of the head. As an adult, a man was required to show his religion by his dress and by his hair.

When my brother Kartar was going to see action in the World War II, we were concerned that a bullet would penetrate his turban just like flesh. A steel helmet on the other hand could make a difference between life and death if a bullet struck his head. Kartar's views on religion had changed since the days when he was in school, and he no longer saw much value in keeping his hair long and wearing a turban. He sometimes pointed out the absurdities and superstitions in religions. He talked about the old stories of Hindu soldiers not being willing to shoot at an enemy hiding behind the painted image of a cow or behind a stuffed cowhide, because the cow was a holy image and during the Mutiny of 1857 the British tacticians took advantage of that fact. He talked about Muslims refusing to use some war materials because rumors circulated that fat from pigs was a constituent in those materials; even the mention of the word "pig" was an unholy occurrence for a Muslim. Kartar would say, "Why make so much fuss about the holy Granth (Sikh bible)? It is just a book that costs less than my boots; why should people bow to a book?" Such talk upset my devout father, but what could he do to a grown-up son, on whom he himself was becoming dependent and who was a King's Commissioned Officer in the British Indian Army! On hearing such irreverent talk, my father would just step outside in disgust instead of arguing with Kartar.

One day, before going off to war, Kartar declared that he was going to be clean shaved. He said he would cut his hair and would wear a helmet instead of a turban. He said, "Isn't it better to try to save your life in war by using protection than to be blindly religious and get your head blasted?" This time my father tried to explain calmly and said to him, "Many Sikhs gave their lives in defending the right to keep their hair uncut. Without God's order, not even a leaf moves; go as you are, and no bullet will touch you. And if God turns a harsh eye, no helmet can save you." Then Kartar told my mother about his thoughts about cutting his hair and about the choice of wearing a turban or a helmet. My mother, not being particularly religious but still a believer in God, said, "Son, if you think a helmet will save your life, you may cut your hair and get clean shaved. Of course I know that with your cut off hair and your face shaved, you will look ugly; *tera varg mara jae ga* (the cut hair will kill your looks); all the clean-shaved people look so ugly! Now you are an impressive *sirdar*; if you cut your hair you will be defaced and will look like a *bania* (shopkeeper) boy!" But Kartar was just experimenting with expressing views contrary to those of his parents. He went into the war with hair, beard and turban intact like a Sikh, and he did return alive after World War II. My parents were pleased to see Kartar return safely, still maintaining his appearance as a Sikh.

There were many discussions in our house about hair; and my father held to his convictions, saying, "Hair is natural. God must have created hair for good reasons. It is a part of God's scheme to create hair for his creatures when it is appropriate. He created leaches, snakes, frogs, worms, fish and such without hair, according to his design. A lion has a mane of hair around his head; other animals have fur according to their design and need. Would a lion look proper without his mane? If God wanted you without hair, he could have created you without hair. It is not by carelessness that God created man with a beard and mustache; nothing in nature is without God's design and intentions; even the pores of the body have functions. All prophets, holy people, saints, *rishi* and *moni* had uncut hair. Jesus had uncut hair and beard; Mohammed had a beard and long hair. Budha is shown with a topknot on his head and so are Ram and Krishn, the Hindu prince gods. God in His wisdom has given men the beard to distinguish from women who have more luxuriant hair on the head. If God wanted men to look like women, he could have created them without facial hair. Keeping hair is just following God's plan; and cutting hair is like violating God's creation and intentions." Then my father would start stretching the belief by saying, "Keeping hair promotes good health, prevents diseases, promotes courage, promotes integrity, promotes holiness, prevents mischief...." and he sincerely believed what he was saying. My father did not have too much body hair, unlike me and my maternal uncles; but he had a full head of long hair and untrimmed beard until his death.

Hair as Identity; Beard a Mark of Honor

Little Sikh boys of observant parents had hair combed, sometimes arranged with braids, leading to a topknot. When I was about five years old, I started insisting on a simple topknot without the braids, because I did not want to be teased for having braids like a girl. There were varying methods to manage Sikh boys' hair, such as tying it with string, with a kerchief, mini turbans (called patka) or full turbans. All were cumbersome until the boys became old enough to tie their own turbans. Very few rural boys wore turbans before the age of seven, and very few went without turbans after the age of twelve, when they also stopped cutting their hair. Uncut hair on the heads of boys in the land of heat and dust provided a perfect shelter for lice. For those who dunked frequently in buffalo ponds and did not clean and dry their hair, it was a continuing problem, and that is why Jat Sikh boys who grazed the cattle often had cut hair. But people like my father thought that hair was a gift from God and therefore not to be cut. In the cities and among the educated Sikh families, they did not cut the young boys' hair. After the 1930s the cutting of hair became rare even among the rural boys, and only the low caste and non-Sikh boys had their hair cut.

Since Sikhs were the majority in our village, it was odd to see any adult with cut hair and a naked head in public. Before the 1940s, most rural Hindu and Muslim men in Punjab wore turbans but did not always have uncut hair or a beard. Going with a bare head in the village would have been like going out partially undressed, being unfortunate and not respectable, among all religions. Moreover, in the early days a grown man without mustache or beard was not considered manly by the village people. And when a man would say, "I will cut off my mustache if I can't do such and such thing", he would mean, "I will humiliate and disgrace myself." People could say to a grown man, "Aren't you ashamed of yourself; you have a beard on your face, yet you still did a lowly thing like this?"

In his memoirs, the Turkic/Mougal conqueror Babar wrote 500 years ago that he once humiliated some of his nobles for their shameful behavior; he ordered their faces shaved and made them walk in the streets without beards as a public disgrace. In Punjab if a man committed a shameful act they would shave his head and face, color his face black, and make him ride a donkey to humiliate him. Beard and honor went together in some circles of the old rural society, although not so the hair on the head, which was usually hidden by a turban.

Sikh wrestlers and some badmash (bad characters) usually trimmed and even shaved their beards, but they kept the hair on the head and the mustache intact; some younger men imitated them. A trimmed or shaved beard on a Sikh suggested a nonconformist or suspicious character, although the shaved face of a Hindu might be just the modern look. Therefore a Sikh with a turban but with trimmed or shaved beard was more likely to be suspected of crime and might be stopped and questioned by police, whereas a man with untrimmed beard would not be stopped without serious evidence. Just as certain styles of turbans were suspicious in the eyes of police, in those days a trimmed or shaved beard on a Sikh man might indicate that he was likely to engage in some dangerous behavior.

As modern times and Western influence arrived, men who were not Sikh started getting clean-shaved, with an *Angrezi hejamet* (English haircut), while caps replaced turbans. Gradually a bare head and a haircut became fashionable even in the rural areas. The practice of cutting the hair has been becoming more common since the 1990s among Sikh teenagers and adults. In 1984, following the assassination of Prime Minister Indira Gandhi, Sikhs outside Punjab, even Sikh soldiers traveling in military uniform but with no weapons, were massacred by Hindu fanatics all over India. For some time after that most Sikhs considered it risky to keep uncut hair in India outside Punjab. Now, watching the fashions from movies and the urban world, where all the famous people are seen without hair, Sikh boys want to look like them. And many inside Punjab are also adopting the cut hair and shaved look. In fact when I went to our Mehraj village school in late 2003, ninety percent of the Jat Sikh boys had cut hair and were without turbans. I assume that a similar pattern is developing in other rural areas of Punjab, so mine might be the last generation to look like conventional Sikhs with turbans. In the future, only priests or orthodox Sikhs will have long hair and a turban, whereas during my youth any Sikh without hair and turban was considered an oddity.

CHAPTER 9

A DIALOGUE ABOUT SPIRITUAL MATTERS

Bikker: Our friend Patrick died in a car accident.

John: That is so tragic! I will pray for him to the Merciful Lord who has taken Patrick at the young age of 34.

Bikker: Where I come from, they believe that the total number of breaths one is allowed in life is predetermined and that every grain you are entitled to eat has your name written on it. When the allowed number of breaths is complete, then God sends Yum Raj (Grim Reaper) to take you away from this world. But how can we blame God for the accident and death of a human? Is God in the business of causing accidents? Do you really believe that there is a merciful God who favors humans, because they are made in his image, but also causes pain, suffering and violence?

John: I believe that He punishes people for their sins. Don't you have similar beliefs?

Bikker: I used to listen respectfully to what I was told about God when I was young; now I like to think for myself. Some of those things I still believe to be reasonable, while others do not seem to be consistent with observations. God would not want me to believe in a religion if it appears to be false. So my rule is to live by the things that are believable as true, keep an open mind about things that may be true but are not provable, and refuse to believe things that are contrary to reason and observation. Some organized religions propagate superstitions and falsehoods as miracles. These miracles usually involve a violation of some law of God and reality, and must be merely deceptions and falsehoods designed to impress gullible believers.

John: Miracles can be performed only by God or by people to whom God gives special powers. God does not have to follow any laws; He can do super natural things and so can some people. If you don't believe in miracles, then you don't believe in religion or God. You may not be a Christian, but are you an atheist?

Bikker: No, being an atheist would be an arrogant stance, ignoring the wonders all around us. I believe in a God that created the universe and made its laws, but organized religions may not be able to use such a realistic God to snare believers. I don't want to dismiss all religions, because any spiritual practice can be a positive influence in the personal lives of people. Most of the rituals and celebrations in our lives—weddings, deaths and festivals—take place through religion. Our ideas about morality and justice came through religions initially. Religion can provide support to the mind and aid the practice of ethics.

But the main problem is that religion can generate hostility and hatred in the mind of a believer against the followers of other faiths; most religious people consider other faiths to be damnable or at least misguided. For example Christians think that all non-Christians will burn in hell; Muslims have similar beliefs about non-believers; and if you don't practice Hindu dharma, you could not be reborn as a human but as some worm or animal. Some thinkers have argued that religion can become a disease of the mind, and once a religion infects such people severely, they have no choice but to detest the people of other faiths. If Osama bi Laden, the prominent jehadist of Islam, had been born a Christian, he would have wanted to kill Muslims or to subjugate and convert them to Christianity; and some Christians would have lauded his efforts.

Truth is not acceptable to people with extreme religious attitudes, if it contradicts their religion. Religions can acquire a vested interest in enforcing pernicious developments in their beliefs, regardless of what is truthful and beneficial to humans. Religions become like biological and corporate entities, and even like empires; they want to survive, flourish, be powerful, and want to dominate and control. Many tribes and societies in ancient times felt that they were God's chosen people and that other races and tribes could not enjoy God's favor. Even in modern times, to some people their religion is like a club, team, clan or tribe favored by God; many feel that their religion must dominate over others and possibly convert or destroy them. Religion has been used frequently as a tool for political power and to motivate the faithful to conquer, destroy or enslave the followers of other religions. The religion of Mohammed was spread mostly by conquest. The Christian sect out of Judaism had major success only when, after three hundred years of struggle for survival, they converted the Roman Emperor Constantine. Subsequently that religion was spread by the power of the Roman Empire. When religion is combined with the powr of a government, there is a probability of suppression or even elimination of religious minorities and restriction of individual liberties. Although they may have started with good principles, most religions become some combination of unnatural beliefs, superstitious rituals, power consolidation schemes and vehicles of hate against other faiths and free thinkers. In our Sikh gurdwara they used to say *"Raj bina dharm nahi,"* that is, "without political power, religion cannot flourish"; so they wanted to combine religion with politics. Fortunately, in the last few centuries some bold thinkers have tried to break the stranglehold of religion on society. The farsighted founders of America tried to limit the power of religion to infect government. But even now, religions want to inject themselves into government and strive to have their tenets promoted by political power.

John: But why would intelligent people accept a faith that is not based on truth?

Bikker: There are always people with the need to believe in some power that will shower blessings on them and will protect them. Humans also find a sense of security in a community of like-minded believers; they consider such a community to be their power base and defense against others in the world. Then they have the urge to impose their beliefs on others, because the satisfaction and validation that comes from someone else accepting your belief is like psychological conquest. For a believer, any new convert adds to his power base, improves his security, and removes threats. Religion becomes like one's family, clan, club or team against others. Once a religious belief is implanted in the mind of a human, it becomes his point of view, and he closes the door to any truth outside it. Then that human is willing to defend this point of view and to promote it at all costs, and he considers the unconverted as alien "others." In some humans, success in converting others fulfills the urge to win and to dominate; in others it fulfills a sincere and natural human desire to help other people.

A believer feels happy when his religion can dominate over others. A contemporary English author has written, "The conquest and raj of India was one of the highest attainments of *Christian civilization*.", as if it was really the religion and not weapons or superior military power that gave them victory. Even nowadays, some fanatics volunteer to sacrifice their lives in order to kill those of other religions. They believe that God is waiting with rewards of a variety of treats for them in paradise, if they die while killing people of other faiths. On 7 July, 2004, I heard a Muslim cleric on British TV saying that "Allah is pleased with the suicide bombers that kill others who don't obey the will of Allah." Another Muslim leader in Germany being interviewed on TV said, "It does not matter whether Bin Laden advocates the killing of Jews and Crusaders; the Quran itself tells us to fight those who don't live according to Allah's rule." Then he said that the best solution for Europe was to follow Islam, rather than live in the current 'immoral ways.' Another preacher was seen on American TV, saying that the flag of Islam must fly over the American capital and over Europe. Those Muslims may appear more fanatical, but the strict believers of other faiths are not much different. A conservative Christian writer who supported the war making policies of American president G.W. Bush, suggested during a television interview, the way to deal with the 'Muslim terrorists': We should invade their countries, kill their leaders and convert the remainder to Christianity. So religion can become a vehicle of hate instead of devotion to God.

Religion moves some people to defend their faith till death, because to them belief is dearer than life. So instead of spiritual uplift, the role of religion can become the promotion of prejudice and hate. Scriptures can be used to justify violence against infidels. You feel validated by anyone who supports your belief and feel violated by anyone who contradicts it. Besides, the god of your ancestors may have a special place in the core of your heart. A strong believer may think of other religions with contempt; thus there maybe a seed of fanaticism and hatred in him. And in the process of consolidating their power, religions accumulate many falsehoods and superstitions. Courtesy may prevail outwardly in modern times, but by its essential nature, every religion is in competition with all other beliefs and is hostile to all truths that are threats to its power. The fact that it is illegal in Saudi Arabia to practice any religion accept Islam shows how much tolerance religious humans show when they have the power.

Most religions preach that their own scriptures came directly from God or were revealed to their prophets, and that the scriptures of other religions may be worthless. A religion may claim that its prophet was the true messenger of God, or God himself in human form, and you are insulting that prophet if you don't submit to his religion. The reality is that some unjustified assertions may be contained in any holy book. What was said or written by a devoted believer in the past, because holy for his followers. But some scriptures may contain falsehoods, either because truth about a matter was not understood when they were written or because the writer was blinded to truth by his faith. God provides scriptures for religions only in the sense that He creates enlightened writers, just as He causes crime, disease, rain, or earthquakes.

John: You have a cynical view of religion. And if you don't believe in miracles, how can you believe in prayers?

Bikker: I am willing to accept some value in religion, but even more in meditation, prayers, and various spiritual practices. I think prayer can soothe and sustain the mind, and meditation can reduce anxiety. Socially coming together and providing mental comfort to each other, is a great benefit of religion. Prayer, meditation, rituals and other spiritual practices might benefit the mind and body, even if God does not listen. Religion can enforce ethics and good behavior or can provide motivation for selfless actions that are useful to humanity. When I saw catholic nuns and priests for the first time, I thought they were the holiest of all people, as they served humanity selflessly. And since they never married, they would not be subject to the common human failings like lust, greed, anger, attachment or pride.

John: You say you believe in God. But you seem to have some abstract view rather than the flesh and blood God who, we Christians believe, came to earth and died for our sins. Is your God kind, forgiving, and merciful? Does He grant wishes and cure diseases?

Bikker: I do not like to refer to God as He, because that word implies that God is a male human. For me, "It" or "That" is a better term of reference. I do, however, use the word He for the sake of convention in the English language. God has no known form, nor any particular location; 'above the clouds' is the most miserable environment, not a good location for God. Names like Zeus, Yahweh, Allah, God, Indra, Brahma, Waheguru, and others are all cultural preferences; 'Creator' or 'Highest Master' describes Its powers and functions more appropriately. God could not be human or any other creature, because all biological entities change and die. God's laws about the gravitational force or electrical properties in nature are never violated, so He is Omnipotent. He is Omnipresent because His power operates everywhere. He may be Omniscient, but He does not really need to know, because everything is guaranteed to happen according to His laws. The Creation and Natural Laws are God's essence, everything in nature follow automatically from those laws, and the laws are enforced automatically and continuously. The remarkable thing about God is that He is on duty keeping the universe running, even when I sleep. If gravity were turned off even for a short time, all of us would fly off the surface of the earth to some unknown abyss, because the earth is spinning at 1,000 miles an hour near the equator and moving at a velocity of a couple of million miles a day around the sun, which itself is moving within the Milky Way galaxy. The same is true of God's other laws as they operate uninterrupted. And these natural processes are the true miracles! When you watch the grandeur, the beauty, the intricacies, the elegance, and the order and consistancy in creation, you have to believe that there is some force behind all this. The nuclear fusion that creates energy in the sun, the electromagnetic nature of matter that creates light and colors under the right conditions; the design and functioning of animal bodies, plants and flowers; the urge in biological organisms to survive, reproduce, dominate and want love—all are the miracles of God.

But unlike Muslims, Christians or Sikhs, I do *not* believe that compassion, forgiveness, mercy, partiality, or intervention to help worshippers, are God's traits. God is probably not forgiving, because that would violate the law of cause and effect. God does not seem to be merciful when the innocent and the helpless suffer. God is without enmity or

208

prejudice, so He can not favor any individual, tribe or race, although by *the law of chance,* some individuals or races may have better gifts or situations than others. And if God is watching any evil, cruelty or suffering, there is no evidence that He tries to intervene, whether the victim is holy like the Pope or some unfortunate leper. He does not change the course of events or the laws of nature because of anyone's prayers. The truth is that God is unconcerned with individuals. He allows bad things to happen to even His supposedly favored people. He also creates people and things that may have random or extreme defects. And the New Age platitude "God is Love" is off the mark if taken literally, "God is unconcerned", may be more accurate.

The Semitic religions insist that God favors them and not any pagans. When they see suffering and misery among themselves, they explain it by the concept of original sin, that is, *the knowledge of good and evil* that Adam and Eve acquired and that causes suffering to the humans of today. I think that acquiring *the knowledge of good and evil* is the true worship of God. I still fail to understand the concept that Christ died for our sins. Does it mean that he has already paid for all our sins, when we had not yet committed them? By giving his life, did he stop people from sinning ever again? Actually, he did not even stop all of his Popes and priests from sinning! It might have been better for humanity if a good man like Jesus had lived longer, instead of being killed.

The Orientals also have a strange view of suffering and calamities. The Hindus say that the real world is the world of soul and this *maya* (material world) is just an illusion, a *leela* (play) arranged by the gods for their own entertainment. The gods enjoy drama so much that pain, pleasure, murder, suffering, victory, defeat, disease, famine, war, earthquakes, and floods are all the manifestations of *His leela* (drama) to keep the world from getting placid and boring. There can't be much drama without conflict, violence, selfishness, anger, greed, cruelty and suffering. But why should God make an innocent child suffer? They say that that suffering is a consequence of karma, the reward for the deeds done when the child's soul was in a previous body. The *karmic law* makes it difficult for your soul to escape the consequences of your actions, although your good deeds may wash away the consequence of some of your evil deeds. So the apparently evil person, enjoying good fortune now, has it coming to him. And karma has consequences for the soul even in later incarnations, assuring misery for creatures and plenty of drama for the enjoyment of the gods. The Buddhists also do not count on any "merciful lord" to eliminate suffering. According to them, suffering is a part of life and is exacerbated by man's attitudes, attachments and wants; so right attitude, right thoughts, right deeds, and discipline of the mind, along with limiting needs, expectations and attachments, are the best approach. I do not know enough of Hinduism or Buddhism to endorse any of their beliefs, but next to my native Sikh thought, I consider the Buddhist approach to be quite honest. I personally believe that some of the drama of life is caused by the forces of nature, and some of the suffering is caused by humans whom God creates with defects; but all humans can do better if they adopt humility and compassion toward others and follow some spiritual practice.

John: Bikker, you don't have a caring, personal God like I have; do you have any kind of devotional practice?

Bikker: I don't believe there is any such thing as a personal or caring God. The stories of God appearing as a human and walking with, advising, helping or testing the faith of the early day patriarchs are just fairy tales. God is not a human, and neither hates anyone nor favors the devotee.

Prayer may be beneficial, but people don't always pray with the best of attitude and intentions. People pray before a football game in order to have a better chance of defeating the opposing team. In India, a sect called Thug, whose creed was to rob and murder people, prayed to their goddess before starting on their evil missions, so that the goddess would bring more victims in their way. Ancient warriors called upon their gods to smite their foes. People with a religious bent of mind may think that prayer can move mountains and can turn stone into wax; but in reality the only possible changes are within one's mind. Our mind can adopt a devotional stance and be transformed gradually; it can imagine healing and sometimes be healed; it can believe in courage and can sometimes act heroically. That is why religion, meditation and prayer can have value, as they work on the human mind and benefit the individual, regardless of their inability to change the mind of God. Meditation and prayer may also be effective because the human mind can benefit from meaningless rituals and repetition. And after your parents, friends and relatives have left you, God can always be there to pray to.

As for my own spiritual practice, some day I hope to start a routine of scripture recitation like my father's. The only practice I have at present emphasizes mind and body rather than scriptures or prayer to God. Some years ago I learned the ability to go into a state of relaxation, to experience body sensations and during the process to detach from existing anxieties and concerns. Thereby I had developed the ability to create a feeling of well-being in my mind and body. With a variation of that process I could also clear minor pains and ailments from any part of my body. Initially I learned this procedure just to fall asleep within seconds, when I needed to. Later, I learned to extend the process. My procedure goes like this:

Sit in a comfortable position. Lying down is an option, but in that position one can fall asleep unintentionally. Breathe in as deeply as comfortable and hold the breath for four seconds. The advantage of holding the breath is that the release occurs more effectively then, as it does with a sigh. Slowly exhale for many seconds, with a sigh or groan; some people are taught to produce the primal sound of Om or Ong during the slow and complete breathing-out, and even press the stomach muscles and the diaphragm to exhale forcefully at the end. Before breathing in again, hold for three to five seconds and pull the stomach muscles up. This is good for stomach awareness. People who practice yoga seriously do not let their stomachs get out of control, and my own waist size at 76 is the same as it was at the age of 18. After a few breath cycles like this, release any effort, strain or tension, and let the body go limp but stay aware of your breathing. Consciously letting go of all stress, tension, or effort in the body is very important. Then one can start from either end of one's body and experience every part and organ in the body successively as one breathes in and out. For some muscles of the body, it may be helpful to tense a part first and then release it, to feel the difference.

Starting with the toes, put your awareness in your toes and then in the front of the foot and feel any *sensation, strain, pain, tension, tingling* or other effect that may be present; dwell in that region and experience whatever is happening as long as necessary to make the sensation unimportant and insignificant. Then move your awareness along the bottom of the feet to the heels as the mind experiences those areas one spot at a time; later, move

210

the awareness to other parts of the feet. In the same way experience the ankles, legs, knees, thighs, genitals, hips, stomach, kidneys, liver, heart, spine, shoulders, arms, hands, neck, up the back of the head to the forehead and all the muscles and cavities in the face. One should cover all the organs of the entire body sequentially, experiencing the feeling in each organ thoroughly and dwelling in each location as long as it takes to experience the sensations there. When the mind is engaged in this process it is totally detached from other concerns of daily life. This process should remove any tension, pain, or minor ailment from the body. Before ending the process, once again I check to make sure that the body is limp and I am not holding or tensing up any part of the body.

A relaxation process of this kind can be a part of the routine for people who practice yoga, those who meditate, and those in the process of self-hypnosis, guided imagery and other practices. Then the practitioner may choose his own path. One may make positive affirmations to improve well-being, examine barriers that stand in the way of achieving one's goals, or visualize oneself performing according to one's goals and plans. Some may pursue thoughts that are liberating, empowering or uplifting. Some may recite a mantra or ritual words sacred to them. One useful procedure is to visualize yourself performing according to your goals, not with anxiety but with total trust; some may focus on having a part of the body undergoing the changes that they desire, to achieve healing, reduce pain, etc. I usually recite the first five *pauri* (stanzas) from the Granth, because I remember them by heart.

I read somewhere that meditation and relaxation are beneficial because they prompt the organs in the body to produce helpful chemicals, to make them function as though whatever your mind imagines is actually happening. The organs of the body can be stimulated by one's mental state to produce hormones and chemicals that reinforce changes in feelings as well as in the functions of the body. Just as hormones and chemicals in the body affect our mind and behavior, conversely our intentional behavior and rituals can affect the production of beneficial hormones. Although the latter process is less subject to one's control and may be slow to produce results, changes in mind, in behavior and body physiology are possible. A body and mind that have been habituated to operate in a certain way cannot change their operations quickly like turning a switch. But with some form of meditation, your body can change from producing the chemicals that lead to anger, hate and anxiety to producing those that promote serenity, love, tolerance, pleasure and health. When I used to practice such mental processes, I felt elated and powerful for a while, as if from a new relationship, new discovery or new acquisition. I used to be able to create a state of extreme pleasure, and I thought I could also cure some minor ailments. But of course one should not depend on such a process if a serious illness in the body develops to such an extent that the attention of a physician is necessary. One must never ignore physical realities, because one's mental powers may be inadequately trained or may be exercised too late to change the outcome. Prayer and meditation have no effect on anything except the human mind, and there are no guaranteed results because every individual may not be able to develop the proficiency to effect the changes, just as all people are not equally hypnotizable. Even when this kind of practice works, it is more like pushing a string than turning a lever by force. But there is no doubt that almost any spiritual practice provides sustenance, serenity, stability and clarity to the mind and removes anxieties and fears.

In the physical world there is no apparant or obvious evidence of any effects caused by prayer, meditation, or the exercise of mental powers. That is why the petitionery prayer might be useful because in it the mind is engaged, but intercessory prayer may make no difference. You cannot cause rain by praying; you cannot kill your enemy by wishing him dead, and you cannot stop a bullet by just praying. Worship, prayer, meditation, self-hypnosis, chanting and many other rituals may all have beneficial effects, but dependence on prayer alone can build false expectations and may disappoint in some situations. Praying to the Goddess of Smallpox may not prevent the disease; a vaccination guarantees better results. One of my friends who was a cheerful and vivacious lady died of breast cancer recently because her church told her to refuse treatment from doctors and just pray to God; instead she was encouraged to go to a Tony Robbins retreat. The chance of changing God's mind by prayers is practically zero. We are on our own, as God is not an interventionist.

John: But Bikker, don't you think those worshippers of idols and false gods are doomed?

Bikker: Because I heard so much preaching against idol worship in my younger days, I used to think that idol worship was useless. But now I believe that worshipping some god made of wood or stone may be about as useful as worshipping the "God in heaven," provided that the worshipper is sincere and convinced of its divinity. The effect of the ritual can be just the same in either case, as the human mind is perfectly designed to benefit from rituals. Some repetitive rituals can be good for the soul.

John: If God does not watch or care, why should people consider being moral and ethical? According to your thinking, they are not going to please or displease God or change His mind anyway.

Bikker: Yes, morality, truth, ethical behavior and the Golden Rule are good things to practice. If you believe in the karmic law of cause and effect, that is alone a good reason for ethical behavior. There are also mundane and practical reasons to be ethical. At some level, a normal human innately knows that unethical, selfish, and immoral behavior will result in deterioration of the society of which he is a part. Therefore, even the motive of self-preservation requires ethical and moral behavior. We may be selfish, but we can't be happy with our wealth or achievements unless we share the joy with others; we cannot be happy when others around us are miserable and suffering. At some level we understand that we will hurt ourselves if we create a society of evil-doers. The ancient Greeks said that whatever harm a man does to society harms the man himself.

In addition to the idea explained above, we know that the evolution of the brain has given humans more power than to other animals. And with this power seems to have come ethics, morality, conscience, and the ability to think about the consequences of actions. A lion has no capacity to reflect when it needs to kill a deer. But a normal person's conscience will torture him when he does something for selfish gain, with harmful consequences for others. A normal person has a conscience that feels connected to all creation; such a conscience enjoys harmony and abhors destruction. When in the process of achieving your goals you do something destructive or evil, you injure a part of your conscience. An injured conscience is a damaged self, because however much you try to suppress or ignore it, your conscience feels the injury. Without conscience there is no mind and no humanity. It does not matter whether or not you have been caught doing the consequences of your actions, even when there is no immediate punishment, so the human conscience is a useful watchman, even if it is sometimes negligent.

John: That sounds like a flaky theory of conscience deciding good and bad actions. How can the conscience make people do the right things? Did Hitler have a conscience?

Bikker: What feels correct to the conscience can be influenced by cultural context, selfish goals, or defects of the mind. Some religions believe that God created man with a free will; I think God created man with built-in selfishness and man has to learn to function in the world of conflicting interests. God has also designed some peoples' minds with extreme defects and perversions, so much so that some of them feel the need to kill others, or even to kill themselves! Unfortunately, defects are created continuously by natural laws, along with the normal things. And some people do suppress their conscience when some other goal, motivated by desire or success, appears to them more important than doing the right thing. Unfortunately, the self comes before everything else. A conqueror who kills many innocent people may be considered an honorable hero by his own people, even by his priests. A dishonest manipulator, who cheats or deprives many others of their just rights, may be honored as a great achiever. Such motives and rewards can warp a man's conscience and derail him from a conscientious path. Usually there are adverse consequences when this happens. There is a record of how tortured and mad Hitler became in his last days, although you wish the God of the chosen people had intervened to stop him before he caused death on a biblical scale. Some psychologists now believe that the soldiers' syndrome, like that suffered by some Vietnam War veterans, Gulf War veterans, and the veterans of the two World Wars after the wars were over, is a result of injured conscience. During the wars they killed because they were taught to hate the enemy, or just for self survival. But later, on reflection, they felt revulsion for what they had done.

So it is unthinkable that you as a normal human would not feel bad when others suffer. Your conscience favors the good and abhors the bad, even when others are doing it to others. That is why it is possible to sympathize with the hero in the movies and despise the villain, although they did nothing good or bad to you personally. It can feel as if those good or bad things are happening to you. It is remarkable how the entire world opposed the apartheid policies of the South African government after the world had developed awareness of the facts. Sometimes people do commit horrible acts for selfish gain; and it may take generations to reject the prevailing injustice, as ordinarily people just go on with their lives, trying to survive in their own circumstances and struggles. It may take courageous thinkers to initiate the process of abolition of the injustice. But whatever is happening to others in the world, your conscience can never be neutral about it; in some way, it is also happening to you.

John: What is the *Purpose of Life*? Why am I here? Should I Expect *Life after Death*?

Bikker: Most religions believe that the purpose of life is to recognize its source, which is God and to worship that Creator. Hindus believe that the gods created life in order to have activity and drama in the world for their own entertainment. Semitic religions believe that God made man in his own image and created all other things for man to exploit. I personally think that *life is merely God's experiment with molecules and cells*. Life had no choice about coming into existence when conditions became suitable for complex molecules, amino acids, proteins, reproducing cells and organisms to form. Normal life is programmed to protect and propagate its DNA, the DNA of its kin, and its species, in that order. You had no choice about being here; you are a part of God's experiment with the nature of molecules, cells and organisms that express themselves according to their traits and properties. And living organisms have traits such that each life, from ants to lizards to crows to elephants, considers itself to be the most important entity. It wants to survive, reproduce and promote itself; in the higher forms it also wants to dominate over others and seeks pleasure, love, approval and glory. Selfishness, fear, anger, enmity, greed, pride, and hate flow automatically from the nature of human life. Without such a design for survival and selfishness, evolution would not have occurred. But this nature can be perilous for evolved humans if it is not controlled with understanding and proper regard for all creation. And because of its self-importance, life looks for some *special meaning* for its existence and may call itself 'the image of God.'

As for life after death, you have to decide for yourself. I am expecting neither much fun nor any misery after I die. My attitude is to keep an open and aware mind. I want to understand how the world works and not to have a destructive relationship with any of God's creation.

John: Isn't all this suffering in the world due to sins? What is the Key to Happiness?

Bikker: The Muslim holy book Quran begins with the word, "In the name of Allah, most compassionate and merciful." and every chapter in the Quran begins with the same words. Some faiths like Budhism suggest that life is about pain and suffering, as if God purposely creates miseries and disasters. I personally think God is unconcerned, and suffering is a result of some natural and some man-made factors that interfere with the desire of an organism to survive, reproduce, and to seek pleasure, love, power and glory. *Change, Chance and Defect*, which are inherent in God's design of nature, will assure frequent misery and occasional disaster. People understand change and chance, but they may be reluctant to believe that God creates *defects*. In reality nothing can exist without defect; even the most perfect crystal will develop defects due to natural causes. Of course humans are created with varying degrees of defects of mind and body, that can create plenty of suffering, disorder and destruction. As my mother used to say, "No person is perfectly good; only God's *naam* is perfect." There is also the unfortunate fact that nearly all life lives by exploiting and usually by devouring some other form of life. So God's laws and phenomena can cause suffering, if one is caught in an unfavorable situation, and people with defective minds can add to the misery in the world.

As for the key to happiness, the ingredients of good health, satisfying work, and loving relationships may keep ordinary people happy. In reality it is impossible to have everything go right for everyone at all times. If you are lucky enough to have the above ingredients but are still unhappy, there may be physiological or mental disorder, or just unrealistic expectations and misconceptions; therefore some professional intervention might be helpful. If the problem is not serious, you may find a remedy by examining your feelings, clearing the cause of anxiety, and eliminating the fear by clarity of thought. Anxiety may be a part of human design; anyone whose survival is threatened or who wants to impress others with a high-ranking job, big house, notable achievements, famous friends, brilliant children, and who would be embarrassed to appear ordinary, has seeds of anxiety in him. If one can acquire an understanding of what *is* and then struggle to change and improve things, the process itself might make one happy. Instead of obsessing about self, if one could engage in the struggle to help others and improve the world, the anxieties might disappear. To prevent the mind/body from damaging itself by existential angst, it may be useful to learn the technique of *detachment* and be an *observer of self*. Werner Erhard, the founder of *est*, used to say that the key to happiness and power is to want what already *is*. But real humans don't follow such path; they want *what is not*. Wise men say that attachment is natural for humans; it may be a cause of pain, but it also makes life joyful; human existence without attachments can be boring. Holy men say that the only way to relieve the problem of attachment is by attaching oneself to something perfect and everlasting, like God.

John: Bikker, do you believe in the Immortal Soul ?

Bikker: Ancients believed that the soul enters the human body as it takes the first breath and it leaves the body at death. Hindus say that every creature has *atma* (soul), which comes from the great reservoir of souls called *Parmatma* (Highest Soul), another name for God. Our atma has been given a body and sent into this world to create activity and drama for the entertainment of gods, because the gods don't want a placid and boring world. Our body is just the vehicle for the atma and will die, but the atma itself is immortal. The purpose of one's atma is to play its part and go back to merge with Parmatma by achieving nirvana (liberation), and not be stuck in the cycle of transmigration by births and deaths in the form of different creatures. But because of worldly distractions and bad karma (evil deeds) in life, one may pollute one's atma, and it may not remain fit for merger with Parmatma. Being unfit to achieve nirvana, it may be reincarnated as a human of some level or even may be reincarnated as an animal if the soul has deteriorated to a much lower mentality. One may be condemned to the cycle of *transmigration*, suffering in one animal life or another, until one is fortunate enough to be born a human again. Then one may have another opportunity to wash away bad karma by doing good deeds, thereby purifying and redeeming the atma and achieving *mukti* or *nirvana*.

The quality of your soul and your record of karma will determine the life form in which you will be reincarnated. If you lust for wealth, you might be reborn as a snake, since in the Indian myths snakes lived on buried treasures. If you are unduly greedy, you might come back as a hog. If you beat your ox cruelly, your soul might return as an ox and will experience being beaten according to the *karmic* law. In the village if someone was hurting a creature, his friends would say, "In your next life, you are going to be born as that creature and the same thing is going to happen to you!" If your soul cultivates nobility it may be reborn as the offspring of a gifted Brahman or a ruling monarch. And if you cultivate lower mentality and behavior, you would be reborn as a lower caste or as some animal or worm, appropriate to the state of your cultivated mentality. My friends in our village wanted to be reincarnated as stud bulls, because their only job would be to have sex, they would be free to roam in the open, and be treated as holy by everyone.

Some Hindus believe that the soul of an ordinary dead person may be just put on hold, and that the Great Judge may not decide its fate, until the survivors perform various rituals and offerings; then the idle soul can be assigned to a new body instead of being free as a ghost to create trouble. When some hurt, loss, or disease occurred in a family, they believed that the soul of the dead ancestor was still not assigned to its next role but was unemployed and free to cause trouble. Their Brahman would give the family a prescription for offerings to appease the gods on behalf of the soul; the bigger the bribe, the better the assignment that your ancestor's soul might get. What is left in the mind of survivors can play tricks to create a variety of feelings and visions, and those feelings and visions are the stuff of superstitions about spirits, ghosts and spooks. Even in the West, some people are tempted to believe that a *medium* can communicate with the spirits of their dead loved ones. Our family did not believe in any wandering spirits of ancestors.

What I have just said about the soul is really a part of the ancient Indian beliefs, which I neither endorse nor understand fully. Nanak, our Sikh Guru, preached about truth, ethical deeds, the love of God and against irrational, hypocritical practices in the name of religion; he did not invalidate the concept of soul. Budhists and Jains also believe in the nature of soul somewhat as the Hindus do, including much of the vocabulary describing its worldly suffering, transmigration and possible nirvana. But the Budhists don't posit any god to take care of your soul. That is why they don't ask you to worship their god but urge you to release your soul from selfish cravings and attachments.

I understand that according to the Semitic religions (Judaism, Christianity, Islam), humans are the only creatures that have souls and the destination (heaven or hell) of the soul is determined on the day of judgment. That is about as reasonable as the claims of other faiths. But they also believe that the day of judgment is going to occur only when their respective prophet or messiah comes down from heaven to earth. It was supposed to happen soon after their scriptures were written, but they are still waiting for such a day (Qyamet for Muslims and Rapture for Christians). They believe that their prophet will take the bodies out of graves and fly the good believers to heaven with him, while all others will be condemned to hell forever. The part about the messiah transporting them out of the graves may be about as true as their story of creation.

John: So, Bikker, do you think you may be reincarnated as a snake in your next life?

Bikker: I find the logic of it fairly elegant, and the system of rewards and punishments for the soul quite logical, but I have an open mind about the possibility that there is a soul that survives after an organism dies. Maybe the soul is just the deeper aspect of the mind; it is operative only when you live and vanishes at death; after you die, only the dust of atoms and molecules is left as the cells of the body decay. According to traditional beliefs, I may pay lip service to soul, but one cannot believe soul to be separate from the body if there is any truth to science. Logically, if a human has a soul, then so does a pig, a lizard, a tiger, and a cow; they are all biological entities and are created and die like humans. I believe that God would be pleased with me only if I follow the truth; and if I do not know the truth, He will prefer me to have an open mind rather than fanatically to follow some religion. God may not punish false beliefs, but false beliefs are wasteful and I consider waste to be immoral. If a false belief leads to evil action or destruction of others, then God should surely disapprove such belief.

John: When we suffer the death of a loved one, does his/her soul experience pain, anxiety or torture? Do they come back after death, to haunt the places they liked? Do they try to hurt those who had displeased them? What can the survivors do to make things better for the souls of the dead?

Bikker: The survivors can either take the empirical approach or the faith approach. The faith approach provides assurances from authority figures, who usually tell you that the soul of the deceased has gone to heaven, and you can thus be consoled. This is a good approach for most people, since no human is comfortable with the idea that nothing of him will remain afterwards; once we have been created, we want to exist forever.

The empirical approach is a bit but in my opinion it is closer to truth. This approach may simple lead to the conclusion that we are just like other living organisms in a world of continuing change. In the eyes of God, a human is about as special as an elephant, a bird, or a virus. When an organism dies, its mind and soul die with it; the body cells are left to decay into a dust of atoms and molecules, and there is no soul left to suffer or to go to heaven. And since there is no unemployed soul, it is unthinkable that it is wandering in its old haunts or trying to make trouble for anybody. A higher commitment to truth is required to accept that death really means the end of the functioning body, mind, and soul.

John: Bikker, there is no hope for you from the merciful God; but summarize your thoughts so that I might remember some key points.

Bikker: I think of God as the power that created everything and whose laws govern the operation of the universe; He does not listen to prayers or change things to favor His worshippers. *Change, chance and defect* are as much the laws of God as is gravity; they are responsible for the good and bad things in our lives. Religions exist because humans have the need to worship something absolutely powerful that controls their fates, and to enjoy the protection of their religion's power base; but then some get attached to their beliefs and want to impose the beliefs on others or to destroy the believers of other faiths. People who preach the religion can acquire power and prestige.

Any earnest meditation, ritual, or prayer may be a beneficial practice, but to insist that beliefs from a particular prophet should be imposed on others amounts to pernicious fanaticism. I don't believe that you are going to meet your prophet after you die, or that others who don't follow your prophet are going to burn in hell for eternity. A "man of faith" does not automatically get my respect; a man of high ethics, humility, and compassion does. If you don't have any other passion that gives you great joy, a spiritual practice can improve your life. The highest worship of God is to acquire knowledge of good and evil and to act in harmony with the truth, so as to minimize destruction, suffering or hatred, and to promote health, harmony, love and enduring pleasure. Humans are just functioning collections of molecules and cells with predictable traits. All life is driven by the desire to promote itself, and the engine of selfishness runs the world, but one achieves greater internal peace if one can detach from one's own desires and works to improve the condition of God's creation. After the death of an organism, only the decaying body cells are left, and you can make your own guess about soul. I hope to live ethically and in harmony with all of God's creation; its destruction and waste is sin. When some destruction is inevitable because life lives on life, and destruction of the evil may be necessary for preservation of the good, I should always make the least destructive choice.

CHAPTER 10

Castes and Occupations

It is awkward to discuss how the lowest castes used to be treated before the Independence of India. Nowadays it is unlawful in India even to mention a person's caste, although the Indian government still uses caste as a criterion to determine a person's right to run for election, to gain admission to schools, to hold jobs in government, and so forth, in order to give preference to the formerly untouchable castes. But this narrative is about the 1930-50 time, when castes were tied to hereditary occupations and when one's caste was either a great barrier or a great privilege. This account is purely historical and should not be taken as an offence by anyone.

Hindus believed that a soul was assigned its role in life according to its karma and was born into a family appropriate to its natural gifts and tendencies. Superior souls with good karma were born to become Brahmin or Kshatri; less deserving ordinary souls came into third tier caste and those with bad karma were born into the lowest caste. Mannu, according to his understanding of the Vedas, formalized the rules of Hindu society, the rituals of life, and the following four castes: (1) the highest were the Brahmin (or Brahman) who were the priests, scholars and teachers; (2) next were the Kshatri, the warriors and rulers; (3) after them were the *Vesh*, the traders, farmers, artisans and all others not classified in the lowest caste and (4) lowest of all were the *Shudra*, the leather workers, night soil removers, and untouchables in menial occupations, who were not allowed to touch the body, food or water of a higher caste person. It was believed that the quality of a soul would determine the occupation it undertakes and the family to which it is born and the caste assignment was decided by God. The touch of an untouchable caste person was supposed to bhrisht (mispronounced as bhitt in Punjabi), that is, pollute, defile or desecrate a high caste person. Sikhs and Muslims were not supposed to have castes, but in reality everyone in Punjab was described by his caste and occupation, and it was still a controlling fact of life in the 1940s in our villages. The Sikhs did not totally abandon the castes of their Hindu origin, and all Muslims were labeled by their occupations, or tribes of origin, but they did not have well defined classifications like the Hindus did. A Muslim of a tribe that considered itself superior would rather kill his daughter than let her marry a Muslim of undesirable caste. A Sikh could marry a Hindu, but only if their caste level was the same; when I was a child, caste was more important than religion, except to Muslims. In our village anyone could be described by his first name and his caste, for example Midda the Bania (shopkeeper), Ramji the Brahmin, Buggha the Sheikh, Bullhu the Nai (barber), Roukher the Soniar (goldsmith), Jamala the Chhimba (tailor, dyer), Jalali the Mirassi, or Ahmet the Jullaha (weaver). Addressing someone in person just by his caste or religion alone was considered rude, except that a Jat felt proud to be addressed as Jat; and some Jats (although they were not high caste) would call themselves by that moniker comically or playfully. You could not address even the high caste Brahmin by calling him "O Brahmin," because people used that mode of talk when they wanted to be abusive.

The upper caste Hindus were not allowed to eat anything touched by anyone of the lowest (untouchable) caste or by a Muslim. The Brahmin considered the Muslims to be desecrated humans, not fitting into the purity of Hindu system. And since the Brahmin had to be able to eat from the house of a Jat (third tier caste), the Jat better not pollute himself by letting a Muslim or the lowest caste Hindu touch his food or water. Though the Jats were not very conscious of sacredness, they would not eat any food touched by a Muslim unless it had been cooked afterwards, as fire was supposed to purify things. If a violation of the caste purity occurred, your parents had to find someone who had some bottled water from the holy Ganga River to purify you. A sprinkle of the *Ganga jal* (Ganges water) was supposed to restore the purity of a person if he were polluted by the touch, food. or water of anyone from an untouchable caste. The Ganga *jal* used to be brought home in bottles by anyone who went to the banks of the Ganga at Hardwar when he took the ashes of a cremated relative for ceremonial disposal in that river. They would use only a little sprinkle, so as to conserve the holy water. From the touch of a low caste person you could just wash off and usually be OK, but on eating or drinking from their vessels, the purification had to be done by Ganga jal. Whenever there was a lapse, people talked about it for years afterwards.

When water was delivered by the Muslim waterman in a leather bag, it was not considered polluted; but to drink from a container from his house was strictly unacceptable. The irony of the situation was that the Muslims and the low castes provided many services even though it was not acceptable to eat anything touched by them. Hindus, specially the Brahmans, made a fetish of cleanliness and bathing; they would wash themselves before every important task. And they thought the Muslims and the lowest castes were inherently unclean with no possibility of improvement. In towns, cooks and dish cleaners in restaurants used to claim their caste to be *Pahari* (mountain) Brahmin. No Jat or Kshatri would take such a job; and the lowest caste was not allowed to touch the utensils, because their touch would pollute and violate the dharma of patrons of the restaurant. The village people were sloppy in their pronunciation of Sanskrit words (from which the Punjabi language is derived), and they would call such a desecration *'bhitt'* instead of *bhrisht*, whenever someone's body, utensil, food or any other object was touched by any one of the untouchable caste. I remember some children who had unknowingly swallowed a low caste person's water, and they were spitting and washing their mouths afterwards when they learned that they had been polluted. I used to hear Jat women complain about their clothing or body being bhrisht (desecrated) by the brushing past of a low caste woman who had come to do some odd job and had accidentally made contact with the higher caste woman's things. My father did not

219

believe in the reality of such desecration or purification except as a matter of cleanliness, but such voices were few and did not make a dent in the practice in the overall community. He could not break the barriers singly, because if he did, then no upper caste family would eat from his hand or touch him.

Uncle Tiloka used to tell stories about the *Vishnoi* people in the desert. He would say, "If there is a caravan of hundred camels, so that the nose string of each following camel is tied to the tail of the preceding camel, and if the Vishnoi's food is loaded on the 100th and the last camel; and if a low caste person touches the nose string of the first or the leading camel, the Vishnoi's food would surely be *bhrisht*, even one hundred camels away." The irony is that the food was loaded on the camel, which was not believed to pollute it; yet a human touching a string 100 camels away could pollute that food. Of course the same bhrisht would result if the shadow of a low caste person fell on the Brahmin's food or body.

On the outskirts of every village, separated by some distance, there were colonies of low caste Chuhra farm workers, *Chumar* leather workers, transients, and others who did unpleasant or menial jobs. The higher castes did not want them to live nearby. On the periphery of our village there were five colonies of the Chuhra (sweepers, latrine cleaners, and farm laborers). When I was a few years old, it was a long walk to go from the village to the Chuhra colony. For a couple of centuries the population did not grow much. But during my lifetime the Jat population started building more houses, extended up to the Chuhra colonies of our village, and then started to pass them.

When Jat boys entered the buffalo pond to swim, the untouchable low caste boys could not be in the water in their vicinity, to avoid desecration. Ironically, a Jat boy could lean against a buffalo without any concern of being polluted. Needless to say, the low caste people were not allowed to enter temples or to draw water from the village well. They generally worshipped some aboriginal gods according to the teachings of Balmeek, their ancient preceptor. For worship, they had a small mud platform called a *thaan*, with a tiny mud hut the size of a dollhouse on it. They performed animal sacrifices to please their deity. The ceremonial pig they designated for sacrifice was decorated with bells and ceremonial *khumni* string necklaces and was pampered for many days before the actual day of sacrifice.

My Turn to Beg for Food While Traveling

Even though trains had arrived in Punjab nearly fifty years before I was born, most rural people still traveled on foot or on animals. Women rarely took a journey other than to visit relatives; but sometimes men went on trips lasting for weeks. People who took the *phull* (ashes of a cremated person) to be immersed in the Ganga river at Hardwar had to walk a couple of weeks to get there and back. It was customary to provide food and shelter free to anyone passing through the villages. That was considered such an act of punn (charity, piety) that some villages would set up free food and drink stalls for the benefit of those traveling to special fairs and pilgrimages. If a traveler was uncertain about which house to go to, he could go to the *sutth* (plaza) or *chauk* (square) where men would be sitting at any time of the day or evening. The traveler would describe his needs to the people there and would be sent to an appropriate house to eat and stay the night.

Sometimes people walked to places as far away as Balhotra and Nagaur in Rajputana to buy oxen or camels; it would take them many weeks to get back. During the journey, there were no commercial places to eat or sleep. Some travelers carried flour, *daal*, salt, and a utensil and griddle to cook simple meals during the trip. Most went to some house in a village and asked to be fed. A traveler needing food was not treated like a beggar; people felt sympathy for a traveler as he was a *perdesi* (foreigner), far from home and in need of help. Cattle dealers sometimes passed through our village. They would come to the village sutth, and someone would say "Send them to Tiloka's house; they have lots of space and the capacity to feed the cattle." The cattle dealers were not even Punjabi-speaking people; but Uncle Tiloka was always sympathetic to such travelers, as he himself had passed through strange places sometimes. So my family would provide free food for the men, free fodder for the oxen, and a place for them to rest overnight. You could not very well let the men or the animals go hungry as that would be *paap* (sin), and the custom of payments for such feeding had not yet developed. Besides, this was not a routine occurrence, and the traveling cattle dealers would be there only for one night and would be gone the next morning.

Once in 1944 I was sent with our fourteen-year-old worker Khushia, son of a potter named Dullah (short for Abdullah), to drive some cattle from Mehraj in Punjab to Talwara, just inside Rajputana. We went through the experience of begging for food during that cattle drive. After covering the first 25 miles, we spent the night in LaleAna in the house of my maternal uncle, Sohna, who had a big yard for sheltering the cattle. On the second day, much of the territory was desert without significant vegetation, and the trails went through sand dunes or barren land. After covering about twenty miles by sunset, we came to a house in Chor Mar village belonging to a family whose daughter was married to a man in our village. According to the custom, that daughter's family were obligated to honor even a donkey from our village, so we and our cattle were given good care in that house. But that was the limit of the Punjabi-speaking areas; on the third day the journey would be through the desert where people of different culture and language lived. We had to bypass the Muslim villages and find a Hindu village when we needed to get food. Although the Muslims were well known for their hospitality, in those days I could not accept food from a Muslim household, because I held to the concept that it would be a desecration of one's person to eat Muslim food. My Muslim companion could eat food from an ordinary Hindu house where I got my food, but I could not eat any food touched by his hand. For this reason, I was the one who played the role of beggar. Khushia watched the cattle while I went to a suitable house at mealtime. The houses of low caste untouchables were always outside a village, usually some distance away, so there was not much chance of an error. Having never begged, I found it extremely awkward to beg for food, but there was no alternative. I went to a house with a big door, where they gave me some simple *roti*. I brought it back and shared it with my companion. That day we were determined to reach our destination, instead of having to spend another day and night in strange territory and having to beg for food. It was getting dark when we reached the Rajputana border and the Ghagger River. About sunset, to my great relief, we came upon Uncle Tiloka waiting at the border to escort us. Although we had to travel some distance in the dark, finding Uncle Tiloka gave us a feeling of comfort and relief. We passed through the dry bed of the Ghagger River and reached my uncle's place in Talwara late at night.

No Escape from Caste

Some low caste Chuhra people in Punjab had adopted the ways of the Sikh majority by taking *amrit*. They were called *mazhabi* Sikh (Sikh by religion) and thus avoided discrimination while in the gurdwara, although they still suffered discrimination outside the gurdwara. The question arises: Why would a person accept the caste system that demeans him, that labels him unclean, untouchable, and lowly, and that ties him to a degrading occupation, while the same system entitles the high caste people to lord over him and to exploit him? Our farm workers used to say, "God made these caste barriers; it would be a sin to break them; we have to follow our role according to dharma." They believed in the caste system just as Christians believe that the Bible is God's word. In those days, though, the low caste people did not really have a choice. If a low caste man in the village acted up, he might not be physically beaten to "straighten him out," but he would face everyone's wrath for trying to break out of the role that God intended for him. They would say, "God could have given you birth in a high caste family if He so intended. If you act uppity, where will you go to shit, as all the land belongs to Jat landowners?" "Blocking their shit" was also a metaphor for having the power to make life of a low caste person uncomfortable if he did not conform to his traditional role. Since major industry as a possible source of employment was unknown in the villages, people of low caste depended for every aspect of life on the landowners, and it could be uncomfortable to displease people higher than you. Besides, if you believed in karma and dharma, behaving according to your assigned caste role in life was your best course. By violating the role to which God had assigned you, would get you in trouble with God as well as with society. Even the low caste men would say, "God has made these barriers; he could have given me birth in a raja's house if my karma had allowed it." They pretended to believe in the sanctity of the caste system; but if they had had any choice, they might have discarded it instantly.

If a low caste person went somewhere else to start a new life, other people would treat him as an unknown entity until they determined his caste. It was their dharma to not pollute and degrade themselves, even unknowingly. They would not hate the person, but until his caste was known, their interaction with him would be at the level necessary for labor or business transactions only. Usually they would be able to guess his caste, because appearance was an indicator of caste. Castes were not made by God, but most likely what happened was that the tribes who at some ancient time fell into the lowest castes were those starting with a disadvantage in making war, in capabilities and in knowledge. A low caste person was usually obvious from his facial structure, skin color, mannerisms, clothing, and speech. In fact the speech and accents of different castes was usually different even after they had lived and worked in the same place for generations. Each caste had its own section to live in, and the tones and accents of the low caste speech were distinctive. Dark brown or black skin, together with a flat or wide nose, thick lips and coarse features, generally indicated lower caste, although there were always exceptions.

Brahmins, Fetish of Purification and Bathing

One of the differences between the lowest caste and the upper castes was the general cleanliness. The Brahmin made a fetish of washing hands of bathing before any important activity. But the hands and even faces of the low caste people could have visible dirt on them most of the time. The low caste boys would defecate and then just such a little dirt on their butts before begining other activates. Clean water was not easily available to them. Most of the year the only bath that such boys had was in the buffalow pond where the buffalo dung and other pollution was entering frequency. In fact one difference between lowest castes and others was the easily visible dirt on their hands, faces and clothes. So apart from low birth, such contamination of the bodies of the lowest castes made other castes squeenish about touching them. In our village, our people had similar beliefs about the "unclean ways" or poor Muslims, whereas upper caste Hindus and specially Brahmins, were fastidues about washing and purifying. So the relatively unclean life of the low castes also promoted untouchability and the need to avoid contact.

Affirmative Action and Revenge of the Untouchables

Starting in the 1950s the caste disadvantages turned to privileges as the laws were passed by the government, not just to prohibit caste discrimination but to give preference to the previously untouchable castes. Since India became independent, low caste people have been espousing Hinduism, because there are political and monetary rewards and job reservations for people classified as low caste Hindu, but not for Sikhs or for those castes who converted to Christianity. There is now reverse discrimination and preferences to such a degree that having a low caste ancestry has become a political, monetary and career asset. In our village some higher caste people have tried to bribe government officials to classify their children as low caste untouchables, because that classification could be beneficial for all future generations. Nowadays, a judge, the chief of police, or the deputy commissioner in a district is as likely to be low caste as anyone else, whereas that would have been unthinkable fifty years ago.

It seems extremely unfair to me that the new Indian laws do not allow anyone in my ancestral village to run for any state or national political office unless he is descended from the untouchable low castes. All elected positions in our district are reserved for the untouchable castes, regardless of their wealth or educational qualifications. And even though they are a small fraction of the population, and most of the people in the district are Jat Sikh, my people are forbidden from exercising political rights because we are not classified as low caste. It is illegal to mention the word caste so they have to use some euphemistic word, but it is also impossible to ignore caste, because the lowest castes insist on being recognized as having untouchable caste ancestry so they may enjoy priorities and privileges. No politician can dare to propose to disregard the caste system because he could be voted out by the low castes, who now want to perpetuate the caste system. In fact recently the Indian government has proposed increasing the reservation of medical college seats from 22% to 49% for the untouchable castes.

There are cases where a low caste servant may have power over his employer, because the employer being higher caste may be forbidden by law to run for public office. For example Tinki, the wife of my nephew Sukhdial, had a girl servant named Bhikhi, whose ancestors had been working in the house of the young bride's family for generations. Tinki liked her servant. So when Tinki got married in 1989, the maid came with the mistress. Later as this Bhikhi became nubile, her mistress arranged her marriage

223

to a same caste boy from our village. Then the mistress asked Bhikhi to run for our village council, because she herself did not have the right to run, as the seat was reserved exclusively for the untouchable low castes. Of course no one treats the servant as an untouchable these days, but her rights are permanent because of her ancestry. And when she was elected the maid could make rules in the council that might affect the life of her mistress. The maid can run for the parliament of India if she wants to but the mistress has no such right in her home district.

Caste Decided Occupation

Apart from being in the military or some other government service, it was rare for any individual in a rural area to follow an occupation other than that dictated by his caste. Caste was tied to hereditary occupation, even if one was not currently practicing that occupation. Industrialization had not yet touched the countryside to eliminate the castes, and democratic voting did not exist before World War II to equalize political power. Caste was synonymous with occupation, so a carpenter's son became a carpenter, a weaver's son became a weaver, and so on. The occupations were hereditary to such an extent that even the profession of prostitution, singing, dancing, and entertainment was confined to a caste called *Kanjer*. The Kanjer would marry into their own caste; their daughters would be trained to be prostitutes, or dancers or singers, and their boys could play musical instruments to accompany the entertainers or be their managers. Since the audience and customers were men, only the Kanjri women were in demand as entertainers, and some of them were clever, sophisticated and glamorous. Before the Independence and partition of India, I saw many Kanjri women riding in *tonga* carriages in Bhatinda with their heavy makeup, jewelry, and fancy clothes. Since the Kanjer in Punjab were Muslim, all of them left for Pakistan after the partition of India, but in other provinces there were non-Muslim Kanjer also.

Officer Candidates Visit Kanjri House

In the early days any one who entertained and provided means of pleasure for money was considered morally degraded. The Kanjer caste provided prostitutes, singers, dancers and entertainers. Respectable people would not even pass through the street of the Kanjer, who, like other castes, would have a colony of their own. But pleasure-oriented people, some habitual drinkers and sometimes daring and wild young men, would sneak a look into those streets.

Once in 1952, I went to be interviewed for a career in the military, to the city of Merutt in the province of Uttar Pradesh, east of Punjab. The interview involved three or four days of aptitude tests, including some practical problem-solving and leadership skills. There were dozens of candidates, and we all stayed in the military services mess in the cantonment area, with little to do after-hours. In the evenings we could go into the city for entertainment. We suspected, although wrongly as it turned out, that the interviewing officers were secretly watching all our moves, manners and behavior at all times in order to weed out those with bad character flaws and morally unfit to be officers. There was always one interviewing officer at every dining table. We felt that we were being watched and evaluated in our table manners, whereas in reality the officers

224

were just trying to be informal and friendly in order to make the candidates feel welcome. At the dining table some candidates would try to be talkative and charming in order to impress the interviewing officers. The candidates also feared that the officers followed them into town in disguise, in order to discover any ungentlemanly conduct; so it was considered risky to wander into the questionable areas of the city of Merutt. But some of the boys from Punjab thought this was their opportunity to see the seamy side of life, as there were no Kanjri left in Punjab after the Partition of India. As curiosity got the better of caution, a group of us candidates reached the Kanjri street by traveling in rickshaws. We wandered through many Kanjri houses. The whole scene was unexciting and made me somewhat uncomfortable, because it was not considered suitable for proper people from good families. Nevertheless, I was not going to be a sissy and leave the group.

The Kanjer men were playing musical instruments and were polite and businesslike, and the Kanjri (female) in their best clothes were sitting on a raised area on carpets with huge pillows behind them. In some places they were singing or making small talk and trading glances. One of the Kanjer, when questioned, quietly explained, "This one is 10 rupees; the other one is 12 rupees; you can have the oldest one for 5 rupees; but this pretty one will cost you 20." If anyone had wanted to, they could have made a selection from among the Kanjri, paid her rate, and taken her to a back room. There was no charge for looking and listening to their music, but you had to pay for a drink if you wanted one. The boys in our group were merely out for curiosity, and no one paid for the services; some had drinks in a couple of establishments, while the others just looked and listened to the music. In one house, the Kanjer said, "Some people come here only to sit around, listen to songs, and possibly to have a drink. This girl does it with any paying customer; the other one is reserved by a rich man and has relations only with him and with no one else. This very young one is scheduled to be initiated by another wealthy patron who is going to pay a huge amount of money for the privilege...." One could not attach much importance to what he said, as it might have been just a part of his marketing tactics.

Only the wealthy, and usually urban, people would hire the Kanjri to perform on the occasion of weddings or other celebrations, and these performances were attended by men only. Attending a Kanjri performance was borderline risqué, but it was not thought to be much worse than drinking alcohol or eating meat. Such indiscretions were considered the prerogative of the rich if they could pay enough to hire the Kanjri. But no respectable woman would come near such a show.

Other kinds of entertainers, who sang, danced, or performed comedy, and so on, were generally not considered respectable either. The attitude was that if you were performing for money and for the pleasure of others, you were not respectable. Attitude toward pleasure and entertainment were so negative that "respectable" families in rural Punjab discouraged their children from learning to dance, sing or play music. Most singers were Mirassi and lower castes. I heard that in southern and eastern India, people used to be more relaxed or liberal about such things, and therefore people in those areas were more advanced than Punjabis in arts, music, dance and performances.

Earning Power of Entertainers

In the villages, every kind of entertainment was usually in the open and was available free to any passerby. The system of controlling access, performance in enclosed spaces, and charging admission was not developed in the rural areas. Most entertainers were like the street performers, the monkey showmen, the bear trainers, and the magicians. A performer was paid only when some viewer was especially pleased with his act. Circus owners were the only ones who controlled access, by means of the sight barrier of canvas walls. With no control over admission, and with a limited market, entertainers were seldom prosperous or respected, and they also had little incentive to develop their talents. For these reasons, and given the belief that some entertainers appealed to prurient interests, theirs was considered the lowest of professions, although they were not the lowest caste.

By the 1930s many Kanji prostitutes, who had been singers, dancers and performers by hereditary occupation, achieved higher status, and their daughters excelled in songs, entertainment and in the movies. Some say that many of the first actresses in India were not from respectable families but were the daughters of Kanjri. With the mass markets of the silver screen and the growth of movie houses for entertainment, the resulting wealth attracted other talented people, trained in drama and theatre, to the film industry. With modern technology and facilities, and with mass marketing and communications, the earnings of entertainers in India became lofty, and consequently their prestige became enviable. As the profession of entertainment gained wealth and respectability, the educated middle class joined the profession. Entertainers are effectively the aristocrats and royalty of the modern day, even in India.

My Aspirations to be a Music Maker

Attitudes toward professional entertainers also affected the image of amateur musicians in the village. Ordinary people who tried to make music for their own pleasure were considered a little risqué and nonconformist. Younger people used to admire the musicians; but the older and religious people thought that singing anything other than the religious *shabad* was like a vice. It was believed that playing music would lead to other vices and might ruin a man. It was rare for a son of a Jat landowner to become a professional musician. People who played music used to be lower status, miscellaneous castes and sometimes even untouchables. The only singers who were respected were the Punjabi poets called *kavisher*, who composed and sang their own songs. Yet many young Jat boys wanted to play music in the rural style.

In my rebellious days, I once threatened to learn to play the *sarangi*, a stringed instrument. I wanted to learn it only for personal pleasure and as another way to bond with my friends. I arranged to learn it from a man named Sohna of the Sadhan family. The stylish Sohna, much older than me, sometimes sat with the boys in the open area outside the village on summer nights, where no women or children would hear our music. There, some of us would sing *kalian*, and Sohna would play the sarangi, late into the warm night. Sometimes he also sang and played the sarangi during the daytime under a grove of trees, surrounded by friends. Playing the sarangi and singing was his private hobby, not entertainment for payment, so no one really looked down upon him because of it. I thought it would give great pleasure and be an accomplishment to be able to play the sarangi as Sohna did, so I arranged with Sohna to learn to play the instrument.

My family was outraged on hearing that I was scheming to learn to play the sarangi. They thought I would be disgracing the family by playing the crude rural music, an act suitable only for less respectable or somewhat wild and nonconformist people. My father said, "Why does this boy always think of wrong and perverted things? What has gone wrong with his mind that he wants to play the sarangi! Why is he frittering his time away in disgraceful activities?! He should go to college, instead." My family even sent word to Sohna not to ruin their son by teaching him to play rural music on the sarangi. Even my friend Nawab Din, who was otherwise quite balanced and wise, said to me, "Playing the sarangi is not a suitable pursuit for men from good families. It has brought misfortune and ruin to every landowning Jat who tried it. First, the sarangi was played by Lukkerwalia; he was murdered by his enemies while he was drunk, and the door of Lukkerwalia's house is locked forever, without any heirs. Then the sarangi was played by Chand of Bukken Ka; he became a pauper and died in rags. Then the sarangi was played by Munshi of Baghail Ka; he is still rotting in jail. Then the sarangi was played by.... Playing the sarangi brings only ruin and bad fortune to men from respectable families; it is a pursuit fit for the lower level people who have nothing to lose." Although the stories of the ruin of those Jat men who played the sarangi were well known, I thought the cause of their ruin was not the music but their other habits and activities. I still went to take sarangi lessons with Sohna, but I was not a natural at playing the sarangi. I could have made progress, but soon the disturbances related to the Independence and the Partition of India upset every body's life, and we could not think of such frivolous activities as playing the sarangi. No one was playing music in the midst of the massacres in Punjab during the Independence of India in 1947.

Miscellaneous Castes in Our Village

One of the under-valued and versatile professionals in the village was the Tirkhan or *Kariger*, literally an artisan or craftsman. In the village a good kariger had to be a designer, engineer, bricklayer, carpenter, cabinet maker, blacksmith, cart and wheel manufacturer, or house builder. Every Kariger was expected to be able to build a brick wall, a plough and yoke, a sickle, an axe, or a spear. Some might specialize in making shovels, hoes or spinning wheels, but any village Kariger could make any of these things when required. If you could describe something to them, they would build it. Each Kariger in our village had a furnace with double leather bellows, because he had to heat, beat and sharpen the tips of plowshares every evening for all the farmers of the village. Some Karigers were like independent businessmen, but each village also had a Kariger retainer for jobs required by the farmers, like making a plough, sharpening plowshares or sickles, or fixing a broken yoke or a bed frame. Every six months, he would be paid in grain at the time of harvest according to the number of ploughs that a farmer ran, regardless of how much work the family got out of the Kariger. The Kariger were the equivalent of Jats or traders in caste, but since they depended on the farmer Jats for wages, their status was not commensurate with their usefulness. Since the Jats owned all the land of the village, they considered all others, including the Brahmins, shopkeepers, carpenters, barbers, and others to be miscellaneous castes and minorities who lived in the Jats' village. In the rural society, compensation for labor was not always in cash. Some castes were paid in grain only, once every six months at harvest time.

The landowner Jat and the laboring Chuhra were necessary for starting a farming village. For other castes to be present, the village had to be well established. The village of Mehraj, having been long established, with four patti (domains), had its share of castes. Our patti Sandly had no Chamar (Hindu leather worker) but had one Mochi (Muslim leather worker) named Qamri, who quit shoe repair to become a chowkidar (watchman); his son Billoo was not much good at any work. We had a Muslim weaver named Ahmet with a young wife named Karima, although he also had an older wife named Fatima. Weavers were an important caste, because every house needed the homespun *khadder* cloth for routine wear. Some of the spare time of adult women, and much of the time of young girls and older women, went into spinning and preparing the yarn for the weaver. We had Sikh and Muslim dyers and tailors. Two Muslim Mirasi families acted as messengers, announcers and singers; their wives did hair for women. We had a Sikh carpenter and a Muslim cowherd. There were Muslim water carriers whose wives roasted grains in the late afternoon. The family of Imam Din, the Araeen vegetable farmer, had migrated a generation earlier from another village. At first they worked as hired farm hands, but later on they became independent sharecroppers. Our Patti Sandly had no Brahmin, but the Brahmin could come from other parts of the village to those nominally Sikh houses who still needed their services. There was a clan of Hindu shopkeepers named Roru Ke, who also used to own an oil-powered flour mill. They were all driven out of the village, partly due to enmity of a Brahmin named Ram Partap who threatened to destroy them with the help of outlaws, although such an act would be totally uncharacteristic of a Brahmin. Then there was an armed robbery in the house of Roru ke. Although none of their men was killed in the robbery, the dozen or so members of their clan subsequently left their fine brick houses empty and scattered to different towns, never to return. A Jat would have to die rather than leave his village where he had his house, land and brotherhood. But they used to say "a shopkeeper belongs to no village; he can take his *takkri-butta* (balance and weights) and set up a shop anywhere." Another shopkeeper named Shiv Ji, with sons older than me, had a small shop, but his family left the village in the late 1930s to live in the security of a market town. Only the less ambitious shopkeepers were still running their shops in the center of our village in the 1940s.

In the times before trains and electricity, the difference between a village and a city was only a matter of size; the big villages had shops and other facilities just as small cities did. Our village had a bazaar in the 1930s, with many shops in Kotli Street selling cloth, sugar, tea, hardware, general merchandise, women's bangles and makeup supplies, and so on. In addition to the Kotli bazaar, there were small shops scattered throughout the village. When the trains came and electricity followed, cities provided much better facilities and security, and most shopkeepers moved to the new market towns. The Hindu shopkeepers, like those in our village, never committed violent crimes. Their men never participated in physical games, in singing songs, in drinking alcohol or in any kind of outdoor activities; in the macho Jat culture they got about as much respect as women or religious people did—not very much.

Potters in the village were as essential as the weavers and the karigar, since every house had to have many water pitchers to fetch water from the well and to store it. If we lost a potter or kariger, we had to find another one quickly from some other village and had to provide a house for his family. I remember that once our *patti* settled Dullah the potter in the house of Chuhi the kariger when the latter died childless. Those houses had very little value, and in the old days people did not usually buy or sell houses in the village. A house abandoned by a Jat would belong to his kin, and a house abandoned by other castes would belong to the village. Until we got a new kariger, our family had to use the services of one from another patti for fixing and upkeep of the farm implements. But when our patti did acquire a new kariger, we had no house available and had to settle his family in the *dharmsala* (village inn) up to the year 1947. I remember Dullah the potter had his flywheel with a little pit near its periphery. He would put the end of a rod into the pit of the flywheel to make it rotate at high speed. As the flywheel kept spinning for long periods after the initial rotation, the potter could keep making utensils from the clay positioned at the center of the wheel. Pots for cooking *daal, saag,* milk or buffalo feed, bowls for eating and many other pots were made of clay and baked in the outdoor kiln. People depended on cooking utensils of clay in the villages. But when all the Muslim potters departed to Pakistan during the Partition of India, there was a rapid change from clay vessels to metal.

In our Patti, there was a *Sonyar* (goldsmith) family, who ran their jewelry-making operation in the front portion of their home in Kotli Street. They were probably Hindu, but they were indistinguishable from the Sikhs because their men had turbans and beards like the Sikhs and they all had village names that were not specific to any particular religion. In the villages there was little difference between Hindus and Sikhs up to the 1930s, castes and occupations were the main difference. The elder goldsmith named Roukher, with a big turban and long white beard, had become mentally deranged in old age. Roukher the Sonyar would be dressed in a heavy ragged coat even in summer, limped as he walked, and always dragged a tree branch everywhere he went until his death. Although the children were scared of his strange appearance and the dragging tree branch, Roukher was never violent. When he and his younger brother both died, and his wife Ghuppo the Sonyari had no other means of support, she cooked at weddings and did other odd jobs for Jat women until their whole family died out. When the Sonyar family were still running their jewelry operation, my mother took me once to their house to cut off my steel *kara* (bracelet), which I could not take off because my wrist had grown too big over time.

The Brahmins and shopkeepers practiced the Hindu religion, and the Muslims indicated their religion by their names and their clothing; but most Jats and people in the miscellaneous castes such as Nai (barber), Soniar (goldsmith), Kariger, Baziger (gymnast, performer), and Sansi, just had non-specific customs and clothing. We thought that the barbers, carpenters, and soniars were all Sikhs because they looked and acted like Sikhs; their old-fashioned names did not distinguish Sikh from Hindu; and before 1930s the difference between Hindus and Sikhs seemed unimportant. In our patti there was also a Nai (barber) who, being in a Sikh village, wore a turban and had unshorn hair and beard like the Sikhs. His name Bullhu indicated neither his religion nor his caste. Although cutting hair was his hereditary profession, he made his living by working at weddings to prepare sweets. The Jat Sikh men could have their beards trimmed, though not the mustache or the hair on the head. Some young ones had their eyebrows and beards shaped by the barber to look sharp. Before the harvest, some Jat boys would get together and ask the Nai to shave their legs because they claimed that leg hair would interfere with their work and could cause pimples during harvesting. The Nai would clip nails, shave the heads of little boys, and even use the razor for minor surgery. He would supplement his income by carrying messages, preparing sweets and providing other services during weddings, while his wife, called the Nain, would style ladies' hair. And traditionally the Nain always accompanied a new Jat bride as her personal attendant during the three-day visit to the bridegroom's house after the wedding ceremony.

The other three pattis of Mehraj had the Muslim shepherds called Sheikh, the *Teli* who crushed mustard seeds to extract oil and ginned cotton to make it suitable for spinning, the Chhimba or Darzi (tailor), and the *Lalari* (dyer) who colored turbans and other cloth. Most of the necessities of life were provided locally by the different castes. As my father used to say, "Except for metals and salt, we can produce everything we need to live, right here in the village. If we had salt and iron, we would be self-sufficient."

Except for the farmers and some shopkeepers, the people of different castes worked in the front portions of their own homes, and generally people of each caste and occupation lived in their own colonies, separate from other castes. Different parts of towns were described by the occupations of the castes living and working there. In bigger towns there would be *Lohar mohalla* (the blacksmith section), *Kanjer mohalla* (the prostitute section), *Dhobi mohalla* (the washer man section), Chumar mohalla (the shoemaker neighborhood), and so forth. People would go to the houses of the potter, the shoemaker, the goldsmith, the oil extractor, the weaver, the tailor, the barber, or the carpenter to get their work done. People worked every day of every year, as feeding cows, herding sheep, sharpening plowshares, or removing cow dung were not optional activities. If you had to be away, you had to find someone to fill in for you. Since people lived in big families, such temporary absences did not create many problems. But usually no one went away anywhere except for fairs, weddings, and deaths.

In addition to the ones mentioned above, some castes followed no particular occupation and lived by hunting, begging, scavenging or stealing. Some castes were even officially listed by the government as " Juraim Pesha", that is, criminal occupation, and had the reputation of committing minor crimes.

Motivations to Upgrade the Caste

Regardless of the ranks of the various castes, it was fashionable to think that one's own caste was better than others and to speak disparagingly about the other castes privately. Even a low caste could deride and say unflattering things about the Brahmins. Nowadays we admire anyone who came from a humble background and achieved prominence, but in the old society you could not get much respect without proper ancestry, hence the struggle for a community to upgrade its caste. The Brahmin and Kshatri were at the top of the caste heap and therefore were happy with the status quo. Sometimes a third tier caste, labeled with a hereditary occupation that was not considered high prestige, made an upward transition; the whole community would upgrade together, following a meeting of their brotherhood. The Klal caste, whose traditional profession was to deal in alcohol beverages, a pleasure industry and therefore not considered respectable in the old days, had become educated, prosperous, and powerful as they went into prestigious professions. It is said that in a certain year they declared themselves to be descendents of some Rajput or a famous ancestor. One of this caste had been the revered Jassa Singh Ahluwalia, the head of a Sikh missl (militia) that ruled a territory; he was also highly respected for his good judgment and fair treatment of colleagues, a rare trait among the Sikhs. His achievements certainly helped to upgrade the Klal caste. The name Ahluwalia became so prestigious that in our village even some Muslim Klals took the name Ahluwalia for themselves, although they had no connection to the famous Sikh general. Aroras and other castes similarly tried to upgrade and some consider themselves to be the equals of the Kshatri caste. The process of upgrading was easier when a community acquired professional, economic or political power, as the Jats did in the eighteenth century when they became the rulers of various states. Ranjit Singh, the ruler of Punjab, was merely a Jat by caste. But the Kshatri would never consider such upgraded castes to be their equal; and from the point of view of the Brahmin, the whole caste structure was being abused by these changes.

Haughty Jat and Humbled Brahmin

The caste system in Punjab had not been turned on its head then, as it was after the Independence when the lowest castes were put in the highest places and given preference in schools, jobs and elections. But in rural Punjab the holy Brahmins had been dislodged from their position of privilege. Centuries of Muslim rule had diminished the prestige of Brahmins. In the Muslim ruler's eye, the Brahmin was just a kafir, to be humbled for not following the religion of Mohammed. The village Jats still had some reverence for the Brahmin caste; some nominally Sikh families still would feed a Brahmin as an act of charity and piety. Some of the older generation still addressed any Brahmin man as *devta* (demigod); some still believed that the Brahmin could predict if there was a *grauh* (gods' wrath, impending calamity) on their family and could suggest preventive measures to minimize the effect. Brahmins in urban areas and in other provinces were still literate and could teach, perform ceremonies, tell fortunes, and so on. But the automatic entitlements because of their caste had diminished in Punjab. This was also the result of Sikh teachings, which had the effect of loosening the hold of Brahmins on society. Gone were the days when the Brahmin were considered the most valuable of human beings, with knowledge of spiritual matters as well as of the material world; when they would train princes in the art of war and council kings in matters of statecraft; when they had knowledge of science and medicine.

In our village a couple of Brahmins were my teachers. But by the 1930s, some Brahmins in the rural Punjab were reduced to fortune-telling, begging door-to-door and working as cooks or servants and even as workers and sharecroppers on the Jat's lands. For example, after I left Mehraj for college and my father did not want to make the effort to cultivate the land, our family land was then cultivated by Brahmin sharecroppers in the decades of the 1950s through the 1980s. They might not have been able to produce the best crops, but they were gentle and easy to deal with. Punjabi Brahmins were the gentlest and the most civil people to talk to, and they lacked the rudeness of the Jat farmers. Many of the servants and pot cleaners in the restaurants would call themselves *Pahari Brahmin* (hill Brahmin), because a low caste person could not be allowed to touch the utensils. Of course the urban Brahmans and those in other parts of India retained their old status pretty much undiminished.

The second highest caste, the Kshatri (in Punjab usually mispronounced as Khatri or Shatri) fared better, since their livelihood did not depend on religious teachings. The Kshatri of Punjab gradually went from being warriors to being government administrators, educators, industrialists, traders, and practitioners of various professions. Nanak, the founder of the Sikh religion, was a Kshatri of the Bedi clan, and in fact all the Sikh gurus came from Kshatri families. The Bedi name lost some of its luster as Guru Nanak's sons tried to set up a competing guru-ship, when Nanak passed away after naming one of his disciples as his successor. But the Sodhi, having the same lineage as the tenth guru, Gobind Singh, became the most revered name among the Sikhs; they had practically the status of a holy family among the Jats. Because of this special status, some of the Sodhi families were given charitable gifts of land by the Jat chiefs and rajas.

But in the Punjab of the eighteenth century, it was the erstwhile ignorable Jats, ranked third in the Hindu caste hierarchy, who ascended in power and prestige. Those who wanted to snub the Jats could even say that the cultivators of the land, being manual workers, should be the lowest caste. But at school we were told that the Jat were the third lowest caste, and Hindu scriptures confirm that the farmer caste level was equivalent of traders and artisans. The Jat did not have a tradition of learning, but in Punjab they became the biggest followers of the Sikh gurus and supported the gurus' political and military struggles against the Mughal Empire and its governors. In the unsettled times of the decay of the Mughal Empire, some Jats conquered territories and became rulers of states. After the Sikh *missls* (militias) dislodged the Mughal power, the missl of Ranjit Singh, a Jat, consolidated their power and extended his kingdom from the Sutlej River to the boundaries of Tibet and Afghanistan. The Phulkian Jat princes ruled territories south of the Sutlej up to the Jumna River.

Since the Jats had become kings and rulers in Punjab by the end of the eighteenth century, they acted as though they were the highest caste. After the English conquered Punjab, some English writers called Jat Sikhs "the noblemen of the late Sikh Empire." Specifically, such statements as "Jat Sikhs at the top, and the Khatri and Arora Sikhs below them" written by the English recorders characterize the power relationships of the Sikh Empire days and thereafter. In the eighteenth century the predominant warriors, conquerors, rulers, maharajas and sardars in Punjab were never Brahmin; some were Kshatri, but mostly they were Jat Sikhs. The caste system was still in force among the Jats, in spite of the Sikh gurus' preaching against such barriers. Caste might theoretically have been unimportant to the Sikhs, but the Jats had become so proud that they acted as though they were better than the Brahmins and the Kshatris. The only Kshatri whom the Jats considered higher were the Sodhi, who were revered like a holy family. Our family, the Sidhu Brards, had descended from the *Rajputs* of the *Kshatri* caste, but since they had been marrying into the *Jat* tribes of Punjab for generations, they had been degraded to the third tier Jat caste. According to folklore, many of the landowning Jat tribes like Gill, Dhillon, Sandhu, and Maan, etc., claim histories similar to the Sidhus.

In Punjab the Jats owned most of the agricultural lands that were not under Muslim control, and land ownership was what gave permanence and prestige to a tribe or clan. Brahmins, shopkeepers, and other castes had no roots or much of a clan or community;

they were isolated families in the villages of Jat landowners. Our family had lived in and owned the land of village Mehraj since its founding in the early seventeenth century and expected to live in our village forever. Other castes in the villages provided services to the Jats and were therefore dependent on them. Being the princes, rulers and landowners of Punjab, it is no wonder that the Jats acted as though they were above other castes. In later years, the rural Jats started feeling that they were the real Sikhs and that the Kshatri, whose ancestors were the founders of the Sikh religion, were like Hindu Sikhs. This perception in the minds of Jats, was due partly to the fact that in the Indian Punjab when you hear a Brahmin family name it is surely Hindu and a Punjabi Jat name is surely Sikh, but a Kshatri family name, can be either Hindu or Sikh, even within the same clan. Before the Independence of India, many Hindu families in the western part of Punjab raised some of their sons to be Sikh and let others stay as conventional Hindu who could follow some Sikh practices. But after the Independence in 1947, as a consequence of the majority Hindu rule it became disadvantageous to be anything other than Hindu. Therefore, if a Kshatri Sikh boy were to get clean shaved, his reversion back to the Hindu fold could be nearly complete, as some of his relatives and clan might already be Hindu. But if a Jat Sikh boy were to cut his hair, it would now be considered merely a change of lifestyle, and he would still be considered a Sikh. In the twentieth century, being a Jat Sikh had cultural and ethnic components even more significant than religious ones. A Punjabi Jat would have to take a drastic step, like becoming a Muslim and changing his name to Mohammed, to avoid being considered a Sikh. Just as an orthodox, a reformed, or an atheist Jew is still considered a Jew, a Punjabi Jat in any form is a Sikh.

From Untouchable Low Caste to Fashionable Christian

After the British occupied Punjab, some missionaries tried converting the local people to the Christian religion. They did this not only because they considered the Indians to be misguided pagans, but also because it was automatic for the rulers to have support from people of their own faith. The loyalty of people of other religions could be commanded only by force. In fact, one reason the Sikhs north of the Sutlej River lost their kingdom to the British, might be the fact that the Sikhs amounted to less than ten percent of the population in their own kingdom. Anyway, there were efforts by Christian missionaries to convert the natives, but their success was generally limited to the untouchable low caste people. In Punjab it was rare for anyone from the higher castes to become a Christian, although in the rest of India, individuals and whole tribes from the higher castes did so sometimes. With promises of better jobs and status it made sense for the low castes to get out of the Hindu system to become Christian. The joke used to be that the untouchable sweeper Fatto became Miss Fatto and the latrine-cleaner Booda became Mr. Booda by becoming a Christian. Over time the status and awareness of the converts improved relative to others, as they were usually urban and became educated. But the number of Christians in Punjab was never significant.

In our village of Mehraj in the 1930s I used to walk to my fields past the mud-walled courtyard of the Catholic padres, located across from the untouchable Chuhra colony. It was called *Padrian da Kotha* (padre's house). Some activities, probably including religious instruction, were conducted inside the padre's house. Some low caste women went to them because the padres treated them respectfully and not like untouchables. But the

233

padres were realistic enough to not aim at the Jat Sikhs or high caste Hindus. After World War II the padre house was abandoned, and gradually the house and the mud-brick wall of the padres' complex fell to the ground; there was no trace left of any conversions. The padres failed because in the rural areas and close knit communities, whole tribes had to be converted together, as the Muslims did. Superior ideology aimed at individuals could fail, but converting the influential and powerful elders would have given them control over whole tribes. Generally, the conversions were a result of economic and political incentives or of major threats to life and not of the superior principles.

Unintended Interbreading Among the Castes

The mixing of racial strains was quite infrequent, although one of our elders took a Muslim Pathan woman as a wife; half of his sons also were given Muslim sounding names and they have villages of Muhabbet and Beg named after them. But unintentional mixing of castes was not easy to stop, even in a society where the touch of a low caste person was an unholy occurrence. Many a landowner's son obtained carnal knowledge by being with a sweeper woman, and many a landowner was tempted by the easy conquest of a laborer woman. Sometimes a high caste woman with raging hormones took risks to fulfill her desire with a low caste man. The dharma and the restraints of conscience or the fear of family and social condemnation deterred some; but for the lustful and adventurous it was only the lack of opportunity that was the deterrent. Some teenage girls sought sex at any risk, even though their parents tried preventive measures, close supervision and severe restrictions. Some landowners' girls managed to have clandestine sex with their low caste farm workers, of whom they had no fear and who could be accessed in the cattle corrals and feed storage buildings. I have known of girls in different villages who had sex with their hired farm workers. After they were married off, their habits might not change, but their marriages provided good cover for any of their babies fathered by the low caste men. Thus the seed of the low caste men was propagated in the Jat landowner community in spite of caste restrictions, and some low caste women carried babies sired by Jat men. Occasionally a Jat baby looked like a low caste Chuhra and a low caste child looked like a Jat. If a child looked quite different from his mother and father, it might be due to recessive genes from earlier generations, or it might be that his mother was playing around. When a Jat child had coarse features, people explained it away by saying, "The mother might have countenanced (*matthe laga*) someone of such appearance while she was pregnant; her looking at such a person affected the appearance of her fetus." People even believed that if a pregnant woman looked at pictures of beautiful people and images, it would make the baby beautiful. They believed that a pregnant woman should avoid seeing ugly images and encountering ugly people; many did not understand that any damage occurred at conception.

My teacher Kesho Ram, who himself was a Brahmin, used to say, "If a Brahmin has a black complexion and a wide or flat nose, he is surely the seed of a non-Brahmin." But the features like nose and lips were considered more important indicators than color alone. The Brahmin and Kshatri were usually the fairer castes, and most people in the third tier castes were not much different from them. But because of the presence of low caste farm workers in proximity to Jat landowner households, racial mixing among them appeared to be more prevalent than among the carpenters, shopkeepers, tailors, barbers,

234

or other groups. When people noted such variations they would remark, "That Chuhri looks just like a Jat woman; if she had better clothes, she could pass for a Jatti." The Jats in the village used to say that if a low caste person was trying to be uppity, he must be the seed of someone from a higher caste and not of his father, that is, he must be a bastard. Differences in appearance among different castes are still noticeable, but because of mixing over time, one cannot be sure of a person's caste from looks alone any more.

Chuhri fights

People of the lowest caste were not usually constrained by the niceties of social behavior, particularly when they were within their own neighborhoods, called *vehra*. Although they interacted with other people for centuries, their pronunciation of words and the tones and accents of their speech could be different from the standard speech of other local people. Among themselves, the low caste women were uninhibited about using obscene words that would make others cringe. It was expected that they would quarrel fairly regularly, either within their families or with their neighbors. It seemed like necessary therapy, as some Chuhri women seemed not to go without a fight for very long. Their language was often so raw and pungent that I cannot describe it exactly, as the equivalent obscenities and expressions are not known to me in English. It would be routine for a father to call to his playing children with language like, "Oh my son Pillo, where are you? Oh son of a pimp, seed of a dog, procurer of your sister; son of a daughter-fucker; oh may plague and leprosy strike you...." Their women would routinely call their daughters "Oh *ghore di rann* (mate of a horse), *gaddan yaddhi* (fucked by donkeys), oh *bahel* (whore), you are sitting there with dilated rear...." This was not said in anger but as routine talk.

Their women could start a fight after returning home in the afternoon and before sunset. They would stand in front of their houses that faced the common vehra and would challenge their opponents, sometimes as a continuation of the previous day's harangue. I remember that one Chuhri named Motor would say to another woman named Budhan, "Come on you filthy whore and mate of horses, it is time to take your inquiry. You are so common and cheap that every dog and cat has fucked you. You were fucked by Diala in the millet field; you were fucked by Paul under the Tahli tree; you were fucked by Natthu for two ears of corn; you were fucked by Nikku in exchange for mustard leaves; the Numberdar (village revenue collector) fucked you when you went to his house to sift food grain; the Babu fucked you when you went to get your letter read; Lekhu fucked you in return for wood fuel.... If we were to turn you over and shake you, a basketful of penises would fall out of you." The retort from Budhan would be equally graphic and full of biting and filthy vocabulary. Their men would not join in the women's fights but would sit around, listen, and only occasionally growl to their wives, "Enough now; get me something to drink," or something of the sort. For other men just watching and listening, it was like entertainment unless their name came up as the participants involved in the acts mentioned above. I saw and heard a few such performances when I was near the scene for one reason or another. Sometimes boys would say to their friends; "Hey, let us go and watch the Chuhri fights." Genteel women from other castes would not go to the Chuhra colony when the Chuhri were fighting.

Among the Chuhra boys, abuse and obscenities naming the mother were considered mild. To really hurt, cut, dishonor and incite the rage of a boy, naming his sister was the ultimate abuse. Their boys would abuse each other, shouting, "My penis on your sister's clit.....; may a donkey's penis go into your sister's vagina; I will pull your sister's pubic hair," but these abuses lose something in translation from Punjabi. Those little boys did not even know the meanings of many of the words they used, but they had heard them so often that it became their staple vocabulary. Even I did not understand the significance of some of the words until I became much older. They wanted to be uninhibitedly graphic in describing the acts they would do to the sisters of their opponents.

Nomadic Lives and the Menace of Ode

Until the mid-twentieth century, there was an abundance of migrant and nomadic tribes in India. Some tribes believed that it was a sin for their race to live under a permanent roof. In conversation, they used to say that they would get bored living in one place and that God did not intend their race to live under a roof. One of them said to me, "Don't ask why I am not tired of moving from place to place; let me ask you why you are not bored living in the same place all the time." The weather was sometimes harsh, but the nomads had no roof to repair, no plumbing leaks to patch, no termites to worry about and no wall to plaster. And when conditions demanded, which might be on the third day or the seventh, they would load their possessions on their means of transportation and be on their way to their next destination. They could easily bear the summer heat; and except for the month of January the winter climate was not too harsh. In those days there was plenty of unused common land around the villages that was available for temporary occupation without the permission of the village elders.

The nomads who most often passed our village were the *Gadi Wale* (wagon people). They would arrive in wagons made with ornate metal decorations and drawn by healthy looking oxen decorated with *ghungral* (necklaces of bells). They dressed and spoke like a variation of the Rajputana desert people. Their women wore multi-pleated, knee-length skirts of dazzling prints and striking colors, not the Punjabi dress or the saari of India. Their blouses were just elaborate brassieres, very ornate and colorful, from breast up to the shoulders, with bare midriff between the brassiere and the skirt. The women wore a veil for the head, but they did not cover their faces from strangers. The Gadi Wali women also had elaborate tattoos on various parts of their bodies, as did many other transient tribes. In a culture where married women did not expose their faces in public and exposing legs was totally unacceptable, the Gadi Wali women with short skirts made quite a spectacle; but we expected unusual behavior from strange races. The women were usually assertive, uninhibited, verbal, and full of humor, and they could talk freely with strange men, as it was their business to sell and trade. Their men made crude implements out of steel, and the women sold the steel gadgets, going door to door in the village and bargaining aggressively while making jokes and showing humor. Starting with little kitchen implements, such as spatulas, scrapers, and tongs, they could also make items according to specifications. In return they wanted money, but they would accept grain, or even a bundle of fodder for their oxen or whatever you could negotiable.

The Gadi Wale men were good at bargaining and were experienced traders of oxen. They would trade their ox for your ox plus some money, and they would come out ahead in any deal with a simple-minded farmer. Anybody who bought an ox from a Gadi Wala was the butt of jokes, because he was surely taken. They might try to take advantage of you in a transaction, but these people were never violent, vicious or criminal; so they were never resented by anyone. The village attitude used to be that everyone has a right to exist. The land was not crowded yet, and the villagers were glad to see new people. You expected other people to be odd and to speak a strange language; but still they were God's people. The Sikligar tribes also made odd things to sell and moved from place to place; but they were not as numerous as the Gadi Wale.

Ode were ferocious nomadic people and provided a contrast with the Gadi Wale. Our people thought that the Ode were destructive, belligerent and violent. The Ode men wore their hair and clothing in the Muslim style to indicate their religion. They would load their *sirki* (straw mat) tents and other belongings on donkeys and let the women and children drive the donkeys while the men herded large numbers of goats and sheep with the help of their fierce dogs. Their men and women, with sunburnt faces, were tall and strongly built. Milk and meat were the principal part of their diet, because of the abundance of their goats and sheep, and they supplemented it with flour, daal and whatever they could steal from the fields. They were not afraid of the landowners and were aggressive in taking whatever they wanted from the land as they traveled. Nobody could stop them at night; so each farmer could only pray that the Ode would not cause too much damage to his crop as they passed by. The Ode passed only through the fields and wild areas and usually stayed far away from the village population.

Our people would watch the Odes' dogs with curiosity and envy. In the days when security was precarious, every householder wanted a big, reliable, and murderous dog. The dogs of the Ode seemed to be more vicious than the common village varieties, and every house coveted one of those dogs. Once while grazing cattle, I watched some of our people try to corner and catch an Ode dog. Bachan, the son of Bhakku, who had a reputation as a tough fighter, decided to capture an Ode dog with the help of his friends. They placed themselves in two groups, one on each side of the irrigation canal that passed through the fields of our Mehraj territory. Two of Bachan's friends separated the Ode dog from the herd of sheep and cornered it against the canal bank with the hope of grabbing and chaining it. Instead of being captured, the cornered dog jumped into the canal and swam to the other bank of the canal. On the other side, Bachan and a friend were waiting and hoping to grab the dog. When the dog reached the other bank and Bachan tried to catch it, the dog bit Bachan's hand and escaped. That episode increased our fear of the ferocious Ode dogs, but it intensified even more the desire among others to own one. There was little chance of developing a cordial relationship with the Odes or of making a deal with them as one could do with the Gadi Wale. The Ode would not sell their dogs readily, and the Jats were too stingy to pay very much; they wanted to just steal one. Some talked about capturing an Ode dog as a puppy, when it would be easier to control, but not many were successful.

Some semi-nomadic tribes grazed cattle and lived in straw huts near river banks. There were hardly any controls over large areas of the wild and uncultivated grazing lands in those days. If conditions for grazing got worse near the Ghagger River and nomads heard that grass was still good on the banks of the River Chenab, the whole tribe would move, driving their cattle to live near Chenab. That river is in Pakistan now, and in any case that lifestyle has died out because there are no free grazing lands anymore. I had the experience of watching the working of one such tribe called *Jamoun ki Dhani*

237

near our Talwara land in Rajputana. There the seasonal river Ghagger passed through the lake bed called Talwara Jhil, and further down the territory the river dissipated in the desert. Uncle Tiloka had moved to Talwara after the breakup of our joint family. I was then a teenager and was sent to assist him just after finishing my matriculation examination in the first week of March 1946. It was like going to a foreign country, as the people there spoke variations of Bagri, Punjabi, Junglee and other tongues. Uncle Tiloka could usually understand the languages; he would instruct me about what words to use for what things if he sent me on an errand.

One day Uncle Tiloka and I wanted to buy some *ghee*, which used to be considered a necessity for good health in those days. We used it for frying foods and added it to already cooked foods in order to improve the taste. Uncle Tiloka took me to Jamoun ki Dhani. We purchased the stored ghee from the Muslim families of Jamoun ki Dhani. After weighing it, we transferred it from their vessel into our own container. I commented that the Muslim ghee was green in tinge compared to what I expected; but Uncle Tiloka assured me that the green color was due to their cows' diet of grass, and that the ghee was good otherwise. Then I asked, "And how about the fact that they are Muslim and we are going to eat Muslim food! Won't it desecrate and pollute us?" Uncle Tiloka said that ghee was a borderline kind of commodity. It might desecrate a strict Vishnoi, but for us it was tolerable, because it could be heated after being purchased and before being eaten. Unlike other houses, my father and uncle were never overly concerned about caste pollution.

The trip to Jamoun ki Dhani was a new cultural experience for me at that age. Those people were good looking, healthy, simple and friendly. Their language had the longer vowel sounds and the lilt of the Lehndi language of western Punjab, which has always been more pleasant to my ears than our own Punjabi. In fact I still have a fantasy about living in a territory near the river Chenab where they speak such a language, but unfortunately it is in Pakistan now. Their women did not cover their faces and wore the same sarong like lower garment that their men wore, which would have been considered risqué or scandalous in our area of Punjab; and they spoke with a frank expression and an easy smile. The formality and inhibitions of middle-class Punjabi women had not touched them, nor did they practice the purdah system of urban Muslims. To me theirs seemed like an idyllic life, with little work for the men except grazing cattle, and no worries! Later I would talk to their boys who grazed cattle nearby. I would ask how they got their drinking water, how they made their clothes, and so forth, and I took delight in the accents with which they answered my questions.

Beggar Castes and Traveling Traders

Begging was natural for the *sadhu* and other holy men, but the holy men never begged for money because they did not want to acquire or own material things; they only begged for food. As a child I never saw a Sikh beggar. A Sikh did not really need to beg; he could live in a gurdwara for the rest of his life if his family did not take care of him. Beggars in the village were rarely Punjabi; they usually came from other provinces and spoke Hindustani. The word Hindustani means Indian, but in Punjab this word was used to describe the Hindi-speaking natives east of Delhi, also called Poorbia (meaning eastern). Those beggars would come to the door and start bestowing blessings and piling on praises: "Oh mistress of the mansion, fortune-loaded queen, blessed of God, may God keep you *sohagan* (with husband), may God keep your offspring healthy, may your fortunes increase, may milk be abundant in your house, may your granary stay full..." They would tailor their words to suit the circumstances.

One Poorbia beggar used to claim that he was a Brahmin from Uttar Pradesh and a *jotishi* (predictor). He would tell fortunes and read palms for the women. Although he would get just a lump of grain like other beggars, he was more effective because of his verbal skills and ability to tell fortunes. The foreigners were more effective fortune-tellers, because they spoke a different language (even the uneducated village Punjabis could understand Hindi) and their accents increased their credibility. Women trusted their power to predict, while a Punjabi-speaking fortune seller would sound too ordinary. Women would say, "That Poorbia *panda* who told fortunes last summer has come again." The old fellow would describe things about his own life to the curious women: "After I collect some money I am going back to my *desh* (country). I have a grown-up son who got married last year, and I gave a gold necklace for his wife. My own wife is a nag; that is why I take to the road and come to this country."

Sellers who came to our doors, hawked things at street corners, or staged street shows, all spoke strange languages and came from elsewhere; our Punjabi people were never good at these miscellaneous occupations. If you had a backache, your knee hurt, your eyes remained swollen, or you had a bad sore on the leg that did not heal, a traveling leech-keeper could help. He would take the leeches out of his jar, stick them to your flesh one by one in a circle around the selected area, and you could watch them bloating with blood. Later, you could watch the loaded leech pulled off, and the dark blood squeezed out of the leech right there on the ground. Another healer was the suction-horn man, who would make a few nicks in the flesh with a razor and then would apply the suction horn on the nicked skin. He would suck the air out of the horn through a small hole in the top with his mouth and would very carefully apply some dough or paste with his tongue before he removed his mouth from the horn, taking care that air did not leak back into it. The application of the suction horn would thus pull some blood through the nicks on the skin. All the "bad blood" extracted by the leeches or the horns, was there for everyone to see, and the patient would invariably say, "I already feel better." The placebo effect probably made the patient feel good temporarily.

In our streets there were traveling magicians, snake charmers called yogi blowing *been* (pipes), monkey showmen, bear showmen, Afghan sellers of raisins, almonds, dates and other dry fruits, sellers of lemon, *dela, amla* or mango for pickles, vegetable and fruit sellers, cloth sellers with bundles on their backs, ear piercers, bangle sellers and miscellaneous medicine sellers. Many of them would accept measures of grain instead of cash. Women at home did not always have cash in their control, but grain was always there in storage. Some men thought that the women were easily fleeced by these traveling salesmen, but in general the women were on their guard and in the company of other friends, so outright *thuggi* was rare.

CHAPTER 11

Sexual Mores and Taboos in Punjab

The subject of sex was not open for conversation in respectable environs, but sexual scenes of copulating animals were everywhere in rural Punjab; little children learned a few things while watching animals. Most village boys knew the basic facts of reproduction by the age of seven. Buffaloes and cows used to be brought to the stud bulls whose resting places would be the open areas at the periphery of the village; there they copulated in full view of the public. The bulls did not belong to anyone; they were not penned or tethered, but wandered about; so the females were brought to them. Donkeys, being disproportionately well endowed, were a sight to behold when in the erect state. Any woman passing by a donkey in that condition would cover her eyes with veil or turn away her face in embarrassment. Teams of stray dogs would chase after a bitch in heat. After some chase, the female and the dominant male dog started the mating act. As penetration proceeded, the front end of the penis of the male dog somehow became stuck inside the female, presumably due to further swelling of the front portion. Then from the humping position the male sometimes flipped one leg over, to face in the opposite direction, a maneuver that seemed quite unnatural. When the male and female dogs were thus joined but pulling in opposite directions, little boys would try to break the connection between the dogs by throwing rocks at them. Some cruel little boys would try to hit the junction point with sticks; some wanted to cut the junction with an ax. But the dogs could not get disconnected easily and it was also hard for them to run away while still connected and facing in opposite directions. Older people would say "Hey kids, leave them alone; it is a sin to break them apart when they are in the act."

With such events happening all around, every boy knew the connection between mating and the birth of the next generation. I imagine that girls, being more sheltered, learned the facts of life at a much later age. Extrapolating the notions about the mating process from animals to people was not difficult, because a lot of the farmers' curses and abuses of their animals, of even friends, consisted of verbal expressions rich in terms dealing with copulation. Men in our family observed proper decorum and avoided this sort of vocabulary, but there was always some neighbor with a filthy mouth whom the boys would hear. In their early years, young boys used the obscene words against others in fights without knowing their true meanings, as their fathers, uncles, and other adults

240

used such vocabulary pretty casually.

Among the young cattle-grazing boys, far away from girls and women, nothing was too vulgar or dirty. While grazing cattle, it was not unusual for them to urinate on the ground or on a bush in others' presence, and sometimes even to stand together in a circle to urinate. Occasionally a smaller group of boys would sit together in a circle, showing off and measuring their penises against little twigs or with their fingers and comparing penises with one another. When near puberty, some even masturbated together to see who could ejaculate the quickest and shoot the farthest. And some shameless ones tried copulation with animals, although most boys were too shy for such bestiality and only watched. A female donkey or goat was an easy target, as it was easy for the young boys to reach. They would ask their friends to hold the animal by the ears and go at it turn by turn. These activities were kept secret only from the elders and from women

Young farm boys fantasized about having a penis as big as that of a bull, and better yet, that of a horse. Among the cattle-grazing boys, before they were put to the plough, everyone's penis size and shape were known to his friends. If there was a Muslim boy, it would be obvious from the lack of foreskin. Boys in some families had the reputation of having big ones. If a boy had an average size penis, he could be just ordinary. If he had a large penis, he might feel proud, or he might consider it no better than having a long nose or big ears. But if he were abnormally small, he might be teased and be the butt of jokes.

One young boy nicknamed Pheena in our village had a penis that was not much bigger than a peanut, and other boys teased him for not being a real male. They tried to scare him by saying that the *khusra or heejra* (hermaphrodite) were going to take him by force and make him live in their colony. The khusra "men" used to shave their faces and wore women's clothes. They tried to act like women and made a nuisance of themselves by their singing until you paid them to go away. So this little boy Pheena felt socially uneasy because of his small penis, and sometimes he expressed his fear of being taken away by the khusra people. He was slightly cross-eyed and short, and that did not help matters. But as he grew a little older, Pheena did not let this issue define him. He grew up to be a competent worker, good natured, of imperturbable temperament and not easily offended, although his penis was still below average in size. Because he was quite stable and dependable, when he grew older, more boys wanted to be his friends rather than tease him. It seems that he worried unnecessarily. Pheena's penis became a non-issue when he became a teenager. He was married to a pretty girl, had three children with her, and had a normal family life.

In spite of the boys' occasional deviant acts of open exposure, masturbation was considered sinful and supposedly sapped one's strength and ruined one's eyesight. Older people would advise young boys to refrain from all sexual activities including masturbation, claiming that it would ruin their health and eyesight and was bad behavior. But some boys did it many times a day when they were teenagers, because of the wave of pleasure that ran through the body. Younger ones, envious of the talk of older boys, also kept trying until the day when they could ejaculate. When the boys grew past the mid-teen years, the intensity of this activity tapered off. But in schools and cities the boys' behavior was more controlled and supervised. The boys in such situations were far behind the rural boys in the knowledge of the facts of life. When boys with rural background went

241

to school with town boys, they thought the town boys were girlish and had awkward spoke in such matters.

Quite contrary to the impression one might get from the ancient Indian sculptures of erotic nature, or from books like Kama Sutra, in our society the subject of sex between men and women was suppressed. What can be heard on American TV would have been forbidden in the presence of women. An ordinary man in Punjab was trained to act as if his mother, sister, or daughter could never have any ideas or desires regarding sex, except in the context of a marriage, and even then it was not anything to think about. When it came to sex, they thought of their mothers and sisters the same way as Christians think about the mother of Jesus. Female cousins were treated like sisters, too, as their chastity reflected on the honor of the extended clan. In polite circles one never talked openly about sex even between married people, and all other sex was unacceptable. So whatever the boys learned, came from their peers and from older boys. Not many in the Punjab villages knew how to read books like *The Kama Sutra*. And the word for illicit sex was "the bad act" or "the evil act." Gossips and whisperers would say, "So and so is said to have done the *evil act* with so and so."

The elders preached the rule to "Treat all women, except your wives, as if they are your mothers, sisters, or daughters." Simple people tried to adhere to this rule. Failure to do so earned one the reputation of having a bad character, brought disgrace to one's family, created a risk of physical harm from the men of the family whose woman one might try to seduce, and severe shame and humiliation in making an unsuccessful attempt. It was not permissible to form a friendship and to develop a relationship with a woman. It required a shameless mind, a thick skin, and reckless disregard for consequences to attempt to approach a girl of one's own village. As one would expect, any unlawful rewards went to the shameless rule breakers.

In addition to the risks and prohibitions, girls were also watched and protected, not only by their mothers and families but by everyone else in the society as well. People felt as if it was their duty to prevent "evil acts." Girls were married off as soon as possible, frequently between the age of 12 and 16. Apart from really young girls and widows, almost all women were married, since there was always a shortage of women, after generations of female infanticide. Even after the killing of girl babies slowed and stopped, it took at least a couple of generations for the numbers of marriageable women to catch up with the numbers of men in society, as older men took younger wives. The fact that some men had more than one wife and the reverse was unthinkable, also created a scarcity of women.

Boys talked about their own sisters and close cousins with reverence, but they considered women of other houses to be fair game and thought that for such girls, chastity was just due to lack of opportunity. Some individuals did break the strict rules. Depending upon who the involved parties were, the consequences ranged from negligible to very severe. The involvement of an unmarried sister of adult brothers, for example, might result in murder; but a consensual act with a married low caste woman might have little consequence, as no one might even gossip about the latter act. Much of my knowledge about this kind of illicit behavior among people in the village came from hearing stories from a few of my adventurous friends in the 1940s. How did other people find out about the illicit affairs? They were always watching, suspecting, and drawing conclusions, even

242

though they were not supposed to think such thoughts. Some fellows heard such things from other women. They minded everyone's business, as if allowing anyone else to do it would hurt them. The superstition used to be that the sin of such "evil acts" of the few would bring the wrath of God on everyone.

The Revered Status of Celibacy

According to tradition, the sex act was considered to diminish the purity and spirituality of a human being. Celibacy, or the never-married state, was synonymous with sacredness. All the holy men, the *sadhu, bhagat* and *sant*, were expected to be celibate. To propitiate and please certain divinities, some of our rural people fed and gave offerings to virgin girls and less frequently to unmarried men, as these categories were assumed to be sinless. Ancient scriptures divided man's life into four stages: *brahm-chari, grhist, ban-prast,* and *sanyas.* An ideal man at young age was supposed to be a student, living a celibate life, in the pious status called *brahm-chari,* implying intact virtue and physical strength. In the *grhist* stage, he could get married, had the license for sense gratification, raised a family, and led a worldly life. It was believed that a man in *grhist* (the married state) could not be without sin, and he also might compromise his morals in the process of acquiring material things. In the *ban prast stage,* one was expected to counsel others and to be free from daily struggles, and in the *sanyas* stage he was expected to renounce worldly life and concentrate on spiritual matters. But the point is that the celibate (brahm-chari) state was assumed to preserve a man's physical, mental, and spiritual powers at a high level, and sexual activity was presumed to degrade all these powers and to leave him impious, with diminished virtue and diminished strength. If a family needed to propitiate the gods or to please the soul of a dead ancestor, they selected an unmarried and therefore "sinless" man to feed, as a surrogate for the dead ancestor. Since females had less freedom of movement and action, every unmarried girl was presumed to be a virgin and therefore to be more sacred than a boy. She also did not normally commit any gross acts of cruelty or mischief, so her sacred and sinless status as a virgin was generally accepted. That is why feeding virgin girls on the days of fasting was a ritual as sacred as feeding the Brahmins or the holy men.

If one wanted to be accepted as a holy person, a virtuous person, or a person with miraculous powers such as the power of healing, it was advantageous to be unmarried. Even a politician who was not married, enjoyed greater respect and trust than did those with wives and families. Nehru, the first prime minister of India, had become a widower at a young age and remained unmarried for the remainder of his life. His celibacy is one reason why his prestige and integrity were totally unchallenged in India as long as he was alive, although now some people think his policies damaged India. Even Mohandas K. Gandhi lived away from his own wife and presumably led a celibate life to enhance his status like a holy man. According to written reports, however, as an old man Mahatma Gandhi insisted on sleeping with nubile young girls at night, claiming that thereby he proved that he had the self-discipline to resist the temptation of the sex act. His handlers and the party workers constantly tried to cover up and to prevent the public from learning of his sleep practices, because much of the public would not accept Gandhi's daily contact with young flesh in bed.

There were legends about brahm-chari (celibate) men with great physical prowess who lost their strength as a result of being seduced into the sex act. The superstition preached among village boys used to be that it takes 100 drops of milk to make one drop of ghee; that it takes 100 drops of ghee to make one drop of blood; and that it takes 100 drops of blood to make one drop of semen. Since milk was a scarce commodity to begin with, and because it was considered the chief source of health and strength, so any waste of a drop of semen was considered to be a million times worse than spilling milk and a tremendous waste of strength. Therefore, masturbation was considered bad not only because it was a sex act but also because it wasted semen and was supposed to rob you of your strength. Village people would make comments about married boys: "He can't lift the *mugder* any more; his strength has been drained by his wife."

Affairs In Spite of the Taboos

Affairs did happen, but talk about them was hush-hush and was heard only in limited circles. Sex with an unmarried girl could result in the murder of the man involved. In our village the problem was compounded by the fact that most landowners there were related to other landowners through a common paternal ancestor. Therefore, a "shotgun marriage" was not even a possibility. A daughter of the village could not become a wife of the village all of a sudden, and start covering her face with the veil or wearing the ghagra (big skirt) like a bride! Every girl in the community was a cousin and was called "sister," and her chastity was a matter of honor for the whole clan. Even though this did not apply to other castes, still it was the custom also to address girls of other castes as if they were related, particularly if they had lived in the village for a generation.

The strict code of behavior forbade even verbal contact between unrelated girls and boys. Under the surface, however, feelings sometimes ran hot. Sometimes these feelings found expression, and some people took horrendous risks to have affairs. It was considered a less serious violation, though, if the woman in the affair was married and the lovers were not related in a strictly forbidden way. Casual jokes and banter in some relations between men and women were considered *thaan sirr* (an appropriate situation) and were accepted to some extent. Thus, teasing and flirting with a *bhabi* or *bhrajhai* (brother's wife) was considered harmless fun. If a man slept with his bhabi, and the relationship was consensual, no one thought of it as an evil. In such cases, the husband either did not show concern or was ignorant of the affair, and the wife, in subtle if not blatant ways, might have the dominant hand in the marriage. An unmarried younger brother of a husband, called a *deor*, sometimes acted as though he had some rights in relation to the older brother's wife. Even in the holy epic Maha Bharat, the mother of the five Pandu brothers tells her sons to share the one wife that the oldest brother had married. In some Jat families where the bride price had been paid from common family resources to obtain a wife for an older brother, there might be an unspoken assumption of rights by the younger brother. If the wife did not tolerate such thoughts, the deor was out of luck; but if the two developed a consensual relationship, there was no scandal. Even if the relationship did not involve actual physical contact or acts, a lot of open banter, suggestive conversations, and jokes, might be exchanged regularly and openly between a deor and his bhabi without occasioning comment. Of course, every family situation was different, and every married woman observed a different degree of propriety, exclusivity, and piety in such matters.

Another sanctioned activity was the risqué conversation between a married man and his wife's sisters, girl cousins, and girl friends. A wife's sister was considered like a half wife (*Sali, adhe ghar wali*), although not for a physical relationship. And since the married man was only a temporary guest and did not live nearby, this was not a serious issue. Another situation arose when a man's married sister had sisters-in-law in her in-law village. In such a situation, when a brother was visiting his married sister he did not need to be too careful about the modesty of those in-law girls when in conversation with them. He could treat them as a Western man would treat women in a bar, but politely. My friend Bikker, visiting his sister's village, tried to connect with one such girl named Nikki who was about his age and constantly teased him. One day as he encountered Nikki, he gave a hint with a gesture that he was going to the upper-story *chobara*, where the rest of the host family did not ordinarily go. He did not have any special expectations, but after she went to her own house, and as soon as she found the opportunity, Nikki came walking from the roof of her own house toward the upper-story chobara where Bikker was waiting for her. Walking from one flat roof to another connected roof was a common way for lovers to meet, out of sight of other people. This happened during the daytime, though, and Nikki's mother had been watchful. The tryst was cut short prematurely by the voice of Nikki's mother, who had climbed the stairs up to the roof, right behind her daughter. The mother shouted for her daughter to return immediately. Later, when Nikki's mother came to Bikker's sister's house, he anticipated some consequences of his "bad intentions." She could have shown her anger at him for trying to seduce her daughter, but she handled the matter smoothly. So without showing any anger and in a teasing tone, Nikki's mother asked Bikker if his "mind was starting to stick (*dil laga*)," that is, if he was starting to enjoy his stay in their village. She said this because before that time Bikker had always complained that his 'mind was not sticking' (dil na lagna) in their village during the visit and that he wanted to go home soon. He was a bit embarrassed, but he had not behaved in a disgraceful or shameful way, because his contact with the girl was not in the category of "strictly forbidden," although if the two had any sexual contact, their action would have been considered immoral and dangerous.

There were gradations of forbidden-ness in the relations between men and women depending on whether or how they were related. Blood relatives on the father's side were the most forbidden, because as long as men and women had the same family name they were considered brothers and sisters, regardless of how remote the genetic connection was. Ironically, a boy or girl could marry anyone with the same family name as their mother's ancestors but not anyone who had the father's surname. This custom may have evolved to discourage any romantic intentions of boys toward girls of the same village but the mother's clan, being in another village, was not open to many possibilities.

Since an open relationship or marriage was unthinkable in almost all cases of premarital contact, boys usually did not develop an attitude of possession, commitment, or exclusivity when they had sex with a woman. Some boys did develop an attachment to "the one and only," even when they did not have an intimate relationship. Some would sigh, swear to die for them, would frequent the girl's street with the hope of catching a glimpse, make up poems or rhymes, sing romantic songs in the loved one's name, and gave gifts and did other things that love-struck people do. But most boys had the attitude of "catch as catch can." And if another fellow "got a little" from the same woman that you were with before, their attitude was that "there was still plenty left." In some cases, even sequential sharing and gang-bangs occurred.

One also heard of many variations of non-consensual sex, sex under duress, and rape with cruelty, and such acts sometimes were committed by people in positions of power. Such a stigma was attached to rape, as well as any other form of extramarital sex, that a victim would not usually discuss it or complain about it to anyone. But if the act was observed by a third party, the victim was expected to scream and shout. As everywhere else in older societies, the woman frequently was thought to be at fault and suffered the most shame for any such act.

Subtle Winks, Clashing Eyes, and Passing Words Through

Under the circumstances of strict controls and forbidden contacts, boys were always hoping to trade a glance with, and possibly make contact with, some girl with raging hormones like their own. They just had to hide their intentions from the general public. They would sit at strategic places where they expected the women to pass by while fetching water from the well or doing other tasks. A boy had to maintain an appearance of having no interest in women. A look or a smile from a woman is what they hoped for. A sideways glance or furtive smile, and in rare cases some indirect word, was a way for a woman to indicate interest. If a girl looked casually at a boy, asked a direct question, or had a request, it might just mean that she was confident and assertive and not necessarily an easy mark. But if she smiled without talking, there was a big potential. Most of the time, as a girl passed any unrelated man she would lower her gaze or look forward only, as though she did not notice or care who was sitting around. It was against social customs for an unmarried girl to cover her face; only her head was covered. She was in the village of her brothers and uncles, and she was expected to treat all boys like brothers. An older woman could look any way she wanted. Younger married women usually covered their faces with a veil, as there might be a man older than the husband in the vicinity, and it would be a violation for the older man to see her face.

Those who were looking for a romantic relationship had to start with eye contact. If a girl was intensely interested in a boy who was sitting alone, she could sometimes fix her gaze on the fellow for a moment, and of course the boys were always looking. That would be signal enough, but sometimes he, and in rare cases she, would wink an eye to show interest unmistakably. If the wink was reciprocated with a wink or smile, it was called *"ankh larri"* (clashed eye), and that would indicate clear acceptance. Stories and songs about initiating affairs mentioned "ankh larri," which meant that the couple had a good rapport and shared strong feelings.

Sometimes, while pretending to be talking to a companion or even to himself, a boy might say "loaded" words actually meant for the ears of a passing woman. He might say to his companion, "O *yaar* (friend), I wish I could find you alone sometime" or, "O friend, what a knockout dresser you are!" When no one else was around, a really brazen young man might say something like, "O good looking, cast a glance of kindness on us." Some guys even said things to their ox or camel with the hope that the woman passing by would take the hint and react. A boy might say to his ox, "O my favorite, beautiful one, I like the style of your walk, but I wish you would show a little more energy and courage." The words would be neutral enough so that he could not be accused of addressing the woman, unless she wanted to react in some way. Or he might say to his ox, "Oh youthful one, why don't you pay attention to what I say?" or even, "You sure are acting difficult! What do I have to do to please you?" Such a ruse was called "passing the words *through* someone or *through* something," instead of talking directly, but most of the time it was blatantly obvious what the speaker was doing. Some stupid fellows trying to copy the clever ones could really foul things up. For example, when a pregnant woman walked by, it was tactless and transparent for a fellow to say to his ox, "Move, oh youthful one; you have become so heavy after drinking too much water." But it was even worse when his stupid friend, trying to one-up him, said to his ox, "Oh my ox, you have become too thin after giving birth" when another woman passed by. Such a stupid fellow was likely to be abused for his remark, instead of receiving any favorable attention.

If a fellow could generate a favorable glance, a smile, or any words from a woman, his next step would be to say some something to her more directly when no one else was around. If he was able to start a conversation in the absence of other people, then he might feel he had a green light, and the next step would be to create an opportunity to meet privately. It might take days, weeks, or even months, but human ingenuity and changing circumstances would always provide an occasion if there was sufficient interest on both sides. That is one reason why some people did not want girls to be literate; they feared that it would be easy for a girl to pass secret notes to her lover when they were forbidden to talk freely. And of course they feared that the girls could become interested in boys by reading romantic stories. Most ordinary boys, who did not have looks, style, or initiative, just kept hoping to run into a promiscuous woman, some day, somehow. For the good looking, clever, and reckless ones, there were more possibilities. There was always some woman who was a bit clever, cunning, and unafraid and who had a need for more male contact than she was getting. Perhaps the men folk in her family were old, unaware, or in denial, and they might not be too threatening even if they found out something "disgraceful." Some women took small risks to connect with a fellow who was good-looking and smooth. Although my friend Juggoo had neither of these qualities, he still arranged to have an encounter with a girl named Debo, as he described to me later.

Debo Turned into a Nymphomaniac

Debo was the first-born daughter of a somewhat older father in our village. Her mother had not been obtained in a traditional marriage but had been purchased in the 1920s and had a prior history of unconventional living. In those days, a woman in unhappy circumstances could run away with a man who was willing to "abduct" her and to help her escape from her situation. Such an "abductor" could not usually keep the woman but "sold" her to some needy "husband." Of course, if she did not like the new situation she could always arrange another abduction, but once she had disgraced herself like this, she could not go back to her parents' village.

People always took a dim view of "purchased" or non-traditional wives, and some refused to deal with houses that included such a wife until the passage of time gave the situation some legitimacy. If the purchased woman was from a lower or unknown caste, the problem was worse. In the house of one Jat landowner in our village lived a purchased woman who was rumored to have belonged to the *Chumar* caste. The woman actually looked as sophisticated as the best in the village; she had the speech and graces of high castes and was more beautiful than all those who were rejecting her. But for decades, and even after her children had grown up, the house of her husband was labeled with her caste, "Chuhar ki Chumari," meaning "the leather-woman of the house of Chuhar." People designated her husband's house, animals, land and family with her rumored caste, forgetting all other names and references for that family. Even as her daughters grew up to be graceful women, the appellation stuck to the family. It took a couple of decades before the brotherhood dealt with them freely.

It was a common belief that a daughter might inherit the loose character of her mother; families with such mothers and daughters tried their best to prevent the possibility of promiscuous behavior in the growing daughter and the consequences of such behavior. Debo's father was a fairly clever man, and her mother, although purchased, was of the acceptable Jat caste. The concerned father tried to keep history from repeating itself by marrying Debo off at the age of thirteen. Debo was a good-looking girl, tall, slim, with large, limpid and expressive eyes; but she did not seem to be too bright. Her father found her a husband who was about three years older than she was and still without a beard. He was the only son of his parents, and they had good land holdings. Although most families checked a bride's mother's background as well as her father's reputation, a good matchmaker or relative was sometimes able to smooth things over to make the match. Besides, her mother's history was nearly two decades old by the time of Debo's marriage. Her father did his best to perform a fine traditional wedding and gave a respectable dowry. He expected his daughter to live happily with her husband in his prosperous household.

But within two years of the marriage, Debo's husband and his family became frustrated with her. Debo was always on the prowl among the *goharas* (pyramids of dried cow dung patties) or in nearby crops to get laid, and she never missed an opportunity. As the husband and the in-laws gradually found out about her activities, they were upset with her. So at the age of about fifteen, they sent Debo back to her parent's house. That was the equivalent of a divorce, since people rarely went through any legal proceedings, and wives were rarely given any property at separation. If the husband did not come to take the wife back to his own house after she was sent to visit her parents, she was an abandoned wife with no rights. Then the troubles were just starting for Debo's mother and father after she returned to live with them. Debo never did anything vicious or defiant, and she was good about doing housework, but if an opportunity for sex came along, she rarely passed it up. From the stories going around later, it appeared that she did not care if it was wrong. Village boys who found out about her tendencies were either scandalized or were looking for ways to get together with her.

My friend Juggoo would pass by Debo's door daily, as her parents lived on the way to his house, and thus he could watch her comings and goings. The way to approach her appeared easy, even for the clumsy and inexperienced Juggoo. He was sixteen and had never been with a woman, but he had heard of the sexual exploits of his older friends and was jealous of them. He wanted to make his mark somehow, and Debo seemed like a good prospect. So one day when Juggoo encountered Debo, he hummed a nonsensical tune and noticed her smile. Surely, this was the green light, he thought. The next time they passed each other, Juggoo grabbed her hip from behind, but not with a hard pinch. Her reaction was a mild protest like, "Don't touch me, you shameless one." It was not the words but the tone that counted, and the tone was not angry. People used to say that when a woman says "No" she means "Yes." Some the apparently angry words would also save her skin if someone else saw the incident. With Debo's mild reaction, Juggo felt the light was intense green and he started thinking of an opportunity and a rendezvous.

A couple of days later, Juggoo and a few others were sitting at the chowkri near the village well, as was the custom among the boys. This was a place to shoot the breeze and discreetly to watch the world go by. This day, Debo came to get a pitcher of water from the well. When a woman had filled a pitcher, she usually needed someone's help to lift it up and to place it on the *innu* (doughnut-shaped pad) on her head. Usually a woman companion would help her, but if she was alone, she could call to someone, "O uncle, please help me lift the pitcher." Under those circumstances, it was perfectly normal and innocent for her to ask for help from whoever was around. Any fellow who was called to help would be willing, and in most cases there was no illicit intention on anyone's part. This time Debo was alone and the opportunity was ripe. She called Juggoo for help in lifting the pitcher. As he went over to the well and before he helped her lift the pitcher, she purposely rubbed her body against his and even stepped on his foot without saying anything. Now the signal was unmistakable, and he thought she was ready for action, even though no other words were said.

A couple of days later when Juggoo was not working in the fields, he decided to see what Debo was doing. In the afternoon he observed her washing clothes at the village well, as women did frequently in the afternoons after they were finished carrying water home. Again this time she was alone. He saw his opportunity and walked by the well, not looking at her so as to avoid arousing suspicion from anyone else around. As he walked by her, he whispered loudly, "Come to the *barra* of Fattah; I will wait for you there." These were the first meaningful words he had ever spoken to her, and the words had to be brief. Juggoo had arranged with his friend Mehtab of Fattah for the use of his family's barra, which is like a corral where farming families keep their cattle, fodder, fuel, wood, and miscellaneous farming necessities and products. Sometimes the barra also had a mud-brick shed, but people did not live there.

Juggoo was not quite certain whether Debo would come to him. A woman, even when she was interested, had many considerations and fears and couldn't just walk over nonchalantly like a man. Meeting privately with an unrelated man was an illicit act and severely forbidden. She had to watch for anyone else who might become aware of her movements and might report to her folks. To Juggoo's surprise and delight, Debo arrived at the barra very soon after he himself got there. Juggoo quickly let her in, looked in the street to make sure no one else had seen her approaching, and bolted the door. He had never been with a woman before and his heart was thumping. His guilt, nervousness, excitement, and fear of being found out were all working against him. Uncomfortable smiles, but few words, were exchanged. Both knew what they were going to do, but Juggoo did not know exactly how it was going to turn out. All he knew was second-hand information from older boys. But Debo appeared relatively unconcerned. He led Debo to the feed storage room where the *toori* (wheat chaff) was packed about knee deep and quite soft. Without many preliminaries, her *salwar* (lower garment) was off and he was naked too below the waist. They spread the clothes they had taken off on the toori to make the surface, which was already soft, more comfortable and to prevent the toori

249

from getting into her hair. Along with his urge to do it, Juggoo was uneasy about how it would go. Was his penis big enough compared to what she had been used to? What if she did not like his body? The big boys used to shave off pubic hair, although not their beards; Juggoo was in the natural state and thought that might turn her off. Will it work? What if she changes her mind or does not like it and hates him afterward?

But Debo was experienced and confident; and she smoothed his way. She lay on her back and gently pulled him on to her as she reclined on the clothes spread on the toori. There was some fumbling about, but Debo took his erect member into her hand and guided it to make the entry quite easy. He thought she was beautiful, soft, and enthusiastic and seemed to be enjoying it as his thrusts continued. Her attitude made it all the more comfortable and enjoyable for both. For Juggoo it was an incredible milestone. Here he was actually doing something he had only heard about from the more sophisticated boys. Before ejaculating, he pulled out to avoid pregnancy, as he had heard about such a possibility. He had also heard about a woman's orgasm, but he was not thinking about that then, and she did not have one. Both of them enjoyed mutual good feeling, though. She used a part of her own salwar to wipe off the ejaculate, saying, "Don't worry. I will wash it off at the well before going home."

Before she was fully dressed again and ready to depart, Juggoo's friend Mehtab arrived. He had known what was happening because he had given Juggoo his permission for the use of his barra. He had just jumped over the wall to come into the barra; then he asked Juggoo if he too could have sex with Debo. When Juggoo looked at Debo, she did not say anything but just smiled. Obviously she was willing and ready to go again. They did not even ask Juggoo to go away or ask for privacy. They went at it as Juggoo watched in amazement at how relaxed Debo was about the proceedings and how shameless Mehtab was, with his bare ass. Men never showed their behinds to other men in that society, but there was that shameless Mehtab, butt-naked as he pumped away at it! Juggoo was more embarrassed than the two fornicators were. He himself could never have done it in the presence of a third person. Pretty soon Debo and Mehtab were done. After they had ushered her out of the barra, the two boys talked and laughed about the whole adventure. They made plans to ask Debo to come again sometime soon. They intended to plan it better next time and to make it a nice party without any anxiety, now that they knew it was possible. They had no fear of her old father, and there was no strong young man in her house. But things changed rapidly thereafter, and that was the only time Juggoo and Debo ever had an encounter.

Not long afterwards, Juggoo found out that he had not made any difficult conquest. Debo had became even more active after that event as more people discovered her inclinations, now that she lived permanently at her parent's house and was not just visiting there. Pretty soon people started counting the names of those who had sex with Debo. There was a rumor of a gang bang when Debo was invited to an unoccupied toori storage room belonging to Santokh the *Fauji* (retired military man) without his knowledge. According to the gossip, when all the boys in the group were done with her, she was rumored to have remarked, "Some of you were alright, but you guys are still just boys; none of you is a real man like Dyal. Next time I want to get together with Dyal."

The year went by and Debo increased her activities with boys of the village. Her behavior became more and more excruciating for her father, as such carryings-on never remained a secret in a small community. Too often, Debo was absent from the house when she was cavorting with some boy, and inevitably there was some gossip among women. Now, her father could hardly show his face in the sutth (plaza) or speak authoritatively, whereas in earlier times he used to be a witty fellow who could liven up the sutth. Finally he could stand it no longer. With the help of friends and acquaintances, he found two unmarried brothers in a village twenty miles away. These brothers did not have much land but they were hard-working. Her father gave Debo to one of them as a wife when she was about seventeen. Even then her extra-marital adventures did not stop completely. Many times, Mehtab of Fattah, who had sex with her after Juggoo did in the barra, went by her village and dropped in to "pay his respects." It was considered a good deed for a man from a married girl's parents' village to drop by at her in-law house to cheer up the daughter of his village and to carry messages from her parents as well. But when Debo's husband was out working in the fields, she went to bed with Mehtab. Thereafter Mehtab stopped there many times "to pay his regards," as her village was on the way to his other relatives' village where he visited normally. The Punjabi poet Waris Shah says, "Nasty habits don't die, even if you cut bit by bit."

Debo was an exception. Most village girls were required to be chaste in their behavior, and most girls considered it immoral and degrading to have sex without marriage. Those who were adventurous were usually in circumstances in which they did not have to fear any male authority. But they still had to be very discrete and cautious, because the consequences of discovery were so horrendous and the disgrace to parents, brothers, and even to cousins would be most humiliating. In my estimate, more than ninety percent of the girls never had any male sexual contact before marriage, and the stories about some of the rest also might be rumors. Such contact was more likely to happen when a girl went for an extended period of time to visit relatives, especially *nanke* (maternal grandparents' house). At the nanke house she would be pampered, privileged, and spoiled and would not be related to the boys, except to immediate cousins. Even so, opportunities to find a landowner's girl alone were still few, unless she herself had an intense interest and an active imagination. Unmarried pregnancy was extremely rare among the landowners, as it could mean death for the girl, one way or the other. If an unwanted pregnancy did happen, the girl would be sent to some relative far away "for a visit." After an abortion or live birth, she would return several months later without any sign of a baby, but there might be whispers. The rarity of pregnancy among unmarried girls in the days when there was little awareness of birth control, may mean that perhaps illicit sexual activity involving unmarried girls was less prevalent than the talk of it.

Another amazing thing was the rarity of sexually transmitted diseases in the village. I never heard of any one of my friends catching anything, and news of such a disease could spread fast. They used to talk about people in the cities having diseases like *garmi* (heat), *atshik* (burning like fire), syphilis, or sores that broke out in the skin. One would read the advertisements in newspapers by various kinds of quacks about cures for such diseases. Cities were where prostitutes were and where such diseases were heard to exist.

Precocious Binder and His Adventures

Some boy in the village might tell his very close friend about his secret sexual adventures; most had not much to talk about. One adventurous fellow was my friend Binder, about a year and a half older than me in age but many years ahead in awareness. Binder was a good-looking boy who was usually well dressed and had a sharp mind. He was so precocious that he had already started experimenting sexually and talking about it before the age of eight, when I got to know him. A year was a long time at that age, and every day there were opportunities for us to learn new facts. By the age of ten, Binder had stuck his penis into every animal (except a cat and a cow) that he could gain access to, from dog to goat, from buffalo to horse, from donkey to camel, and he proudly described these activities in detail to his friends. He was never shy about sharing the details of his exploits; in fact he described them proudly just as a man shares his hunting and fishing adventures.

During the cotton picking season, little children were encouraged to stomp and romp on the piles of cotton stored in their houses, in order to compress it. For the neighborhood children it was a part of normal play, and innocent fun, but Binder used such occasions in various houses to get physical with girls of his age. Binder described to me his acts with girls in his neighborhood, who were ten and eleven year old. As he grew older, he grew bolder, and some girls found it easy to trust and play with a good-looking, assertive, and familiar boy. He had a knack for finding girls who were willing and whose parents were careless of their whereabouts. If the girls were reluctant, he talked convincingly to them to persuade them to comply, as he later described to me sometimes. What would be considered serious child molestation was just horseplay and sport to Binder. It was incredible to me that those innocent little girls ever agreed to such activity, whether during the stomping of cotton piles in the house or in the unoccupied upper-story *chobara*. The parents never suspected that such things were happening. Since scandals or tragedies involving young girls were rare, some parents could become careless. The girls did not go to school, and mothers and relatives were usually with them, whatever they were doing. But all that Binder needed with those little girls was being around the house but out of sight of their parents. The mothers never expected any suspicious or nasty behavior from a pretty young boy like him. The only one whom he spared was his uncle's daughter, and of course he was fiercely protective of his own sisters' chastity. I was totally retarded in this respect and did not think such things were possible.

Binder once described to me his adventures with Beebo, a girl who lived some houses away from him. They were teenagers by then, and he had been playing with Beebo as with other neighborhood girls for years. One summer day he told Beebo that he would come to her bed in the dark night while she was sleeping on the roof of her house. That night he climbed a wall a couple of houses away from her house, as the wall was not too high to climb at that location. Since the roofs of all the houses were connected, he was then able to walk on top of the flat roofs up to her bed. He took his shoes off and got into her bed under the covers. According to him, Beebo said, "You sure are a *kachcha* (raw, inexperienced) lover! What if someone walks by on the roof and sees a man's shoes here!" She picked up the shoes and put them on the bed under the covers. He stayed with her all night. He told me that in the dark, early hours of the morning, her brother, who was sleeping out of sight on the other side of the chobara, actually walked by the bed as he went downstairs before he went to work in the fields. But Beebo had wrapped herself completely around Binder under the covers to make it appear that there was only one person in her bed. Any false move, a cough or a sound, would have caused a major disaster.

But such dangers never stopped Binder. Before and after that event, he had encounters with Beebo many times. They did it at her home when no one was expected there and in the millet crops near the village, where a woman walking with a jug of water was assumed to be going to answer the call of nature. He told me he had also slept with her elder sister a few times, but that the sister was getting married soon. He said he liked both sisters equally for different qualities, even though the older one was too skinny and tall. He would tell in detail how their lips felt, how beautiful their breasts were, and how the older one said, "I love you this much and some more" when she embraced him tightly. It seemed that whichever girl Binder approached, she was ready to play with him. Even some married ones did, whereas I never had the courage to try any such thing. But it is also true that there were some girls near Binder's house about whom he never made any claims. Those girls must not have encouraged him, because he was not the kind to shirk from adventure or from talking about it. Even when he could play with several girls, he was always looking for new ones to have sex with.

I think that Binder was a very uncommon person. I never knew any other boy like that. I just happened to be his classmate and heard his stories. After his teenage years, Binder completely abandoned this behavior and became a successful, respected family man. Like most of my friends he died some years ago.

I was younger than my friend Binder by year and a half and that was a big difference when I was ten years old. Also Binder had a precocious and active mind, while I was somewhat slow in every way. He was as smart as I was in school, but he was much more aware about the world. He would tell us "the facts of life," such as how babies are made (man's ejaculate is deposited on a flower inside a woman; then the flower closes and the baby develops from that deposit in the flower). He told me that women have periods of menstrual flow once a month and have to use a special cloth, and that is why the word 'kappre' (cloth) is used for that time of the month. He told me the rumors about who was having an affair with whom. Other boys were not shy about playing with their penises in the presence of friends, but Binder started masturbating earlier than his peers and was the one who fully described the details of his experiences to us. He told us that if a boy continues to masturbate, at first nothing happens except the usual excitement and pleasure, but after he has tried for a long time a wave of pleasure runs through the body with no discharge of any kind. Although ejaculation starts after you are twelve or so, Binder did not want to wait until that age of twelve, when he would have matured and his body would be ready. After practicing for a few months, he worked up to a point where a small quantity of thin ejaculate would appear at the end. Then he thought he had become a man and boasted to others about it.

Binder described his 'wet dreams' like fish stories. In one dream he found a woman, flirted with her, and had intercourse with her. In reality, after the nocturnal emission, he was just left with a wet lower garment. When he woke up, it felt like an egg had broken in it. He said that when the ejaculate dried and hardened on the garment, the cloth became stiff, as if with heavy starch; and the portion with the ejaculate stain looked like the map of Punjab. He would have been embarrassed to have his mother or sisters wash the affected garment, so he cut out the "starched portion" of the clothing with scissors and wrote a note on it saying, "In the memory of my dear son, who died for lack of a mother." He saved the note for some days before throwing it away. Other boys had similar sexual dreams off and on, with infinite possibilities: sometimes they cavorted with vaguely familiar faces in dreams and sometimes with total strangers; sometimes they lost one partner, then found another; and sometimes the dreams were interrupted when they were awakened. Few boys talked about their dreams, but Binder talked about such matters without shame or shyness. He told me that you are more likely to have such dreams if you have eggs, meats, or other "warm foods" in your diet and less likely if you eat simple vegetables and grains. In a man's teens and twenties such dreams were inevitable, even if he were married, although with lower frequency with advancing age. The dreams had nothing to do with the quality of his relationship with the wife but were affected mostly by his physiological condition, diet, and other circumstances of his life. It is only after middle age that men may start waking up from such a dream before a sexual encounter is concluded, and thus they wake without having a wet dream. Wet dreams were indicators of a man's physical condition but they were also embarrassing. We used to wonder if holy men also had wet dreams.

Binder and Billu Mess Up

One morning, there was news in the village that some robbers had tried to rob Katy (pronounced Cotty) during the previous night. Katy was a married girl who was back in her mother's house because her husband was in service somewhere at the time. The story was that as Katy was sleeping on the roof of her house, two robbers had tried to choke her and to take her gold necklace and earrings. When she started shrieking, the neighbors awoke and came to her rescue, and the robbers ran away. One of the robbers even attacked a pursuing neighbor with a sword before making his escape but did not injure him. One of the pursuers thought he recognized one of the "robbers." A couple of days later, the whispers started going around as the truth became known about the supposed robbery. The whispers said that it was not really a robbery but an attempted sexual assault. Then the whispers said that the girl knew the "attackers" and it was merely a miscommunication between illicit lovers. A gruff, outspoken, distant uncle of the girl from the same street made the remark, "If a bitch is in heat, the dogs will come; the dogs this time are some local boys and not from another patti." From then on, there were two stories: polite people spoke of robbers who had tried to rob a nice girl because her brothers were living somewhere far away, while the less polite but more savvy people said that the episode was just a matter of poor communication between illicit lovers. As usual in matters of sex, it was as if there were two parallel societies in the village.

Katy was a gorgeous, fashionable, articulate and assertive girl. Binder once told me that a girl friend of Katy named Bunti shared a daring experience with her. He said Bunti had arranged to have her husband Karnail sleep with Katy. This was a one-time encounter, as a favor to her husband and to her friend Katy, when the husband had come to visit her parents' house. The two girls were good friends but Katy was the cleverer and the more daring of the two. She wanted to have sex with her friend Bunti's husband, as her own husband was away in service. There was no risk for Bunti in arranging this, because in that society it was impossible for a husband to leave his wife and take up with another woman in a different village. And there was little fear of pregnancy for Katy because she was married. Binder said that Bunti herself guarded the door of the chobara (upper story

254

chamber) while her own husband and Katy did it. I have no idea how Binder found out about such secrets of the women, but he probably learned it from his own many contacts with the neighborhood girls. Those of us who heard such things thought that Binder's street must have been a den of sin. We thought there were no such girls in the rest of the village.

A few days after the attempted "robbery" of Katy's necklace, Binder told me the truth about how his friend Billu's plan got fouled up. Katy had told Billu that she usually slept on the roof, as is the custom in summertime, but that her mother slept downstairs in the courtyard. Billu had told her he would come during the night by climbing a convenient wall and would walk up to the roof where her bed was, but they had not arranged any definite time. He thought that since Katy was going to be alone, he could just show up at night and then negotiate, and there was no need to plan in detail as there was very little danger. So Katy was not lying awake or waiting for him. Billu took his friend Binder along as a favor, and they climbed up to the roof where her bed was. She was alone and sound asleep when Billu put his hand on her shoulder and neck area. Katy woke up startled and saw the two men in the dark, who appeared menacing. Before she could recollect herself, she started shouting, "robbers, robbers, help, help,..." Then Billu said to her, "Hey Katy, we are no robbers. It is me, Billu, and this is my friend Binder." She said, "I am sorry; it is too late to talk now; you better run or the whole neighborhood will be upon you and I will be disgraced." The neighbors came to aid pretty quickly. So Binder and Billu jumped off the roof into a vacant yard as the neighbors rushed to apprehend them. In such situations men would take great risks to apprehend an offender. A neighborhood boy jumped off the roof right after them in order to catch them. At this point Billu attacked the pursuing boy with a sword, but he did not injure the boy, who was strong, alert, and armed with a stick. Both the "robbers" escaped, but someone among the pursuers thought he recognized the robbers even in the dark.

The neighbors soon forgot about the incident; but for Binder it was not over. Those who recognized him told his older brother Jinder about who the robbers were. Jinder was an upstanding, hard-working, well-behaved fellow, just like his father, whereas the younger Binder was adventurous, more like his own mother. Anyway, Binder told me that Jinder threatened to smash his bones, but he managed to avoid the older brother. The brother accused Binder of engaging in immoral actions and bringing disgrace on the family. Regardless of how common it was, illicit sex was considered *paap* (sin) and thought to have consequences beyond the physical. Binder had to spend a few days away from the village with his relatives until his brother's rage cooled down. Fortunately for Binder, his brother did not know much about his other exploits.

Tragedy of Tejo

In the village population, very few unmarried girls dared to have sexual affairs, and those who did, had to be exceptionally adventurous. A love affair in the modern sense happened only in fairy tales. In the village, opportunities for illicit lovers to be alone were hard to create as open contact or conversation was not allowed, and everyone feared the social disgrace that would result from such activities. Low caste woman, however, moved about relatively freely, as they came to the farmers' fields to collect the means of subsistence, such as mustard leaves to cook, or fuel, or fallen kernels from the field after the farmer had harvested. Some farmers always left a small corner of the harvest, called *bodi*, as charity for the low castes to pick. Thus, it was not difficult to arrange an illicit meeting with a low caste woman. On the other hand, a meeting with a woman of the landowners was risky; it usually had to be brief, and there was not much time for preliminaries. Talking was not a high priority, and people who met this way were not looking for a long-term relationship. The only thing that the parties could meet for was a "quickie." For most girls an affair was not worth the risk, and the consequences were not pretty, as the following story of Tejo illustrates.

Tejo was a teenage girl of sensuous beauty, with a vibrant personality. She was from another village, but I had seen her a few times when she visited her relatives in our village Mehraj. I admired her slim body, smooth skin, bright eyes, and perfectly even teeth. Tejo was so vivacious and appealing that everyone noticed her, and many boys in her village wanted her. She was also adventurous and full of life, but creating the opportunity to meet a boy was risky. Finally Tejo made a connection with a handsome guy named Dhanna from her village who was strong, daring, and a budding *badmash* (bad character), not terribly afraid of any consequences.

The one place in the villages that affords an opportunity for a secret meeting is the *barra*, where people keep their oxen or buffaloes when they don't keep them in their own courtyard. The barra was often a hundred yards or more away from the residence. It was the travel between the house and the barra, and having to spend time to perform some task there, that created the opportunity. Some barra had a closed room for storing *toori* (chaff) and animal feed where illicit lovers could meet, but the fear of being seen and found out was always present. Tejo's family had a barra a short distance away from their house, and sometimes Tejo went there to milk the buffalo. Although the family was usually careful not to leave her unsupervised for long when she could be vulnerable, it was impossible to send guards with her at all times, and of course they trusted her to be virtuous and chaste. Her beau Dhanna used to sit on a log along the way to the barra. After some glances, smiles, words and familiarity, Tejo and Dhanna got involved. With the excuse of milking the buffalo and doing other chores, pretty soon Tejo was having a hot love affair with Dhanna.

If Tejo had not become pregnant, this affair could have gone the way of other unknown events. It would have stopped later when she would be married off to someone else. She could have been married in a year or two, and no one would have known the difference. But the fact that the unmarried Tejo got pregnant became known relatively late in the term, and it struck her parents like a bolt from the blue. They were bewildered and felt disgraced. Abortion was not easily available in villages, and she would have to be sent to live in some other village if it could be arranged, in order to hide the fact and minimize public dishonor. But perhaps it was already too late for an easy abortion. It is said that too much time had passed before the parents detected the problem of Tejo's pregnancy and she was starting to show. It is hard to know the details of what trauma the family went through. It was mentioned that the family had thought of killing her. Her lover Dhanna was a really tough and violent guy and was not afraid of being killed by Tejo's family. And if they could only threaten and not kill the guy, then it would have been an even bigger, public disgrace.

This was the time of the 1947 religious massacres related to the Partition of India.

256

Many people were absorbed in different struggles of life and death. In the middle of those disturbances, and in spite of the increased difficulty and risk of travel, Tejo's family had to find a solution to the condition she was in. A regular marriage was unthinkable under the circumstances. They found a house with two brothers who were willing to take her as a wife. Under normal circumstances, these were not the kind of people that Tejo would have considered even as servants, but now she did not really have a voice, after disgracing her family and being big with an illegitimate pregnancy. There was no marriage ceremony; she was just "seated" in the house of the two brothers by the parents in a hush-hush manner. Initially, the "husband" did not let her stay in the house where the neighbors could see a pregnant bride. He kept her in their cotton fields until a baby boy was born. I was told that they disposed off the newborn baby; and some days later the husband brought the childless bride Tejo to his home. They told anyone who wanted to visit and meet the bride that she was slightly unwell and unable to meet any visitors for some time. Since she did not have a regular wedding or *moklava*, there was no question of community ceremonies like "seeing the bride and her clothes." Of course they could not hide the facts completely from other people. I who lived many villages away was told the complete story Tejo's by someone who was quite reliable; and by that time others must have known the story too. The fact that there was no marriage ceremony and that a beautiful girl like that was just "seated" and given to a house informally was itself suspicious. Knowing Tejo's personality, I felt that she deserved better and that her life would not have been wasted like that if more compassionate and tolerant social attitudes had prevailed. As Tejo's fate indicates, the consequences of premarital affairs were dire enough so that such cases were rare.

Among college girls and boys, the situation was slightly different. In their environment it was possible for girls to talk to boys publicly, although only the bolder ones spent much time together. Some of them progressed to meeting where they could be alone and things could progress to touching, kissing and beyond, but sexual intercourse among college girls was perhaps as uncommon as it was in the villages. In the cities the opportunity to talk together was easier and was socially accepted. There were no crops or goharas to hide behind, but there were activities to provide an excuse to be away from home, and inventive minds could not be stopped completely. Then there were also young city girls of "loose character" who sometime roved in twos on their bicycles in gaudy clothes, with bright lipstick and makeup, throwing glances at boys they thought were attractive and might be rich. It was believed that such girls were ready for a party any time. It was the behavior of such bold girls that the village people had in mind when they talked about the loose morals of educated city girls.

Homosexuality in the Old Society

Homosexuality as a topic of conversation was not as delicate as the talk of sex between men and women was. There was going to be no murder over this issue. Such talk was used for jokes and abuses among men. Ridicule was piled only on the submitting male partner, that is, the one who performed the female role and was called *londa or launda* (slave, submissive). Less serious stigma was attached to the man in the dominant role. From olden times many people were known to engage in such activities. Baber, the Turkic/Mongol conqueror of Afghanistan and the founder of the Mughal Empire in India, in his memoirs from 500 years ago, gives some stories of homosexual activities among the elite of their Muslim, Turkic society. Some powerful and influential men in places like Samarkand, with harems of wives, also kept young boys for sex. Baber relates the story of how as a young prince he himself was hopelessly in love with a boy and how he would feel weak at the sight of him but was too embarrassed to let any of his guards and attendants know about it. Here are some excerpts from Baber's memoirs: "Uncle Sultan Mahmud Mirza never neglected his prayers, but he also kept boys for pederasty, the very sons of *begs* (*nobles*), his own foster brothers....For the fleeting enjoyment of this transitory world, whenever he saw a handsome boy, he used every means to carry him off....Such currency did the vile practice gain in this time that every man had his boy; to keep a catamite was a creditable thing and not to have one, was regarded rather an imputation on a man's spirit." In another passage he relates: "There was a lad belonging to the camp bazar, named Babari. I became wonderfully fond of him, nay, to speak the truth, mad and distracted after him. Never was a lover so wretched, enamored, so dishonored as I. Sometimes he came to visit me and from shame and modesty, I found myself unable to look him direct in the eye. How could I converse or disclose my passion.... One day while passing with attendants, at the sight of him I almost fell to pieces with great confusion and shame."

In our Punjabi society, however, homosexuality was considered unnatural and degrading. We considered it to be immoral behavior but were less shocked by it than by illicit heterosexual sex, which had more serious consequences. Apart from the morality, the submitting boy was considered effeminate, soft and dirty; people sneered and snickered at the mention of his name. There were cases where young boys were coerced, bribed, influenced or talked into such roles by older boys or men. Such *londa* (submitting) boys were gradually victimized by more people, once their tendency to consent became a habit and became known. If a boy was good looking, of light complexion, and not too well protected, others would try to train him to be a londa. Since it was forbidden to have female company or friendship, except as a relative, many more boys fell victims at a young age than might have been expected. Ordinary people thought that in *londa bazi* (homosexual activity), the dominant one who entered, was just behaving badly; but the londa, the one who submitted, was considered lowly, dirty, and degraded as well. There were no exclusive relationships at young age, and there could be many londa baz (dominant one) for each londa. Since polite and religious people never talked about such activity or acknowledged its existence, they could never condemn homosexuality. In holy places it was just unthinkable to talk about such things. So the homosexuals were not hated, and nobody wanted to hurt them; they were just ignored by respectable society and their activity was considered unmentionable.

In our village there were a few boys who had londa tendencies, but most boys would rather have died than submitted to an aggressive approach from anybody. Parents of boys had to be protective of their sons. Once when I was 14 years old and relatively small, it was considered preferable for me to stay in Rampura Phul in winter while studying there rather than come home to the village every night. The days in winter were short, and it could take four hours to travel back and forth, so my father arranged for me to eat my meals by monthly contract at a Punjabi-style *dhaba* (restaurant) in Rampura Phul. Then my father noticed that the owner of the restaurant, a tall fat fellow, was particularly sweet-talking and a flattering guy. My father warned me, "Gurnam, beware of people like him. He may be ok, but some people like him may have the habit of londa bazi (homosexual activity)." My father had never before spoken such words or anything about sex to me, but he thought fit to warn me then. As it turned out, the restaurant owner was just a gregarious flatterer and a pleaser, unlike the village people, and he never bothered me as I ate two meals daily at his restaurant for some months.

In any area, any londa boy quickly became known for his tendencies. One of my classmates, Inderjit, was well known to submit to other boys and to older men in homosexual acts when he was young. He was a pretty boy when he was a child. His mother dressed him in silk clothes for school to complement his good looks, whereas the homespun khadder shirt was the regular wear of ordinary boys like me. Perhaps more important is the fact that he was precocious, had tremendous interest in sex of all types, and had little sense of fear and shame. He had submitted to many older boys and had also experimented with smoking drugs with low caste Muslims in exchange for submitting to them. He was known to have had sex with a low caste Sansi and also with a Mirasi school teacher named Akbar. This young unmarried teacher would ask his students to come to his house to study at night, and the boys would sleep there overnight. Only Inderjit, who was good looking and was known to be a londa, was "victimized" by the teacher; other students just provided the cover for this activity. My father would not let me go to study at any teacher's house at night, because he thought there were enough hours in the day for studying. Inderjit would mention to me how much fun they had overnight at the teacher's house and how they had become friends with the teacher. I thought I was really missing something. So one night I got permission to take my quilt to the teacher's house to study and to stay overnight. If there was any studying done, it did not take very long. The rest of the night, the boys heard *boli* (romantic ballads and risqué songs), jokes, and the teacher's stories of his exploits. The teacher Akbar and his brother inhaled cigarette smoke, shook it in their mouths violently, and brought egg-like balls of smoke out of their mouths to deposit on the table. These "smoke eggs" collapsed gradually after a long time. There were other silly and wasteful activities that night, much partying, but not much studying and not enough sleeping. I was never allowed to go there again, although I found it interesting. Inderjit would not openly discuss it, and I could not ask questions about such a subject, but he never feared or cared that anyone would find out about his homosexual habits. Sometimes he even exploited that habit to get something he wanted from others. To me his behavior seemed surreal and under-worldly, and other boys talked about it, but Inderjit never seemed to be afraid of getting a bad name as a londa.

It may not seem credible to modern-day readers, but the truth is that Inderjit had abandoned his homosexual behavior by the age of 15 or so. Once he got older, sex with women became his main interest and he was wildly successful with women also. His success might have been due to fact that the male members of his family were known to be particularly well endowed; but more likely it was his uninhibited behavior, his lack of fear of getting a bad name, and his ability to talk effectively with girls. Later in life, he became a respectable, prosperous landowner with a big house and many children, and with a great deal of influence in his community. All his history as a londa was forgotten.

I knew of another londa boy who used to graze cattle in our village where his mother lived after being abandoned by his father. It was humbling for him to be the son of an abandoned wife and not to be living in his father's village. With no father or other man to supervise and protect him, this boy became an easy target for any cattle grazers that wanted to force themselves on him. A woman could do a fair job of protecting her son in a school, but out in the fields, grazing cattle, it was a different world. He became known as a londa to every cattle grazer, and they had no fear of his family. After he became a teenager though, he went to live in his father's village. There he became prosperous with inherited land, was married, and lived a normal family life afterwards. So it appeared that some londa boys had just succumbed to the aggressive demands or persuasions of others and never really wanted to be in the habit. Most such boys quit the londa habit and adopted heterosexual patterns of life as they grew to be teenagers. Later they were married and never reverted to the "evil habit."

The main difference in my days from the present times was that the marriages of most boys were arranged by their parents during their teenage years, whether the boys and girls liked it or not. Much of the homosexual habits and tendencies were thus curbed or covered up by the heterosexual marriages. A few men still continued this "habit of londa bazi" in adult life, rather secretly, but such londa, known to others in the village, were less than one in a hundred in the adult population, although more might have been latent or hidden. Unlike the modern day homosexuals who openly display 'gay traits' and want to be recognized as a group to be protected and be given rights not previously entitled to, in those days they lived unobtrusively. The polite people would never even think about their "deviant habit," while the aware people whispered and snickered about them. They were not hated and there was no violence against homosexuals. Our preachers never talked about sexual matters much less homosexual matters; they would only mention loyalty to one's spouse.

The fear of being a victim or of being labeled a londa was such that no man was willing to be naked in the presence of another man or to show his behind. It was perfectly acceptable for women to be naked in the presence of other women, because homosexuality among women was unthinkable in the old rural society. These customs were exactly opposite to the customs in Western societies, where men in gym facilities can walk around naked, but I have heard that women do not get naked in the presence of other women. In my circles, since we all knew that there was no homosexual among us, physical touching in public among grown boys and men was common, casual, and caused no concern. Some college boys held hands when they went for a walk, whereas in America such behavior among men would be considered deviant. Frequently young boys put their hands on each other's shoulders like oxen in a yoke as they walked. Kissing among men was unthinkable, but hugging and other forms of physical contact were considered a sign of affection and closeness. Many times I went to visit my friend Amrik, who was a student in a law college in another city, and the two of us slept in one bed overnight without any concerns. But we would not have wanted to touch or be too near a man if he were known to be a londa, as we would be uneasy about his "unclean" homosexual body. But a londa baz would not be squeamish about contact with another londa; after all, other people did have sex with low castes or even with animals.

Not Lesbo Land Either

The concept of women loving women did not seem strange in that society, but was considered natural and innocent rather than sexual or dirty. Women had the role as loving creatures, starting with dolls and then with their children. Women hugged, physically touched, and kissed one another and their children; but Indian women never kissed a man in public. It was common and socially acceptable for women to be completely naked in the presence of their women friends and relatives while trying on clothes, taking baths, and so on. It was not considered unusual or odd for two women to sleep in the same bed, as they might do so for convenience and as a sign of closeness to be admired. Lesbianism, which is feared in the Western world and was initially considered a product of the angry women's movement, had no significance in our old society. There, the women were required to be married unless they were widowed. In fact if a woman was never married, she would be revered for being a "virgin."

If there was any homosexual activity among girls, it was not a significant practice or a topic of concern in polite circles. It could not be carried into adulthood, when they were required to be married. We never heard of or even thought of such possibilities when we were in the village. But once there was a rumor among boys in our college that some girls in a women's college did things to one another. There was also a rumor of the confiscation of strap-on cocks from the dormitory of a girls' college in the city of Jullunder. But no parent was told about such activities as the authorities would find it too uncomfortable to discuss such 'violations.' All this might be just a false rumor The boys who heard it considered it a naughty play and perhaps an isolated deviant act, but not likely to become a damaging habit.

But one college-age girl in India told me that when she was younger, she slept with an older girl relative one night and that the older cousin put the nipple of one breast into her mouth and asked her to keep sucking on it. Both of these well-educated girls became well placed professionals; later they were married and had children; and they lived without any sign of deviation from the norm. But if any girl had refused to get married to a man, had asserted her homosexuality, and had acted in other unconventional ways, people there also would have become fearful of lesbianism.

CHAPTER 12

Punjabi and Sikh Names

Sikh names are derived from the Punjabi language, which is based on Sanskrit, but has an abundance of Persian words in it. When Guru Gobind introduced the *amrit* ceremony for his special brand of Sikhs in 1699, he added the word 'Singh' (lion) to the first names of all male Sikhs including his own, and then Sikhs started naming their sons accordingly. Similarly the word Kaur was attached to the names of Sikh girls. In fact most Sikh names for boys and girls became the same, with Singh or Kaur added to distinguish male from female. Nowadays, there is a trend among urban Sikh parents to give diverse Hindu, Muslim, and foreign names to their daughters, to fit cosmopolitan life. For example, my nephews' daughters in India are named Mandeep Kaur, Amanat, Natasha, Jaspriya, Azmat, Reet, and so on, but the boys' first names still end with Singh. Before the Partition of India, more Hindus and Sikhs had names derived from the Arabic or Persian, with attachments like Singh, Ram, Mull, Das, Chand, Raj, Kumar and Lal added, to distinguish them from Muslims. The Muslim names had Islamic attachments like Deen or Din, Ali, Ullah, Mohammed, Ahmed, Khan, Beg, Hussein, Shah, etc., or were preceded by Abd-ul, Zia-ul, Ghias-ul, Mohammed, and other Arabic words. Since the official language was Persian or Urdu and the rulers had been Muslim for several hundred years, Persian and Arabic first names were inevitable. After the Partition of India, old-fashioned names or names from the Muslim culture were given less frequently to Sikh children. Nowadays, Indians are getting highly creative with the language to form new names. Unlike the European custom, an Indian family tries to give its children the names that no one else has in their circle of friends and relatives.

Informal first names, before Singh or Kaur was added, suggested the sex of the individual. In the early days most names ending with either a consonant or with the "a", "u" or "er" sound were masculine, as, for example, Karta, Boota, Gyana, Kapura, Dhanna, Buddha, Nikka, Dharma, Karma, Atma, Kishna, Bishna, Brahma, or Jugga; or Persu, Mittu, Chittu, Nandu, Beeru, Telu, Bansu, or Nathu; or Gujjer, Inder, Ishwer, Joginder, Gheecher, Bikker, Sunder, or Pakher; or Sirdool, Mullen, Bukken, Chunnen, Thummen, Nanak, Manak, Jodh, Arjun, Gobind, or Chand. On the other hand, names ending with "an" (where the "n" is only pronounced so as to create a nasal sound), such as Jindan, Indran, Kaulan, Acchran, Meeran, Taran, Jeetan, Ranjitan, Roopan, and Sodhan, were always feminine, whereas outside the Punjab such girls' names ended simply with the "a" sound and not with the nasal "an" sound. Most names ending with an "ee" sound, such as Rami, Nikki, Nandi, Santi, Bunti, Rakhi, Rajji, Bibi, Indie, Kaati, Rupi, Nihali, Dhanni, Nanki, Janki; or those with an "o" sound, such as Gulabo, Punjabo, Tejo, Rajo, Bunto, Chinto, Maro, Nando, Billo, Indo, Dilipo, Rupo, Dhanno, Kishno, and Kahno, were all feminine. From the root word Jeet (win or winner), Jeeta and Jeetu would be boys but Jeetan, Jeeti or Jeeto would be girls. In the last couple of decades, however, names do not always follow these rules; nowadays many girls are also given names ending with 'u' or 'a'.

All Names Have Meanings

It was rare to find a Punjabi first name without a meaning. Thus Jawahar means "precious stone," Moti means "pearl," Naginder means "jewel of the God Inder," Kirpal means "the kind one," Gurdial means "God's gift," Shiela Banti means "embodiment of gentleness," and Shanti Devi means "peace goddess." Among the names of Muslim origin, Jang Bahadur means "war brave," Gulab Din means "rose of faith," and Mehtab means "moonlight." Some parents chose unabashedly pretentious and bombastic names for their children. Among the Hindus, choosing the name of a god or goddess for their children (Shiv, Krishn, Brahma, Vishnu or Bishnu, Inder, or Ishwer; and Devi, Lakshmi, Durga, or Sita, for example) was considered virtuous. Guru Gobind Singh chose the word "Singh" (lion) to attach to the name of every Sikh male with the aim of raising their morale, after removing the attachments like Ram, Lal, Chand, Das, Dev, Kumar, Anand, and Parkash from the names of Hindu origin. Then the boys could be given names like Garh Tor Singh (fort breaker lion) and Daljit Singh (victor over armies lion).

People used to joke about the pretentious names and mock the irony they sometimes created. For example: "The boy is afraid of jackals but he is named Daler Singh (Bold Lion); he forgets his loin cloth by the pond but he is named Suchet Singh (aware lion); and he has not a penny in his pocket, but he is named Dhanni Ram (wealthy god)." Millions of Punjabi people, specially the Sikhs in the last hundred years, have the word Inder or Jit compounded into their first names, as, for example, Inderjit, Rajinder, Devinder, Mohinder, Harinder, Narinder, Joginder, and Satinder; or Harjit, Diljit, Baljit, Manjit, and Kanwaljit. They just thought of a word and stuck Inder or Jit to it, resulting in a proliferation of such compounded names. Hindus would stick the word Dev (god) or Devi (goddess), Ram or Krishan into the names of their children, with the wish that their son or daughter would turn out to be like an avatar (god born as human) or have god-like powers. Giving a child the name of a god or goddess was considered virtuous and wishful, rather than pretentious, just as so many Mexicans name their sons 'Jesus', and Muslims name many of theirs Mohammed.

Names suitable when a child was young, sometimes changed as the person grew older and/or more important; names were most likely to be changed before they started to be written. The saying "Persu, Persa, Pers Ram, *es maya ke tin nam*", means that the name changes from Persu to Persa to Pers Ram according to the amount of wealth the person acquires; or from little, to bigger, to powerful, as the person grows in importance. Similarly there were Desu, Desa, Des Raj or Parbhu, Parbha, Parbh Das or Hansu, Hansa, Hans Raj progressions. The ending with 'u' was informal, the 'a' ending was worth

263

noting, but removing the vowel ending and adding the second part to the name made it formal and more respectable. A servant or familiar person could be addressed with one name, but a master or a respectable person had to be addressed with two names, with "Ji" also added for extra respect.

As one went from Punjabi to Hindi, some alterations in sound and changes of accent were inevitable. South Indians usually add an "m" or "n" sound at the end of names to make them sound like Sanskrit. The Hindi-speaking Indians, especially the pretentious ones, add extra vowels like "a" or "ya" into their words; they also seem to emphasize the sound "a" at the end of most words. For example the name Chander in Punjabi sounds like Chandra in Hindi-speaking areas; Ram in Punjabi becomes Rama in Hindi; Krishn becomes Krishna; Inder becomes Indra; Buddh becomes Buddha; Shiv becomes Shiva, Rajinder becomes Rajendra, and so on. My father had the habit of signing his name as "Nagendra Singh" instead of Naginder Singh, since he had learned Hindi and Sanskrit when he went to school in Bhatinda in his childhood and the teachers wrote his name the way a Hindi-speaking person would pronounce it. It is common for Punjabis to 'eat vowels' and sometimes even consonants from Sanskrit words. Sound replacement is also common, for example from V to B, from Y to J, from SH to S, and from KSH to KH or SH.

Family names, originally called *gotra*, or just *gote* in Punjabi, were not normally used in the village, as most landowners in our village had the same family name anyway. But in other places people added the family names for better identification. Everyone's gotra name was known to others because it indicated your lineage, and it generally determined your caste and excluded you from marrying someone from the same family. Literate people referred to family names as *zaat* (race, kind) or sub-caste; and in Punjab a family name could indicate your religion, caste, occupation, place of origin and possibly your social status. For example in Punjab, a Gaur, Kaushal or Sharma is a Brahman; a Sodhi or Khanna is a Kshatri; an Aggarwal, Goel or Gupta is a shopkeeper caste; while the family names Sidhu, Sandhu, Dhillon, Gill, Brard, Birk, Maan, Bhullar, Garewal, Dhaliwal, Deol, Aulakh, Chahal, Mahal, Cheema, or Randhawa, are Jat Sikhs. As a result of conversions in the past, some Muslim Jats with similar family names can be found in the Pakistan part of Punjab. Some educated people, especially writers and poets, gave themselves new last names (*tukhallus*) to indicate their town of origin, personalities or ideals rather than indicating their family or caste.

If you didn't know a man in Punjab, you could address a Sikh as Sirdar or Sardar, a Hindu as Babu, Lala or Seth, and a Muslim as Mian or Khan, as everyone made sure that his religion was obvious from his hair and dress. The word 'Ji' could be added at the end of the name for additional respect. But in modern times, the word 'Sahib' after the name, title, or address of any man or woman has the most flattering effect.

CHAPTER 13

SUPERSTITIONS IN OUR VILLAGES

The lives of village people in Punjab were continuously affected by superstitions. Uneducated people were somewhat more gullible than others, but literacy was no guarantee of freedom from superstition. When as a child I was told by a fortune-telling Brahmin that "Washing your hair on a Tuesday would bring bad health and misfortune," it was imprinted in my mind for the rest of my life. I don't dare to take a chance and wash my hair on Tuesdays, even now. We were also told that the position the stars at the time of one's birth determined one's health, wealth, occupation, love life, achievements, adversities and ultimate fate. Although my father had become an amrit dhari Sikh, and we were not supposed to believe the Brahmins, our culture of the 1930s was still permeated with the old influences. The Brahmins were not just the purveyors of religion; some of them had developed the system of *jotish* (divining, predicting) to tell people what was causing their misfortunes. Then they would suggest preventive steps or remedies—which usually included giving a feast and a donation to the Brahmin! It was in their interest to promote superstitions, because their livelihood was tied to such beliefs; but the Brahmins themselves were also victims of superstition.

The Brahmin might predict *grauh*, a period of impending misfortune, in the future of a family or individual. His prediction would indicate how long the grauh was going to last, but by tradition the duration specified could be one of the following: a short period of grauh was predicted to last for a few weeks, a medium length one for a year and a quarter, a severe one for seven and a half years, and sometimes a very long grauh for twenty-two years. These grauh periods of varying duration and severity might depend on the configuration of the stars and planets relative to their configuration when the individual was born, or even on the configuration when the spouse or other family members of the individual were born. The grauh might be caused by the karma of one's previous life; it could be caused by *paap* (a bad act) or by negligence in performing *dharma* duties. If a family complained to the Brahmin about a misfortune that already occurred, he would suggest appropriate mitigating measures.

For a Hindu family, a Brahmin would prepare the horoscopes for a boy and a girl about to get engaged. If their horoscopes were "clashing, incompatible or inauspicious," the match could not be made. In some cases the Brahmin could work out a dispensation

265

for a fee and certain other required acts, whereby the effect of the stars could be diminished. I remember that a traveling *jotishi* once predicted some mild grauh for me; he told my mother that the harmful effects could be minimized if I would feed some dough to cows or to crows every Tuesday for a three-month period. My mother gave him some grain for his advice, but I never followed up on his recommendation. By the 1930s, hardly any Sikh family worried about horoscopes, but affluent Hindu families felt they had to consult their Brahmin about the most auspicious times for important undertakings like a wedding or the construction of a house. A boy and girl might seem well-suited for one another and the families might want their marriage, but if the Brahmin said the marriage would not work due to clashing horoscopes, his word could be decisive.

My father used to mock the Brahmins' practice of *jotish* with this little rhyme: *Rahu Ketu bael hamare, sarh satti hai kheti; patri hamari bari shikaren, mar liavay chheti*. This may be translated as: "Rahu and Ketu, the stars of omens, are like our oxen; the 'seven-and-half year curse' is like our crop; our divining calendar is like a great hunter; it brings in the kill pretty fast." The Brahmin's prosperity depended on his predicting evil influences and impending doom for his clients. The potential victims of these predictions of grauh would have to follow his prescriptions and rituals for mitigating the evil effect, with appropriate donations and periodic charity to him. The family felt grateful for the support they got from him, although it was impossible to measure the benefit. If a disaster still happened, they felt that the Brahmin did the best that he could, but the grauh was too severe for the preventive measures they had taken. Guru Nanak, in his Sikh teachings, preached against such superstitious beliefs and practices, but some rural Sikhs continued to hold to these superstitions. Women in particular wanted to be on the safe side by performing the rituals they had learned from their mothers, and they avoided acts, times and situations that they feared could cause misfortune for themselves or their families.

Some women propitiated the Goddess of Smallpox (called *Mata Rani* or Mata Devi) so that their children won't get the smallpox, or would recover from it undamaged if they did get the disease. In some regions, the God of snakes had to be kept happy so that he would not send any snakes to occupy your nooks and crannies. If the spirit of your dead ancestor was angry, it could get into your buffalo so it would kick the bucket when you tried to milk it. An angry spirit in the form of a bird might fly over your ox, killing it on the spot. Your son might get a stomachache if someone cast an evil eye on him. If the god of rain were unhappy, he might withhold rain and kill your crops with drought. Just as a good lawyer can save you from bad legal problems, a good Brahmin was supposed to be able to predict the cause of the evil influence and suggest remedies. And you were expected to give a donation for this service even if he didn't demand one.

A dead ancestor could cause trouble for a family if they were not doing enough to provide comfort to his soul. Some families used to build a *mutti* (a small tomb about four to five feet in height) near the cremation grounds in the memory of a special dead ancestor, for him to rest in. Then periodically they offered *prasad* (consecrated food) at the mutti. On certain days, the family would prepare special treats, sweets, and take them to their ancestor's mutti to make the ritual offering.

This mutti was like a sacred place of worship for that family. Children playing about the neighborhood who became familiar with this pattern of offerings, would follow the dish-carrier to the mutti. At the mutti, the offerings were made with ritualistic prayer; then the sanctified food was distributed among the people gathered there and to any others on the dish-carrier's way home. The children who received the treats thought this custom was rather nice; but our family never built a mutti, nor did we make offerings to any dead ancestor.

It was believed that the spirit of a dead person could "enter into" someone and drive him mad. Sometimes, a borderline schizophrenic would go into mad fits and would start shouting strange things. His family might believe that the spirit of some dead person had entered him to drive him mad. Such a mad person might be chained, and might claim that he or she was such-and-such dead person who was angry as hell. The mad person might say something like, "I am Bogha, and I had an untimely death. I will devastate your household; I will pull your roots...." The things the mad person said were seldom coherent or specific but were just sporadic outbursts that were interpreted as demands from the dead ancestor. The families felt impelled to look for special clues behind his every word. Even when such a crazy person was not clear and said nonsensical things, they hung on his every word to interpret the meaning. The frightened people felt that it was an opportunity to learn about the wishes of the ancestor through the mad person into whom the ancestor had entered. Afterwards, in order to propitiate the angry spirit of the dead person, they might build a mutti or they might just distribute offerings, give to charity, feed the Brahmins, the sadhus, the cows, the virgin girls and other "sinless" persons, according to the advice of the Brahmin or of some wise person. They thought that the mad person, who had hardly any control of his senses, could not fabricate things. According to these beliefs, spirits always spoke though innocent, ignorant, guileless, naïve or even crazy people and not through clever people, so words spoken by a child, by a crazy person, by a holy man, or by someone from a revered family were considered ominous.

Chela Khelda by the Temple

Some old practices still lingered in towns and larger villages. One evening I saw beside a Hindu temple in Rampura Phul an activity that I had heard about but had never seen before. It was called "chela khelda" (disciple play?). There outside the temple a man acting as a chela was in some kind of frenzy or trance; a large circle of curious, spellbound onlookers had surrounded him. Most of the time he was shouting mindlessly, and once in a while he also made pronouncements. People believed that the "chela khelda" person had established connection with a goddess and that he had the power to see and predict what other humans could not know. The chela had to cultivate the power to establish contact with higher spirits over time, in order to get into such play. When the chela was making various pronouncements, it would appear that he was mad. But you could ask him a question and hope to get an answer, which would come from a higher spirit. This kind of "play of the chela" was not a regular event but would be staged by a special chela only occasionally, usually at night, at some well-recognized place. People used to say, "In such and such village there is a chela khelda. You should go there if you want to get to the root of your problem." Some would travel to such a village in the hope of having

267

their questions about the problems of their lives answered by the chela. It might all be just an act by the imaginative and clever guy to pretend and play the chela, and thereby to get gullible people to believe in his powers. It might look like a show, but to the believers in need of help, the chela khelda was no joke.

Bhoot, Churail and Spooks

Stories of spooks and spirits were abundant in the old society. It was always someone from the past who was said to have seen the ghosts, not someone you could ask personally to verify their story. Neither I nor anyone in my family ever saw a ghost, even though our Outer House was at the site of *Pukka Barra* (a haunted corral). People claimed that there used to be ghost dances and terrifying shrieks at night in that place outside the village in earlier times. Unlike the Western concept of ghosts without bodies, the village spooks were said to appear in physical bodies, but only in special situations and not routinely. According to the local descriptions, the male *bhoot* (ghosts) were supposed to be big, black, ugly and hairy. The *chrail* (female spooks) had tall and skinny bodies, big eyes, big mouths with thick and bloody lips, big widely-spaced teeth and very long nails. My friend Mukand used to say that the chrail had breasts that were two feet long and that the chrail folded each breast to throw it back over each shoulder. But the description of bhoot and chrail could vary. According to the superstitions, a bhoot could choke you or take out your liver, as they had abilities beyond the physical. Our neighbor, Uncle Tope Wala, in the days before he went to East Asia and then to America around the year 1902, was reported to have seen a whole tribe of bhoot and charail one dry, hot summer night as he was traveling to his fields. Other people related visions of walking flames, shrieking bhoot, and dancing churail in remote, hot, dry areas. Some people said they had heard cries and shrieks from the Muslim graveyard and that the bhoot were raving about how thirsty they were. The bhoots were believed to be able to drink blood only and no water; they were always thirsty, since they never had enough blood to drink. The bhoot avoided water because they could be destroyed by water; so people would try to keep some water in their vicinity, for protection from bhoots.

Village people also believed that those traveling *barola* (whirlwinds) with a lot of dust and debris had malignant spirits in them and could kill little children. The barola were also believed to cause physical or mental problems for adults who might be caught in them. Little boys used to believe that if you urinated in an old shoe and threw it into the whirlwind, it would be filled with money after the whirlwind had passed. I tried the urine-in-the-shoe trick with whirlwinds a couple of times while grazing cattle in the fields, but no bhoot were ever generous to me. Only a wet shoe with dirt and sand in it, but no coins, was left after the whirlwind had passed.

On dry hot days when the sun was at the meridian (*sikher dupehra*), the bhoot were supposed to be in their element. That was one of the times to avoid cemeteries, cremation grounds, dry areas and reputedly haunted places. The night time, except for the early morning hours, was also considered a time of freedom and power for the bhoot. Water and lush green areas were what the bhoot avoided. Muslim graves containing dead bodies were considered worse than the Sikh and Hindu cremation grounds. It was believed that the Jinn (Muslim word for bhoot) could pop up any time from the graves, although most Muslims believed that bodies were not supposed to come out of the

268

graves until *Qyamet*, the Day of Judgement. Each Muslim *Qabr* (grave) near our village was covered by an oval mound of dirt about six feet long and a foot high when fresh; the dirt would gradually be washed flat by rains in a few years. No headstone or anything else marked the graves of those poor Muslims; only the rows of oval dirt mounds indicated that there were bodies underneath. In 1937, when the Muslims abandoned the old Qabrstan (graveyard), there was no trace of any grave, as the dirt mounds had been eroded by rain. But I was still afraid as I passed by the old Qabrstan on my way to our fields at night or at noon. My heart would be pounding as I approached the Qabrstan; I would be alert for any sound or sight of a bhoot approaching, until I was well past those grounds.

People in the village usually died at home, but it was not advisable to keep a dead body at home overnight. There was real urgency to cremate a body on the day of death. You could not sleep on a bed near a dead body, as it was believed that a ghost would surely tilt your bed to throw you down. It was an ill omen for anyone in the family to eat solid food until after the body was cremated. It was desirable to keep water handy, since the bhoot avoided water. Another object useful for warding off the bhoot was anything made of iron. It need not be a sword or knife; even a steel bracelet was supposed to be protective. Young Sikh boys would say, "If I see a bhoot, I will immediately flash my steel *kara* (bracelet), so it can't hurt me."

After grain had been extracted from the harvest and made into a *bohel* (pile), special precautions had to be taken to avoid the harmful influence of bhoot. There were stories about bad things happening; such as a body part of a dead animal being discovered in the grain bohel; or blood, bones, rags and other strange objects found inside a bohel that had not been protected from evil effects. The grain pile at that stage had to be attended and guarded with water, steel objects, and pitchforks, especially overnight. No one with uncovered head was allowed to come near a harvest pile in the threshing ground. No grown up woman was ever allowed to come within a wide circle around the harvest grain pile, though young girls were not forbidden.

Laddhoo ka Jand and Other Haunted Places

There was a famous *jand* tree in the sand dunes far from the village beyond the irrigation canal. For our people the word *Nehro Par* (across the canal) always brought to mind the image of hot, dry desert and sand dunes. This tree named Laddhoo ka Jand was believed to be *pukka* (haunted). Gyana Kamla (Gyana the Insane), who was middle-aged and had turned mad some years earlier, died of unknown causes under that tree in the summer of 1935. Some guessed that it was the heat and thirst that killed Gyana Kamla; others said the bhoot took out his liver at high noon. People used to claim that on dry summer nights they had seen sparks and heard shrieks from that Luddhoo ka Jand tree from a mile away. No one had any reason to go within a mile of that location at night, although people did farm near there during the daytime and seasonally. Some other old trees and some abandoned buildings were considered haunted too.

There is a story about a charismatic holy man, a sadhu who lived near the village of Bhagta a few miles north of our village. This sadhu reputedly had control over bhoots and employed bhoot labor to build a brick-lined well in one night, when every-one else was asleep. I cannot say much for the truth of that story, which may just be based on the expression "It was built overnight." Nevertheless, that well is still considered sacred by the superstitious people, who believe that the whole project was built by the labor of ghosts under the command of the holy man. Such stories of bhoot were much more common before the days of irrigation; people believed that ghosts appeared less often when water became more readily available. Be that as it may, now the entire environment has changed, no barren lands are left, all old trees have been cut, awareness and education have increased, and with the pressure of population, the bhoot have few places to hide.

Stories of bhoot and chrail were sometimes told as bedtime stories; they probably had some adverse effects, as the children acquired fears even if no one ever tried to frighten them. Young boys playing outside the village after dark would be frightened when the older ones ran away, leaving them behind and saying, "aee bhoot chrail," meaning, "bhoot and chrail are coming to get you." I was afraid of bhoot up to my teenage years, so it was never comfortable for me to walk by graves or in the wilderness in the dark. My father would say, "There are no bhoot anywhere; dead people can't rise and become ghosts; if they have that ability, then the idea of death is meaningless! I will go to any place at any time and let us see if a ghost can get me." But most people would not tempt fate with such talk, because they believed that bhoot might be eavesdropping without your knowledge, and it would not be good to challenge a bhoot or to make it angry.

Bhoot were the obvious suspects when something struck your ox dead or caused the buffalo to quit giving milk. When someone went crazy, people would say, "A bhoot has entered him." There were people who specialized in eliminating bhoot out of mad people, but that exorcism mostly consisted of beating the affected person, and it was not always an unqualified success. When superstitious people suspected that a known dead ancestor had "entered the person" and made him crazy, they had to try some measure other than beating.

It was good to talk pessimistically about a matter, if you were worried that it might not turn out favorably, whether it was your crop, your milk buffalo, or your child's health. Speaking positively and confidently might cause the result to turn out bad, they believed; this may be similar to the Western concept of a jinx (caused by a jinn). Spilling milk was considered bad luck, but spilling *ghee* accidentally was considered a good omen, even though ghee was 15 times more expensive. In fact, when laying the foundation for a building it was customary to pour a little ghee in the foundation for good luck. Pouring mustard oil at your door on an auspicious occasion was also supposed to bring good luck. Many parents, while beating their misbehaving little boys, would say, "A bhoot has entered you; I am going to extract the bhoot out of you."

"Moon of the Fourth" and Inauspicious Days

It was important to see the new moon no later than its third day each month. Whereas in modern urban societies one rarely sees the moon or stars, and some people don't even see the sun, it was not easy to avoid seeing the moon in rural Punjab. Seeing the new moon for the first time in any month on its fourth day was supposed to bring misfortune. People avoided facing the 'moon of the fourth' if they had missed seeing it in the first three days due to clouds or other causes. But it was OK to see the moon on the fifth day or thereafter if you missed it for the first four days. Someone would say, "I don't know what *chauth da chand* (moon of the fourth) I have encountered; everything is going wrong."

It was considered unfavorable to travel in certain directions on certain days—for example, "Don't go east on a Monday." Wednesday was the auspicious day to begin the sowing season; Tuesday was the proper day to begin harvesting. A brother could not depart from his sister's house on a Thursday. Tuesday was the proper day to ward off misfortunes by feeding dough to crows and cows, but bad for washing your hair. "Even a buffalo does not dip its head under water on Tuesday," one fortune-telling Brahmin told us. My mother thought that washing the hair on Sunday was bad, because that is the day when the unfortunate prisoners had leave to do so. Sunday was considered a bad day for everything except routine work. Saturday was not a particularly good day to begin an important task either. And if you began something on lazy Friday (*Jum'a Jillha*), it would not be finished expeditiously. But Wednesday (Buddh Var) was the most auspicious day for most tasks and Monday was the second best. The saying *"Budh, Kam Shudh"* means: "Wednesday, task clear"; so you would be safe to begin any task on Wednesday. Many of these beliefs were established long before the impact of Western civilization or of the Muslim religion so the fact that the Semitic religions of Christianity, Judaism and Islam consider Sunday, Saturday and Friday, respectively, to be holy, had no effect on Indian superstitions.

If one of your shoes was lying upside down, it could indicate that you would be getting into some kind of trouble. If one of your shoes was lying in front of the other so that both shoes were facing the same direction, this could indicate that some unwanted travel is going to be necessary. Travel was always fraught with danger and was something to be feared. Crows sitting on a roof edge and cawing continuously suggested the imminent arrival of guests. Women would say, "The crows on the roof edge are going crazy, we are sure to have some guests pretty soon." If you shout at a crow and ask if your loved one is coming home, and the crow flies away, it suggest that the loved one will be arriving soon.

The Concept of Nazar

There was a strong belief in *nazar*, a gaze of the eye that may cause adverse effects. According to this superstition, if something was really good or beautiful, someone's nazar could destroy it. This is not quite the European equivalent of the evil eye, because the gazer does not have to wish ill for the nazar to have its destructive effect. Some people were believed to be particularly dangerous in this respect, and families made efforts to avoid the effect of the gaze of such people on precious objects or persons. It was believed that those who are deprived or who are envious are the ones whose nazar is the most destructive, but anyone who was not a member of the family was considered a potential source of nazar. So the relatives of a beautiful person or the owners of a beautiful object tried to make it look less beautiful and avoided praising and admiring it. If you had a beautiful child, you put a little black mark on its cheek or forehead to make it imperfect, to prevent nazar. A beautiful bride had to be protected from nazar by various rituals. If you had built a new house, you put a black pot on corner of the roof to prevent someone's evil eye from collapsing the house. A black pot was also considered helpful in protecting an exceptionally good crop.

271

If you believe you have been hit by someone's nazar and want to relieve its effect, you could follow this procedure: Collect the dust from the footsteps of the suspected person; if you don't know the exact person who caused the nazar, then get the dust from a crossing, since everybody passes through there. Burn the dust in the *chullah* (stove), collect the ashes of the dust, beat the ashes with a shoe, and throw the ashes back in the crossing; that should reduce the nazar effect. Sometimes when you want to determine who caused the nazar, you wave a piece of alum over the head of the victim and throw *the alum* into the chullah fire. As the alum fuses in the heat and forms into a shape, from that shape you try to guess the identity of the person who caused the nazar. For example if the fused alum piece looks like a pipe, it is probably a person who smokes; if it is a shapeless blob, it could be a fat person among the suspects. Then you beat the fused alum with a shoe, you curse the nazar-causing person, and then you throw the ashes at a crossing. Another procedure to remove the effect of nazar was to wave over the head of the affected person some money or cloth, or something else that you are willing to donate, while reciting ritual words, and then donate the waved money or object to charity. To determine if it is really nazar that has caused the problem or the disease and not some other factor, women waved red peppers over the head of the affected person and threw the red peppers into the fire. If the fumes from the peppers drive you crazy, which would be normal, then nazar may not be involved; but if the fumes don't feel too pungent, then nazar is confirmed. Not everyone had the eye that could cause nazar; but the eyes of some individuals had the reputation of having the severest effects. Women usually hid their pretty babies and beautiful objects from such people.

There is a story of a man who was walking behind his buffalo that had an amazingly big udder. He passed with his buffalo through the village *sutth* (plaza) where people were sitting around as usual. A big udder would be the sign that the buffalo was a very good milk producer. One of the sitting men, who had a reputation for severe nazar, cast his gaze on the udder and said, "Wow, what a buffalo!" It is said that the buffalo went only a few steps further, collapsed, and died on the spot because of the nazar. The death of the buffalo infuriated the owner. It turned out that the buffalo's owner also had an eye with strong nazar. The angry owner walked back to the plaza, faced the man who had gazed at the buffalo's udder, and said, "Wow, what fantastic eyes you have!". The man who had just looked at and praised the buffalo udder, immediately turned blind because the owner of the buffalo caused nazar to the gazer's eyes and destroyed them. Of course this is more in the nature of a joke rather than a true story, but it does indicate the extent to which people believed in nazar.

And it was not just the eye, but even the tongue that could cause damage. If some person praised a thing or a person, it could have an adverse effect just like nazar. Some people in my family believed that my erratic behavior and unwillingness to go to college to study were the result of nazar. Since I used to be good in school, they thought that some evil person might have praised me, causing the whole problem. In fact my sister Maro's husband was so convinced of this possibility that he went to the holy sadhu in his own village and got a *taveez* (charm) from the sadhu to counteract the effects of nazar on me. I was asked to wear the taveez around my neck in order to cure my mind so that the bad influences would disappear and I would go back to college. But I could never be persuaded to follow such rituals.

When I was young, we used to see strange objects, such as colored threads, broken clay pots, or rags, thrown down at a crossing, presumably by someone who had done some *toona* (voodoo) rituals. We were scared to touch or even go near such things lying at the crossings, fearing that they could affect us. Those objects were strange and scary. People believed that you could be the next victim of a calamity if you stepped on them, as the person doing the toona expected to unload his misfortune on some new victim.

Amulets, *Taveez* and Protective Measures

Most people in the village would go to some holy man, or to an ordinary wise person who had the reputation of giving amulets or talismans to guard against nazar or for other benefits. Some of my Muslim classmates wore such amulets called *taveez*, usually encased in steel, copper, or silver around their necks. Taveez and nazar are Persian words, as our language took nearly half its nouns from that language. Sometimes young boys and toddlers wore the taveez in *tiragi* strings around their waists, along with beads and other decorations. Many boys in my grade school, wore taveez around their necks to maintain good health, but my father would never let us wear such a thing. Some taveez were given by holy men to wear just for good luck. Lovers would obtain taveez and put it around the neck of their beloved so that he or she would always remain true and faithful. Then there were people who would obtain taveez to wear so that its magical power would make them irresistible to the person whom they loved. Wearing taveez became such a common custom that they became ornaments. Women sometimes wore necklaces of taveez with gold cases as jewelry but without any charm enclosed.

Sometimes amulets and taveez in wooden holders were put around the necks of favored buffaloes, oxen and other cattle to prevent disease. On a larger scale, to protect the cattle against an epidemic and sometimes to prevent hoof and mouth disease, some person with the reputation of having miraculous powers would perform *toona* (voodoo). Then the toona performer would hang a pot wrapped in cloth and containing magical objects, like a banner across the main street entrance to the village. Since all the cattle of the village would have to pass under that banner, they thought the cattle would be automatically protected against the disease because of the toona.

Some people specialized in *hathaula* (hand ritual). Hathaula might involve the touching with the hand, but mostly it was just waving of the hands to effect a cure. It usually included some mumbled and inaudible words and the performance of gestures and hand movements. Once when I was about four years old, my mother took me to an old man to get relief from swollen glands an the side of my neck due to *canadu* (possibly mumps). He was a Muslim water carrier in our village. He just mumbled a few words as he rubbed ash with his thumb lightly on my neck and sent us home with a blessing.

Such rituals provided assurance for people, but there was no way to find out if they did any good to the cattle or to people, or what would have happened without the toona or hathaula. If things did go wrong, it was assumed that the toona performer did his best to intervene, and the rest was up to God. Others believed that without the toona the results would have been worse, or that the disease was too severe for the performer's art and discipline. My oldest sister's husband, who is in his eighties and is an illiterate farmer, has started doing toona for snake bites, even though his own son is an allopathic doctor in a city. I asked him how he could dare to risk people's lives by claiming that he can cure people, if the snake was really poisonous. He said, "In most cases people heal after some suffering. But if someone dies, it just means that I did my best, but I have not accumulated enough merit by cultivating the art." Nobody was going to sue him if someone died. People assumed that the toona performer just did his best, and the rest is your *kismet* or up to God. The superstition was that his power would not work if money was involved; his reward was just thanks and respect. Many of the people in the villages who performed toona and hathaula were ascetics like sadhu, and their image had some good effect, but a performer of toona could also be any ignorant, poor and inarticulate person; if he acquired a reputation as a performer of toona, people flocked to him from far and wide.

Auspicious Departures

Leaving home was always fraught with some risk and uncertainty. If you were going on an important journey, it was best to have the *shagun* (omen) and conditions as favorable as luck would allow. While stepping out of the door for an important errand or departure, it was considered good to encounter a Chuhra (low caste), but meeting a Brahmin or village *numberdar* (headman) was a bad omen. Encountering a person with *uncovered head* would be a disaster. Meeting someone carrying water, milk or ghee was good, but one with an empty vessel was very bad. Encountering someone carrying greenery or flowers was good; meeting someone carrying fuel was considered disastrous. To encounter a married woman, specially a pregnant woman, was very beneficial; seeing a widow 's countenance was the kiss of death. Usually someone was sent out of the door ahead of time to forestall the departure of the loved one, in case some undesirable person was likely to encounter the traveler as he or she went out of the door, and to delay him or her until better conditions prevailed for departure. My mother and sisters were always anxious when Kartar had to go back after his leave, as his well-being was critically important to our family. They also put something sweet (gur or laddu) in his mouth just before he left, but not milk, because milk was supposed to attract bad spirits. Letting a loved one go away without feeding him was considered inauspicious. My mother used to say that God gives food only to those who are already full when they leave home, and to leave while hungry was to invite trouble. There was so much emphasis on feeding that forcing a guest to eat more and more was considered just good hospitality.

If some one sneezed in front of you as you departed, it was bad, but a sneeze from behind was considered encouragement. A second sneeze also neutralized the bad effect of the first. A cat crossing your path, or a dog vigorously flapping his ears (as if it had flees), were bad omens. Kites or vultures circling overhead for an extended period signified impending doom over the community. A cat meowing loudly and continuously at night was the harbinger of misfortune. Three men would not start on a journey together at the same time; they staggered their departures and could get together later if they needed to. If you see a snake on the way, you are going to have severely bad luck, but if you could kill the snake, you would be successful in your mission and might proceed. Even dreaming about a snake implied that you were going to be trapped in the snares of some dangerous person, possibly a crafty woman. A calf born in the month of Bhadon (after mid-August) or a buffalo calf born in Magh (after mid-January) was a bad omen and might bring untold disasters upon the owners. Tales of miseries visited upon the owners of such animals would scare off a buyer. No one would be willing to stick his neck out and buy such a buffalo or calf. You had to wait to sell until the calf grew older and others could not determine the month of its birth with certainty. For a child to be born in the month of Kattak (after mid-October) was an unfortunate occurrence, possibly because that was the busiest time of the year, and calling someone "Kattak-born" was a form of abuse. A baby born in the eighth month of pregnancy was bad; it was comparatively better if the premature baby was born during the seventh month. An owl on the roof edge shrieking continuously at night would bring death or destruction. In fact unlike the Western world, where people associate the owl with wisdom, our people regarded the voice of the owl as a bad omen, because the cursed owl is reputed to seek ruins and deserted places. My mother said that the night before her son Hardial died, two owls shrieking loudly and continuously on the roof edge really worried and scared her. The next day her baby Hardial, who was already ill, died, confirming her fears.

CHAPTER 14

COMPLEXITIES IN RELATIONSHIPS

The Punjabi words for father are Bapu, Peo, or Pitta. The words for mother are Ma (ending with a nasal sound) or Mata, and in some families Bebe or Bibi. In polite families one added the word Ji while addressing any relative senior to oneself. The words for son are Putter (puttra in Hindi), Poot, Beta, Munda (boy) or Larka, and for daughter are Puttri, Dhee, Beti, Kuri (girl) or Larki. The words Shohra or Shokra for a boy, are sometimes used playfully.

In English, the siblings of parents, and their spouses, are just generic aunts and uncles. But in the Punjabi culture, there was a real difference in entitlements and obligations, depending upon what kind of uncle or aunt someone was. *Taya* was an older brother or male cousin of your father; he was never entitled to see the unveiled face of your mother. But your mother would not need to cover her face from *Chacha*, a younger brother or cousin of your father, who could joke around and be quite informal with her. *Mamma* (your mother's brother) had the responsibility of taking care of you; he had to show respect and had low status in relation to your father. In fact, he had lower status than anyone in your father's clan. The wives of *Taya*, *Chacha* and *Mamma* were called *Tai*, *Chachi* and *Mammi*, respectively.

Masser, the husband of your *Massi* (mother's sister), was the equal of your father in prestige; he would be polite to you, but he had no responsibility for you or power over you. But *Phupher*, the husband of your father's sister (*Phuphi or Bhua*), being the husband of a daughter of your village, would get the utmost respect from everyone in your village. He could lord it over any in-law and he had all the privileges; he had no responsibilities except to be polite. Among cousins, the offspring of a daughter of the village, while visiting the *Nanke* (mother's parents), commanded privileges and affection from everyone. *Dada* and *Dadi*, the father and mother of your father, respectively, had to be respected more than your own father and mother; you were their *Potra* (grandson) or *Potri* (granddaughter). Your *Nana and Nani* (parents of your mother) would never lord it over you; their job was to pamper and spoil you as you were their *Dohtra or Dohtri* (grandson or granddaughter). In the Punjabi language, to make any relation "great grand," one adds the word "Per" in front of the relationship, for example, *PerDada* means great grandfather. In general, a girl from the paternal side was to be treated with the utmost respect, and all relations resulting from her marriage had to be honored more than others.

The word for 'brother' varies in the different regions of Punjab from *Bhrata* to *Bhra*, *Bha*, *Bhau*, *Bhai*, *Veer* or *Bier*. A *Bhrajhai* or *Bhabi*, is the wife of brother or cousin. If she is the wife of his older brother or cousin, then he is her *Deor*, her "younger brother-in-law." The relations between Deor and Bhabi can be open, easy, and playful. If, however, she is the wife of his younger brother or cousin, then he is her *Jeth*, her "older brother-in-law," and she must keep her face covered when in his presence. The relations between this Jeth and Bhabi have to be formal, not playful. Thus the position of a Jeth was not as enviable as that of a Deor, and sometimes an age difference of a few days would forever alter his relationship with the wife of a brother or cousin. Occasionally, an older man (a Jeth) could "negotiate the release of veil" with his Bhabi if there was a sufficient excuse.

In the Western world, the catchall term "in-law" implies the equality of everyone involved. In Punjab, not only is the word different for every kind of in-law, but the status, privileges, responsibilities and rights are very different depending on their relative positions. The parents of bride and of bridegroom are each other's Kurm. A *Juvayee* (the daughter's husband was treated like the most privileged person. All his in-laws and their close family were required to please, respect, honor and serve him, although he would visit them quite infrequently. In fact, when someone wanted to abuse anyone severely he could say, "I will be your Juvayee" and be ready to face the consequences. The daughter-in-law (*Nooh*), on the other hand, had no privileged position, as she lived in the house of her *Sohra* (father-in-law) and *Sass* (mother-in-law). The worst in-law relationship was being someone's *Sala* (wife's brother) or *Sohra* (wife's father). Calling a man "Sala" was a form of severe abuse, whereas in the Western world the word brother-in-law is quite neutral. You would not call anyone Sala or Sohra, even if that were your actual relationship to them, because these words are humiliating to them and are usually used in abusing. A Sala was supposed to be at the service of his *Bhenoia* (husband of *Bhen* or sister) to please and honor him at all times, without expecting any reciprocity. No wonder that people considered having a baby girl as a major problem for the future, because some day she would make her brother and father somebody's Sala and Sohra, respectively. A *Sali* (wife's sister) was considered like a half wife ("*Sali, Adhi Ghar Wali*"), who had some freedom of speech and could tease and joke within boundaries. A husband's sister (*Nunaan*) also had a somewhat privileged position over her *Bharjhai* (brother's wife). Within the limits of politeness the relationship of a boy with a sisters nunaan was an informal one.

Nowadays, some of the strict customs of these in-law relationships are being relaxed with increased education, urbanization and the advancement of women. But they are nowhere near the comfort, unconcern and informality of Western in-law relationships. *Sala-Bhenoia* relationship, between a man and his sister's husband is still the most delicate of all relationships among the Punjabis. Although all three of my sisters' husbands treat me decently, my sense that their status is above mine, controls my behavior toward them to this day.

But Honor Thy Sister Even More

In the Western world there is a perception that women's status in India is miserably low.

Surely, peculiarities and even horror stories are not hard to find, but some stories distort the true status in relationships. Every girl was also some man's daughter, and her well-being was of great importance to the parents during her whole life. And in Punjab, if she was lucky enough to have a brother, she had even more power at her service. Protection and dignity of daughters and sisters was a serious matter of honor. In good families of the rural Punjab an unmarried girl was treated like a sacred person, and her honor and safety were the responsibility of everybody in the brotherhood. A daughter's word or wish was not usually turned down, if there was way to fulfill it. This may be partly due to the fact that, unlike a boy, a girl would not be unreasonable. If a baby girl reached the age to walk and talk, she was treated with greater care and courtesy than a boy. Starting at about the age of three, many girls were given gold ornaments for their hair and tikka or bindi jewelry for their foreheads, especially by their maternal grandparents. I remember that our next-door neighbor Aunt Hernami, who still believed in the traditional Hindu rituals, used to feed the *dhyani* (maidens from the neighborhood) on the sacred days related to fasting. My friend Dr. Meji Singh told me that his mother used to wash the feet of such maidens before the feast. The girls were given gifts of money after their meal and were treated like holy people. A man attending a wedding in another village would find out if there was any daughter of his own village already married into this other village, and if he found one he would have a dish of sweets sent to that daughter's house. In fact our old society held the following four entities to be sacred: a maiden, a Brahmin, a sadhu (ascetic), and a cow. It was believed that God would reward you many times more if you give something to a daughter; any gift or donation to a girl was considered *punn* (a sacred act). When little boys were horsing around on the furniture, they were told, "Don't ever let your foot touch your sister; it is a sin to touch a virgin with your foot." The girls were given priority on most social occasions. For a man, there could be no bigger disgrace than any hurt or dishonor to his sister. All this may seem contradictory, when situations could be found where girls were unwanted and resented.

But unlike the case of his sister, it would not do for a boy to be too sensitive if someone said anything jokingly to his mother. This sometimes happened because the husband's brother could take some liberties with his brother's wife, although only for routine social conversations. Male cousins of the husband, even distant ones as long as they were of a similar level, were free to joke, banter, and talk in informal, teasing language to their brother's or cousin's wife, and vice versa, without any particular consequences. People thought that such kidding and teasing was the spice of life as long as the wife did not object. But since everyone's mother had some brothers-in-law, such loose talk from these men was embarrassing to the mother's growing sons. They just had to tolerate the custom, although some reacted with anger. A little boy had to put up with the embarrassing words said to his mother, and a man could not be too sensitive to things that his cousins might say to his wife.

Whereas a European thinks that a sister-in-law is like a sister, in the Indian system the wife's sister or a brother's wife was considered like a half wife. So a husband speaking to his wifes sister could be a source of some embarrassment to any brother of those sisters. For these reasons, brothers and fathers kept out of the way when a girl's husband came to visit.

But sisters and unmarried girls were in an entirely sacrosanct realm, and they were always spoken to and treated with reserve, respect and honor. Little boys sometimes engaged in verbal abuse and even physical fights with their playmates. When they wanted to hurt somebody, they would abuse him in the name of the opponent's ancestor or even mother. But when they were reckless and ready for real violence, they would abuse him in the name of his sister, because that was the ultimate hurt and insult. Sometimes there were murderous fights between men and it would be dangerous to intervene. But a sister of either man or a daughter of the village could come in between the fighting men and sometimes could even stop the fight. No body could hurt her; she was honored, unlike a boy who would be treated like a rival.

When a girl was married off, it was a matter of honor for brothers to make sure their sister was not mistreated. Fathers were usually helpless in such matters, but any husband who mistreated a sister of powerful brothers could expect punishment from her brothers. I know a couple of brothers who severely beat up their sister's husband and brought her back with them, because her husband was mistreating her and physically abusing her. It was more than a year before reconciliation could be arranged, but then the husband never again abused her physically. A brother was an invaluable source of support for a woman.

Although girls were loved and respected, power was in the hands of the men. The value of a human still depended on the ability to kill and subdue enemies, and on the ability to earn a living. In that society before widespread education, mechanization and technology, and the imposition of law and order, women were at a disadvantage in strength and were usually helpless dependents. Each class of men treated their women according to their custom, so the status of women was never uniform. The lower the socio-economic class, the lower was the status of woman. The people at the lower economic levels were also not too sensitive about their daughters' future. Some would marry the daughter off only if the groom's people paid money as a bride price. Then people would whisper, "So and so must have gotten money for his daughter" when a girl was married to an older man or to a poor boy. This was called the marriage of *kharch* (cost). When parents received money in exchange for their daughter. On the other hand, a man worried about his prestige would pay the maximum possible in cash, gold and other dowry, if he could arrange to marry his daughter into a prosperous family. This was called a marriage of *punn* (pious deed). Such a dowry was a nearly universal requirement in upper and middle class houses. Some grooms' parents could consider themselves slighted and dishonored if their daughter-in-law did not bring as much in dowry as they felt was appropriate to their status. Terms of the dowry were negotiated before the betrothal ceremony and usually were made known among members of the clan. Also, it was a matter of honor if a parent could pay a big dowry to marry his daughter into a house more prestigious than his own. When some house married their daughter into a lower level family or received money secretly, people would say, "They have sunk their daughter." The prestige of a house was tied to how well their daughter was settled.

His Pride in Jeopardy, If He Begets a Daughter

Among the upper and middle classes the status of girls and women was higher, and their wishes were respected more often. But in those classes, a daughter could also be a source of continuous worry and pain until she had grown children of her own, preferably male.

279

Anything that hurt her, would hurt her helpless parents and brothers even more. The greater your sense of honor, the bigger the pressure and anxiety to see your daughter settled into a respectable family of equal or better status. This anxiety and burden were the major reason why people did not want to have a daughter. You would be responsible for protecting her physical well being from the time of birth and then finding someone suitable to marry her. You had to be humble before those to whom you might give your daughter in marriage; you were at the mercy of other people who would determine your daughter's happiness. So in that society, your pride was lowered the instant you had a daughter. Being the brother or father of a wife was the most humbling situation. They used to say that a man could not twist his mustache upward if he had a daughter, because the mustache turning upward at the ends signified pride, arrogance and invincibility, whereas the mustache turning downward indicated humility and pessimism.

Apart from the anxiety and expense of having girls, the status of everyone who was from the wife's clan, was lower than the status of anyone from the husband's clan. The visiting husband of a girl of the village could act like a lord over the girl's family. Although most husbands were polite, but if a shallow and nasty one could get drunk and speak foul language, no one would dare to say anything to stop him, unless his wife could. Calling someone *sala* (wife's brother) or *sohra* (wife's father) was a serious form of abuse, and to say, "I will be the *juvaee* (son-in-law) of your house" was to invite serious violence. In such an environment, not many would be willing to be someone's sala or sohra if they had a choice! This was another reason that most people did not wish to have baby girls.

There were other issues that tipped the balance against girls. A son was considered the real maintainer of the race. He could get a wife from anywhere, even an off-caste woman. But without a son and a male heir, "the door of their house was going to be locked." In the Hindu tradition, only a *puttra* (son) could perform your final rites at death in order for you to secure a proper place in the next world. And the old songs said, "There is no name (trace) left without sons and there is no security without brothers." According to the old laws, girls could not inherit property, and male cousins, even your sworn enemies, had a greater right to inherit your land after your death than your daughters did. Sometimes they could legally prevent the sale of your property to others if you did not have a male child, claiming a priority right by ancestry. For that reason the death or disappearance of an only son would start the rivals itching to obtain your property. In some vicious situations, they could try to arrange the death of a single son in order to inherit the land. Most people accepted daughters, as they believed that raising a daughter is a pious deed and wipes out any bad karma; but without a son there would be no family left afterwards.

In a middle-class house, the feeding, care and protection of the female child was not the major issue. The over-riding issue was: How would they be able to find a suitable husband for her, and what would they be able to give at the time of marriage to make her acceptable? What if they could not find anybody suitable to marry her, while she kept getting older? Even though there was a shortage of girls because of female infanticide in earlier decades, and many men could never be married, some families still had difficulty in finding a suitable match for their daughters. In our village, a girl named Sodhan was unmarried until her late thirties. People continuously condemned her family for not making enough effort to marry her off. She was nearly middle-aged when she was married off to a younger man, and miraculously she had a baby boy during her forties. It was not like Western societies where an adult girl was expected to leave the house and find herself a job or a husband. An unmarried older daughter sitting at home, although rare, was the ultimate heartache and caused feelings of failure and disgrace for parents. Even when a daughter was married off, the parents would worry, "How can we be sure she will be happy? What if her husband or in-laws don't treat her right?" Being the daughter's father was the ultimate worrying and humbling experience in life, and your honor, prestige and happiness were tied to her fortunes and her well-being. If your son was a bum, it was not so bad. He could graze cattle starting at age seven, and later on he could plow the fields or be sent into the army. He would need minimal clothing and no protection. But having a daughter was a responsibility for the rest of your life. In the village you could not be haughty, arrogant, cavalier, or even tell a dirty joke, if you were the father of an old unmarried daughter. The family into which a girl is married would have a leg up and a superior position over the girl's family forever, and the latter would have to act humble in relation to the people of her husband's clan.

The Rajputs and Jats took such matters of honor and pride with morbid seriousness. They thought it was better to kill a new-born daughter than to be anxious and humiliated for her whole life. Motivations of 'honor' among Rajputs were also responsible for *sati* (burning a living widow with her dead husband), because the deceased Rajput and his clan would be disgraced if his widow were taken over by anyone else. Therefore his family would force the widow to burn (sati) herself on her dead husband's cremation pyre. To others they would just say that the wife did not wish to live anymore without her husband. But in reality the widow was not given any choice and was forced to burn herself in sati ceremony if she did not have any children. Such customs prevailed only in some regions and castes, or among high profile families, and they were abolished by law in the nineteenth century.

Plight of Widows

Even where sati was not practiced, a widow was considered an ill-starred person whose cursed association killed her husband and who could bring only misfortune if she were anywhere around you. No one of any substance would marry a widow among the middle class and upper castes of Hindu society. If you happened to encounter a widow as you embarked on an important task or journey, it was regarded as a bad omen. A Hindu widow had to wipe off the *bindi* (beauty dot) from her forehead and never wear that mark again as it was meant only for the blessed, joyful, married women. Bindi was originally a religious mark, and therefore Sikh women did not wear one; but nowadays, its religious significance is usually ignored. A widow could not braid or do her hair for the rest of her life but had to let her hair hang loose. She could not wear ornaments or any face makeup. So the first thing she had to do on hearing of her husband's death was to wipe off the mark from her forehead, undo her braids to let her hair loose, remove all jewelry and ornaments and change from the usual bright clothing into simple white or drab colors. It was like preparing for a mental death. White or colorless clothes, loose hair and no ornaments were the signs of a widow and people avoided seeing her face on important occasions in order to avoid bad luck.

Sometimes if her deceased husband had a brother, even if he were not of compatible age, the elders in our communities would try to convince him to take the widow as a wife, in the process called *chadur pauna*, after the period of mourning was over. But if she had half-grown children or no available brother-in-law to take over, she had to grow old with her diminished status. If she had no children and was still young, she usually went back to her parent's household to live. Among the Jats, who were not as rigid as the Rajputs or Brahmins, she was sometimes given to some needy man in *karewa* (getting a woman without marriage) but not in a regular marriage ceremony. Although she might get lucky in the karewa situation, she could not be married into any family of substance. Most unmarried widows grew old in unenviable circumstances. That is why *boodh suhagan* (till old age, be in marital bliss) was a commonly given blessing, and *randi* (widow) was a term of cruel abuse among fighting women. Facing such a miserable future as a widow, it is easy to understand why sometimes women willingly committed sati, although most of the time they were not allowed a choice. The British made laws to abolish sati within territories under their rule, but such laws did not apply in the princely states where most of the Rajputs lived. Similarly, the custom of female infanticide also ended only gradually, even after it had been legally banned.

Un-divorced First Wives

However unhappy they might be, the women in Punjab would not divorce their husbands, except among the Muslims. If a wife was sent by her husband to her parents' village and he did not go to bring her back, she was an "abandoned woman." The word "abandoned" was applied to a wife who was no longer living in her husband's house, and it was considered disgraceful for her and her parents, not for the husband. The custom and rules of divorce did not exist in the Hindu society of those days; so that system was more unfair to women than to men. In rare cases a daring or reckless woman would run away with someone else if she were unhappy. But after that, the "abductor" could not keep her in the same village; she had to be willing to be "sold" to some needy person. There was no question of a formal marriage for a used wife, but just a *karewa* (takeover); and the "abducted" woman was just "seated" in the house of a new husband.

A woman who had not been given in marriage by her parents but had been obtained by other means would not be truly respectable in the community. And if she had run away with someone else, she could not come back to her parents' or brothers' house, since they would feel disgraced. She was usually placed or seated with some undesirable fellow who was willing to pay the price to her "abductor." In my younger days the going price for a good abducted woman was a few hundred rupees (about two or three times the price of a camel), depending on her age and looks, and also upon how old or needy the new husband was. For a "respectable" woman unable to get along with her husband, the usual choice was to go back to live with her parents or brothers and not to run away with someone else. A woman's parents or brothers were always willing to take her in; it was the matter of their honor. In the parents' village, she would not be considered a cursed woman, as a widow would be, but hers was not considered a blessed life.

The idea of going to court to enforce the rights of an abandoned wife was unthinkable to ordinary people. No wonder that people were afraid of having daughters who would need to be married some day, perhaps under unfortunate circumstances.

No official records were kept of weddings or deaths; there was merely a social recognition by the families and the community. Records of births were kept, but the mother's name might not be written in the record at the birth of a child. If a dispute arose she would have a hard time proving that she was someone's wife or mother. For example, my birth records in the district office included only the name of my father and not of my mother. And my father once had to go to court to testify that he had read the Sikh scriptures to perform the marriage of Kando, the our neighbor Aunt Harnami's daughters, to an Indian man from Canada. Kando's husband had died of cancer within two years of the marriage when they were living in Canada. After she returned to India, Kando had to prove in an Indian court that she had been married to the man according to the usual customs and legally was the widow of the deceased.

Prosperous husbands could marry additional wives in those days, without divorcing the first. When such affluent men took second wives, the first wife could continue to live in the same house if there was no severe hatred, or she could go to her parents' house. There was still a shortage of girls because of female infanticide in earlier times, and many poorer people could never get a wife; yet many parents would give their daughter gladly to an affluent man as an additional wife, and they provided a big dowry in addition. My classmate Mukand had been married at the age of thirteen or so; later, when he was sixteen or seventeen years old, he wanted a second and prettier wife. Since his family had a fair amount of land, he thought he could get a second wife and an additional dowry; he wanted to keep the first wife to help with the housework. In fact a woman in the village was willing to bring her niece to him as a second wife. For a few years, Mukand's wife felt the insecurity of not being wanted, but the husband's family was quite pleased with her because she was a wonderful person. Without complaining about her husband's behavior directly, she used to say to me in Punjabi rhymes, "My intelligence is of no help, as the dark complexion is sinking my fortunes...". She could speak to me about such matters as it was considered quite proper for a wife to talk freely to a *deor* (younger brother or cousin of the husband), though it would have been improper for her to speak so to any man older than the husband. I was a couple of years younger than her husband, but we were not closely related. Apart from the disapproval of his own family, Mukand would also have incurred the wrath of his wife's brothers if he had tried to hurt her. After some years of such thoughts, he settled into the marriage, which strengthened in time. When he was about twenty years old, they had a child or two and other matters became predominant on his mind. Later, he became more prosperous and respected in the village, but a new wife was not a priority for him by then. Several men of moderate means in our village had two wives each. And some parents would give their second daughter to a man if their first daughter, married to the same man, did not have any children. They would think that the cause of infertility was the woman and that if he was going to get a second wife anyway, it was better to have their second daughter in his house than to have some other wife competing against their first daughter.

After 1950, the law changed so that a man could not marry a second wife without divorcing the first. This reformation, called the Hindu Code Bill, made it illegal to have multiple wives, except where the multiple wives already existed. Muslims in India were exempted from this law because it was their religious right to have up to four wives at a time. Politicians were always afraid of the Muslims, who might have revolted ferociously if anyone had tried to curtail their right to have multiple wives. The Hindu Code Bill also gave property inheritance rights to daughters. Indians would have opposed such a law under the British, considering it a violation of their customs by a caste-less, foreign race; but in 1950, shortly after Independence, Prime Minister Nehru could do no wrong in the eyes of Indians. In rural areas, laws granting equal property rights to girls are still resisted and circumvented in various ways by landowning families, to prevent girls from inheriting paternal land. Courts can enforce a girl's rights, but this can be a complicated effort. Officials and lower courts in India are notorious for corruption and delays, and land cases can take decades to decide, incurring big expenses and the danger of violence. So unless the parents give possession of the land to a daughter while they are still alive, she may not be able to get it afterwards.

Conquering Heroes and Women's Rights

Worries about future of the girl child were one reason for preferring boys. The other reason was the male's physical ability to commit violence and to subjugate enemies more effectively. Where the law was not likely to provide protection, lack of physical power to defend oneself could be fatal. Beauty and intelligence were worthless in the face of the ability to kill. Parents might love their daughter as much as their son, but without sons to safeguard the family, she would be a source of burden and worry. In the olden times, when a marauder with horses and swordsmen could come and kill all your men or occupy your land, the male power to kill and defend was valued for good reasons. After killing the men, the marauder could acquire all the "beauties" he wanted and could take them home as slaves for life. At the village level where law was largely inaccessible, physical force was still very important in my day, to keep life and property safe, to exercise your water rights, and generally to protect your family and livelihood; and hence families continued to prefer baby boys to girls. The lower your physical strength, the less your value as a human being, unless you had some other exceptional talent. Romantic tales of women who heroically defended against enemies are just isolated and exaggerated examples of special circumstances. The right-belongs-to-might realities were largely responsible for the inequality of rights for men and women before a society of laws became established. Muscle power maintained a decisive advantage before machines replaced men and new technologies made female employment equally effective. In earlier times there was a preference for males in Europe too, although not to such an extreme. King Henry VIII divorced or killed some of his wives when they failed to produce a male heir for him; and in the process he became the head of the church in his country.

Western women who have lived in law-and-order societies, where technology makes physical strength unimportant, cannot understand why those backward countries did not raise the status of women. They have little concept of being subjected to brute force. In an actual conversation, one Western woman remarked to me that "it would be romantic and adventurous to be captured and carried away by some marauding, conquering hero." She neglected to imagine the scenario where all her family and relatives could be butchered, she could be one of the hundreds in his captivity, pushing one of his mules to his destination; her fate might be to feed animals and remove manure for the rest of her life or to be one of many "wives," rather than any grand romance. How was she going to secure any rights there? According to the book *Ain-i-Akbari*, the Mughal Emperor

Akbar's harem included a total of 5,000 women. Raja Man Singh Kachhwaha had 1500 wives who bore him 4,000 children. Nadir Shah of Persia and Afghanistan, after conquering Delhi in 1739, ordered a general massacre of all Indians in that city, looted 150 million rupees in cash, took the famous Peacock Throne and the Koh-i-Noor Diamond, and took the princess of his choice from the house of the vanquished emperor as an additional wife. He ordered that his soldiers was to take "no more than twenty women and twenty mules each" with them back to Persia. Conquering heroes were not nice guys, and you had no rights without the ability to kill effectively.

In the new Indian society, where physical strength no longer determines your value as a human, and where technology, education and the new laws can make a woman as effective as a man, girls are starting to be valued equally. Girls can achieve academically as much as boys, are better at communicating verbally, handle human relations better, and have access to all the top desirable jobs now; so the attitudes toward girls have started changing in India. But the old society feared having girl children, and some backward thinking people still do.

No More Female Infanticide

Before my time, some people in North India would kill their new-born girls rather than go through the life-long anxiety of raising them. Older women in my village used to tell us the daughter-killing stories; even in my days those stories did not shock anybody, though it was considered a sin to kill a baby. The tribes and castes that considered themselves superior and proud felt that having a daughter was the ultimate humbling and painful experience. A wife who had girls in succession was despised; if her husband was prosperous, he would marry a second wife, thinking that it was his wife's fault, not his, that she gave birth to daughters. A Rajput would say, "Accursed be the day when a female child is born to me." Books and stories from the eighteenth and nineteenth centuries indicate that the Rajput and the Jat (Sikh or Hindu) were the worst offenders, although other castes practiced female infanticide to varying degrees. The low ratio of girls to boys alive in their population was a clear indicator. In my own family, there had not been any living girls in two or three generations before my own sisters, but my father's mother did not have or kill any daughters. Even in my days, people accepted newborn girls grudgingly by saying that the suffering you endure and sacrifices you make in raising a daughter is *punn* (pious deed), which could wipe off some *paap* (sin) that might have been done at some other time during life. My mother told me that parents never tried to hide the fact of killing female babies but openly discussed it as a matter of practical necessity. But whenever bad things happened to families who had killed babies, people prophesied that the paap (sin) of killing innocent babies would sink (*gharq*) those families. Even when I was young, some people were suspected of having killed their newborn girls when they said the baby was stillborn. But if a baby girl survived for the first couple of days of her life, then she would become a person known to them, not an easily disposable mass of flesh. So the day of the birth was critical for a girl.

We were told that if they did not want to keep a newborn girl, women used to put a lump of *gur* (solid raw sugar) in the mouth of the newborn and a *pooni* (roll of cotton) in her hand and they would say the rhyme '*Gur Khaeen, Puni Katteen; Aap Na Aeen, Veer*

285

nu Ghatteen' as they sent her to the next world. The rhyme means: "Have a treat of gur, and spin the yarn from this pooni to keep busy; but don't return yourself in the future, send a brother instead." Sometimes they choked the newborn or just put her in an earthen pitcher without killing her, covered it with a lid, buried the pitcher and told every one that the child had died at birth or was stillborn. Whenever people dug the ground around an old house and found a clay pitcher, they always looked for baby skull and bones inside it.

To kill the baby girls, some people just gave a combination of the well-known poisonous plants, such as *akk* or *dhatura*, by applying them to the mother's breast or administering them in other ways. Giving opium to the newborn was the most common way to kill. Most children were given opium in the first year of their lives anyway, in order to keep them in "good health and good humor," so overdosing was easy. Some women cursing their grown-up daughters, even when they were not seriously angry, would say, "I should have overdosed you with opium, instead of keeping you." My father had forbidden the practice of giving opium to the babies in his house. But people would tell my mother "If you had more sense you would give the baby a little opium daily to keep the baby cheerful, and to avoid sickness; it would make your life easier." Aunt Harnami's children and her daughters' babies as well, were given small daily doses of opium. Apparently, there were no long-term adverse effects upon the babies from the low doses of opium in infancy. The killing of baby girls might have been partly responsible for keeping the population in check, although diseases made a bigger difference. The population of our village did not change much for 100 years starting from the mid nineteenth century; but subsequently the population of India has at least quadrupled in the last 65 years.

In my time girls were allowed to live, but they were accepted grudgingly. And some girls knew that they were resented as a burden. Some people considered baby girls as a punishment to the parents from God. Many girls were cursed for being born and suffered verbal abuses. Sometimes the girls themselves would say: "I am sorry that I was born; I am such a burden and source of worry and pain to you." Many such girls were given undesirable and despicable names by their parents to express their displeasure at having female children. Some girls in our neighborhood were named Murro (one who should die), Akko (poisonous, tiresome, annoying), Kaudi (bitter) and Mukko or Mukk Jani (one who should end). Boys would never be given names like that. In anger many mothers would say to their daughters, but never to their sons, "I wish you would die." I wonder if this unwanted status caused much harm to the personalities of those girls; many such that I knew turned out to be cheerful, outgoing and likeable as they grew up. They would laugh, play and joke with their friends. Some of them just never knew that there were better ways to be and laughed through it all. I attribute their survival to the resilience of the human spirit, their low expectations, their acceptance of the prevailing conditions and their belief that this was their *kismet* and no one's fault. They compared themselves with others in similar circumstances and knew that some girls were just luckier than they were. The continuous physical closeness among all members of the clan also helped, so that there could be plenty of complaining, consoling, celebrating and other distractions.

Dealing with In-Laws

Life for an unmarried girl in a middle-class family was relatively good. For a married woman life was sometimes a lot worse. Life was certainly bad if the husband were abusive or dysfunctional. Occasional wife-beating occurred in at least twenty-five percent of the houses. Uncle Bhan Singh, being a wise man, never beat any of his wives. He never liked the first one, who was about half his size; he was married against his wishes, so he abandoned her quickly. His second wife was sweet and cheerful, but she died accidentally; his third wife had an air of nobility and dignity about her and not of the beatable kind.

Most married couples lived in joint families, where there would be less of a danger of being beaten severely. But the wife had to live in the house of her in-laws, who controlled the resources, the land and the house. In ideal circumstances she would be admired and adored by her in-laws, but only a few brides were so lucky. Personality problems could create a powder keg in a family, and there were always sources of conflict. The approval of a mother-in-law might hinge on a wife's looks, manners, speech, ability to perform tasks, on the amount of dowry she brought, on how affluent and well-connected her parents were, and on the mother-in-law's comparison of her with other wives in the neighborhood. More often than not, the mother-in-law made her daughter-in-law's life miserable. Hostility and ill-will toward a girl's mother-in-law is proverbial, part of the vocabulary, folklore and songs of antiquity. The mother-in-law had the power in the relationship, at least for the first few years, until the daughter-in-law felt some kind of stability. Having a male child was one way for the daughter-in-law to gain power, as it would be harder for her husband to abandon a wife with a son. Having some control over her husband was another possibility, and the wife's control usually increased with time. And if the wife had powerful brothers, it would be harder for anyone to mistreat her; they would not tolerate such effrontery to their honor, although it was still a delicate situation for the use of force.

Touching of the Feet and *Matha Tekna*

Perfect obedience was expected from a wife, and obedient behavior was cultivated in girls from childhood. A wife had to be obedient not just to her husband but also to her in-laws, who had the real power. She had to conform to the wishes of her mother-in-law. whose presence was continuous. For a new bride, the act of reverence started with the gesture of touching the feet of her mother-in-law with her hands and sometimes also the feet of her father-in-law, but not those of her husband or any of his brothers. This practice became less frequent as time passed in the marriage, particularly when they started quarreling; but touching of the feet was still expected whenever they met after some time of separation. The bride's touching an end of her veil to the feet of a senior woman was considered as good as touching with her hands. To the more remote senior women, a wife might simply say the verbal greeting, "*matha tekdi ha,*" which literally means "I place my forehead at your feet." For saying *Mattha tekna,* she was given a verbal blessing by the recipient with words like: live long; be in marital bliss till old age; may your body be strong; may God bless you with a son; may milk be abundant in your house; may your children thrive, and similar sentiments, depending on the circumstances.

A wife was not obliged to greet any senior man except for touching the feet of her father in-law for the first meeting after a long absence. She would never utter any words when touching his feet, and she would never show her face to him. Any actual communication with him could not be direct, but through other relatives.

Although the practice of prostrating oneself before a superior had been discontinued, younger men sometimes said *"paeri paena"* (at your feet, I place myself), particularly to senior women. Boys did not touch the feet of any man; they just gave a verbal greeting to the men. But boys and men were expected to touch the feet of all senior women relatives, such as the mother-in-law, mother's sisters and other women, at the first meeting after an absence. As time passed or familiarity set in, they could just say " mattha tekda ha" or "paeri paena." I personally said "mattha tekda ha" to older women and sometimes touched their feet when meeting them for the first time. To men I would say only the traditional Sikh greeting, "Sat Sri Akal." It was a custom to show more respect to women than to men.

The one gesture that a senior person receiving all that respect and adoration was obliged to make, was to issue some words of blessing. In cases where the relationship was close, the senior person also touched or petted the head of the younger person. This gesture of petting the head of the younger person was called *sirr pilosna* (head soothing or petting). In some situations, the elder just touched the shoulder instead of the head of a youngster, as a quicker and less formal gesture; he also added some flowery words of blessing to show affection. But if it was not a close relationship, then merely some reciprocal words of greeting, without sirr pilosna, would be adequate.

The Privileged *Juvayee*

As mentioned before, son-in-law was the most privileged person in that society. If he went to the wife's village, every one would honor him like a lord, not just the immediate family of the in-laws. It was customary for girls of the village to gather and talk to him. For example, they would say to their friends, "Binni's husband is visiting; let's check him out." Those girls were the only people who did not have to respect him; they were free to tease, ridicule or make fun of him, to listen to his wit, to challenge him with a riddle, to recite a *doha* (couplet) as a challenge to see how he responded, to speak in rhymes and see if he could answer in any clever way, and banter of that sort. They could even talk a bit nasty and could have a no-holds-barred conversation. So a fresh bridegroom had to memorize some poetry, riddles in rhymes, some boli (ballads) and a good number of spicy doha couplets before visiting his wife's village and facing a battery of clever girls. If he brought along a companion, usually a bachelor, that companion could add to the conviviality and banter. But these would be just two guys against a dozen girls or more. No one had to watch his or her words; they could be as brazen as they wanted to be. Some of the fast girls really dropped their inhibitions, while the shy ones felt scandalized and covered their mouths and noses with their veils to hide their embar-rassment. These gatherings could be as long and as frequent as the situation permitted, and no parents or elders were expected to chaperone or come near such gatherings. I had the experience of accompanying my friend Mukand to his in-law's village once or twice. I was not verbally gifted, but still the entertainment in those gatherings was tantalizing for me.

The Western custom of hostility between son-in-law and mother-in-law is in complete contrast to Punjabi rural customs. The mother-in-law treated him as though he was dearer than her own sons, as his attitude and behavior were a factor in the happiness of her daughter. In fact a *sass* (mother-in-law) said only the most polite, gracious and affectionate words to her son-in-law; harsh words were unthinkable, as he was equally respectful to her. Nothing was denied to him, and the in-law family was constantly thinking of the ways to please him. The rural saying could be translated as, "There is no joy at the in-laws without sass as there is no rain without clouds." The house of a man's in-laws was like paradise for him. The in-law men usually remained out of the way and he was entertained exclusively by women. He in turn conducted himself with respect in the senior in-laws' presence. But with his wife's sisters and cousins, he could be as free and informal as he wanted to be.

He was treated to the best food the women could prepare. The best bed and the fanciest bed covers and pillows were set up for him. Sometimes they would provide him with alcohol and meat, even if no one in the in-law house used such things. There was always a man attending on him wherever he went outside their house. If he wanted to answer the call of nature, which was almost always out in the fields or wilderness (the local expression for that activity was "going to the jungle"), a boy or a brother-in-law would carry water for him to the fields to allow him to wash himself afterwards. Everybody spoke to him with respect, because he was the husband of a daughter of the village. A wife of the village did not enjoy such respect, but a daughter of the village was nearly sacred, and her husband was a notch higher. As they say, he could "eat fabulous and speak foul."

For a married girl, it was usually a big relief to be able to get away from her in-laws, back to the house of her parents where she would be honored and respected by everyone. She would have been important enough as a virgin, but now she was treated like a guest also. And if she had any children, those children would have a privileged existence in the house of their mother's parents, called *nanke* (pronounced naan kay). Time spent at the nanke house was better than any vacation of modern days. A child in the nanke house was fed the best foods and was pampered and spoiled, and no one would discipline or say any harsh words to him/her. Everyone in the community would treat him/her with more respect than they would treat any local person. The nanke would buy gifts for him/her and would try to please in every way. Since very few children went to school, some could spend parts of their early lives at the nanke house away from their own parents. A child raised in the nanke house was expected to be spoiled. One of the reasons that as a child I never had a toy was that my *nana* and *nani* (maternal grandparents) were not living. Whereas it was common for little boys to talk glowingly of their nanke and to show off the things they received from them, I never visited my nanke until I was sixteen years old, except once during a wedding. So I felt underprivileged compared to other children. I also craved for the freedom and privileges that came with living at the nanke's house. Two sons and a daughter of my sister Maro lived in our house while they went to school in our village. According to custom, my father did not punish them as he disciplined us. A vacation in the modern sense was unthinkable for village people; visiting relatives was the closest thing to a vacation for them. And visiting nanke was better than visiting any other relatives.

There was a fairy tale in which a wolf catches a little girl and wants to eat her. She uses a ruse, saying, "I am too skinny and have very little flesh on me to satisfy you. You should wait, because I am going to the nanke house and will surely be returning fat and juicy after being well fed there; it will be a better time for you to eat me when I return from the nanke house." There was a game where you lifted a little child high over your head "to show his nanke," as the child was too small to look far away. In a Punjabi child's mind, nanke was somewhere between fantasyland and paradise.

The Relationship between a Husband and Wife

In my days a bride and her groom never met before their wedding, and officially they did not see one another's face until *moklawa*, the ceremony that came some weeks, months or even years after the wedding, depending on the circumstances. Moklawa was not like a honeymoon, but the period when for the first time the bride spent some days or some weeks in the husband's house. For the first few years of her marriage, a wife who was young or had not yet had any children would spend a good part of the time back at her own parent's house. This turnover was considered good for the couple's relationship, as people said, "Even the *roti* can burn on the griddle if you don't turn it over timely."

In a large household a new wife was not expected to talk much with her husband, and being lovey-dovey in the presence of others was an absolute no-no. She would talk to him only when they could be alone. She was not supposed to say her husband's actual name and instead depended on words like "*woh*" (he), "your brother," "your son," "my child's father," "*ghar wala*" or "my owner" to refer to him. It was considered inauspicious, or immodest for a husband or wife to say the actual name of his or her spouse. Superstitious people thought it would reduce the life span to say the name of the spouse. Some words used in those days, such as "owner" for husband, would be considered offensive and politically incorrect nowadays, after women's liberation. But in my day, a woman would routinely say, "When my *maalik* (owner, lord) comes home from the fields, I will ask his opinion" or "My owner is so bad tempered, I dare not talk to him about this matter." Most expressions in those days implied that a woman was her husband's property, although in practice and usually after a few years of marriage the situation was not so skewed in favor of the husband. Needless to say, the same vocabulary is not used much in educated circles now, and many independent girls are not even getting married anymore.

In many families the new bride was initially treated well and was adored by women of the extended family and the community. She was dressed in the best of clothes, since most brides got a couple of dozen new suits of expensive clothes for the wedding. She was not allowed to do any hard or unpleasant work for a few months. People considered that the bride had just come from the house of her parents where she was pampered, and it was not proper to require her to do any work. She might do some embroidery or other delicate work but nothing difficult or dirty. For a good part of the first year the bride spent a portion of the time back at her own parents' house and not at her in-laws'. Everyone among the in-laws wanted to be in her good graces; they wanted to show off their bride to the community women and wanted to be proud of her. So the first year could be the best time of life for a bride. But after a year or two, the novelty wore off and usually the mother-in-law and her daughters got on the bride's case. They sometimes became hostile and belligerent; they might start picking faults in her and in some cases might start to torture her mentally.

290

CHAPTER 15

MARRIAGE CUSTOMS IN PUNJAB

When my parents got married, probably around 1916, their wedding was performed by a Brahmin according to Hindu rites, as most weddings in our area were performed then. With the reforms of the Singh Sabha movement in the 20th Century, the defining change from the Hindu to the Sikh wedding ritual was that in a Hindu wedding, the couple walked around the sacred fire as a Brahmin gave a recitation in Sanskrit, while in the Sikh rites the couple walked four times around the holy Granth with recitations from the Granth. Most other wedding traditions and customs remained unchanged. In my day, persons of different religions or castes were seldom included in wedding parties. I never saw a Muslim wedding, but it was supposed to be a quick and simple affair. I heard that the only thing the Muslim groom and bride had to do was to say "*qabool,*" meaning "acceptable," in the presence of a *qazi*; their wedding ceremonies took just minutes, not hours or days. Similarly all a man had to do to dissolve his marriage was to say "talaaq" three times. I was invited to only one Hindu wedding and that too in my college days, because in the villages it was not customary to invite people who were not one's caste, clan or kin.

The betrothal process in our society was usually quite elaborate. It was negotiated by the parents without any involvement of the prospective bride and groom. It could start in any of a number of ways. The most likely matchmaker was some aunt of the bride or of the groom or some other activist lady from the village who knew both families. Subtle inquires about the possibilities of a match were always going on. Cold-call approaches, based on secondhand information, were also not unthinkable. In some cases a Brahmin, or even a Nai (a barber, who would not be cutting hair in a Sikh village) would be sent by the girl's family to the prospective bridegroom's parents for initial inquiries and to evaluate the boy, the house and their land holdings. Being good observers, the Brahmin or Nai were able to evaluate the prospects quickly and would not feel uneasy or awkward. Then a relative of the girl, possibly her father or maternal uncle, would go to the boy's house, without invitation or prior warning. It was considered perfectly normal to arrive unexpectedly, broach the subject to the parents of the groom, and say that they had come to "look at the boy," as if to buy an ox. They would be treated hospitably and with courtesy even in cases where there was not much mutual interest. Some old men who were good talkers and had plenty of leisure, made a habit of going to eat at the homes of prosperous families and getting special treats, even if they had only a remote niece as an excuse to look for a prospective groom. If such an old man had impressive personality, he would be treated lavishly, depending on what kind of story he could concoct about "our beautiful and virtuous girl." During one year, my family sent me to several strange villages to look for marriage prospects for my sister Karo, who was actually older than me. I was of college age then, and it was easier for me than for my father to make initial enquiries. The families of the prospective bridegrooms that I visited were usually courteous and hospitable. One of the families just gave me a picture of their boy as he himself was not at home. When we showed the picture to my sister Karo, she said she was not impressed. She said the fellow had a skimpy beard, suggesting a poor constitution and bad health; we dropped that case immediately. If the initial impressions were positive, then some more responsible person, such as the girl's father or the maternal uncle, would take charge of negotiations. Maternal relatives (called *nanke*) were highly important in such matters and would try their best for their nieces.

Before the betrothal, both parties would try to show their best side, but the situation was not reciprocal. Everything about the boy was open to inspection and questions. The prospective bride could never be seen by any man from the groom's side. In the upper stratum of society, she would be seen by women from the groom's side, but being seen by any man from the groom's side would be considered an insult. Of my three sisters, Karo was the only one whose prospective husband came to see her before marriage; and since he was educated and our family considered itself modern and progressive, this was permitted from a distance. Questions about land holdings and other assets of the prospective bridegroom would be asked.

Some people tried to exaggerate and even misrepresent their assets in order to make a good impression and clinch the deal. In our neighborhood, Uncle Assa, an eccentric and a funny man of the village, used to make us laugh as he told us the story of how he fooled the people who came to check out his middle-aged older brother Massa as a marriage prospect. Uncle Massa had returned penniless from Hong Kong, and it was difficult to find a wife for him as he was older than my father. His family did not have much land, but fortunately he was quite fat, so that wrinkles on his face were smoothed out, and in those days being fat also created an illusion of prosperity. I remember that before he was married, one night Massa came to our house drunk, although our house was far away from theirs. He was very loud and talkative. My father handled him politely, as it was proper to be hospitable to a visiting person from the neighborhood in the evenings. My father did not drink anymore, but we had a bottle of whiskey that he had received while attending a function of the Maharaja of Patiala. Massa was drinking our whiskey and making noises that seemed really scary to me as I was only six years old.

When the bride's people came, his younger brother Assa (who himself had never qualified to get a wife, nor had their third brother Preetam who had also returned from Honk Kong) practiced every kind of deception to arrange his older brother's betrothal. Assa pointed to someone else's vacant lot where some bricks were piled up and said that his brother was building a new *haveli* (mansion) there with the money he had brought from Hong Kong. Then he took the visitors to the farms and waved his hand, saying,

"All that land belongs to our family," when in reality that land belonged to many other families in the clan, and his own parcel was miniscule. Then in his house he showed the visitor a few pitchers of clay which were full of grain, but he had covered the grain in the pitchers with silver rupee coins. He told them, "These pitchers are full of silver rupees. The rest of Massa's money has not yet arrived from Hong Kong." He had instructed the neighborhood children not to address the prospective groom by the word *taya* (an uncle who is older than one's father), but to call him *chacha* (younger uncle), so that the groom would not be perceived as an old man.

Fortunately for Uncle Massa, the deceptions worked. The people who had come to arrange the match took the bait and he was married in 1936. Although I was too young to be sent, my brother Kartar did go with the bridegroom's party. At the wedding house, Kartar was rebuked once when he accidentally addressed the bridegroom as "taya" (older uncle) and forgot to call him "chacha" according to the instructions.

Friends and family used to tell a prospective bridegroom to dress in his best clothes to face the visitors when they came to "look him over"; the visitors did not always talk to him, but just saw from a distance. In the village, when some fellow was being overly fussy about his clothes and appearance, people would say tauntingly, "Why are you being so particular and fussy about your looks! Are any betrothal people coming to look at you?" And frequently there were stories about the enemies of a prospective bridegroom providing unfavorable information to a visiting match seeker. Such adverse information was called *bhanni* (a deal breaker, with unfavorable information). To be credible and not an obvious attempt to prevent the match, the bhanni had to be executed carefully. Here is a story of one such bhanni, which starts innocently, without apparent ill will, so as not to betray any malicious motive, but builds up slowly and ends with a harsh conclusion.

A Bhanni against the Onion-Eater Boy

A Brahmin was dispatched by a Jat family to make inquires about a prospective bridegroom in another village. He went to that village and as he wanted to make a careful check, instead of meeting the prospective groom's parents he started making enquiries of a man in the neighborhood. He asked the neighbor about the habits of the prospective bridegroom and about the status of his family. Their conversation went like this:

Brahman: "Please tell me what this boy Ghudder of the Birk family is really like. We are looking for a suitable boy for the daughter of our *jajman* (client in religious matters), who is a respectable landowner."

Neighbor of the boy: "Oh, that Ghudder of the Birks is alright, but he does have the habit of eating onions."

Brahman: "That does not sound bad at all; I don't see any real problem with eating onions, except some temporary smell. These days it is hard to find a boy who has all the good habits; eating onions should be no problem."

Neighbor: "Oh, Ghudder does not eat onions ordinarily. He eats them only when they are nicely fried and cooked with spices and with meat of some kind. You should know that this boy does eat meat."

Brahman: "I realize that Ghudder may not be entirely virtuous. He may have the vice of eating meat; but we are not looking for a holy man. Young boys do indulge in eating meat sometimes; I don't see this bad habit of eating meat as a major issue either, if there are no other problems."

Neighbor: "Oh, Ghudder does not eat meat every day but only when he drinks a lot, since eating meat and drinking alcohol go together; he is quite fond of whiskey and sometimes he drinks in excess."

Brahman: "Now this may be serious, but most young landowners do eat meat and drink whiskey; and they usually quit such vices later when they become householders. To me Ghudder still sounds like a wholesome average boy."

Neighbor: "Frankly the Birks don't have that kind of money, to afford drinking whiskey and eating meat frequently. Ghudder drinks whiskey only when he has committed theft and is flush with cash."

Brahman: "Oh, Ram! Ram! Ram! (God! God! God!). I am glad you told me this. That boy is a thief too? There is no way I am going to present this as a possibility to my jajman!"

Neighbor: "Ghudder used to be a good boy. But when his father Jhandu was in jail, the boy started keeping company with bad characters who smoked *chilm* (tobacco pipes) and drank alcohol. They got the boy into bad habits and in time he also joined them in committing thefts."

Brahman: "Oh Sri, Sri, Sri, (holy, holy, holy). This is horrible; you mean to tell me that this boy is a thief and his father was in jail! What kind of family are they, anyway!"

Neighbor: "Oh, Jhandu Birk, the father of Ghudder, was in jail for breaking the leg of the lover of Nandi, who is Ghudder's mother. He had discovered that Nandi was having an illicit affair with the other man."

Brahman: "Oh, Hari! Hari! Hari! (God! God! God!) Ghudder's mother had an illicit lover? This family is rotten!"

Neighbor: "Oh, you might already know that in the early days the Birks were even poorer than they are now. No one would give his daughter in marriage to someone like Jhandu Birk. So Jhandu had to purchase his wife Nandi and he had *karewa*, not a regular marriage. Nandi had run away from some previous husbands and Jhandu used to know the bad characters who dealt in runaway and abducted women. Nandi had quite a reputation before she was purchased by Jhandu. And then she had this child Ghudder, who is now grown up and a big dangerous boy."

Brahman "Oh, thank you for telling me all this about the boy Ghudder and his family. Surely, such a house is not suitable for the daughter of my jajman, who is a respectable landowner."

And so the bhanni about the onion-eating boy was built up slowly. Since everybody knew and minded every one else's business in the village, many people used to suspect such bhanni possibilities in various situations. They would suspect some malicious bhanni by enemies and rivals, when a boy was rejected for a match, when an ox did not sell, or some other critical deal fell through. There was always a shortage of girls because of female infanticide in older times; so ordinary families of prospective bridegrooms could not afford to reject a girl. Only the rich parents of boys could afford to be selective. Among average families it was the girls' parents who were discriminating. Not all men could get wives, and when someone's son was rejected, they suspected a bhanni.

Often, in earlier times and in some parts, the boy's parents asked for the girl's hand, hence the word *mang* (beg, ask or request), or mangna or mangni for betrothal. But gradually as times changed and more baby girls were allowed to live, the shortage of girls eased. This shortage took a couple of generations to ameliorate because the younger girls were married to the large number of unmarried older boys over time. As the proportion of girls increased, the marriage market changed, so later on, it was the girl's parents who had to make extra efforts to get her into the best possible situation. The couple themselves still did not have any input into the decision as they did not ever see, much less talk to, their intended mates before marriage. Most people saw a marriage essentially as a relationship between two families, in which the bride and groom were like commodities. The two youngsters might be told what was happening and where the prospective mate lived, but they usually did not have enough awareness, reason or information to rebel against the proceedings. Besides, it was the custom for children to be obedient to the wishes of their parents, and the religious belief was that one's *sanjog* (sacred relationship) was predetermined by God and written according to one's karma and kismet. The young people also had no choice, since dating or having a romantic relationship with anyone was not the accepted custom; having such contact with a person of the opposite sex would be considered illicit, highly immoral and a violation of sacred rules. The boy and the girl could only hope for the best, since their parents were completely in charge of the transaction.

In later times, with the increase in the number of marriageable girls, parents felt the pressure to find the best possible matches for their daughters. They offered the biggest dowry they could afford. Girls' relatives tried in various ways to convince the prospective groom's parents of the desirability of the match. Sometimes matchmakers exerted pressure on the groom's parents to accept the match, and if rebuffed they developed ill-will and expressed their displeasure: "They are acting uppity; don't they have daughters of their own? We are not talking to them anymore. We should wrest control of that plot of land which they hold in mortgage and damage them economically." The family of Ishwer Singh and Jung Singh, who were prosperous and influential in our village, were once annoyed with my father because he did not accept their proposal for the marriage of their relatives' daughter to his son Kartar. Fortunately they did not become our enemies. While other people in the village were strengthening relationships and negotiating dowries with those who wanted to arrange matches for their relatives' daughters, my father actually became the object of hostility a couple of times for not considering such offers for his sons. He always said, "When they are educated and independent, the boys can decide whom they want to marry." But such talk sounded foolish to the traditional people, who would say, "Just arrange the marriage now; the boy and the girl will grow up in time. She is a girl from a *gharana* (good house); she will bring good fortune to your house and will work as a daughter-in-law in your house while your boy is away at college." But my father never wanted any of us to be stuck in a marriage before compliting our education; all of his sons arranged their own marriages.

No Luck with Seebo

Offers of marriage were made even for me when I was sixteen years old, though I was unproductive and not particularly well behaved. Our neighbor Aunt Harnami hinted many times about her niece Naseeb Kaur, or Naseebo, shortened to Seebo, from AliKe village. Seebo was about my age, or possibly a bit older. I was sixteen, had dropped out of college, and was not doing anything useful or according to my family's wishes. Aunt Harnami suggested to our family that I would probably mend my ways and act responsibly if I were married off. It was a common belief that a boy starts to tame his behavior after he is entangled in the relationship of marriage and is burdened with a wife. I had seen Seebo once or twice when she came to visit her aunt. I thought she was vivacious, beautiful, talented and perhaps too good for me. Seebo was tall and slim, had an attractive face, smooth skin, and dancing eyes; she was bold, energetic and good at singing and dancing. She had such presence, looks and verbal assertiveness that I was totally mesmerized by her personality. She was uneducated, but education was of no importance to me at that time. She was smart and much more sophisticated than I was, in spite of my education. I liked her a lot, but I was also a bit intimidated by her looks and personality. And one was supposed to treat every girl as one's sister until and unless he was married to her. And this was neither the first nor the last such upheaval in my mind.

Once in 1946, Seebo visited our village as a part of the *nanka meil* (wedding guests from the bride or groom's mother's village) for the marriage of Aunt Harnami's son, Chand Singh. Our Inner House had a common *vehra* (courtyard) with Aunt Harnami's house, so I was in their house all the time during the wedding days, except to sleep. On an occasion like a marriage, helping, socializing, eating together, talking, laughing and celebrating together for several days in the groom's house was normal. Although I had been invited to go with the *junj* (groom's wedding party), I missed my ride with the party because I was tardy. Thus I was one of two boys left behind. The other was Kartar of the Sadhan family, who was a very close friend of the bridegroom. I felt pretty bad about having missed Chand's wedding party which went to Dyalpura. That could have been great fun for three days. On their return, my friends told me of all the happenings in Dyalpura, and of the girls that they traded wits with. Even my good friend Nawab Din the Araeen, though he was a Muslim, went with the Junj. A Muslim would not normally be in a Jat wedding, and it was an awkward question whether to treat him like a low caste Araeen, when he was such a good friend. The reason he was included was that the Araeen maintained their ox carriage for hire on such occasions.

Anyway, although I missed going with the groom's party, I had the consolation of observing the singing, dancing and other antics of the *nanka meil* in Aunt Harnami's house, in the absence of all the men who had gone with the wedding party. In those days, men were not permitted to participate in the women's song and dance, but even hearing the songs from a distance was exciting. Seebo, the object of my fascination and part of the nanka meil, was in great form in those days and the celebration of the wedding provided a perfect outlet for her talents. She was the life of the party and sang the raciest songs of the Punjabi language of those days, with outrageous, titillating themes and provocative words. That singing party on the first evening lasted well past midnight, and Seebo's married but equally bold and vivacious sister Dialo took up any slack in the singing and dancing. Those songs of Seebo and Dialo rang in my ears for many years afterwards; and I have still not forgotten them.

During the second evening of the nanka meil activities, everyone was involved in the hustle and bustle of the wedding. I was sitting alone casually in front of Aunt Harnami's *chullah* (hearth) to keep warm. Seebo came over and sat right next to me on a *peerhi* (low seat) in front of the chullah. That move by Seebo could have been considered either quite innocent or very bold, considering that there was no one else with us. We had exchanged glances before, but we had never spoken to one another. Just the previous evening, I had heard her tremendous repertoire of songs, some bold and risqué and others romantic and sentimental; now all kinds of things were going through my mind. She looked ravishing and sophisticated, with silky soft skin and shiny clothes, and she was a girl, unrelated to me, just the right age and unattainable. I felt like a dull-witted dunce compared to her and was awestruck and overwhelmed by her presence so close to me. With just the two of us alone in front of the fire that evening for some time, tension was high and the silence was thick. If either of us had spoken, it might have become light and innocent, but I was totally frozen and did not have the courage to utter a single word. Seebo may have felt that she had already done too much by coming alone and sitting next to me with no one else around. If we had been educated or city people, this kind of meeting might have been considered routine and casual. Or if she had been directly related me, we could have laughed and talked without any charge. But under the circumstances, even sitting near an unrelated girl, without a good excuse, felt like a violation. Being cold could be some excuse, but a girl would not ordinarily sit next to an unrelated boy, as it could be considered flirting and making oneself available. And I just felt that she was too sophisticated, and clever, and would surely reject me if I said anything. I was not exactly being virtuous, considering the thoughts that were going through my mind. It was like a novice deer hunter with the excitement of seeing a deer in his gun-sights, unable to pull the trigger and failing to shoot because of nervous excitement. I was not smooth enough to make small talk with Seebo, although I had had plenty of free conversations with her older, married, and therefore "safer" sister Dialo, whose husband had gone with the groom's party. The married sister even had a drink with me that evening; I was only sixteen but had a bottle of whiskey with me. This was a daring act for Dialo, since women were not supposed to drink alcohol; but no one else knew about the drink, and nothing else happened between us anyway except some spicy and tasty talk. Many times far-out things did happen at wedding celebrations, when women were in an uninhibited state of mind, although such things would not be thought of in the busy workaday life. Village people used to say that a woman is in an entirely different state of mind during a wedding celebration, especially if she is in the nanka meil party for a few days.

Three days after I spent that time with Seebo and Dialo, the nanka meil departed, singing sad farewell songs of departure through the village streets: "Hey anyone, anyone, keep us here a couple of days more!...We are not too demanding as guests... Just give us simple daal-roti!...We love your village..(and so forth)." But as expected, Seebo went back to her own village. I felt a great void, a sense of loss and longing, as if I had lost something precious. I felt bad that I did not develop a speaking relationship with her. I was sad and unhappy for several days and felt lonely in the midst of the hustle and bustle of the family and of the village.

Once I contrived to make a stop at Seebo's parent's house in AliKe village with the excuse that I was on my way to buy an ox at the cattle market at Tappa, some miles beyond. Going to the house of the relative of a neighbor was as good as going to your own relatives; so I was not doing anything unusual. I ate dinner and spent the night in her house. She served me food, as her mother was cooking and I was the guest. But even there I never got a chance to talk much to Seebo. And she had to act properly so as not to arouse the disapproval of her family; she might have felt that showing an interest in me would have led to no good consequence. The next day I went on to the cattle market in Tappa and bought an ox. Later, on reaching home, my father with rare frankness and in a slightly disapproving and teasing manner, remarked to me, "With your stopping in AliKe village, that might have become a really expensive ox for us."

I used to wish my father would change his mind and agree to my marriage with Seebo, as Aunt Harnami had suggested and as even her son Chand had mentioned to me once. I didn't dare to say anything directly to my father about such a matter. My father wanted me to be educated, not to be burdened with a wife or to waste my life in the village. Marriage at that stage would have closed any possibility of education for me, and thus it was unthinkable from his standpoint. His motto was, "When this boy makes his own life, he can find a wife." He had previously refused to act on such offers for his older son Kartar. A year later, in 1947, Seebo's life went in an entirely different direction, but to this day I am convinced that my life would have never lacked excitement if I had had Seebo's companionship Seebo.

Amrik Betrothed While a Toddler

Some boys and girls were betrothed at very young ages. In a society with shortage of girls due to female infanticide in earlier times, not every body could find a wife. So it used to be a matter of pride to say, "Our boy was betrothed while at the teat," that is, while still suckling on his mother's breast. Some affluent fathers who had sons, would start planning early, negotiating with people from good families who had daughters. The farmers always said, *"bald laane da; dhee gharane di,"* which implied that a daughter from a prominent house has the best traits. So a parent would consider it wise to "lock up" a prospect from a good family before the girl was promised to someone else. Although it was a matter of honor not to break such promises, with changing times things sometimes went in unexpected directions. This reminds me of the true story of my close friend from college days, Amrik Singh Aulakh.

We used to joke that his given name meant American Lion. He was born in the LylePur district, in the part of Punjab that later became Pakistan as a result of the partition of India. The towns of LylePur and Montgomery were settled about the beginning of the twentieth century, in the heyday of the British Raj in Punjab and were apparently named after distinguished British administrators. Amrik's mother had died before he was old enough to remember her. His father subsequently betrothed him to the baby daughter of an acquaintance in a nearby village, about the time when both would have been toddlers. In 1947, Amrik's father was forced to flee from what became the Punjab portion of Pakistan and came to the Indian part of Punjab. The girl's family also escaped from Pakistan and settled somewhere else in India as refugees. In those days people never lost track of their friends, regardless of time and distance, and all relationships were forever.

It was common for young children to be raised by their mother's folks if the mother died. So Amrik lived in the *nanke* house of the cousins on his mother's side, who had land and mango orchards in the vicinity of Hoshiarpur. Amrik went to the grade school and high school there. In the 1950s, he also went to Punjab University College in Hoshiarpur, where he and I became best friends. I lived in the college hostel; he commuted on his bicycle and spent much time with me after school and on Sundays. We would go into the city, walk around Model Town, and go to the movies or to college functions together. Amrik was the most wonderful friend to have. He was very polite, dependable, sincere, loyal, humorous, generous with his time, and not easily annoyed. Later still, I joined the Physics Honors School of The Punjab University in Hoshiarpur and Amrik joined law college in the city of Jallunder, only twenty-five miles away. We visited each other frequently with groups of friends over weekends. Girls were a frequent topic of conversation among the bachelors.

Amrik was tall, slim, witty and an extremely likeable guy. He treated me with great regard, and being his guest felt like being in the lap of comfort. He started meeting educated girls from good families, when he was invited as a guest by various friends. He would come back and describe to me his various encounters: "This one is extremely beautiful; her manners are so elegant; her voice is so delicious that when she talks, one feels as if she is singing. She is my friend's sister, so I have to think of her as a sister; but she would be perfect for you. Let me invite you there some day." Although he was serious about his suggestions, and the girls' families would not discourage such explorations, I just laughed the suggestions away. Although I was in my mid-twenties then, it would have been fruitless for me to chase such stories while I was still a student.

A couple of years later in 1956, when he was completing law comn, Amrik met a girl in the resort town of Simla. This used to be the summer capital of British India, where the Viceroy used to stay in the hills of Punjab. Some affluent families also went there to spend summers in the cool climate. Amrik had arranged to spend a couple of summers there even while he was a student. This girl's family had invited Amrik to dinner a couple of times, and a mutual interest had developed between Amrik and the girl. Even in educated urban families, young girls were not allowed to be alone with any unrelated man, but it was acceptable to socialize in groups. They even went to a movie accompanied by other young friends. Amrik said the opportunity to talk to her felt like slice of heaven. "She is so classy, so beautiful and still willing to be my friend," he would write to me in his letters. He wanted to marry that girl, but he was still unsure about the consent of her parents. He thought her parents might not consider him up to their standard, even though the girl was favorably disposed toward him. "Maybe after I have been practicing law for a year they will think I am OK, and then they might agree to my proposal," Amrik told me. But an unexpected obstacle came in his way.

About that time, the family of the girl who had been betrothed to Amrik before the creation of Pakistan, when he himself was a toddler, spoke again with Amrik's father. Now her refugee clan was living in a farming village in the district of Karnal. Amrik could not have seen the girl after the creation of Pakistan, and in fact he may have never seen her at all. Her people were uneducated farmers, and of course the girl was completely illiterate too. Since she had already been spoken for, some twenty years earlier, by Amrik's father, her family was not in any hurry or panic. But now that their daughter was over twenty years old, they wanted Amrik's father to make his word good. Betrothal used to be like a sacred promise as if ordained by God and not to be violated. His father broached the subject to Amrik, who had perhaps never considered this matter of betrothal. He had not even lived much with his father after his mother had died. As close as we were, he had never mentioned to me that his father had made such a commitment on his behalf. He never talked much about his paternal family, and I used to think his father lived somewhere near Hoshiarpur, where his mother's folks lived; but in reality his father lived far away near Sangrur, south of the Sutlej River. Now that Amrik was trained as a lawyer, how could he be married to an illiterate village girl whom he had never seen! And his heart was set on the Simla girl with whom he was keeping in tone.

The old man said that he could not go back on his sacred word of betrothal, and Amrik would have to marry that girl. Amrik was just beginning his law practice in the city of Patiala which is not very far from Sangrur, where his father was. To avoid a confrontation with his father, and hoping the problem would just go away, he left his place in Patiala without telling anyone. He came to stay with me, as I had become a Lecturer in Physics at Khalsa College in Amritsar by that time. Amrik's father was perplexed and did not know how to find his son. First he visited Amrik's lawyer friends in other towns, and after making enquiries from them, he found out my address. Then the father headed to my place in Amritsar in order to trace Amrik. In those days, telephones were rare even in big cities; one had to travel in person or write letters for any communication. But in the Punjab of those days it was easy to find someone even in a city, if you knew his name and approximate locality. Even in the cities, people still minded everyone's business just as they did in the villages. It was still not a crowded society, unlike the India of today, where the population has tripled since then and city life has become more congested and impersonal. After he was told that I was in Khalsa College, Amrik's father located my residence in the on-campus apartments where some of us bachelor "professors" lived. The father showed up at my door and asked for Amrik. I invited him in and they sat together inside and discussed the matter of Amrik's marriage to the village girl, in my presence. The father wanted my support in convincing Amrik about what was a matter of honor. But I could not very well speak against my friend and his feelings, even though I had to be respectful to the elder.

There was an emotional but civil exchange of views between the father and the son for a couple of hours. Amrik was respectful to his father, as he was a gentle guy anyway. But he expressed his views frankly this time. He said that if the father could not violate his word, he could not violate the wishes of his heart. He suggested that his father should express helplessness to the girl's folks, saying that his educated lawyer son was not under his control. The father listened, and then he went over the history of his family, the death of Amrik's mother, the Partition of India and being forced to leave home and land behind in Pakistan, the difficulty with which he had saved from his farming income to pay for Amrik's education, the importance of keeping one's word, and the virtues of daughters from good families. Then he described some of the despicable ways of the educated, slick city girls and the disgraceful and immoral modes of behavior that he believed were prevalent among educated girls. He gave specific examples of scandals as reported in the newspapers and even heard by the illiterate, as such scandals were spicy bits in the village *sutth* gatherings. Then Amrik's father said, "I cannot go back on my word, as a man's *zabaan* (tongue) is the measure of his morals; breaking a pledge is sin in the eyes of God and also shameful in the brotherhood. If you do not agree with me, then come before the brotherhood, and when the girl's folks are invited there, tell them with your own tongue that you cannot marry her. Then I can prove to the brotherhood that I am helpless and have done my best." The old man's words were convincing and not easy to reject. Amrik wanted to avoid any further confrontation or capitulation and he said to me, "Gurnam, can we go for a walk to the Company *Baagh*, please?" The old father, on seeing that Amrik was trying to escape the situation, made it clear that if his pledge of betrothal was broken, he would never see his son's face again, and their relationship would be severed forever. Leaving his father at my residence, Amrik and I went to walk in the Company *Baagh*, the fashionable recreational area of Amritsar in those days.

The word "Company" refers to The East India Company, which ruled India before the British Crown took direct control of its colony; and 'Baagh' meant a garden or orchard, and more commonly a park. When the Company was like a sovereign with its own army, navy, treasury and administrative services, the British made park-like areas near their cantonments and residential colonies in many cities. There was a Mall Road in the Jullundar cantonment area also, and Company Baagh existed in some other big cities of India too. The Company Baagh and Mall Road in Amritsar were the places where the Indian gentry came for evening walks in those days after the British had left. Doctors, lawyers, professors, judges, businessmen and high government officials with their families came there. Boys in groups, married couples, college girls, wives and daughters of prosperous people dressed in their best, the glamorous and the fashionable local people all walked there before dark. Everyone who was anyone wanted to be seen there and would go to walk on the *Thandi Sarak* (cool road) in the late afternoons and into the twilight hours. Some families would come in horse-drawn *tongas* or hired vehicles; some in motor carriages and then they let the driver wait some distance away, as they themselves walked in the Company Baagh.

Amrik and I walked near the Company Baagh, but Amrik was in a sad mood, which was quite unlike his usual self and incongruent with the scenery. When it was dark, he told me to go back to my place alone, as he himself did not want to confront his father. I left him in the Company Bagh and came back to my apartment alone. Amrik's father, who was still at my place, said that he was disappointed in his son. He said he was going back to his village but he was not giving up yet. As his son was not expected to come back soon, the father wanted to catch a train back to his home without spending the night with me; the old man left my place immediately. Later that night after his father had left and it was safe, Amrik returned to my place and stayed there for a couple of days more. On the third day, Amrik's father showed up again at my residence with three other elderly men, all of whom had big beards, strange accents and turbans of the style of rural Majha (middle Punjab). Like his father, all those elders were uneducated people. Amrik himself did not have their accent in his speech, because he had been raised by his maternal relatives. After many arguments with the elders and after much convincing, the upshot of the discussion was that Amrik agreed to go to his father's village and to face the girl's folks, who would be invited there. Then, if he did not want to marry the girl, he would announce his decision to the brotherhood. He did not have to go to the village immediately, however; if he consented to the marriage as planned; his word would be enough. Amrik was acting like a modern educated man and a lawyer, determined not to give in. So he agreed to go to the village, face the folks of the girl and the entire brotherhood, and announce his decision there. At the Amritsar train station before his departure, we walked around on the platform, apart from the elders. Everything in India happened slowly then, and it was not uncommon to wait at a railway station for an hour or two. Amrik was slightly anxious and stressed but still confident that he could stand up to all the village people and not be coerced to marry someone against his will. He said to me, "Gurnam, wish me luck. This matter will affect the rest of my life." After that we shook hands and he boarded the train, sat down with the elders, and went to his father's village.

I fully expected him to stand his ground and refuse to be forced to marry an unknown girl. But within a week I got a telegram: "Arrive at the Sangroor train station on May 8th; Amrik's wedding party departing on 9th; marriage date May 10th, 1957." I was surprised by the change in Amrik's intentions. He had seemed to be totally determined and unmoved before he left my place, and now he was being married to an unknown person against his will! This was the traditional pattern of life among our people, but he had been trying to be an exception. The elders' persuasion had won over the lawyer's arguments. I took the train from Amritsar to Sangroor to attend his wedding, and someone from their family received me at the railway station. From the Sangroor train station, I was taken in a carriage to Amrik's father's village that afternoon. I joined Amrik's friends, including Iqbal of FaridKot and Onkar of Bhadaur, and other law college friends. There was plenty of drinking; many old jokes and stories created an atmosphere of conviviality.

The next day the groom's party drove in hired buses and carriages along the dirt roads of the countryside to the bride's village in the Karnal district. Her people lived in huge brick houses, with vast common courtyards, left behind by Muslim landowners who had been forced to migrate to Pakistan nine years earlier. The bride's people were dressed in garbs and strange turbans in the style of west Punjab rural people. They were handsome, pleasant and hospitable. The next day the marriage took place according to the simple Sikh rites, and on the third day the bride was taken to the groom's village, unaware of all the struggles and negotiations that the two families had gone through. The newlyweds had never seen one another before that time. All went well and the next day I went back from Amrik's village to my place in Amritsar.

A month later, I was rushing to make arrangements to obtain a passport in order to go to school in America. Obtaining a passport in India was not an easy matter in those days. On my way from our village, I stopped at Amrik's house in Patiala briefly, to say hello and possibly to see Amrik's bride. In rural society in those days, men on the in-law side were never allowed to see a bride's face at the wedding. Among the in-law men only those who were junior to the husband could see a woman's face after her marriage. Since Amrik and his wife were now living in the city of Patiala and the husband was an educated lawyer, it seemed possible that I might see her face, unless she had decided to keep to the village customs. Amrik said that his wife was totally illiterate, but he was extremely happy with her. He said she was a very beautiful, good-natured girl with light brown hair and blue eyes. Some people in Punjab did have blue eyes, sometimes called 'cat eyes'; in fact I knew four or five blue-eyed men even in our own village population of five thousand. Amrik said he was extremely pleased with her sweet nature and had had no idea he would be lucky enough to have such a wonderful wife. He said "Fate works in mysterious ways. I fought this possibility as hard as I could, but I am fortunate that I lost and am now married to this precious girl." Either his wife was not home, or it was not his intention to let me see her; his wife never came into the living room for the short duration that I was there, and I did not ask to see her. People in our society sometimes changed their views after marriage and became reluctant to let their wives be seen by others, as if they were protecting some precious assets from robbery. Anyway, I could not stay at Amrik's house very long that day, as I had to catch the train to reach Delhi for an appointment to obtain my passport.

Not all arranged marriages turned out as well as Amrik's did. It is also hard to leave such a personal decision in the hands of others. Although matchmakers tried, according to their own judgments, to arrange marriages in which the couple would be compatible, horror stories of matches-from-hell were not hard to find. That was the last time I saw Amrik, as I left for the U.S.A., two months later. About two years later, when he stopped replying to my letters from America, I was annoyed at the change in his attitude and his failure to respond. I thought it was just a case of "out of sight, out of mind," or the fact of Amrik being a lawyer, or the urban mentality. But I did not expect this from my friend Amrik; he used to be so trustworthy! When I returned to India more than nine years later, I learned that he had died unexpectedly from pneumonia or some illness a couple of years after I left India. I never found out what happened to his wife. If I felt a loss, what did the young, uneducated, helpless widow in Indian society feel! I don't know what I have learned from his fate, except how unfair God can be, how temporary and uncertain life is, how the things that one opposes fiercely can turn out to be good fortune, and how we can struggle for the good life, only to have it all vanish due to things beyond our control. Although he died decades ago, the Amrik of my Hoshiarpur days is still in my memory.

The days of arranged marriages changed for the generation born after World War II. As people started getting more education, became employable in occupations other than farm work, and began to be economically independent, they did not have to depend on their parents property or to be under their control. They became more aware and assertive in the choice of their mates and started resisting purely arranged marriages. First, they insisted on seeing their prospective mates before deciding to marry them, even when the marriages were arranged by their parents or other relatives. Most educated people now find their own mates, and some don't get married at all. The new system and the choices people make are not without problems and heartaches, however.

Betrothal Ceremonies

There used to be elaborate engagement ceremonies called *mangna or mangni* (ask, beg, request) and sometimes called *chohara* (dried date). I don't know why the chohara was symbolically so important, but it probably came from the Persians or Arabs. "Placing the *chohara*" in the palm of the betrothed groom symbolized the pledge to give him one's daughter. The mangni ceremony took place after the conditions of dowry had been agreed upon by the parents. For the boy this ceremony was like being crowned by the girl's parents. The boy was seated on a cushion, chair or *charpai* bed, and the girl's people gave him gifts, sometimes gold coins, sweets, nuts, dry fruits, specifically including the dry date called chohara. Relatives and people in the community waved a rupee coin over the head of the betrothed—waving something over the head was considered a sanctifying

303

motion—and put the gifts in his lap. The brotherhood and relatives also made a formal contribution of money called *neonda*, but such neonda was more substantial at weddings, when it was even recorded in the *behi* record book. A family kept a record of how much neonda others had contributed, because that was like an obligation, although voluntary. A substantial gift package was then also sent by the boy's side to the girl's house, to honor her. Of course any such occasion was an excuse for teams of women from the community to sing songs appropriate to the occasion. Although the mangni started the countdown to marriage, the actual marriage might not take place until months or years had passed, depending on the ages of the betrothed and other circumstances. Breaking such an engagement was considered a very unworthy action, almost as bad as divorce. For the girl, then, preparations started for her "hope chest" and for all the things she would be taking to her husband's house as dowry.

Invitation by Sending the *Gandh*

In the rural areas in those days, all important messages had to be carried by messengers and were delivered verbally. Even after the trains were running and a postal system was functional, wedding invitations were never sent by letter in the rural society. Although some people in the village could read and write, a letter would not be considered a serious invitation. In fact a wedding invitation by letter might be taken as an insult, a snub or indifference. A letter invitation would be sent only to those whom one did not particularly want to invite. All genuine wedding invitations were made by sending the *gandh* or *gatth* (knot). The gandh messenger was usually a Nai (a barber, unemployed where the Sikhs did not need haircuts) or a Mirassi (praise singer). The gandh were just knots in pieces of cloth, sent to different villages for each relative to be invited. There might be some object and reminder in each knot, but the main object in the Gandh was a hemisphere of crystal sugar (*missri da kooza*). This missri da kooza was the size and shape of a half tennis ball, made from lumps of sugar in crystal form called missri (which looks like transparent rock candy). As he delivered the gandh invitations, the messenger would get a verbal response from the invitees. Usually they would say something like *"bari khushi nal awan gey"* (with great pleasure, we will come). They would tell everyone joyfully that the "knot has arrived" for the marriage of so-and-so and would make plans with excitement.

Each invited family received a formal knot delivered by a legitimate message carrier, not just a verbal message through a third party. Some people would invite even very remote relatives to a wedding. For example at my sister Maro's wedding in February 1942, the family of my grandmother's sister's son from the village of Mohi in Ludhiana district was invited by sending the knot through Sudhu the Mirassi, and they were highly appreciative. But a knot was also sent to the house into which my great grandfather was married in the village of Khuddi, that is, where my great grandmother was from. That family gave a rude response to our Mirassi, something like *"saada qui Mehraj katta viaha hai?"*, literally, "What calf of ours is married into Mehraj!" That sarcastic and insulting rebuff suggested that they didn't give a damn about their relatives in Mehraj. They may have rejected the invitation because of some past hurt or because the relationship was considered too remote to keep up; but most likely it was because our Mirassi just talked to some gruff old man in their house and not to any women. In general, the response to the gandh was very enthusiastic. After delivering one knot, the knot carrier would then take the next knot to the next relative in another village and mentally record their response, and so on. After World war II, the custom of sending the knots began to wane, and nowadays some people do not even understand that the expression "sending the knot" means to send a genuine invitation. Even in ordinary conversations, friends used to say: "Don't be such a stranger! Do I have to send a 'knot' to invite you to come over?"

Song Parties, Wedding Sweets and Nanka Meil

Starting about two to three months before the marriage date, women friends and neighbors would get together in the evenings in the groom's house to sing the old wedding songs. Similar song parties would be held at the bride's house. Each song was sung by a group of at least two and possibly many women, both to overcome shyness and also to harmonize like a chorus. These songs were the harbinger of a wedding and created a festive environment in anticipation of the wedding. About a week before the wedding day, sweets called *laddu, jalebi, panjiri*, and less often *balu shahi, sukkerpara* and *barfi*, etc., and an abundant supply of *pakora*, were prepared for the guests. They were cooked in large quantities in fifty- or hundred-gallon steel woks called *kraha*, the smaller woks called *krahi* being used for auxiliary purposes. A kraha was so heavy that even when empty it required two strong men to lift it. The main ingredients in laddu were noodles of chickpea-flour paste, fried in *ghee* and then dipped in thick, hot sugar syrup. After the fried noodles had been taken out of the syrup, these syrupy bits were later formed into the *laddu* balls while still warm. The *jalebi* were made from wheat-flour batter, a thin stream of which was slowly poured into frying ghee to form pretzel-like shapes; the fried jalebi were then dipped in hot syrup and later put on a grill to drip dry. The *panjiri* was a powdery mixture of flour and sugar, dry roasted in ghee with some other ingredients. The *pakora* of rural Punjab were just very thick noodles of fried chickpea paste with some mild spice or salt. For this purpose the chickpea paste was squeezed through a sieve with large round holes into boiling mustard oil. But in urban India, the same word pakora is used for different kinds of vegetable pieces dipped in spicy batter and fried in oil. During the wedding, the sweets were placed on cloth sheets, spread on the floor or on a *charpai*, as they needed to be served to the guests in large quantities. Any sweets remaining after the wedding were stored in containers. Some sweets could be kept for months, as the sugar was a good preservative, but they hardened with time.

It was the established custom to distribute the sweets (laddu, jalebi, pakora) to every house in the community. This was always done for engagements and weddings, but sometimes also for other occasions like births, and even for the deaths of special people who had lived to ripe old age. After wedding ceremonies, women volunteers from the brotherhood would distribute the wedding sweets by going from house to house in the whole community. We used to distribute sweets to our entire *patti* of Sandly and to some chosen houses in other pattis. They were given even to the houses that might not be on speaking terms with the wedding house, as the women volunteers who went to distribute the sweets were not always from the wedding house. The low castes were excluded from the regular distribution, but they would get sweets directly from the wedding house if they were their bigari (hereditary dependent workers). For children, in whose homes fat and sugar were not easy to get, the arrival of sweets from the wedding houses was a big treat.

305

Depending on the closeness of their relationship, the wedding guests, called *mel* or *meil* (meeting), started arriving at the houses of the groom's and the bride's families two to five days before the wedding. The meil party from the clan of the mother of the bride/groom were called the *nanka* meil. They were the most important, most numerous, and most rambunctious guests and added most to the festivities. They were the ones who did most of the dancing, sang the most memorable songs, and had license to exceed the norms. Their women also did the "*jago* tour" of the village streets at night, with a vessel fitted with a number of lighted mustard-oil lamps, carried on the head of a woman. They sang songs to announce the arrival of *jago* (the awake one), the sleepless, restless girl bent on partying.

In a wedding, the bride's side awaited the arrival of the bridegroom's party at the bride's family home and prepared to serve them when they arrived, usually the day before the actual wedding. The ceremony took place on the second day after their arrival, and the bridegroom's party usually left on the third day, escorting the new bride to the bridegroom's family's house. The meil guests often started leaving after the bride had departed, but depending on the closeness of their relationship, some meil parties might stay for a week. On the bridegroom's side, the meil guests stayed at the wedding house for the three days that the bridegroom's party was away at the bride's village, and then after the bridegroom's party returned to his village, they stayed for three more days while the bride was at the groom's house. After three days, the bride returned to her parents' house and the meil guests returned to their own villages. Thus, most meil guests stayed for one week at the groom's house. It should be understood that the meil that came to attend a wedding stayed only at that house and did not go as guests to the other house.

The guests who arrived many days earlier, before the wedding sweets were prepared, did not always get any fancy food. But something sweet in large amounts had to be provided according to custom. Sweets were not just a minor addition to a meal, like dessert in the West; they were the important and major part of the meal. The early meil might get just something like krah (pudding of ghee, sugar and flour) or kheer (rice cooked in milk) if the wedding sweets were not ready yet. Sometimes they did *gote kanala* (platter of tribe), which is the term for feeding of a clan sitting around one very large platter of food. In old times the ceremony of a gote (tribe, caste) sitting to eat out of one kanala (large platter) was used to denote acceptance of a man in the clan. But in my days such rituals were not observed, and gote kanala was mostly for the meil guests.

Junj, the Bridegroom's Party

Wedding preparations on the bridegroom's side were similar to the activities at the bride's house, but they had only to entertain their own *meil* and to dispatch the bridegroom's party to the bride's village. The bridegroom went through an elaborate ceremony of rubbing vatna (yellow concoction containing chickpea flour, turmeric and oil) on his skin. Then he was bathed by the clan wives and by other women relatives. He would be bathed ceremonially by the women under a canopy of a *phulkari* held by many women as they sang the appropriate songs. He got dressed, and tied a turban of some striking color, usually covered by a golden band and with a *sehra* (visor of dangling golden threads). Then he mounted his horse to depart with his junj party, accompanied by his *sarwala* (best man?). Before departure, in the *jandi-vadhen* (chopping the jand tree) ceremony the bridegroom walked around a jand tree several times and ceremonially, but lightly, struck his sword against the jand tree as he circled it. Women sang the appropriate songs during this ceremony and all during the process of departure. Then he mounted his horse and departed from the crowd of singing women with his junj party on its way to the bride's village. The departure had the earmarks of going on a campaign. No women went with the groom's party in those days. The bride's place was usually less than a half-day ride for him and his party of horse and camel riders, but it could take longer for the canopied, four-wheeled ox carriage called a *rath* that they took with them to bring back the bride. The two-wheeled ox carriages called *gadi*, although also canopied, were for less formal occasions.

The arrival of the junj at the bride's village was a colorful and noisy affair, in a normally quiet village. In the late forties, I had the opportunity to go to such an affair as an independent teenager with the junj party of Muddhoo from our village. I had decorated my black camel as best as I could. Whatever decorative equipment I did not own, such as the camel's knee bells, the flowery snout decorations and the decorative caparison, I borrowed from other people. It was the duty of the groom's family to arrange rides for anyone who did not have his own, but I had my black camel. I was accompanied on the camel by Mohinder son of Bhag Singh, Gurkhi Ka. He was about my age and was the most handsome boy in our village then. So we thought we were hot stuff and we acted accordingly! We started drinking even as we started the ride from our village and were somewhat intoxicated by the time we reached the bride's village, which luckily was only about ten miles away. The bride's folks had arranged for us to be lodged in the community *dharmasala* (inn), which is not a posh accommodation, but which is maintained in each village and is usually free to everyone. Some selected, important people in the junj (but not the bridegroom) were accommodated in the *chobara* (upper story) of the houses of the bride's family friends. In most houses the upper story was for guests or special occasions and not for routine family use. At the inn, volunteers of the bride's family had set up *charpai* beds which were borrowed from various houses of the community. The bedding consisted of a lower quilt (*gadella*) for comfort and an upper quilt (*razai*) or cotton blanket as cover. The beds and bedding, collected and set up at the lodging place for the bridegroom's party, would be returned to their owners after the wedding party departed. Although the village families gave their best beds and bedding for this purpose, one could not be sure that they were unquestionably clean. Sheets were usually not provided in those days; and not all of our people in the junj were terribly conscious of cleanliness and hygiene.

But we were not in any hurry to get to the lodge. The point was to have the camel strut his stuff and jingle his knee bells in front of the village people and to impress the women sitting on rooftops. We raced our black camel back and forth to make its knee bells jingle loudly. In our intoxicated state, we also shouted all kinds of exclamations, trying to show off, as other junj riders were showing off in their own ways.

A junj party from a substantial house used to bring its own brass band, but in our case the bride's people provided a brass band leading our way. The band marched along and played every time the junj went from the lodging to the bride's house for two meals a day, lunch and dinner. Breakfast was usually supplied at the lodging facility to anyone who had recovered from their hangover from the previous night's drinking. Some of the men were totally drunk for all three days, as free liquor was provided by the groom's people; so they did not care for any breakfast. For the customary three days the entire entourage was housed, fed and cared for, along with our horses, camels and oxen, by the clan volunteers from the girl's family. We just gave our camel to them and forgot all about it for the three days.

Sometimes, the groom's people used to bring along professional entertainers, singers and comedians; those entertainers usually played in the open in a public area for the benefit of everyones. Only the very affluent would hire a *Kanjri* (female entertainer, singer, dancer, prostitute) from the cities for entertainment at weddings. It was a respectable thing to hire the Kanjri for entertainment, but visiting a Kanjri's house was considered immoral. The traditional singers of *kallee* (Punjabi ballads) were men; they were allowed to perform in the Sutth or plaza. But *naqlia* (comedian), *nachar* (male dancers) and *Kanji* were not considered dignified enough to play in the Sutth, as some daughter or sister might pass through there and any off-color words would offend her dignity. The *naqlia, nachar* and *Kanjri* had to play in some out-of-the-way location. After 1950, with the advent of electronic sound systems, human entertainers were hired less and less often for weddings. Now the annoying practice of playing film songs through loudspeakers at high volume well into the night makes the villagers resent that unwanted noise.

On the second day the actual marriage ceremony took place at the bride's house. The ceremony in our Hindu period was performed by a Brahmin, sometimes at night, and was called *pheray* (circling around), because the couple went around the fire as the Brahmin recited the sacred words. For the Hindus, fire was one of the sacred things and was called *Agni Devta* (fire god), just as there were gods for sun, water, grain and air. In the Sikh era, the pheray around the fire was changed to *anand karaj* where the couple circled around the holy Granth four times, and the granthi recited the prescribed four passages from the holy Granth. The father or a senior man closely related to the bride would tie the knot of the bridegroom's ceremonial piece of cloth to the bride's veil, and the bridegroom would lead her slowly during the rounds as various family members assisted her walk. The bride was just like a package wrapped in red clothes and not to be seen by anybody at that time. Before and after the pheray ceremony, they chanted additional *shabads*; words of advice from a preacher or from an elder; some parting words from a friend might also be included. But the wedding couple never spoke a word, and the bride never showed her face. After the formal ceremony was over, friends and clan members would wave money over the heads of the couple and put it into their laps. Most people just watched what everyone was wearing.

At every mealtime, the girls of the village gathered around the junj guests and sang taunting and teasing songs, called *sithnian*, aimed at the bridegroom, his friends, and his relatives. Since the ceremony was usually held in the bride's courtyard, rows of singing women also sat on the roof edges and aimed their songs at the wedding party. All the work of feeding and caring for the *junj* and the *meil* (wedding guests other than the junj) was the responsibility of the men and boys of the clan. The women's job was to prepare the bride and her clothes, and to sing songs; the older women made sure the supplies were available for the men to use. The junj party stayed on for the second night and entertainment of various types continued.

Some of the songs by girls of the village had the function of "binding" the marriage party (*junj bandhni*) so that junj party had to stop eating and all acts. And some witty man from the junj party had the task of coming up with clever verses to "release" the junj, so that they could resume eating. The bridegroom had to bring along some poetic fellow who would be able to get up and recite clever rhymes to release the junj; otherwise their clan would be thought dull and witless. Some of the women's songs were about welcoming and praising the guests, but the girls also sang numerous teasing, taunting, and deriding songs, directed at the bridegroom (possibly doubting the morals of his sister, berating the habits of his mother, or belittling his friends and his clan) to get a rise out of them. If some fellow had the wit to get up and respond in rhyme, the more credit to him. Sometimes the girls played pranks, like hiding the shoes of the groom or of the best man, when they took their shoes off as they were seated to eat. Then later on they would have to negotiate with the girls for the return of the shoes. A myriad of such customs prevailed in different areas. On the third day, after early lunch, the groom's party prepared to depart and to take the bride with them.

Loading and Unloading the Bride

In those days, the *rath* carriage transported only the bride and her female attendant, but not the bridegroom. Traditionally a *Nain* (barber's woman) accompanied the bride during her travel to, and her stay at, her in-laws house, when she went from her *PeKe* (father's) to *Sohray* (father-in-law's). In still earlier times the bride used to climb into a canopied enclosure called *palki* (palanquin), *doli, or dola*, furnished like the seating portion of a carriage. This doli with the bride inside was carried on two horizontal poles by four men called *kohar*. The word doli or dola was still used later for "dispatching a bride" in a *rath* or for "giving away a daughter." The terms 'pheray' and 'doli' were so symbolic of the bride that nasty boys when fighting, would use these words for abusing like this: "May I have pheray with your sister; may I take your sister's doli." At the bride's departure, many of the women, children, and some men of the village would gather in the open; some songs would be sung, and the band would play. There would be parting hugs, and it was customary for the heavily veiled bride to sob and cry for a while before entering the doli or rath. Her face was covered; so all she had to do was to make the crying sounds. Some men would whisper that the bride was faking, but brides had no difficulty in turning on their tears at the time of departure. Older women usually said, "Don't cry dear; you are going to your own new home," but the bride's mother and possibly sisters would also cry a little bit when the doli departed. In more recent days, after the 1950s when educated brides started going with uncovered faces and smiling instead of crying at the departure time, older people whispered about such shamelessness and brazenness. Not acting shy and not pretending grief at the separation from her family used to be inappropriate behavior for a bride. Anyway, she was completely veiled and placed into the doli like package.

When the bride got into the rath, the groom's father (bride's *sohra*) and other elders had bags of coins ready. They showered those coins over the rath/doli carriage of the departing bride, whom they were preparing to take to their own village. Poor people and their children dove into the crowd in search of coins as the showers began. No Jat landowner would disgrace himself by picking up these coins, because that would be like taking from charity; but some children did it anyway. The one throwing the coins would pretend not to want to stop the coin shower, to show off his joy and big-heartedness, and the bride's people would pretend to restrain him by saying, "Oh, that is much too generous; this should be more than enough." Usually the bridegroom's elders showered enough money, so that most children and low castes could gather a little spending money; they all enjoyed the process, anyway. Most rural weddings of ordinary people were within one day's ride from home, even at the slow pace of the oxen pulling the rath. The groom and his men rode along on their own mounts like guards; a groom was not expected to sit in the rath with the bride in those days; only her female attendant, could sit in the rath.

At the bridegroom's house there was an elaborate ceremony of unloading the bride from the doli. Again she was treated like a packaged gift. This was done by the groom's sisters, wives of the bridegroom's brothers, and other wives of the same generation, to the accompaniment of traditional and appropriate songs. Before the bride could be taken through the door, the bridegroom's mother (bride's *sass*) poured oil or even ghee on the door frame as a sanctifying and welcoming ritual and put something sweet in the bride's mouth. Then the groom's mother took the *piala*, a ceremonial drink, waved the glass over the bride's head, and took a sip. The mother-in-law repeated this act of waving the drink over the bride's head and sipping several times to show her unbounded joy. Then the bride, covered in wraps of phulkari, was escorted by her sisters-in-law to the appropriate room or a corner of the house.

Traditional songs were prescribed for each step of the wedding: to welcome the bridegroom's party, to bind the junj, to load and unload the bride, and numerous other aspects of the celebration. The marriage customs, including the songs prescribed for each occasion, were fairly uniform in rural Punjab, and most of them have survived up to modern times. Once I saw a documentary program on Indian TV which covered many aspects of the Punjabi wedding celebrations, including exactly the songs that I had always heard. Evidently, all those traditional songs have been recorded without alteration.

Veil, Purdah or Ghund

The custom of the *ghund* (veil) specified that no "in-law man" who was older than the husband was allowed to see a wife's face. Wives did not have to hide their faces from a *deor* (any younger brother or cousin of the husband), however. Sometimes the bride might require a gift even from a deor before "releasing the *ghund*," and only after he had provided the gift could he see her face. When she was in doubt about a man's age, the bride could ask others or use her best judgment about whether to cover her face before a particular man. Once a man had seen her face, it was useless to cover her face before him. Therefore, most new wives gave themselves the benefit of doubt and covered their faces in any case, and a fellow could negotiate the release of the veil if he were truly younger than her husband. But wives did not need to cover their faces against a "public person" or a complete stranger, as he was not a relation of her in-laws. Most men who were not from the clan of the in-laws of the bride were considered in the category of her brothers, and she had no need of a covering veil against strangers. In general the newer the bride, the fancier her clothes, the more she would cover her face from others of the in-law village, and the more curious and tempted they were to see her face. She would reduce the coverage of her face gradually.

Sometimes a shy woman found the veil to be a convenient device, because she could see others but the others could not see her face. But some women thought it was a real inconvenience to have to pull the veil forward all the time in the presence of senior in-laws. So as not to catch the wives unaware, it was obligatory for any senior in-law to indicate his arrival by khangoora (fake coughing or clearing the throat) or by saying something not directed at anyone in particular; it was not considered proper for them to speak directly to the young wives. The system had become so rigid that it was considered acceptable for a woman to have a naked breast in front of everyone while nursing her baby, but at the same time to have her face covered. Some women who were not new brides would fulfill the obligation by holding just an edge of veil in the mouth to partially cover one side of the face, if their hands were not free for pulling the veil forward.

Giddha, Bhangra, and Boli

When the bridegroom's party departed and was away from his village for three days, the crowd of women in his parents' house had no duties except to sing and dance to celebrate; the same was true on the bride's side after the bride departed to go to her in-laws. At these times, other boys from the village would gather for the gidhha (clapping, song and dance) sessions at the marriage house. Women of the *meil* and even the local wives were obliged to join the giddha circle in the courtyard, but any unmarried girl would not be permitted to dance in such a giddha dominated by men. Unmarried girls could only join in the giddha that was performed exclusively by women.

The giddha was a performance where one person recited a *boli* (ballad, song), and with the last couplet of the boli, every one joined in the chorus. They clapped rhythmically while repeating the last couplet of the song several times. Usually half of the participants in the circle would repeat the last couplet and then the opposing half would repeat it. They repeated that last couplet alternately until someone else was ready to sing a new boli. The married women of the meil, and other wives danced to that rhythm for the duration of that refrain, until someone started another song, and this pattern of song and dance was repeated. Since the women were obligated by custom to dance, they would not be considered bold and shameless, although at times they still pretended to be shy. That was one day on which they could dance in a provocative manner if they chose; all their men would be away, gone with the junj, and most of the men present were strangers from whom they had little to fear. Young wives, and sometimes older ones also, usually in pairs, danced in the giddha circle. In any wedding giddha, dancing was the women's role, and singing, clapping and music making was the role of the boys from the village. Men and women never danced together as couples in those days. The clapping with hands gives it the name giddha, although sometimes the fellows could use small drums or other simple instruments in addition to hand clapping. This might last for hours and occasionally for two successive days. The guys who had good voices were admired for their effective delivery. I remember that once a dancing woman was so pleased with the 'boli' song of a fellow named Devan that she came to pat him on the back. This was a bold gesture and showed that she was highly impressed, because the dancing *melen*

311

usually acted shy and coy in such situations. I myself had acquired a repertoire of a hundred boli songs, but I did not have the courage to sing in the giddha where talented guys like Devan and the sons of Chand the Rosha (blond) showed their talents.

Bhangra was originally the male song and dance among some rural tribes of western Punjab, while in the eastern Punjab giddha was either exclusively the girls' song and dance during the Teeyan festival, or the performance at a wedding house as described above. In fact men in the eastern Punjab villages used to consider it unmanly to dance, and dancing was considered an effeminate activity. The only time they saw a man dancing was when the *nachaar* men dressed in female clothes with lipstick, face powder, long skirts and artificial pigtails and veils, entertained in the shows. Those dancers were not considered respectable in the rural Jat culture.

But after the creation of Pakistan in 1947, when some refugees brought the custom of bhangra dances from western Punjab, it quickly caught on in the cultural shows and on college campuses. In Pakistan, then they may have abolished the bhangra but it now thrives in Punjab & India. In 1955, when the Soviet party secretary Nikita Kruschev and premier Bulganin came to inspect the construction of Bhakra Dam on the Sutlej River in Punjab, a cultural show was staged in their honor. College authorities had invited some of us from Punjab University to assemble near the Bhakra Dam to cheer Kruschev and Bulganin. Also some teams of Bhangra dancing boys and girls had been gathered by the government from the colleges of Punjab, to perform the dances to entertain the Russian leaders in the evening. There I saw fellows like Manohar and other boys and girls participating, and they later introduced the Bhangra dance into Indian movies. Then bhangra became acknowledged as a great cultural contribution from Punjab at the Republic Day celebrations, because of its vigor, energy, and rhythm. Nowadays the distinction between bhangra and giddha is disappearing, as urban boys and girls dance together in the bhangra style at weddings and parties, just as they all dance to the film music and to popular tunes.

Women's Hairstyles

In the villages, a woman's hair was always braided and gathered, regardless of what style it might be; unbraided and loose hair was the sign of a cursed widow. The most common village style was the one with braids starting from the front and sides, with smaller braids being criss-crossed, ending in one large braid in the back. Married girls had a distinctive hairdo of braids with *saggi-phull*, the *gold* ornaments on top of the head. In the days before the 1950s, saggi-phull were an essential ornament for the front center of the head of a Punjabi rural bride; only old women or unmarried girls could be without saggi-phull. The saggi was a hemisphere shaped cup, about the size of a half orange, made from a molded layer of gold with filigree work, mounted on a silver hemisphere. To this saggi were added the phull, which were two smaller matching hemispheres, one on each side of the saggi that appeared like horn buds of gold. That saggi-phull ensemble was highly attractive on a bride's head, although it was usually covered with a veil. The new wives in the village always wore the saggi-phull for the first few years, unless they were in mourning. They could remove the saggi from the head at night, but they did not remove the phull, except when washing their hair. Unmarried girls seldom wore the saggi-phull, although some doting nanke (maternal grandparents) would have them made for their little granddaughters. Over time, a married woman might stop wearing the big saggi, but she would continue to wear the phull for at least ten or fifteen years after marriage, unless she became a widow. The saggi-phull hair-do included a highly attractive plait about three inches wide, called a *pranda or prandi*. The pranda was interwoven with the hair braids, embellished with black yarns, and wrapped with a final layer of hot pink yarn. This *pranda* plait extended from the front, at the saggi-phull, up over the crown and all the way down to the back of the head..It required special skills to be able to do the hair with the saggi-phull, and sometimes a lady had to call the Mirassi woman or the Nain (barber's wife) for a proper hairdo. A woman whose hair was not braided was either a widow or very old and unkempt. Of course no woman in Punjab would ever have a haircut in those days. Hindu women in towns wore the saggi too; it seemed strange that some of them wore the phull at the back of their heads instead of the front but still wore the saggi at the front of the head. Urban women stopped wearing the saggi-phull during the 1940s, but rural women continued to wear it a couple of decades longer.

Delousing Sessions

Lice were a fact of village life in the 1930s. Anyone who washed his hair as often as once a week was considered fashionable. Those who had to sweat much and were often in dust and dirt, needed to wash their hair frequently, but many could not. Cleaning the hair was not always easy. Heating water on the mud stove with cow-dung fuel was not the difficult part; but the available cleaning agents were most unsatisfactory. I had not seen or heard of shampoo until my brother brought a bottle in the 1940s. Heated buttermilk was the only hair-cleaning agent available in the village in those days. Ordinary soap made the hair sticky and gummy because of the hard water. After washing the hair with buttermilk, a little mustard oil was applied to the hair. Sometimes mustard oil mixed with buttermilk was heated and then used to wash the hair. Occasionally, some people washed their hair with the peel of reetha (a bitter, poisonous nut) boiled in water with the hope of killing the lice. Winter was a bad time for long hair because drying full-length hair took a long time in that season. A woman or a Sikh man would have to sit in the winter sun for quite a while waiting for the hair to dry. It was not uncommon for rural people, especially young boys, not to wash their hair or change their clothes for a couple of weeks in wintertime. Many such people had lice—big ones, medium-size ones, and lice larvae. Lice eggs, or larvae, that were white in color would stick like miniature beads along the length of a strand of hair. Clothing lice were usually white with a dark red abdomen containing human blood, but head lice were usually black or brown, although a red one might be found sometimes. Women would sit in front of one another, sometimes in tandem, to remove lice from the heads before or after washing the hair. There was a stigma about having any kind of lice, and calling someone jooan wala (lice carrier) was a form of abuse. Common lice were a serious annoyance, and the itch from their bites could keep you awake. My mother used to say that proliferation of lice was a harbinger of *zehmet* (disease) and possibly a bad omen that might indicate that some bigger calamity was about to occur. So even if one could put up with the annoyance of itching, there was some urgency about removing the lice.

As time progressed and girls started going to school, they stopped making the

313

numerous small braids. Those braids were too much work for the girls who washed their hair often. Therefore the educated ones started having only the one big braid in the back. Even that style with just one braid was called *loose hair* in the 1940s. Some city schoolgirls started wearing two braids instead of one, and people thought that was a provocative fashion. Educated women then began to think of the saggi-phull and the numerous braids as just primitive fashions, and they stopped wearing the saggi-phull even at their own weddings. They also stopped covering their faces with a veil at the time of marriage, although they still covered their heads. Educated girls started wearing their hair loose, without any braid. When I was young, such loose hair was the sign of an unfortunate and cursed widow whose countenance or presence could bring you bad luck, but after the 1950s, loose hair became common in the cities.

People used to say that whatever clothing or hairstyle the Kanjri (prostitute, entertainer caste) women wore, eventually became the fashion for all women. At first, a few daring women copied the entertainers' style, and a few years later the rest of the culture followed those fashions. The prostitute caste was accused of being the fashion trend-setters in the land as the movie stars are now. My father used to say deridingly that all new fashions are started by the Kanjri women, and therefore it was immoral for the girls from good families to follow the new fashions.

Jewelry and Ornaments for the Bride

Before her wedding day a bride was expected to dress unobtrusively in drab, unattractive clothes. Her ears and nose would have been pierced many years earlier, and frequently she would wear inexpensive fillers in her pierced ears and nose. For the wedding day, her hands and feet were colored with *mehndi* and her skin got a special massage with *vatna,* mentioned earlier. Mehndi is the powdered leaf of a plant made into a paste that produces the *henna* red color if left on the hands for some time. The longer the mehndi paste was left on the skin, the more intense the color became. There was a superstition that the more intense the mehndi color became, the more control the bride would have over her husband and her in-laws. Nowadays the custom of mehndi application has become even more elaborate. Mehndi was not for men or boys. As a rebuke, fellows would say to a reluctant worker, "Why can't you grab the tool; is there mehndi applied to your hands?"

I don't know the complete details about the preparation of a bride, but she was loaded with ornaments, her hair was done with saggi-phull, and she got the best *red* clothes the family could obtain for the marriage ceremony. Other ornaments were optional, but a bride without red clothes, saggi-phull, ear and nose ornaments, and some kind of necklace was unthinkable in Punjab villages in those days. There might be a whole row of rings for the rim of each ear, called *murkia*n; other earrings called *nuttian* and *tungle,* and the large hoops called *baley* or *balian,* were worn in the earlobes. Sometimes a woman wore golden 'sleeves' called *boojli* in her earlobes, and then the *dandian* hoop rings could pass through the boojli sleeves. There were several possible ornaments for the nose. A *koka* was a small gold pin on one side of the nose, usually temporary and replaced later by the larger golden *teeli* or *long.* The *nutth* was a large nose ring with gold leaves, passing through one side of the nose and sometimes tied to the ear by a silk thread to prevent entanglement. The nutth ring was cumbersome and therefore was worn only for the first few days of marriage or for special occasions. A *machhli* was a ring with gold leaves dangling from the central septum of the nose and partially hiding the mouth.

Wherever there was a suitable space on a woman's body, there was an ornament for it. The golden necklaces called *kunthi, hussli,* and *haar* were of various designs and embellishments; a *hamel haar* was a necklace of gold or silver coins. For the fingers there were the *chhaap, chhalla or mundri* rings. Bangles and bracelets (*bang, churi, kangan, kara*) for the wrists came in various designs. Toe rings were not common, but there were *jhanjer, pattri* and *pazeb* pairs of anklets, made of silver and with tiny bells; from the sound of the tiny bells on the pazeb you could tell if the bride was coming your way. I was most fascinated by the intricate construction of the *pazeb* (foot ornament), a wide band of links with bells at the bottom that went all around each ankle of the bride.

My mother wore most of those ear and nose ornaments in the early days but had mostly empty holes in her nose and ears in later years. Her brothers had given her much more jewelry than other houses ordinarily gave to their daughters, but her jewelry was gradually sold off by my father, and the proceeds were used for major purchases. My father turned against jewelry when he got initiated as an amritdhari Sikh and did not allow any of his daughters even to pierce their ears. After marriage, his oldest daughter, Maro, got her ears pierced at her in-laws' house. In her in-law village, going without jewelry would have been considered very unfortunate for a woman. What distinguished a wife of the village from a daughter or a widow were her jewelry, her colorful clothing, and her *ghagra* (big skirt).

A girl could wear *bindi* on her forehead or a *tikka* ornament with three golden leaves dangling at the center of the forehead. The *kanjri* women had started wearing *shingar* as a head ornament and no longer wore the saggi-phull. Later, some sophisticated women also wore the *shingar* chain going back along the parting of the hair.

Bride's Clothes and Dowry:

In addition to jewelry, utensils, bedding, and the *sandooq* (a large four-legged wooden box), personal clothes were the major item of dowry in a marriage. Girls would start embroidering and making other items of clothing, even before they were nine years old. The *phulkari* and *baagh* were the veils and covers, made from home-made thick cotton cloth, colored maroon, and embroidered in various patterns with silk thread called *putt* or *rayshem.* The baagh was just larger and was embroidered more densely than phulkari and could be used as wrap over other clothing in winter. For most women, the phulkari and baagh were not worn much after the first couple of years of marriage, and were usually given to others as gifts or to girls in the next generation. Ample supplies of *chunni* or *dupatta,* the veils of finer cotton, or silk, with or without embroidery, sequins, or appliqués of the golden tape called *gota,* were a must for every bride. The dowry sometimes also included home-made *durri* carpets and cotton blankets called *chuttahi* and *khes* for spreading on beds. Men could use the khes to wrap around their bodies in cold weather. Some brides took *razai* and *gadella quilts* to her in-law's house.

There was great emphasis on expensive suits of silk and other shiny or luxuriantly soft cloth in dazzling colors. The number of such suits given to the bride could be as many as two to four dozen. Parents felt that they had to provide enough fancy clothes so that she would look like a new bride every day for several years. That is why it is not unusual to see women laborers in India sweeping the streets in dazzling, expensive-looking clothes. Even in remote villages women knew of various kinds of cloth such as bulbulteen (velveteen), China silk, chenille, georgette, and gornat; I never learned the meanings of all those names. To children the whole wedding scene seemed like part of an unreal fairy tale, the clothes were so dazzling to see, so smooth to touch and rub, and the bride and newer wives were so beautiful, a great contrast with the conditions of everyday life in the village. Now I am impressed the same way when I see the English royalty of the Victorian period in cinema scenes. As well as the bride and groom, every member of the wedding house and the meil guests had new suits of clothes made for the occasion. In the modern affluent society new clothes are routine, but in those times a new suit of clothes was a big deal for village people.

Moklawa, the Final Step

The engagement and wedding were just the preliminaries, and not yet the time for the wedding couple to get together. Right after the marriage ceremony, the bride came to the bridegroom's house for only three days. During that time, she was continuously surrounded by women of the household and the *meil*, and she was guarded by the *Nain* (barber's woman) who was the attendant sent by her parents to look after her. So much was going on at the wedding house that the bridegroom would not usually have any chance to see her or talk to her; and custom dictated that the bridegroom not be in her company until *moklawa*. "Moklawa" literally means opening up or getting comfortable and was put off until a later time. During the marriage visit she was like a possession of the groom's whole family. Very adventurous husbands would bribe the Nain and get a chance to speak to the bride when no one else was around, but usually the Nain acted like a gatekeeper and just said, "The bride is too shy to talk." And that was considered an acceptable excuse, as shyness was considered a virtue in a bride. About the third or fourth day the bride with the attendant Nain would return to her parents' house.

Depending on the situation, weeks, months, or even years could pass after the marriage ceremony before the *moklawa* was arranged. That was not like a honeymoon in the sense of going somewhere on a trip following the wedding; it was the time when the bride finally went to live with the husband's family. This additional step of moklawa was necessary partly because some boys and girls could be married before the age of twelve. The parents were always in a hurry to perform their children's marriage. Much of the dowry (except jewelry), such as clothes, bedding, and the sandooq, were given not at the time of wedding but at the time of moklawa, to be taken to the groom's house. This time no female attendant came with the bride, but a brother sccompanied the bride and groom during the journey; and then the brother returned after leaving her in her new home. In modern times, the interval between the wedding and moklawa became shorter, and frequently it became a "combined wedding and moklawa." More recently, the moklawa as a separate event has been dispensed with; now the young people marry when they are ready to live together.

Ghori, Jori, and Kantha for Bridegroom

It should be remembered that other than clothes and possibly some gold jewelry, the dowry items were not supposed to be in the control of the bride; they were supposed to be given to the house into which she was married. The husband's family could do whatever they wanted with the dowry assets, although if there was no disharmony, there would be no problem. In the villages, a substantial house would expect that the bride's family would give at least three items to the bridegroom: a ghori (horse), jori (two gold bracelets), and a kuntha (men's gold necklace). These items were usually given to prosperous bridegrooms in addition to any other negotiated dowry items. The horse given by the in-laws was a matter of great pride for a man, but he would not wear the jori and kuntha routinely.

Showing the Bride and Her "Clothes"

When the bride first came to the groom's house following the wedding, a *Mirassi* or caller was sent to all houses in the community to invite the women to come and "see the bride." Of those coming to see the bride, only the close friends and family members would wave a rupee coin over her head and put it in her lap; a rupee was three or four days' wage for a laborer then. The veiled bride did not smile or talk in such situations; the women would line up to lift her veil one by one, so that only one of them at a time could see her face. There were always comments about how the wife looked, but with all the decorations and jewelry, the bride was seen at her best, so the comments were generally favorable. As long as she was not too skinny, women would describe her as beautiful. Most women just talked about her complexion, her gold jewelry, and her clothes. Sometimes a naughty fellow put on a ghagra skirt, donned a veil to hide his own face, and sneaked into line among the women. He could lift the bride's veil to look at her face, and his guise might not be discovered until it was too late. If the guy was younger than the husband, most people could just laugh it off, but if he was older than the husband it was considered highly improper and a serious violation to pull such a prank.

While the bride and her jewelry could be seen at the time of marriage, the "clothes" were shown at the time of moklawa. The Mirassi caller would again be sent to every neighborhood to tell the women to "please go and see clothes of the bride of such and such house." The custom of showing the clothes, utensils, bedding, furniture, the sandooq, and all other things that the bride brought from her parents' house was pretty well standardized. The clothes and all the goods were spread on portable charpai beds or placed nearby. Women did not forget for years what someone's wife had brought as dowry. Everything except cash was displayed on the beds in the courtyard. Even children could accompany mothers and sisters to such events and would look at the shiny, colorful clothes with amazement. As a child I had gone with my sisters to some showings and was in awe of the apparent splendor of the wedding clothes, as I touched and rubbed the soft silks and shiny chenille between my fingers. I would be tempted even to rub the silky and shiny clothes that the newer wives were wearing on those occasions. Sometimes I rubbed their salwar cloth between my fingers secretly, when they were not aware; I had to be careful not to actually touch their legs or torso, because I could have got into trouble.

Rural weddings were not just sober, private affairs. Although food was provided only for the meil guests, for the closest members of the clan, and for the groom's junj party, the larger community shared in the event to some extent, either as volunteers, spectators, singers, dancers, or organizers of entertainment. They certainly received the sweets distributed to every house. Giddha/Bhangra was staged by the boys of the village with the cooperation of the nanka meil women guests. Uninvited girls of the village would come in groups and would sing songs as the groom's wedding party ate lunch or dinner. Just about all activities and ceremonies related to marriage were accompanied by singing of songs. Crowds looked down from rooftops since many of the activities were in the courtyards and sometimes under canopy-like covers. Whether the groom's party was leaving or returning, or whether the bride was being loaded or unloaded from the carriage, there would be crowds watching the whole spectacle, and the women would be singing. In such an event, some castes would be on the periphery looking for handouts. And if the wedding was in a famous house, some undesirables like the *khusra* (hermaphrodite) groups, dressed as women, refused to budge and insisted on being paid, or they would raise a stink with their songs.

CHAPTER 16

DEATH AND MOURNING RITUALS

Untimely death was pretty common in our society, as it was without modern medical care. I heard that life expectancy in India was only 26 years when I was a toddler in 1931; the life expectancy had gone up to 32 years by 1941. People could become grandparents in their thirties; fifty years was considered old age, when many people died, although a few lived beyond eighty years and even into their nineties. Small dead babies, below the speaking age, were just buried in the earth, but a dead adult had to be cremated with proper rituals. Indian culture considered burial to be degrading to a human. They thought that putting a body under dirt to be trampled over, and perhaps even urinated upon by animals forever, was demeaning. Offering the dead body to the God of Fire (Agni devta) was a sanctifying action and was considered the appropriate last rite for a human.

A dead man's body would be given a bath by men of the family; a dead woman's would be washed by women. Then the deceased would be dressed in new clothes, put on a ladder-like wooden contraption called a *seehri*, and covered with a new white cloth. The word for the burial clothes was cuffin, probably from Persian. Then the corpse on the seehri was carried by sons, nephews or younger men to the cremation grounds. It was inauspicious to have anyone older than the deceased as a pallbearer, since that would imply that he/she did not leave any younger males behind. As the dead body was placed on the funeral pyre, recitation of some passages from the Sikh scriptures and final Ardas (prayer) was performed by one of the elders, and then the pyre was lighted. In our area there was no custom of a Sikh priest performing the last rites, and we had abandoned the Brahminical customs at least a generation earlier. Every attempt was made to cremate a person on the same day that the person died, although this was not always possible; cremation at night was inauspicious. Unlike births, deaths were not officially recorded.

In our culture it was forbidden for family members to eat as long as the dead body was waiting to be cremated. That is why there was some rush to proceed with the cremation immediately after death, if there was any daylight left. Also, sitting on furniture was a taboo when there was a dead body around or when you were in serious mourning. During the mourning process, people had to sit on the ground, usually on a carpet-like *putti*, sometimes covered with a sheet. For months afterwards, whenever anyone came to console and condole, he would begin the visit by squatting on the ground as a mark of mourning before exchanging many words. Then the bereaved family quickly provided a mat or something for the guest to sit on the ground, and they themselves would also sit on the floor. Only some time later, at the urging of the family, would the visitor sit on a *charpai* or other furniture. In ordinary situations, if someone was sitting on the floor, except while praying or doing work that required sitting, the women would say, "Please don't sit on the floor; it is a bad omen!" In mourning, in prayer, and in some mass gatherings one could sit on the ground but not ordinarily in the house.

While men made the funeral arrangements, it was the women who did the heavy mourning, wailing, keening, and crying. *Siapa* was the general word for mourning activities, and *pittna* was a form of physical expression in which women would beat their thighs with their hands repetitively while standing and sometimes while walking. Less frequently, they would slap other parts of their bodies to display the feeling of extreme pain and loss. Siapa was accompanied by anguished verbal expressions. The siapa and pittna activities were sometimes intense and extreme in the initial stages of a mourning session, which was then followed by more verbal wailing and *baen* (dirges). The baen were performed by women of the community gathered in the house of the deceased, producing stylized, slow, mournful sounds with varying tones. In the baen, the chorus would produce one vowel tone at a time, "Ooooo...oooo," for many seconds and then switch to another vowel tone, "Aaaaaaa..aaaaa," then to "Eeeeeee..eeeee," then to "Uuuuuuu..uuu," and so on. Then one of the women would eloquently recount the loss to the family, or the fate of the young widow or widower, or the children left behind, the deserted *haveli* (mansion), the acres of land and crops, and sometimes even the thirsty oxen or buffaloes waiting for him. The lead woman usually described one fact in a sentence at a time; then it was followed by the collective baen of all the women repeating the vowel tones. Then the same or another woman could start another sentence, followed by the collective chorus of baen. If a woman was experienced and verbally skillful, she would tailor the elegy to suit the situation, and at the end of her elegy the whole chorus would join in the slow baen. Then another woman would recount the memorable deeds, the associations, and the unfinished tasks of the deceased, and at the end of each item she would be joined by others in the collective dirge. Experienced mourner women of the neighborhood who were creative and poetic in their recitations, were expected to come and join in the dirges. This could go on for hours and could be repeated for shorter periods during the following days and weeks.

But the really heart-rending baen came from the wife or the mother. Right after the death, the mother and the wife were too overwhelmed by grief to verbalize; but in the following days, or when someone came to express grief, they could burst with emotions. Once I went with my friend Mukand to express grief to his wife's cousin who had become a widow at a young age, when her husband died in an accident. The wailing of that young widow was hard for me to bear, and her words in Punjabi went like this: "Oh light of my eyes, why did God shut you down in your prime; why did you struggle so much, only to have the best years stolen from you! Who will your young children turn to; why did God inflict this tragedy on your wife! All these houses, fields and property are worthless without you; all gold and silver are worthless without you; I am pushing my life away as it has no value without you; this world looks dark and deserted without you, O son of my father-in-law...." Her grief was so overpowering and she was so eloquent, that sixty years later I still have not forgotten her words of pain.

It was obligatory for a *mukaan* (mourning party) to go to a deceased relative's village to express grief. When women of the mukaan party approached the house of the deceased, they started beating their thighs in siapa and uttering the standard sounds and words of mourning loudly. The mukaan party usually chose some experienced and articulate mourner to go along, so younger people were never a part of the mukaan. If an old person had died and the mukaan was merely fulfilling a ritual, the women of the mukaan party could laugh and tell jokes on the way until they got close to the house; but for an untimely death, this was an unpleasant duty. If it was a distant relative, just one person could go to perform the ritual of mukaan and fulfill the obligation; but for an important death, the mukaan consisted of a team of several men and women mourners. Men would just sit quietly or say something simple; it is the women who appeared to dramatize the scene. It would be a serious social error not to go for mukaan in a timely fashion.

A siapa aroused the emotions and was disturbing to hear. It sometimes happened that some vicious and derelict women, after being angry with a family, tried to cause them serious hurt. She could not beat them up, so she would try a mean tactic. She would stand in front of their house at night and would start the siapa by wailing and pittna (by slapping her thighs.) And she would shriek, declaring that she had come for the mukaan (mourning the death) of their sons. Although no sons were dead, and she did it just as a form of severe abuse and a curse, hearing such words would be extremely painful and upsetting for the house. And since she would usually do such shrieking at night, it was doubly shocking and disturbing. But sometimes nothing could be done to prevent the defying and abusing old woman. In fact the humiliated and traumatized family feared the escalation of her activity if they retaliated, because such a woman, without any family or assets, would have nothing to lose. Her abuses and curses declaring the death of sons were hurtful and not merely annoying. That was the one situation when people with sons were vulnerable, as no one would wish death to their daughters.

Sometimes when young girls got into mean fights with other girls, they would slap their own thighs and say, "*Tere veer da siapa kardi haan*," or "*Tere bhaian nou pittdi haan*", which means, "I am doing the siapa (mourning) of the death of your brothers." Boys were considered precious, and families were always concerned for their health and safety, so the ultimate hurt or curse to a family was to wish death for their sons or to act out by saying that their sons had died. When a young girl got angry, she could abuse the opponent by calling her "*Bhra nu* Pittni," which means "mourner of brother." No one would abuse another by saying, "mourner of sister."

Cremation Ashes taken to Hardwar

Some Semitic religions believe that without proper burial a person will not be resurrected when the Savior comes to wake the dead. In the Punjabi tradition, cremation was the sanctifying act, because Sikhs and Hindus believe that once the soul leaves the body, that body is never going to live again; the soul will just enter another body. And if the ashes of a dead person were not cast into the river Ganga at HarDwar, it was felt that the survivors in the family had not honored the dead person. God would not be pleased with those who remained behind, as they did not do their dharmic duty. Some even believed that the soul of the dead person might trouble the descendents if they did not

321

fulfill their last duty to him. So on the third day following the cremation of the deceased, the remains of the burnt finger and toe bones and some additional ashes were collected from the cremation residue. These ashes of fingers and toes, called "phull," were usually put in a jar with a lid, and a piece of cloth was tied over the lid to keep it sealed. A few weeks to a few months later, someone had to undertake the journey to a place called HarDwar (God's door), in the Himalayan hills on the bank of the Ganga River, before the Ganga descends into the plains. There, the ashes of the deceased were poured into the Ganga after some rituals. It was a journey of many days each way, as the one carrying the ashes went on foot in the days before the trains came and many did so even later.

As schism developed between Hindus and Sikhs after the partition of India, some Sikhs decided that the Sutlej River, a tributary of the Indus in Punjab, was as holy as the Ganga River; then the Sikhs began to cast the ashes into the Sutlej at Kiratpur. After the June 1984 attack the Golden Temple in Amritsar by the Indian army and the massacre of Sikhs all over India after the assassination of Indra Gandhi, many more Sikhs began to cast the ashes of their dead into the Sutlej instead of the Ganga. But the history of the Jats is tied to HarDwar, where there are Brahmins whose hereditary profession has been to maintain the record of deaths. Those Brahmins have records for the Sidhu Brards of Mehraj for the last 400 years. This is partly because the Maharajas of the Phulkian states, whose ancestors have dominated southern Punjab for 250 years, have a common ancestry with our Mehraj families. Each Brahmin of HarDwar maintains records for specific villages and families. Any time someone goes to immerse ashes into the Ganga, he is steered to the appropriate Brahmin who does the rituals and handles the records for that family. And that Brahmin updates the information about all the deaths, births, and living individuals of the bereaved family. The Brahmin expects a donation for his services, so he is always courteous and solicitous. When my father died in April 1984, before Indra Gandhi ordered the army to attack the Golden Temple, we took his ashes to HarDwar on the Ganges. But in November 1995 we took the ashes of my mother to Kiratpur on the Sutlej river. The Sikh recorders there do write down whose phull were brought for immersion on what date, but they do not maintain genealogies of the families.

There was a feeling of loss at any death in the immediate family, regardless of the age and circumstances, but when a person died at a ripe old age, the rituals were quite different. If the deceased was over fifty years old and did not leave any unmarried daughters, his obligations and tasks in life were considered complete. If he had grandsons, he surely had reason to leave the world satisfied. If he was wealthy and influential, his sons considered it a matter of pride to distribute the *gadaura* in his name. Although gadaura was only a hard cake made mostly of sugar, its distribution was an uncommon ritual in the villages. It was distributed not merely to every house in the village of the deceased but also in the wider area as a mark of the prestige and prominence of the dead man. Not many families felt qualified to distribute gadaura even if they could afford it financially, since it would be considered pretentious to do so. Therefore, the distribution of gadaura was quite rare. The expression used to be, "Why are they acting so uppity! Has their family distributed gadaura?" Nevertheless, even an average family celebrated the death of an older person, if it occurred at the appropriately ripe age, and if that person did not leave any unmarried daughters behind. Sweets were prepared after such a death, as if for a wedding, and they were distributed in the village. Even we distributed sweets in our village at my mother's death. People shared food and gave alms to celebrate a well-lived life and a good end to an old person's life.

Doll Cremation and Mourner Training

Like everywhere else, young girls played with dolls and in Punjab such play activity involved the life cycle of dolls. They dressed and undressed the dolls, and they performed the marriage of boy doll and girl doll with all the rituals and songs. Dolls had babies and some dolls died. In early summer, about a month before the *Teeyan* festival, there used to be a young girl's activity, lasting for a good part of a day, in which a female doll was supposed to have died. Groups of girls used to go through the rituals of doll death, preparation for her last rites, the activity of siapa, pittna, wailing, dirges, taking the doll to the cremation grounds for proper rites, building a pyre, placing the doll on it, and setting fire to the pyre. Then they came home wailing and performed the baen and dirges according to their abilities, followed by the conclusion of the mourning rituals. This was a way to act out the rituals related to death and mourning. The impact of death was felt frequently by people, since everyone knew most other people in the village; life expectancy was short, and people died from time to time. So it was useful for a woman to be able to manage such situations rather than feel like an ignorant dunce. The play and ritual of doll cremation provided some training for the young girls, just as the Teeyan festival provided training in the singing and dancing activities.

CHAPTER 17

FESTIVAL OF TEEYAN, CELEBRATING RAINY SEASON

Village people used to hold Yugg (a charitable feast) in the name of the God Inder with the hope of rain. Young girls would sing, "*Bhaian ne bandh le pour, oh meenh pa de Rabba,*" which means, "Oh God send some rain, as the brothers have tied *pour* to the plough and are ready to sow." The rains start first in southwest India with the arrival of the monsoons. Later, these monsoons hit the mountains of northeastern India. As they are stopped by the Himalayan range, sometimes the storms turn west. Then these nearly spent but eagerly awaited clouds reach the Punjab plains by mid-July with the meager leftover moisture. That is why rains in Punjab are chancy, scanty, and unpredictable. The rains of the month of Sawan (after mid-July) also provide some relief from the heat. So nothing was received with as much reverence and joy as the rain in the semi-arid Punjab before the advent of irrigation canals. One would watch the monsoon clouds as they came over the horizon from the east or north, usually in a broad front that was gray or white. Girls sang joyful songs about the kali ghata (black cloud front) as a welcome sign. Unlike the European climates, good weather in Punjab was the one with lot of clouds and some rain or drizzle. Such a cloudy duzzly day could inspire the school principal to declare a "fine day" holiday.

Sometimes the rain came down with full force, with a lot of thunder and lightning. It was a common superstition that lightning seeks certain kinds of people. For example, a little boy and his maternal uncle being together were considered the most vulnerable to a lightning strike. Farmers liked it best when the rain fell in a slow drizzle for many days, since that soaked the ground better without washing it away. But any rain was welcome, as it filled the ponds and allowed the ploughs to run by softening the earth; the farmers could not plough, much less sow, the un-irrigated lands without rain. During the summer rains, little boys used to stand under the water pouring from the spouts off the roofs; in the heat, any contact with water was a joyful experience. When the water first accumulated in the ponds, young buffaloes pranced about in excitement. The air was washed clean, and the trees appeared greener as all the dust was washed off. We all felt elated during and after the rain. All of a sudden the universe appeared benign and comfortable. Women cooked *gulgula* (deep fried sweet dough) and *poora* (sweet crepes) to celebrate the rain. Within a couple of days of the first rain, a myriad of creatures appeared from nowhere. One always wondered, where did all those teams of frogs come from, when there were none a few days ago! Some people said the frogs had gone to the underworld (*patal*) and the rain had just called them back. Locust-like crickets on *akk* plants and large, soft bodied, scarlet beetles on the ground appeared from nowhere, along with fireflies and a zillion other creatures. Within a week, plants started sprouting everywhere. The farmers were happy to welcome the sacred rain and their daughters started the *songs of Teeyan*.

Teeyan was the girl's festival, possibly originating from a celebration of the first rain of the season. Teeyan came officially on the *Teej* (third) day of the month of *Sawan* of the Bikermi calendar, just after mid-July. Young girls started going into groves of trees before the Teej of Sawan and launched their rope swings, anticipating the season. During the day in the Teeyan season, the girls gathered under the trees on their own side of the village to play, sing, dance, and gossip. In our side of the village, sometimes they staged simple skits and plays under the trees. No one objected if little boys, below seven years or so, went to watch them. Once I watched a mock wedding, complete with a girl with a turban acting as the bridegroom and a more articulate older lady acting as the Brahmin performing the marriage ceremony according to Hindu rites. She recited rhymes in praise of "my jajman (client), *satyvan* (powerful), prosperous landowner, generous, owning many milk cows and donator of pearls." In the 1930s the Punjabi village culture was still permeated with Brahminical customs. Some girls brought small portable *charpai* to sit in groups in the shade of the trees, and the older ones embroidered or knitted as they enjoyed the gatherings. Young tomboys would climb high tree branches, and others would tie ropes to tall pipple or neem tree branches to make long swings. This was also the time when many newly married girls and those not yet completely bogged down in their married life chose to come back to visit their parents' village and to have reunions with their old *saheli* (girl friends). Since Teeyan was a season lasting weeks and not just one day, it was therefore a time for the girls' reunions as well.

Later in the afternoons and into the twilight hour, the main Teeyan gathering became a big affair, when girls from all sides of our village, numbering in hundreds, gathered in one location. The designated Teeyan grounds were an open area north of our village near the House of Padres. The girls who chose not to walk that far also had a smaller gathering on their own side of the village for singing and dancing. There was no age limit, but the crowd tended to be younger, including the visiting married girls and some relatively new wives of our village who could not manage to go to their own parents' village for the Teeyan season. Many people felt that the Teeyan festival in Mehraj was better than anywhere else in Punjab in those days, so some young wives chose to stay in Mehraj instead of going to their own parents' village for the festival. A daughter of the village could go, no matter how old she was, and could meet old friends there. But a wife of the village could also be escorted there by the girls if she was newly wed, just to check out the scene and to show off her clothes and jewelry. There was more than one giddha circle for singing and dancing in the Teeyan grounds and perhaps some other entertainment arranged by the girls themselves. The principal activities of the festival were singing, dancing, people-watching, and gossip. Girls caught up on everybody's news and found out who was doing what. Some got to boast about their new lives. When they came home, girls always commented on the clothes and jewlry of the fashionable girls and of the newlyweds. For the rest of the year, they continued to talk about the happenings at the Teeyan gathering and described who the prettiest and most popular girls were.

On the periphery of Teejan there were vendors of fruit, candy, and ice cream, etc., but men were not allowed to go into the festival itself. A visiting husband of a girl, being in a privileged position, could sometimes wander through the Teeyan festival casually without violating any one's sensitivities, but a man from the same village could not go close. The festival would last three to four weeks, depending on the whims and dictates of the popular and influential girls. The girls would go to the Teeyan in small groups of friends, but they usually returned in large groups, walking through the major streets, singing songs of joy and celebration, of clouds and rain, of flowers and crops and of the blessed village of their brothers and elders.

The most conservative old men decried the prolongation of this 'frivolous, senseless carnival.' Some said it took the girls away from housework for too long; some said they wasted money buying glamorous clothes for the Teeyan and got bad ideas about fashion and such things. Others said that the reason too little rain was falling was that the girls' continued the extravagance and laughter for too long and that God did not like such frivolity and laughter. My father was against the frivolity of Teeyan, and used to say, "the Muslim rulers encouraged Teeyan; that way they could see who was going out to Teeyan and could pick the best looking girls to take away forcibly." Speaking against another religion and the oppressive invaders of the past was fashionable; in reality Islam was not in favor of such pagan celebrations as Teeyan. Under the influence of my father, at the age of about twelve, even the otherwise gentle Kartar tried to prevent our older sister Maro from going to Teeyan, thinking that he was carrying out his father's wishes. One day there was a dragging, crying, scuffle between Kartar and Maro as she stepped out to join her friends to go, and Kartar tried to prevent her. At the time, I was too young to do much about my sister's shrieks, but some elders of the village who witnessed the incident, said harsh things to Kartar for interfering with his sister's departure, and Maro went crying to the Teeyan festival that day.

As the girls' groups coming back from Teejan passed through the Sutth, the elderly men sitting in the plaza would say, "Bibi, please perform the *ballho* (ceremonial conclusion) of your Teejan festival tomorrow; it has already been too long!" The girls would say that it was not in their control to end the Teejan, and that the popular and influential girls from the other side of the village did not want to end the festival yet. When they did end the season, it was done with songs of protest about the pressure from the killjoy, elderly men to "shorten the festival by so many days." Once I heard their song of protest as they were returning through the plaza. Some rhymes of the song translated from Punjabi, went like this: "Black cloud front came climbing, Oh brothers in your raj; We have come home after playing the Teeyan, Oh brothers in your raj; but the Teeyan festival was reduced by six days, Oh brothers in your raj," and so on.

CHAPTER 18

DIVERSITY OF DRESS MODES

In my younger days, clothing was not just to cover the body; it used to be a statement about one's religion, caste, or status. For a man the turban was the principal indicator of who he was. Before the 1940s, men of all religions in our village wore turbans; the turban was essential for being dressed, respectable, and respectful to others. Sikhs, Hindus, and Muslims had slightly different styles of turbans, and an educated man would not tie his turban as rural people did.

Mystique of the Turban

There was a saying, "You can judge a man by *Raftar, Guftar, Dastar.*" These Persian words mean that you can judge him by his *walk* or *mannerisms*, by his *speech*, and by his *turban*. It is true that the turban usually represented the essence of the man. The kind of cloth, the skill in winding the turban, and especially the style in which it was tied, could indicate religion, caste, social status, education level, character, tendencies, expected behavior, and the region the wearer came from. Whatever else a man was wearing, the attention of others was first drawn to his turban and mainly the turban determined how others treated its wearer. Clever fellows sometimes gained access to favorable situations just by tying the turban in the appropriate style to look respectable, rich, or sophisticated. If someone was not skilled at tying a turban, he would get someone else to tie the turban for him on a special occasion like marriage, in order to make a good impression. A man could be stopped by police for questioning just because of the wild, or suspicious style of his turban, while another man with a proper *Patiala Shahi* turban walked by unquestioned. As with turban profiling, there were cases of beard profiling, in which the police might consider a Sikh with shaved beard as a suspect character.

People in locations 50 miles apart could have turbans of radically different styles, and the turbans of educated urban people differed from those of rural people. The turbans of the Malwa region south of the Sutlej river were different from those in Majha (Middle Punjab). Fashionable Muslims used to wear a *qullah* under the turban. The qullah, a conical hat, served as the foundation and was stiff enough so that the turban wound around the qullah base could be removed and put back on the head without collapsing. The *Rajputs* had a distinct style of turban and so did the Pathan traders. Some orthodox

Sikhs, like the *Kookas*, wore the rounded turban of olden times. The Sikh Gurus were usually pictured with the same round, free style of turban, starting with a *pech* (turn, round, layer) at the forehead and building the successive pech to cover the head with the rest of the cloth. Local prejudices led people to think that those visiting from other locations had funny-looking turbans, and they always had strange accents as well; their accents and turbans were a dead giveaway of their origin. Sometimes a young boy tried to look funny by tying his turban 'like a foreigner' and imitated the strange accents of other regions to entertain his friends.

A turban could be given as a gift, to honor a man, or as a symbol of succession (a son succeeding his father). The turban was also used in many symbolic acts, such as coming in abject humiliation and apology, or begging a favor by taking one's turban off and putting it at the feet of the person being appeased and conciliated. 'Putting one's turban at the feet' of anyone was like putting one's honor at the mercy of that person and begging his favor. Even the expression "I am ready to put my turban at your feet" was considered the ultimate in humility and appeasement. On the other hand, 'to take somebody's turban off in an assembly', was a way of dishonoring the person and was the ultimate insult. Removing and 'throwing one's own turban off' meant being furious, outraged, or blowing one's top. Symbolically 'exchanging turbans' with a very close friend would mean sworn, faithful, lifelong friendship. Exchanging turbans was a serious pledge of friendship and loyalty, and it was not done frequently or lightly. When a fellow said, "The sardar of such-and-such village is a turban-exchange friend of my father," it meant that the sardar would do anything and make any sacrifice for his friend. Although I never had a "turban-exchange friend," my relationships with my friends Nawab Din (though a Muslim) in the village and later with Amrik Singh Aulakh (in college) were as close as that. Tragically, both died in their twenties. Even some girls and women would exchange *chunni* (veil) or d*upatta* with their *saheli* (girl friend) as a mark of faithful friendship, but turban exchange was a far more serious matter.

Notwithstanding all of the above, a turban was merely to protect the head and to cover the hair. Except when you were engaged in strenuous or athletic activities, having a bare head in public was considered informal, undressed, bad manners, or disgraceful, depending on the situation. It was an omen of bad luck to encounter a bare-headed person while starting on an important journey or task. It would be *avgun* (the opposite of virtue) for a man or woman to serve food when he or she was bare-headed. Even women said in derogatory tones to their daughters, "How disgraceful! You are sitting around with *nanga jhatta* (bare hair)!" A Sikh could not go into the gurdwara with a bare head. It would be very insulting to a dignitary if you bared your head in his presence. Usually, a bare head meant that you were undressed and were exposing an important part of your body without any reason. The turban certainly provided protection from sun, wind, cold, and minor blows to the head. Your hair might be messy, dirty, or disorganized, you might have gray or completely white hair, or you might even be completely bald, but no one could know what was under your turban. A woman I knew used to say, "A turban covers a lot of sins!" During the 1940s, some younger Hindus and Muslims in the village stopped wearing turbans, but Sikhs *had* to wear the turban to manage their hair. Hence, the turban has become a religious symbol for Sikhs in modern times, although there are no commandments in the holy Granth to keep long hair or to wear a turban.

The turban (variously called *Pagri, Pug, Safa,* or *Dastar*) can be made of cotton or *tusser* (silk), but now most turbans are made of fine cotton cloth. It can be plain white for respectable old men, red for bridegrooms and celebrants, black for mourners or protestors, blue for *Nihang* warriors, orange or pink for happy fair-goers, special colors for military regiments or corps, saffron or gold for some types of religious Hindus or Sikhs, or multicolored prints (*chint*) or tie-dyed (*cheera*) for the daring and fashionable. Most of the time, however, the color of the turban was a matter of personal preference without special meaning. The style of the turban surely told a bigger story and classified a person more definitely. A *turra* (plume) of the starched end of the turban, sticking up vertically on top of the head, signified pride or exuberance; young villagers on special occasions wore that turra style and so did some Punjab police officers. My father was strictly against a turra on the turban, because it was associated with the wild, *badmash,* rustic, or arrogant and not with humble or gentle people. They used to say that once a fellow has a daughter, the plume of his turban gets lowered, i.e., he can no longer act proud and arrogant after he has a daughter.

The Patiala Shahi Turban

Turbans of rural people used to be irregular and varied. The villagers usually had a *taura* (the free end of the turban) which could be used as an air filter during a sandstorm, a water filter while drinking from a puddle, to tie and secure a valuable object, or for any other purpose. Then in the nineteenth century, the Sikh princely state of Patiala made their *Patiala Shahi* turban fashionable and prescribed that style for the Maharaja's army, police and courtiers. The Patiala Shahi style had a uniform, arched appearance in front, no taura loose end for miscellaneous uses, and no turra plume on top. The different *pech* (windings) of such a turban, layer staggered on layer, also became more orderly, whereas in earlier times the winding of the turban could be plain or rounded in front and quite irregular. Simultaneously with the turban change, the Patiala armed forces also started requiring Sikh men to roll the beard into a knot and tuck it under the chin. Later, the beard was required to be rolled around a string which went under and around the jaws and was then tied on top of the head. The British Indian army adopted the Patiala Shahi turban style for their Sikh troops. The rural people still kept the individualistic styles. But as time passed all educated Sikhs started following the Patiala Shahi style, which has become the standard most followed everywhere now.

From Cotton Plant to Woven Cloth

Before World War II, most cloth for routine wear in the village was made from home-grown cotton picked in our own fields. Women performed several operations by hand to turn cotton into cloth. First they put the cotton through a hand-operated rolling machine called *belni*, to remove the seeds from the fiber. Then the cotton fiber was taken to the *teli,* who would *pinjh* (fluff) the cotton fibers with a teasing string device called *tada*. Women would then make the fluffy cotton into *pooni* (rolls), each about seven inches long and one inch in diameter, by rolling the fluffy bits of cotton over a thin reed and then removing the reed. Then they would spin yarn from the cotton pooni with the *charkha* (spinning wheel). Spinning was easy work for old women or young girls. The girls usually sat together in small groups from the neighborhood and conversed, reminisced, told jokes and stories, gossiped, and laughed as they operated their charkhas. These social gatherings while they were spinning, called *tiranjan*, were so important to the girls that they sang many songs about them and exchanged reminiscences about them later in life. It took many pooni to make enough yarn on the *takkla* (spinning needle) of the spinning wheel before a useful size *glota* (roll) of yarn was formed.

Next, the women wound the yarn from many glota onto big hollow reeds called *nurra*. They then set poles in the ground in four rows about eight inches apart and extending for twenty to thirty yards, with a pole every yard or so along each row. Finally, a team of two or four women ran the yarn from the nurra holders, for many yards along the rows back and forth between the vertical sticks to make the *tana* (warp), for the weaver's loom. The weaver treated the *tana* with a starchy solution called *paan* and mounted the yarn on his loom. As the weaver wove the cloth, the women kept him supplied with the *peta* (weft) yarn. The weaver had to schedule the successive jobs according to his capacity, as he could weave only a few yards a day. Thus a roll of the coarse *khadder* cloth would come off the loom after many days of work by the weaver.

The khadder cloth was used to make ordinary clothes. All the *chutahi* (bed covers), *khes* (blankets), *razai* and *gadella* (upper and lower quilts), *phulkari and bagh* (embroidered veils), and all other cloth for routine use was made this way. Only special clothes for weddings, clothing for brides, and clothing to visit relatives or for festivals and celebrations, were made from cloth purchased from the market. Sewing was done by women by hand, with thread and needle, and they also did any dyeing that was necessary before or after sewing. There were dyers in our village, and some tailors had acquired hand-operated sewing machines by the 1930s, but most village people were not affluent enough to spend even pennies to pay the tailor and the dyer, unless the clothes were for a marriage or some other special use. In the late 1940s, my brother Kartar purchased a hand-powered Singer sewing machine for my sisters; that made it much easier and faster for them to stitch shirts or other clothes.

All those operations to turn cotton into cloth employed the least capable, from little girls to old ladies. For this reason, old ladies were always useful to have in the house, while old men were just a nuisance unless they could be sent to watch the crops. It is understandable why Gandhi thought the *charkha* (spinning wheel) was both the solution to India's unemployment problem and the means by which the country could end its dependence on fabrics made in British factories. He prescribed the coarse khaddar clothes and cap as the appropriate wear for the patriots and freedom fighters of his Congress Party. However, anyone who took Gandhi's advice about the spinning wheel seriously would surely have starved in the machine age. In Punjab there are no professional weavers any more, as they were mostly Muslim and migrated to Pakistan in 1947. Later, some women learned to weave cloth as a hobby but as girls gain education with the prospect of becoming doctors, professors, or government officials, no young girl with any ambition is expected to spin yarn or weave cloth in modern times.

Punjabi Dress for Women

Punjabi women's dress (*salwar, chemise and chunni*) was apparently a variation of that worn by women in Afghanistan and was quite different from the *sari* of India. A salwar was a loose, pantaloon-like garment with a drawstring, as was worn by men and women in central and western Asia; some variations of this were the tambi, the sutthan or a tight pajama hugging the calves. Chemise was the long blouse or shirt; it would be considered immodest and inappropriate if the chemise were tucked in and the exposed behind of the salwar showed. The *chunni* or *dupatta* was a head cover or veil and it could be worn in various ways. Some variation was possible, but every time the women started wearing a slightly different style, the older and religious men were outraged. If the cuff of the salwar changed from six inches to thirteen inches, or the shirt would change from mid-calf length to knee length, some people would think it was an outrageous attention-getter. If hem of the shirt was high above the knee so that the dangling end of the *nala* (drawstring) of her salwar was showing, it might be considered a provocation to men. But after a few years when the new fashion would become the norm, some other variation in dress style would displease the older generation.

The *nala* was an accessory of some importance; brides had ample supplies of nala in dazzling colors and of various fibers and designs. The importance of the nala was that it tied and opened the lower garments for women. The nala for a *ghagra* (big skirt) could be embellished with flowers made from silk thread, with sequins, even with tiny bells, and with other decorative items at both ends. Most of the drawstrings used to be knitted bands with elaborate knots like macramé on the ends. If you stretched the width of the nala, you would see various patterns and interesting knit figures, although in its usually folded condition, when the nala looked like a rope, such patterns were not visible. Some of this decoration was not for efficiency or show, but for the girl's own pleasure in making the nala with such patterns.

After World War II, the one item of dress that started disappearing, even from the rural areas of Punjab, was the outer full skirt called *ghagra or lengha*. When I was young, no married woman, unless she was a daughter of the village, would step out of the house without wearing the ghagra in addition to her regular garments. The ghagra covered the legs down to the feet, practically touching the ground, and women wore their shirts on the outside of the ghagra. Brides would have the fancy ends of the drawstring hanging by the side of the ghagra skirt to show them off. The ghagra skirt for a woman could take from twenty to thirty yards of cloth to make. Lighter versions called ghagri might be worn for some occasions, or indoors. Women of the shopkeeper caste frequently wore the chenille ghagri, sometimes even without the salwar. When inside the house, a rural woman did not wear the big skirt, as the salwar was considered appropriate enough while indoors. But for stepping outside in public, fetching water, visiting the hospital, or taking yarn to the weaver, she would feel immodest without the ghagra, as if her suit of salwar/camis were just the intimate garments. Newer brides would wear the ghagra even while carrying lunch for their husbands in the fields, but they would take it off when they got away from the populated areas. Other people would "talk" if they saw a wife of the village out of the house without the ghagra, because the ghagra and face covering distinguished a wife of the village from a daughter. Once she stepped outside the territory of her in-laws, it would not be necessary for the woman to wear the ghagra; her regular clothes were appropriate.

At my brother Kartar's wedding with Jeet in 1954, someone created a commotion by telling her people that Kartar's clan of Mehraj, *in the Jungle area*, were uneducated people;

331

and that the Mehraj people might make Jeet the bride, wear a ghagra when she was taken there after the marriage. They worried that the backward fashion of ghagra would be an imposition. They had to be assured that being the wife of a high official, Jeet would not be subjected to the ghagra custom.

Rajputana women wore colorful skirts and blouses while women in other parts of India wore some variant of the *sari*. In earlier times some women in Punjab south of the Sutlej River must also have worn the flowery skirt and blouse of the kind worn by women in Rajputana. My sisters sometimes took out grandmother's clothes from the old *sandooq* and laughed at the strange and colorful skirts and blouses. My sisters would say mockingly, "These are just like *Thalli Wali* (desert women's) clothes!" No women in our area wore short skirts.

There were Muslim women in Mehraj whose clothes were no different from the clothes of others, as none of those poor castes observed the custom of purdah. But we sometimes saw Muslim women at the Bhatinda railway junction, traveling between Delhi and Lahore, wearing the *burqah*. The burqah covered a Muslim woman from head to toe; its eye-holes had screens so that no one could see even her eyes. Women wearing burqah seemed like walking mini-tents. Some times you could see their hands. Boys fantasized and speculated that the woman inside the burqah must be extremely beautiful. Once in a while, though, when we caught them unaware with veil lifted, some of these women's faces were a real disappointment.

Men's clothing in northwestern Punjab and in urban areas consisted of a shirt, a *kurta* or *chemise* for the top, a salwar or pajama for the bottom, and a turban or some other headgear. The kurta for men might vary some in length, but it usually went to the knee and was to be worn outside the dhoti, pajama, or the salwar, to cover the buttocks and front for modesty. It was quite shocking to the village people at first when educated boys adopted the western wear, showing the contours of their buttocks in pants, with no shirt outside the pants to cover them. In time, however, the tightly clothed buttocks have come to be regarded as no more shocking than knees or shoulders.

In our rural areas, most men wore a style of *dhoti* or *chadur* instead of the salwar to cover their legs. The dhoti is an unstitched cloth that goes once around the waist like a sarong and covers as much of the legs as the wearer thinks proper or fashionable. Just as religious Hindu women wear the unstitched sari, the Hindu masculine equivalent is an unstitched cloth dhoti. Some said that the dhoti and sari were religious symbols, because a Hindu could not perform religious worship while wearing any stitched cloth, but perhaps that rule is applicable only to a strict Brahmin. The style of wearing the unstitched dhoti changed in the territories toward Delhi, in Rajputana, and beyond. In hot weather the loose dhoti made sense, but to allow for any agility in movement, one had to learn to cope with its inherent awkwardness or to tie it like a diaper as the Indian laborers outside Punjab did.

Fashionable Punjabis, the wealthy and the influential, wore coats called a*chkan*, a collarless, mid-calf length coat with many buttons all the way from the neck down. A shorter version of the achkan has come to be known as the Nehru Jacket, but it is probably of Persian or Turbic origin. For weddings or ceremonial occasions, the achkan could be made of some showy cloth and bright colour such as red, silver, or golden in color and of silk or brocade. An official or lawyer might wear just a plain black achkan with a white tight pajama, and less commonly a loose pajama called *tamba* with it. In the old days it was unthinkable for a village farmer to wear the achkan coat or the pajama bottom.

Janghia, My Coveted Underwear

To perform physical work, the Punjabi farmers just took off their sarong-like dhoti. While doing strenuous farm work they wore only the *janghia*, or *langota* under their long shirt. The janghia was made from thick cloth, cut and stitched into a triangle, with cloth strings at two corners of the triangle and a strap four or five inches wide at the third corner. The triangular janghia was put over the buttocks, and the wide strap was brought forward between the legs to cover the genitals. Then while tying the janghia, a boy would hold the end of the wide strap in his mouth, tie the side strings around his waist over the strap, and pass the remaining end of the strap back over the genitals to be tucked in the back of the janghia. A properly fitting janghia looked like a woman's bikini bottom, but it always gave one the feeling of agility and readiness for athletic activity. A langota used even less cloth than a janghia and barely covered the genitals. The janghia was worn in Punjab by farmers, wrestlers, athletes, young cattle grazers, and uneducated workers, who needed to be ready to tackle a physically demanding task. Educated or city people would never wear the janghia. They wore either a dhoti or a variation of a pajama or salwar; the work of educated people did not require the removal of any clothing.

Sikhs who became *amritdhari* (formally initiated by taking the amrit) wore *kachehra* (loose short pants to the knee with a drawstring) as part of the practice of their religion. They had a great aversion to, and prohibition against, wearing a janghia or dhoti. Village Jat boys in turn made fun of the amritdhari Sikhs wearing the kachehra with a little insulting ditty. A farmer went to the fields or pursued vigorous activities wearing only the janghia. As times changed and more people were educated, the janghia and dhoti gave way to clothes resembling pajamas, and more recently some kinds of slacks, following the fashion among educated people worldwide.

In the villages it was common to see little toddler boys naked in summer, wearing nothing but a *tiragi*. The tiragi was a string of thread around the waist, sometimes with a few beads and possibly including a *taweez* (a talisman or charm capsule). This custom of boys wearing the string around the waist probably came from the sacred thread of Hindu tradition. I remember wearing a black and sometimes a pink tiragi, usually with a *chugga* (shirt) on. Later at the age of about four, I graduated to wearing a little *kachha* (shorts, underwear). It was customary for cattle-grazing boys to wear a janghia, but schoolboys were not allowed to wear the janghia; they had to wear the kachha shorts. I always wished I could wear a janghia like the cattle-grazing boys and athletes did, but my father, being an amritdhari Sikh, was strictly against the janghia and dhoti. My uncle Tiloka wore the janghia and dhoti; he dressed that way because he was not an amritdhari Sikh and also because he was illiterate. Later, as a rebellious teenager and a grownup, I wore the janghia once in a while; but each time I felt as if I were violating a sacred commandment by doing so; it felt as though I was doing something illicit.

Men's Jewelry and Tattoos

Jewelry for women has been described in the section on weddings. Before World War II, in the rural areas of Punjab it was common for men also to wear jewelry. Around the neck some boys and men wore metal jewelry, a *taveez* or talisman or a packaged charm; these were usually worn on a black string (called *gaani*) like a woman's choker. *Kuntha*, a necklace with large gold beads, was a prestigious thing for a man to wear. It might have several beads of the size of a grape, made of well-designed gold shells, with shellac fillings. The remainder of the string that passed through the beads of the kuntha was braided with golden thread like a work of art hanging at the wearer's back. The men's kuntha was not for routine wear; it was for special occasions only. Many men wore the gold *tungle* (earrings), some with one to three colored beads in them. Some men wore just the small *nutti* or *mundri* earrings without any beads. Rich men sometimes received a kuntha and a pair of gold bracelets, called *jori*, from their in-laws as gifts on the occasion of their marriage, but they rarely wore the bracelets. Most ordinary men just wore a steel *kara* bracelet, which was also an indication of their Sikh religion. Most rural men wore only earrings and a black *gaani* string with a small taveez around the neck; very few wore them after the 1950s.

In my rebellious days at the age of 16, I had squirreled away some money with the hope of having a kuntha made for my neck. I was always timid about fashions, though, and I did not dare to have my ears pierced for fear that my father would run me out of the house for such a disgrace. I never wore even a simple gaani string around my neck, and I was never tempted to wear anything in my ears. My father was against ornaments even for women; jewelry for boys would be like a red flag and a despicable sight to him. A kuntha might have been easier for him to tolerate, since it did not require any body alteration and was meant to be worn only for special occasions. I tried to push the limits and actually went with a friend to a goldsmith in Phul to have a gold kuntha made for me. I had almost enough money, but then my friend said that I should think some more before spending all of it on the kuntha. I never got my kuntha made and never had my ears pierced, just as I never learned to play the sarangi music. That is because the disturbance due to the approaching Partition and Independence of 1947 put an end to my frivolous thoughts. Our men never wore any nose ornaments, except in special cases when a wise man prescribed that a boy have his nose pierced and wear something in it to prevent some disease or misfortune. Such boys were always named Nathu (one with a nose artifact). After the 1950s, rural boys and men stopped wearing jewelry.

Tattooing different parts of the body was common among the men and women of nomadic tribes and the transient castes; their women would also customarily expose more parts of their bodies in public. Some Jat boys, and a very few girls, did get tattoos on their hands or wrists, but a tattoo on any unexposed part, like the leg of a Jat girl, was unthinkable. Some boys, especially wrestlers and body builders, would get tattoos of peacocks, snakes, the sun, flowers, and other objects on the front of their thighs. Many of these wrestlers and athletes had the bodies with minimal hair growth on their legs, so that the tattoos showed even on their unshaved thighs when they paraded around the arena. No one in my family would ever have dared to get a tattoo, although some of my classmates had tattoos on their hands and thighs. For example, Mukand, a Jat Sikh boy, had the word "*Om*," the Indian symbol for God, tattooed on the back of one hand and something like a star of David on the other hand. Those were the easiest symbols for the tattoo artist at the fair to make. Another classmate, the good-natured Ghoke the Mirassi, had tattoos on his thighs and his wrists, but it would have been a sin for a Muslim like him to have the word Om or the star of David tattooed on him. I was too scared of my father to get a tattoo. I was very timid when it came to styles and fashions; so I was never tempted to have a tattoo.

Minimal Clothing; Shoes Optional

Most poor young boys wore only a shirt, which would be washed once or twice a month; they might also have an older shirt into which they could change temporarily. In winter it was common for children to sleep in the same shirt that they had worn during the day; a separate sleeping suit was something unheard of. In summer in the villages it was common to see little toddler boys naked, with only a *tiragi string* around the waist. Little girls had to wear both top and bottom clothing even when the parents were poor. A naked boy was nothing unusual, but a naked female was strictly against the social norms.

Thorny trees and bushes were abundant in our area, and thorns piercing the feet were a common source of pain. It was not always possible to extract a thorn broken under the skin, when no portion of the thorn was visible or sticking out of the flesh. People applied various concoctions, like packs of salt and gur (raw sugar), to the bottom of the foot with the hope that the concoction would soften the flesh and bring the thorn out. The body expelled the thorn only after the puss formed. Anyway, we all hoped that the soles of our feet would become impervious to thorns, like a camel's feet. Unlike the hard hoofs of cows and buffaloes, a camel just has hard pads as soles and it can't hurt you too badly if it accidentally steps on your foot. Tahri Khan, who was our farm worker for some years, never wore shoes in his entire life except for a few minutes on the day when he was married. He had the reputation that he had hardened his feet so thoroughly that thorns would not pierce his feet when he stepped on them; but I doubt if this was strictly true.

Except for hot sand, which had to be avoided, the earth was soft and comfortable to walk on without shoes. Many little boys were encouraged to walk barefoot on rough or hot ground and later in the stubble of harvested fields to harden the soles of the feet. They wanted to develop *Pukka Paer* (hard feet) like a camel's sole so that later on they would not need to wear any shoes at all. Young boys thought of shoes as a hindrance and a nuisance. They appreciated the freedom from shoes, because new moccasin-like shoes pinched and hurt, and they caused blisters. They were not made specifically for the right and left foot and had to be broken in; when they wore out, their heels collapsed and they dragged like slippers. Many boys would take their new shoes off and carry them around, and generally considered the shoes to be a burden. They had to remove shoes in order to run or play, because on the soft earth, shoes just impeded movement.

The village shoemakers used two basic varieties of leather. One was the thick, rough, uncolored variety with a natural tan, and looked like the leather for shoe soles. The tough and hardy lower classes and farmers wore shoes with the uppers made from this coarse leather called *dhauri*. The other variety of leather, called *khall*, was thinner, softer, and usually colored red. Women and gentle people would wear shoes with the upper part made of khall. Rarely did anyone in the village wear what they called chrome leather, similar to that of modern-day shoes. After the Independence and Partition, the modern style of shoe became common because it is more comfortable than the older styles and is now easy to obtain from stores. Fashionable men in the village, as well as brides and newlyweds, wore shoes with the upper leather embroidered with *zarri* (golden or silver thread). An upward-curving front of the shoe ending in a 'tail' of leather at the toe was a stylish feature. A variation of that feature is depicted in cartoons to give shoes the Arabian Nights look. I always wanted the khall shoes with zarri and tails, but my father was against a tail on a shoe; he considered it superfluous to have shoes with tails. And of course the expensive zarri embroidery on a shoe was a forbidden luxury for us. Other boys had zarri shoes with tails made or received them as a gift from their maternal grandparents, but I never had such shoes until I was 37 years old, educated, and wearing western-style clothes. Janghia underwear, khall shoes with zarri and tails, and the turra plume on the turban were some of the things that were not allowed for the boys in our house.

Although boys liked the freedom of not wearing shoes, their parents felt that being shoeless indicated poverty, informality, backwardness, and low class status, so they tried to provide shoes for their children. Like some other boys, I carried my new shoes around with me because they hurt and caused blisters. I would place the shoes somewhere while playing or before walking into a pond. Sometimes I forgot where I had left the shoes, or the shoes were stolen. When I returned home without my shoes, I would be severely scolded for many days for losing the shoes. Then I felt incompetent and worthless for having lost them. Parents were always occupied tending to the needs of oxen, buffaloes, farm implements, and crops. They could not always attend to the need for new shoes timely. If I lost my shoes, which happened frequently in the days when I was under 10 years old, then the whole cycle of scolding, planning, seeking the shoemaker, and waiting for weeks, started all over again.

A second pair of shoes was more difficult to obtain than a second shirt, which could be stitched easily from the home-made khadder. First you had to find a shoemaker who could make a pair for you; there were not many shoemakers in Mehraj, and there was none in our *patti*. Sometimes shoemakers would come from other villages to our houses, because women could not travel to the shoemakers. They measured our feet in finger widths; and since they could not read or write, they had to just memorize the measure for each person. On their next trip, two or three weeks later, they might bring the shoes for some of us if they had had time to make them. If the shoes fit poorly, we either accepted them or waited in the hope that the shoemaker would make another trip. It could take weeks before another pair could be obtained.

As a teenager, I walked to Phul many times to give my measurement foot to the shoemakers there. A colony of Chumars lived outside the walled village of Phul; such untouchable leather workers were not allowed to live inside the village boundaries in earlier times. It took half a day for me to walk to the shoemakers of Phul and to return home; if I was distracted eating wild *ber* from the trees on the way, the trip killed nearly a whole day. A week or two later, depending on the promise of the shoemaker, I again walked to Phul to check if the shoes were ready. It was not like the modern days when you can make a phone call; you had to walk to the other village even to get a negative answer. The shoemakers, like those in many other trades, were notorious for breaking their promises about the time of delivery. If the shoemaker had other orders and could not make mine on time, or if the shoes were too tight, I had to come again. It could easily take weeks before I could get my not-so-perfect pair of shoes and start breaking them.

CHAPTER 19

CRIME AND LAWS IN PUNJAB

When Sikh dominance and rule was established in Punjab late in the 18th century, the insecurity of being butchered, or subjugated by foreign invaders ended. But law and order had always been a problem, and internal crimes were frequent even during my childhood. Our area of twenty-two villages had been operating as an independent territory for some time. The English author Lepel Griffin wrote a paragraph about "The Republic of Mehraj" in one of his books. Even the maps of Emperor Akbar's time from the late 16th century show our area to be *la qanoon* (without his law). When the British became dominant in eastern Punjab in 1835, our twenty-two villages, along with the Phulkian states, allied themselves with the British, years before the British conquered the rest of Punjab in 1849. So this pocket of Mehraj villages, surrounded by other princely states on all sides, was attached to the British district headquarters of Ferozepur, 70 miles away, with just a police post and a revenue officer in the village of Nathana. When a crime was committed in Mehraj, someone had to travel about seven miles through the wilderness from Mehraj to the police post at Nathana to report it, and the travel was risky except during daylight hours. The police would then schedule a trip to Mehraj, the delay depending on the seriousness of the crime and on their other preoccupations.

The mounted police were autocratic and harsh and they extorted bribes from the public. The usual procedure of the police after arresting a person was to start with verbal abuse. Then the policemen would start beating the person, unless he was a man of some status and influence who could cause them problems. If the crime was not serious, the person would be released after a beating and a bribe. If they felt that more beating might be necessary to make the person confess, or to extort a higher bribe, they were in no hurry to release him. There was no limit to the length of time they could detain a person; they could take him to Nathana if they chose to make his life miserable. The police were not always keen to search for serious criminals, for doing so might be dangerous. And violent criminals would not pay bribes, so the police had little motivation to beat hardened criminals.. Uncle Tiloka used to say, "Criminals are the natural allies of the police; they guarantee the police jobs and are dishonest just like the police."

337

Police Raid on a Gambling Party

Once, on a summer day in 1940, some twenty men were sitting in a gambling circle under the trees by the pond, not far from our Outer House. The gamblers did this every day at some location in the village and they played against one another rather than against any establishment.. If the men were gambling in someone's cattle yard, the winners gave the owner of the yard a bottle of whiskey in appreciation. Over time, such a host also got a reputation as a *badmash* (bad character); and that had some intimidation value in the village. That afternoon, the grove of trees by the pond was a neutral gambling venue, not hosted by anyone. As usual, some winners were having a peg or two of whiskey, and the scene was jolly but orderly. I was playing in the trees with some other young boys and watching the gamblers, who were throwing dice. Onlookers became excited as the dice throwers invoked Gods' help, saying things like, *"shikka Malika, shikka!"*or *"paon, Bazan Wale, paon,"* meaning, "sixes, O Lord, make it sixes" or "snake eyes, O Keeper Of Hawks, make it snake eyes for me." When the inevitable disappointment came from the throw of dice, they cursed the dice, saying, "Oh, *tera bera ghark!*" or "Oh, *tera satya nas!*" meaning, "Oh, may your boat sink!" or "May you be utterly destroyed!"

While the gambling was in full swing, all of a sudden, the mounted police arrived and rounded up everyone including the onlookers. Young boys like me were free to watch or to run away. The mounted police ordered the apprehended persons to lie down on the ground and started beating them, according to their usual procedure. One of the gamblers there, a man named Mahindra who usually did not do any farm work,and lived on his family assets, was a regular in the gambling circle. Mahindra attempted to escape and ran toward our house to hide from the mounted police. It was customary for our people to leave the doors open during daytime. So Mahindra raced in through the front door of our house. But a policeman on his horse chased right behind him through our front door, through our veranda, and into the courtyard. They both ran out through the other gate of our courtyard, as the horseman caught up to Mahindra and began beating him with a stick. In that society, a policeman did not need your permission to stomp through your house on his horse; you were lucky if he did not also abuse you for allowing a gambler to hide in your house. Anyway, the mounted policeman chased and whipped the running gambler, driving him back to the grove of trees. There, Mahindra was laid on the ground where the rest of the gamblers were being beaten. The policemen trampled on the prostrate men with their boots as if they were crushing a grape harvest. They beat the arrested group with sticks and horsewhips while the victims shrieked and begged for mercy. Later, every one of the apprehended people had to pay a bribe to the police before they were released. Some who were just out on errands and did not have any money with them had to send for their relatives to pay and release them. For the police it was like a good day's hunt that provided a moderate income. This was typical of how they handled petty lawbreakers. The police could arbitrarily call any activity a crime if they chose to do so. Even if some poor man was just keeping a pig, a Muslim policeman might treat it like a crime, because the sight a pig was offensive to Muslims, for religious reasons.

Opium, Whiskey and Other Excuses for Bribes

Opium and whiskey could be sold only in licensed shops under *theka* (contract, license) from the government. The *thekedar* (liquor license holder) was usually not the gentle type; he frequently had good relations with bad characters. The licensed sellers of opium were mostly Hindu shopkeepers and straight businessmen, but alcohol was more often related to violent crimes, so the Hindus avoided such business. It was legal to use opium and whiskey, but if someone in our British territory was caught with the stronger (*pukka*) form of opium that could be purchased legally in the princely states, he could be arrested and taken to jail. Then he had to pay a bribe to be released. The same was true if the police caught anyone with a sealed whiskey bottle from a princely state. The princely states were treated like independent foreign countries for this purpose, although they were under the thumb of the British. Our Mehraj villages, which were British territory, were completely surrounded by the three princely states of Nabha, Patiala and FaridKot. The nearest market towns were in the princely states; so we continuously passed through the states to buy and sell things, but opium and whiskey from those states were prohibited in British territory. The police would stake out a point on the way and occasionally searched men returning from the market town or from a fair in one of those states. Anyone who was gaunt and thin (one sign of opium use for a long time) was searched. Those who looked fat, prosperous, or young were usually waved through without being searched. Unlike my brothers, I used to be pleasantly fat as a teenager, so I always enjoyed favorable treatment from everyone. Anyone possessing the strong kind of opium or an unopened bottle of whiskey was arrested for transporting contraband from a princely state into the English-ruled territory. If the bottle was partially empty and you were already drinking, you were allowed to go on, but any amount of the wrong kind of opium was always a violation. If fellows returning from the fair at Selbrah suspected that there might be a police stakeout further down the road, they ate or threw away any remaining opium, and they opened the whiskey bottle and drank a little bit out of it before proceeding toward the police, because an open bottle was not illegal.

A policeman in the rural areas was never a welcome sight. Even if you were the victim of a crime, you might have to pay a bribe to get their attention, and they might still mistreat you. Minor crimes in the village were rarely tried in court; the police usually decided on the spot how much of a beating and bribe was appropriate for each case. For a more serious crime the offender was taken to the police station in Nathana, and then it took a longer time and a bigger bribe to be released. When a murder was committed, the person arrested or punished was not always the one who had committed the crime. It depended upon who was able to influence the police with a bribe and who could be enlisted as a witness. The police could make a case against anyone, sometimes even against a person who had never been anywhere near the crime scene. They would find someone who would agree to be a witness because of enmity with the accused or someone who often testified for money, even without actually seeing the crime.

A police inspector (a couple of ranks above the lowest level policeman) in a rural area could get rich within a few years; but even the low-level policemen had plenty of opportunities to enjoy luxuries. Police inspectors would try to get transferred to those rural areas where murders over land and water disputes or family feuds were frequent.

These policemen *themselves* paid bribes and used influence with higher authorities to secure transfers to the lucrative, high crime areas. Corruption and bribes were common in all the police ranks except at the top posts which were held by British officers. In earlier times, the British practice was never to appoint an Englishman to a post below a certain rank where an Indian could serve. Later on they did allow some capable Indians to be appointed above such a barrier. After Independence when the British left, the system became even more corrupt, and it was not just police inspector who became immensely rich; the bribes flowed all the way to the top officials and up to the cabinet ministers.

In addition to the police, the most consistently corrupt official was/is the land records officer, called the *patwari*. You could never have a land sale deed recorded without a bribe. In some cases, the patwari might mess up your land records and show someone else as the cultivator of your land for years. Then it would be nearly impossible for you to get justice through courts, because the lower-level judges were usually corrupt and some could be bribed through lawyers. Sometimes it was possible to buy off the lawyer of the opposing party and weaken the opposing party's case. The system has been made even more intractable by the new land laws; now if a person gets possession of a property, he cannot be easily dispossessed, regardless of who the actual owner of the property may be. A patwari can do a million tricks with land records, and there is no way you can straighten out the mess without his cooperation. Horror stories of land disputes aided by patwaris are abundant all over Punjab, and it can take a lifetime to untangle such problems. In our own family, we have owned and cultivated one parcel of land for more than 70 years, but the names of some of the former owners were not removed by the patwari from the record at the time of purchase. Even though we have petitioned the courts through lawyers for years, and there is no counter-claim of ownership from anybody else, the courts have repeatedly refused to ratify our ownership, with some excuse or the other. We can continue to be in possession of the land but we are not recognized as its owners. A patwari's written word is still very difficult to undo, so you don't dare to deny him a bribe.

Armed Robbers and Petty Thieves

In the 1930s, armed robbery was a frequent crime in rural areas. People who were believed to have cash or gold jewelry always felt insecure. Anyone traveling through the countryside with money was an easy target. A gun was very scary, but before my time even a robber with any steel weapon or even a dang (bamboo stick) could intimidate and rob people. No one could keep a gun without a license; in those days only the *zaildar* (an official who assisted in law enforcement) and a couple of other people in our village had the license to own shotguns. Nobody had a license to own a pistol, revolver or rifle. Illegal guns were also rare; only a few famous outlaws had them, and they usually picked bigger targets. Most became robbers not because of poverty, but because they had killed an enemy. Since such a killer had little hope of escaping a long prison sentence or death, he become an outlaw and either stole or took a gun by force or deception from a licensed person. The names of these robbers were well known and romanticized; all little boys wanted to take the names of the well-known *daku* (robbers) when they played cops-and-robbers games. Some daku had become such legendary heroes that "poetry pamphlets" were published about their exploits. I used to say, "When I grow up, I am going to become a daku."

I remember one robbery in Mehraj in about 1942 in the house of ManneKe, who were believed to have a lot of cash. The ManneKe family were simple farmers and lived unpretentiously. They sometimes lent money to people at relatively lenient rates compared to the regular money lenders. Hindu shopkeepers who lent money had been moving into towns during the 30s and 40s and they would not readily lend money in the villages anymore, because many borrowers had declared bankruptcy during the economic depression. Anyway, one evening about two hours after dark, gunshots were heard in the village. A gunshot was rare because it would reveal illegal ownership of a gun, and police would hound the owner until he was put in jail. But it would be natural for a robber to discharge a weapon to scare his victims into quick compliance. On hearing those gunshots, everyone in our neighborhood climbed on his roof, because getting on the roof was the quickest way to hear what was happening. My neighbor, standing on his roof, said, *"ManneKe, Daku Pae Gae,"* meaning, "robbers have fallen on ManneKe house." No one had the means, courage, or inclination to do anything about it. The robbers could have taken all night if they had wanted to, because there was no chance of anyone informing the police until the next day. That night the robbers took some money but they did not kill anybody. The next day the ManneKe men appeared pretty traumatized, and for months thereafter they were somewhat depressed. The saving grace in the robbery was that no one from the younger generation fell into the hands of the robbers. They usually would not kill or kidnap anybody old, but there was always the danger that a younger man could be killed. In very rare cases, an unmarried girl could be taken away by a notorious robber, if he had an enmity with the victim's family and wanted to disgrace them. The loss of money was bad enough, but the black mark of having an unmarried girl taken away would be difficult for a family to bear; such a stigma stayed for generations even if the girl could be found later. The robbers would not ordinarily take away a married woman.

In the 1930s there was a famous *daku*, called Baziger because that was his caste; people were frequently called by their caste behind their back. This Baziger was reputed to have armed companions, including a woman. He lived in the cover of crops south of Mehraj near an irrigation canal. He did not bother ordinary people, and people were reluctant to help the police in killing him. Hazura Singh, the Zaildar (official who watched and assisted law and order, but had no authority to arrest) tried to do his part to apprehend Baziger, since he personally would be a natural target for the outlaws. One day Hazura led the police to the Baziger's hideout. The siege started early and lasted all day, and dozens of policemen were involved in the effort. The police had to even set fire to a sugarcane field to flush out the *daku*. Before the end of the day, every one of Bazigar's party had been killed by police gunfire. A year or so later, the Zaildar himself was murdered by someone unrelated to Bazigar. His skinny thirteen-year old son Harnam was three or four years ahead of me in school. Weighing less than 100 pounds at the time, he inherited the rank of Zaildar. Such a rank used to be hereditary, So Harnam, although barely a teenager, quickly learned to ride a horse and shoot a gun, which were the requirements of the job, but he did not have enough meat on him to command much respect. As an adult, Harnam became quite tall, and fat enough to look respectable.

Modha, The Daku Mar

Gold jewelry was a tempting target for robbers, especially on the highways. For instance, once around 1937, a daughter of our village was returning from her husband's house after her *moklawa*. The moklawa was the first time the bride lived her husband's house after the initial visit at the time of marriage, and she would be loaded with jewelry at that time. That afternoon she and her escorts had landed from the railway train at Rampura Phul, and she was traveling in a *rath* (a canopied, four wheeled, ox-drawn carriage) through the sand dunes to Mehraj, a distance of about five miles. Halfway between the train station and the village, the rath was stopped by a robber with a pistol. The robber ordered the attendants to remove all of the girl's jewelry and hand it over to him. They had to comply for fear of the bullets. After taking the jewelry, the robber was walking away when a young man of our village named Modha caught up to the party and asked the attendants what had happened. They pointed toward the escaping robber and said that he had taken all the jewelry of their sister. Modha shouted at them, "Why do you guys have beards and mustaches if you will let a sister's jewelry be robbed?" Modha immediately ran after the robber, but he had only a *khoonda* (a bamboo rod with a hook at the end) in his hand. In those days, it was illegal to own even an edged steel weapon; only an *amritdhari* Sikh, dressed as a *Nihang*, could carry a steel weapon as a religious right. Any cutting tool made of steel might be confiscated by the police, and the owner might be penalized unless he could prove that the tool was essential for farm work or his profession, and it had a handle which was less than three feet long. Anyway, Modha ran with his khoonda rod and caught up with the robber. The robber fired a couple of shots at him but missed each time. Then Modha hit the robber with his khoonda, felled him, and took his pistol away. They tied the robber's hands behind his back with his turban and leashed him to the rath. Then the robber had to walk to the village tethered behind the rath with one man walking behind him to make sure he did not escape.

After arriving in the village, they tied the robber in the open, to the steel bars of a window for public display. I myself saw him tied with a rope to the steel bars, outside the *bethak* (sitting room) of SadhanKe, who were Modha's friends, as Modha himself did not have a proper house in those days. Modha's house was not prosperous before the 1940s, and he did not work much either. In fact he used to play cards with us under the trees during the daytime instead of working, although he was twenty years older than we were. As the robber was tethered like an animal to the steel bars, anyone from the village who came by to see him, was able to slap and abuse him if he wished. My friends and I were too small to slap him; we were even too scared to get close. The next day he was taken to the Nathana police post, seven miles away. He turned out to be a low caste whose father had been in the military, and that was how he had acquired the stolen pistol. In those days, a low caste was unlikely to become a robber, although he might become a thief. After that incident, Modha was called Daku Mar (robber killer), and he was treated like a hero for a while, for saving the honor of a daughter of the village. But Modha was modest about it, saying, "How could I show my face in the village if I had let this robber go unchallenged after he robbed my sister's ornaments." She was not really his sister, and not even from our side of the village; but we treated every girl of the village like a sister in those days.

342

While rich people feared *daka* (armed robbery), the less affluent were likely to be victims of *chori* (theft). Theft of animals was quite common in the villages before World War II. Camels and horses were stolen most often because they could be ridden away, while good oxen came next. It was not easy to steal buffalo, as they walked slowly, required more maintenance, and were harder to sell for cash. Even so, a notorious thief did steal a buffalo from the corral of Sirmukh Singh's family one night; then they had to pay some informers to recover the buffalo from the village of Kalyan. Punjabi cows were considered so worthless by the 1940s that people were abandoning them; there was no question of any body stealing a cow.

Our family never suffered a robbery or theft. We were not rich enough for robbers, and thieves would have been afraid of our big family, our vicious dog, and the presence of many men. The presence of men was a great deterrent to robbers, while the presence of women would just make a house vulnerable; so it is easy to understand why people wanted sons and not daughters. The fact that my father had three brothers was a big safety factor. Moreover, thieves were surely deterred by our fierce family dog, Bhoora. Our dog was so protective that even during cold, blustery nights he could be seen walking on top of the perimeter walls of our courtyard. Uncle Bhag used to say, "We had jobs as guards in Hong Kong, but we were not as conscientious as your dog Bhoora. We sometimes dozed off or went inside to rest, but this dog never neglects his duty." All our women cried when our dog Bhoora died. Fortunately, by that time the number of crimes had started declining because of the Second World War and the resulting prosperity.

Thieves could cut through the wall of a house at night to enter and steal money, jewelry, and other valuables. This was most likely to happen in summer, when people slept on rooftops or outside in the courtyard, and in houses whose walls were not common with other houses, but were exposed. It was not just rich people who were victims of theft but rather the most vulnerable ones, whether rich or poor. Uncle Viceroy and his wife Gulabo had the exposed wall of their house broken by thieves in the late 1930s. The thieves then entered through the opening in the wall and took whatever cash, jewelry, and clothes were in the *sandooq* inside the house while the family slept in the front courtyard. The next day I saw the mud bricks and plaster that the thieves had dug from the three-foot thick wall to gain entry into the house, as well as some debris scattered outside the gap in the wall. For me that gap in the wall was a depressing sight. In the morning, neighbors gathered around the gap in the torn wall to express sympathy. Uncle Viceroy and his wife Gulabo were already poor; the theft was just another blow.

It was believed that a *bheti* (possessor of inside information) is often involved in any theft. The family of my friend Mukand, son of Sirmukh Singh, had a buffalo, an ox, and camels stolen at various times, because Beeru Khan, the brother of Allah Ditta, was their enemy and a friend of many thieves. Beeru was feared and notorious, but he did not confront his enemies; he acted only when they were absent or unaware. When Beeru did not steal the cattle himself, he encouraged his criminal friends to do so and told them the easiest ways to steal animals from his enemy's house. Beeru had once attacked Sirmukh Singh with the intention of killing him while the latter was sleeping in his own *barra* (animal corral). Beeru inflicted severe cuts on Sirmukh Singh's body while the latter was sleeping. Afterwards, my father helped Sirmukh Singh to recover by cleaning his wounds and applying medicines for several months; my father had done such voluntary

343

service for others also according to the custom in villages. Beeru Khan was never caught or punished for that crime. He frequently committed crimes, since that was his only occupation, and he was always hiding from public view and from the police. Although his mother Manno lived merely hundred yards away and his brother Allah Ditta lived by the pond outside the village, I never in all my life saw Beeru except a little glance of him from behind once, when I was about seven years old. I saw him with long loose hair, jumping over a wall while the police were chasing him. Beeru climbed over the wall, but the police horses could not jump over the wall and so he escaped. Although friendship with that low caste Muslim was not socially desirable, some aspiring *badmash* (bad character) Jat boys wanted to cultivate their acquaintance with him in order to intimidate others. Once in 1946, Harnek Palleka boasted to me that Beeru came to visit him in his barra sometimes at night and that he was going to get an illegal pistol from Beeru. Other men, like Bachan of Bhukku, also cultivated a friendship with dangerous criminals like Beeru. Fortunately, like other Muslims, Beeru left our village when Pakistan was created in 1947.

One day Mukand's older brother Chand, working in the fields of RajjoWali (all the fields had names), had to surrender his camel to the well-known armed robber Mangat of Marri village. Mangat came to him in the field and said he needed to ride the camel to escape the police who were coming after him. Robbers did not usually threaten people of their own region, but Mangat claimed that this was an emergency. He pointed a gun at Chand and told him to hurry up and build a temporary saddle (called a *soondka*) of straw and brush, and to secure it with a rope on the camel. Chand had to comply or be shot. As Mangat was riding away, Chand asked if he could hope to get his camel back, since he was helping Mangat in that emergency. Mangat promised to leave the camel a few miles away, but that camel was never recovered. Mangat probably sold it to some of his criminal friends.

Khoji, the Hoof-Mark Tracker

Sometimes stolen animals were recovered through persistent investigation. Mukand's family did recover a stolen buffalo once from the village of Kalyan. News of a theft spread quickly from village to village, and some people became informers if they suspected theft. The receiver of a stolen animal usually had to hide it or to explain away and lie to his neighbors about where he had gotten that particular animal. It was a custom among village men to visit their neighbors without an invitation to inspect or admire a new camel, horse, ox, or buffalo, just as women went to inspect a new bride, her clothes, and jewelry. Recovering a stolen animal required good guesswork, a knowledge of thief psychology, the tracing of the animal's footmarks on the ground, and, hopefully, an informer. The skills of a *khoji* (detective, expert at tracing footmarks) were valued for good reason. If summoned soon after a theft, he could find the animal by tracing its footmarks in the dirt, because each animal's tracks were distinctive.

Even we cattle grazers were amateur khoji and became familiar with the tracks of each of our animals in order to find them if they strayed or got lost. Some of our animals found clever ways to escape so that they could feed in someone else's crop or even go to the village of the previous owner. It was a major headache if a cattle grazer lost any of his animals. A stray animal eating someone else's crop could be taken to the *phatak* (gate, impound) by the owner of the crop, although this was not done frequently. You would have to pay a penalty to the phatak official in order to have each animal released. Therefore we had to learn to find a lost animal by tracking its footmarks before we got into trouble. We all routinely observed the foot tracks of animals and of people to determine what had been happening in the area recently, or which way someone had taken his herd, or what kind of animals had been eating our crops. A hunter would look for fresh tracks when he was looking to trap or kill a wild animal.

If the footmarks of a stolen animal "died" in one location, the khoji could pick them up a little further along and follow the tracks again. A thief might walk the animal through a pond to lose the footmarks, but the khoji always found them again where the animal left the pond. Most land was sandy and soft, so footmarks were hard to avoid and were useful unless too much time had passed or sand from a dust storm had covered them. From the contour of a hoof track or from the traces of worms, or objects partially covering the tracks, he could tell how fresh the tracks were. Like the fellow who set broken bones, or the one who performed *toona* (voodoo) or *hathaula* (hand healing), the khoji did not always get paid in cash; he usually did it for honor and gratitude, and nobody's time was too valuable in those days.

Homicide was a common occurrence in our rural areas. People did not kill strangers; the most common reasons were land or water disputes, but continuing feuds and spur-of-the-moment anger were also sometimes the cause. My uncle used to say, "Zar, Zoru, Zameen" (gold, woman, land) are the causes of violence, and many examples bore that out. Killings were committed to defend one's "honor," out of enmity, from sudden anger, or to assert one's dominance. One of the ways a reckless young man with aggressive tendencies established his credibility and created fear in the minds of others was by committing a murder. When the man came out of prison after serving jail time for murder, people deferred to him. The only people who would then be willing to mess with him would be those who had less to lose, or those with many brothers and no women to worry about. There were gradations of fear depending on the nature of violence for which the man served jail time. Usually theft and clandestine crimes accumulated no credibility, but anyone who killed another in combat after a challenge was generally feared.

Crime dropped considerably during World War II and later. Robberies and thefts occurred less frequently in rural Punjab after 1943 as the economic conditions had changed. Men were needed for the war effort, and unemployment became less common in the village. Coincidentally there were good rains in Punjab in 1942, and some years of bumper crops occurred after that time. More men in Punjab were then occupied gainfully and were too busy to commit crime. Crop prices went up as the war progressed and this increase ended the price depression of the 1930s; workers became harder to find and more expensive to employ. Land prices rose. Financially inept or careless people who had mortgaged away their lands in the past were able to get most of their lands back by encumbering or selling only small portion of the land to pay off the fixed debts. Some formerly desperate families became prosperous. The prosperity induced by the war diminished the robberies and thefts, although violent crimes and corruption were as prevalent as ever.

Velli and Badmash

The *badmash* (bad characters) in the villages were the tough, aggressive, and borderline criminal fellows. They would assert their clout and importance, and could commit violent crimes, but they were rarely treacherous to their friends. The serious badmash were not gregarious or articulate; some talked as little as possible. A man could not afford to act nasty if he had a wife, sister, or daughter, since having such female relatives would make him vulnerable. The badmash were not womanizers, as frequent association with women would make them appear less dangerous. And you could count on them to stand up for their friends, right or wrong. The badmash usually violated the social proprieties when it came to drinking alcohol, eating opium, and sometimes smoking intoxicants. For that reason many were also called *"velli"* (one with vices), a term they considered a compliment but the general public considered it self-destructive behavior. In fact "velli" implied a fellow addicted to some kind of stimulant or intoxicant. Most of them had served a term in prison for a violent crime, and this jail time afforded them some status in their circles. They took pride in violent crimes but not in thefts or minor crimes.

This reminds me of a story that an American wife once told me. She was visiting distant relatives of her husband on their farm in India in the 1960s. Someone there pointed to a middle-aged Muslim worker at their farm and around the household, saying, "That is Badru; he is a pretty reliable worker, though he had committed fourteen murders before he came to work here." The American wife shrieked, "Oh my God; get me out of here; I can't bear the thought of being near a serial killer!" They said, "Oh, no problem; don't worry; he is very loyal and very honest; he killed all those people only to help his friends; and that too was in his younger days." You had to compromise your own morality a bit to associate with them, but in a lawless society, such badmash were useful to have on your side; and they were usually trustworthy.

Security and Fortifications

In the old days, many bigger towns had perimeter walls, with gates that could be closed at night or in time of outside danger. A small town usually had four gates that were manned and controlled during the day and were closed and watched at night. This system kept robbers and strangers out. In the olden times, the populations of towns did not increase rapidly and spill out beyond the boundary walls. The village of Phul, three miles away, had a 20-foot high mud brick wall all around it, with four gates. Actually the wall was that height only as seen from the outside and the low, moat-like ground outside the wall made the apparent height more impressive. The outside of the town wall had to be maintained with a coating of mud plaster only once every few years, as there was not much rain in our region. In the 1930s and 40s, the entire population of Phul lived inside the wall, except for the few houses of the leather workers; the untouchable caste people traditionally lived apart from the general population everywhere. The boundary wall of Phul had the Mehraj Gate to the west, the Rampura Gate to the south, the Sidhana Gate to the north, and the Dhobali Gate to the east. For the extra security of the ruler, there was also a brick fort in the center of Phul. In the 1940s the Phul fort was used as a jail and for government activities, since the Raja and his capital now were 50 miles away at Nabha, far from our sandy desert area.

346

The train station of Rampura Phul and the market towns there were established, when the trains came, at the common boundary of the territories of Rampura and Phul, belonging to the two princely states of Patiala and Nabha respectively. The boundary walls of the market town of Phul Mandi had more than four gates, as it was built in modern times when major outside threat was not very severe. But even during the 1940s, all the boundary gates of Phul Mandi were locked by the police after dark, and the residents had to plan their activities accordingly. Such security was the reason that so many Hindu shopkeepers, including many from our own village, had moved into Phul Mandi when I was young. When a train arrived at the Rampura Phul railway station after dark, then one gate of the town was opened by a guard to allow the train passengers to enter the town. Another gate was opened to allow train passengers to travel out to their respective villages at night, and the gates were locked again.

Similarly, starting in the 1930s Rampura Mandi was built by the State of Patiala on the other side of the railroad tracks next to the railway station. It was built a bit late to rival Phul Mandi, but it had its own boundary wall and gates. The shops and houses in Rampura Mandi were largely empty in the early 1940s and the rents were negligible. Nabha, being a smaller state, had made early and intensive efforts to settle the merchants in Phul Mandi as it represented a larger part of the Raja's assets and a gateway to his ancestral village of Phul. But Patiala, being a bigger princely state with other important cities like Bhatinda, Sirhind and Patiala, had neglected the development of Rampura Mandi. During the 1940s I had the experience of living in the market towns of Rampura Mandi and Phul Mandi while getting an education from my teacher Kesho Ram. I had started studying with him in Phul Mandi, but then he moved to the low rent Rampura Mandi on the opposite side of the railroad tracks. For a while he tried teaching in the front room of his own house. Then he found an abandoned *gurdwara* (Sikh temple) out in the farms, some distance from the town walls, to use as a classroom. Sometimes when he coached his special students, he went back to his house late at night after the gates of the town had been closed. He could not always find the watchman to open the gate, so he would climb over the tall steel gates of Rampura Mandi illegally. In such cases, it was important to cultivate the goodwill of the *chowkidar*/watchman and to request him to be at the gate at the appointed time to allow entry to the town.

Phul Mandi was where I saw an electric light bulb for the first time, because the town had built a *bijli ghar* (electricity house) with an oil-powered electricity generator. There I also had a taste of having to deal with the restriction of liberty imposed by the boundary gates and by law enforcement, compared to the freedom of the village. Our village Mehraj in the English territory, although bigger than Phul in population, had no maharaja, no perimeter wall, no gates, no importance, and no security. But I liked the feeling in my village. The presence of police and the lack of freedom due to locked gates in the townships felt like confinement. I always thought in my mind: How can those people live in the same place where there are police; they might not die of fear but the presence of police surely must kill their spirits! There could not be any joy or celebration in the presence of the Indian police!

In our English territory, the police station in Nathana, was seven miles from our village Mehraj. Considering the difficulties of travel, that was like another world, and we did not see the police often. When the mounted police did come, they were cruel and they threatened, beat, and extorted bribes from people at the slightest pretext. Some people brought milk, chickens, bottles of whiskey, and other supplies to the visiting police to stay in their good graces; others were ordered to bring such things. Whoever housed the policemen and served as a host to them gained influence in the village. Before 1934, when the police "descended" on the village, they stayed in a government building for from the village, close by the *dera* (abode of Hindu holy man) of Tilk Rai. Later, when the dera became a gurdwara, the managing committee went to court, claiming that the government building was on the land of the dera and should therefore become the property of the gurdwara. The claim succeeded, so the police stopped using that building. Later on a literate Muslim named Ahluwalia played host to the police. Some years later when the police would "descend," they stayed in the mansion of the Kapoore Ke family. Later still, a shopkeeper who was Hindu but had changed his name from Gopal Mal to Gopal Singh began hosting the police. He had acquired some agricultural land, rode a horse, and kept a beard and turban like a Sikh, to establish his credibility. Having the police come and stay in his house gave him additional prestige in the village. Not every family had the desire or the social skills to play host to the police.

When the crime rate was high the village *chowkidar* (watchman) named Qamri wandered through the streets at night in our village, shouting, "*khaber dar; jagte raho!*" which meant, "beware, keep awake." His shouts were worthless, and his watch had no noticeable effect on the crime rate. People complained that it was absurd to shout, "Beware, Keep Awake!" in the middle of the night when they wanted to sleep.

CHAPTER 20

LIVING ON A CUL-DE-SAC

In the village we were highly motivated to live close together so as to not expose our house walls to potential thieves. Every effort was made to have the outside walls of our houses covered by other peoples' houses and structures. The fronts of the several houses of our clan that shared side walls, opened into a community courtyard, with an outlet to the street on only one side. Our home, which we called the Inner House, was in the middle of three contiguous houses. On our left lived Aunt Harnami whose husband Buggoo died when I was young; her son Chand and daughters Chand Kaur, Nand Kaur and Mukand Kaur were all older than me. Buggoo had become Harnami's husband when his older brother Arjan died. On our right was the house of Uncle Bhan Singh, whose parents died when I was young; his brother Bhag Singh returned from Hong Kong in 1939. We did not have an enclosing gate for the 'courtyard;' the street just ended in front of our houses, forming a cul-de-sac. The *vehra* (courtyard) of lower-status people was just the shared space created by a group of houses opening to a common area, where outdoor living, playing, and resting took place. Some families had trees in their vehras and animals in adjacent areas, but our own cattle were kept in a corral on the periphery of the village. The houses of some big *sirdars* had the apartments of family members on all sides, enclosing a large courtyard with a big *darwaza* (door, front structure) and possibly a *bethik* (sitting room) on either side to entertain strangers, who were not to be admitted into the inner quarters of the family.

In our vehra, the women of all three houses were in close company of each other while cooking, cleaning, spinning yarn, fetching water from the well, washing clothes, and doing other tasks. Loneliness was rare and sympathy was always at hand when someone was in distress. Many of the tasks were done cooperatively with other women. Women sitting together would make noodles called *sevian* from wheat dough. Similarly, spinning the yarn was done by young girls sitting in groups with their spinning wheels. Even to make the warp component of the yarn for the weaver or to wash clothes at a pond, the women usually worked in teams and in the company of others. Girls and women were almost never alone, except by plan. As was to be expected, there were verbal quarrels among the women at times, but these were soon forgotten. Quarrels among the men of the neighborhood seldom arose, because they would have been too

349

serious and violent. Men's fights were usually with people farther away. Men would normally not join women's fights. Houses were not as enclosed as they are in cold climates; some parts and living areas of a house were open to free entry by anyone. Even in a neighborhood where houses did not open into a common vehra, people interacted closely most of the time; they freely walked into each other's houses to talk or socialize without invitation, prior warning, or permission. Asking permission to enter someone's house to visit would have been considered odd and peculiar.

The Structure of Our Inner House

Our Inner House was modest even by the standards of a Punjab village; it was probably built in the mid-nineteenth century by my great grandfather Sajjan. It was adjacent to the ancestral house that his brother Wazir had inherited. Three centuries ago that was probably the sites of original house of our ancestor Sandly, because the houses of different branches of the clan went outward from that high spot; rainwater flowed from there in all other directions.

In those days, rural people of ordinary means used to build one main structure called a *svaat* as large as one's pocketbook allowed. Then they built substructures inside that main svaat according to their needs, and some added a veranda in front. The main svaat of our Inner House had mud-brick walls and no windows. Four *thumm* (pillars) made of small kiln brick supported three large wooden *latain* (beams) which were really complete tree trunks cut to size and squared off to make the beams. The beams supported many wooden *shahtir* (rafters), which in turn were spanned by the smaller *kurri* rafters in between, all made by the local kariger (carpenter). The kurri rafters supported the ceiling of *sirki* (bamboo grass mats) made from soft reeds which were available pre-assembled from the market. The smooth sirki was covered with coarse bamboo reed on top and then by a dry bush called *khipp*. A plaster of straw-reinforced clay finished the flat roof, and finally a layer of earth was poured on the top. Once every few years the outer sides of the walls were re-plastered with clay mixed with straw. The inside walls had smoother mud plaster and were coated with a yellow clay solution called *poacha*, which was a "yellow wash" instead of whitewash. The floor was also coated with straw mixed with mud, resurfaced every few years. Our svaat was divided into two main parts by a row of cabinets called kothi across the width of the svaat. The veranda in front of the two doors of the svaat had a facade of the small kiln brick, which in the nineteenth century indicated some degree of prosperity, as such brick was not produced locally. One half of the old veranda was later replaced by my father and his brothers with a slightly larger veranda in the early 1920s, just before my brother Kartar was born. The arches of this new veranda were made with common brick as the small brick was no longer available.

The more prosperous people would build a *darwaza* (frontal building) and possibly a *bethak* (sitting room) in front of their courtyard, and separated from the main living svaat. We did not have a darwaza or bethak, nor a separate kitchen or an upper story for our Inner House. Great grandfather was not rich, and moreover he did not have enough land in that location. The svaat floor was about 18 to 20 inches deeper into the ground than the outside veranda level, and that, aided by the yard-thick walls and no windows, kept the temperature more comfortable inside the svaat than outside, both in winter and in summer. Since the house nestled against other people's houses on three sides, they would say, "This house is like a strongbox; security is worth the inconvenience." But on rainy nights in July and August, it was hazardous to walk from outskirts of the village through the muddy and slippery gullies to reach our house.

Of those two levels of *kothi* cabinets that divided our svaat, one set had furniture-quality doors, while the older two sets were unattractive. The upper levels of these kothi were used to store grain and had big holes on the top to pour in the grain. When the grain was poured into the kothi from the top, the front door of the kothi had to be kept locked. Below the door, the kothi had a hole with a rag stuffed into it. You pulled out the rag to pour grain out of the kothi hole and stuffed the rag back in when you wanted it to stop, but this was a tricky maneuver. The newer kothi were used for the storage of foodstuffs and edibles. I was constantly raiding the new kothi for *gur* (solid brown sugar), butter, or any sweets delivered as gifts from someone's wedding in the village. Unlike other houses where they protected and locked the edible things, my mother never locked our kothi.

The partition of the main structure of our house allowed the one side (about one and a half beams in length) to be used for living quarters and the other side for agricultural products and overflow activities. In my great grandfather's time, the two portions may have been divided between his two sons, or the second portion may have been used to shelter animals in cold weather. In my lifetime all our cattle were kept in the barra (corral), some distance away from the village. Inside the living portion of the svaat, there were two small rooms on one side, each with a mezzanine on top. These rooms were called *kothri* (a slight variation from kothi), and only the newed kothri was big enough for a couple of beds. The newer kothri was used seasonally for storing cotton or grains. In winter it was used for sleeping or for a girls' all-night spinning bee. The older kothri with the lower ceiling was dark, during day or night, and had strange and dirty wood, metal, and leather objects in it. Little children were scared to go into this old kothri as they believed that *bhoot* (ghosts) lived inside and could strangle or kill you. The fact that there were bats nesting in the old kothri did not help matters. There were also mouse or rat holes in the earthen floor of the old kothri. Now that I think about it, that dark kothri was a perfect breeding place for rats and plague; no wonder that both of my grandparents died of plague within a week of one another, a hundred years ago. Descendents of the rats that killed my grandparents might still have been living there in my days.

We used two types of traps for rats. In one of them the rat got crushed in the spring-loaded trap as it reached for food. In the other, the rat entered an enclosure to get food but could not get out. The rats trapped thus in the cage were later taken to an open space outside the village. A group of boys would follow the cage carrier when they saw the cage loaded with rats. As the rats were released one by one, the boys competed in killing as many escaping rats as they could. If a rat found a hole to hide in, before anyone could kill it, the boy who had been chasing it was shamed by the others.

Objects in the attics above our two kothris, were also intriguing. There was an old grandmother's *sandooq* with musty, useless stuff in it. There was a *patiar* basket, about 3 feet in diameter and one foot deep, lined with leather, containing odd things such as a thick dog-eared book so old that the Gurmukhi script in it looked hand scribed, a dull small dagger without a sheath, a tarnished metal dish, dried-up army boots, parts of an old milk churn, and so forth. On the mezzanine above the new kothri, there was a large old bed with *rangeel* (painted) posts and striped webbing instead of string webbing. In

351

autumn, cotton was stored in the kothri, and as more was added day after day, its level reached from the floor to the mezzanine. We children were encouraged to climb, play, and romp all over the cotton in order to compress it so that more could be stored.

The Chullah, Hara and Tandoor

In many families, the *chullah* (mud stove, hearth) was in the sacrosanct part of the house. The chullah was made of clay, about a foot high, shaped like a horseshoe to accommodate cooking pots on top and to feed fuel from the front side. In some houses it was in a proper kitchen called chullahni, or in a veranda, or outside on a platform called a *chauka* (square platform), which was slightly raised. Workers of the untouchable caste were not allowed to step on the *chauka* on which the chullah was located. If it was outdoor, the chauka had a *kandholi* (short, thin wall) for privacy. About once a year, women applied a fresh coat of clay or mud mixed with cow dung to purify the chauka. Many traditional women would not allow meat to be cooked on their chullah-chauka, since they considered the eating of meat to be sinful indulgence. They also thought that cooking meat emits a bad odor and felt that the meat would desecrate their hearth forever. Many did not allow shoes at the chauka. But our old house had only a chullah but no *chullahni* (kitchen), or even a kandholi like that of our neighbors Aunt Harnami as we were cramped for space. The chullah, molded from clay and built right on the ground in our old house, was just outside one of the doors of the veranda. We also had another chullah inside the old veranda for winter or for rainy days. We also had a portable clay chullah which could be put anywhere for cooking. Our old Inner House had no darwaza (frontal building), bethak (sitting room), or chullahni, for lack of space. The fact that our house lacked these amenities also indicated that my ancestors were not prosperous.

Adjacent to our outdoor chullah were twin clay ovens called *hara* with their own roof, about six feet high. As a child, my sister Karo once fell off our veranda roof while playing, but as she landed first on the roof of the hara, which broke her fall, she was not seriously injured. Milk was usually heated slowly for half a day in one of the hara while simultaneously in the other hara, things like cotton seed and chickpeas or ground wheat and *khull* (a residue of mustard) were cooked for the milk buffalo. The hara oven was the same shape as the clay oven called *tandoor*, which is used for cooking *roti* or *naan*. The main difference between them is that the hara was kept at a low heat and cooked slowly, while the tandoor was raised to a high heat to cook food quickly. In addition, the tandoor had to have clean inner surface where the dough came in contact with it. The surface of the hara, by contrast, had a horrendous tar buildup after daily use. The cow-dung patties used as fuel in the hara gave off much smoke as they smoldered with a limited air supply for long periods, whereas the tandoor fuel burned much cleaner, to generate higher temperatures for baking. The tandoor was usually built in a common area and shared among several houses. Women from neighboring families cooked roti or naan in the tandoor cooperatively and in rapid succession when the tandoor was heated and ready.

Brick-Making Bee and Elementary Construction

In the *barra* (corral) outside the village, my family built walls from the mud bricks that were used for all sorts of structures in those days. A few years before I was born, my father and his brothers had acquired barra land outside our village to keep cattle, and for this purpose they put up a thorn fence to make a corral. Eventually, they decided to replace the fence with a wall.

For any work that required a lot of manpower and needed to be done rapidly, such as making bricks, installing a roof, or harvesting a big crop in danger of spoilage, sometimes it was impractical to hire paid labor. Instead, it was customary to arrange a *mang* (working bee) by announcing the day of the project and requesting the participation of the village clan and friends. This way you got the best and strongest young men for the mang, and no hired laborers could match their enthusiasm and cheerfulness during the project. There might be between 20 and 40 men, depending on the project and on one's influence. During the mang party the workers had the opportunity to show off their strength and ability as well as to tell jokes, laugh and socialize. The work day would be followed by a big feast in the evening, at which only the men of the host family did the serving. By tradition, the mang feast always included one half pound of *ghee* and two and a half pounds (*sawa ser*) of *suker* (raw brown sugar) for every man. Some young men could eat their share of the suker and ghee sitting right there, along with whatever else was served, but a few took their leftover suker and ghee to their homes. In a society in which there was never enough fat and sugar in the diet, this was their reward for the hard work during the bee. The practice of the mang became less common after World War II as the society became less cohesive and more individualistic.

Uncle Tiloka commanded a lot of respect from the young men of our community and could gather as many volunteers as he wanted for a task. We had held a mang for harvesting a few times, and for other projects as well. So my family held a mang for making mud bricks from the sticky clay that forms at the bottom of a pond over time and that solidifies and hardens better than ordinary mud. The process was fairly simple; all it required was manpower.

When the pond was drying but the clay at the bottom was still quite wet, it was worked and homogenized with *kahi* shovels. The clay was mixed with as much additional water as necessary to make the mud soft enough to be moldable but not so thin as to flow easily. Once the mud had been worked, it was carried by men out of the mud pit using *benghi* (a barrow board with handles in front and back) and was poured on level ground. Then one of three processes was chosen for the next step. One method was to pour the clay into a brick mold, pat it to make the top surface smooth, and then remove the mold, leaving the brick to dry slowly. A more precise process was required for bricks intended to be baked in the kiln. For kiln bricks the clay was pressed into a shaping mold with a bottom plate that might have a trademark pattern on it, and then the mold was overturned to remove it from the brick. Five sides of the mud were thus shaped by the sides and bottom of the mold to make a brick intended for the kiln.

But a *rough and rapid* process was by pouring the mud in long rectangular piles, to flatten it to the height that one wanted the brick thickness to be, and then to make the top and side surfaces of the rectangular pile as smooth as practical. The final step, when the clay had dried somewhat but had not totally hardened, was to cut the rectangular pile, length-wise and breadth-wise with a sickle, like brownies in a pan. The thickness of the bricks was determined by the height of the mud pile, and the cutting blade was used to determine their length and width. This rough and rapid process was used by my family to make large, rough bricks at the pond near our barra (cattle corral) outside the village. Not only were the bricks made by the help of young friends in the village, the perimeter walls of our cattle yard were also built with those bricks by a similar *mang* party, under the supervision of an artisan. With that many men, it took just a couple of days to enclose an area of approximately 50 by 60 yards. Thus the old fence of thorny bush was replaced by a three foot-thick mud brick wall.

This enclosure was originally intended only for our cattle and for the storage of agricultural products. When the wall was first built, my family never imagined that with changing times it was to become the bearing wall of our future residence. The plot of land it occupied was of little value and was some distance from our village. Moreover, it was near a Chuhra colony, and when they acquired the land our people did not expect actually to live away from our fellow Jats and near the Chuhra colony.

The walls rested on no real foundation, as they were intended to be merely an animal corral. A decade later it became the bearing wall for our first *svaat* at that location, which I saw being built there in 1935. I still remember the names of the artisans, Sunder Singh and his sons Bachna and Bhajna, who built it. We stored animal feed in this Avaat. In time more buildings were erected and supported by that perimeter wall. Mice and rats could dig from outside through the sand foundation under the wall. Before we built the buildings, I used to climb on top of this three-foot wide wall with my friends and jump on to the sand dunes outside, for fun and excitement. To get to the top of the wall, we either climbed the gate or climbed the high pile of dried plant matter leaning against the wall.

In 1935, when we built the first *svaat*, we also installed a pipe well with a hand pump on the property to obtain water both for our cattle and for humans. In the prior decades the water table had been rising in the wells, so during the 1930s some families in the village installed pipe wells with hand pumps. Before 1935, like everyone else we used to depend on the common village well for water. The image of my mother wearing her big *ghagra* skirt with a water pitcher on her head, making many trips daily to and from the village well, is still imprinted on my mind. But in 1935 we got our own water source with that pump. Then in 1937 we constructed a more substantial house at the corral, with a brick veranda, some additional rooms, and a small *chobara* (second-story room) as well as a regular *chullahni* (kitchen), although we did not live there yet. My uncle Mohinder had returned in 1937 from Hong Kong; we were fairly prosperous in spite of the economic depression, and we needed a new house.

In 1938 we still lived in the old Inner House; but every night after dinner I had to escort Nihalo, my newlywed uncle's wife, from our Inner House to the chobara (upper story) of this Outer House. The newlyweds needed privacy, and the Inner House was crowded. Uncle Mohinder never escorted his wife himself and usually arrived there late, depending on what other things he was busy with, so I had to take his bride there every night. Even though the distance was not great, returning from this Outer House to our Inner House in the village in the dark was scary for me.

In 1939, the family built another svaat at this outer location and then our entire family moved there from the old house, which was getting very crowded. By this time there were four adult brothers, two wives and my parents' six children. In 1941, my youngest brother Kirpal was born in the Outer House. In time, Uncle Mohinder and Nihalo had six children, about one every year or two.

After our joint family broke up in 1945, the Outer House was not large enough for our separated families, so my father's family moved back into the old Inner House that had been abandoned some years earlier. It was in 1949 that with Kartar's resources we built a new house for our family in our half of the divided *barra* (corral), without changing the sand foundation. Then the old house built by my great grandfather was abandoned. For some time we gave the house free of rent to a refugee woman, who was working as a nurse in the local hospital and living with her daughter. She was a beautiful, cultured woman with patrician features and had lived the life of an aristocrat in the days before she was forced out of Pakistan as a refugee. Now she had to support herself by working as a nurse, and she became a friend of our family. A few years later, the Inner House was again neglected. In one rainy year the roof collapsed and later the walls also collapsed. The Outer House, built in 1949, was our family home from then on. Until the death of my father in 1984, this was the gathering place for his sons and daughters whenever they returned from the pursuits of their lives; we usually coordinated our visits to gather at the same time. It is not an exaggeration to say that the time up to the death of my father felt like the golden years for our family. My father's house was like a dreamland where all of us and our sisters's children played, were nurtured, and entertained. The gatherings there every evening were memorable, as neighbors and friends would come and sit with us late into the night, nibbling snacks, analyzing issues, relating experiences, telling jokes, or singing songs.

The Village Well and Bathing Facilities

Before the irrigation canals were dug in the latter part of the nineteenth century, sources of water in our area were few and not easily accessible. Underground water was very deep; a community had to be substantial and well-established in order to afford a deep well. About the time our village was founded early in the seventeenth century, people had to find a pond to obtain drinking water. If the pond dried up, they were in a precarious situation and had to get water from somewhere else until the next rain. According to local lore, the well in our village was built, or rather funded, by Alla Singh, the founder and first raja of the State of Patiala. Since Mehraj was the village where his grandfather Phul had been born and grew up, it was natural for Alla Singh to visit his ancestral village and his cousins sometimes. It is said that on one of his visits, a wife of his Mehraj cousin from Patti Sandly taunted him, saying, "What kind of *raja* are you, when your *Bhabi* (cousins' wives) are drinking water from the ponds!" They say Alla Singh then ordered the construction of that well, which was made of small bricks and smooth plaster. Its diameter at the mouth was nearly twenty feet. They built three *biddh* (the access areas for drawing water) on the rim of the big well so that each branch of Patti Sandly could have their own waterman draw water independently. Biddh was the place on the edge of the well where the catcher of the *boka* (a huge water bucket of leather with a steel rim) stood under the mounted wheel. A thick rope tied to the boka went over the wheel, and after the boka was lowered into the well and full of water, two oxen or a single camel pulled the other end of that rope to lift the boka full of water from the bottom of the well. After each lift, the boka was emptied into a reservoir, from which the water was diverted into different drains and pipes. The pipes went to the various outlets around the well, where women opened the rag plugs from the mouth of an outlet to fill their pitchers with the well water. Pipes and drains also went to the many hauz (small pools) around the well. The well water felt relatively warm in the winter months, as it came from a great depth in the earth; so a bath in winter was quite comfortable even with the unheated water fresh out of the well.

Very rich people had small bathing pools, called *hauz*, in their homes if they had their own source of water. We had only the community well, and by the time I grew up, very few people were using the hauz at the well for taking baths. The waterman would leave the hauz full when his day ended, but it was not customary for men to jump into the hauz. To leave the water clean for others, most men just used their buckets to get the water out of the hauz to bath by the well. Women used the hauz only as a source of water to wash their clothes at the well. It would have been unthinkable for women to bathe in the open in those hauz at the village well. Women were reluctant even to go to our *talab* (big pool), although there was a walled and secluded portion of the talab for their bathing and swimming.

The moderately rich had a *ghussal khana* (bath chamber) or *hammam*, but hot and cold water for the hammam had to be provided by their servants; they usually did not have running water. For those who did not even have a separate kitchen, a hammam was out of the question. When we had a tub, it was made of galvanized steel. Usually it was portable and small; and it was just used as a source of bath water while the bather sat on the *pattra*, a wooden seat. The used water drained into the street, but the climate was so hot and water was so scarce that this water did not travel very far before drying out. Most of the time, women took baths in a corner of their own courtyard. For privacy, they would just put a *charpai* in front, setting it up sideways as a sight barrier. A woman sat on the wooden pattra and used a bucket of water and a cup to take a bath. In severely cold weather, they sometimes took a bath indoors sitting in a *kanali*, a sort of portable, flat-bottom, shallow, clay bathtub. After the bath, this water was discarded outside; so the kanali could not be very big and the amount of water used indoors was limited by the size of the kanali. Soap was a luxury that was available only for the rich or fashionable people. The poor village women just used a *jhama*, a plate of baked clay with a rough surface, as an abrasive to rub off dirt from the skin.

Washing clothes was subject to the same limitations as washing the hair. Soap was not available to all people. Many people washed their dirty clothes in the water from the well, the pond, or the talab. Just as the jhama was used for rubbing dirt off the body, a *thappa* (paddle) was used for beating the dirt out of clothes; village people did not have many delicate clothes. The wet and rinsed clothes were placed on a wooden pattra and beaten with the thappa until the dirt was not very visible. Professional laundrymen in cities did use cleaning agents and washboards, and a few village families could buy soap, but most poor people in the village did not use much soap before the 1950s.

Our Village Talab

In addition to the hospital and the school, the gurdwara (Sikh Temple) became the third entity in this complex, situated about a quarter mile from our village. Before the 1930s, this was a *dera* (holy man's place), but after the Gurdwara Act, it changed from a Hindu dera to a Sikh gurdwara. Near the dera there was a government guest house where police and other officials used to stay when they arrived. But after the gurdwara committee obtained control of the dera in the early 1930s, they claimed in court that the guest house was built on dera land. They won the lawsuit, took possession of the government building, and used it as their gurdwara until they built a newer building in about 1938 and much later another building on the high ground.

Between the school and the gurdwara there was an enormous talab (pool of water), and the gurdwara committee got control of the talab too because all those fifty or so acres of land were deemed to belong to the dera. The enormous talab occupied more than an acre of land, with about 20 brick steps going down into it, but the bottom of the pool was just natural clay. When it was full, the water could be 200 feet across and 30 feel deep. A few times in my lifetime, the talab was filled to the top by bringing canal water into it; and two long tunnels were meant to bring water to fill the pool, but the tunnels were also used by daring school children to play hide and seek. There were two brick ramps about thirty feet wide going down to the bottom of the talab on the north and south sides. On each side of each ramp there were long runways and jumping platforms to dive into the pool. When I was young, people used to bring their buffaloes down these ramps to bathe them in the pool. But when the gurdwara authorities got firm control of the property, they put a stop to the washing of buffaloes.

In one portion of the talab there was a women's enclosed area called a *pona*, about fifty feet square with 15-foot high walls above the water for privacy; but water flowed freely between the main talab and the women's pona, through the small holes in the walls. Anterooms were provided for the women for shade and privacy, although all women there undressed and walked naked freely in front of other women without any sense of shame or self-consciousness. In exact reverse of Western customs, it was common for women to be undressed in other women's company; but it would have been considered very shameful for a man to be naked in the presence of another man. The walls and arched doorways of those anterooms were coated with very smooth plaster and had interesting murals on them. I remember as a four-year-old being in this women's pool, and I remember seeing a tall wife promenading naked on the inside ledge along the wall all around, high above the water, and then diving in, as other women were bathing on the steps. I have no memory about who she was; I remember only that she was tall, and naked.

In the late 1930s as hand pumps were being installed in homes and cleaner water became available, women stopped using this talab for bathing. They also stopped using the talab for washing clothes. After that the pona enclosure was used by young boys to climb up the walls of the pona and dive from there into the main pool. There were hexagonal kiosks with domes at three corners of the pool; but there were no trees nearby in the early years because leaves from the trees would have made a mess in the pool. It was a tradition for newlyweds and even for ordinary women to take some earth from the bottom of a sacred pond and ceremonially place it on a mound nearby, as an act of virtue. Such *mitti kadhna* (taking out earth), regarded as an act of piety or virtue, was practiced at many other shrines in Punjab also; so the mounds of excavated clay were frequently found near ponds considered sacred. Our talab was at the site of the dera of Tilk Rai, a Sidh or holy man from our own clan, who lived some centuries ago; therefore the site was sacred to our people and sometimes our women carried a little bit of mud from the pool to deposit on the mound. When the pool was full of water, they had to request someone to dive for the mud from the bottom. Once every few years the bottom of the talab was excavated by men of our community, in order to remove the accumulated mud and to maintain appropriate depth. The depth of water could be 20 to 30 feet, but the talab was not always filled to the top.

Going to the Jungle, Not to the Latrine

The problem of answering the call of nature could be quite an inconvenience, depending upon how fussy and squeamish one was. Ordinary village people did not have any places to defecate or urinate in their houses. The activity of defecation for men was called *Jungle jana ve* "going to the jungle", from the practice of earlier times. When a guy said he could beat the jungle out of another, he did not mean trees and plants. For women it was called *"baher jana"* (going out). It was common for a village woman to say "bacche ne jungle phiria hai; potra badl de," which literally means, "the baby has wandered the jungle; change the diaper." But all defecation by adults had to be done outside the village boundaries; the notion of shitting in your own house would have felt very strange and dirty to a villager. The more special a person thought he was, the farther from the village he wanted to go, and somewhat farther than other people had gone before him. The center of an average village was usually not more than 150 yards from its boundary in those days, but finding privacy was not always easy. Usually there was some common village land around the boundary with *kreer* or other bushy growth, which was left uncultivated and for such use. Every family also had a *roori* (dump) just outside the village boundary, to throw cow dung and trash, which was later used as fertilizer in the farms. There were also the *gohara* pyramids erected from dried cow dung patties, which provided a sight barrier. Some women went to urinate behind those gohara pyramids, but that could be some walk from the house. Crops in the nearby fields could also be high enough to provide a sight barrier, but when there were no crops, one just had to go farther away, a comfortable distance from any foot paths. It was normal and expected that a person could go into anyone's crop, but that was a long distance to go from the house just to urinate. To urinate, most women just used some empty lot in the neighborhood where houses had collapsed long ago, or where nothing ever had been built. Some even went up to their own roof-tops to urinate. But to defecate, it was necessary to go outside the village, unless the person was severely ill and immobile. The villagers used to build a *khatta*, an enclosure with earthen embankments, on a fraction of an acre just outside the village, so that the women could defecate inside the enclosure. Many women, however, did not like the idea of going near other piles of shit, except in an emergency, and they would rather go into the crops or in the open fields farther away.

It was a ritual for women friends to gather in groups, with water containers in hand, to go to the *nyaee fields* (fields close to the village). In fact going baher (out) was a sort of a social occasion for most of them to get together every day just about sunset, whether they needed to go or not; for some of them this was the only time of absolute freedom. They would go with friends and squat near each other and talk on all kinds of topics for long periods while defecating. With a new bride, there could easily be a dozen women and girls, to accompany her to the fields in addition to the principal companion carrying water for her. The new bride would take off her *ghagra* (big skirt) and hand it to one of the attendants, while she herself walked some distance further in ordinary clothes to do her deed. Men in that society could never be naked near one another, or sit exposed near each other, much less talk under such circumstances. But it was a common practice for women to be naked in the presence of other women and talk in many situations. The men were working in the fields most of the day, so they could "go to jungle" anywhere during those times.

One scavenger of all the piles and rolls of feces was the sheep. The shepherds, who in our village were Muslims called Sheikh, would bring their flock to those areas which they expected to be abundant in shit, whether fresh or dried up. Although the shepherd had to stay discreetly out of sight, the sheep were pretty aggressive; and sometimes a sheep would dart right behind a person squatting to defecate and gobble up the excrement as fast as it came out. So the expression "going like sheep to shit" was used as a derogatory term in Punjab for an overly eager and greedy person grabbing for something. That is one reason the village people considered sheep to be dirty and stupid animals. Women used "sheep" as a word of abuse toward other women, just as the abusive word "donkey" was used against boys. But as a clean-up crew, a flock of sheep was hard to beat.

If someone was severely ill and unable to move, ashes or sand would be spread in a corner of the courtyard behind a barrier, and the person would have to squat there. But ordinarily the idea of anyone shitting at home or pissing in a pot was unthinkable. In the warm climate there was no need to keep anything like a chamber pot under the bed. Even at night you could just walk out of bed and go some distance without worrying about being cold. Furthermore, in the warm climate one had to urinate less frequently, because water evaporated rapidly from the body. One of the derogatory things the village people said about 'the effeminate, soft, affluent city people' was that the city people shit at home. Little boys teased the still smaller boys about shitting at home, calling them "ghar huggna", i.e., home-shitter. That insult motivated the little ones at an early age to be trained to go outside the village. There was no training to use any potty.

The more affluent and those not engaged in farm work, started making toilet facilities in corners of their courtyards or in spaces nearby for their women. The rich, the nobility, and prominent people in big cities had facilities for eliminating waste. In our colleges, the toilets used to drain into huge containers which were removed and changed periodically by sanitation workers. In the military officers' mess in Ahmednagar, where I went to visit my brother in 1949, there was no sewer system. For the British officers, there were removable pots fitted into holes in the seats of wooden chairs. When the pot in the chair was partially full, its cover was lifted and the pot was removed, emptied, and cleaned or exchanged periodically. Low caste people had the job of removing such waste and cleaning latrines on a regular basis in the cities. To avoid calling them by their actual castes, they were called by euphemistic names like bhangi or jemadar. In the bigger cities there are sewerage systems now. Even in the villages, now some people have facilities in their courtyards. But the toilet facilities in the villages are still unsatisfactory without the municipal sewerage systems, and the "septic tanks" often are not maintained properly.

Ukhli to Crush and *Chukki* to Grind

On one side of the veranda of our Inner House there was a large mortar and pestle, called *ukhli* and *moohli*, respectively. The ukhli was sunk into the ground and was about thirty inches wide at the top, tapering to a rounded cone about a foot deep. It was made of a durable mortar with small stones embedded at the bottom. A typical ukhli could hold 40 to 50 pounds of grain or other foodstuff to be crushed. The wooden moohli (pestle) was about four feet long and about five inches in diameter, but narrow in the middle for a hand grip. Either end of the moohli could be used for crushing and pounding the materials in the ukhli since the grip was in the middle of the moohli. Sometimes two women faced one another sitting on opposite sides of the ukhli and struck alternate blows down into the grain with their moohlis. Most of the time the ukhli was used for crushing animal feed, particularly milch-buffalo feed such as cooked cotton seeds and chickpeas. But sometimes human food needed to be prepared in some way in the ukhli, such as to remove the residual husk from barley or millet before cooking. The ukhli could be used to crush or separate many things.

Chukki, the hand-operated flour mill, was the bane of women before machines started grinding grain into flour. Even when animal driven flour-mills, called *khrass*, were available in larger villages, only a few people took their grain to the khrass to be ground. In the 1930s, the first thing most wives did after waking up was to grind grain into flour with the chukki. Prosperous families got low caste women to come to their houses to grind the grain. A typical chukki consisted of about a forty pound circular upper slab of stone with a hole in its center, on top of a similar stone at the bottom with an axle at its center. There was a handle near the outer edge of the upper stone slab, and at its central opening there was a wooden fitting through which the axle of the lower stone passed. As grain was fed in at the central opening of this upper stone slab, the gram was ground between the stone slabs and it moved outward with each turn of the chukki, getting finer and finer, until it spilled into the space on the periphery of the slabs. There was a clay wall around the chukki to contain the flour in this peripheral space called *maat*. One could easily sleep through the groaning and soothing sound of the chukki, but that sound was more conducive to sleep if it was running in the neighbor's house fifty feet away, rather than just a few feet away near your bed. From farther away it was a pleasant, soothing hum that drowned out other morning noises. It was hard, sweat-producing work for a mother to rotate the forty pound slab of stone continuously to produce enough flour for her family; she had to rotate the upper slab of the chukki for a long period to grind the quantity of flour required. Unmarried girls were not usually put to such work, as they were protected from most hardships.

Some types of grain were ground only to a course grade called *dalia*, for feeding animals. Sometimes the chukki was used to grind beans so course as to barely break each bean into its two naturally equal parts called *daal*. These broken beans were used to cook the dish which was also called *daal* (spiced bean soup), to be eaten by humans. The word daal refers to the splitting of the beans into two parts, and hence the food prepared from it also got the name daal.

Men made up all kinds of justifications as how good it was for a woman's health to work the chukki. My father would say, "A woman who grinds the chukki, first thing in the morning, will never have any diseases. The flour of the chukki is better for health than machine-ground flour. Machines burn the nutrition out of flour; so people should eat only hand-ground flour." When I was young, our village had a few animal-powered kharass (probably a Persian word for a donkey-powered chukki). But in Punjab the kharass were run by oxen or by camels, because a Jat considered it degrading to own a donkey. When we took our camel to the kharass to grind a sack of wheat into flour, his eyes were covered with blinders. He would go around and around as he pulled a

360

wooden lever tied to gears that were connected to the axle of the grindstone and thus powered the kharass machine. Two or three oil-powered machines also had been put up in Mehraj during my childhood, and people from other villages also came to grind their grain there. We thought that kharass flour was almost as good for health as the chukki flour. But everyone spoke about the evils of machine flour, because they believed that all the nutrients were burned out of it, since the flour felt hot when it came out of the machine. People had a tendency to put the blame on something for their diseases, so the machine flour was blamed for the modern diseases.

About four miles away from our village, there were hydro-powered mills called *ghraat* at the waterfalls of the irrigation canal; there a small portion of the canal water was diverted to power a row of flour mills. People thought the flour ground by hydro-powered ghraat was the best quality and nearly as good for health as the chukki flour ground by women. A trip to the ghraat for grinding flour had to be scheduled by the men in this free time; in the busy season it was difficult to go to the ghraat. Furthermore, the irrigation canal was dry, off and on during the year, since the limited amount of water had to be diverted to other branches of the Sirhind canal going to other regions. If there were no waterfalls, then no ghraat ran, and then people had to depend on the oil-powered machine, on khrass, or the woman-powered chukki.

Despite all these other possibilities, sometimes my mother had to grind flour to feed the whole family and workers when the men folk were too busy to go to the powered mill to grind the wheat. For making daal from beans like chickpeas, moong, mah, moath or masur, the *chukki* was the only method used. Any grains that needed partial grinding for feeding the animals, were also ground by women with the chukki. Partial grinding was not so laborious; it was the fine flour that required prolonged and difficult labor. The flour to make roti was needed every day, at least twice a day. It is easy to understand why it made practical sense for a conqueror in earlier times to kill all the males of the enemy and carry the women off as slaves, not just to gather fuel and water, cook and clean, but also to grind flour with the chukki for the rest of their lives. In my childhood, prisoners in India were made to grind flour, especially in the princely states. They say that even Nanak, the founder of the Sikh faith, was captured and imprisoned by men of the Mughal conqueror Baber and was put to grinding flour with a chukki along with the other prisoners until they discovered that he was a holy man. Sikh legend says that the chukki in front of Nanak ran automatically, without his hand touching it! This miracle is about as true as the ones about his stopping a mountain landslide with the palm of his hand or his going on travels to faraway lands instantly, simply by closing his eyes.

Our Pots and Utensils

Before the village people acquired water pumps in the 1930s, every family had many water pitchers of baked clay called by various names such as *taura, muggha, matka, matkna, chatti, ghara,* or *ghari*. I remember that our family used to have a dozen pitchers (each about 40 pounds' capacity) sitting full of water in two rows. They were used not only to bring water from the well but also to store water; because on some days the waterman did not work, and being caught short of water was not a happy situation. Milk was churned in a similar clay vessel called a *rirkna*, fitted with a wooden device called a *kur*, through which passed a *madhani* (churn) with four blades at the churning end. The madhani was rotated with a *netra* (rope belt) wound around it, that had wooden handles (*dhindi*) at both ends. As one pulled the rope wound around the madhani alternately with each hand, the madhani rotated back and forth inside the churning vessel. For cooking, in addition to the usual *Kujja* pots baked of clay, our house had brass *pateela* pots and even a large pot called a *deg* of about six gallons' capacity that was made of *kansi* (white metal).

Our main eating vessels were *thali* (a platter), *chhanna* (a flat bottom bowl), *kaul* (a small bowl) and an even smaller *kauli* bowl, all usually made of *kansi* alloy, although in earlier days some were made of brass. The tumblers were made of brass plated with a metal coating that looked like dull silver. Those coated brass utensils were called Moradabadi. In earlier times, vessels of brass without the coating were used. But the kansi alloy came to be preferred since the brass utensils became etched and stained by most kinds of food and the health hazards of brass vessels became a consideration. When this hazard came to be feared, brass surfaces that came in contact with food were coated with a tin-like metal that gave the surface a silvery or aluminum appearance. Many families neglected to coat their brass utensils and later worried whether someone's sickness was caused by poisoning from the utensils. I don't know if there was ever any definitive study to determine the effect of brass and other metals used for cooking and eating. Adverse effects would have been slow and permanent rather than acute and temporary. People went by the word of the itinerant men who came by and offered to 'tin-coat' the brass utensils for a better look and good health.

Clay pots were always made in the village, while metal ones had to be purchased from the market, as were most eating utensils. The clay utensils were safe to use, but they were harder to clean and broke easily. People used large serving spoons made of metal or wood, called *karchhi* and *doey*, respectively. Most village people ate with their fingers, except the very few progressive families who might know the use of the spoon and who provided spoons for guests in later years. The use of forks was unknown except to some high class, urban and anglicized people in big cities. A knife for eating was unnecessary as there was no meat to cut and most cooked food could be eaten without cutting. Paring knives were owned by very few people. Most people had just the large kitchen *daat* with a pedestal, which served as the cutting tool for fruits or vegetables but was very awkward for general use as a knife. Our kitchen and household tools were crude and of poor quality steel, and they were usually made by the Gadi Wala nomads. After the partition of India, most of the potters, being Muslim, left for Pakistan, and in our area Hindu potters were rare. Later, the village people came to depend upon the metal utensils. As time went by and people became more prosperous, most of the utensils were made from stainless steel.

Charpai, The All-Purpose Piece of Furniture

An average family in the village would have several *manja, manji* or what in Hindi were called *charpai* (four footed) portable beds. Most four-post bed frames had string webbing to sit or sleep on. A family would have one charpai for each member to sleep on and one or two fancier and larger *palang* (large bed) for guests. The strings of poor peoples' beds were made of the fibrous bamboo-like grasses called *moonj*. More affluent families used the strings made from hemp or cotton thread for greater comfort, better appearance, and a more durable bed. The posts of the manja (bed) for adults were about two feet high;

362

there were smaller manji and *panghoora* for children. Some fancy palang beds had *rangeel* (painted) posts and webbing of woven cotton-thread stripes called *nevaar*, instead of string webbing.

Although the charpai was mainly for sleeping, it was also the principal piece of furniture on which men sat, indoors or out in the courtyard. An important guest would be seated on a large, fancy palang. A small manji bed could be carried to a shady tree for resting or to play cards with friends. On summer nights, men lifted these beds up along the wall of the house, and then someone on the roof would catch it and place it on the roof for a family member to sleep on. Many men sat on a charpai to eat their meals, brought in a platter, as no family in the village had tables and chairs in the 1930s. So the charpai was the all-purpose furniture, not merely for sleeping, but for sitting, socializing, playing cards, eating meals, and for doing some kinds of delicate work by women.

It was a social error for a wife to be caught sitting on a charpai in the presence of men, possibly because she was expected to be busy getting things ready in anticipation of their arrival. This is exactly the opposite of the Western society, where a man is not supposed to sit when a woman enters the room. A wife usually would not sit on a charpai in the presence of men, even if she was free from work. She would not need to jump off if caught sitting on a bed, but would quietly get down and be engaged in some domestic work when her man arrived. Women could sit together on charpai beds while doing embroidery and similar tasks, when no men were around. A daughter could do whatever she wanted, as she was the privileged one in her father's house.

The proper furniture for a woman to sit on was the *peerhi*, a smaller, two-foot square version of a charpai, and about 5 to 7 inches high. The peehri seat was closer to the ground and that allowed a woman to sit while cooking, cleaning, and doing other chores. It was nearly a taboo for a man to sit on a peerhi. Women felt very uneasy when their sons sat on a peerhi except to keep warm in front of the chullah, the cooking stove or hearth, where it was impractical to place a charpai. My mother would just say that it was *avgun* (the opposite of virtue) for boys to sit on a peerhi. Avgun was just meant an unworthy act and was not a misdeed. The peerhi was a necessity when a woman was cooking or sitting at her spinning wheel, as no other furniture was as suitable.

In the 1940s some educated families in the village started having the local carpenter build tables and chairs of solid wood, for entertaining guests. When they saw government officials or the doctor using such furniture in their offices, they wanted tables and chairs for themselves too. But it would have been considered pretentious and incongruous for a village farmer to own tables and chairs in the 1930s. Table and chairs were much above their standard of life, so the charpai served as a multipurpose piece of furniture. A dining table was also unnecessary, because the families did not sit together for dinner. They would eat in succession if they wanted to eat the roti hot and fresh as it was being cooked. As the wife was cooking, the children were fed according to their needs or in the order in which they arrived. A wife never sat with her husband to eat. It was considered a minor sin for a wife to eat before feeding her husband, regardless of how late he was in arriving home; she would feel guilty if she ate first.

The *Sandooq* was the personal furniture that a bride brought from her parents' house as a part of her dowry. She kept all her private, precious, or expensive things in the sandooq, safe from others' hands and eyes. The sandooq was a large wooden container, about five foot cube, with a small lockable door in the front panel. It might have elaborate designs, paint, metal, and/or mirror decorations depending on how much expense the parents could afford for their daughter's wedding. One important feature of the sandooq was that it would have four legs, eight to twelve inches long. Where there were mice, rats, and other vermin and the floors were earthen, separation from the ground was helpful. In later years some people started getting large metal and wood trunks, called *petti*, either in lieu of a sandooq or in addition to it. But the petti without legs was not traditional for a bride. Steel trunks were also a modern invention. In earlier times some village people had the round *patiar*, which was a leather-lined basket with a lid. For temporary storage or the transportation of goods, large open baskets called *tokra* were used. These tokra baskets were made from flexible mulberry tree shoots that were lopped off when the branches were about nine month old and used when still flexible, before they dried up. Smaller baskets called *tokri or bohti* were made from the thinnest tree branches of mulberry and from other materials for miscellaneous uses.

Heat, Light and Power

Our houses were heated or cooled only by design and physical orientation. Even the chullah (hearth) or the cooking stove was outside the main house and not in the living or sleeping areas to provide heat. In that climate, keeping warm was easy, except between December and February; but keeping cool was difficult. Summer heat in Punjab was as oppressive as in the worst of places on the globe. A house facing north or east, with thick mud brick walls shared with adjacent houses, minimal ventilation so as to keep hot winds out, with its floor somewhat deep into the ground and large trees situated south and west, all helped to keep it cool. But many people were negligent or did not have a choice. Some might build a house with doors facing south or west because that is where the street was, and thus they suffered for generations. My mother used to say that it would bring misfortune to have a house facing south as the Dubboo's house did. The summer sun entered their svaat door a good part of the day and it was not possible to cool the house much, except by sprinkling water in front of the door and in the courtyard in the late afternoon. Women used hand fans; a man would just sweat, as he could not admit to being hot and would not ordinarily use a fan.

It was very cold near freezing point on some days in January even in the Punjab plains, and in rare years small puddles of water froze overnight in some areas until the sun came up. Western-style coats and pants were not common there. The village people would just wrap themselves in cotton blankets (*khes*) when going about. Some people would wear *bhoongi,* a hood that went from the top of the head down to mid-calf and could be gathered to cover the front of the body. Some men had jackets of quilted cotton and pajama bottoms of some thick cloth to cope with the cold. Children spent time in front of the chullah fire before they went to bed. In the bed people slept on stitched quilts with rag fillings inside, called *julli*, and for the top cover they had a quilt filled with cotton, called *rezai*. In later years, people began to regard the julli quilt as demeaning, because it was filled with old rags, so the julli became an object of ridicule. Many started to use a maroon-colored, cotton-filled quilt called *gadella* for the bottom on the bed and usually a paisley print quilt for the top, both made from the home-made and village-dyed cotton cloth. It was also considered a low-class habit to carry a quilt wrapped around you; only the poor and non-Punjabis carried their quilts about, even in trains and other places in winter. *Julli Chuck* (quilt carrier) was a term of derision in Punjab, implying low class and unfashionable.

Diva (non-Punjabis may call it deepa), the mustard oil lamp, was a very small clay cup with a notch for the cotton wick. For light in the house at night, most people in the early years used mustard oil diva lamps (the word Divali for the festival of lamps, comes from diva.) During the 1930s, some families had kerosene lanterns, but a kerosene lantern was a luxury for the poorest people of the village. It gave more light than 10 mustard oil lamps when its glass chimney was clean. It was less affected by wind, although nothing could stay lit during a hurricane and raindrops could break the heated glass chimney. In some years such as during World War II, when the supply of kerosene was scarce and uncertain, we again depended on diva lamps using mustard oil, which was a domestic product. The "gas lamp," in which petroleum vapor under pressure was sprayed on a special wick, was spectacularly bright, but such lamps were seen only in later years in the gurdwara and at the weddings of affluent people. Some bigger towns installed oil-powered electricity generators in the 1930s, but electricity in those years was used mainly for lights and not for appliances or other purposes. After I left India, electricity from the hydro-generators on the Bhakra Dam was brought to the villages during the 1960s and the mustard-oil diva became history. When hydroelectric power from the newly built Bhakra Dam was abundant in the 1960s, the government encouraged its use, and for some time there were no meters to monitor the amount of electricity used by the rural families. Later, electricity was supplied to the villages for lighting, heating, and motors at a minimal cost. Many village people paid very little for the use of electricity, until the demand from the burgeoning cities like Delhi grew rapidly.

In the 1940s some rich and progressive farmers in a few places used imported tractors, but in the 1960s and 70s farm mechanization started seriously in Punjab. The use of animal power was mostly eliminated in Punjab by the end of the 1970s, by which time one did not often find oxen and camels pulling ploughs or carts in Punjab.

Household fuel in the village consisted of cow dung pathi or dried up cotton plants or other kinds of plant matter. Burning wood for cooking was fairly common when I was young in the 1930s when any house could cut down a tree or two from their own property and used the logs and branches to burn as fuel. The Beri tree was the preferred fuel for cremation of the dead, because being fruit wood it was hard and burned slowly. But after the pressure of population became greater, trees became scarce. With that scarcity the rural Jats used wood fuel only for large-scale cooking, for yugg, or for weddings and such activities. They had plenty of cotton plant matter from their own crops to burn for routine cooking. Shopkeepers, Brahmans, and other castes who did not have farm products to burn, continued to burn wood for some time longer, but those in the cities were switching to burning coal or oil in stoves. The use of compressed gas did not become widespread until after the 1960s. Nowadays, the village people may still burn farm product residues, but in the cities the compressed gas or electric stoves are now commonly used for cooking.

CHAPTER 21

OUR FOOD IN THE VILLAGE

Roti, the unleavened flat bread, was the staple for our people. When one thinks of farm life, visions of fresh foods and healthy meals come to mind. But our food in the village was a far cry from the cuisine of modern Indian restaurants. In the 1930s our food was plain for ordinary people and scanty for poor people. An average farming family could afford only three things: flour to make *roti, daal* from lentils or some vegetable, and simple spices to make it all palatable. People were poorer in the 1930s than they are now. Small farmers had milk, but it was neither abundant nor continuously available through the year. Some counted the months and weeks from conception, before their only buffalo or cow would start giving milk after calving.

Uncle Tope Wala (hat man), who had returned after living in America for 43 years, used to lament, "In this country it is the same boring roti, morning, noon and night; there is no variety in the food in rural India." But he *could* afford better food; for ordinary villagers the only possible variety was that instead of wheat flour for the roti, occasionally it was a mixture (missi roti) with barley, maize, millet, or chickpea flour. Daal (lentil soup with spices) to accompany the roti might be *mung, mah, massur, moath, chhole* (chickpea), or some rarer varieties of beans. Before canal irrigation started in the late 19th century, even wheat was a precious and scarce commodity. In the desert areas, barley, millet, and chickpea flour were more readily available than wheat for making roti.

What you got to eat with the roti depended on your prosperity level, and the imagination and skills of the women in the house. To make the roti palatable, daal was almost always a part of our every dinner. When cooking vegetables, the more skilled cook fried the vegetables with onions, garlic, ginger, and a selection of spices, and then the resulting *tarri* (sauce) could be tasty. Eating meat was generally for the rich or the hunting *sirdars,* and infrequently for adventurous younger guys who could slaughter some small animal. Meat was usually not roasted but cooked like the vegetables, with spices, and again the quality of sauce was determined by the skill of the cook. There were no regular sources of fish in rural Punjab. In cities you could get cooked fish at food stalls; usually it was deep fried and highly spiced.

Only some creative and caring wife brought anything elaborate to the fields for the workers to eat. Most workers just swallowed their roti with a raw onion, a pickle, or *chutney* sauce. The chutney of the villagers was a mixture of salt, peppers, onions, and possibly some other herb or spice added and crushed with mortar and pestle. As a special treat, some mothers would make *choori* for their sons' lunches when they were sent to graze cattle or even to school. Choori was the word for broken bread mixed with ghee and brown sugar when hot. It was usually made into balls to prevent drying.

Sometimes in the busy season, our evening meal consisted of a bowl of *dalia* (porridge) taken with milk. At other times it was cooked *khichri*, the best one being a mixture of moath beans and bajra (millet) that was taken with milk when hot in the evening. The following morning, the cold khichri was best either with yogurt or preferably with raw milk fresh out of the udder. City people thought khichri was poor folk's food, but the khichri of moth-bajra is still a pleasant memory for me. It has become rare in modern Punjab because its ingredients like moath can not be grown much anymore.

For poor people and sharecroppers who could never afford their own buffaloes, any milk products would come from the generosity of the landowner's wife. For the poor, the only milk product available free was the *lassi* (buttermilk), because the landowners had little use for it after the butter had been extracted from the milk. Some people thrived on drinking lassi, but the fashionable ones avoided it, because it was free. There was a common belief, perhaps false, that the lassi caused *vadi* or *vat* (an imbalance in health according to the Vedic system of medicine), even to cattle. Vadi was considered responsible for creating excess of fluids in the body, making joints ache and swell, or making people and animals lethargic and sluggish. Tea and opium were considered to have curative effects, opposite to those of lassi on the body. An opium user would never touch lassi, because it would dull the effect of opium. The village people thought that sugar, milk, butter, ghee, nuts, and meat give strength, while grains, vegetables and daal are good only for survival; that spices have no health value but are mainly for taste, and that tea and opium are like tonics for short term use, but could be addictive. Since buttermilk was the product after the precious *ghee* had been extracted out of milk, some people treated buttermilk like a waste product and tried to make the animals drink it.

Most landowners in our village never sowed vegetables intentionally, although some vegetables could grow in the midst of their crops due to stray seeds. Many pulled out the vegetable plants from their crops whenever they saw any. Some unintended seeds, like okra, squash, or pumpkin, would go through the garbage heap which was later used as fertilizer, and could grow as vegetable plants. A few people might sow some vegetable seeds like pumpkin, gourds, zuccini, squash, cucumber, okra, or *tindo*, but then they could not always prevent others from stealing the vegetables and trampling their main crop in the process. So, for most families, homegrown vegetables were sporadic and unplanned, as the farmers thought that they interfered with the regular cash crops. Women usually bought vegetables or fruits from street hawkers in exchange for grain or cash; the stores rarely sold vegetables or fruits in our village.

At some stage in their growth, many ordinary crops could be cooked with appropriate spices to prepare vegetable dishes that were tasty and healthful. For example mustard leaves, tender stems, and other leafy plants were used to prepare *saag*. Tender green chickpea beans, instead of peas, with potatoes or cauliflower were a good seasonal vegetable. Even the lowly camel feed like the green *gwara* bean pods could be fried and spiced to become a delicacy. But crops like carrots, radishes, turnips or cauliflower that required extra care to grow were avoided by most farmers, as they wanted to cultivate only the cash crops that they could sell through brokers. Selling vegetables in retail was considered a menial occupation and below the dignity of Jats. Growing vegetables and other crops to be sold at retail, was the occupation of other castes like the Araeen, and in our village this was done infrequently. Their attitude was that anything grown for eating at home was a waste of resources, and growing anything for selling in retail was for the castes that were not respectable. Our family sometimes gave land to Imam Din, an Araeen sharecropper, to grow vegetables or sugar cane. But we considered it a frivolity, since such things were only for personal consumption and were not cash crops.

The food in our house was ordinary compared to that in other homes. My mother cooked in bulk for everyone including the farm workers. It was only when my sisters grew up that they learned to prepare dishes that were better-tasting. Consequently, I don't have any real longing for my mother's cooking, but I have always enjoyed being a guest at the homes of my sisters Karo and Choti. The skill of a cook was measured by how good a sauce she could make. Women used not just salt and pepper but fried onions with garlic, ginger, coriander, cumin, turmeric, cinnamon, fenugreek, fennel, nutmeg, cardamom, and other rare spices to make the Punjabi style *turri* (sauce) for meats as well as for vegetables.

In our house, there were no particular food prohibitions, but meat was not a part of the regular diet in most rural households; they did not spend time hunting or raising animals for meat. They were of two minds about eating meat. They believed that eating meat made bodies strong and fat; but also believed that, like many other pleasures, doing so was sinful, and you had to kill one of God's creature to get meat. Hindus and Sikhs would not eat cow meat. Some people kept chickens as a hobby, but more of the lower castes did so because they were not squeamish about the resulting filth in their homes. Hunting was common among affluent landowners who did not normally work in the fields. Low caste people, who were considered polluted anyway, could eat whatever meat they could get. Some low castes could also eat parts of a dead animal after they hauled it away from the farmer's house, and removed its hide to sell to leather workers, as the Jat caste was not expected to touch a dead animal. This image of the lower castes eating dead animals increased the contempt for meat in the minds of the upper castes. Eating meat was considered more sinful than drinking alcohol, but some younger men defied conventions and indulged in eating meat even if their families did not. When women would not permit the desecration of their kitchens by meat, the landowners' boys would buy and slaughter a goat or chicken, or they would buy the meat and cook it in a wife-less house and shared it with their friends along with whiskey. This was mildly frowned upon by their families as impious indulgence, but the younger Jat men defied the families. Once Chand and his friends were even accused of stealing some shepherd's sheep at night and eating it at a wife-less house. The prohibition against eating meat varied from family to family. Professional butchers were found only where there was a significant Muslim population, such as in the village of Phul; so some Jat boys traveled to Phul to buy meat. An animal slaughtered according to the *helal* (Muslim kosher) rituals was a forbidden food for the Sikhs, but any Jat Sikh landowner who ate meat was violating some rule of piety anyway; so they did not worry too much about the prohibition against the helal meat.

When I was a teenager, I myself raised a male goat and slaughtered it when it was about 15 months old. I got a little help from my sharecropper named Santu, who knew how to skin and gut it and knew how the different organs of the slaughtered animal were useful. There was no refrigeration, but since it was the winter season, a part of the carcass was just hung in a cold room in our house for many days until it was all used up. My mother was used to cooking meat from her younger days when her adventurous brothers went hunting with the Sirdar of Talwandi. The Sirdar and his wife visited the home of my maternal uncles occasionally since they were good friends, but the Sirdar would never associate with ordinary Jat farmers.

Animal sacrifice were a part of the religious rituals of the low caste Chuhra people until the 1950s, when they gradually started abandoning traditions. For those ancient rituals they would raise a pig themselves or buy a ceremonial pig from somewhere. They would have the animal decorated with ritual *khumni* threads and bells for a few days. Then on a certain day, right in front of the small mud platform called thaan (their sacred space) with a tiny mud temple like a doll's house, they would slaughter the pig and share the meat with their kin and friends. The Muslim police officers would go into an abusive rage and would order the low castes to stop keeping or eating pigs. Even the sight of a pig was considered an unholy occurrence for a Muslim, and being the powerful policemen, the Muslims could not stand the effrontery to their religion from the lowly Chuhra who kept pigs. In fact even uttering the word pig in the presence of a Muslim in Punjab would cause a major fight, and saying "eat pig" to a Muslim could result in murder, just as saying "eat cow" to a Hindu could do. After 1947 there were no Muslims left in the Indian Punjab to enforce the ban on the slaughter of pigs.

Desi Khand and Ghee

In those days, refined sugar in white powdered form, called *desi khand* (domestic sugar), was a costly item, saved for special occasions or for special guests. It was mixed with heated ghee and served as the choicest treat, constituting the first course of a meal for a special guest. Brown sugar that was called *suker* in powdered form and *gur* in solid form, was less expensive as it was produced without special refining. Granulated sugar was quite unpopular before the 1940s. Some people believed the rumors that there were ground-up cow bones in the granulated sugar and that the desi white-powder sugar was purer. This would make it a sin to eat crystal sugar and kept its price lower in the earlier days. The more informed people realized that granulated crystal sugar was in fact the purer form, because it was easier to add impurities to the powdered sugar than to the grainy crystals. With some unease at first, they began to use granulated sugar for preparing sweets for weddings and festivals, as no one could tell what kind of sugar was used in their preparation. Later in the 1940s it became common knowledge that crystal sugar was just as good as powdered sugar and did not cause any sin. In the 1950s the use of the desi powdered sugar started declining and the granulated sugar became more common.

My family sometimes bought a 200-pound bag of gur (solid brown sugar) to feed to our oxen because they believed that sugar promotes strength and good health. They regretted the fact that I ate too much of the sugar stealthily, when it was meant for the oxen. They would say, "Gurnam, you are eating too much *gur* secretly; the worm will eat your teeth." But I was addicted to sugar all my life and never worried about my teeth.

Like everyone else, I believed that sugar, ghee, and milk were good for health, as indicated by the resulting fat. Nuts of all kinds were even more prized than sugar, ghee, and milk, but nuts were expensive not a domestic product and available to even fewer people.

For wedding feasts, sweets like *Luddoo, Jalebi, SukerPara* and *Balu Shahi* were prepared with white sugar. On the evening of a *mang* (working bee of volunteers), the host would provide two and a half pounds of suker (brown sugar) and half a pound of ghee as the prescribed amount of mixture for every volunteer to eat after the hard day's work. For an important guest, the best treat was a mixture of desi white sugar and ghee, usually eaten before roti, daal and other things. The guest's *lagi* (a hereditary dependent of lower caste), if accompanying the master, would get the brown suker and ghee and not the precious white sugar. Women usually kept a hidden supply of white sugar for unexpected guests, because to be caught without such a supply would be embarrassing.

Rural people were unable to go routinely to market towns to buy things to eat, so home-grown commodities were consumed by most people. For example, *sevian* were the noodles rolled at home from wheat dough. For this purpose a team of women from the neighborhood would sit on mats and clean sheets, with the round surface of an inverted pitcher in front of each woman. A ball of dough would be put on top of the round surface of the pitcher. With the palms of the hands pressing back and forth, a woman would roll thin noodles out of the dough. A pile of noodles gradually accumulated on the sheet on each side of the inverted pitcher. Periodically the pile of noodles was removed and hung on the branch of a dried kreer bush to dry in the sun, and later the dried sevian would be stored in a container. The sevian dessert was prepared by simply boiling the noodles in water and adding some sugar and ghee.

The more aware families started serving sweet dishes like *kheer* (rice cooked in milk), and *krah* (pudding of flour, sugar and ghee) to their guests. They served these deserts after the main meal instead of the traditional white sugar and ghee before the meal. But there would be 'behind-the-back' talk from old-fashioned people who felt they had not gotten proper treatment without the sugar-ghee mixture to begin the meal. Rice was considered a delicacy since it was not grown in Punjab in those days, as it later came to be with the abundance of water. Things like *gulab jamun* and *rasgulla* were the milk, sugar and flour products, mostly in the cities. *Khoa* (milk cooked until it became solid) with sugar and possibly some nuts was another highly valued food, prepared for strength and good health. Families supplied ghee and khoa to their sons to keep them fat when they were sent to a boarding school or college.

When the rainy season started, women cooked *poora, gulgula* and *pakora*. The poora were just the equivalent of sweet crepes. Women started with liquefied wheat batter containing brown sugar, poured it on a heated griddle coated with oil, and spread it on the griddle with the folded leaf of a pipple tree. The poora was turned over once after the first surface was cooked adequately. The gulgula were made from the sweetened or spiced dough by deep frying the blobs of the dough in boiling oil. The Punjabi village pakora were just very thick noodles made from the dough of chickpea with very little else added. The chickpea dough was continuously squeezed through a sieve with large round holes, into frying oil to make the pakora. But the word pakora is used in the rest of India for other deep fried foods made from various vegetables dipped in spiced chickpea batter.

After giving birth, and to regain her strength, a woman received about a 40-pound load of *punjiri*, which was a cooked mixture of flour, sugar, ghee, various nuts, dates, raisins, seeds, and dry fruits, and some mild herbs or spices (*kamarkass, sundh*, four kinds of *goond, supari, ajwain*, and so forth). Sometimes the punjiri could be made into balls called *pinni*, but it could be also stored as compacted powder in a clay pitcher. Punjiri was traditionally sent by the in-laws to the wife, when she had her baby at her own parents' house.

Ghee Equals a Hundred Medicines

Ghee (in our area it was called *gheo*), the clarified butter, is made by melting butter and separating the fat from any milk residue. The advantage of making ghee from butter is that this clarified butter does not turn rancid easily and can be stored for a long time even in warm climates. In modern times, ghee may be considered dangerous animal fat that may cause clogged arteries, but in my time ghee was considered the key to good health and heavenly taste. As a catalyst to improve taste and to provide better nutrition, every roti was coated with ghee when it was still hot. The ghee brought out the taste in all those spicy daals, vegetables, and saag that were eaten with the roti. The saying, *"Gheo Banawe Torian, Vaddi Bahu da Nam"* means, "It is the *ghee* that makes the zuchini/squash taste good, but the senior wife gets the credit." By the way, *senior wife* implies the wife of the oldest brother in a big household, and not multiple wives for one man. In winter, when buffalo milk was more abundant, rural boys built their bodies with exercise. Some were given quantities of ghee that their families had pledged to them as rewards for good behavior or hard work. A *panjseri* (five *ser*), about 10 pounds of ghee, was a good reward. Since gaining weight and getting fat was the objective (and not always easy), most fellows would just drink a small bowl of the melted ghee daily to rapidly build up fat. Belief in the nutritional value of sugar, ghee, and milk was so strong that even draught animals were given brown sugar in the heavy work season. Animals like the oxen of our house were given wheat dough mixed with raw sugar. After a severely stressful day of racing under a heavy passenger load, a camel would be given a dose of sugar and alum (aluminum sulfate?). In extreme cases of stress, the camel might get some hot milk and ghee "to relieve the shock to his body", because of the belief that ghee gives strength and heals any damage to the body. The proverb, *sau chacha, ik peo; sau daru, ik gheo* (One Father = Hundred Uncles; One Ghee = Hundred Medicines), was believed true for humans as well as for animals. Apart from its value in improving health and increasing strength, ghee was used for ceremonial occasions and for *shagun* (a good omen). For an especially important or sacred occasion, a lamp of ghee, instead of oil, was lit by a family. That was also done in honor of a new bride or a special guest, and it created a pleasant smell. Sometimes mustard oil was poured at the door, and rarely some ghee was poured as a special guest entered the door. A small amount of ghee was poured in the foundation when the construction of a new house was started. So ghee had a special place in the lives of village people.

People also believed that garlic was good for health and could prevent diseases. But to make it even more effective, they would fry the garlic in ghee because then the fried cloves of garlic were not so pungent. After eating the garlic cloves, they would drink the residual ghee. When I was a teenager, I stealthily ate gobs of solid ghee, without mixing it with anything, and thinking that I was absorbing pure strength. On the days when my Uncle Tiloka was not feeling his best or felt somewhat sick, he would ask my sisters to fry some garlic in ghee for him to drink. He thought that the ghee would keep him strong and healthy while the garlic was additional insurance for health. In retrospect, the ghee may have clogged his arteries and may have contributed to his early death by heart attack at the age of 73; my father, who was never given enough ghee, lived fifteen years longer. My mother used to tell my father that his body was skinny and withering and he should eat some ghee; but my father always said that he would make the sacrifice to provide the ghee to his children instead. There was never enough ghee in an average family and those who had lower priority would get very little of it.

Glorious Opium and Lowly Tea

More people in Mehraj drank whiskey than drank tea during the 1930s, as the drinking of tea had not yet become common. People used to think that tea could be addictive and thus a bad habit. But not many drank alcohol regularly either. Ordinary people drank whiskey only on special occasions such as weddings, fairs, festivals and celebrations. People who had addictive personalities drank to excess on such occasions and then could not stop drinking for days after the special occasion. Drinking alcohol was considered a habit of self-indulgent and pleasure-loving people, and drinking to excess was the cause of jokes. It was acceptable for young men to drink alcohol occasionally, since people felt it was the time of their lives to enjoy themselves before they got bogged down with family worries. There were always quotations about how transitory life was and the exhortation to "enjoy life while you are still young." If one never drank alcohol, one might be considered odd and weird among his peers. In rural families, drinking alcohol was not considered as much of a sin as eating meat, because alcohol might involve pleasure but not killing of any animal. The main disadvantage of drinking was that it made some people belligerent, as they did not feel inhibitions or have full control of their mental faculties in that state. No woman drank alcohol openly, except as *medicine* to cure some minor sickness or cold.

No wine or beer was sold in the countryside in those days, and you could buy whiskey and opium only at a licensed shop. Practically, there was no age limit for buying opium or whiskey. When as a 14-year-old I used to walk to my teacher five miles away to the market town of Rampura Phul, my Aunt Hernami would sometimes give me money and request me to buy opium for her. Aunt Harnami was not considered an addict and did not look like one, as she was not skinny. She just believed that she was taking opium to maintain good health and to prevent minor aches and pains. She also had given opium daily to all her babies until they were a couple of years old. She felt that opium kept minor diseases away and kept the babies in good health and a good mood. Feeding opium to babies was a fairly common practice even among people who themselves did not take opium. Only my father had forbidden opium strictly for his children.

People who were well known to be addicted to opium, acquired the designation of *amli* (addict; user of stimulants); it was considered perfectly polite and friendly to address them, "Oh Amli, how are you today?" Such an amli would be more talkative and entertaining after taking a pinch of opium than without. At fairs and long, continuous activities, an amli would offer opium to his companions, saying, "Take this pinch of opium; you will enjoy the fair more." or "With a little opium we will walk the distance in better time." and there was some truth in that. Eating opium was considered more benign than drinking alcohol, although opium was more addictive. The amli thought the glorious opium was like a gift from God; it made them feel better immediately and took away pain and fatigue.

One day in the summer of 1946, my father, my two uncles and I had gone to the town of Gidder Baha to a court. We were done early, at about noon, and the elders were going to take the train to get back home that evening. I decided to walk from Gidder Baha to my village Mehraj, a distance of about 35 miles. I was 16 years old, and in those days I felt that nothing was too difficult for me. I started from Gidder Baha about noon along the bank of a canal and asked people the best route to Mehraj as I progressed. On the way an older man grazing cattle on the bank of the canal asked me where I was heading, as people usually tried to be helpful to a traveler. When I told him that my destination was Mehraj, the old timer said, "Young man, Mehraj is in the roots of the sky! You better take this pinch of opium if you hope to travel that far; then you can walk faster and won't get tired too quickly." There was some truth to what he said. After taking the opium, I was partly walking and partly running for the rest of the day. By that night I made it to Nathana, about seven miles short of my destination. It was too dark and late to continue, so in Nathana I went to the village *sutth* (plaza) and asked the people there for a place to stay. Three of the men sitting in the sutth offered to provide me food and bed. I went to the house of one of them for the night. This man was a widower raising a 10-year-old son, and he was a *badmash* (bad character). I remember that he was a little mean and threatening to his son and cursed him for not doing his chores. But he knew another badmash acquaintance of mine named Nathu from another village. This man had shared some adventures with Nathu in the past, so it turned out to be a pleasant evening of sharing stories, a modest meal, and a nice sendoff for me in the morning. But it was the opium that made my travel easy.

In the 1930s, some twenty percent or more of the men in our village were regular opium users (amli); others were occasional users. They (amli) were also some of the first to experiment with tea in the twenties and thirties; once the appreciation of tea developed, every opium user also became a tea drinker. In the minds of our village people, tea was considered addictive because it was first associated with opium eaters and every opium eater drank tea regularly. They would boil the tea for a long time to make it really strong for the extra kick and to feel energetic. In the 1940s, our family started serving tea to our workers at harvest time, because tea was considered a stimulant that made them work better. It was also necessary to please the workers because of the labor shortage caused by World War II and by the resulting prosperity. Gradually the workers started demanding opium along with their tea, saying, "When we work for such-and-such house, they always give us opium. We need opium to keep up our energy." In fact, as owners we took a pinch ourselves as we gave opium to every worker so that they would work faster. At the end of the harvest season, the non-addicts had to quit taking opium. We suffered a couple of days of withdrawal, but no new addicts were made this way. All the non-addicts quit cold turkey, although for a couple of days there was a feeling of heaviness and lethargy in the body, a feeling of excessive fluids in the mouth, mild aches and pains, and the joints felt like they did not want to stay together. After the Independence, the Indian government banned opium completely, and the number of known addicts may have gone down somewhat. However, the number of new young addicts increased fifty years later, although most had taken to the modern drugs and chemicals instead of opium.

In earlier times when a guest arrived, the first thing a hostess would offer was hot milk, usually with some sugar added. Starting in the mid-forties, tea became the first thing offered. At first, some puritanical people decried tea as an evil which was bad for health, addictive, and perhaps worse than alcohol and opium, since it was cheaper and easy to get without going to a government licensed shop. They would say "Peoples' health is not as good as it used to be, because they have been ruined by drinking tea." All such thoughts, about tea being bad for the health, have changed since then. Tea became the routine drink of the masses in Punjab until the sixties, when its importance was diminished by soda pops among the young and fashionable. The village people did not know much about coffee.

Cannabis or marijuana, locally called *sukha* (comfort drug?), was used by some holy people by grinding the leaves and putting them in a drink; but the general public never gave it much consideration. Of course *smoking* the cannabis would have been frowned upon, since smoking anything was prohibited among the Sikhs; only Muslims and Hindus could smoke. But cannabis never caught on, except with some holy people, who used it to enter a different state of consciousness as a part of their spiritual practice. Even some *nihang* (traditional Sikh warriors) and a few common people might take a marijuana drink occasionally. Sometimes in the summer, a gathering of friends would make the drink *thandiai* (cooler), which normally had some herbs, rose petals, *kaskas*, exotic seeds, almonds, and sugar. Occasionally, the boys would grind in dry leaves of cannabis for a special effect and to feel some disorientation resulting from the cannabis-loaded thandiai. This practice never became widespread, though, because cannabis did not provide the punch and the high that whiskey did. After the 1950s, the use of cannabis became even less prevalent, although I am not sure if there was any legal prohibition against it, because it was growing in abundance in many places near water.

Smoking any thing was strictly forbidden among the Sikhs, and this is the only rule about eating and drinking that was observed pretty universally by the rural Sikhs. People in the village who did smoke were some *velli* (with vice) and *badmash* (bad characters), the untouchable low castes, and some Muslim and Hindu men. Tobacco was considered so filthy that a Sikh child was not allowed to touch even a fallen cigarette butt on the ground, not even with his shoe. A Sikh had to get little twigs to grab a fallen cigarette butt in order to dispose of it. As far as Sikhs were concerned, the old concept of not touching any impure thing or person, in order to avoid defiling your own being, applied to tobacco. The Sikhs would not sit near anyone who smoked, nor could they eat anything touched by a smoker's hands.

CHAPTER 22

LEISURE ACTIVITIES AND PASTIMES

In spite of the harshness of life, the village people found ways of entertainments, pleasurable activities, and celebrations in the midst of dire poverty, physical misery, and occasional calamities. The younger generation enjoyed many distractions. These included engagements and weddings, fairs and festivals, *giddha* and *teeyan*, ballad recitations and instrument playing, *naqlia, nachar* and *jalsa* performers, sports and games, exercise and body massage, grip testing, wrestling and *tallian*, competitions and matches, camel or horse racing, monkey shows and bear shows, magic shows and bazi, story telling and joke sessions, watching *Gadi Wale* nomads and *Nihang Singhs*, visiting relatives and partying with friends, and so on. Such activities had a way of brightening life. They made me happy to be in my village and snared me so that I never wanted to leave there. It would take a separate book to describe all the activities, but I will describe some of them briefly.

Older people did not see any value in sports. They had a negative attitude toward entertainment, pleasure, games, and all celebrations except religious ones. Most fathers thought that playing and sports were a waste of time, that they were not merely a distraction but fostered an unhealthy outlook in children; and that playing games promoted frivolity and had no virtue. Since a game could become a habit, and a deviation from productive pursuits, it was considered a wicked addiction, not good for a man's future. So, it was best to prevent good children from playing. Only the young and the *badmash* (bad characters) on the fringe of society, who were neither influential nor respectable, considered sports important. Many times it was the badmash and the velli, the violent and the misfit, who encouraged and promoted sports, competitions, and entertainment in the villages.

Little children played games such as *luk michai* (hide and seek) and *peecho bakri* (hopscotch) like children everywhere. In our village, there were no modern sports like cricket, basketball, football, baseball, hockey or soccer, for the local population. The grade school did provide a soccer ball to the boys, and the teacher watched them play during the noontime recess, but even this modest support was neither provided regularly nor continued from year to year. Volleyball was played more frequently after school hours, but it was mostly for the older and taller students, who were outnumbered by the younger teachers, grown-up former students, a peon or two, and any other adults who were hanging around the school.

Khuddo-Khoondi: A game played in good weather by boys who did not go to school was *khuddo-khoondi* (ball and hockey stick). The game resembled field hockey and was played with a ball made from rags and strings and a stick with natural curve at one end. Some trees produced shoots with a curve at the point where the shoot grew out of the tree, and while grazing cattle we tried to find and cut the branches that were already shaped like a khoondi. Commercially made hockey sticks used in the cities and high schools were unknown to the illiterate village boys. The vacant pirr grounds were the natural place to play khuddo-khoondi. I joined the village boys in khuddo-khoondi off and on. Although I was one of the smallest, until I finished grade school, I used to get quite excited about the game and never wanted it to end.

Gulli-Danda: The other popular village game was *gulli danda*. A *gulli* is a piece of wood, five to eight inches long and about an inch in diameter, and the *danda* is a stick of comparable diameter and about a yard in length. The ends of the gulli are tapered, so that if the danda hits the tapered end of the gulli when it is lying on the ground, the gulli bounces into the air. The active player hits the tapered end of the gulli with the danda to make it bounce into the air; and while it is still up in the air he hits it hard with the danda to make it go flying away. This bounce-and-hit action is called a *buggh*.

To start the game, the gulli is placed on the ground over a narrow slot called a *raab*, which is also the base for the game. The active player puts the lower end of his danda into the raab slot behind the gulli and pushes it up forward with the danda so that the gulli flies far away. The opposing player tries to catch the gulli in flight. If he succeeds, the hitter is out. If he can not catch the gulli, he picks it up and throws it at the danda, which has been placed at the raab base. If the thrower is skilled or lucky and hits the danda with the gulli, the hitter is out and the opposing party takes over. If he misses, the hitter tries to shoot a buggh (described above) to make the gulli go as far as he can. If the opposing players do not catch the gulli and it falls to the ground, they throw it again, trying to hit the danda at the raab base. If the gulli still does not hit the danda, the hitter executes another buggh. If the hitter is good, he can continue to drive the gulli farther and farther from the raab base with each buggh, until the gulli has gone so far that the opposing team has no hope of hitting the danda placed at the raab. At that point, the catching team admits defeat and the hitting team wins. With children playing the game, the catching team had to give the winners a ride by carrying them on their backs from the spot where the gulli finally landed, back to the raab base. Grown-up players did not expect a ride but merely the acknowledgement of defeat from the other side. I played gulli danda whenever I could escape my father's supervision. I was rebuked, but never beaten, whenever I was caught playing, because like candy, playing was considered a temptation to which children were expected to fall victims easily. He just said that gulli danda and all games were the habits of illiterate non-achievers and a waste of time.

As might be expected, everyone wanted to be on the hitting side, not the side that had to catch or retrieve the gulli. In this and in all games mentioned below, the "obligation to perform" was called daavi; that was also the word for the safe base in some games, so the word daavi has two meanings. In a game, the boy who was "it" had the daavi obligation. When a little boy wanted to quit a game while he had the daavi obligation, older boys bullied him and did not let him quit. They said, "No, you can't quit as long as you owe a daavi." They even beat or abused him (with the usual abusive rhymes) if he did not fulfill the daavi obligation, until someone else was "it".

Kabuddi: Simply pronounced *kaudi* when spoken rapidly, this was a game between two teams of several players each. It was usually played on soft ground, which was abundant around the village. During the 1930s, except for the small area of cleared *kuller* or *pirr* where the grain was threshed after the harvest, all the land for three miles east of Mehraj toward Phul, three miles southeast toward Rampura-Phul Mandi, and two miles south toward GuruSar was sandy desert. In this game, a line defines the two teams' territories. To begin the game, a player from one team runs across the boundary into the other team's territory, continuously saying, "kaudi, kaudi, kaudi," as the word "kabuddi" is too cumbersome to utter when you are running around. He tries to touch the players of the other party without himself being captured, and he tries to return to his own territory across the boundary *before* his breath runs out. He has to attack and touch members of the other team within the duration of one breath, as signified by his continuous utterance of "kaudi, kaudi, kaudi." If the other team catches him, he tries to break loose with as much force as necessary, but he has to escape within one breath. If he is caught and held by the other side until his breath runs out, he is "dead" and is eliminated. If he returns successfully into his own territory before his breath runs out, all those he touched within one breath are "dead" and are eliminated. Then a player from the other team makes a similar "attack" into the first team's territory. The game ends when players of the losing team are all "dead" and one or more players of the winning team survive. In a variation of the game, some members of a team could be resurrected under certain conditions.

Lallah: This is a game where a group of boys occupy, with their toes, small round holes called *lallah* they have dug into the ground. The game starts when the boy who is "it" throws a khuddo (rag ball) to hit one of the players. If he hits successfully, the target boy is out. Otherwise the boy nearest to the spot where the ball lands hits the ball as far as he can with a stick without abandoning his lallah. The "it" boy tries to do one of three things: to occupy a lallah that is temporarily vacant, or to catch the ball in flight, or to hit one of the boys occupying a lallah with the *khuddo* ball from wherever it stops. If he can do one of those things, the boy whose lallah he has taken, or whose throw he has caught, or whom he has managed to hit with the khuddo, becomes "it,"; the boy who was formerly "it" occupies the vacated lallah. If the "it" boy cannot catch the moving ball, he picks it up when it stops, and then throws it from that spot at the occupant of any lallah. If he misses and the ball stops near the occupant of a lallah, that boy may leave his lallah to drive the ball further away, to be safer, or he may bring it close enough for a strong hit. When leaving his lallah to hit the ball, he may risk losing his lallah, so he may have to let the ball stay where it is and risk being hit by the "it" boy from that close position. If the "it" boy tries to hit one of the occupants and throws with too much force and misses, he has to go further away to retrieve the ball and has little hope of hitting the occupants of the lallahs from so far away, or of occupying their lallah. Thus, the players must continuously form judgments and decisions during play.

Kundle: This game is similar to the lallah game in concept, but the boys occupy circles instead of holes, and they hit the ball with a *ballah* (paddle) rather than a khoondi stick. The boy who is "it" does not hit the occupants but tries to either occupy an abandoned *kundle* (circle), or to have the ball stop in a kundle, or to catch the ball when it is in the air. Any of these events will oust the boy who hit the ball, and make him "it"; one who was formerly "it" gets his kundle. The kundle game has to be played with a bouncing ball; There are rules about not rolling the ball into a circle and not hitting it sideways but up or down with the bat, so that it may bounce and give the "it" boy a chance to catch.

Bander Killa: This is a game of little boys, where one boy sits at the center, holding one end of a rope or of turban and another boy, holding the other end of the turban, runs or walks around in a circle whose radius is the turban. The rest of the players roam outside the circle. They try to enter the circle randomly and touch or hit the shoulder of the boy in the center with a hand. If the second boy, circling with the outer end of the turban, touches any of the intruders in the process, that intruder becomes "it" and sits at the center; the boy at the center takes the circumference end of the turban from the second boy, and that second boy himself joins the outside players.

Kotla Chhupaki: The *kotla* is a soft whip made of clothes, and chhupaki means hiding. Boys sit in a circle, and the one boy who is "it" goes around the circle and surreptitiously drops the kotla behind one of the sitting boys. But he pretends that he still has the kotla hidden under his shirt so that no one will suspect that he dropped it behind him. A boy was not allowed to look behind his back to see if the kotla had been dropped behind him, but if he suspected without looking that the kotla was behind him, then he could pick it up and run to beat the "it" boy with the kotla before the latter makes it around the circle and reaches the empty spot. The new boy in control of the whip becomes the "it" boy. If the victim does not know that the whip had dropped behind him, then the next time the "it" boy comes around the circle, he picks up the kotla, and starts whipping the unsuspecting boy behind whom he had dropped the whip. That boy then gets up, runs around the circle of boys ahead of the whipper, and reoccupies his own spot as fast as he can. The "it" boy had the privilege of whipping him as long as he was sly enough to drop the whip and could still give the impression that he was hiding it.

Daavi and Karkanda: This game was played mainly in the trees and was called *karkanda*. Some trees, like the *pipple* and boher (bunyan) had big, slanting, and at some points nearly horizontal branches, so that a boy could even walk on a tree branch. Many *pipple* branches were low enough so the boys could hang down from them and land safely. To begin the game a boy would throw the karkanda stick as far as he could, but he had to throw it under his leg. The boy who was "it" had to go and pick up the karkanda stick thrown by the first boy. This gave the other players time to climb the tree. The "it" boy had to fetch the karkanda, place it at the specified *daavi* (base) location, and then try to touch any one of the players while they were on the tree branches or anywhere away from the daavi base. The first boy who was caught or touched became "it," and then it would be his turn to bring the karkanda back and try to catch one of the others. When played without the karkanda or a tree, the game just involved hiding or running, and then it was called simply daavi. In all games, reaching the daavi meant that you were "safe," and the "it" boy could not touch you.

Nili da Sowar (blue-horse rider): In this game, one team of two to four little boys were the horses bent forward in line, connected in tandem, and leaning against a wall; the other team were the riders. A boy from the rider team would take a running start and try to jump on to the backs of the team of "horses" as far forward as possible without falling. The remaining riders would also try to jump on to the "horses" behind him. Any mishap, slip, fall, or touch of any rider to the ground entitled the horse team to become riders and vice versa. After some time if no one fell or touched the ground, the game started again.

Ghutti: This game was played with marbles, small *kaudi* shells, walnuts or just pebbles. The first player takes a pool of marbles from all parties and tries to toss as many as he can into the ghutti (hole) by throwing them from a specified distance. After his throw he can take only the contents of the ghutti pit, if any. Or he can risk all and try to hit, with a marble piece in his hand, any of the remaining marbles that did not go into the ghutti. If he succeeds in striking any marble outside the ghutti with his marble, he wins the whole pot; otherwise he loses all including the contents of the ghutti. There were many variations in the rules in this game. Sometimes the contents of the ghutti belonged to the thrower and the second player got to try his luck by collecting the marbles remaining outside the ghutti. The process of tossing marbles into the ghutti or striking any outside marbles with the shooting marble could be repeated.

Washing Hands: This was not really a game but more like suffering punishment for losing a game. In some games, after the game was over, the loser could retrieve some of his lost marbles, shells, or pebbles from the winner by a process called "washing hands." This consisted of the loser rubbing his folded hands, as though washing them, continuously in front of the winner who would try to slap the folded hands. The loser could avoid being hit by swiftly moving his hands away. If the winner missed hitting the folded hands in any attempt, the loser won a single marble back, and he would keep washing his hands in order to win the rest of his marbles. Unhappily, the winner was usually the swifter and more skilled and would attempt a strike only when he was sure of hitting the folded hands. Thus the swift winner delivered a lot of punishment to the usually younger loser and did not give back the marbles easily. Sometimes the winner just pretended to be ready to strike (did not actually swing but made a threatening jerk) to scare the loser, who fruitlessly pulled his hands back, but did not retrieve any marbles. Undoubtedly, in this and in other games there was an element of cruelty in the way the winners treated the losers, who were usually younger, slower, and therefore the object of ridicule in other ways also.

In one game, which we played while grazing cattle, we dug two parallel rows of five holes each, and one hole at each end of the two rows. Pebbles or similar things were distributed in the holes before the game started. The pebbles were moved to the different holes by the parties alternately according to their strategies. The object, of course, was to win the most pebbles. The rules of this game varied from place to place.

Games like *shatranj* or chess, *pasa* or checkers, cards, and other games of strategy, chance, and skill, were played by serious adults for pastime. The younger boys played cards quite frequently. My father considered the playing of cards to be nearly as sinful as gambling, and we were not allowed to own or to be caught holding the cards.

Wrestling and *Tallian:* Wrestling was an honored sport in the villages. Most teenagers and young men who had large and fat bodies tried wrestling. They had to be bigger than the average man in order to get any respect in a society where being big and fat was not easy. All people, except the religious and the educated, admired a wrestler, called *mull* or *pahlwan*. A wrestler was identifiable by his bulk and from his walk with outward-spreading arms and legs. In our area, all the pahlwans were Jat Sikhs; there were no Hindus athletes, although sometimes I did hear a Muslim name at the Selbrah fair arena. No pahlwan was expected to keep a full beard. It was acceptable for a Sikh pahlwan to shave his beard, but very few shaved it off completely. No pahlwan would shave his mustache, as the mustache was a symbol of pride. Most Sikh pahlwan kept full-length hair in a topknot on the head. In the villages a Sikh would have a better chance of getting donations with full-length hair, as he would look strange and weird without the topknot of hair.

Tallian was a physical competition that required a combination of strength, skill, speed, and agility. *Talli* (plural: *tallian*) was a hit or push on the chest of the opponent. In fact the combination of wrestling and tallian was called *ghol khel* (wrestling play). Some of the men with the best-shaped bodies competed in the tallian game. I personally admired the talli players more than the wrestlers, because their bodies were well shaped and they would not be freaky fat like the wrestlers. They were usually tall, well built, and not very fat, although some fat was necessary in order to be taken seriously and to receive any donations from viewers. Viewers would just laugh at a skinny man, pretending to be a pahlwan, rather than admiring him or giving him donations. To the well-built fellows promenading around, they would give donations gladly and say, "The heart is glad on seeing a *juvan* (youth) like that."

I used to watch the talli players with great interest and admiration. The talli hitter slicked his body with mustard oil to become slippery and he ran backwards as he hit the chest of the catcher who was chasing him. If the catcher grabbed hold of him, or put a stranglehold on him with his legs, or otherwise detained the hitter for several seconds, the catcher was declared the winner. But if the hitter was not caught but escaped after delivering a few talli blows, the prize went to the hitter. Since it was hard to catch a man of equal strength slicked with oil, the benefit of the doubt went to the catcher. As could be expected, hitters were plenty, but good catchers were few.

When I was young, one good catcher was Joginder of village Jalaal. Even better was Mehr Singh from our village Mehraj, who was a tall, sinewy guy, with a taut body and well defined muscles. Like most pahlwans, Meher Singh trimmed and sometimes shaved his beard. He kept a full up-turned mustache and kept his full-length hair in a topknot. Like all other Pahlwans, he wore a turban when he was dressed and not competing in the arena or promenading before the public. People used to say, "Mehr Singh is a great pahlwan, but he is too bogged down with farm work and *qabil dari* (family life). He is too skinny and needs to eat more ghee to gain weight and strength; otherwise this may be his last year." But the "skinny" Mehr Singh would surprise everyone again the next year with his winning performance. He was admired and valued because good catchers were so few. From our own neighborhood, Banta son of Sauni, who was short and chunky, and Kartara son of Channan, who was tall and slim, both entered the regional competition once. They were not the best, but they looked good enough so that Banta collected two rupees and Kartara collected three rupees during the promenade. A top player could collect ten to twenty rupees and a champion winner might be given much more.

Athletes' skills were not mass marketed in those days. Every show and display was free and open to every body in the *akhara* (arena), without restriction or the charging of

380

admission. The only reward the winner gained was the viewers' voluntary donations as he promenaded by.

Thaapi is a gesture I have never seen among competitors in the western world. In our rural areas, thaapi was a gesture of bravado and arrogance, a challenging and intimidating noise, an assertion of strength against the opponent, and a declaration of readiness to fight. The most common mode of thaapi by a wrestler was to strike a cupped hand to the front inside of his thigh or to strike the cupped hand to his arm folded at the elbow. The thaapi noise could be quite loud and intimidating. The *mull* or *pahlwan* slicked with mustard oil, wearing nothing but a bikini-like *janghia*, promenaded by slowly, pushing the sand back with his feet like a challenging bull as he walked. He would stop occasionally, tilt his head back and strike a thaapi on his thigh and more frequently on the folded arm near the elbow as if to declare that he was invincible. But he would not speak unless someone asked him what village he was from; it was considered unmanly and even ridiculous for a pahlwan to talk too much. Everyone wanted to know which village produced a man like that, and he was a source of pride and notoriety for his village. Some individuals would honor him with one rupee; a rupee coin made of silver was a week's wage for a laborer in the early days. People who admired an athlete would keep putting rupee coins in his hands even before the contest began, just for appearing and promenading. In fact some of the *juvan* (youth) never competed at all because a suitable opponent for them could not be found. These fellows just promenaded in the hope of receiving donations. People would say, "What a great juvan! My heart is made happy by looking at a youth like that." Some skinny specimens hardly ever collected a rupee.

Wrist Clutching and Strength Tests: It was common for ordinary men to test each other's strength by gripping an opponent's wrist with both hands and having him try to break the grip. Then they reversed roles. I myself was pretty good at gripping and releasing even as a teenager. At age seventeen, I tried grip matches with fellows like Banta, who was a legitimate pahlwan for a while, but at that time he was stronger than me. In later years, I never met anybody else who was a better gripper than me, but of course I never competed with real champions; I usually tried it against my close friends and even my older brother.

Young men used to engage in body building during the winter months when the oppressive heat did not sap their strength. Also there was more time fro leisure and usually a greater supply of milk and accumulated ghee available in winter. Being fat was synonymous with being healthy, strong, prosperous, and respectable. Conversely, the word for thin, weak, bad, and poor was the same: *mara* or *lissa*. Sometimes boys would get together and massage their own bodies with oil as they did various exercises like weightlifting, pushups (*dund*), and squats (*bethak*), and some could do these movements hundreds of times. I was never big, strong, or motivated enough to get into massage, body building or any other exercise program. I was not thin, but I was small in height and not strong and muscular like some other village boys were. Some pahlwan exercised with *moogli* (solid wood barrels with handles) by holding one moogli in each hand and swinging them alternately. *Mugder* was a weight made of wood, stone, or iron, sometimes with a handle. Only the strongest competed in lifting a mugder, while the mugder was lying near the sutth or common gathering place, all winter. In a competition, weightlifters would go from lower weights to the higher weights until a winner was determined.

A few fellows in the village flew kites with some degree of sophistication. Some attached bells to their kites and others hung lights or shiny objects from large kites as others watched them from rooftops during late afternoons, evenings, and sometimes into the night in summer time.

Some boys made bows from mulberry tree shoots and arrows from any kind of thin stick. We put a little wax at the tip of the arrow to give it weight and momentum. Most of us were pretty incompetent with those homemade bows and arrows. Only some skilled guys like Gurdev MeanyKa tried to put metal tips on their arrows, to use them for hunting.

Gopia was a sling with a wide portion that could hold a pebble or ball of clay. A fellow would swing the gopia with the load many times to give it speed and then release one end of the sling to let the load fly away. But the gopia was not an accurate weapon. Most of the time the gopia was used to scare or shoot birds that were eating the millet crops. An ordinary fellow could not expected to kill a bird with a gopia because the sling was nearly impossible to aim with any precision.

Gulail was a small piece of wood in the shape of "Y" where the ends of a wide band of rubber could be tied to the top of the Y. A small pebble or rock could be placed in the center of the rubber band and pulled hard. When the pebble was released, the tension in the rubber band propelled it some distance. The chance of hitting a bird with a gulail was not very good; the chances of unintended injury to nearby people was high with the shot of any gopia or gulail.

Pigeon Keepers: In the olden days prominent people kept hunting hawks and other birds. The last Sikh guru, Gobind Singh, was well known as a keeper of hawks. People in our village aspired only to keeping pigeons as a hobby. My father considered keeping pigeons a frivolous activity and a mild vice, not fit for people from farming families. Usually the misfits, the *velli*, or idle people had such hobbies, not the working middle class. The *kabooter baz* (pigeon flyer) would have a square platform called a *chhatri* (umbrella) mounted on a long pole on his roof, and his pigeons would land on that chhatri after their flight. In those days many chhatri would be visible above the houses in village, like radio or TV antennas of later times. The pigeons were normally kept in an enclosure, safe from cats and other predators, but when released to fly, some of them went away for many hours. Then in the late afternoon when they were tired he would coax them to come and settle on the chhatri; later he would feed and cage them. Pet pigeons were of many interesting colors, and some owners bred them for special traits. An unmarried old man with a white beard, nicknamed Dhatti (that means a guy with bad habits), who lived on the street going to our Inner House, had many pigeons. As a young boy, I would stop at his open door and wished I could take a closer look at or even touch his kabooter. But old Dhatti was gruff and irritable, not the one to humor little children.

One of my classmates named Ghoke (his real name was Mohammed Ismael) of the Mirasi caste used to keep pigeons. Ghoke was a few years older than me, but he had failed many grades in school, and younger boys like me had caught up and then passed him in grades. Ghoke eventually dropped out of school after failing the sixth grade several times and then started helping his father, who was the local postmaster. The Mirasi were considered low caste in our village, but his family was from some other region and his father's being the postmaster gave them some standing. Ghoke was a good-looking, happy, friendly, and pleasant fellow. He smoked cigarettes even before the fifth grade, but smoking was acceptable for a Muslim, although drinking alcohol was not. Everyone in Ghoke's family including his father Nabi Bakhsh and brothers Akbar, Asghar, Rafi, and Shafi smoked whatever was available. Ghoke had tattoos on his body, and he was a good singer, jester, and flatterer as the people of Mirasi caste were reputed to be. Ghoke was a glib talker and could do various tricks with his face. So keeping pigeons was not any special vice for Ghoke. My knowledge of pigeons, their habits and diversity, their special diets, and so on came only from Ghoke. My father would have considered it a disgrace if any of his sons had ever tried keeping pigeons. Besides, we did not put much value on pets and hobbies since we owned so many animals, with many of whom we had 'relationships' for life. People who had to work on the farms could not waste time keeping pigeons.

Animal fights, although not routine, did take place. Some boys purposely tried to bring together rival bulls from different pattis of the village so that they could watch them fight. A buffalo bull would not quit fighting his rival. When one was defeated and ran, the victor still wanted to kill the other and would not abandon the attempt to kill it until he got tired of chasing it. Of course the vanquished had the greater need to run in order to survive. A Brahma bull would also show great spirit in fighting but was not as determined to kill the opponent as a buffalo bull would be; he was content just to win and then to coexist with his competitors, but not so the buffalo bulls. Some roosters fought until they were bloody, sometimes losing their eyes or parts of their crowns and suffering other damage in the process. Some dogs also were pretty vicious and tore their opponents in fights, but not every rooster or dog had the urge to fight another.

Racing horses for short distances (a few hundred yards at the most) and camels for longer distances sometimes provided entertainment for the villagers. I raced my camels against other peoples' camels many times informally, but I never owned a horse of my own.

Floating logs as boats. Younger boys could make a game and entertainment out of anything, without equipment and without cost, as long as they could get together. In summer time when the pond was full of warm rainwater, we used floating logs as boats to ride from one end of the pond to the other. In other games, we jumped from the branches of the pipple tree into the pond. We tried to catch frogs, turtles and other water creatures.

We went out to collect wild *ber*, *pinjhu*, or *peelu* berries, or wild *chibber* melons. In those days we had to walk only half a mile from the village to collect a good variety of wild ber fruit from the various beri trees. One could pick ber from any beri, regardless of who its owner was. There was so little population pressure that some ber were left unpicked day after day. The population of the Indian sub-continent has gone up by a factor of four or five in my lifetime, making everything scarce. *Khakri* were sour melons with a wonderful taste; the similar chibber melons, varying in size all the way down to the size of a walnut, were a delicacy too, and they were free if you could find them. If one had to pay, then one would go to a sweet melon field of some Araeen and eat as many on the spot as one could.

We went lizard hunting in the bushes to see how many lizards each of us could kill. We might find a stray donkey and take turns riding it. We found beehives for honey and sometimes even an occasional yellow-jacket nest whose hive contained a substance resembling candied sugar called *missri*. We pulled up chickpea plants and roasted their green pods by placing the plants on a burning bush to make *holaan* to eat. At other times we roasted ears of corn to eat in the fields. The chances of mischief, injury, fights, and blame resulting from the actions of the young boys were always a source of worry for the parents. In general very few parents knew the whereabouts of their boys when they were not at their assigned tasks. At the age of seven or eight, if I did not return home from playing until midnight, I just went to bed when everyone else was already asleep as there was no locked door; no one was worried when I was missing at night before they went to sleep.

Girls' Games

After the age of seven or eight, girls started playing separately from boys. About that age, the boys started cattle grazing and the girls started spinning yarn, usually under the supervision of someone older. Since they did not go to school, everyone of the same sex in the neighborhood was generally available for playing in the late afternoons. Grownup girls' singing and dancing are described in detail in the section about the festival of *teeyan*. During teeyan, grownup girls would swing on the *peengh* (long swing) like great athletes. Sometimes two girls got on one swing facing each other and pumped alternately to make the swing go as high as possible. Usually they went high enough to reach and grab leaves from the tall trees on which the swings were mounted or even to pull leaves from the trees close by. The act of pulling leaves by swinging up high was called uprooting the mother-in-law's hair (*sass da jhatta*), enacting the traditional hostility of girls toward the future mother-in-law. Girls were naturally skilled in dancing, and they did this starting young, with kikkri kreer di (like ring around the roses). The simple dance started with two girls holding hands, with outstretched arms, with feet close to one another but with their torsos and heads leaning back, and moving rhythmically in a short circle. Another dance was by rhythmically striking the heel to the ground, while clapping and making noise with the mouth. The older ones sang and danced the girls' *giddha*, at weddings and during the teeyan festival.

Many of the young girls' games involved the life cycle of dolls, like dressing, weddings, babies, and deaths of dolls, and thus they learned the appropriate and customary rituals, songs, clothes, and vocabulary for such occasions. Girls also played coordination games, at which they were better than boys because the boys would not even attempt those games. One such game was *thikrian* (pebbles), which is like playing jacks.

CHAPTER 23

ENTERTAINMENT IN RURAL AREAS

Giddha and Bhangra were the energetic Punjabi songs/dances for women and men respectively. These activities have been described in the section on weddings.

The Baziger Performances

Bazi was a show of gymnastic feats and athletic skills by the people of the Baziger caste. The Baziger in our village used to stage a performance about once or twice a year. For some days before the bazi performance, their drummer would announce the event, to encourage donations of goods, grains, and cash. My mother had donated *phulkari* (embroidered covers), grains, and other things to the bazi in our village. For this performance, their men would be dressed only in their *janghia* (bikini-like bottoms), which had all kinds of embroidery, sequins and appliqués on them. They also wore a belt of bells during the performance, and the bells jingled as they jumped and did somersaults and other acrobatics. One old Baziger would beat the drum to create enthusiasm. A slanting board would be fixed in the ground with ten or fifteen feet of the board sticking up in the air. The performing Bazigar took a running start, ran up to the top of the slanting board, and then sprang high into the air above a barrier and did as many summersaults as he could before landing on the softened earth. Then the barrier would be raised. Whoever cleared the highest barrier and did the best summersaults would be the winner. There were many other feats of skill but not necessarily of strength. Then the winners, and sometimes even the losers, promenaded before the audience and did summersaults and after tricks while walking, with the expectation of voluntary donations, because there was no charge to attend such events.

Kavisher, The Rural Punjabi Poet

A *kavisher* (*kavi* for short) was a poet as well as a singer; he composed his own songs, ballads, and poems. His specialty was clever rhymes, because rhymes were necessary for most kinds of entertainment. During performances, the kavisher might have one or two accompanists who would be aspiring poets and had memorized his songs for the performance; the songs always sounded better with two or three other singers harmonizing with the principal singer. Sometimes two singers would sing alternate rhymes of the same song, and sometimes they sang duets with opposing roles in a song. During performances, some of this poetry could take a couple of hours to sing; but they had to memorize it all, because no one was expected to read during a performance.

Some of the kavi published little pamphlets (called *chittha*) of their poetry, which might be about philosophy and wisdom, some admirable work or some injustice, some heroes or lovers, signs of the times, ironic or humorous twists, or an address to someone; it might arouse emotion or motivate people to action, or it might be a comedy. A man named Chand the Kavisher was a highly popular and admired kavi in Mehraj from the 1930s through the 1950s. Another kavi named Arjun was somewhat lower in wit, vocabulary, and skill, and there were also other aspiring kavi in the village. To Chand, who was a landowning farmer, poetry was a hobby and a distraction from the farm work. I was full of admiration for Chand's choice of incisive and humorous vocabulary and the potent words that expressed his philosophy. He was gifted, but he had probably never attended any school and had learned the Punjabi letters from some elder. His depth of thinking, his speculations about nature, his humor, his descriptions of unique events, unusual people, or the spirit of the times, were comparable to the best of poets. He even published a pamphlet of boli for giddha, and another one for junj-release rituals for weddings. Even now, I wish I could find some of Chand's poetic works, which I heard as a youngster, and which are probably long lost as his sons were neither literate nor inclined toward poetry.

Writing for business and correspondence in plain prose was acceptable, but to get the attention of the reluctant listener, and to make a strong impact with the message, it was most effective to recite things in verse. People had learned in ancient times that to draw the attention of humans and to motivate them to act or to memorize, the subject matter had to be put in rhyme. Quotations and proverbs used to be in rhyme; there were hardly any quotations in prose. Plain prose just fell flat, but if said in verse, the same idea could sound pungent, memorable and powerful. Most religious writers composed their thoughts in verse. Nanak, Kabir, Farid and most other religious preceptors had preached in verse, and the Granth of the Sikhs is in the form of poetry.

In the Punjab of the nineteen-thirties and -forties, even political messages were propagated in rhymes. When World War II started, the British Indian government enlisted the help of local kavishers to compose poems that would motivate young men to join the military. Enlistment in the army was voluntary, so motivation was necessary to make the men go to war. The kavi were hired by the government to hold free music concerts in the countryside and to sing their songs to bring out the martial spirit in the listeners. I went to one of these concerts in Nathana village when my uncle had taken me there for another reason. One song of the kavisher had a refrain that translated like this: "What difficulty could a lion like you have in winning against a jackal like a German?" Another song was an argument in a family that was trying to prevent their boy from joining the "fires of warfare," but the young boy was witty and courageous. His retort, translated, went like this: "I want to go to war; you get back and go home. I will bring the severed heads of the Germans and the Japanese....". The young man in the song could not be dissuaded from joining the army, and he fantasized about defeating Japan and Germany.

Even the politicians of those days set their propaganda in verse. The communists were the most talented, most dedicated, and best organized for such purposes. They held poetry contests during their campaigns and conferences. The poems and songs were all about arousing the "slumbering laborers and peasants." They sang about the virtues of sharing wealth, about redistributing the land among the have-nots, and about eliminating the exploiting capitalists to bring joy and power to workers. All this was more effective and memorable when sung, and not just said in plain language.

Natchaar, Naqlia and Kallee Singers

Whereas a kavisher was the respected poet and singer, the *natchaar* and *naqlia* entertainers were denigrated by conservative people. Ntachaar were male dancers dressed up as women, complete with hair braids, face makeup and lipstick, colorful veils, ankle length skirts and even bells around their ankles. They sang, danced, and did comic acts. The natchaar could gather a circle of people whenever they set up to perform at a fair. Some people would bring the natchaar to a village for performance, and sometimes they were hired by a wedding house. More often people would hire the naqlia (imitator, comedian) who had dramatists, singers and the natchaar dancers among them. In the earlier days the naqlia were mostly men, some of whom were dressed as women if the part called for it; but in later years they started including women. They told jokes and humorous stories; they danced and performed little skits. Sometimes they staged musical plays, usually based on the famous love stories such as Heer-Ranjha, Mirza-Sahiba, Sohni-Mahiwal, Leila-Majnoon, Sassi-Pannu and others, which were the Punjabi equivalents of Romeo and Juliet. They tried to make even serious stories into comedies. When the story was too tragic to permit comedy, they would perform comic acts during the intermission. Like other showmen, the naqlia performances were in the open and attendance was free. If it was night, they performed by kerosene or gas lamps. No women were ever in the audience during the performances of nachaar or naqlia. The generic word for the gatherings of nachaar or naglia performances was *jalsa*.

The kavisher poets appealed to the thinking people, the naqlia and natchaar were risqué or romantic, while the *kallee* singers were for the common farmers' sons. Those kallee singers usually sang in groups of two to four. At the Selbrah fair, four miles north of our village, there used to be several circles of kallee singers, and even at the Rampura cattle market there would be such a circle. They could be hired by a wedding house or sponsored by some fashionable guys to perform in the village. One of the singers played the *sarangi*, a multi-stringed instrument with a plain rectangular wooden sound box. Each of the remaining singers would play *dhudh*, a miniature drum held in one hand and struck with the fingers of the other hand. The kallee (songs) were mostly about lovers; their staple was the ballads of Heer and Ranjha, the quintessential Punjabi lovers in rural folklore. A few sang about Mirza and Sahiba (in Punjabi there is always a nasal sound after the female names ending with "a," so Sahiba is pronounced Sahiban), Beeja and Kaulan, and about Dullah Bhatti the brave. Unlike Romeo and Juliet, Heer and Ranjha of the Punjabi ballads were not fictitious characters. Heer was the daughter of the Sials of Jhang and Ranjha was a Jat of village Takht Hazara. They probably lived in the 15th century. Although they were Muslim, our Sikh Jats thought of Heer and Ranjha as if they were our own people, because the cultural aspects were more important than religion. In fact in the story, when Ranjha was depressed as he had lost Heer, he became a disciple of a Hindu yogi named Gorakh Nath to cope with the loss of his beloved, and to attain mystic powers. In the present-day Wahabi-dominated Islam, such a deviation from Islam would not be tolerated, but rural lives were simpler then, and people tried whatever suited their circumstances. Heer and Ranjha were immortalized by Damodar who was their contemporary, and later by Waris Shah who could be called the Shakespeare of the Punjabi language. The love stories of Sohni-Mahiwal, Leila-Majnoon and Sassi-Pannu were not sung in kallee style; Heer-Ranja was the staple of kallee singers, while Mirza-Sahiban, Beeja-Kaulan, Dulla Bhatti and sometimes Pooran Bhagat, were added for variety. All the kallee songs and stories (except Dullah Bhatti and Pooran Bhagat which had other conflicts) dealt with the struggles of unrequited love, the obstacles and oppression of parents and society, or their tragic deaths; there were no "lived-happily-forever-after" stories.

The kallee of Dullah Bhatti, who supposedly rebelled against and defied Akber the Mughal emperor, used to create problems sometimes. The songs of Dullah Bhatti got some of the listeners, especially the drunk ones, so excited emotionally that these songs were blamed for fights among the young toughs. The singer aroused the emotions by reciting how the brave and defiant Dullah Bhatti tried to defend the honor of his family, and was not afraid to face the powerful ruler. And the drunken Jats felt that they too were brave and wanted to fight and defeat someone. The elders used to tell the singers, "Please don't sing a kallee of Dullah Bhatti; otherwise there will surely be a murder, since the boys are drunk."

As mentioned in the section on weddings, the Kanjri female dancer/singer/prostitutes were not a village phenomenon. Only the very affluent would hire the Kanjri from the cities and bring them for entertainment of the general public. Such entertainment could be held under a large tent or in the open but far away from where any lady of the village could see the Kanjri entertainer. Whereas the kavi performances did not need to be restricted, the natchaar dancers, the naqlia comedians and the female Kanjri entertainers had to perform in out-of-the-way locations.

My observation was that all the activities mentioned above were only for the Jat boys and men. The Brahman, the shopkeeper castes, the religious people or our women did not come out of their houses to participate in such activities, in sports, or in other entertainments; they also did not drink alcohol. Muslims joined some activities, but they were too insignificant to matter. We felt as if other castes were in our village just temporarily or were not meant to participate in the social life; so our Jat community felt different from them. Maybe they felt that such activities were crude or risky and not consistent with their family cultures. Keeping within one's own caste or ethnic group was the custom in those days, and apartheid was a virtue.

Sutth, the Village Plaza

In the villages, *sutth* was a place where you could go at any time of the day or night to sit around, talk or be entertained. This location was usually at a prominent street crossing or plaza; sometimes it was called *chowk* (square) or *chowkri*. The sutth could have seats made from tree stumps, crude benches or just a simple clay, brick or cement platform. Sometimes a part of the area would be roofed for protection from sun and weather. And sometimes the village *dharmsala* (place of dharma, free inn) would be in the same location as the sutth. All community meetings used to be held in the sutth, and decisions by the brotherhood were taken there in the open, usually standing up. Anyone could call a panchayat (village council), that is, request a meeting of the brotherhood, to settle a dispute with another, to redress a grievance, to discuss the distribution of canal water, to get rid of some menace, to plan for a new project, or to conduct some other community business. In earlier times, the goodwill of the brotherhood was so important that they considered the decision of the panchayat to be sacred. In the 1930s and 40s, village people still respected the decisions of the brotherhood, but in later times, courts became the preferred places to settle serious disputes. In the 1940s the panchayat meetings were still called to make decisions on matters such as the disposal of stray cows, the distribution of canal water, the collection of funds, holding a yugg with the hope of rain, or digging a water channel. In earlier years, everyone had equal voice and there was no head of such a community council, but after the 1940s, the panchayat councils became formalized and regulated by the government.

Momentous things were not always happening, so the sutth was mostly a place for entertainment, a club without membership, for shooting the breeze about everything. The conversation could be about the little kid who went by hopping and skipping; it could be about the best place to buy oxen; it could be about the lack of rain or too much of it somewhere else; it could be about a festival celebration or about someone's marriage; it could be about the crazy new fashions; or it could be about a crime committed in the area. Everyone was careful to observe proper decorum; you could not afford to gossip or say something disrespectful about others openly. One had to use proper language, but funny and humorous chatter was welcome. No stranger, however important, would pass through the sutth without saying a formal greeting to the people that were seated there. There was an ever-present opportunity for pastimes, entertainment, and exchange of information. Anyone who did something disgraceful, would avoid the sutth but some religious people would also consider the sutth gatherings as a waste of time. For older men, for visitors, for those unwilling to work and living off their assets, or for those unfit to work, the sutth was a great escape from boredom and loneliness. There were always people with humorous stories, sanitized jokes, people boasting of past adventures and daring deeds. Bets could be made or challenges could be thrown; they could discuss crime, morality, deflation in crop prices, the heat wave, police arresting someone, or a robbery somewhere.

The village sutth was like an all-day and all-evening party, every day of the year, although the number in attendance varied from time to time. There were the regulars, the boasters (paadi mar), the jokesters, the complainers, and the guppy. The word guppy literally means "liar," but it could be used for anyone who talked a lot or told tall tales; so "guppy" was not considered an insult. In fact the guppy and the jokesters were considered good company, whether you were sitting around or traveling together. Many men in the sutth just sat and listened to the others. Some complained about how bad life was, and it seemed therapeutic to express their feelings to others. Some were philosophical and resigned to the way the life was. For examples, an old fellow might ask his friend, "Oh Dasondha Singh, how is your life these days?" And Dasondha might reply, "Oh friend, nothing important is happening; I am just busy in *bringing the day of death closer.*" Or he might say "O brother, what is there to worry about? I have passed the greater part of my life; only a little time remains and that will pass too." But some young, optimistic types would exuberantly say: "*Teeyan jaise din, Divali jaisean rataan,*" which may be translated roughly as, "My days are like the festival of Teeyan and my nights are like the celebration of Divali." This meant that they were extremely happy with life.

Some brought rolls of hemp fiber or animal hair and kept spinning strings from the fibers while listening to or sharing stories. Occasionally, some would bring a more elaborate task to perform, such as assembling a rope with the help of two other persons, from the already prepared fiber strings. Some might even bring materials to string a new charpai bed, but most such productive work was frowned upon in the sutth, except for spinning the strings from fibers, which required minimal attention. For most people the sutth was just a place to relax after work, to sit, see friends, talk and listen. There was no unseemly gossip in the Sutth. If a group of younger men wanted to talk about things that were not of a respectable nature, they would move to a far corner of the place or agree to meet at some bachelors house.

CHAPTER 24

FESTIVALS AND FAIRS

Divali, the Festival of Lamps

The word Divali is formed from the word *diva* (lamp), and it was celebrated by Sikhs and Hindus all over India. Even the orthodox Sikhs used to celebrate it as they related the Divali festival to a day of liberation in the history of one of their gurus that coincided with the Divali day. But Divali is really a traditional Hindu celebration. It commemorates the return of the god/prince Ram after fourteen years of exile that had been ordered by his father the king, at the urging of Ram's stepmother. According to mythology, about the time the exile was supposed to end, Ram's wife Sita was kidnapped by Ravan the king of Lanka (now called Sri Lanka) by trickery. So Ram retrieved his wife from Ravana's captivity, and the celebration of his return became Divali. It can be in late October or early November, because the timing is tied to the phase of the moon so that the night is pitch dark for this festival of lights. About that time the summer harvest is also secured and the season is pleasantly cool.

In the days before electricity, rows of mustard oil lamps on top of perimeter walls, on door fronts, on village wells or on temples, looked quite impressive. Some families would go to place lamps on the tombs of their ancestors and on other places of importance. Some people traveled a hundred miles on foot to see the spectacular arrangements of lamps at the Golden Temple in Amritsar on Divali evening and to see the hustle and bustle related to the event. I know this because there was a poem about a man named Gullu from our village who had gone there, more than a hundred years ago. Gullu became a hero because he fought a bunch of Majha hoodlums to free a girl whom they had tried to carry away from the Divali fair in Amritsar.

On Divali evening, the sweet shops had dazzling displays and elaborate arrangements of sweets in their storefronts, and even watching them was a delight. Firecrackers and fireworks were going off everywhere as children of every family, even in the remote rural localities, would had been gathering them for the big day. Each young boy prepared for weeks to assemble his *masaal*, a sort of portable torch. The masaal was a clay bowl that the potter made specifically for this occasion. This bowl was fitted at the end of a forked wooden stick, and inside the masaal it was traditional to put chopped *gidder peerhi* (a wood-fungus) and mustard oil. Then the boys with burning masaals gathered in groups and went from house to house all evening long and asked every house to put oil in their masaals to keep them burning as late at night as they could. One sees masaal-like torches in movies depicting ancient night scenes, but in a Punjabi masaal there is always hot oil that burns slowly, and a boy had to be careful to keep it from spilling.

Since girls could not go out of the house at night, they would have *ghroundi*, a baked or unbaked clay structure. The ghrundi was like a miniature temple or pyramid painted and decorated according to the owner's skills and had space to put lamps inside and/or outside, and possibly some sweets inside. With adult help, girls sometimes worked for weeks before Divali to construct, paint, and decorate the portable ghroundi; but the simplest one for a small child might just resemble a jack-o-lantern. Some potters made ghroundi if a family requested, as Aunt Hernami usually did for her young daughters. It is possible that the ghroundi and masaal were merely rural customs, because I never saw anyone in the cities with one of these things. But of course I never saw a city household until I was in my twenties and some old customs were dying out by then.

Many rural people, nominally Sikh but with residual Hindu traditions, believed that on Divali evening, Lakshmi the goddess of wealth and happiness, comes into those houses that have lit their lamps and are celebrating enthusiastically, but that Lakshmi would turn away from those doors that didn't have their lamps (diva) lit.

The Lohri Festival

In the villages, Lohri was as important a festival as Divali, in my days. It came in the dead of winter, and every neighborhood of the village made its own community fire in the street for this festival. In our neighborhood a shallow pit was dug at a street corner and in that pit a pyramid of dried cow dung *pathi* (patties) was erected. Each family contributed a pathi to the Lohri pyramid. Young kids went from house to house with a basket, and announced in rhyme, "*Mai ni mai paeen pathi, tera putra charhuga hathi,*" flattering the woman of the house while requesting her to donate a pathi for the Lohri fire. At night all the neighbors sat around the Lohri fire, usually on low *peehri* seats. First there would be general talk and gossip about what other neighborhoods were doing. Later at night, serious classical tales were told by elders and by skilled storytellers. I still remember the words from one fable that Uncle Nick used to tell every year. He was not the articulate or talkative type, so people were even more curious about his stories. These stories would go on till past midnight. Some people ceremonially threw sesame seeds in the fire and recited the rhyme, "Ishwer aye, delidder jae, delidder di jerr chulhe pye," which meant, "Come God's blessings; go away lethargy and sickness; let the root of malady be thrown into the fire." There might be gods and myths related to the Lohri festival, but I do not know enough about them. Some mischievous children would "marry up" the Lohri from another neighborhood, that is, get a stick burning in the other neighborhood's pyramid and bring the flaming stick from the others' fire to their own pyramid.

The elders in the *sutth* (plaza) would have piles of *gur* (solid raw sugar) spread on sheets and blankets. They distributed the gur, and sometimes coconut and sesame seeds as well, to everyone who went to the sutth during the Lohri evening. For this purpose, many ten pound *bheli* of *gur* (mounds of solid brown sugar) would have been donated by each of the families who had reason to rejoice. If a family had a newborn son, a new bride, or some other welcome event in their house during the previus year, they would donate a bheli of gur to the sutth. This donation was to recognize the blessing to their family and hoping an equally good fortunes in the future. The value of raw sugar is hard for modern day people to appreciate but to us children deprived of sugar, at that age it was a real treat. During the Lohri night, mothers prepared *kheer* (rice cooked in milk) in big vessels overnight for their families to eat in the morning. As festivals go, Lohri was quieter and about neighborhood gathering, relating, and being thankful. It is possible that the Festival of Lohri was not celebrated in the cities; now Lohri may be fading in the villages as well, because the elements necessary for it are disappearing.

Besakhi, The Indian New Year Day

On Besakhi day, the winter harvest is ripe but it is usually not fully secured yet. Besakhi, sometimes written as Baisakhi, was the first day of the first month, Besakh, according to the Bikermi Calendar. This calendar was started in the reign of King Bikram during one of the ages of prosperity in India. The Sikhs also celebrate Besakhi because that is the day when Guru Gobind chose to initiate the Khalsa, his new breed of saint soldiers, with the *amrit ceremony*, with five symbols, and the word Singh added to every male Sikh name. The Bikermi calendar year starts on 13th April, when it is 58 years ahead of the European calendar; on January 1 it is only 57 years ahead.

When I was a boy, every event was cited and discussed according to the Bikermi calendar. In the villages, the date, month and year of birth, the year of big rains, the year of famine, the year of the *Ghadar* rebellion against the British, and so forth, were remembered according to the Bikermi Calendar. My mother knew the children's birthdays according to the Bikermi calendar only. Now, with the adoption of the European calendar, the Bikermi calendar is becoming less important even in India. But Besakhi is still celebrated by Sikhs and Hindus by going to fairs, bathing at sacred places, and holding feasts. On Besakhi day there are traditional *mela* (fairs) at many places, as well as family celebrations. I remember that in 1947, several of us from our village traveled 25 miles overnight to reach the Besakhi fair at Talwandi Sabo gurdwara.

Dasehra Festival

Dasehra is a celebration of the victory of god/prince Ram, with the help of the mythical monkey/general Hanuman, over the 'evil king' Ravan of Lanka and the recovery of his wife Sita from Ravan's possession. Dasehra has to precede Divali by three weeks, because the battle and the victory had to occur before Ram could bring his wife home on the day of Divali. Dasehra also means the 10th day, which follows the nine dark nights. Many big cities had elaborate *mela* (fairs) on Dasehra day. As a youngster, I may have gone to some rural Dasehra fairs, which were mostly about buying sweets and seeing various feats and tricks, hustle and bustle. But once in 1946 on my way back from Amritsar, I happened to get off the train at FaridKot where the Raja of FaridKot used to sponsor a big Dasehra fair. Then in 1952 I went to college in Hoshiarpur, where I saw the biggest Dasehra celebration. There, in the fair grounds, huge thirty or forty foot high effigies of Ravan and his generals with cruel, grotesque, and demonic faces made from colorful paper, had been erected. Some people were dressed with Hanuman monkey masks and 'monkey troopers' were prancing around. Near sunset, with elaborate ceremony the blazing arrow from the bow of the person impersonating Prince Ram set ablaze the paper effigies of Ravan and his generals. I heard that sometimes there were incendiary materials and firecrackers stuffed into the effigies to create a more spectacular effect. This created delight and cheers in the crowd and then there was revelry and rejoicing at the destruction of the 'evil forces.' Religious people had intense emotions about Dasehra activities in those days, just as Christians have about Easter. But to us as children it was just like another secular mela to go to.

The Festival of Holi

This festival comes in early March, just before the harvest is ripe. There is some associated myth about an arrogant king who wants to be worshipped as God and orders his son to be burned when the prince refuses to recognize the king as God; but the prince is saved by the King's sister Holika. In the villages it was just an occasion for throwing *gulali* (color) at someone whom you wanted to tease or to get the attention of. There was some trickery, deception, and playfulness in throwing color at your intended target, frequently between men and women, but it was intended to express your playfulness and liking rather than hostility. Clever methods were used to bring people into situations where colored water could be thrown on them. For many people this provided an opportunity to open up to some others in a sanctioned way. The wife of a brother or cousin was a legitimate target for a boy to throw color on, and vice versa. People picked on someone with whom they could be expected to have a playful, teasing relationship, but there were a few occasions where a stranger too could be a target.

Sikhs celebrated all the above festivals, but also the birthday of Guru Nanak, two weeks after Divali, and the birthdays of Guru Gobind Singh and other Gurus, all called *gurpurbh*. The celebrations usually included recitations of the *Granth*, and preaching and singing of *shabad* inside the gurdwara. At the conclusion of the Granth recitation in the early morning hours firecrackers would announce the birth. The best part of the celebration was the *jaloos* (procession) of the Granth through the village on the afternoon before the birthday. The jaloos had singers accompanying the Granth, the Nihang Singhs in uniform with steel weapons walking in front of the Granth, others showing their skills in fencing and swordplay, people on horses behind, acrobats, people shooting firecrackers, and music makers. For me the Sikh religious celebrations were not as interesting as the traditional Indian festivals.

In addition to the above, there were other important days for the Hindus, like *ShivRatri* (Shiva's night?), and *Basant Panchmi* (fifth of Spring?). *Rakhri*, also called *Raksha Bandhen* (protection band), was an occasion for a sister to tie a wrist band on her brother, her protector. *Shradh* were the days to feed the Brahmans as act of piety, and *Karwa Chauth* were the days when women fasted to prolong the lives of their husbands. In the 1930s, some village Sikhs, like Aunt Hernami, observed some of these Hindu practices, but in our house we never recognized their importance. It was believed that if you did not celebrate those festivals enthusiastically, the particular god or goddess associated with the event wouldn't bring his/her favors to you. Such days might not have much religious significance for the rural Sikhs; they were just cultural traditions from our Hindu past. I look back with nostalgia and warm feelings on the celebrations of those days.

Muslims usually did not celebrate any Indian festivals; I think it was sinful for them to participate in anything that was not of Arabic origin. They had two kinds of "Eid" and the Ramadan month of fasting, which came in different months and seasons in different years because they were scheduled according to the lunar calendar. Since there were not many cultural links between the Sikhs and the Muslims in our area, and the Muslims in Mehraj were insignificant in number, I never saw any Muslim celebrations; I only read about them. There were no Christians in rural Punjab. During the British rule my mother used to say that my brother Kartar was coming home for "the holiday of Big Day." From that name I used to think that the Christmas holiday occurred because the days were expected to get longer after the shortest day had already passed. It was only in college that I became aware of the meaning of the term *Big Day* as Christmas.

Yugg for God Indra

The *yugg* was not a regular event on any particular day; it was a charity feeding event that the village planned and performed. The purpose of the yugg was *punn*, an act of charity by the community, usually at the encouragement of a holy man, and it involved a feast to please Inder (Indra), the god of heaven and rain; and to ward off famines, locusts, diseases, disasters, and other unfavorable events. Several 50 to 100 gallon steel *kraha* (wok) of rice cooked with raw sugar were prepared to feed everyone who could come by that day. Rice was a scarce and valued commodity in those days in our area, not for regular daily meals. After the yugg had been announced by the village drummer, everyone in the village would be aware of the event; so poor people in the nearby villages also learned of the coming yugg feast. Normally, girls from landed families would not be enthusiastic about such feeding, and the sweet rice was not exactly a delicacy for them; but the feeding of virgins was considered an act pleasing to God, so the elders would make a special pleading to the girls and invite them to come, "Bibi, zaroor ao; punn da kam hai". So the girls walked in groups, sometimes more than a mile, to the yugg to increase its effectiveness, as this was an event for punn, to make rain. Men prepared and served the rice, and the drummer kept beating the drum to keep things lively. Usually the drummer was a part of the additional project of digging and deepening the water pond at the same time; the yugg was always held beside a pond that was dry in the yugg season before the rains. The deepening of the pond was also considered an act pleasing to God and a preparation for his blessings of rain, because all his creatures, tame and wild, would drink from it. So the yugg was a feast, held by a pond, usually at the urging of a *sadhu* (Hindu ascetic), and it was an all day affair of feeding and digging.

The measure of a successful yugg was to see how close it came to raining. If it rained, people felt validated and happy, and the holy sadhu got some credit. If not even a cloud showed up on the day of the yugg, the sadhu might say, "There is major *grauh* (Gods' wrath) on this land; people have not been living by the *dharma*; too many people have been committing *paap* (sin); more *punn* has to be done to alleviate God's wrath." In dry years there would be many more yugg. Other parts of the village and other villages would hold their own yugg on different days, hoping for additional success. Poor people could depend on eating at some yugg for many days during the season, if they were willing to travel some distance. The elders' feeling used to be that even if it did not rain after performing a yugg, this was an act of propitiation that God would recognize, and it would wash off some of the sins of the land. Apparently this custom of yugg has died out after the 1940s.

395

CHAPTER 25

ANIMALS IN PUNJAB?

In our village a farmer kept his animals in his house, either in the courtyard or in a separate part of his house. Even those who had separate place for animals might keep the milk cow or buffalo in the house, for convenience. If there was a separate place for animals, some adult male of the family had to sleep near the animals to prevent theft and other problems.

How holy was the cow?

From ancient times, Indians have revered the cow for important reasons. In the old society, milk had the status of a sacred commodity and was considered the most valuable food for human health. And the source of milk, after one's mother, was the cow. During my childhood the Punjabi Hindus called the animal *gow mata* (cow mother). The Brahma variety might not be the best cow for milk, but it was hardy enough to tolerate the harsh heat of India. It could subsist by foraging in the relatively unproductive land and required minimal maintenance.

An even more important reason for worshiping the cow was that the Brahma bull was the main source of power in India before the advent of the internal combustion engine. Male calves grew to be draught oxen after they were castrated at about the age of two years (possibly to make them more compliant); otherwise they became stud bulls. Oxen were necessary for plowing the land; for running most machines like the oil extractor *kohlu*, the sugarcane crusher *ghulari*, the wheat grinding *khrass*; and for transport by oxcart. A horse was too delicate and 'high-maintenance' for such tasks in the Indian climate. The camel was very useful in certain geographical regions but had its limitations in others. Thus, before trains and motorized transport became common in India, the ox was indispensable for a productive society. Not much could be grown if the ox did not pull a plough; and he dragged the carts of harvested crops to bring the wealth home. Our gratitude to the ox ran deep, since the ox was the creator of family food and fortune. Men sang praises to the abilities and loyalties of their oxen: "Dhann gow da jaiya, jis da khaeay kamaya," which means approximately, "Glory to the cow-born, whose earnings we eat!" Hindus treated all life as sacred, and the cow was at the top of the list. Going beyond the concept of God as an abstract, they showed appreciation for all things that they thought were God's manifestations and blessings. They worshipped the sun god, without whom life could not exist; the wind god for bringing clouds and other comforts; the fire god for energy and for the power to purify; and the water god and the grain god for obvious reasons. Reverence for the cow was part of the same thinking.

The cows we had in Punjab were mediocre at producing milk and did not make the best draught animals either. Therefore, stud bulls were imported from other areas such as Hissar, or from Nagaur in the Rajputana desert. It is because of thinking in a rut with no spirit of innovation, that no one abandoned the Punjab variety of cow altogether, to breed the Hissar and Nagaur variety, which had trimmer and more muscular bodies. In fact, from the reputation of Nagaur oxen, the adjective "Nagauri" came to signify superior, top notch, or high caliber, even when describing things other than oxen. The expression "What Nagauri do you think of yourself?" was a common taunt among the quarreling village boys. With poor oxen, plowing was drudgery; and if your loaded oxcart became stuck in mud or deep sand, you had to call someone with a stronger team of oxen to pull the cart out.

It took two oxen to pull a plough or an oxcart. The number of oxen, and therefore the number of ploughs, was a reliable measure of a landowner's cultivable land, since each plough could cultivate 20 to 40 acres, depending on the quality of land. Thus a man's land holdings could be determined by the number of oxen he owned. When looking for a prospective bridegroom for their daughter, the parents would ask, "How many ploughs does his family run?" or they could just count the oxen. Some of our laborers who had worked for the Sirdar of Badal previously, used to say that the Sirdar owned rows and rows of oxen that stood along very long continuous mangers. A middle-class family in our village would run at least two ploughs, while two oxen and a single plough were considered bare subsistence farming.

How sacred was the cow?

Apart from its milk, farming, transport and other uses for power, the *goha* or *gober* (dung) of the cow was useful as fertilizer; alternatively it was made into pathi (patties) and dried for use as fuel for household cooking. The *gohara* (pyramid of dried cow dung patties) on the periphery of a village was an indication of the prosperity of the village. The saying, "You can judge the substance of a village from its goharas" was not really a joke, because the amount of cow dung produced indicated the number of animals owned and the quantity of fuel consumed by the residents of the village.

They used to say that even when a cow dies, its hide and bones are useful, whereas the human body is good for nothing after it is dead. Western people may recoil at the thought of cow dung being used to "purify" the kitchen floor in India, but cow dung mixed with clay was used as a coating for the floor. After it dried, cow dung mixed with clay was not any worse than other materials used in the village. What is more, if the holy Brahmin followed this practice of using cow dung and clay mixture for purifying his own kitchen area, others could not be too squeamish. There were even cases where children's hair was washed with cow urine to cure scalp diseases.

For all the reasons given above, the cow was considered sacred. When a wealthy person wanted to perform a great act of charity, he would donate a cow (*gow daan*) to a Brahmin. Some fellows would say to a friend, "Oh, why do you need to take a bath right now; what cows do you have to donate?" That saying referred to the fact that one had to wash and purify oneself before making such an important donation. And just as people used to swear by God, by their son, by their eyes, and so on, many would swear by cow, because the cow was sacred.

When I was growing up, our house kept buffaloes rather than cows for milk, but sometimes we kept a cow or two anyway, because we hoped to raise a male calf to become an ox. When I was a little boy, my family had four huge oxen, named NaiWala (bought from a *Nai*), Landa (with a cut tail), Gora (blondish red) and Sava (bluish gray). The last three were born of our own cows. Gora and Sava, born of the same mother, were fast in their movements and had an inborn tendency to threaten strangers and children. NaiWala and Landa were white, gentle, and very strong. They all had different traits, abilities, and habits. Except for the Gora ox, which was sold to a GadiWala nomad in a bad year (I felt a pain in my heart when that ox was sold and taken away from our house; but adults could be hard-hearted about such things.), we kept all our oxen for their entire lives. As a little boy, I was fascinated with and in awe of our powerful, magnificent, and impressive oxen. During the 1930s, they pulled our two ploughs. When we needed to transport loads, Landa and NaiWala would be yoked to the oxcart directly, while Gora and Sava would be yoked in front of them and their yoke was connected to the cart by a very thick leather rope called *nard*, to provide additional power. A good, healthy calf that was about three years old could be yoked for farm work. Most oxen lived to be sixteen to eighteen years old; the stud bulls that were not castrated, lived about the same amount of time, as did the cows and buffaloes.

A healthy pair of oxen were a delight to watch, under yoke or just standing at the manger. Most people had great affection for their oxen, since a normal ox would give his all to a task when called upon to do so. The ox is a gentle and cooperative animal, and it was natural to be grateful for his traits and abilities. A cow does not like a bath, but lifts its tail in delight if you scratch its skin; unlike the buffalo, a cow never sits in water. Some stud bulls, but not all, were very gentle and when we got near them they would come to us to be petted and scratched. People raked and cleaned their oxen's fur and massaged their skin with metal brushes called *kharkra*. They oiled the horns of their oxen; they tried to fatten the oxen with extra grain and feed; and they would put either a single *tully* bell or a multi-bell *ghungral,* which was a leather necklace with round *ghungru* bells, around an ox's neck. Some also put a leather strap around the roots of the horns and hung little decorations over their foreheads. My family owned several ghungral bell-necklaces from the days when my uncles and their oxen were young. Later, when my uncles grew older, those ghungral and the leather nard just hung on the pegs and hooks in our Inner House. The noise of a ghungral was like music to the owner's ears when the young oxen would run fast while pulling a cart. Whereas plowing with weak oxen was drudgery, it was pure delight and a source of pride when your plough went through half an acre of land by noon. For an owner, to pass the slower cart of another was a matter of great pride. It was not just some lifeless car engine, it was a flesh and blood competition. If someone's oxcart was stuck because his weak oxen could not pull it out of sand or mud, an owner with stronger oxen would be very proud to be able to pull it out.

Most houses owned only one or two cows, and it was impractical to send an adult to graze a single cow. So each village had a *vaagi*, a herdsman, whose job was to graze the vugg (herd) of cows of the village. In our village there were several vugg, one for each part of the village. In the morning, a family would take their cow to the vugg location on the periphery of the village where the cows were gathered; the stud bull of the village also was usually to be found there. The vaagi took the herd to the wilderness to graze during the day. Even though sometimes there was not much to graze on, sending the cows out with the vaagi gave them a chance to wander about, to keep them from getting restless after being tethered continuously. Some cows were unmanageable and hyperactive, so the owners and the vaagi tied a wooden *daha* (pole) that dangled from their necks and dragged between their feet. This daha was about four to five feet long, and the handicap of that dragging daha made it difficult for the cow to run; she had to be cautious even while walking to avoid stepping on it. But restless and erratic cows had to be treated this way until they started to behave better. The cowherd tied a big bell to the neck of the best-behaved cow with the hope that other cows would follow that one, and you could hear from a distance when the vugg was coming back to the village. One way to describe the time of day was by the return of the vugg after grazing, because at that time the sun was about three ropes high above the horizon. Women would say, "It is *vugg vela* (vugg time) and I should set the *daal* to cook, so that it will be ready by dinner time." At vugg time each cow went to her own house, and the stud bull just hung out at the designated spot. In later years when more people started owning buffaloes, some families sent their young sons, starting at the age of seven or so, to graze buffaloes and cows together, and some even included a goat or two. This was automatic employment for young boys, as most of them never went to school.

By the 1940s, cows were getting to be of little importance in Punjab, and people started abandoning them. The unwanted cows became a problem because the Punjab variety cow was not as good for milk as the buffalo was, and its calves did not make as good oxen as the Nagaur variety did. Butchering a cow was unthinkable for non-Muslims. In fact many of the conflicts between Hindus and Muslims were because the Muslims wanted to eat the cow, and the Hindus felt that the cow was sacred and had to be defended. At the same time, the sight of a pig was an offence to a Muslim. The difference was that the Hindus loved the cow, while the Muslims hated the pig. A fellow trying to convince others of his honesty would swear, "As cow is to a Hindu and pig is to a Muslim, *anything illegitimate is similar for me*; I will not take anything dishonestly!" Some notorious outlaws became heroes in the eyes of village people by rescuing cows from butchers. Rich Hindus in some larger towns built *gow shala* (cow houses) for the care and maintenance of unwanted cows as an act of punn (piety). The cows in gow shala were well fed and healthier looking than those owned by individuals. In the villages, however, there was no provision for unwanted cows. As the Punjabi cows became less and less useful, they were abandoned more frequently. There emerged the menace of unwanted stray cows turned wild, euphemistically called "Ram Gow" (God's cow), even before the Muslims left in 1947. A herd of hundreds of the wild Ram Gow lived a couple of miles from our village in wild lands near the boundary of Phul territory. They were so dangerous that even men on horses feared them, as they feared tigers or lions, because the cows could just charge and even topple a horse. If they were coming your way, you were lucky to find a tree to climb. They usually traveled to feed just after sunset, damaged crops overnight, and returned to their place before sunrise. In those days, the Ram Gow were destructive and were feared more than any wild animal in our area. When the village people got really tired of the stray cows, farm boy volunteers just drove the herds of cows across the border to Pakistan, where the meat-eaters were probably salivating. I think the Ram Gow might have met their fate there.

Nowadays, stray cows are mainly found in the cities, because the farmers cannot tolerate them in the countryside and make efforts to get rid of them. I read in Chandigarh Tribune newspaper when I was there in November 2003, that two people in that city were killed that week by cows; religious people prevent any action against the cows to reduce such deaths. The increase in the numbers of unwanted cows and a decrease in the provisions for the care of cow has left many stray cows. Ironically, now such stray cows are found mostly on the roads and pavements of the big cities; there are no stray cows in their natural habitat in the Punjab countryside.

Cruelty Even to the Holy Animal

In rural Punjab, cruelty to animals was so common that no one considered it odd. For some, that Indian idea of all life being sacred and the cow being holy, was only theoretical. When a farmer's oxen could not pull the oxcart stuck in the sand, both oxen would be beaten continuously to make them pull harder. The oxen would use all their might to move the cart a few feet and might be exhausted, but the beating would not stop. Yokes sometimes caused the necks of oxen to become swollen, bleeding, and infected from improper use and excessive stress, but not every farmer took pity on his ox and let its neck heal before putting the yoke on it. The ox makes no noise when it suffers, except in extreme situations. There was always a stick to hit the ox. The ploughman used the *prani*, a stick with a leather strap tied in front; the prani was a relatively gentle way to get the attention of the ox, to make it move faster. But some cruel fellows had a nail into the front of the prani to pierce the skin of the ox, to prod it to move faster or pull harder. A healthy ox will move faster if you merely touch its skin; but weak and sickly oxen might be stabbed hard with the prod nails when they were strained to the limit and could not pull any harder. Some fellows could be sadistic to an animal, so that it was hard for onlookers to witness their cruelty. Sometimes other people would plead with the owner to not be so cruel and to have mercy on *gow da jaia* (one born of a cow).

In 1979 when I went to visit Punjab, I saw rows and rows of healthy oxen lined up as I passed by the train station at Rampura Phul. From the condition of their yokes it looked as though they had not been put to work for some time. I asked an old Hindu man why those beautiful oxen were standing there. He said, "Don't ask such a question; it is painful for me to describe their fate; they are waiting to be loaded on the train and may be going to extinction." Whereas during my childhood the number of oxen in rural Punjab was roughly equal to the number of adult men, there are no oxen to be seen there any more. Tractors and trucks have completely replaced oxen and camels in Punjab.

The Milch Buffalo

After the irrigation canals came and feed sources and water were assured, the more prosperous people started keeping buffaloes for milk instead of cows. My father told us that when he was a little boy in the beginning of 20th century, very few families owned buffaloes; most of them could afford only a cow. Buffalo milk was sweeter, richer, and tastier than that from the Brahma variety cow, and buffaloes gave more milk per animal than cows. But the buffalo does not tolerate intense sun; it does not have the protection of fur as a cow has, so our people could not use the buffalo males as draught animals. Later on, even the Brahmins and the shopkeepers in our village started to maintain buffaloes rather than cows for milk.

The buffalo milk flowed only after calving; so the birth of a calf was a much-anticipated event. As a boy, I was sometimes left to guard a pregnant buffalo that was about to give birth. It was feared that the buffalo might eat the "afterbirth" and umbilical cord, and there was a superstition that either the buffalo would die from eating them or that it could be a bad omen that would bring some other disaster on the family. If the buffalo was restless and got up, the birth would be delayed. The buffalo had to sit down before the *mutandi* (amniotic sac, water bag) would show. In some cases, the front hoofs of the calf might show even before the water bag broke. I would start pulling the front hoofs only after the snout of the calf started to come out; and then I would see the calf's head. In fact pulling was not even necessary, but most owners got anxious and wanted it to happen quickly. If the snout did not show, then the orientation of the calf might be wrong and it would be dangerous to pull the calf's hoofs. Sometimes the birth was quick; sometimes it took hours from start to finish. If there was any complication, I was supposed to alert some knowledgeable adult. Once the calf's head passed, it was a smooth exit. I was always squeamish about the umbilical cord, which among animals breaks automatically; it does not need to be cut, and any remainder dries up and just drops off the calf's navel after three to four weeks.

Everyone used to hope for a female buffalo calf, because it would grow up to give milk, while male buffalo would be useless except for butchering, which our people never did. Male buffaloes as draught animals were considered a laughing matter in our area, although in the Majha region some people used them like oxen. On the other hand, a male cow calf was a useful draught animal, whereas the Brahma cow female was inferior as a milk animal. So people prayed for a female buffalo calf and for a male cow calf. Sex preference was nothing new in the rural areas, but no one could do anything about it except to wish and pray.

Buffaloes and cows in heat used to be brought to the stud bulls whose resting places, after grazing in the fields, were in open spaces near the boundary of the village. There they copulated in full view of the public. Sometimes a bull would seek out a female in *heha* (estrus) just by the drift of the smell of the female; at other times, owners searched for the bull. The tethered female animal in heat indicated her condition by extreme restlessness, sometimes to the extent even of breaking the tether rope, and by calling loudly and continuously (the call of a cow was called 'rhamb' and the call of a buffalo was called 'ring') until she was brought to the bull. There was also some clear, viscous flow from the animal for one or two days, but it was so subtle and minimal that a negligent or clueless owner might ignore it or miss seeing it. If the owner did not take the cow to the bull during that period, or if the impregnation was unsuccessful, he would have to wait for the next time she was in heat. Unlike the case of wild animals, the time of estrus of cows and buffaloes was not predictable or according to any regular timetable, and not even seasonal. Owners would coax the bull and say, "Come on, be a hero; it is just one push for a champion like you, but it means milk and butter for our family for a whole year." Some would even use their hands to guide the bull, and they would be cheerful at the successful conclusion of the act. Many people encouraged the bull to repeat the performance several times to make sure of the impregnation.

In the villages it was neither customary nor socially acceptable to buy and sell milk. Near big cities some people, with a degree of embarrassment, started selling milk to sweet and tea shops. In earlier times milk was considered a sacred substance, and selling milk was considered an immoral act, akin to prostitution. Only the *Gowala* caste could sell milk, just as only the *Kanjer* caste could be prostitutes and entertainers. They used to say "milk and a son are God's blessings; to sell the sacred milk is trivializing God's gift and a sin." A common blessing used to be: "May God grant you milk and a son." This song to a beloved indicates the importance of milk: "Some people pray for milk; some beg for a son; I just beg for your daily séance...." In my childhood no good Jat family would disgrace itself by selling or buying milk. If you needed a lot of milk for a wedding or to prepare sweets, everyone in the community who knew you, brought milk to your house, usually without your having to ask for it. Some people used to bring milk to our house when they found out that we were all visiting and thought our family might need more milk. Selling ghee was acceptable, and people did store and sell ghee; they just could not sell milk and still be respectable. But after World War II, some people started selling milk even in our village, although both the buyers and sellers felt a bit uneasy and tried to be secretive about the sale. In later years, milk was sold just like any other commodity.

Families would give milk to a sadhu, to their workers, or to the temple volunteer. In general, though, the only milk product given free was the *lassi* (buttermilk), of which there was usually plenty in prosperous households. The lassi was treated like a waste product, useful only to feed to an animal or to wash hair with. Because of its sour taste, like most children I hated buttermilk, although my father insisted that it was good for health. The men in our house drank lassi when they were young; but some village people made jokes about that practice because it was considered a cheap habit. Eating and drinking were not very private affairs in the village; everyone knew who ate what and how, and our men got the unflattering reputation of drinking lassi. Although *lassi-peena* (buttermilk drinker) was not as insulting as *julli-chuck* (quilt carrier), no one in the village wanted to be teased about it. Once people got accustomed to tea, they did not drink lassi any more, because lassi and tea were considered opposite in characteristics and incompatible. Some people thought lassi made people lethargic and sleepy, and led to excessive *Vat* (an imbalance of the elements of *Vat, Pit, Cuff,* in the body). For that reason some people would not feed lassi even to their oxen or camels. Washing the hair with lassi was its most important use. Only a few people drank it and fed it to their animals. Lassi was the only milk product that the poor low caste people could get free from a Jat house.

The Versatile Camel

In regions close to the desert, the camel was more useful and versatile than the ox. Whereas the ox was a domestic product in Punjab, a camel raised in the desert cost more;

it ate more and did not function very well in mud. But a camel also had many advantages. It could pull a plough as well as two oxen could, it could run machinery, it could be harnessed to assist the yoked oxen in pulling an oxcart or could pull a camel cart without the oxen, and it could carry loads or passengers. When a farmer was tired after his day's work, he could load the camel with animal fodder and ride it home. If you didn't have a camel, you had to walk behind your oxen carrying all your paraphernalia on your head. For a farmer in the desert-like areas of Punjab, a camel was somewhere between a necessity and a luxury. You could ride a camel to the market and transport your purchases home on it instead of carrying them on your head. You could put it to power the flour-mill and grind your wheat, to power the water wheel to draw water from the well, and for numerous other tasks. Most camels in our village were used for pulling the plough, for pulling oxcarts, for transportation of loads and for riding. Some camels could be trained for smooth rides or even for fancy stepping, much as a horse could be trained. Even the British Indian army had regiments of camel riders called the Camel Corps. Even after the British rule ended and up to more recent times, the Indian military kept camels.

The camels used in our area were usually born and raised in the desert of Rajputana, south of Punjab. They were the single-hump dromedaries, like the camels of the Arabian countries. Many Americans say that a camel can spit at you. I don't know the habits of two-humped camels, which is the kind that Americans seem to know about, from Bob Hope's movies such as "Road to Morocco." I only know that our single-hump camels did not have the trait of spitting, unless the dropping foam during the masti season can be called spit. Our family usually had one and sometimes two camels in addition to the oxen. Our *Kala Untth* (black camel) was bought in 1937 when he had not yet got any permanent teeth and was *kheera* (having milk teeth) at the age of about two. He could pull a plough easily even before he became *duga* (having two adult teeth) at the age of about three. As a *chauga* (four adult teeth at about four years), *shigga* (six teeth), and *nesha* (with canine teeth) at about seven years of age, he was known for his legendary strength. Front teeth are a measure of an animal's age, but farm animals, except for the horse family, grow only the bottom teeth in front; they do not grow front teeth, except the canines, in the upper gum. As milk teeth in the front drop, the larger permanent teeth that take their place indicate the age of the animal. Camels have chewing molars at the top and bottom like most farm animals; in the front they get a total of six biting teeth at the bottom only. Male camels also get the longer canine teeth (nesh) at maturity, while female camels do not get the big canine teeth.

Some male camels may bite. And even though they do not have upper cutting teeth, their canine teeth can penetrate human flesh easily. A mature male camel can cause serious injury with his canine teeth (although most don't dare to do such a thing), but more fearsome is the fact that a male camel sometimes tries to crush a human with its chest, if it is in a state of *masti* or *musti* (intoxication?). Bakhtaur son of Inder Singh in our village, was crushed by his camel one day when he had carelessly turned his back to the camel as he got busy cutting fodder. The camel apparently had been holding a grudge against its owner and found an opportunity to kill him. His camel would have killed Bakhtaur by grinding and crushing him under its chest, but he was saved by men from the neighboring fields when they sensed something was wrong and ran to rescue him. It took more than a year for Bakhtaur's broken bones and internal injuries to heal, and his body never recovered its strength completely. Killings of owners by their camels happened very rarely. In the *masti* season, owners learned to take preventive measures like *shikli* (a muzzle), *neol* (steel foot hobbles), and fresh holes through the snout area to pass the *lahti* (fittings) and *nakail* (nose string) that could hurt the camel and make him obey. Camels are usually timid, obedient, and harmless, except for the few males that get out of line during the masti season. Only a small fraction of male camels are really dangerous, but usually they are also the strongest ones. The owners just have to watch their behavior to prevent unpleasant surprises.

From mid December to late February and sometimes a little longer, most mature male camels get into a state of *masti* (senselessness) intoxication, when the camel feels intoxicated, wild and mad. The degree of masti can be mild in many of them, possibly determined by the intensity of their individual hormones and their health. A camel's state of masti is flagrantly obvious, as indicated by his *bukken* (roar); they never roar like that during the rest of the year. Another physical indication of masti is that the top of the head of a *mast* camel appears swollen. He shows little interest in eating when he is *mast* and he looks slim at the waist. Usually the mast camel does not even chew his cud, as he is not in a relaxed mental state then. Also, any time his attention is drawn to another camel or to a person, and even to some noise, he begins *bukken* (roaring). A roaring mast camel blows a large, pink, oval, balloon-like structure out of his mouth and starts foaming at the mouth. While in masti, he grinds his teeth furiously and lashes his tail forward and backward rhythmically (*mukkrah* motion) and energetically between his legs. He may walk with his hind legs spread apart, and he can spray his urine about with his tail in mukkrah motion unless the owner is careful to bend and tie the tail. The male camel is designed so that ordinarily the stream of his urine flows backward and falls several feet behind him. Most mast camels are merely exuberant and playful and are still quite obedient to their owners. A few, like our Kala Untth, get really senseless, uncontrollable, and in some situations totally murderous. Even the fresh pins (lahti) through the side of the snout and strings through the nostrils, that normally hurt him enough to make him scream with pain, were not enough to make him obey when in the masti state. A mast camel is out of his mind and becomes careless of his own well being.

Many owners of mast camels were proudest of their animals when they were in the masti state, when the camel would roar by blowing the pink oval balloon out of his throat. The *bulken* sound of a mature camel can be quite interesting to hear; it resembles the sound of escaping air from a pitcher dipped in water but is more powerful and loud. The owners showed off their mast camels in various ways at the fair, sometimes by riding them and sometimes by just parading the decorated animals around. The roaring, foaming, and mukkrah-tail swinging animal with the swollen head, walking by spreading the rear legs wide apart, and ringing the mukkrah bells with his tail, made a spectacle of itself. The turban and shoulders of the camel owner would get loaded with the foam dropping gradually from the mast camel's mouth. Some were proud that their camel was so powerful and dangerous. Even when the foam from the roaring mast camel's mouth fell on the turban and shoulders of the owner, he did not act squeamish about it; he just kept getting loaded with the foam and full of pride. Not every mast camel was normally disobedient or dangerous; most would only be just difficult enough to be interesting. The healthier and more robust male camels of all colors (and particularly the black ones) turned mast in the mating season. You could get a female camel without any danger of masti; but in general the females were not as strong.

My Black Camel in Masti

Our Kala Unth (black camel), when in the state of masti, seemed to have unlimited strength; he became uncontrollable and disregarded pain. Most of the time he was still manageable and we still used him for work, but the risk with most mast camels in winter was real. Once when I was eighteen and I was a farmer in our village, I loaded my Kala Untth with animal fodder from the field. The camel was in the masti state, but I had control of his nose strings to make him obey. He gave me no trouble while I was loading him all by myself in the field; later we started for the village. He was quite obedient while walking the nearly two miles toward the village. But when were within about 100 yards of our house and it saw some other camels, my camel became aroused, went out of control, and started running after me to attack. In order to indicate that it was my intention to go faster, I ran even faster, pretending that I was in control and that I was pulling the camel's nukail to make the camel follow even faster. Dropping the nose string at that point and running away would have meant that the camel got the upper hand, and then he would have been even more difficult to control afterwards. Abandoning control of the nose string and running to safety would have given the camel a "win event" against me and would have affected his future relationship with me. A mast camel with a "win" against its owner is difficult to control without being tied up or disabled. Thus, instead of abandoning the camel I had to pull the nose string as if I were commanding the camel. The camel was not fooled, however; it felt its power and wanted to crush me. The front gate of our courtyard was open and I led him by the nose string as I ran inside, with Kala Untth chasing after me. I got behind the fodder-chopping machine for protection. The camel, unable to get behind the machine, tried to crush me by pushing it and toppling it over on me. The machine was about five feet high with a flywheel but was not firmly fixed in the ground, so it was not sufficient protection. But several people had seen this camel with a bad reputation, running out of control in the attack mode. Those people ran into our courtyard without being asked to help. I threw the camel's nose strings for them to catch and to pull, and they got additional ropes and sticks to tackle, pull, tie, beat, and control the camel. In a few minutes my safety was assured. If the camel had decided to attack me while I was loading it alone in the fields, the result of the attack could have been quite different. Anyway my Kala Untth had experienced the power against me that day. This experience made it somewhat harder for me to control him in the future until the masti season passed. Kala Untth had created many other memorable, scary, and publicly known incidents prior to this, and we were aware of his habits.

One method to get back some power from the camel is to put a muzzle on him and to tie up his bent knees while he is sitting. This maneuver can be executed by a couple of skillful people with a rope. Then one can hold the nose string and approach him, all the while making sure that he can not knock you down with his neck as you fearlessly get close to him. If he tries to attack, the owner beats him hard with a flexible stick that causes no permanent injury, until he no longer has the will to attack. After extensive beating, when the camel no longer attacks you, the feeling of powerlessness will register in his brain, just as in the brain of a drunken man. After that he recognizes the power of his master somewhat, but there are no permanent guarantees until the masti season passes. And if he is the type that holds a grudge, you could get into trouble even later when you are vulnerable and unaware. During most of the year, male camels give no trouble if their keepers have a strong will and exercise caution. But some camels in the masti state constantly test their owners' will.

Our Kala Untth had many virtues that made my uncle its proud owner. Apart from his legendary strength, for which he had a reputation in the area, Kala Untth knew exactly how the master wanted him to turn each time, in every situation. After he was trained, he did not just turn in the most convenient, lazy way, as oxen would. He had learned that the most convenient way was not acceptable to the owner to plough the corners of the field or to lead the oxcart around corners. So he made sure to move more precisely, to turn widely at bends, and not to cut corners, even in the masti season. Once he was trained, he formed a permanent habit and did not need continuous direction. He would lead the ox cart to the correct field, which the oxen probably could not even find without his lead. The oxcart driver could fall asleep on the cart and trust the camel to take him to the master's field or destination, choosing each turn correctly out of all the alternate routes. Where there were two possible previously known destinations, he would choose the one taken more frequently. Kala Untth did all these things correctly out of habit even when he was in the masti state; many such qualities made him valuable and admirable.

Our Kala Untth with his circular *churna* (manger) in the center of the animal area was the pride of our family. He could sit anywhere around it, and we always spread some sand around the churna for his comfort. For this purpose we occasionally took the camel to a sand dune and loaded it with sand to bring home for the comfort of the animals. When he was not in masti, he sat in the courtyard chewing his cud in peace. The sound of his chewing could be heard from some distance away, and like the tick of a big clock it was nearly hypnotic. It was fascinating to watch the mass of cud travel like a wave from his stomach through his long neck to his mouth and then, after a couple of minutes, watch the wave of cud traveling back to the stomach after it had been chewed, all this happening automatically and effortlessly. Buffaloes and other animals, except horses and donkeys, chew their cud too, but they don't have a long neck where you can watch the wave of the traveling mass of cud.

In the less busy season, fashionable young fellows made great efforts to outfit their camels. They put a decorative caparison, a fancy saddle, and flowery nukel strings tied to the decorative lahti nose fittings. Many 'flowers' and bulbs made from silk and other colorful fibers were tied to the nose string as decorations. Some added the decorative *dhaliara* (rope frame for snout) and tied a colorful handkerchief to the dhaliara. They added bells for the knees and would bend and tie the camel's tail to the saddle with a decorative mukkrah stripe, which also had many bells on it. That is how a fellow rode in style to a fair or to visit his relatives. When the fellow went to bring back his wife from a visit to her parents, the decorations had to be elaborate to impress the wife's relatives. The ultimate in camel decorations were called for if you were going to join a *junj*, the bridegroom's wedding party. You gave a little extra spur to make the camel jingle those knee-bells with extra speed. For wedding parties and for going to fairs, it was not uncommon to encounter a masti-intoxicated camel loaded with three or four riders intoxicated with liquor. Sometimes they just kept the camels circling with fancy steps back and forth, even after reaching the destination point, just to show off with the jingle of knee bells. I have heard that some fellows gave their camel a shot of whiskey on such occasions, but I never gave any whiskey to my black camel.

Horses, Ponies and Donkeys

Only a few families in Mehraj had horses during my time, because a horse did not fit the lifestyle of an ordinary working farmer. My family had a horse when my father was young; also my father kept a horse when he had retired from farming. Possession of a good horse increased the prestige of the rider and put him in a different class compared to camel riders and oxcart drivers. It implied that the rider had other people working the farms for him and that he was prosperous; so he would be treated with some respect, and the police were ordinarily not rude to him. Many of the guests in Aunt Hernami's house, including the husband of her oldest daughter Chand Kaur, used to arrive on horses. None of our relatives ever arrived on horseback. My sister Maro's husband did own a horse, but he lived far away, and it was more practical for him to come by train.

We used to talk admiringly of those who had good horses, and I always wished I had a horse good enough to win races against others. Gurdev of Meeny Ka always had a horse or two. He also kept hunting dogs, steel weapons of many descriptions, and occasionally played some musical instruments. Another Gurdev, of Kapoore Ka house, kept horses, as he was from one of the richest families in the village. The *zaildar* always rode a horse in order to fulfill his official duties, and some traveling government officials and the mounted police had horses.

But a horse was not considered worth the trouble of maintenance for an average farmer; a camel was stronger, more versatile, and practical. There was a rhyme, "*Dekho, Jat di aqel gaee, bhens bechkay ghori laee; dudh peeno gya, lidd chakni paee,*" Which can be translated as, "Behold, the Jat has lost his senses; he sold the buffalo to buy a horse; he lost the opportunity drink buffalo milk, and now has to remove horse manure.

Horses were not a part of my life while I was growing up. But once in my teenage years, I borrowed my sister Maro's husband's horse, because I wanted to acquire and transport some illicit liquor from their village to ours, 25 miles away. It was easier to borrow the horse from my sister's house than to borrow their camel, because a horse was not important to the farming operation. Their village was in the princely State of Patiala, where the administration was lax, not in the English territory like ours; so people used to distill illicit liquor in their village. Through my brother-in-law, I had gotten to know a fellow named Nathu who distilled liquor. Nathu was a self-proclaimed *velli* and a violent *badmash* (bad character), but yet a sincere friend. My brother-in-law himself was a teetotaler; his joy in life was opium. But after Nathu became my friend, he offered me drinks of the various grades of distillation to show the difference in the punch from bottles of the first cut relative to the mildness of the batch near the end of the distillation. When I flinched and reacted to the harshness and strength of the first-cut alcohol, Nathu would say, "Gurnam, you are still too tender to drink like a man." Anyway, Nathu obtained some home-distilled whiskey for me to take from their village to mine. I would have gotten in trouble if I had transported the illegal whiskey on the train, so my brother-in-law offered me his horse to ride and to transport the whiskey.

I found the 25-mile ride though the winter-green countryside rather refreshing and fun, but it gave my untrained behind a condensed dose of the riding experience. My bottom was not just sore but had blisters for many days afterwards. Such things had happened to me before after riding horses without good-quality saddles, but a camel ride was always relatively benign, even without a saddle. Anyway, for months thereafter my friends enjoyed the illicit whiskey, which was much stronger than that available from the licensed shops in our English-ruled area. The laws were lax in the princely states, but if some official decided to catch and punish you, their system of justice was harsh and merciless compared to that in our English territory.

For sheer hardiness and the ability to carry three or four people, the camel was a better choice, but a good horse gave the rider more prestige. For short distances it could run faster than a camel. People with horses rode in the parade on the Guru's birthday; no camel could be allowed to enter the parade. The biggest and the best-looking collection of horses in Punjab were in the Boodha Dal (elders army) of the *nihang* Sikhs. Some lower castes, like the Mirassi and Sansi kept horses, but theirs were small, decrepit, damaged, or discarded ponies and were deridingly called *tattu* or *taer*. The taer were not much better than a donkey.

Except for isolated cases, people who owned donkeys were primarily from the potter caste. They used the donkeys for hauling unbaked pots and fuel to their kiln, to transport the baked pots back from the kiln after a few days, and for many other transportation needs. Potters and their teams of donkeys were also frequently hired to transport bricks and other loads. Poor people sometimes kept a donkey, but farmers considered it below their dignity to own one. They considered the donkey to be a stupid, dirty, lowly animal that grazed on trash heaps after it was released from its load. Riding a donkey was considered degrading unless you were a potter and the donkey fitted your occupation. One of the humiliating punishments was to shave a man's face and make him ride a donkey through the village. Teachers frequently used "donkey" as a term of abuse and an insult to their students. Calling someone a donkey was more degrading than calling him a pig. Young boys in search of mischief sometimes rode a stray donkey while playing outside, as donkeys were usually let loose by the potters to graze on garbage piles. But the boys' mothers felt that their children had been defiled when they learned that the boys had been riding the donkeys.

Dogs and Cats

Although feral cats were all around, nobody in the village had a pet cat. Cats were thought of as undesirable nuisance. A few people kept dogs for *shikar* (hunting). Sometimes, the low status people officially classified as criminal castes without any specific occupation, like the Sansi or the Bauria, might also hunt. A sophisticated sirdar might keep Alsatian (German Shepherd) dogs as they had the reputation of being watchful, loyal, and threatening. Village people kept dogs primarily for protection and security. Dogs as mere pets did not get much consideration, though, since in a society with little wealth and plenty of other animals around the house, the value of a dog as a pet was minimal. A good watchdog, on the other hand, was considered better protection than a human guard. People wanted the meanest and fiercest dog that could be kept chained during the day and be released in the courtyard at night. In the village, there were always numerous un-owned dogs that raised a ruckus at the slightest sound on a quiet night. If you were walking a lonely path during a dark night, the continuous barking of stray dogs told you how far and in which direction the village was. In the wilderness, the possibility that there was human life somewhere within a mile or two in some direction was indicated at night only by the sounds of barking dogs, since there were no electric lights in those days. Once in a while, there was a commotion in the village because a mad (rabid) dog was on the loose. Many times as a youngster I watched the young men of the village running after a rabid dog in order to kill him, to prevent it from biting any human or other dogs.

Sheep and Goat

In our village there were Muslims of the Sheikh caste who kept sheep and goats in their fenced *barra* (corral) on the periphery of the village. The Sheikh may have been an honored caste at one time, but in our village they were poor, low status people. They had to be humble, as they had no land of their own and grazed their sheep in the stubble fields belonging to the Jat landowners. The only time any farmer sought to flatter them was when he wanted the Sheikh's sheep to spend the night on his land, so that the sheep droppings and urine would act as fertilizer for the land. On those occasions the farmer provided food for the shepherds in the field, where they kept watch at night.

The sheep also acted as scavengers of human waste, and the Sheikh circulated them around the fecal piles every morning or evening for such purposes. Contrary to the European attitude, in Punjab a goat was considered a cleaner animal, while the sheep was considered to be a filthy animal that ate human waste. Consequently, no one except the Sheikhs or some other low caste would keep sheep. Wool might be prized in cold climates, but in the hot plains, cotton was more useful for most of the year. Sheep was a term of abuse, insult, and contempt among fighting women because it implied stupidity and slovenliness. The other reputation about sheep was their tendency to walk by keeping the snout near the tail of the sheep in front, which implied following blindly. So the expression *bhed chaal* (sheep walk) meant doing what others were doing or following others, without thinking. Elders used to say *bhed chaal* when they decried the masses following fads and fashions mindlessly.

Whereas there was no point in keeping just one or two sheep, it made sense to own a single goat. A goat was likeable and in fact was a cute animal, able to eat every kind of vegetation. Poor people kept a goat or two, and sometimes even the Jat landowners kept one. Like a pet, the goat would follow you to the field; unlike the sheep, it could feed on thorny bushes and tree branches as well in the crops. A well-trained goat ran to its owner like a dog when he called it. With an accompanying goat, there was a ready supply of goat milk at tea time in the fields for the farm workers away from home; our rural people never drank tea without milk. Some Jats, however, felt that a goat caused too much damage to a crop, so that the convenience of having milk available was not worthwhile. For example, a goat might eat the tender cotton pods before they opened or it gobbled the bean pods or kernels from crops. For this reason most farmers avoided keeping a goat unless it could be sent to graze with their other animals or joined with a goat herd. The families who kept goats, arranged to take them to a goatherd's flock, just as they took their cows to the cowherd. Our family kept a goat or two in the early years; when Uncle Nick used to graze our cattle, he would take the goat along with the buffaloes and cows. The goat's milk was like a bonus and not some thing we depended upon, though, so we never kept a goat after 1942.

Pigs and Chickens

Pigs did not fit the lifestyle of Jat farmers, because eating meat was not a high priority among them. Not keeping pigs also avoided offending the Indian Muslim officials, for whom seeing a pig was like committing a sin. As a child I saw pigs when I accompanied my uncle to the low caste colony to arrange laborers for farm work. The Chuhra caste kept pigs to sacrifice for their religious rituals once or twice a year. My father used to talk about hunting wild boar on his horse when he was in the military service of the State of Patiala in the second decade of the twentieth century. For most Jat Sikh people in our village, the sight of a pig was a rare event.

One would think that keeping chickens would be a natural thing for a farmer. For the mostly vegetarian Jats, this was not the case. Some landowners, men of leisure, and those fond of eating meat and eggs, did kept chickens. Chickens of the bantam variety used to look so colorful and attractive that we children hoped they would not be eaten. Our family considered keeping chickens a frivolous activity, only slightly better than keeping pigeons. Chickens fed on the trash piles and on the diversity of worms that thrived year-around in that climate. At night their owners secured the chickens in enclosures to protect them from stray cats. Frequently, the low caste and poor people kept chickens, and the Jats just bought a chicken from them for slaughter or bought eggs from them for a special guest. Sometimes my father used to talk about his plan of a large profitable chicken farm in the fashion of American chicken farmers, but the village people dismissed such thoughts as impractical and wild schemes.

Race and Beauty at Cattle Fairs

To the unaware, one animal looks just like another of the same species and may appear of the same value. This perception is due to lack of proper attention. I remember the time when I was so ignorant and unaware that I thought it was hard to tell the difference between one oriental man and another; to me they all looked alike. And I have met Americans who think that it is hard to tell the difference between different Sikhs, as they all have turbans and beards. I still think all sheep of the same breed look alike, but I can still remember most of the individual animals we owned over the years because of their distinct looks. To the farmer and to those experienced with animals, the body structure, the horn shape, the skin texture, quality of hair, length and shape of the tail, shape of the snout, droop of the ears, size of the udder or of the hump, and color of the animal all provide information about the value of each animal. They are distinct individuals, and each animal may have different abilities, traits, and advantages. Because animals are less complex than humans, an experienced person can predict with high accuracy what performance and benefits to expect from a particular animal. For example, a certain race might be good for speed, another breed might be better for strength, and another for durability. A certain race of buffalo might be better for milk, and a certain variety of

410

camel would be good for speed. Animals of appropriate races, breeds, and features were priced accordingly at the fairs, and those with undesirable looks were hard to sell.

A black or reddish camel was considered to have greater strength and endurance than camels of whitish-beige color, which usually lacked spirit and speed. A drooping snout and floppy ears were considered ugly and undesirable on a camel, and such camels were used mostly for caravan loads, not for riding, if one had a choice. Only the very poor would buy a *thulla* (drooping snout) camel with floppy ears, but these camels were not too delicate and they required minimum care. While shopping for a camel, we wanted one that looked hefty with wide chest, had all features in proper alignment, a straight or upward snout, small lips, alert eyes, vertical and close-fitting ears, and reddish brown or black coloring.

We wanted buffaloes with small horns that curled in tight spirals not much bigger than a human fist. The color of a buffalo was not critical, but the top grade went to a *ballhi*, the black buffalo whose forehead, tail, and all feet were marked white. It was a pleasure to look at the markings of a ballhi buffalo rather than a plain black one. The *bhoori* (blondish brown) buffalo was preferred slightly compared to a plain black one, but it was not considered as pretty as a ballhi buffalo. Thin, shiny, and hairless skin and thin long tail were the mark of a buffalo that might be expected to yield a good milk supply. Thick skin with thick hair might be hardy but was considered undesirable for a buffalo. Most important for a buffalo were its udder and teats. A large udder indicated that it would provide a high milk yield and the longer teats were a good feature for show purposes, although both could be deceptive. That is partly because the sellers, when they took their buffaloes to cattle fairs, would purposely not milk them for a while so that the udder and teats would be enlarged and would seem ready to burst with milk. A buyer had to come to a firm agreement on price before verifying the milk yield. When the buyer decided to milk the buffalo to determine the yield, the buffalo thus loaded from overdue milking would naturally give more milk.

Once my Uncle Tiloka and I took a buffalo to sell at the animal market in Rampura Phul. We did not want to be at a disadvantage compared to other buffalo sellers and wanted to draw attention to our own buffalo, so we had kept our buffalo loaded by not milking it for the previous period; so it could barely walk to the fair. Because of the huge udder, a buffalo dealer was especially interested in our animal. My uncle came to an agreement with the buyer on the price for the buffalo, but the milk yield had to be verified before we could walk to a government clerk to register the transaction. Then the buyer pointed out that the milk was dripping out of the buffalo as she walked; that was highly abnormal. We were a bit embarrassed, because the cause was obvious, but I was also afraid that our buffalo had some kind of disease or defect, causing the milk to squirt out spontaneously. The buyer could have backed out; but he was an experienced dealer and after showing some reluctance and balking a little bit, he agreed to conclude the purchase anyway. The additional feature that added value to our buffalo was that it had a female calf.

In bullocks, we looked for relatively small, upward- or forward-curved and symmetric horns; backward-pointing horns were not desirable. Most of our oxen were white, some were grayish blue (sava), and a few were reddish blond (gora); but the color made no difference in the quality of oxen. The size, body structure, and general health were

411

scrutinized carefully by the buyer. For an ox, a wide chest and posterior without a big tummy were indicators of strength and speed. A thin tail, tight skin, and no hanging folds of loose flesh, were indicators of quick temperament and rapid movement. Thick and loose skin, a fat tail, and long fur often indicated sluggishness and less sensitivity to stimulation when the owner spurred it to go faster. To tease a man, his companions might call him "*moti poonch wala*," that is, thick-tailed; that was a mild insult that meant dull, slow, or insensitive. Usually it was enough just to touch the skin of a good ox to make it go faster, but you had to hit a dull, sluggish ox with the a stick to make it move. If an ox did not lift its ears at the slightest sound or other stimulation, you were stuck with a sluggish animal. Oxen from places like Hissar and Nagaur in the desert had the more desirable characteristics compared to the non-descript mongrels of Punjab, although the Punjab oxen were somewhat bigger and stronger.

To make their animals look attractive at the fair and fetch higher prices, owners would put decorative accessories on them. Bullocks had their fur groomed, their horns oiled, and leather crowns and straps were put on the front of their heads at the base of the horns. Owners put *ghungral* (a necklace of ghungru bells) with wide leather collars, and in winter covers of beautiful cloth with decorative patterns were draped over the oxen. Camels had their own accessories that have been described earlier. Buffaloes were just washed and their horns and skin oiled. Of course no owner took an animal to the fair without first removing any *chitcher* (parasite, animal lice) the animal might have. Buffaloes, cows, and even camels could have chitcher parasites in the sheltered parts and folds in the skin. These lice not only sucked blood but detracted from the looks of the animal. One variety of chitcher was the size of a peanut when loaded with blood, but the second variety was just a larger version of common lice.

Rows and rows of traders' oxen would be tied in one area at the fair, camels would be in another area, and buffaloes in another; but individual sellers paraded their animals wherever they could get the best exposure. There were plenty of *dalal* (brokers) at the fair trying to make a quick buck by arranging sales. Sometimes you could get a better price through a dalal, even after subtracting his commission, than by trying to sell the animal by yourself. All animal sales were recorded by government clerks stationed in a designated place, and the seller paid a fee for the recording. The clerk would write down the animal's kind, age, color, distinguishing features, purchase price, and the names of buyer and seller. The professional traders would buy large groups of animals of the kind they specialized in, and some took the animals on railway trains to places a thousand miles away.

The sale of a buffalo was concluded after the buyer had a chance to milk it to check the yield. A horse was tested by riding, but very few horses were brought to the fair as they were usually bought through personal contact. A camel was tested by riding, but usually the seller rode the camel himself to show its ability and also to prevent some stranger from just riding it away and never returning. An ox was tested by plowing, before the conclusion of the sale. I actually saw some oxen sit down during the test, refusing to pull the plough; and if you tried to hit or prod the ox to get up, it would just cower down further and stick its tongue out. Some owners tried to sell such oxen with bad habits at those fairs where there were no plough-testing facilities and the buyers would be strangers never to be seen again. It was like passing a base coin. If one sold an animal at one's own house, it was a custom to say to the buyer, "May it cause you much benefit." as you handover the rope ceremoniously, but at the market not many people said such words.

The cattle fair at Rampura Phul, a few miles from our village, lasted about seven days and drew people from far and wide. That fair covered about a quarter mile square and even spilled into the surrounding area and access roads. In those days, cattle fairs were one of the best places to watch a variety of people and animals of different characteristics. Many of us would take a day or two off to go to the cattle fair, just for entertainment. There were also singing circles, naqlia jesters, nachaar dancers, freak shows, candy sellers, roadside dentists, sellers of tonics and miracle cures, tatto artists, circus acts, and many kinds of tricksters and gypsters at the cattle fair.

That pattern of life has gone forever, as no oxen or camels are needed in Punjab any more and no one wants the Brahma variety of cow. In fact the Holstein variety of cow is becoming popular there, and some people have to provide air conditioning for their cows because that North European race is so sensitive to heat. I have heard that nowadays people take their used tractors, instead of oxen and camels, to trade at fairs.

Feed for Our Animals

The type of feed we provided to each animal varied according to its kind and its function. A camel would not eat wheat chaff as an ox did; this factor also defined the preferred geographical areas for the camel. The camel could eat the leaves of many trees but preferred the semi-desert trees like *jand*, kreer, *kikker* or *beri*, as their leaves were spicier than the bland leaves of trees from the irrigated areas. We did not have any available wild desert areas where our camel could feed, so we fed him plants from the *gwara*, chickpea, and other bean crops or spicy greens. The dried husks and leaves of similar bean crops were stored as camel feed for milch off season. The buffalo were never given camel feed, because of the belief (perhaps false) that the husks of beans and spicy plants would dry up the milk. For the maintenance of its health, my uncle would give an occasional mixture of brown sugar and alum to our camel. This was not something the camel took willingly, and it had to be force-fed by a *naal* (pipe) full of the liquid. Every animal liked grain, but grain being scarce was not usually fed to camels; rather, it was fed mostly to milch buffaloes and sometimes to the oxen. Goats liked the same kind of feed that the camels did.

Buffaloes and oxen were usually fed *sunnhi*, a mixture of wheat chaff and ground grain; they would not eat the simple chaff alone unless they were really hungry. The buffaloes also were given a cooked mixture of cottonseed and chickpea, with the expectation of a higher yield of milk and butter. Sometimes milch buffaloes were force-fed some *khull*, which was the residue of mustard after the oil had been extracted from it. In addition, buffaloes and oxen were given various green crops, usually chopped by a hand-cranked chopping machine. In summer the green feed crops were gwara for camel and oxen and *jawar* (a kind of millet) or maize plants for buffaloes. In winter their feed was mustard plants or *chara*, a green crop raised just for feed, and less frequently chickpea plants with nearly ripe beans pods. People tried their best to get the highest yields of milk and ghee from buffaloes by various feeding methods, but I am not sure they understood animal nutrition very well. Oxen were not as pampered as the milch

413

buffaloes but during the hard plowing season, some oxen were fed balls of wheat dough containing brown sugar.

Wild Animals and Birds

With the advent of irrigation canals in late 19th century and the availability of inoculation against diseases in the twentieth century, there was a rapid increase of human population in Punjab; consequently pressure on the land increased. The population of the Indian sub-continent has increased more than 400% during my lifetime! In the 1931 census, the combined population of what is now India, Pakistan, and Bangladesh was 330 million and now it is probably 1400 million, in spite of emigration. The lands that used to be considered worthless, variously called *bunjer, maera, daer, jhiri* or *beed* and left as common grazing or hunting grounds, started shrinking as the land was later cleared for agricultural use. With the disappearance of such lands, even their names have disappeared, and the new generation does not recognize these words. Wild animals were under some pressure even before the 1950s, but there was abundant wildlife as there were still adequate wildlife refuge areas in the 1940s. Very few people owned guns, and killing animals was considered a sin by some people. Hunting was considered the pastime of the rich, of big sirdars, or of the people formerly classified as criminal castes. The farmers considered wildlife as undesirable pests that damaged crops; they just did not make any efforts to eliminate them. But I remember going to see a dead wolf, with its front legs mangled by a trap, on display in the village in 1937. The Sheikhs had trapped it; they said it was dangerous to their sheep. Even then wolves were rare and we were left only with their stories. Foxes, porcupines, hedgehogs, rabbits, and such creatures were still plenty, especially the jackal groups, one-upping each other with their nighttime howls. While grazing cattle, we young boys were always searching for the burrows of wild animals for fun; once in a while we caught one of their young.

In some un-irrigated areas with wild lands that had never been cultivated, there were sandy mounds and hillocks due to the accumulation of sand around hardy bushes such as bush *ber* and the cactus *kreer*. The sand accumulates over long periods, because the bush acts as a barrier to the free flow of wind, which then deposits sand there. These bushes, trees, and hillocks were perfect hiding places for wildlife when all the crops nearby had been harvested and the farms were bare of vegetation. In our fields we saw herds of deer, sometimes in groups 20 to 50 strong, with larger, darker, long-horned males and reddish-beige does and fawns. There were also herds of *rojh*, an animal larger than a deer and about the size of a small horse. The male rojh was slate blue in color with two straight short horns, and the female was close to the color of a deer and without horns. Farmers resented these deer and rojh since they damaged crops, but none of them ever did anything to kill them. Eating a rojh was generally not acceptable among our people, as it was a large animal with hoofs like a cow; but a deer was considered to be in the same category as a goat and was therefore considered edible.

Hunting was so uncommon and game was so abundant that an alert hunter was rewarded quickly and without serious effort. Once in the early 1950s, my half-Chinese cousin Sarwan and I, home from college, accompanied the local doctor who was a bachelor and his friend Gurdev MeanyKa when they went hunting. We started late in the afternoon after the doctor had completed his daily duties. We had only one shotgun. We walked

414

less than a mile to the sand dunes toward the Phul territory. Gurdev, a very skillful hunter, asked everyone to wait near a tree. He himself went around a sand dune, and within a few minutes we heard a gunshot. He had felled a deer. The two Chuhra workers who had accompanied us tied together the front and the back feet of the deer and passed a wooden rod between the ties. Putting the rod on their shoulders, they walked in tandem, one man behind the other with the dear slung in between, to bring it home in minutes. I still have a photograph of that event, taken by my cousin's camera in about 1953.

Among the wild bushes and hillocks there were many snakes, mongooses, *goh* (a fat lizard), and small lizards. The black cobra was the most feared creature, and there were stories (mostly false) in which a snake "owned" a certain path and confronted travelers by lifting his head "canopy" to block the way of people traveling that path. Some believed that certain dead people had been reincarnated as snakes to enjoy their old stomping grounds and were waiting to kill any intruders who trespassed into their territory. My father repudiated such stories by saying that snakes never intend to confront anyone and that they were just trying to protect themselves and avoiding humans most of the time.

As a child I was extremely afraid of snakes during my walks to the fields at night. Surely some deaths occurred due to snake bites. One day, on my way to school I saw two dead young men lying on charpai beds outdoors at the hospital. They had been killed by snake bites while they were watering their field and must have stepped into a nest of snakes as they walked in the water. There were *toona* or voodoo type of healers, but remedies for snakebites were unknown to rural people. The fear of snakes was exaggerated by stories and legends. There were false stories of snakes in some flooded areas being so abundant that there were not enough plants for them to climb and that several snakes were reported to have climbed each plant of the crop to avoid drowning. Once such a rumor started in the villages, it was impossible to correct. Most of the time, we saw big snakes only when they came out of the baskets of the snake charmer *jogi* (same word as yogi). The snake charmer would open his basket and the snake would move its head from side to side when the snake charmer played his pipe. Sometimes a snake charmer predicted that there was a snake around the house and offered to capture it. He played his bagpipe and rigged the appearance of a snake coming out of someone's courtyard. He then caught the snake and put it into his basket. The scared householders had to pay the snake charmer in grain and thank him besides for getting rid of the potential danger. Some people believed that the snake charmer just planted his own snake near the house and then played the pipe to bring it out. I never understood the truth about that.

In that climate every kind of wild bird thrived. Farmers cursed the abundance of crows, sparrows, and other birds. Thousands of birds might come and eat up the unprotected grain from the millet kernels in a ripe crop. Wild pigeons, doves, and parrots were not as big a threat, because they never formed large flocks; and vultures, kites, and hawks did not feed on crops and so they were not resented. The thicker the growth of trees in an area, the greater would be the abundance and variety of exotic birds there. The wild peacock was a loved animal because of its beauty. In some areas, however, there were so many peacocks that they damaged the crops. Peacocks thrived wherever there were trees and a little water, even in desert areas. While grazing cattle, we always

415

wanted to catch a male peacock. In a ritualistic way the male would spread its yard-long feathers in a vertical semicircle and start turning around and around in a slow dance near the female. As soon as it heard us getting near, though, it would wrap its feathers together and run away. Occasionally, the male peacock dropped a long feather, and some people collected those feathers to make baskets and other things.

After the independence of India additional irrigation projects were developed, and because of the population pressure most wild lands were reclaimed for farming. As the wild lands disappeared, so with them disappeared much of the wildlife. The final blow in the eradication of wildlife was the consolidation of holdings and development schemes in the 1950s, whereby the government at first seized control of all lands including the wild patches. The former owners lost all their lands but were given land rights on paper. Then new parcels of land were delineated and issued to all such landowners in different locations, in amounts and quality depending on the value of the adjusted land rights of each family. People who were about to lose possession of their land holdings cut down all trees on their land for their own use before losing both the land and the trees. Afterwards, those who were allotted the lands that were formerly wild and uncultivated had no choice but to clear them of all bushes in order to make a living. Thus no old trees or bushes were left as a result of the government's scheme of 'Consolidation of Holdings.' Without trees and bushes, the landscapes changed. Now there is hardly any uncultivated land in rural Punjab except some small plots for special uses. With no old trees and few bushes left, wild animals became extinct pretty rapidly. The destruction of all those wild animals in just a few years was a tragedy of horrendous proportions!

CHAPTER 26

VEGETATION, TREES AND CROPS

The soil and climate of the Punjab plains could support a large variety of plants and trees. It was mostly alluvial soil deposited over the eons, with a preponderance of sand in the southern part and dry foothills in the north of the plains. The winters were mild; summers started very hot and dry in May and became hot and humid when the rains came in July and August. In the days before the irrigation canals, grains such as barley, wheat, chickpeas, mustard, millet, and beans grew if there was some rain. But in some years the plants burned in the drought before the crop could mature, so starvation of people and cattle was possible in years of such famine. With irrigation the yield became reliable and crops became more diverse; then cotton and wheat became the most important cash crops.

The climate in parts of Punjab was good for some kinds of fruit, but the only fruit that grew wild in our Mehraj area were the *ber*, *peelu* and *pinjhu*. Growing fruit for commercial purposes did not become common or successful for a variety of reasons. Even Phul ka *Baagh* (the orchard of Phul) that the State of Nabha planted was just a show-piece for the Raja and did not have to be commercially successful. That orchard on the boundary of Phul and Mehraj territories was spread over a few hundred acres on the edge of sand dunes, but it had a supply of canal water. It had an attractive design with roads crisscrossing and dividing various sections. It had many native trees like *Jamun*, mango, and the grafted ber, but it also had a variety of exotic and delicate fruit trees and flowering bushes. It had many beds and rows of flowers. Everything inside the orchard was beautiful, well arranged, and awe-inspiring. One got the feeling that one was entering an official and restricted area. An outsider could not wander into that orchard, since there were guards at the gate, but some people got permission to visit, and stroll about the roads in the orchard, and view the exotic fruit trees and abundance of flowers.

At the age of about nine, my friends and I found out about the Phul Bagh (orchard). We learned that sometimes outsiders were admitted to the Bagh to pick the *jamun* fruit, so a group of us would walk through the dunes from Mehraj to go to pick jamun in the Bagh. The jamun looks like black cherry with soft purple pulp, but it is quite tart in taste until it is really ripe. We got paid according to the amount we picked, and we ate the best of the fruit in the process even though we were not supposed to eat while picking.

It was tempting to stay in the orchard after picking jamun, because it was cooler there, due to the irrigation and the shade of the trees. Although the workers were watchful and the possibility of severe punishment for stealing fruit was real, some boys did filch some occasionally to satisfy their curiosity, because the exotic fruits of Phul ka Bagh were really tempting. We would come home by evening after earning a few pennies but with stomachs nearly bursting after eating the free jamun fruit.

The Discomfort of Selling without an *Ahrtia*

Our people in the village did not grow any fruits or vegetables to sell. They were too tradition-bound to cultivate anything other than the routine crops of cotton, wheat, chickpeas, barley, corn, millet, and animal feeds. Everything they grew was either for their own consumption or to sell in bulk through an *ahrtia*, the commodities broker. They grew non-perishable crops that could be stored until the end of the season or even longer if they decided to wait. When they needed money, they took the harvest to the broker in the market town, never seeing their customers. Each farmer had his *ahrtia* (broker) in the market; that broker was also his moneylender, his financial advisor, and sometimes his host. It was not uncommon in those days to go and eat at his house while visiting the market, since the broker made an effort to cultivate the relationship; the broker's wife had no choice but to cook and feed the guests, regardless of how she felt about the uncouth Jats. Since my family provided more in grains and commodities to the market than an average farmer did, our broker was courteous and solicitous. I was invited to eat at the ahrtia's house a few times. Once the broker even told my father that his family would provide food for me for the winter season while I studied English with my teacher Kesho Ram in Rampura Phul so that I would not have to travel five miles each way back and forth to school from our village. Such an imposition on the broker's family would have been unreasonable, though, and my father did not agree to the arrangement. He believed that if you do not pay for something directly, you may have to pay even more indirectly. One could send a son to live with a relative or even a friend in a rural area; some boys of our relatives and friends lived free in our house with my parents for years while they went to school in our village. The mentality and conditions among townspeople were different, though, and a business relationship is not the same as a personal one.

The ahrtia was important because landowners were very uncomfortable with the idea of selling a commodity directly to another individual and taking his money. That was also a reason why they did not grow fruits and vegetables. Taking money for your crop or accepting wages for work done for another individual, were considered demeaning among the landowner Jats. They never sold goods (except animals and possibly some ghee), nor did they ever labor for anybody to receive wages. A Jat had to take his crop in bulk to the broker who handled the sale of the commodity, took his commission, and paid the rest to the Jat. Their inaptitude and the fear of selling kept the farmers from growing any perishable cash crops that had to be sold fresh.

Only the shopkeeper caste sold things for money, and some castes like Araeen sold vegetables, but the Jats did not admire that mentality. The Jats might be poor, but they were stuck in the haughty mentality of their ancestors. They pitied the Hindu shopkeeper sitting in his shop and constantly watching with hope that someone would come to buy his stuff. The Jats also thought the shopkeeper was a parasite. They resented the fact that he sat comfortably in the shade and lived off the labor of those who toiled in the hot sun. The Jats also believed that cheating and deception were a part of shop-keeping. In reality the shopkeepers were not any more dishonest than the general population; but the business of selling is such that you take as much as you can from others, and in return you give them as little you have to, without losing business because of competitors. The Jat commonly believed that all *Bania* (the shopkeeper caste) were crooks and that they got rich by cheating and by clever tricks. It is not just the fear of selling but also their ineptitude and lack of subtlety that kept the Jat from success in marketing anything.

A Jat Opens a Shop

My Brahman teacher Kesho Ram used to tell this story about a Jat. The Jat felt that the shopkeepers just sit comfortably indoors in the shade all day and get rich by selling things produced by other people, while the farmer who worked hard all day in the heat to produce crops got little reward. Someone had told the Jat the secret of how the Bania gets rich by cheating. He was told that the Bania has a hidden weight stuck to the bottom of the scale pan on one side of the weighing balance. When he sells something, it is put in the pan with the hidden weight under it so that the actual weight of the commodity given to the customer is less by the amount of the hidden weight. And when he buys something, he switches the pan, so it takes a greater amount of that commodity to show a certain weight. By switching sides of the loaded balance, the shopkeeper gave a smaller amount of the commodity while selling, but while buying he received a greater amount of a commodity than was shown by the apparent measure. He was told that even if he did not use the hidden weight, it was still possible for the shopkeeper to press the lever of the balance with his little finger in a very subtle way to weigh incorrectly and to cheat.

Anyway, the Jat thought he had found the secret to riches by becoming a shopkeeper, although he felt that he would be disgracing himself by following the demeaning occupation of a shopkeeper. But he was going to cheat not just in subtle ways like the Bania, but in a major way, to get rich quick! So he glued a one-pound weight under the bottom of the pan on one side of his balance. Equipped with this balance he opened his shop. An old farmer woman brought some cotton to the new Jat shopkeeper to trade it for sugar. The cotton was a only about half a pound and the Jat shopkeeper put it on the normal side of the balance as he would put measuring weights in the pan with the hidden weight. The woman asked, "How much is the cotton worth?" The Jat shopkeeper said, "Lady, even if you bring this much more, it will still be worth nothing in my shop." With his balance it would take a pound of cotton just to show zero weight. Needless to say, the business of the Jat shopkeeper did not thrive. He knew no subtlety and wanted to cheat in a big way to get rich quickly.

It was believed that a Jat could never be a successful businessman, because he would not know how to deceive and flatter people, as these traits were commonly attributed to a shopkeeper. My teacher used to tell another story about a Jat who tried to beg but did not know how to flatter. Instead of singing praises and using euphemistic words, he would say in a straightforward manner, "Lady, bring some chickpeas quickly so I can get them roasted." Needless to say, he got rebukes instead of alms.

419

Few Old Trees and Their Extinction

Our area, with its scanty rains and its location on the edge of the desert, did not have an abundance of trees. There were few trees; every big tree was valued as a refuge from the scorching sun, and every old tree had a name. *Pipple, boher,* and neem were the trees that were planted for shade near ponds or wells as acts of *punn* (piety) so that humans or animals could take shelter from the sun. Pipple trees were never planted on an individual's property because of the superstition that they bring misfortune if they grow on private property. Pipple leaves are heart-shaped, shiny, and three to four inches in size; the boher (banyan) leaves are coarser, thicker, oval in shape, six to ten inches long, and several inches across. Some old boher could send adventitious roots, called beards, from their branches, and these dropped-from-above "beards" gradually reached the ground and took root. In time these beards became secondary stems supporting the tree. Boher trees used to spread laterally, their shade was dense, and they grew to be the biggest trees around. The fruits of boher and pipple trees resembled a small fig, but never seemed to become mature or sweet. Although there were legends about some boher trees lasting from the ancient times, it is hard to confirm such stories, because in my lifetime in the southern Punjab, all the old trees died because of the ecological changes. Boher trees with multiple stems or beards in other parts did live long lives, and Buddha is supposed to have meditated and gained enlightenment under one of those boher trees.

A *neem* tree was frequently planted with pipple and boher to make a *triveni* (three trees), and triveni were the day-time gathering places for men on summer days. Girls had the exclusive use of such trees during the festival of *teeyan;* men were not allowed under the trees during the teeyan season. Before and after the teeyan, the shade of these trees was used by men to sleep on portable *charpai* beds through the summer heat, to play cards during the day, to play music, to socialize, and so forth, and the groves were used by little boys for climbing games. Sometimes cattle sheltered there from the sun. There might be an illegal gambling game or a singing arena under these trees. Sometimes a transient tribe would set up camp there for a few days.

The neem tree had uses other than just the shade. We tried to eat its fruit, called *neemoli,* when it was so golden ripe that it was more sweet than bitter; but the neemoli was deadly bitter when still green. People thought the neemoli was like a tonic and prevented diseases; I doubt if there was any truth in that. Neem leaves were very bitter and had many medicinal and antiseptic uses. My father used to boil the neem leaf in water to clean and heal the wounds of people who came to him with such problems. And of course a banner of neem branches was tied at the top front of the door when a baby boy was born in a house. Nowadays, some pharmaceutical companies are trying to patent drugs or pesticides that can be made from neem, so more uses of the neem tree are still to come.

The fruit called *ber,* from the tree called *beri,* had numerous varieties in size, shape, color, taste, pulp, pit size, and ripening time, but there were three principal classifications of the fruit. Paindu, the variety that was cultivated and possibly grafted, had a prolate shape and had green to golden or reddish coloring, with a large fraction as pulp and a small, elongated pit. The second variety was the wild tree *ber,* usually round in shape, smaller than a cherry, and with the greatest diversity in taste, color, and pulp size. You never knew what the next wild ber was going to taste like; it could be anything from divinely sweet to tart or a sour "throat choker." Certain trees had the reputation of producing the best fruit, and from the taste we could tell which beri tree the fruit came from. Some ber started ripening in November, others ripened as late as March, and people would still shake some trees for the leftovers in April. My mother's sisters, who lived in the desert territory in TaruAna where ber was more abundant and the population was sparse, collected, dried, and stored them in clay pitchers; they occasionally gave us dried ber as a gift. Nowadays, the idea of drying ber is unheard of. The third category was the wild ber from *mallah*. The mallah were thorny bushes, generally three to six feet high, and they grew uncontrollably along property boundaries. They flowered in late summer and their ber ripened in October or November. Mallah fruit was similar to but smaller than the "tree ber," with even a smaller proportion of pulp to pit.

Wild ber trees thrived in the near-desert area of Punjab and were abundant in areas south of the Sutlej river, well into the reaches of the Rajputana desert. The trees did not really require canal irrigation but tolerated some of it. The unwanted mallah bush ber grew spontaneously in the wild lands, on the boundaries of the fields, and along the footpaths going to other villages. When walking to the next village you could just stop at a mallah bush on the side of the path to collect some ber, or you could go to a larger beri tree in the middle of a field to collect a small bundle for your pleasure or to take to the children. The cattle grazers usually brought ber home for children at the end of the day. An outing in any direction to collect ber from the fields was a common pastime in my younger days, when the ber were abundant and there was little pressure of population. All kinds of wild ber have become practically extinct in our region since the 1950s land consolidation schemes. People cleared most bush ber from their lands when the consolidation schemes were implemented by the government. Of course, the wild ber might have died anyway because of the rise in the underground water table that occurred in subsequent times. There are no wild ber in Punjab anymore, but the cultivated paindu ber variety can be purchased from the markets now.

Another common tree in our area was the *kikker*, a kind of acacia with long thorns (up to three inches), spicy bark, miniature leaves, yellow flowers, and long, flat *tukka* (bean pods). The tukka pod could be used for pickling while it was tender green; but after it ripened its dry hard seeds were of no use. Pickles of acacia pod were uniquely delicious, as the added spices turned its harshness into a delicacy. In some respects it was comparable to the *amla* pickle, whose characteristic aftertaste is the stuff of quotations. Unlike the European acacia, the Punjab kikker was considered anti-allergenic, and people chewed its bark for that reason. People used the green twigs from kikker branches for brushing teeth. All one had to do was to chew an end of the twig to create bristles for brushing the teeth. Goats and camels loved the kikker leaves, and especially the tukka pods, which were considered medicinal for the animals as well as for humans. Sometimes the kikker bark was used as a dying agent. Its wood was not as good for construction or furniture as wood from the beri or the *tahli* tree used to be.

Tahli was a thorn-less and highly water-dependent tree with small round leaves of about one inch in diameter. It came to our area with the arrival of canals. In the hierarchy of qualities of timber grown in our area, tahli was the most valued for construction or furniture, although there was not much lumber to choose from. Beri was next, but smaller in size, and the kikker was the least desirable.

Jand was the king of the desert and a hardier cousin of the kikker tree, with deeper roots, small thorns, and miniature leaves that were the delight of camels. In those years when in the miserable dry heat the jand tree was still luxuriant with new green shoots, old-timers would say, "That damn jand tree looks so happy and lush green; it is going to be a year of drought and famine!" because jand was one of the trees that thrived even in the draught. The ripe bean pods (*khokhe*) of the jand were sweet tasting, and they were even sweeter when completely dry. Children would try to pick the khokhe, either by climbing the jand tree or sometimes just by throwing sticks to hit the branches and fell the dry bean pods.

Kreer was a kind of cactus tree that thrived in our area before the days of canal irrigation. A kreer could grow to be a hemispherical dome about fifteen feet in diameter but low to the ground. The bark of the kreer was bitter and was ground for some medicines. Its stem was small and its wood was of little importance, except to make the cross-shaped head of a *madhani*, the milk-churning device. Because of its bitterness, a madhani of kreer was assumed to be good for health. Its thorns were miniature and insignificant, and those leaves lasted for only a few days in spring. The kreer flowered with the most dazzling, intense pink and red colors. Then its green fruit called *dela*, the size of a blueberry, was set. The dela was used for pickling. But if the dela is not picked when green it ripens into a bright red fruit called *pinjhu*, with some sweet pulp but mostly seeds. It was common for kids to go gathering ber or pinjhu in the bushes after school, as there was a wild area of nearly quarter of a square mile near our local school. But the two fruits ripened at different times of the year; the ber began the winter and the pinjhu started the summer.

Bunn or *vunn* was another hardy but thorn-less tree with branches and leaves like the willow. Its fruit, called *peelu*, was distinct from the pinjhu of the kreer tree and ripened from green to golden to red or bluish purple. The vunn was not as hardy as the kreer, and although it was somewhat draught resistant, it tolerated water quite well. There were groves of vunn trees near some water ponds in the wilderness. The vunn tended to spread its very dense willow-like branches low to the ground and thus the vunn groves provided heavy cover and hiding places for small armies, bands of robbers, or wildlife. In some cases you could set up camp in a vunn grove and not be visible to any spies from a distance. The clusters of vunn trees were often found in land reserves called *jhirdi* or *beed*, like an oasis of the near desert, and ordinary travelers feared going into such areas, even during the daytime. In the 1940s there were still many wild acres of vunn and kreer in a place called Maari near our village. This was reputed to be the original camping place for the Sidhu Brards when they first arrived from Bhatinda and Bidowal in the early seventeenth century for the purpose of settling in this new area. Although Maari was on the direct path from Mehraj to Rampura, yet ninety-nine percent of the people followed a path that skirted around this jhirdi (jungle) for safety sake. Sometimes I used to stop at the Maari *vunn* trees, on my way from my teacher in Rampura Phul, to collect and eat the pinjhu and peelu fruits. Another such vunn cluster was around GuruSar, three miles south of Mehraj, where the Sikh Guru, Hargobind, had fought a battle with the Moughal General Lallah Beg about the time our village Mehraj was founded. There were numerous such reserves in my early life, but a *vunn, kreer* or *jand* tree is not easy to find anywhere in southern Punjab now. The virulent growth of *booey*, and *pohli* shrubs, and less so of *khipp* and *hermal* were a real nuisance for farmers to weed out from their fields.

Most varieties of the semi-desert trees have disappeared from our area over the last sixty years. After the Indian government's consolidation schemes and redistribution of land, most of those trees, except tahli, kikker and neem, have become practically extinct in the Mehraj area. Old trees were cut down when the owners realized that their lands were going to be assigned to other parties. Another reason for the extinction of some of these trees may be the rising underground water table which in the Mehraj has crept up from one hundred feet deep to about twelve or fifteen feet during my lifetime—a horrendous ecological change! Rains appear to have increased, vast sand dunes have gradually disappeared, and the water table has risen due to irrigation by canal water for more than a century. Of the above list of trees, the tahli survives because of its affinity to water and because of the value of its lumber. The kikker survives because of its overall hardiness and the neem because of its perceived medicinal value; and of course all three kinds of trees are able to survive with a high water table.

Since 1950, the eucalyptus has been spreading everywhere in Punjab. In the 1940s it was an object of curiosity with its young, smooth, white trunk and was found only along the streets of English residential colonies and cantonments in the fashionable areas of cities, after being imported by the British officials. Now it grows virulently everywhere. With the shortage of every kind of wood and the relatively rapid growth of eucalyptus, it has a new economic value, and its planting is encouraged by the government.

CHAPTER 27

BAAT AND STORIES

The telling of stories at night, called *baat*, was an important feature of village life of the 1930s and 1940s, as there were few other sources of entertainment in the dark, in the times before electricity. Now bedtime stories may be told only to children, but when I grew up there even the adults were listeners and beneficiaries. Usually older people recited baat to younger ones, and women told or listened to baat more often than men did. Regardless of the number of listeners, one person was usually selected to respond to the recitation of the story by *hangara*, which was the listener's frequent acknowledgement or response to each sentence uttered or each event described in a story. This indicated that the listener was keeping up with the progress of the story. The hangara responder sometimes asked a question to clarify any confusion about the story or any unfamiliar words. Some people used to fall asleep right after the baat started, and in the dark it was difficult to tell without the hangara if anyone was listening.

Lohri festival evening was an occasion when experienced storytellers told baat while sitting around the outdoor community fire. My sister Karo had accumulated a repertoire of many baat at a relatively young age, and she was good at relating them. In summer when people slept on rooftops, many children dragged their *charpai* beds to a neighbor's adjoining roof to sleep near a good storyteller. The stories were usually about foolish kings, wicked queens, wise *wazir*, brave princes, beautiful princesses, clever witches, stupid or lucky people, *bhoot* and *chrail* ghosts, angels and fairies, birds and animals that talked, buried treasures, snakes, magic, miracles, good people suffering but winning later and wicked people losing ultimately. In fairy tales, everything did not have to be logical or true; the storyteller would just say that in the ancient ages, birds and animals could talk and other strange things happened. It is impossible to translate the funny words, repetitions, and expressions from one language and culture to another; so the effect may not be as pleasing as in the original Punjabi, but a sample of some baat is given below.

Sheikh Chili and His Daydreams

Once there was a man named Sheikh Chili who was not good at doing anything worthwhile and was clueless about how to find a job. But he had an active imagination, an unquestioning mind, and a habit of daydreaming and talking to himself. In difficult

424

times, no one would hire him for any job. One day an out of town wealthy merchant hired him to carry a pitcher of milk to the carriage-stand and promised that he would get one *rupiah* coin for that labor. Sheikh Chili was overjoyed to get the job. He put the heavy clay pitcher full of milk on his head with the help of the owner and started walking toward the carriage-stand, which was far away. He had a long walk ahead and started daydreaming about what he was going to do with the one rupiah wage he was going to get. He said to himself, "Wow, a whole rupiah! That is a lot of money! What should I do with this much money? Should I buy candy? No, I am not going to spend that money on candy, though I would like to. Should I buy shoes? No, I can go barefoot. I think I should increase my wealth by investing this money. I think I am going to buy a dozen eggs with this money. In about three weeks, little baby chicks will hatch out of those eggs, and in a few months, when they grow bigger, I will have a dozen chickens. Those chickens will then start laying more eggs, which will turn into more chicks and chickens. With all those chickens laying more eggs, I will have even more chickens... even more eggs... even more chickens...Pretty soon I will have so many chickens I won't know what to do with them. So I will sell all those chickens for a lot of money. And with that money I will buy flocks of goats and sheep. Those goats and sheep will have little kids and lambs, which will grow up to be more goats and sheep, which will give more kids and lambs, and pretty soon I will have so many goats and sheep that I will have to sell them all for even more money. With all that money I will buy cows and horses and then those will have calves and foals, which will grow to be more and more cows and horses, and pretty soon I won't know what to do with so many cows and horses. So I will sell most of them, and with all that wealth I will buy a lot of land and build a big house. Everyone will want to marry his daughter to me, but I will pick only the prettiest one, or maybe I will marry two or three wives. The wives will have children who will grow up to take cares of all business, as I will be too rich to bother about daily work. I will just sit and spoil myself and will act very important and temperamental to everyone, even to my prettiest wife. Sometimes she will beg me to come and eat dinner; but if I am not in the mood I will show my temper and just shake my head and shout, 'No, I don't want to eat yet!'"

As Sheikh Chilli said the word "No," he also shook his head in a gesture of refusal. As he shook his head, the pitcher of milk fell off his head and broke, spilling the milk all over the footpath. The owner of the milk was very angry at losing many rupiahs' worth of milk. He wanted to have Sheikh Chilli beaten and sent to a debtor's prison for the loss that Sheikh Chili had caused him. But Sheikh Chilli said, "You small-minded trader! You are crying over the spilled milk. And here I have spilled all my eggs and chickens, all my sheep and goats, all my horses and cows, all my lands and houses, all my wives and children. I am the one who has lost everything. I am the one who should be angry and shouting, and not you shouting at me!"

Ghudda, the Clueless One

Once there was a man who was known by the people of his village to be particularly tactless, stupid, and unaware. For that reason they called him by the nickname Ghudda, which means "clueless," although his original name was Sulakhan (smart, artful). He resented the nickname Ghudda and had gotten into many fights with people who called him by that nickname. As he got sick and tired of being called Ghudda, he decided to go to another village where nobody would know that name, he thought, much less call him that. So he went to this new village and stood at the corner of a crossing. Village women carrying the pitchers of water from the well to their houses kept passing through that crossing.

Just as he was standing at the corner purposelessly, a sharp and witty woman with a pitcher on her head walked by. Ghudda was so impressed with her walk that he stared at her and fixed his gaze on her continuously, without any subtlety. The woman with the water pitcher was not the shy type. When she became conscious of his persistent stare, the woman said, "What are you staring at, oh Ghudda?" And Ghudda said, "Ethe bhee koi aakay bhain grhah gya!" which means roughly, "Which sister-fucker came here already and told what my nickname is?" The moral of the story is that you can't hide your real self; you take yourself with you wherever you go. You disclose your true self by your behavior, and people will treat you accordingly.

Seven Bhoots and Seven Manni

Once upon a time there was a shiftless, poor, boy named Mannu. He was almost a grown man but he still had no job. His father had died and there was nobody in his house to earn a living. Mannu's mother was always nagging him to go and earn some money, but Mannu never had any luck anywhere in his own village. One day his mother decided to force him to go somewhere far away to seek his fortune. She made him seven *manni*, which are loaves of unleavened bread, much bigger than a *roti*, containing sugar and other ingredients in addition to flour. She packed the seven manni for him, so that he could start in search of a job. His mother said, "These manni are so big that one will be enough for you for each day, and they should sustain you until you find a job. So Mannu departed to seek his fortune. He walked all day and got tired and hungry. As the night fell, he decided to rest and sleep under a pipple tree by the pond near a village. He did not know that the pipple tree was haunted. It was already dark and he opened his bundle of manni and started counting: "Should I eat one? Should I eat two? May be I will eat three; may be I will eat four…. I am so hungry, I think I can eat all seven!"

Now, it so happened that on this pipple tree there lived seven *bhoot* (ghosts, spooks). Those bhoot heard Mannu counting and thought that he was planning to eat all seven of the party of bhoots, although Mannu was actually talking about eating all seven of his manni. The head bhoot, still hiding in the tree branches in the darkness, said to Mannu, "Will you please spare any at all?" And Mannu said, "No, I am so hungry that I will eat all seven." The bhoot said, "What if we give you something magical; will you spare some then?" Mannu said, "Well, then I might spare some or not eat any at all; and I will even go hungry if your offer is good enough." So the bhoot dropped a griddle, a pan, and a *karahi* (wok) and said, "When you say the magic words *"khana banao,"* these utensils will prepare a grand feast of delicacies instantly and will serve as many people as you like." So Mannu took the magic utensils given by the bhoot and came home with his new acquisition. He said the magic words "khana banao," and a great feast was created. He and his mother had a wonderful meal. Next time they even entertained their relatives and friends lavishly. So the times had turned better for them and they were quite happy.

But Mannu still did not have a job, and they still lived in a dilapidated shack. All he and his mother could do was to eat and get fat. His mother wanted other things for him, too. So she again packed seven manni and dispatched him in search of a fortune. Mannu again walked all day, got tired and hungry, and reached the same haunted pipple tree by evening. After a little rest, he started counting his manni: "Should I eat one? Should I eat two? May be I will eat three; may be I will eat four or five or six.....I am so hungry, I could eat all seven." The leader of the seven bhoot still hiding in the tree branches said, "Will you spare any at all?" Mannu said, "No, I think I am hungry enough to eat all seven." The bhoot said, "What if we give you something magical?" Mannu said, "Then I might spare some and might not eat any at all." The bhoot said, "Here is a magic box. When you say the words *"dhan-e-dhan"* it will become full of gold, silver, and money." Mannu collected the magic box and reached home the next day. After returning to his house he said the magic words "dhan-e-dhan" and created a lot of gold, silver, and money with the magic box and became a very rich man. With his new wealth he built a palatial house, and with the magic utensils he prepared a great feast for all his relatives and friends in his grand house. He became rich and famous!

Unfortunately, the officials of the raja (ruler, king) got wind of his good fortune and took away all his possessions, including the magic utensils and the magic money box. They said he must have stolen the money from somewhere and also had not paid any taxes. The raja's soldiers slapped him a few times, occupied his house, and threw him out. Mannu lost all his wealth and became poor again. His mother had to send him away again with the seven manni, to seek his fortune. By nightfall, Mannu reached the same haunted pipple tree again and started counting his manni, "Should I eat one? I think I will eat two; no, I will eat three, four, five, six....I am so hungry, I will eat all seven." The head bhoot, still hiding in the tree branches in the dark and thinking that Mannu was talking about eating the seven bhoot, said "Will you kindly spare any?" Mannu said, "No, I think I am hungry enough to eat all seven". The head bhoot said, "What if we give you something magical?" Mannu said," Then I can spare all and can even stay hungry." The head bhoot asked, "What happened to the other magical things we gave you before?" Mannu told the bhoot how the raja's soldiers had taken everything away and how he was helpless against the soldiers who beat him up. The leader of the bhoots said, "Take this *nadi* (rope) and *danda* (stick) and say the words *'lage danda, jood nadi.'* The nadi will bind your enemy, and the danda will strike them until you order it to stop with the magic words *'buss, hutto,'* which mean: 'enough, stop.' So your opponents will have no choice but to submit to your wishes." Mannu took the danda and nadi and reached home.

The next day Mannu asked the raja's officials to vacate his house and to return his possessions to him. The king's men just ridiculed him and threatened a severe beating. Then Mannu uttered the words "lage danda, jood nadi." All the raja's men were tied with the nadi and the danda started beating them. The soldiers begged for mercy and wanted to be released, as the beating by the danda was hurting and was not stopping. When the raja heard this, he sent one general and half his army to capture Mannu. When the general came and tried to attack Mannu, all that Mannu had to do was to say, "lage danda, jood nadi," and all the troops there were tied and were beaten, too. When the raja heard this, he was even more furious and sent his best general and all the rest of his army to attack Mannu. But all that Mannu had to say was, "lage danda, jood nadi," and the whole army was tied with ropes and was being beaten. After this the raja had no more options, and he consulted his *wazir* to find a way out. The wazir went to Mannu and said, "Mannu, you seem to have great power; let us do something good with it. The raja has a beautiful daughter; if you appear before the raja and beg for the hand of his daughter, you can have the princess and keep all your wealth." After the wazir's negotiation, Mannu said the words, "buss, hutto" and released the king's army. So the clever wazir arranged the marriage of Mannu and the king's daughter. There was no shortage of silver and gold, and the magic utensils prepared the grandest feast for the wedding. Mannu and the princess ruled the kingdom and lived happily forever after.

Sonen and Rupen, the Orphan Princesses

Once there was a raja (ruler) who had two daughters, named Sonen (golden) and Rupen (silver). They were *ladli* (pampered, spoiled) princesses and lived in luxury with their parents, who were the raja and the rani (queen) of the land. But the rani died when they were still young, and their father the raja got a new rani as wife. This new rani had a mean temperament and was a cruel stepmother (all stepmothers are mean in fairy tales) to them. The stepmother spoke to them very harshly, made them work like servants, and did not give them enough to eat. In fact, the stepmother would say, "I wish you girls had died with your mother." She would not let their father see them or talk to them. Sonen and Rupen sang the wailing song in memory of their mother: "Ik Sonen thie, ik Rupen thie; oh dono bhenan ladlian….", which means, "One was Sonan, one was Rupen; they both were pampered sisters….they lived in the palace with their mother and father..then one day their mother died..," and so on. The vicious stepmother heard their song and thought the girls were still happy in spite of her efforts to torture them; she wanted them to starve and be miserable. She stopped giving them enough to eat now; so the girls grew thinner and thinner, until they were in danger of perishing.

Then one night when Sonan and Rupan were going to bed hungry, singing their wailing song, the spirit of their dead mother came to them and said, "I know your stepmother is trying to starve you. So I will become a *beri* tree just outside the palace. When you come to me, I will lower my branches; you can pick and eat my *ber* fruit, and you will survive until you grow older and can take care of yourselves." Sonen and Rupen started going to the beri tree every day, and the tree would lower its branches for them. They picked and ate the ber and became quite healthy again. The stepmother became suspicious and sent her ugly, cross-eyed daughter to see what they were eating. Thus the stepmother found out about the beri tree, and she was livid. The rani lay down in bed with a cover of *khan patti* (mourning blanket?) during the day. The raja came home and asked, "Rani, rani, why are you in bed? Why are you morose? Why are you sad?" The rani said, "Don't ask my condition; I am not talking!" The raja again asked, "Rani, rani, why are you sad?" The rani again said, "Don't ask my story!" The raja persisted, "Rani, it makes me feel bad to see you unhappy; please be cheerful; I will do anything you want; I will bring precious jewels and gold for you; I will order the best delicacies for you; just tell me what will make you happy." When the raja persisted, the rani said, "I will live only if you have that beri tree uprooted and burned." The Raja said, "That is a very simple matter; it will be done this very day."

So the beri tree which had supplied Sonen and Rupen with food, was uprooted, and they were starving again. One night again they sang their wailing song, "Ek Sonen thie, ek Rupen thie..." The spirit of the dead mother again appeared to Sonen and Rupen and they told her, "The wicked rani has destroyed the beri tree." Then the mother said, "I will appear as a *bhoori* (blonde) buffalo in the pond; I will stay in the water and no one else will get my milk. But when you come there, I will come out of the pond and you can drink my milk." So Sonen and Rupen would sneak to the buffalo pond when the stepmother was not looking, and they would drink the milk of the bhoori buffalo. Pretty soon they became healthy again. The stepmother got suspicious and again sent her cross-eyed daughter to find out their secret. When she learned about the bhoori buffalo, the rani was furious again. She lay down in bed during the day, sulking, with a khun patti cover. When the raja came home, he asked, "Rani, rani, why are you in bed?" And the rani said, "Don't ask my story; you don't care enough about me anyway." The Raja insisted, "Rani, I will cross the mountains for you; I will dam the rivers for you; tell me what will make you happy." The rani said," I will live only if you capture the bhoori buffalo in yonder pond and have it killed. So the Raja had the bhoori buffalo killed, and the sisters Sonen and Rupen began to starve again. Once again Sonen and Rupen sang their wailing song, "Ek Sonen thie, ek Rupen thie..." The mother's spirit again appeared to Sonen and Rupen and she found out their plight. Then the mother's spirit said, "Every evening I will appear as a platter of laddu and jalebi (sweets made from flour, sugar and ghee) in the cupboard and you can feed yourself from the platter of laddu-jalebi. That is exactly what happened, and the girls ate laddu-jalebi regularly and became fat and healthy again. The rani again sent her cross-eyed daughter to find out their secret. When she found the truth, the rani was very frustrated as her schemes were failing, and she was not succeeding in starving the sisters Sonen and Rupen. This time she had to take a drastic step. So again she lay down sulking in bed with a khan patti cover. The raja came home and asked, "Rani, rani, why are you in bed?" The rani said, "Don't ask my story; you don't care enough for me anyway." The raja said, "Rani, nothing is too precious for you. I will bring riches at your feet; I will fulfill your every desire; just tell me what to do and it will be done." The rani said, "I will live only if the two sisters Sonen and Rupen are killed and their bones are scattered outside this kingdom." The raja did not really want to kill the girls, so he told some of his soldiers to take the girls outside his kingdom and just abandon them there but not to kill them. The raja's soldiers took Sonen and Rupen beyond the boundary of the raja's territory and told them never to return, as they would be killed if they returned, and the soldiers too would be killed with them for not carrying out the queen's wishes.

So Sonen and Rupen were released outside the kingdom and they were completely on their own in the wilderness, without any help. By now they were twelve and ten years old. They had never done much useful work before, because they were princesses and did not know how to obtain food. They sang their wailing song, "Ek Sonen thie, ek Rupen Thie..," but the spirit of the mother did not appear, because it was haunting only the old palace of the raja. An old shepherd grazing his sheep and goats in the wilderness heard their song. He saw that these girls looked like they were from some aristocratic family. When they told the shepherd their story, he said he would give them a part of his flock of sheep and goats and they could live by grazing the animals. He said that they could keep all of the increase in the flock, and later on they could return the original sheep back to him. The two sisters Sonan and Rupan grazed their sheep and goats, and their animals had many lambs and kids, which became sheep and goats, and their flock was increasing. They lived in their own straw hut and sang their sad song daily.

One day as they were grazing the sheep, a prince from this new kingdom came riding his horse while hunting. His horse was startled by a sudden noise from the bushes and bucked suddenly, raising his front legs off the ground. The horse threw the prince down violently and ran away. The prince was injured badly and became unconscious. The two sisters found him and nursed him to health in their hut for several days. Slowly the prince recovered. Men of the prince's father searched for him for many days. Finally they found him in the straw hut of Sonen and Rupen and took him back to the king, who was happy to find his son. But when the prince was back in the palace, he was very sad and wanted to go back to see Sonen, who had saved his life. He told his father that he was in love with the shepherd girl and could not live without her. The king was angry with his son's behavior at first, because he did not want his son to associate with lowly shepherd girls. But the prince insisted he wanted to marry Sonen because he loved her. The king said, "We are the rulers of this land; what do we have in common with lowly, poor shepherds. It is not possible for you to degrade yourself by marrying anyone of low birth and status." But the prince kept insisting on marrying Sonen, and he wanted to find her again. He stopped eating, and his health deteriorated. The king and queen were very worried about his health and happiness. At last they told their soldiers, "Go and find out which shepherd is the father of those wretched girls, so we can talk with him about the future of the girls." The servants made inquires but found out nothing about the girls—no father, no mother. Then the king said, "Go and bring the girl to my court tomorrow."

The next day Sonen was dragged by the soldiers to the court. She scattered mustard seeds along the way as she went. The king noticed that Sonan was a pretty girl and questioned her. She told the king her entire life story, about her father who was a raja, and their mother who had died, and how they had been exiled from their father's kingdom. The king remarked that Sonen looked regal in spite of her raggedy clothes. Then he said, "We are very sorry for your suffering; but your suffering will come to an end if you marry my son." Sonen had already fallen in love with the prince when she took care of him, so she was married to the prince. Many days passed, and Rupen was still living alone in the straw shack, worried and miserable in her absence sisters. It was already spring and new plants were growing. Although Sonen had sent soldiers to fetch Rupen, she was not in the hut, as she had already started in search of her sister. She followed the line of mustard plants that had grown from the seeds Sonen had scattered. Thus she reached the palace of the king. Rupen was invited to live as a guest in the palace and they all lived happily forever after.

The United Family and the Fighting Family

Once upon a time there was a family that had become very poor because of bad crops and other calamities. They had two children and had no way of making a good living to feed themselves. But they had the virtue of being able to unite, cooperate, and work together rather than quarreling with one another, and the children obeyed the parents. Everyone in the house did what the father told them to do. After much struggle and thought, the parents decided to leave their village and go somewhere else to find better opportunities. They locked the door of their house and took their meager belongings with them. The family traveled some distance on the first day, but by late afternoon they were all tired and decided to camp under a big tree for the night. When they were gathered under the tree, the father said to the boy, "Son, go and gather some firewood." The boy said, "Yes, father, I am going right away." And he quickly brought back some dry wood. Then father told the girl, "My daughter, please get some water from the stream." The girl said "Yes, father, I will get it in no time." Then he said to the wife, "Clean the utensils and get ready to make a fire so that we may cook something." And the wife said, "I have already cleaned the utensils and will make a fire right now." Everyone in this family worked cooperatively.

It happened that there lived a bird up in the branches of that tree, and this bird heard and saw everything. In ancient times the birds used to have the ability to speak the human language. So the bird asked the family, "Hey folks, you are gathering wood and water and are making fire, but you don't seem to have any food. What do you expect to cook and eat?" The father said, "If we don't find any other food, we may have to catch and cook you for dinner." The bird thought to himself, "This family knows how to work together. They might really catch me. I better do something so that they will spare my life." So the bird said, "Will you spare my life if I tell you about a treasure?" They said they would, and the bird told them to dig near the roots of that tree for a treasure. They all started digging, and they had to dig hard and deep. After much digging, they found a treasure-chest of riches and were overjoyed to find all that wealth. They were so happy, they forgot all about being hungry. In the morning they returned to their old home. With all that treasure in their possession, pretty soon they started living like rich people.

There was another house opposite to this united family, but the family members in that opposite house were always quarreling with each other and could never work together. When they saw their former poor neighbors living comfortably, they burned with jealousy. They asked where the united family had gotten its riches. When they heard the details of the story of the united family, the wife said to her husband, "This seems so easy, but you are so worthless; why don't you go to the same place so we can have a treasure of our own! We could get even richer than these stupid neighbors of ours." So the fighting family decided to leave even as they quarrelled. It was hard to get the children to go along, but after many abuses and threats, the children of the family were dragged along. The fighting family reached the same tree that the neighbors had described. It was hard to get the children to come together and listen, but the father tried his best. The father said to the son, "Hey boy, go gather some firewood." The boy said to his father, "Why should I? I am too tired; go get it yourself." When the father threatened and abused him, the boy said, "Do you want to burn in the fire, old man?" Then the father told the daughter to go and fetch water from the stream. And the girl said, "I am doing my nails; go and drown yourself in the water." When he asked his wife to make fire, the wife replied, "Oh, don't bother me. I have a headache, and if you were any good you would be digging for the treasure by now."

All this time the same bird had been sitting in the tree listening to their quarreling, and it asked them, "Hey folks, what are you planning to cook for dinner?" They all said, "We are going to catch and cook you." The bird just laughed in their faces and said, "You losers could not catch a slug; there is no way you could work together to catch me; pretty soon you are going to start fighting with one another, and you may kill each other instead of killing me." Then the father said, "Who needs to listen to a stupid bird like that; let us just start digging." But the children and the wife said they were too tired to do anything then. The father dug some shovels of dirt around the tree as he had heard how the good family got its wealth by digging. But finding no treasure, he started cursing the other members of the family and cursing the bird. The bird ridiculed them, laughed some more, and said, "Those who deserved the treasure have taken it." The fighting family returned home furious, and they blamed one another and everything else for their failure. They resumed their fighting life, lived in envy of the united family, and were as miserable as ever.

Owls Seeking Ghost Towns

There was once a very cruel and unjust king; but he had a wise *wazir* (minister, advisor) who was concerned about the fate of the kingdom. One day while the king went hunting in the wilderness with his hunting party, they had to camp out for the night. The king was annoyed by the loud and continuous shrieking of owls. Since he usually consulted his wazir about whatever he himself did not understand, he asked the wazir why the owls were shrieking so furiously. The wazir said, "Your majesty, those are the two parties of owls at an owl wedding, discussing the dowry that is appropriate to be given by the bride's father. Owls love wastelands, and deserted ghost towns are very coveted as dowry items among the owls. The father of the owl bridegroom is saying to the owl bride's father, 'I want at least five ghost towns as dowry. Anything less is an insult to our status.' The bride's father is saying humbly, 'Please, have a heart; I have only three; and three ghost towns are a reasonable dowry in today's environment.' The bridegroom's father says, 'Three ghost towns is an offer below our dignity to consider.' Then the bride's father says, 'Please be reasonable; accept three ghost towns for now, and I assure you that if this cruel king and his reign continue, pretty soon there will be many more ghost towns; and then I will give you several more ghost towns, hopefully in the near future.'" The Wazir was trying to point out to the king in a clever way how his harsh rule was creating unbearable conditions in the kingdom.

On its surface, this conversation among the owls as reported by the wazir just illustrates the local thoughts on the nature of the cursed owl, seeking desolation. But it also can be understood as an allegory for someone to mend his ways. For example, once there was a farewell luncheon for me when I was leaving the work group of my boss Hans Kruger to join another division. I myself had good relations with Kruger, but some other physicists had left Kruger's group after quarrels and disagreements with him. Some believed that scientists were leaving Kruger's group because of his bad attitude and his poor treatment of the professionals under him. I jokingly told this parable of owls and ghost towns as a parallel to the conditions in Kruger's group, suggesting why many physicists had left before. The German-born Hans Kruger got up and said, "We had a parable in Germany that said, "All deserters will be shot."

One Hundred Onions or One Hundred Shoe Blows?

Once there was a foolish man who was passing by an onion field. He thought that no one was watching the field. He decided to steal some onions from the field, but that was against the law. As the owner was watching this theft from behind the fence, the thief was caught with the stolen load of onions and was brought before the alderman of the village. The alderman said to the thief, "You should realize that if people get away with stealing, it could be very bad for our community. We have to set an example by punishing you. But since this is your first offence, I will let you choose your own punishment. You can either take one hundred beatings with a shoe, or you can eat one hundred onions." The foolish thief said, "Oh, this is an easy choice; I don't want any beatings. I think I will eat a hundred onions." So a hundred onions were laid out before the thief to eat. He ate one, two, three, four, four and a half, five... His eyes were watering and his nose was running. He could not stand the harsh pungent onions any more. He said to the alderman: "I have changed my mind; those onions are horrible; I think the hundred blows with a shoe will be easier to bear; I think I will take the shoe beatings instead."

So the chowkidar (attendant) was ordered to start beating the thief with a big heavy shoe. One, two, three ...seven, eight, nine, ten, eleven blows, and the thief was shrieking, "O please stop; this hurts so badly. I can't take even a single blow more; I have changed my mind; I think I will eat the rest of the hundred onions." So he started eating more onions ...six, seven...eleven, twelve ...fourteen, fifteen onions ... His nose was running, his eyes were watering, and he could stand no more onions. He said, "I can't eat even one more onion. They are so harsh; I have changed my mind; I think the shoe beatings are less painful than eating onions."

So the chowkidar again started striking the thief with the heavy shoe ...twelve, thirteen... . ninteen, twenty, twenty-one... and the thief was shrieking with pain. Again he said, " Stop! Stop! This hurts so badly; I think I will go back to eating onions." He ate sixteen, seventeen, eighteen, ninteen, twenty, twenty-one onions..., but his nose and eyes were in serious trouble and the membranes in his mouth were sore. Again he said, "These onions are horrible; I think I would rather take the shoe beatings." The thief just could not stick to one of the punishments and kept changing back and forth from eating onions to getting shoe beatings and back again to eating onions. In this way, the thief ate nearly a hundred onions and also endured all hundred shoe blows, because he was not willing to stick with one hard choice. This example is sometimes used to describe people who suffer worse as they are trying to avoid making a hard sacrifice or a big expense; but they may suffer in two ways and twice as much, by not being decisive.

Our Hotel Room Negotiations

This is a true story of my brothers Gurdial, Kirpal and me, and our three wives with the children Apar, Gyan, and Amrita. We were on a trip from Punjab to Kashmir in late September, 1973. The nine of us were in one car, a 1968 Chevrolet Impala, which Kirpal had imported when he returned from America and which was packed to the limit with our luggage and us. As we reached the town of Jammu, my brothers felt that there was still a little bit of daylight left, and they thought we could cover some more miles toward Srinagar before stopping, although their wives were saying that it was late and dangerous to travel. We had gone a very short distance past Jammu, just beyond the bridge over the river, when the Chevrolet had a flat tire. Kirpal was the doer in the whole group, Gurdial gave verbal support, and I was treated like a guest. As Kirpal was changing the wheel, the car fell off the jack, injuring Kirpal's knee slightly. Although Kirpal escaped serious injury, he said that such injuries usually give trouble later in life even if they don't disable you in your youth. He said, "The body never forgets such insults." Anyway, we again lifted the car with the jack, and Kirpal did manage to change the wheel of the car, but because of all that delay, it was already dark. We could not go any further and returned to Jammu to look for a place to stay for the night.

It was late summer, it was the tourist season in Kashmir, and it was late in the evening. Hotel rooms were difficult to obtain. At the first hotel, the manager said that he could give us three rooms, but we would have to decide immediately, as it was already late. The brothers and the wives looked at the rooms. The rooms were not particularly good and the brothers thought that the price was rather high. Gurdial said, "Let us look elsewhere." So we drove to another hotel. The rooms in that hotel were not any better and the prices were a bit higher than those at the first hotel. So Kirpal said, "This place is an outrageous rip off; even the first hotel was better than this; let's go back to that first place." When we arrived at the first hotel, the attendant said, "I have other people waiting. If you still want those rooms, you will have to pay 25% more than before and you have to decide immediately. Kirpal said, "Those are lousy rooms. I am not paying that much more for those rooms. The original price was high enough, and that is all we are willing to pay." But it was late, and the wives and children were tired. Gurdial said, "The second hotel was not that bad; we should have taken those rooms; let us go back there or look somewhere else." So we drove to the second hotel; everybody was very tired and sleepy by this time. When we reached there, the manager said he had no rooms left. Then we inquired at a third hotel but no luck there either. So the whole group came back to the first hotel. It was very late and we were really tired and sleepy. When the brothers again talked to the manager, he said he had different and similar quality rooms but it would cost us 50% more now. At this time the brothers did not have any choice as the women and children were ready to collapse anywhere. We took the worse rooms at the first hotel at 50% higher prices, after having suffered for two additional hours in the dark driving around. That is when Gurdial remarked "We have eaten a hundred onions as well as suffered a hundred shoe beatings."

Milk Money and Water Money

Once there was a Gowala (cow keeper, milk seller) who had been selling milk in a town for some years. He was making a fair living but he was not getting rich. Then one day he thought he had found a clever way to increase his income. He added to the milk an equal amount of water and thus doubled the volume. Therefore he got twice as much money by selling the diluted milk. If the milk looked too thin, he just mixed a little bit of flour in it to make it look thick. Some customers complained about the quality of the milk, but enough people kept buying his milk so that he made nearly twice as much money as before. Many years went by, and he finally had accumulated enough money. He thought he would not have to work any more. He decided to go back to his village to retire in comfort. In a pack he collected his belongings, and in a big purse he bundled all his silver coins. He started for his village, walking under big shady trees along the bank of a river. After walking a long distance, he was tired and decided to take a rest leaning against his bundle under the shade of a tree, with his money bag by his side. As he was resting, he fell asleep. A big monkey came down from the tree, grabbed the money bag, and climbed back up into the tree. When the Gowala woke up, his money bag was gone. Looking up into the tree, he saw the monkey with the money bag and became extremely upset. From below, he begged the monkey to return the money bag, but with no success. If he folded his hands and prayed, the monkey folded its hands in the praying pose. If he made a fist and cursed the monkey, the monkey made a fist to imitate him. He was afraid to threaten the monkey too much, as the animal might just run away; and then he would have no hope of recovering the money.

After a while the monkey opened the money-bag, looked at each shiny coin, and found that the coins were not edible. Then the monkey started throwing the coins one by one from the tree, randomly in all directions. About half the coins fell in the deep water in the river and about half of them fell on the ground. Then the milk seller collected all the coins from the ground, but he could never recover any of those that fell in the deep river. The milk seller was very unhappy at first. But after some thought he philosophized to himself, "The money that I earned from selling milk is in my possession; but the ill-gotten gains, which came from adding water to the milk, has gone into the water; the milk money and the water money have been separated."

Monkey See, Monkey Do

Once there was a man who made his living by selling hats from door to door, village to village. He always wore a sample hat himself, so that others could see what the hats looked like and would be tempted to buy and wear his hats. One day he was traveling with his bundle of hats from one village to another. It was a hot day and he decided to rest under the shade of a big tree. He fell asleep, with his hat still on his head and with the bundle of hats beside him. It turned out that many monkeys were playing in the nearby trees. One of the monkeys came near the bundle of hats, took out a hat, and put the hat on his head, just as he had seen the hat on the man's head. All the other monkeys also got a hat each for themselves from the bundle. The monkeys were afraid of the man; so when the man awakened, they climbed the big tree with the hats still on their heads. When the man looked around, he found his empty bundle, his hats were all gone, and those monkeys in the tree were wearing the hats. At first the man was angry and upset and expressed his anguish by putting his hands on both sides of his head. Watching him, all the monkeys put their hands by the sides of their heads. Then the man started to beg the monkeys with folded hands to return the hats. The monkeys also folded their hands toward him. Then the man became extremely angry, started abusing the monkeys, and made an angry fist toward them. All the monkeys made fists toward him. Totally angry and frustrated, the man took his hat off and threw it on the ground, saying, "I am ruined; I hate you monkeys!" In imitation, all the monkeys also took off their hats and threw them on the ground. The hat seller collected all the hats, put them in his bundle, and walked away.

Bujharat or Paheli (Riddles)

It was always a comfortable feeling to listen to stories, even the familiar ones. But sometimes people traded *bujharat* (riddles whose answer the listener has to guess) instead of telling stories. They are usually in rhyme, even if they had to add some nonsensical words to it, but not always this made them very enjoyable. Riddles worked best when guests were visiting, because then they would not already know the answers to the riddles. Here is a sample of riddles:

(1) "Teri Bhua da Bhai, Teri Nani da Juvai, Tera Qui Lagya?" This is hard to translate because relations like aunt and grandmother are generic in English, while there are distinct categories of aunts and grandmothers in Punjabi. The riddle asks: "The brother of your Bhua (paternal aunt) and the son-in law of your Nani (maternal grandmother); what is his relationship to you?" And the answer is "Father".

(2) A woman is asked, "Untth te charhendye, nukel pharenda tera qui lagda?" She answers, "Ehda nam mein boldi nahi, mera nam hai Jeean; ehdi sass meri sass, dono mama dheean". Translation: "Hey lady, mounted on the camel, who is the guy holding the camel's nose string?" She answers, "I cannot say his name (because of the delicacy of the relationship), but my name is Jeean; but his mother-in-law and my mother-in-law are mother and daughter." What is the relationship of that man and the woman? The answer is, "Father-in-law and daughter-in-law."

(3) "Chacha Kahe Lagde Nahi; Mama Kahe Lagde Hai." Translation: "They don't touch when you say Chacha, but they touch when you say Mama." What are they?

The answer is: "Lips".

(4) "Untth di Bethni, Mirg di Chaal, Kann Nahi, Poonch Nahi, Dhoohi te Nahi Baal." Translation: "Sits like a camel, hops like a deer; has no ears, no tail, and no hair on the back." The answer is, "frog."

(5) "Kikker te Kuhara, Hethan Pani Uttay Gara." Translation: "Liquid is below; mud is on top. What is it?" The answer: "Butter floating on buttermilk"

(6) "Bhoin Kapre di, Hal Lohe da, Beej Trazeen Toli da, Jehra Meri Baat Na Boojeh, puttr baney meri goli da"

Translation: "The earth is of cloth; plough is of iron; the precious seed is measured by balance." The answer: A phulkari being embroidered with needle and silk thread.

(7) "Ma Patli Patang, Putr Soob Jiha; Ma Gai Nhaun, Putr Doob Gia." Translation: "Mother is very thin, son is big and fat; mother goes down to take a bath, and the son drowns." Answer: The waterman's rope and the big *boka* leather bucket.

(8) "Dekho Rab da Sabab, Heth Pani Uttay Agg." Translation: "See the miracle of God; water is below and fire is on top." Answer: Fire on top and water below in the hookah.

(9) "Aggay Chikker, Pichhay Dheri, Bujhan Wale Teri Teri." Translation: "Pile in the back and mud in front; if you can find it, it is all yours." Answer: Feces and urine from squatting and defecating on earth.

Glossary of Punjabi Words Used

When the English people at first started writing the Indian words in Roman script, they started adding an "a" at the end of many words that would otherwise end with a consonant. This might be due to the pattern of speech of the Hindi speaking people who emphasize such sounds and were more numerous than Punjabi speakers. But the same words of Punjabi are spelled and pronounced without emphasizing the additional vowel sound "a." For example, the words which are spelled by Punjabi speakers as dharm, karm, nirvan, yog, Ram, Krishn, Shiv, and Yum, etc., are written by many English writers as dharma, karma, nirvana, yoga, Rama, Krishna, Shiva, and Yuma respectively.

AMRIT: (1) without death; (2) nectar of immortality; (3) ambrosial drink of the gods; (4) the ceremony of formal initiation for a Sikh, by taking the 'amrit' drink.

AMRIT DHARI: a Sikh who has been formally initiated by taking the amrit.

ANAND: (1) bliss; rejoicing; (2) a portion of the Sikh prayer.

ANAND KARJ: rejoicing ceremony; the Sikh wedding ritual.

ATMA: the immortal soul; based on the this root word, MAHATMA means great soul and PARMATMA means the highest soul (God).

BAAT: (1) a Punjabi bedtime story; (2) anecdote; (3) any matter, thing or problem.

BABA: (1) term of respect for an older man; (2) grandfather.

BABU: an official; now a days, any clerk.

BAAGH: (1) garden; park; orchard; (2) a woman's heavily embroidered shawl; phulkari.

BAHI: (or BEHI): old- fashioned record book.

BAPU: (or BAP): father.

BEBE: (1) senior lady; address of respect from one woman to another. (2) mother.

BEEBEE or BIBI: (1) young girl; (2) a respectable woman.

BER (rhymes with "bail"): a wild fruit in Punjab.

BETHIK: sitting room; a room for visitors.

BHAGT (also BHAGAT or BHAKTA): one who devotes all his actions to God; devotee.

BHAI (BHAU, BHRATA, BHRA, BHA): Punjabi words for brother.

BHANGRA: (1) Punjabi style folk dance; (2) Punjabi song and dance performance.

BHATINDA: an old town in southern Punjab; famous railway junction in the 1930s.

BHEN (rhymes with ban): sister

BHOG: (1) satisfactory completion; enjoyment; (2) completion of recitation of scriptures.

BIBI (same as BEEBEE): (1) respected lady; (2) young girl.

BOLI: (1)spoken; language; (2) song for a giddha or bhangra dance; (3) a ballad.

BRAHMIN (or BRAHMAN): highest caste in the Hindu system; religious ritual performer; Hindu priest class.

CHAR PAI: four- footed; the four- pedestal bed with webbing.

CHULLAH: mud stove for cooking; hearth

CRORE: ten million; one hundred lakh; large number.

DAAL (or DAL): split beans; a spicy soup-like preparation to eat with roti bread.

DADA: paternal grandfather.

DADI: paternal grandmother.

DERA: (1)camp; resting place; (2) abode or lodging of a holy man.

DHARM (or DHARMA): divine law which a person must observe; faith; sacred duty.

DHARMSALA: house of dharma; a free inn for travelers.

DHEE: daughter.

DIN (pronounced DEEN): (1) faith; religion; (2) part of a Muslim name.

DINN RAAT: day and night; all the time.

GANGA: holy river in north India, which is called Ganges by the European people.

GHEE: butter, after being clarified by heating and removing any non-fat milk residue.

GIDDHA: Punjabi girls' clapping and singing; song and dance at a wedding or festival.

GOTRA or GOTE: clan; tribe; family name; heritage.

GRANTH: (1) great book; (2) holy book of the Sikhs.

GRANTHI: one who recites the Sikh holy scriptures; acting priest of the Sikhs.

GURBANI: Guru's word; God's word; Sikh holy scriptures.

GURDWARA: Guru's door; God's house; Sikh place of worship.

GURMUKHI: script for the Sikh scriptures and for the Punjabi language.

GURU: revered master; spiritual teacher; word to describe God in Sikh scriptures.

HAKEEM: one who knows; healer; native doctor.

HAKIM: official; authority; one who orders or rules.

HINDU: (1) originally, of the Indus Valley; (2) of India; (3) follower of the Vedic religion.

INDER (or INDRA): chief god of early Hindu religion; God of sky and of rain.

INDUS: river in northwest India, now mostly in Pakistan; variously called Hind, Ind, Sindh.

JAT: (rhymes with "cut"): the farmer caste in Punjab and nearby areas; cultivator; land owner.

JI (or JEE): respected or dear one; added after a name or title for extra politeness.

JUNJ: groom's wedding party that goes to bride's village to marry and bring her back.

JUVAEE: husband of daughter.

JUVAN: (1) youth; grown up; (2) a soldier of low rank.

KA (also KE, KI, KIAN depending on gender, and whether singular or plural, etc.): of; from; used to indicate relation, connection or possession.

KACCHA (or KUCCHA): raw; uncooked; unripe; poorly done; not strong; not firm, undesirable.

KAFIR: Muslim word of contempt for a non-believer; not a follower of Mohammed.

KARM (or KARMA): deeds whose rewards and consequences go with the soul and affect its later incarnations; consequence of action for the soul.

KHALSA: (1) Guru's own; (2) Sikh initiated by amrit ceremony.

KHUMMNI: tie-dyed, multi-strand thread; used for rituals, for ceremonial or sacred occasions in Hindu homes.

KISMET: fate; luck; fortune; belief in preordained fate

KSHATRI (also KHATRI, SHATRI): warrior, ruler caste.

KANTHA (also KUNTHA): a kind of man's necklace.

LAKH: hundred thousand; a big number; numerous.

MA (pronounced MAAN): mother (in Punjabi there is a nasal "n" sound for female names which end in "a").

MAHA: great, big; used as prefix to make bigger, e.g., MAHATMA

MAHARAJA: great raja; big ruler; king

MALIK: owner; husband; lord; sometimes used for God.

MAYA: (1) wealth; material world; unreal; illusion; (2) in Hindu thought, maya is the trap of the world of senses; only the world of soul is considered real.

MEHRAJ: ancestral village of the rulers of the Phulkian States and of many chiefs.

MEL or MEIL (pronounced 'mail'): meeting; wedding guests who are already relatives.

MELA: fair; meeting; gathering for a celebration.

MELEN or MEILEN: a woman among the meil wedding guests; a woman who dances in the giddha.

MISSL: militia; bands of Sikh soldiers who later became powerful and ruled territories.

MOHRI: a thorny tree branch used to build fence; symbol of settlement; claim of land by fixing Mohri.

MUKTI: end of hardship; release; liberation; Punjabi word for nirvana.

NAAM: (1) name; (2) in Sikh scriptures and spiritual practice, it is God's essence.

NANA: maternal grandfather.

NANI: maternal grandmother.

NANKE: of maternal grandparents; village of maternal grandparents.

NEEM: a tree in India with bitter leaves that may be used as antiseptic or pesticide.

NIRVAN: liberation from the cycle of transmigration of soul; the ultimate bliss, release.

PAAP: misdeed; harmful act; unholy act; sin.

PAISA (or PESA): a coin which used to be 1/64, but is now 1/100, of a rupee; money.

PANCHAYAT: originally a council of five elders; village decision makers, gathering of brotherhood.

PANI (PAANI): water.

PATHI: patty made of cow dung, used as fuel when dry.

PATTI (pronounced "putti"): (1) domain; estate; section of a village; (2) if pronounced with an Indian 't', it means a carpet or sheet made from fibers or animal hair.

PEERHI: (1) generations; ancestral names; also (2) a low seat, usually for women.

PHUL (rhymes with "cool"): (1) ancestor of the rulers of the Phulkian States, born in Mehraj; (2) Flower.

PHULKIAN: the states of Patiala, Nabha, Jind, and the chiefs of Bhadaur, Malaud, Badrukhan, Rampura, Dyalpura, etc., who were all descendents of Phul.

PHULKARI: flower work; a woman's shawl embroidered with silk thread.

PHULL (rhymes with "bull"): Punjabi pronunciation of the Hindi word "phool", which means "flower." This word also means 'the remains of cremated finger bones.'

PUKKA: (same as PAKKA), firm, strong, well bailt, ripe well cooked, opposite of Kaccha.

PUNDIT (or PANDIT): learned; knowledgeable; of Brahmin caste.

PUNJAB: land of five rivers which are tributaries of the Indus; a province in northwest India, part of which is now in Pakistan and part in India.

PUNN (or POON): a good, sacred or pious deed; a charitable act; opposite of PAAP.

PUTRA (PUT or POOT): son; male child.

PUTRI: female child; daughter.

RAJ: rule; kingdom; domination; government.

RAJA: king; ruler (MAHARAJA means great ruler), noble.

RAJPUT: son of ruler; a prince; warrior of Kshatri caste.

RAJPUTANA: land of Rajputs; desert region in western India, later made into Rajasthan.

ROTI: unleavened flat bread; meals; livelihood; feast.

RUPEE (RUPIAH): (1) unit of currency, (2) silver.

SAAG: green leaf vegetable, such as mustard or spinach, cooked with spices.

SADHU: practitioner of sadhna or holy discipline; Hindu holy man; ascetic; mystic.

SAHIB: lord; noble; hence SAHIBZADA: noble born; prince.

SALA: brother of wife.

SAMADHI: a state of deep concentration; isolation of senses from external distractions.

SANDOOQ: box; four- legged container for bride's dowry items and clothes, etc.

SARDAR (or SIRDAR): chief lord; head; now this word is used to address any Sikh.

SATGURU: True Lord; another Sikh name for God.

SATTH (pronounced SUTTH): gathering place; village plaza; a community meeting.

SER: weight measure; about two pounds.

SHABAD: word; holy word; a religious chant; song from scriptures.

SHAH: (1) lord; (2) a wealthy man.

SHRI, SHREE, SRI or SIRI: revered; honorable; used before a name for extra respect.

SIKH: (1) disciple of Guru Nanak; scholar; learner; follower of Sikh religion.

SINGH: (1) lion; (2) part of the name of a man; now-a-days usually a Sikh, but not always.

SINGH SABHA: an organization for reformation and improvement of the Sikhs.

SIRDAR: see SARDAR above..

SUTLEJ: a tributary of the Indus Rriver that is farthest to the east.

TANDOOR: oven made of clay.

VED (also VEDA): (1) Hindu holy book; (2) knowledge.

VEHRA: front yard.

VIDYA: education; learning.

WAH: exclamation of wonder laudatory commendation.

WAHEGURU: Wondrous Master; Sikh name for God.

WALA: (1) owner; possessor. (2) with, of, from, having.

WAZIR (or VIZIR): counselor; minister; advisor to king.

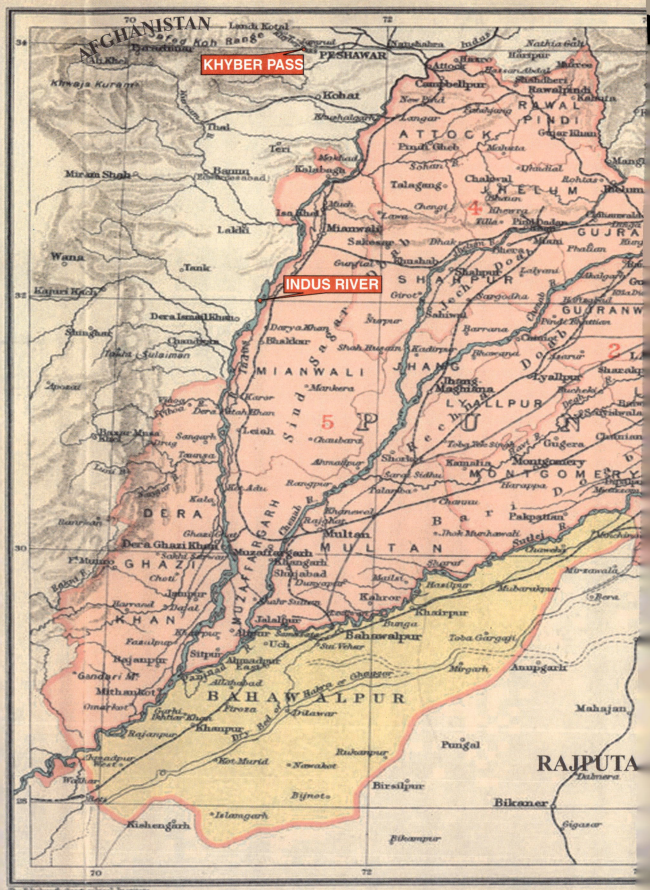